NATIVES *and*
NEWCOMERS

Also by James Axtell

THE EDUCATIONAL WRITINGS OF JOHN LOCKE
A Critical Edition

THE SCHOOL UPON A HILL
Education and Society in Colonial New England

INDIAN MISSIONS
A Critical Bibliography
(with James P. Ronda)

THE EUROPEAN AND THE INDIAN
Essays in the Ethnohistory of Colonial North America

THE INDIAN PEOPLES OF EASTERN AMERICA
A Documentary History of the Sexes

THE INVASION WITHIN
The Contest of Cultures in Colonial North America

AFTER COLUMBUS
Essays in the Ethnohistory of Colonial North America

BEYOND 1492
Encounters in Colonial North America

THE INDIANS' NEW SOUTH
Cultural Change in the Colonial Southeast

THE PLEASURES OF ACADEME
A Celebration & Defense of Higher Education

NATIVES *and* NEWCOMERS

The Cultural Origins of North America

James Axtell

The College of William and Mary

New York   Oxford
OXFORD UNIVERSITY PRESS
2001

Oxford University Press

Oxford   New York
Athens   Auckland   Bangkok   Bogotá   Buenos Aires   Calcutta
Cape Town   Chennai   Dar es Salaam   Delhi   Florence   Hong Kong   Istanbul
Karachi   Kuala Lumpur   Madrid   Melbourne   Mexico City   Mumbai
Nairobi   Paris   São Paulo   Singapore   Taipei   Tokyo   Toronto   Warsaw

and associated companies in
Berlin   Ibadan

Published by Oxford University Press, Inc.,
198 Madison Avenue, New York, New York 10016
http://www.oup-usa.org

Oxford is a registered trademark of Oxford University Press

Library of Congress Cataloging-in-Publication Data

Axtell, James.
    Natives and newcomers : the cultural origins of North America / James Axtell.
      p. cm.
    Includes index.
    ISBN 0-19-513770-1 (cloth)—ISBN 0-19-513771-X (pbk.)
      1. Indians of North America—First contact with Europeans. 2. Indians of North
America—History—Colonial period, ca. 1600–1775. 3. Indians of North
America—Cultural assimilation. 4. North America—History—Colonial period, ca.
1600–1775. I. Title.
    E98.F39 N37 2000
    970.02—dc21

                                                                        99-056089

Printing (last digit): 9 8 7 6 5 4 3 2 1

Printed in the United States of America
on acid-free paper

For Susan
Tolerant and amusing muse

CONTENTS

ILLUSTRATIONS

PREFACE

College textbooks and lecturers like to tell us that when Columbus and his crew splashed ashore on the beach at Guanahaní in October 1492, the "Old World" of Europe, Asia, and Africa met and was bound irrevocably to the (equally old) "New World" of the Americas. Of course, it was not "worlds" that met, except metaphorically, but *people* from those distant and diverse geographies, societies, and cultures. Nor, for all the powerful symbolism of that first meeting, did the Columbian or American "Encounter" (as Quincentenary organizers aptly dubbed it) occur all at once or once and for all. It continued to happen and was reconfigured every time natives and newcomers encountered each other—gladly, begrudgingly, or angrily—anywhere in North, South, or Central America during the hemisphere's variously long colonial periods. Some would argue that the Encounter is still alive and not particularly well today, more than five hundred years after Columbus's fortuitous and fateful find in the Caribbean.

For the past thirty years, I have tried to take the measure of the Encounter between Indians and Europeans in colonial North America and to probe its meaning for the emerging history of the United States and, to a lesser extent, Canada. In doing so, I early recognized that the European focus of colonial ambition and endeavor was not just the thirteen English mainland colonies but the whole continent, whose immensity, infinitely varied geographical features, and particularly its myriad, disunited native polities and peoples constituted the largest and most persistent obstacles the colonists had to overcome. This meant that my courses on exploration and colonization had to include and often feature Spanish, Portuguese, French, Dutch, Swedish, and Russian actors, as well as the familiar English. This in turn obliged me to begin the story not in 1607 at Jamestown or even 1584 on Roanoke Island, but in Europe's medieval exploration and exploitation of Asia, Africa, the Near East, the Mediterranean and its islands, and the eastern Atlantic islands; even the main chapters on North America had to attend to the sixteenth century as fully and carefully as to the two that followed.

Of equal importance was treating the various Indian and European participants with moral and methodological parity. I wanted not only to demonstrate that the cultural changes wrought by the Encounter were mutual, two-way if not always equal, but to treat all the contestants fairly, with as little favoritism or axe-grinding as possible. This was never easy, given the changing political climate and my own intellectual evolution. In many ways the scales were tipped against the Europeans. Particularly during the American Indian Movement's heyday in the late 1960s and early '70s (when I became acutely aware of the academy's and my own neglect of the Indians' historical importance) and, for similar reasons, during the politically charged half-dozen years leading to the Columbian Quincentenary (in which I was heavily involved as a member and then chairman of the American Historical Association's nonpartisan quincentenary committee), it was as difficult for the colonists to receive sympathy or justice as it was for Indians in more conservative periods.

In seeking intellectual tools to enable me to achieve some parity of treatment and, equally difficult and important, to understand the distinctive "otherness" of native cultures, I discovered ethnohistory, the original "cultural studies" approach, which I describe in the Prologue. Six books and most of the articles I have published in the last twenty-five years have been attempts to view the American Encounter through the bifocal lenses fashioned from methods and perspectives contributed equally by history and anthropology.

As one of the earliest historians to practice and stump for ethnohistory, and especially to turn its gaze on colonial as well as native cultures, I have been gratified to witness the proliferation of Indian studies among more Eurocentric colonialists. But their often specialized and narrowly focused studies, as insightful as they often are, are not for beginners. Thus this volume assembles fifteen of my most resonant and accessible attempts to describe and explain the major aspects of Indian-European relations, from French Canada to Spanish Florida, from the sixteenth century (actually 1492) to the eighteenth, for students and readers relatively new to the subject.

This book differs from several older articles and three more recent books that assay either native contributions to American culture or the mutual role of natives and colonists in molding early American culture. Anthropologist Jack Weatherford's popular accounts, *Indian Givers: How the Indians of the Americas Transformed the World* (1988) and *Native Roots: How the Indians Enriched America* (1991), roam all over the Americas in time and space. Historian Colin Calloway's topical treatment of *New Worlds for All: Indians, Europeans, and the Remaking of Early America* (1997), which kindly acknowledges debts to most of the following chapters, focuses on the colonial period in North America but pays scant attention to chronology. All three books make it difficult for readers to follow the specific conditions and timing of causation.

This volume, by contrast, seeks to avoid the *omnium gatherum* quality and unanchored generalizations of the typical "influence" or "contribution" studies and to prevent reader disorientation by paying attention to chronology and, whenever possible, to specific groups of natives and colonists rather than generic "Indians" and "Europeans." It also treats in some degree all the major facets of Indian-European interaction: initial contacts, communication (a topic almost entirely ignored by historians), trade and gift-giving, diplomacy, social and sexual partnering, work and labor, religious and cultural conversion, military clashes and captivity, and disease mortality.

Although my subtitle is "The Cultural Origins of North America," this book does contain one large omission: except in Chapter Twelve, I do not attempt to assess the social and cultural role of the involuntary immigrants from Africa, who played no small part in the historical development of North America, particularly of the United States. Two considerations (perhaps rationalizations) account for this omission. First, others have treated exceedingly well the formative interactions of European colonists and Africans, free and slave, particularly my colleague Philip Morgan and Ira Berlin. Second, relatively little attention so far has been paid to Indian-Black relations, partly because both groups were largely nonliterate and left few written records, partly because even colonial sources about them are scattered and piecemeal, and largely, I suspect, because the groups did not voluntarily mix much until well into the eighteenth century, and then usually in small numbers or as individuals. I can only hope that younger scholars will step in soon to fill the gap.

The following chapters have all been published previously, but in too many places for convenient access. Eleven appeared in three previous Oxford collections of my essays: *The European and the Indian* (1981), *After Columbus* (1988), and *Beyond 1492* (1992). Four (Prologue and Chapters Two, Five, and Nine) are relatively new. I have corrected a few textual infelicities, excised some repetition, and updated the endnotes. Short introductions to the five sections contextualize the individual chapters by describing their origins and relating them to my other writings and to each other. The Prologue was written for a spirited conference on "Methodologies and American Indian History" at Western Michigan University in 1995. I sought to explain to a mixed audience of natives, academics, and native academics the virtues (and venial sins) of ethnohistory as a tool for reconstructing native and intercultural history. A revised version of the essay published in *Rethinking American Indian History*, edited by Donald L. Fixico (Albuquerque, 1997), is an appropriate introduction to a book on the American Encounter.

J. A.

Northeast Harbor, Maine
July 1999

NATIVES *and* NEWCOMERS

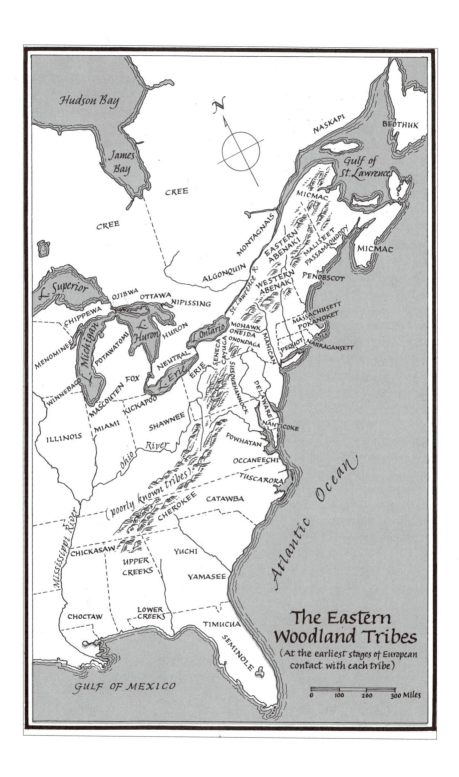

Hudson Bay

James Bay

N

NASKAPI

BEOTHUK

Gulf of St. Lawrence

CREE

CREE

MICMAC

ALGONQUIN

MONTAGNAIS

EASTERN ABENAKI

MALISEET

PASSAMAQUODDY

MICMAC

L. Superior

OJIBWA

OTTAWA

NIPISSING

WESTERN ABENAKI

PENOBSCOT

CHIPPEWA

St. Lawrence R.

L. Michigan

L. Huron

HURON

L. Ontario

MOHAWK

ONEIDA

ONONDAGA

MASSACHUSETT

POKANOKET

MENOMINEE

POTAWATOMI

NEUTRAL

SENECA

CAYUGA

MAHICAN

PEQUOT

NARRAGANSETT

WINNEBAGO

MASCOUTEN

FOX

L. Erie

ERIE

SUSQUEHANNOCK

DELAWARE

ILLINOIS

KICKAPOO

MIAMI

SHAWNEE

NANTICOKE

POWHATAN

Ohio River

(poorly known tribes)

OCCANEECHI

TUSCARORA

CHEROKEE

CATAWBA

Atlantic Ocean

Mississippi River

CHICKASAW

YUCHI

UPPER CREEKS

YAMASEE

CHOCTAW

LOWER CREEKS

TIMUCUA

SEMINOLE

GULF OF MEXICO

The Eastern
Woodland Tribes

(At the earliest stages of European
contact with each tribe)

0   100   200   300 Miles

THE ETHNOHISTORY OF NATIVE AMERICA

Thirty years ago, when I was entering the academic profession, very few historians pursued the history of America's native peoples. Certainly no historians I knew felt particularly guilty for leaving Indian peoples out of their courses and books, for implying that America *had* no history until the advent of scribbling Europeans and that, even *after* 1492, Indians had little to do with the making of American society and culture generally. Indians (the collective generic was invariably used) and their so-called history were relegated to the Anthropology Department, where odd men in plaid shirts and dirty boots attended to all the "primitive" others of the world, who constituted, at best, exotic footnotes to the real history of "civilized" movers and shakers.

Those who were interested in the history of native America, primarily anthropologists, relied almost exclusively on the methodology or investigative procedure known as ethnohistory. So, in 1970, when I belatedly realized that I could not make any sense of colonial America or of the later United States without understanding the role of their native peoples, I turned to scholars who identified themselves as ethnohistorians and convened annually at meetings of the American Society for Ethnohistory. I was drawn initially to that organization because its journal, *Ethnohistory,* published most of the best articles on Indian history I could find in those dim pre-Web days. (The *American Indian Quarterly* and the *American Indian Culture and Research Journal,* were not founded until 1974 and 1976, respectively.) Some articles, I noticed with interest, were even written by people with degrees and positions in history. In the course of attending those relatively small and friendly meetings and reading the journal. I began to get some feel for the theoretical and operational characteristics of ethnohistory, for what it could do well and what its blind spots were.

As I began to include the Indians in my courses, I felt that I needed at least a working definition of ethnohistory, partly to answer in my own mind the voiced and unvoiced questions some of my more traditional colleagues had about introducing such a novel subject to the curriculum. When I turned to the official statement of the society's aims on the inside front cover of its journal, I found three successive definitions that were not very helpful. Initially, ethnohistory was corporately defined as "original research in the documentary history of the culture and movements of primitive peoples, and related problems of broader scope."[1] In 1966 that definition—at once restricted, demeaning, and hopelessly vague—was replaced by another not much better. Ethnohistory, it said, was devoted to "general culture history and process, and the specific history of peoples on all levels of sociocultural organization, emphasizing that of primitives and peasantries, in all world areas."[2] By the winter of 1971 the society's growing sensitivity to nomenclature erased the pejorative reference to "primitives and peasantries" and replaced it with a kinder but equally problematic "non-industrial peoples."[3] Nor would I have been much helped by subsequent definitions. By 1982 ethnohistory had become simply, and confusingly, "the cultural history of ethnic peoples throughout the world."[4] And from 1984 to 1986, when the frustrating official attempt to define the field finally ceased altogether, the society said that its purview was "the past of cultures and societies in all areas of the world, emphasizing the use of documentary and field materials and historiographic and anthropological approaches."[5]

The last definition at least had a familiar ring, because in 1979 I had tried my own hand at defining the field, in part to sort out the different styles and emphases as well as the commonalities of its anthropological and increasingly numerous historical practitioners. To some extent, my characterization of ethnohistory tried to reach a consensus among the many earlier definitions that had been offered by exemplary practitioners such as anthropologists William Fenton, William Sturtevant, Nancy Lurie, Robert Carmack, and Charles Hudson and historian Wilcomb Washburn.[6] But I also wanted to emphasize its distinctive interdisciplinary methods and to avoid the bland vagueness of the society's earlier definitions. As I saw it—and largely still see it—ethnohistory involves "the use of historical and ethnological methods and materials to gain knowledge of the nature and cause of change in a culture [or cultures] defined [ethnologically]."[7]

In probing what such a definition does and does not say, we note first that any culture of any complexity or size anywhere in the world is a potential object of ethnohistorical attention. While the American society and its journal began with an exclusive interest in the native peoples of North America and have since maintained a strong interest in them, nothing about the operating procedures of ethnohistory mandates that it restrict itself to the tribal peoples of the Americas or, indeed, to *tribal* peoples at all. As the journal's articles have shown, particularly in the last twenty years, ethnohistory is perfectly capable of shedding light on the cultural history of state societies, industrialized societies, colonizing societies, and capitalist societies in regions all over the globe—Africa, Asia, Australia, Europe, and the Americas, North, South, and Central. The group or region studied is much less important than *how* it is studied and with what organizing *focus*.

Ethnohistory, like most workaday anthropology, takes as its most proper subject *culture* as opposed to *society* or socioeconomic organization per se. While sociologists and dictionary makers have little trouble agreeing on what constitutes a society, anthropologists have always had a devil of a time defining culture. When I went to the literature in search of a consensual definition, I quickly realized that I would have to concoct my own from many different strands and theoretical strains. What I came away with was a notion that culture is "an idealized pattern of meanings, values, and norms differentially shared by the members of a society, which can be inferred from the non-instinctive [or learned] behavior of the group and from the symbolic products of their actions, including material artifacts, language, and social institutions."[8] In other words, culture is a kind of code by which a people live and which gives meaning, direction, and order to their lives. The code is an idealized construct, imagined or seen in its entirety and complexity perhaps only by a perceptive and diligent outside observer, because the insiders assume or internalize much of the code during their education or enculturation and because different members of the society are privy only to certain parts of the total code, those most appropriate to their particular class, race, status, gender, age, education, ancestry, family position, region, and so forth.

According to such a definition, ethnohistorians must try mightily to see cultures *whole*, as all of their social parts and sub-codes interact functionally and symbiotically to produce a single cultural organism, which is potentially knowable and translatable to members of other cultures. This is somewhat easier to do, of course, the smaller the society, which explains why ethnohistory has habitually focused on the cultures of relatively small-scale, allegedly "simple" societies, particularly tribal societies. Like all students of "otherness," ethnohistorians must also try to understand each culture, initially at least, on its own terms, according to its own cultural code, because that is the only way to understand *why* people in the past acted as they did. Unless we know what they imagined reality to be and their own particular place and role in it, we will never succeed in re-creating the world they really lived in. For as Charles Horton Cooley, the great early-twentieth-century sociologist, reminded us, society—and he might have said culture too—is "an interweaving and interworking of mental selves. . . . The imaginations which people have of one another are the solid facts of society."[9]

This means that the ethnohistorian must take virtually nothing for granted about the social culture under study if he or she wishes to get inside the heads, to break the code, of its constituent members. Students of a historical culture must start from the premise that "the past is a foreign country; they do things differently there."[10] And not just *some* things, but *everything*, beginning with speaking and thinking. Ideally, every ethnohistorian would enter his or her historical country like a child newly born to the natives, through the slowly forming template of language—oral, mental, and bodily. If the descendants of one's historical subjects and their ancient tongue survive, the ethnohistorian would do well to learn that tongue while becoming acquainted with the other aspects of the culture's past and present. But many scholars study groups whose native languages have been partially or completely lost to change and death, and other scholars do not specialize in a single group but explore larger regions, usually across several linguistic boundaries, so the entry to culture via language is partly closed to them. They can and should, however, seek as much access to the epistemology, ontology, and mental universe of their subjects as possible through historical dictionaries, word lists, and grammars and through some familiarity with the grammatical and syntactical principles and operations of languages belonging to the same linguistic family or cognate groups. This will ensure that they do not unconsciously intrude their own mental prospects and processes upon the very different realms and reasonings of their historical subjects.

In addition to language, ethnohistory draws upon an unlimited host of "historical and ethnological materials" to reconstruct the normative codes of past cultures. In theory at least, it was not always so. In the early sixties, both the journal and most theorists described ethnohistory's primary sources as "historical *documents*," by which they meant almost exclusively the written records of literate societies that came in contact with native cultures. Usually the record makers were explorers, colonists, or imperialists who sought and often secured control over, or destruction of, the native peoples. Invariably, their records and observations of the natives reflected their sociopolitical goals and their own cultural biases, thereby refracting or warping to some extent whatever they saw. Despite these evidential drawbacks, the newcomers often left unique and sometimes abundant records of native peoples whose own histories were as fragile as memory and as perishable as sound. While ethnohistorians should always be skeptical of the *interpretations* placed on the natives' words and actions, the outsider's *descriptions* of that behavior are usually indispensable and often trustworthy, if never as thorough or encompassing as we might wish.

One crucial test of reliability of any evidence pertaining to native life, written or otherwise, is to weigh and measure it critically against ethnological knowledge gained from study of the group or similar groups through a variety of methods and materials. It is this new dimension—the critical use of ethnological concepts, materials, and sensitivity to evaluate historical documents—that separates ethnohistory from history proper. For ethnohistorians can bring to bear "special knowledge of the group, linguistic insights, and understanding of culture phenomena," which allow them to utilize written data more fully than the average historian.[11]

At the same time, documentary historians—particularly those who have paid attention to the latest developments in rhetoric, semiotics, and "colonial discourse"—have much to teach ethnohistorians about the contexts, tropes, and discursive strategies that inform any written record.[12] Language always "says" more than it *denotes,* so it is a major job of the document decoder to deconstruct and decipher all of its messages, to listen as well to its silences and static, before giving credence to any one part. So-called facts always come dressed, not naked, and it behooves ethnohistorians to learn to read the sartorial signs as well as to interpret contemporary speech in the contextual grammar of facial, gestural, and body language. Because we are seldom bequeathed evidence of the extraverbal envelope of historical speech, ethnohistorians should pay close attention to the signifying properties of their written evidence in order to maximize the usefulness of its ethnographic contents. When I served on the board of editors of the journal *Ethnohistory* from 1983 to 1990, the major reason I had for rejecting articles—besides literary ineptitude—was lack of any critical appreciation of the limits of historical documents. Too many anthropologists were historically naive and too many historians were ethnologically innocent.

The best way for ethnohistorians to lose their ethnological innocence is to delve into the broadest possible array of evidence left by the group in question, written and nonwritten. If we want to understand the historical culture of an Indian group in colonial North America, for example, we are obviously denied direct access to the people themselves, none of whom are living. Ethnohistorians are no more unfortunate in this regard than other historians whose subjects are also beyond the reach of interview. In fact, students of American Indian cultures are somewhat better off than most historians because they occasionally enjoy three kinds of second-best evidence of life in earlier centuries. Enduring native languages we have already mentioned. Modern native people who speak an ancient tongue still think, to a considerable extent, in ancient ways. Not entirely or consistently, of course, because every language grows and changes with time and circumstance. Modern Mohawk, while it reveals many traditional habits of mind and constructions of reality, nonetheless incorporates innumerable new words and concepts—borrowed from Dutch, French, English, German, and American neighbors—to account for the new worlds the Mohawks found themselves part of in the four centuries since Samuel de Champlain and Henry Hudson.

Even if descendants of our historical subjects no longer speak their traditional language, they frequently provide two other windows into the past. One is enduring cultural customs and ways of living. Like language, these too are subject to internal change and acculturation to external pressures, direct and indirect. It is highly unlikely that an Indian inhabitant of the eastern United States today lives and thinks exactly or even very much like his ancestors did in 1492 or 1607; unless he or she had remained incredibly isolated from the social history of the last four hundred years, and particularly from the accelerated changes of the past half-century, such a person would carry the telltale marks of change and difference that the modern descendant of New England

Puritans and Virginia cavaliers inevitably bear. It is not that ancient customs and cultural patterns do not endure; they do. But they seldom survive in pure, timeless forms or in their original, defining contexts. They come encrusted with accretions and diminished by subtractions, so we must devise ways to peel off the later additions from, and restore the missing pieces to, the original. One such way is to consult every written record of a group's cultural practices, from the time we are studying to the present. This can proceed in either direction—"downstream," with the flow of time, or, at William Fenton's suggestion, "upstream," working back from reliable ethnographic observations among modern descendants through the documents to the desired custom or practice.[13] However difficult it proves, the work must be done if we want to recapture historical verisimilitude rather than settle for an anachronistic substitute.

The other window on the past that native descendants can sometimes provide is oral traditions and memories. Not unlike the written and oral memories of literate peoples, these come in three forms: (in the language of Western scholarship) as *myths* involving spiritual beings and culture heroes; as *histories* concerning events important to the collective definition of the group; and as personal *stories* often involving the moral adventures of friends, relatives, or total strangers. But like cultural customs, oral memories are all subject to change and selective amnesia. So they too must be subjected to critical analysis and cross-checked against other reliable evidence.[14]

Myths provide unique glimpses of native concepts of reality, time and space, causation, planes of existence, cosmologies, and pantheons; but like any part of a growing cultural organism, they can change, thereby altering, perhaps critically, the version we are seeking that was current at a particular time and place. Native oral histories are also keys to our understanding of the natives' understanding of the world they fashioned and inhabited. But again, as we know from even written—and erasable—histories, every generation has reasons to rewrite or manipulate the past to suit its own needs and circumstances. However tenacious and accurate oral traditions can be, native historians were no less susceptible to those temptations to revise. We simply need to double-check whenever possible.

Moreover, native history was not calibrated to Western calendars; what we would call exact (calendrical) dates are usually missing. Nor was native history immune to the propensity of winners to fashion the story they would like their kinsmen and descendants to hear, rather than a more balanced or "objective" account telling about all parties, all motives, and all sets of actions and reactions. But it usually does convey the emotional resonance of the events for the narrator's ancestral group, and often concrete information that can be recovered in no other way.

The most striking example of unique oral information I have encountered came from a series of Abenaki language tapes collected by the late Gordon Day at the acculturated reserve town of St. Francis in southern Quebec in the late 1950s and early 1960s. In telling stories about the famous raid of Major

Robert Rogers and his Rangers upon the French-allied village in 1759, at least two narrators revealed that the villagers had been warned about the raid the night before by one of Rogers's Indian scouts. Many villagers believed the warning and hid themselves and their families in four identifiable locations outside the village. But several villagers disregarded it and continued to celebrate a wedding in the council house. When Rogers struck just before dawn, he caught the unwary asleep and claimed to have killed two hundred, close to the village's whole population. Yet French sources put the dead count at only thirty. The only source in English for this key event in the last intercolonial war—made more famous by Spencer Tracy's portrayal of Rogers in the film version of Kenneth Roberts's *Northwest Passage*—is Rogers's own journal. The conundrum solved by Abenaki oral tradition was how, if Rogers had obliterated the village population (as he thought he had), a large and angry French and Indian army had quickly emerged and chased his ragged forces with lethal efficiency back to New England. Only the Abenakis knew, and no one bothered to ask them for two hundred years.[15]

We know that the natives of America had a very long history before Europeans arrived to observe and record their lives for posterity, which is why we should no longer use the term "*pre*history" to designate the Indian past before 1492. But if we are interested in reconstructing that "pre*contact* history," we are pretty much dependent on just three sources: largely untestable oral tradition; the science and serendipity of archaeology to uncover its material vestiges; and historical linguistics to tell us something about language affiliations, formations, and separations. Each source has serious limitations, but when used together, along with the observations of the earliest Europeans, they often sketch a reliable, if partial, portrait of native culture before Western time and print intruded.

After contact, ironically, our access to native evidence expands exponentially. Artists such as John White, Carl Bodmer, George Catlin, and Father Nicholas Point and, later, photographers such as Edward Curtis and William Henry Jackson have left us indelible visual images of many native individuals, groups, and communities. Although most if not all of these images were staged and composed for purposes that had little to do with the future needs of objectifying historians, they still give us valuable insights into native realities while they alert us to ever-changing Western imaginings and agendas.[16]

The Renaissance penchant for collecting exotica or "curiosities" around the world, including walking souvenirs, soon led to more benign but no less colonialist collections and museums of cultural objects, of which a few large ones were acquired on a systematic scale. Many artifacts were purchased from native owners or trustees; many others were stolen from graves and other archaeological sites. More recently, evidence of the European goods traded in native villages around the Great Lakes has been salvaged intact from the cold-water rivers where wiry *voyageurs* failed to shoot rapids to save another back-breaking portage.[17] If the artifacts come with good provenience, they are immensely useful in revivifying the historical cultures from which they came. Without the collectors' mania for acquisition, no matter how venal or aggrandizing their motives, we would know much less than we do and immeasurably less than we would like to know about native American cultures.

One of the well-documented artifacts I am grateful for, as a sometime student of Indian captivities, is a braided prisoner tie dropped by Caughnawaga Mohawk raiders near Fort Massachusetts (modern-day Adams) in August 1746. If the Deerfield Memorial Museum had not acquired and preserved it, I and the readers of one of my articles (Chapter Eight below) would not know that the tie crossed through itself, like a dog choke-chain, and featured a wider, quill-decorated strip around the throat, like a woman's tumpline or burden strap, of which it was undoubtedly a variation. No written descriptions ever conveyed these interesting and, to me, important details.[18]

Another rich source of native history is maps. Predominantly, these are European products created to serve colonial or imperial ends.[19] But when they do not simply leave all signs of native communities, claims, and properties off or transmogrify them into European turf with new names, they may contain good evidence of native towns and territories, place-names, migrations, battles, economic activities, and sacred sites. Even their decorative cartouches or border designs sometimes harbor reliable images and ethnographic details by eyewitnesses. Yet natives, too, drew maps for the newcomers—with fingers or sticks on sand and dirt, on birchbark, skin, and paper with charcoal, paint, or quill pens and ink. Much of their information was incorporated in colonial maps, which were then used to wrest the continent from the natives' obliging hands. Native maps also reveal native thinking because they express distances not in units of uniform, abstract, Euclidean space, but in time traveled by foot or canoe. The University of Wisconsin, Milwaukee, has in progress a large project to inventory, annotate, and reproduce all of the known native maps in North America. And the latest volume in the impressive *History of Cartography* series, published by the University of Chicago Press, is devoted to *Cartography in the Traditional African, American, Arctic, Australian, and Pacific Societies.*[20]

About other sources for native history we can be summary. The ecological and geographical alterations wrought by native habitations, farming, and hunting can be read on the ground and in records by keen-eyed students of those fields.[21] Art historians and ethnomusicologists can trace cultural codes and changes in the decorative and utilitarian artifacts and in the dances, songs, and chants of historical peoples. And documentary sleuths can tease still more insights into native life from a broader array of written records. Treaty minutes, legislative records, explorers' journals, missionary reports, and captivity narratives are well known and have more to tell us. But we have yet to derive full benefit from such wayward documents as traders' account books and correspondence; military records; slave auction, indentured servant, and plantation records; court records (local and provincial); and writings, newspapers, and other publications of literate natives, who were either self-taught or educated in colonial schools or apprenticeships. In every category of record, we still have much to learn about the gendered approaches and responses of native Americans to their worlds.[22]

As attractive, challenging, and useful as ethnohistory may seem from my not-disinterested description, it has its critics, not a few of whom are insiders who have used or continue to use its distinctive methodology with signal success. Their criticisms fall into five themes; most object to ethnohistory's name and its implications rather than its goals or procedures.

The first criticism is that although ethnohistory is, in theory, inclusive, it is in practice *exclusionary* because it focuses on small tribal societies, on cultural "Others," and therefore "ghettoizes" their history by calling it by a special poly-syllabic and hyphenated name. The ethnohistorical spotlight is seldom turned on large state societies, particularly the colonizing ones that forced themselves upon the world's indigenous peoples to initiate contact. And by effectively relegating native history to a special corner of scholarship, ethnohistory fails to integrate natives into the larger national or global narratives that carry academic weight and inform policymakers.[23] James Merrell, one of its best practitioners, has even argued that historians of colonial America were "more sensitive to Indian history in the 1970s, before much of the literature on the subject appeared, than they are today, when the scholarship on Indians is more abundant." This decline he attributes to ethnohistory's "arcane" methodological pretensions, which have scared off most historians, even though many of them pursue similar kinds of multi- or interdisciplinary history of other groups, such as black slaves, indentured servants, women, and sailors.[24]

There is certainly some truth in this criticism. In the twenty years between 1968 and 1987, *Ethnohistory* published 234 articles on American Indians, and only 110 on all other topics.[25] It is also true that ethnohistory *sounds* complicated because it *is* complicated; it requires bifocal, double competencies both in history and anthropology, narrative and analysis, and their constant integration. It is not a field for the lazy or faint-hearted. If it takes extra time and effort to achieve competence, I and others would argue that the purchase more than justifies the expense. But I would also admit that ethnohistorians have only just begun to revise the histories of Euro-American colonies and states by viewing their cultures comparatively through the lenses of contiguous native cultures. Bruce Trigger and I have long argued that particularly "the colonial history of Canada and the United States cannot be understood without detailed consideration of the role played by Indians."[26] Wielding a prodigious knowledge of northeastern native cultures, Trigger proceeded to knock Champlain and the Jesuits off their Canadian pedestals, and I wrote a counterfactual scenario of "Colonial America without the Indians" to demonstrate their utter indispensability to the forging and shaping of its whole history.[27]

Nonetheless, we should also recognize that the colonizers' documentation regarding the natives does and will always outweigh native evidence on the colonizers, and that scholars will understandably, if not forgivably, gravitate to the fattest books and fullest archives. Only those with extra gumption and imagination will try to buck that trend and write colonial history from the "other" side of the frontier.

A variation on the first set of criticisms comes from those who think their academic oxen are being gored by ethnohistorians. In 1982 Harry Porter, a Cambridge don and, in fact, a former tutor of mine, charged the American practitioners of ethnohistory with constituting an exclusive "club," a veritable "church" of self-elected, self-righteous, moralizing snobs who looked down their noses at "mere" historians of Indian-white relations, Western attitudes toward natives, and the West's civilizing mission and accomplishments. Porter's was clearly a cry of wounded chauvinism because he objected strenuously to the "rather irritating anti-English bias" in many ethnohistorians of early America, who seemed to feel duty-bound "to write exposes of the European way of life in America." His pique was not entirely unwarranted: all but two of the twenty-five authors he reviewed were trained historians, who had lived and written in the United States in the turbulent 1970s and who believed that moral judgments deserved a place in ethnohistory. Readers of his essay might have sensed, but could not know for certain, that it was also an unfortunate skirmish in an academic turf fight. Porter dubbed me the "High Priest" of the ethnohistorical communion not only for my recent attempt to define ethnohistory for historians, but because two years earlier I had published a highly critical review of his six hundred-page book, *The Inconstant Savage* (as had three other reviewees), contrasting what I regarded as his unfocused, eccentric approach to intellectual history with the rigor of ethnohistory.[28]

A third criticism, now dated, is that ethnohistory's penchant for language about "primitives" is not only "patronizing" but "pernicious," because it abets racist and colonialist attitudes toward other peoples, particularly of color. Africanists in particular warned that reserving the term *ethnohistory* for "people without written history" or who are considered otherwise "primitive" would be highly and rightly resented by the peoples of that complex continent.[29] Since anthropologists in general have largely given up the use of "primitive" as pejorative, misleading, or meaningless, ethnohistorians have followed suit, sometimes opting for substitutes hardly more edifying.[30] "Subalterns" (from Asian historiography) or "peasants" (from Marxism) do not seem destined to sweep the field anytime soon, while "natives" has generic utility only in the early stages of contact, before long-time creoles and colonists earn the right to wear the same label. In the Americas, "Indians" is short, carries no pejorative baggage despite Columbus, and is reasonably clear, unless we do comparative, world, or immigration history, which most ethnohistorians do not.

Objections to the name *ethnohistory* flow in two different directions and constitute a fourth category of criticism. Bruce Trigger, even before his adoption as a Huron, argued that "Native American history" would serve better than the segregating implications of "ethnohistory."[31] But this only compounds the problem by suggesting that the methodology has no other applications than in the Americas, which is clearly not the case. Shepard Krech, the former editor of *Ethnohistory*, prefers "anthropological history" or "historical anthropology" (depending on the slant) for two reasons. One is that the newest and most fruitful histories being written are no less hyphenated than ethnohistory; most disciplines and scholarly genres today are hopelessly "blurred" (in Clifford Geertz's phrase) and happily "osmotic." The second reason is that the bilateral borrowings of method and theory implied by the older definitions of ethnohistory are now being supplied by wider venues of stimulation and challenge. "Theory today is as likely to derive neither, strictly speaking, from anthropology nor history but from semiotics, structuralism, Marxism, critical theory, linguistics, sociology, cultural studies, literary criticism, political economy, or world-system theory—or from some postmodern blend."[32] His point is well taken. While I no longer have a strong attachment to the name except in my teaching of new recruits, I would suggest that most students of native American history, young and old, are still not greatly influenced by postmodernity and are quite busy enough trying to master two complex disciplines and to gain some bibliographical control—with or without the Internet—over a vast and growing database relating to their subject. If I am right, "ethnohistory" might still retain some usefulness as a denominator of the methodology best designed for the work at hand.

A fifth and final indictment of ethnohistory stems indirectly from a challenge issued by Calvin Martin to all students of native American cultures. In his edited volume of essays on *The American Indian and the Problem of History*, published in 1987, Martin argued that tribal peoples lived, and perhaps still live, in a mythic world of "biological" time, which is "eternal, cyclical, endlessly repetitive, powered by Nature, and cosmogonic." Western historians cannot hope to comprehend the native worldview unless they use their imaginations to transcend their own limited "linear, remorselessly historical, profane, and anthropological" sense of time. "We historians," he urged, "need to get out of history, as we know it, if we wish to write authentic histories of American Indians." We, too, need to learn to see ourselves as "cosmic mucilage" connecting humans to animals, plants, and the elements, to rewire our heads with "mythic circuitry," and to write our history in "mythic language."[33]

Martin is onto something important here, but he goes much too far. His remedy entails, as Frederick Turner, another contributor to the volume, admits, "conscious abandonment of our Western view of life and human history," a surrender fraught with "threat of loss, of radical disorientation, of intellectual chaos."[34] If Western historians were to swallow Martin's prescription, they would somehow cease being Westerners and would become Indianized tribespeople. They would, therefore, be incapable of writing the kind of history that modern audiences turn to for their understanding of the past. By the same logic, in their new mindset, they would be as incapable of understanding the European invaders as any mythic, time-bound natives must have been. Silence or profound ignorance seem to be the only alternatives.

The way out of Martin's myopic dilemma is provided by Christopher Vec-
sey, another contributor, who reminds us that Western history has long incul-
cated the use of "imaginative double vision." We use deep research and empathy to see other people as they saw themselves, but we also use hindsight and
objectifying scholarship to see them as they could not see themselves, as only
we can. Thus we achieve historical vision, at once "loving and scrutinizing," for
our own human purposes, without needing to commit professional or cultural
suicide.[35]

In spite of its acknowledged imperfections, ethnohistory remains, I would
argue, the sharpest, most comprehensive, most inclusive, most flexible tool we
have for writing and teaching the history of America's native peoples. All of
the other approaches in use today are but facets of the ethnohistorical ideal.
They need to be pursued with every bit as much care and rigor as does the syn-
optic methodology. But if ethnohistory can adjust to the new intellectual
times—and I have no doubt that it can—it will retain its preeminence in the
field. If it becomes more reflexive regarding theory, its moral and political
implications, and epistemology, if its practitioners become more critical users
of documents and records of every sort as well as more tuned to the ethnological resonance of their contents, I see no reason why it should not flourish for
many years to come, even under its old name.

But if it does suffer a name change or an erosion of identity in the fast, new
academic market, I would hope that a few diehard ethnohistorians would preserve and reserve its name and methodology for one major subject to which
both are uniquely suited. I refer to the entwined histories of natives and newcomers in the constantly shifting, contested, polysemous zones of cultural
interaction we sometimes still call frontiers. While it is often difficult to know
where or when they begin and, even more, end, we know that America's multicultural history was essentially, in its longest chapters, the story of a complex
series of successive and overlapping frontiers. If we want to get that story
straight for ourselves and future generations, we had better hold on to the single best instrument we have for uncovering it, particularly if we want to do justice to *all* the participants, not just those who allegedly "won"—or "lost."

PART I

CONTACTS

INTRODUCTION

Before they did anything else in North America, Indians and European explorers and would-be colonists met each other, both in the flesh and in their respective imaginations. The result on both sides was often "amazement and doubt in the presence of the other"—the title of a conference session to which I was asked to contribute a paper in October 1988 at SUNY-Albany. At the conference I gave a brief version of my paper, per instructions, but later submitted an expanded version for publication in the conference proceedings. This appeared four years later in Spanish in *De Palabra y Obra en el Nuevo Mundo, 1. Imágenes Interétnicas,* edited by Miguel León-Portilla, Manuel Gutiérrez Estévez, Gary H. Gossen, and J. Jorge Klor de Alva (Madrid, 1992).

In 1990 I inherited the chairmanship of the American Historical Association's Columbus Quincentenary Committee, on which I had served since its founding in 1985. With it I fell heir to much delayed plans for a four-pamphlet series, "Essays on the Columbian Encounter," designed to acquaint history teachers and students with the major issues, best bibliography, and salient information on the American aftermath of 1492. In order to launch the series without further delay, the committee chose a much extended and revised (English) version of my Albany essay as the first title, and it was duly published by the AHA in 1991. That version was reprinted without change in *Beyond 1492* (1992) and appears here as Chapter One, with only minor changes.

A prelude to that longer description of first encounters in North America was an illustrated essay entitled "Through Another Glass Darkly: Early Indian Views of Europeans," which appeared in *After Columbus* (1988). Growing from a conference paper at Ohio State University in 1986, it employed evidence from European documents, native artifacts, and cross-cultural humor to suggest how various natives and native groups regarded the earliest "white men" they encountered and their societies throughout eastern North American and abroad.* That essay, in turn, was written as a companion to, or mirror

---

*Similarly, "The Exploration of Norumbega: Native Perspectives," assesses some of the reactions of Indians in northern New England to the advent of Europeans. It was first published in *Beyond 1492* (1992) and two years later in *American Beginnings: Explo-*

image of, one of my earliest writings on Indians, "Through a Glass Darkly: Colonial Attitudes toward the Native Americans." The latter was given originally as a lecture at Dartmouth College and then published in the inaugural issue of the *American Indian Culture and Research Journal* in 1974. Its evidence was drawn only from written documents from the Northeast, and it made too small an attempt to be fair to the whole colonial population, most of whom were not bent on harming their Indian neighbors.

Chapter Two introduces the tortured and often laughable subject of how the natives and the newcomers managed to communicate with each other once they met. Strange to say, such a basic and important subject has received virtually no attention from historians and largely specialized treatment by historical anthropologists and linguists, as I discovered when I set out to write a comprehensive chapter for *American Encounter,* the second volume of my Oxford trilogy. Soon after completing the chapter and quietly filing it, ironically, I was asked to chair a session at a conference on "Communicating with the Indians" at the John Carter Brown Library in Providence. Had the organizers, Norman Fiering and Edward Gray, known of my essay on the use of signs, pidgins, jargons, and interpreters from the St. Lawrence and Great Lakes to the Gulf of Mexico and the Mississippi, they might have requested a paper instead. In fact, once they learned of it, they asked to use the full chapter to open their edited volume, *The Language Encounter in the Americas, 1492 to 1800,* published in 2000. It appears here in virtually the same words and signs, though, I trust, without any obfuscating jargon.

---

ration, Culture, and Cartography in the Land of Norumbega, edited by Emerson W. Baker, Edwin A. Churchill, Richard S. D'Abate, Kristine L. Jones, Victor A. Konrad, and Harald E. L. Prins.

ONE

IMAGINING THE OTHER

First Encounters

When Christopher Columbus, "Admiral of the Ocean Sea," stumbled across the Taíno people of Guanahaní island on October 12, 1492, he unwittingly launched the most massive encounter of foreign peoples in human history. More than five centuries later we are still taking stock of that momentous meeting.

Since the late 1960s and early '70s, when the unpopular war in Southeast Asia, the civil rights movement, and American Indian protests shook our consciousness and refocused our imaginations, our interpretations of those early American encounters have become increasingly bifocal and sensitive to native perspectives. We have come to see with virtually new eyes that the Indians discovered Columbus and his world as surely and as importantly as he did them and theirs. With good reason, the theme of the Columbian quincentenary was the *mutuality* of discovery and acculturation during five hundred years of ongoing "encounter."

The theme of the quadricentenary in 1892 was far different. In Spain and the United States particularly, the dominant cause of celebration (not mere commemoration or reflection) was the *progress* of Western technology, Christian religion, and democratic institutions over the Western Hemisphere, particularly among the "benighted" and "primitive" peoples Columbus "discovered" (as if they were lost). The heroic historical stature of the great discoverer himself was symbolized in countless marble statues; the human subjects of his discovery and exploitation were remembered only in sanitized museum cases highlighting their exotic aboriginality or in live demonstrations of their new-found civility, literacy, and industry. Unacknowledged were the cataclysmic ravages of disease, warfare, injustice, and dispossession that were the major (but not only) legacy of that encounter. No accounting was made of the frightful human toll of history, the incalculable costs of "progress," "civilization," and "empire."

Textbook Firsts

Before the reorientation of the '60s and '70s, North Americans knew something of the outlines of the debit side of the encounter (with the exception of disease) from their textbooks. But they tended to assume, with the textbook authors, that any warfare or bloodshed was the result of "savages" hopelessly resisting the inexorable incursion of "civilized" explorers and colonists bent on delivering them from native despotism, false religion, and cultural backwardness. In their collective mind's eye, a vision that many of us still share, they saw countless depictions of intrepid Europeans wading ashore in a hail of flint-tipped arrows and throat-catching war whoops. They remembered all too vividly how the Roanoke colonists were lost to history after numerous attacks by chief Wingina's naked minions in 1585–87, how the Chesapeakes of Cape Henry crept up "like Beares, with their Bowes in their mouthes" to assault the first wave of Virginia settlers in 1607, and how Nauset warriors pelted arrows at the poor Pilgrims who initially landed on Cape Cod in 1620 before finding shelter and religious toleration at Plymouth.[1]

But what the Pilgrims called "The First Encounter" was not, except for them. Fresh from European ports, the Pilgrims could not know that the natives who received them so ungraciously were not acting out of some atavistic racial hatred or primitive xenophobia but from a well-founded sense of revenge for injuries inflicted by earlier European visitors. By 1607 or 1620, when most textbooks before the '70s began the American story, many of the native peoples of the Atlantic seaboard had experienced fifty or a hundred years of contact with European ships, men, and erstwhile colonies. Predictably, many of those contacts ended in suspicion, fear, and conflict.

If we hope to plumb the long-term significance of the cultural encounters set in motion by the Columbian advent in 1492, we must do two things. First, we must search carefully for the very earliest Indian-European encounters, before either party had been forced into pugnacity or unbending distrust by conflict with the other. This will entail a certain amount of chronological backpeddling into the sixteenth century, but because of the uneven character of American exploration, even in the East, it is possible to find such innocent moments well into the seventeenth and even eighteenth centuries. And second, if we hope to recapture the palpable reality of those earliest encounters, we must, like the actors themselves, try to look squarely into the "others" faces and to hear, not just listen to, the halting dialogues—or sad monologues— they carried on. Since "the imaginations which people have of one another are the solid facts of society," we must try to imagine the imaginations that Europeans and Indians had of each other.[2]

This will be no easy task because the great majority of documents we have been left were written by the European invaders of the Americas and not by the Indians. Thus we have plenty of European depictions of the alien faces and conduct they saw and the strange words they heard, but we have too few

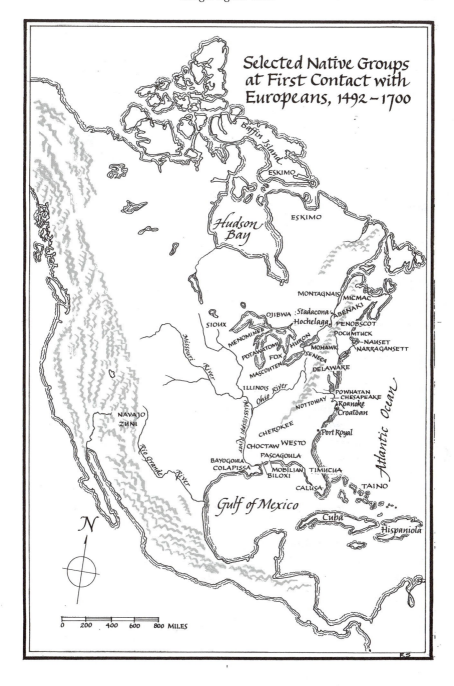

Selected Native Groups
at First Contact with
Europeans, 1492~1700

Indian visions of the European intruders. The temptation is to use what is easily available, but, in this case particularly, we should firmly resist it. For it would hoodwink us to the fact that *all* peoples are ethnocentric, that cultural judgments are always relative, and that every "other" we objectify is at the same time a first-person subject, an "I." When reading early contact accounts, we should keep in mind Michel de Montaigne's sly observation that "Each man calls barbarism whatever is not his own practice. . . . Barbarians are no more marvelous to us than we are to them, nor for better cause." In America as in ancient Greece, language often constituted the first sign of difference. As the apostle Paul warned the Corinthians: "If I know not the meaning of the voice, I shall be unto him that speaketh a barbarian, and he that speaketh shall be a barbarian unto me."[3]

Imagining the "Other"

Before the "barbarians" of Europe and America actually met, they each had some notion of what the "other" would probably be like. Thanks to their own recent experience of peoples and places and to the rediscovered libraries of the ancient world, Europeans had a rich "cabinet of curiosities," accumulated over many centuries on three continents, from which to draw. From Marco Polo's thirteenth-century travels in particular, they continued to learn of immense empires and fabulous riches in the Far East. To resourceful fleets of Portuguese seamen, Africa gradually revealed its cultural secrets. Christian crusaders heading for the Holy City and pilgrims of every stripe left their footprints all around the sun-drenched rim of the Mediterranean. Hot on the heels of all these adventurers were eager avatars of trade, fanning out from the commercial capitals of Europe in search of useful knowledge as well as luxury goods and mineral wealth.

Beneath this growing knowledge of cultures and geographies lay a bedrock of ancient precedent—the Old and New Testaments and the classical heritage of Greece and Rome recently regained by the scholars of the Renaissance—and an even denser stratum of medieval legend. While the second-century Egyptian astronomer Claudius Ptolemy gave sixteenth-century Europeans a workable heaven by which to navigate and the fifth-century B.C. traveler-historian Herodotus a way to write the history of "others," credulous tale-tellers of the Middle Ages topped their imaginations with a bestiary of human monsters, monstrosities, and wild hairy men.

Accordingly, peoples of black, brown, yellow, and white skin, religions as diverse as Buddhism, pantheism, and atheism, and a spectrum of polities from divine monarchy to natural anarchy could be found in the collective wisdom of Europe. But also present, for learned and credulous alike, were strange people who ate human flesh, peered at the world from one large eye in the middle of

Medieval travel books prominently featured archetypal human monstrosities, who presumably lived in exotic, unexplored countries. Among the oddities in Gregor Reisch's menagerie were a sciapode ("who is shading himself under his only foot"), a cyclops, a little dicephalus (two-headed person), an acephalus (with his face in his chest), and a cynocephalus (dog-headed). From Reisch, *Margarita Philosophica* (Basel, 1517).

their chests, and barked rather than spoke from canine snouts. To Europeans, "others" might appear in an infinite variety of shapes, hues, and habits, but they were always and distinctly unlike Europeans and, for the most part, therefore regarded as inferior. Before and after 1492, the occidental wall between "them" and "us" was high, and only a few thinkers like Montaigne in the sixteenth century were available to give fellow Europeans a leg up.[4]

The relatively isolated natives of the Americas, by contrast, were prepared by experience to see in "others" largely faithful reflections of themselves or of the anthropomorphic deities who populated their pantheons. While Europeans found "others" to be different and usually inferior, the "others" the Indians knew tended to be similar or superior. This is not to say that Indian cultures were blessedly lacking in ethnocentrism: they were as hide-bound as the next group. But their human experience was limited solely to other Indian peoples, so their ethnographic categories appear to have been relatively few, perhaps some variation on three.

The Indians' first category consisted of their own immediate social group, whether band, tribe, chiefdom, or confederacy. As if to celebrate their ethnocentrism, the names many, perhaps most, groups (Iroquois, Navajo, Penobscot) gave themselves meant "the original people" or "the true men," in other words, the only folks who mattered. Their enemies and neighbors, on the other hand, were called names (Eskimo, Sioux, Nottoway) that meant "raw meat-eaters," "bark-eaters," or "rattlesnakes." In cultural retrospect, most of these perceived differences were minor or nonexistent and were simply inflated or invented by politics and inherited hatreds. Beneath the reciprocal epithets were brown-skinned Americans whose lives were strikingly similar, all things considered.

Even the third category of "others"—the spiritual beings with whom the Indian people closely shared the world—did not vary greatly from group to group. While these "supernatural" (a distinction they did not make) persons could easily change appearance and voice, particularly when encountered in dreams or induced trances, the Indians of North America shared a belief that all living things possessed "souls" or "spirits" capable of unrestricted movement in time and space and of harming or helping other "persons." Because the magnitude of their power was largely unknown and because they might appear in a strange guise, each "person" had to be treated with respect and circumspection, often in formal ceremonies of supplication and thanksgiving. Thus, when Europeans first appeared at the edge of the water, woods, plains, or desert, the Indians were prepared to treat with extraordinary "persons" whose physical manifestations might be very different from, but certainly not inferior to, their own.[5]

Native Prophecies and Memories

Even before the first white men materialized, they may have impressed themselves upon the Indian imagination. Shamans who were thought capable of seeing into the future and other prescient people may have prophesied the coming of the Europeans. I say "may have" because these prophecies were recorded only after contact with the literate newcomers. In 1540 Francisco Vásquez de Coronado was glad to hear from Zuni elders in the desert Southwest that "it was foretold them more than fifty years ago that a people such as we are would come, and from the direction we have come, and that the whole country would be conquered." It is not unlikely that the natives' memories were jogged by the 1,700 men in the Spanish *entrada*, including 250 heavily armed horse-soldiers. A year later, under similar conditions, six leaders from an Indian town near the Mississippi visited Hernando de Soto's camp, saying "they were come to see what people [the Spanish] were and that they had learned from their ancestors that a white race would inevitably subdue them."[6]

A *wiochist* or shaman had a similar message for the Powhatans as they confronted English bellicosity in early Virginia after 1607: he predicted that "bearded men should come & take away their Country & that there should none of the original Indians be left, within . . . an hundred & fifty" years. Another shaman was somewhat more ambiguous when he informed the "emperor" Powhatan that "from the *Chesapeack* Bay a Nation should arise, which should dissolve and give end to his Empier." While the apparently feckless Jamestown colonists looked on, Powhatan exterminated the whole tribe of "*Chessiopeians*" to hedge his bets.[7]

Confronting a different English challenge, natives in New England were given a prophecy appropriate to their circumstances. During the lethal plague that preceded the arrival of the Plymouth pilgrims in 1620, a Nauset man on Cape Cod dreamed of the advent of "a great many men" dressed in what proved to be English-style clothes. One of them, dressed all in black, stood on an eminence with a book in his hand and told the assembled Indians that "God was *moosquantum* or angry with them, and that he would kill them for their sinnes. . . . "[8]

More prevalent than prophesies were oral traditions regarding the Europeans' arrival, a few collected shortly after contact, most of them several centuries later. When the natives recalled their first encounters with European "others," it was novel "persons" like their own deities whom they remembered. In 1633 a young Montagnais on the north shore of the St. Lawrence related the story his grandmother had told him of the Indians' astonishment at seeing a French ship for the first time. Like many natives before and after, they thought it was a "moving Island." Having seen the men aboard, however, the Montagnais women began to prepare wigwams for them, "as is their custom when new guests arrive," and four canoes bade the strangers welcome. The French gave them a barrel of ship's biscuits and probably offered them some wine. But the natives were appalled that these people "drank blood and ate wood" and promptly threw the tasteless biscuits into the river. Obviously more impressed by French technology than cuisine, the Montagnais henceforth called the French *ouemichtigouchiou*, "men in a wooden canoe or boat."[9]

The Micmacs were equally unimpressed by French fare, as they recalled in the nineteenth century. When the first Frenchmen arrived in the Gaspé, presumably in the early sixteenth century, the Micmacs "mistook the bread which was given them for a piece of birch tinder." When wine was proffered, perhaps a nice Bordeaux red, the natives became convinced that the strangers were "cruel and inhuman, since in their amusements . . . they drank blood without repugnance. . . . Therefore they remained some time not only without tasting it, but even without wishing to become in any manner intimate, or to hold intercourse, with a nation which they believed to be accustomed to blood and carnage."[10]

Further west, perhaps around Lake Superior, an Ojibwa prophet dreamed that

men of strange appearance have come across the great water. They have landed on our island [North America]. Their skins are white like snow, and on their faces long hair grows. These people have come across the great water in wonderfully large canoes which have great white wings like those of a giant bird. The men have long and sharp knives, and they have long black tubes which they point at birds and animals. The tubes make a smoke that rises into the air just like the smoke from our pipes. From them come fire and such terrific noise that I was frightened, even in my dream.

At once a flotilla of trusted men was sent through the Great Lakes and down the St. Lawrence to investigate. On the lower river they found a clearing in which all the trees had been cut down, which led them to conjecture that "giant beavers with huge, sharp teeth had done the cutting." The prophet disagreed, reminding them of the long knives in his dream. Knowing that their stone-headed axes could not cut such large trees so smoothly, they were "filled with awe, and with terror also." Still more puzzling were "long, rolled-up shavings" of wood and scraps of "bright-coloured cloth," which they stuck in their hair and wound around their heads. Farther down the river they finally came upon the white-faced bearded strangers with their astonishing long knives, thunder tubes, and giant winged canoes, just as the prophet had foretold.

Having satisfied their curiosity and fulfilled the prophet's dream, the Indians returned home with their trophies: each villager was given a small piece of cloth as a memento. To impress their neighbors, the Ojibwas followed an old custom. Just as they tied the scalps of their enemies on long poles, "now they fastened the splinters of wood and strips of calico to poles and sent them with special messengers" from one tribe to another. Thus were these strange articles passed from hand to hand around the whole lake, giving the natives of the interior their first knowledge of the white men from Europe.[11]

White Deities

The Indians regarded the Europeans' ability to fashion incredible objects and make them work less as mechanical aptitude than as spiritual power. When the Delawares, who once lived along the New Jersey–New York coast, met their first Dutch ship in the early seventeenth century, they concluded that it was a "remarkably large house in which the Mannitto (the Great or Supreme Being) himself was present." Thinking he was coming to pay them a visit, they prepared meat for a sacrifice, put all their religious effigies in order, and staged a grand dance to please or appease him. Meanwhile, the tribal conjurers tried to fathom his purpose in coming because their people were all "distracted between hope and fear." While preparations went forward, runners brought the welcome news that the visitors were humans like themselves, only strangely colored and oddly dressed. But when the Dutchmen made their appearance, graced the assembly with a round of liquor, and distributed iron and cloth gifts, the natives were confirmed in their original belief that every white man was an "inferior Mannitto attendant upon the Supreme Deity"—the ship's captain—who "shone superior" in his red velvet suit glittering with gold lace.[12]

The earliest European objects of native awe corroborated native testimony about their godlike reception. The gentle inhabitants of the West Indies, Columbus assured his sovereign sponsors, were "very firmly convinced that I, with these ships and men, came from the heavens, and in this belief they everywhere received me after they had mastered their fear." Even the Taínos he kidnapped as guides and interpreters and took to Spain to support his discoveries were "still of the opinion that I come from Heaven, for all the intercourse which they have had with me. They were the first to announce this wherever I went . . . 'Come! Come! See the men from Heaven!'"[13]

Four survivors of the ill-fated Florida expedition of Pánfilo de Narváez (1528) also traded on their reputation for divinity as they walked from eastern Texas to Mexico. After some success in curing Indians with Christian prayers, elementary surgery, and the power of positive thinking, Álvar Núñez Cabeza de Vaca and his three cohorts were regarded wherever they went as "children of the sun." The crowds of native acolytes who accompanied them swore at each new village that the Spaniards "had power to heal the sick and to destroy," just like their own shamans. In order to preserve their tremendous influence over the natives, the Spanish "gods" cultivated an inscrutable public silence, letting their black servant, Estevánico, make their mundane arrangements. The strange caravan of white and black beings, apparently endowed with extraordinary spiritual power and attended by an adoring cast of hundreds, sometimes thousands, gave them "control throughout the country in all that the inhabitants had power, or deemed of any value, or cherished."[14]

Having read the accounts of his Spanish predecessors before launching his own gold-seeking *entrada* into the Southeast in 1539, Hernando de Soto burnished his divine attributes to a high lustre. Whenever he came to a new province and needed bearers, food, and guides, he announced through his interpreter that "he was a son of the sun and came from where it dwelt," that he and his men were immortal, and that the natives could hide nothing because the face that appeared in the mirror he held before them "told him whatever they were planning and thinking about." Only when Soto visibly weakened and took to his bed did a chief near the Mississippi call his bluff, "saying that with respect to what he said about being the son of the sun, let him dry up the great river and he would believe him." Nor, when Soto died three days later, did the natives swallow the Spanish story that he was not dead but had only "gone to the sky as he had often done before."[15]

In the seventeenth century, Indians who first encountered French and English explorers also regarded them as deities from a familiar cosmos. When the English at Roanoke failed to sicken during Indian epidemics and seemed to show no sexual interest in native women—and had no women of their own—several of the local Indians "could not tel whether to thinke [them] gods or men." Believing in general that "all the gods are of humane shape," others thought the English immortal because they "were not borne of women." Likewise, when French traders and missionaries canoed into the upper Great Lakes in the 1660s, the Indians "often took them for spirits and gods." Having heard that the French were "a different species from other men," the Potawatomis near Green Bay were astonished to see in Nicolas Perrot, a French emissary, that the strangers possessed human form and "regarded it as a present that the sky and the spirits had made them in permitting one of the celestial beings to enter their land." Forty years later, wrote a missionary in 1700, the French in Louisiana had some difficulty in disabusing the Bayogoulas of the notion that "we are spirits descended from heaven, and that the fire of our cannon is the same sort as celestial fire."[16]

Welcoming the Strangers

The welcome and treatment the natives lavished on them convinced the Europeans even further that they were regarded as the bearers of divine tidings or at least of special human talents that were nonexistent or in very short supply in native society. It is difficult to tell from credulous European sources when the natives first realized that the intruders in their midst were not gods from another realm but were humans nonetheless possessed of extraordinary "spirits" or "souls," on a par with their own shamans and witches who practiced the black and white arts. In large part, the Europeans were treated as any native dignitaries would have been, but some aspects of their reception were clearly intended to honor celestial rather than earthly visitors.

Europeans first realized that Indians had placed them in a category by themselves when they caused a sensation by walking into native villages. When Columbus sent two of his men to explore a large island town, the inhabitants "touched them and kissed their hands and feet, marveling and . . . attempting to see if they were, like themselves, of flesh and bone." After a five-day stay, the men returned to the ship but had some difficulty persuading five hundred natives not to accompany them in hopes of seeing them "return to the heavens." The southwestern Indians who wanted to touch Cabeza de Vaca's band of wandering medicine men "pressed us so closely," he half-boasted, "that they lacked little of killing us; and without letting us put our feet to the ground, carried us to their dwellings. We were so crowded upon by numbers, that we [escaped] into the houses they had made for us."[17]

The natives of the Great Lakes and upper Mississippi also "devoured [the first Europeans] with their eyes." In the 1660s the Green Bay Potawatomis did not "dare look [Nicolas Perrot] in his face; and the women and children watched him from a distance." About the same time, Father Claude Allouez felt slightly more discommoded by the villagers at Chequamegon on Lake

Superior. "We were so frequently visited by these people," he recalled, "most of whom had never seen any Europeans, that we were overwhelmed" and religious instruction went slowly. He was happier with the visits of the teachable children, who came to him "in troops to satisfy their curiosity by looking at a stranger." Eight years later, Father Jacques Marquette was likewise showered with attention by the Illinois not far from the Mississippi. "All these people, who had never seen any Frenchmen among them," he wrote, "could not cease looking at us. They lay on the grass along the road; they preceded us, and then retraced their steps to come and see us again. All this was done noiselessly, and with marks of great respect for us." When the Frenchmen were walked through the three-hundred-house village after a feast, "an orator continually harangued to oblige all the people to come to see us without annoying us."[18]

Even relative latecomers among the English sometimes had to endure the astonished stares of native hosts. In 1674 three Englishmen in two different parts of the Southeast met Indians who had apparently not laid eyes on their like. At the Westo village on the Savannah River, the chief's house could not hold the crowd that wanted to admire Henry Woodward, a surgeon and early planter of South Carolina. The smaller fry solved the problem by climbing up on the roof and peeling it back to get a clear view. Meanwhile, beyond the Great Smoky Mountains, a town of western Cherokees welcomed two servants of a Virginia gentleman-trader "even to addoration in their cerrimonies of courtesies." The visitors' equally unusual packhorse was tethered to a stake in the middle of town and given a royal diet of corn, fish, and bear oil. Similarly, the white guests were invited to squat on a specially built scaffold so that the natives "might stand and gaze at them and not offend them by theire throng." None of these celebrated Europeans ever talked about his embarrassment or self-consciousness under such exposure, but we can well imagine that even the most self-possessed and arrogant men must occasionally have developed a healthy blush.[19]

An even surer sign that the first Europeans were exalted in Indian eyes was the official welcome they received. Those who arrived by water were first guided to the best anchorages and landings. If smaller boats then could not reach dry land, the natives often plowed into the surf or stream to carry the sailors piggyback. On Hispaniola in 1492, villagers "insisted on carrying [Columbus and his men] on their backs . . . through some rivers and muddy places." French officers in sixteenth-century Florida traveled to an important chief's village perched on the shoulders, not merely the backs, of several Indians who sought to keep them out of the marshy mire surrounding it. In 1535, en route to Hochelaga on the upper St. Lawrence, wiry Jacques Cartier had been lifted from his longboat by a husky Indian and carried to shore in the man's arms "as easily as if he had been a six-year-old child." Having been carted around in a red blanket on other occasions, Nicolas Perrot and a French companion drew the line at being piggybacked. They politely told their Mas-

Indian hospitality to the first Europeans is depicted in this 1556 engraving of Jacques Cartier's approach to the St. Lawrence Iroquois village of Hochelaga (present-day Montreal). Two Indians carry the French piggyback while other natives welcome Cartier and his men at one of the (fancifully drawn) palisade gates. Engraver Giacomo Gastaldi worked from Cartier's written description rather than personal observation, but he captured the spirit of native kindness to strangers. From Giovanni Battista Ramusio, *Terzo volume della navigationi et viaggi* (Venice, 1556).

couten hosts that "as they could shape . . . iron, they had strength to walk." Few other Europeans let pride get in the way of a free ride.[20]

If getting there was half the fun, the arrival must have been somewhat discomfiting to those who had no idea what to expect. As soon as the newcomers were deposited in the village square or the chief's house, a startling round of touching and rubbing began, the import of which was not immediately clear. On their eight-year trek through the Southwest after 1528, Cabeza de Vaca and his comrades received at least two different greetings. One village, after quelling their fear of the strangers, "reached their hands to our faces and bodies, and passed them in like manner over their own." Another group somewhat farther west greeted the Spaniards "with such yells as were terrific, striking the palms of their hands violently against their thighs," a response that would have scared the wits out of Europeans less accustomed to native ways.[21]

Fortunately for most landed immigrants, the former gentle greeting was much more typical in eastern America. On the Gaspé Peninsula, both the Micmacs and the visiting Stadaconans who met Cartier "rubbed his arms and his breast with their hands" in welcome. Fifty years later, in 1584, Arthur Barlowe was greeted at Roanoke by Granganimeo, the local chief's brother, who struck his head and chest and then Barlowe's "to shewe [they] were all one." Several hundred miles away, on the icy coasts of Baffin Island, Eskimo traders were initiating relations with John Davis and his crew by pointing to the sun,

striking their chests "so hard that [the sailors] might heare the blow," and crying "*Iliaoute*" in a loud voice. When Davis stuck out his hand to greet one of
them English-style, the man kissed it instead.[22]

The customary greeting in South Carolina, as the English noted in the late
1660s, was the "stroaking of our shoulders with their palmes and sucking in
theire breath the whilst." In Louisiana the French experienced a variation on
the same theme. At their first camp near Biloxi in 1699, Pierre LeMoyne
d'Iberville and his officers had their faces rubbed with white clay before being
saluted in friendly fashion, which was, he wrote, to "pass their hands over their
faces and breasts, and then pass their hands over yours, after which they raise
them toward the sky, rubbing them together again and embracing again."
Antoine de Sauvole, the fort commander, obviously found one party of
Pascagoulas almost too much for his Gallic sensibilities. "I have never seen
natives [*sauvages*] less inhibited," he confided to his journal. "They have
embraced us, something that I have never seen the others do." The most sen-
sual treatment, however, was reserved for Europeans who had hiked into
Indian country: their hosts massaged their feet, legs, joints, and even eyelids
with soothing bear oil.[23]

But the cosseting had only begun. The visitors were next seated on fresh
skins or reed mats, "harangued" (as they put it) with unintelligible speeches,
entertained with dancing, singing, and games, and feasted to surfeit on such
delicacies as *sagamité* (corn meal mush seasoned with fat) and roasted dog. An
Illinois master of ceremonies, recalled Father Marquette, "filled a spoon with
sagamité three or four times, and put it to my mouth as if I was a little child."
After removing the bones from the second—fish—course and blowing on
some pieces to cool them, the genial host put them in the Frenchmen's mouths
"as one would give food to a bird." They passed on the dog course, as "gods"
had some leave to do, but happily chewed the fat buffalo morsels again placed
in their mouths. Most European guests, however, were allowed to feed themselves and so could take more time to appreciate native foods, upon which
most of them would be dependent far longer than they could imagine.[24]

Becoming Americanized

Next came the serious business of assimilating the strangers into native society, of making the "others" even more like themselves, and securing peace until
the newcomers displayed behavior that was less than "divine" or even, in native
terms, "human." Throughout much of eastern America in the seventeenth and
eighteenth centuries, the major vehicle of peaceful alliance was the calumet, a
four-foot-long wood and stone pipe richly decorated with paint and a fan of
long feathers. (After his Canadian experience, Iberville brought his own to
Louisiana, an iron one "made in the shape of a ship with the white flag
adorned with fleur-de-lis and ornamented with glass beads.") The Europeans

soon learned that possession of a calumet was a passport through even hostile Indian country, and that sharing its consecrated smoke was the major ticket to diplomatic success. To refuse a calumet ceremony—which in the lower Mississippi Valley invariably lasted three days—was to declare war upon, or at least to risk affronting, the offering party. In 1701 Iberville took such a risk in passing a village of Mobilians because he did not have three days to spare. But he managed to unfurrow their brows by distributing several presents and taking a chief with him to receive the hospitality of Fort Biloxi.[25]

As early as the sixteenth century, smoke played another key role in welcoming the godlike Europeans. In native America, tobacco was sacred, and on its smoke prayers were lifted to heaven. The best way to honor any great-spirited being, therefore, was to offer it tobacco or smoke. When Father Allouez advised a Fox man to have his dangerously ill parents bled, the man poured powdered tobacco all over the priest's gown and said, "Thou art a spirit; come now, restore these sick people to health; I offer thee this tobacco in sacrifice." A dusty gown was small enough price to pay for such status, but other Frenchmen paid more dearly. In another part of the Great Lakes, Nicolas Perrot had smoke blown directly into his face "as the greatest honor that they could render him; he saw himself smoked like meat," but gamely "said not a word." With Iberville on the Mississippi, Father Paul du Ru reported that, after puffing two or three times on a calumet, one of the Indians "came and blew smoke from his pipe into my nose as though to cense me." Du Ru may have come off better than the first French captain who sailed to the Menominees on Lake Michigan: he had tobacco ground into his forehead. One of the earliest Europeans to be honored with smoke was too ethnocentric to recognize his good fortune. When some Baffin Island Eskimos tried to place John Davis in the consecrating smoke of their fire, he pushed one of them into the smoke instead and testily had the fire stomped out and kicked into the sea.[26]

If being smoked connoted some kind of religious affirmation, other ceremonies spelled political and social acceptance of the newcomers. At least two European leaders had the honor of being "crowned" by their native counterparts, but the exact meaning of their coronation is still unclear. At the future site of La Navidad on Hispaniola, Columbus was fêted by the paramount chief Guacanagarí and five subordinate "kings," as the Admiral called them, "all with their crowns displaying their high rank." Guacanagarí led Columbus to a chair on a raised platform and "took off the crown from his own head and put it on the Admiral's. In return the grateful don dressed the chief in a collar of beautiful beads and agates, his own scarlet cloak, colored buskins, and a large silver ring. Probably the Indian got the better deal, as did the *Agouhanna* or head chief of Hochelaga in 1535. When Jacques Cartier rubbed the chief's paralyzed arms and legs at his request, the grateful man took off the red hedgehog-skin band he wore as a crown and presented it to the Frenchman. Before he left, Cartier distributed an array of metal tools and jewelry to repay the Hochelagans for their generous hospitality and political friendship.[27]

French visitors await a line of Natchez dignitaries during a three-day calumet cere-mony in early Louisiana. From Antoine Simon Le Page du Pratz (who lived among the Natchez from 1720 to 1728), *Histoire de la Louisiane,* 3 vols. (Paris, 1758).

Cartier's education in native politics had begun even before he left his base near the future Quebec City. In an effort to dissuade Cartier from going upriver to visit the Hochelagans on Montreal Island, Donnacona, the chief of the rival Stadaconans, made him a present of three children, including the ten-year-old daughter of his own sister and the younger brother of Cartier's native interpreter. These human gifts, Cartier quickly learned, were meant as seals on a firm political alliance to prevent any trafficking with enemies. When the French persisted in their travel plans and threatened to give the children back, the Stadaconans relented and put the best face they could on the necessity of dealing with ignorant intruders who refused to play by the established rules of the diplomatic game. But Cartier had already learned enough to accept the eight-year-old daughter of the chief at Achelacy, some twenty-five leagues upriver, an alliance that paid dividends during French difficulties with Don-nacona later that winter.[28]

More than a century and a half later, another French captain was given an Indian child to seal an alliance. In 1699 the chief of the Bayogoulas gave an adopted twelve-year-old slave boy to Jean Baptiste LeMoyne de Bienville, Iberville's younger brother and lieutenant in Louisiana. Perhaps realizing that he was slated to be shipped to France for training as an interpreter, the "poor boy regretted leaving the Indians so much that he cried incessantly without being able to stop." Sadly, he died of a throat ailment just after returning to his homeland "without getting to talk to any of his people."[29]

In native eyes, the integration of the European "others" was nearly complete. Yet one thing was missing. Although the strangers were religiously honored and politically allied, they were not bound by the gossamer ties of marriage or adoption as kinsmen. In the earliest sources, foreign observers seldom distinguished clearly between marriage *á la façon du pays* (according to native custom) and hospitable short-term companionship and even less seldom recognized adoption ceremonies when they occurred. So we have to rely on later evidence to interpret the faint signals left by the first Europeans, who seldom understood their hosts' language.

We know generally that in native society, an unattached person was *persona non grata*. To be accepted as a full member of a tribe or band was to be related—biologically or fictively—to other members. So a European trader, diplomat, missionary, or officer who wanted to exercise any sway over native life had to become part of an Indian family, either by adoption or marriage. More specifically, we know that throughout the sixteenth century the Indians of Florida readily adopted Spanish shipwreck victims, including several women who took native husbands and had *mestizo* children by them. We also know that all over eastern America in subsequent centuries, European war captives and runaways were adopted, married, and treated as if they had been born of Indian mothers. It is therefore likely that many of the chief-ly "harangues," elaborate gift-givings, exchanges of official insignia, and bestowal of Indian names reported by European leaders marked the newcomers' adoption as fictive kin.[30]

By the same token, the bestowal of native women upon the strangers was probably meant not only to betoken temporary hospitality but often to pledge long-term fidelity in marriage, which in Indian society did not require banns, dowries, rings, or a church wedding. On the Mississippi in 1541, the caciques of Casqui and Pacaha offered Soto three of their close relatives as "testimonial[s] of love." Begging the Spaniard to take his daughter as his wife, one chief said that "his greatest desire was to unite his blood with that of so great a lord as he was." The other was willing to give up two of his pleasingly plump sisters, Macanoche and Mochila, to cement relations with the dangerous "children of the sun."[31]

William Hilton was similarly if somewhat more ambiguously propositioned on the Cape Fear River in 1663. After repulsing several minor attacks upriver, Hilton and his crew were called to shore by forty warriors crying "Bonny, Bonny." When the English landed, the natives threw beads into their boat, made a long, indecipherable speech, and presented the nonplussed crew with "two very handsom proper young Indian women, the tallest," Hilton wrote, "that we have seen in this Countrey; which we supposed to be the Kings Daughters, or persons of some great account amongst them. These young women were ready to come into our Boat." Indeed, he hurried to assure his sensitive English readers, "one of them crouding in, was hardly perswaded to go out again." Three years later, Henry Woodward discovered what such a gift entailed. Having been left with the Port Royal Indians to learn their language and to serve as hostage for the return of the chief's nephew, who was taken to Barbados for a similar purpose, the chief gave Woodward a large cornfield and his Indian counterpart's sister, "telling him that shee should tend him and dresse his victuals and be careful of him that soe her Brother might be the better used amongst [the English]."[32]

The sixty men who stopped with Iberville at the Bayogoula village in 1700 undoubtedly would have sold their honor cheap to share Woodward's fate. As the French arrived for the requisite three days of the calumet, the chiefs asked Iberville whether they "would require as many women as there were men in [their] party." Just as he, a non-smoker, was not eager to smoke the calumet, so Iberville "spoiled" what he perceived as his men's sport by showing his hand to his hosts and making them understand that "their skin—red and tanned—should not come close to that of the French, which was white."[33]

The attention and welcome generated among the Indians by the advent of the first Europeans was clearly exceptional; whether gods in human shape or rare mortals, these beings were quite unlike any of the "original peoples" of America. As such they deserved the most respectful treatment possible and required full incorporation into native society in order to harness their assets and to forestall any harm they might do. But what exactly was the source of the Europeans' fascination and power? What did the Indians see in the strangers that was not, or only dimly, seen in their own kind?

White Power

One difference was the whiteness of European skin. On Arthur Barlowe's reconnaissance of Roanoke Island in 1584, the natives "wondred mervelously when we were amongest them, at the whiteness of our skinnes, ever coveting to touch our breastes, and to view the same." Sixty years earlier, the natives of the Outer Banks had been equally astonished by the newcomers' whiteness. When one of Giovanni da Verrazzano's sailors was nearly drowned trying to swim with some small gifts to a group of Indians, they rescued him, took off his shoes, stockings, and shirt, built a large warming fire, "placed him on the ground in the sun . . . and made gestures of great admiration, looking at the whiteness of his flesh and examining him from head to foot." The Biloxi Indians, who first laid eyes on the French in 1699, also gaped at the "white-skinned people" in their midst. "Thus," noted André Pénicaut, the literate ship's carpenter, "we appeared to be quite different from them, who have very tawny skin."[34]

But the close examination that the Indians gave the explorers' chests, faces, and arms may have been focused on the skin's hairiness as well as its pallor. For Pénicaut went on to say that the Biloxis were also astonished by the heavy beards and bald heads among the French, for the Biloxis had "heavy black hair which they groom very carefully" and, like the other Mississippi tribes, "remove the hair from their faces as well as from other parts of the body . . . with shell ash and hot water as one would remove the hair from a suckling pig." Undiluted Indian genes still carry no chromosomes for baldness. Understandably, European beards and tufted chests held an ugly fascination for the smooth-skinned Americans. Before they actually saw a white man, the Potawatomis and Menominees around Green Bay believed the French to be a different species from other men, not because their skin was a shade or two lighter but because they were "covered with hair."[35]

The first Europeans were celebrated less because they were pale or hairy than because they were spiritually powerful "gods" (as the Europeans put it) or *manitous* (in Algonquian parlance), like Indian shamans and conjurers. There were two chief sources of their power. The first was their reputation among the Indians as purveyors or preventers of disease, exactly comparable to native shamans, who were also thought to wield powers of life and death. Jacques Cartier was asked to lay hands on all the sick and handicapped at Hochelaga as if, he said, "Christ had come down to earth to heal them." The three Spanish doctors in Cabeza de Vaca's traveling medicine show were thought to raise men from the dead as well as to cure a variety of ailments. They got into this profitable business—satisfied customers paid them fees of food and goods beyond their ability to consume—when their Texas captors forced them to practice traditional shamanic blowing and rubbing techniques for their keep, convinced that "we who were extraordinary men must possess power and efficacy over all other things." Not surprisingly, the cacique of Casqui thought it only sensible to ask the "son of the sun"—Soto—to restore sight to a number of his blind villagers.[36]

At the same time, the Indians believed that all spiritual power was double-edged: those who could cure could also kill. Only powerful "spirits" possessed the ability to bewitch or to counteract another's witchcraft. When the Roanoke colonists inadvertently carried deadly European diseases into the North Carolina coastal region, they were deified by their hosts for their ability to kill Indians at a distance and to remain unscathed themselves. "There could at no time happen any strange sicknesse, losses, hurtes, or any other crosse unto [the natives]," wrote Thomas Harriot, the expedition's Indian expert, "but that they would impute to us the cause or means thereof for offending or not pleasing us." The Indians had extra cause to worry when four of five towns that had practiced some "subtle devise" against the English were ravaged by an unknown disease shortly after the colonists' departure. The English rivals under chief Wingina deduced that the havoc was wrought by "our God through our meanes, and that wee by him might kil and slaie whom wee would without weapons and not come neere them."[37]

The second and more important source of the white man's power in native America was his technological superiority. As native oral traditions suggest, European ships initially impressed the Americans who piloted nothing larger than dug-out canoes. Columbus attributed his divine reception largely to his clothes and his ships. Arthur Barlowe told Sir Walter Ralegh that the natives of Roanoke "had our shippes in marvelous admiration, and all things els was so strange unto them, as it appeared that none of them had ever seene the like." As late as 1700 many Mississippi Valley tribes had never seen a European sailing ship. So when Iberville returned to Louisiana with the French fleet, Sauvole took four native dignitaries to view the frigates. As predicted, they were "ecstatic to see such big contraptions." When they returned to Fort Biloxi they told waiting tribesmen that "they had been on the ships that went up to the clouds, that there were more than fifty villages on each one and crowds that one cannot pass through, and one made them climb down to a place where they did not see sun or moon." Then they all left for Choctaw country upriver "to teach them these wonders."[38]

Another cause of wonderment was firearms, which Verrazzano noted as early as 1524. On an "Arcadian" coast somewhere south of New York harbor, a handsome, naked Indian man approached a group of the French sailors and showed them a burning stick, "as if to offer [them] fire." But when the Europeans trumped his hospitality by firing a matchlock, "he trembled all over with fear" and "remained as if thunderstruck, and prayed, worshiping like a monk, pointing his finger to the sky; and indicating the sea and the ship, he appeared to bless us."[39]

Not without reason, European metal weapons continued to impress the natives who saw them in action for the first time. When chief Donnacona asked Cartier to demonstrate his artillery in 1535, of which two of the chief's men had given "great account," the Frenchman obliged by firing a dozen cannon into the nearby woods. The Stadaconans were "so much astonished as if the heavens had fallen upon them, and began to howl and to shriek in such a very loud manner that one would have thought hell had emptied itself there." When Pierre Radisson and Nicolas Perrot traveled among the Indians of Wisconsin in the 1650s and '60s, the natives literally worshipped their guns, knives, and hatchets by blowing sacred smoke over them "as if it were incense." Likewise, the woodland Sioux who captured the Recollect missionary Louis Hennepin in 1680 called a gun *Manza Ouckange,* "iron which has a spirit." Understandably, the gun's noise and smoke initially did as much to terrify the natives as did its lead balls, which everyone conceded did more crippling damage to internal organs and bones than did flint-tipped arrows.[40]

Weapons were of paramount importance to the feuding polities of North America, but metal objects of any kind, cloth goods, and cleverly designed or sizable wooden objects also drew their admiration. Thomas Harriot put his finger on the primary cause of the Indians' initially exalted opinion of the white strangers when he noted that

> most things they sawe with us, as Mathematicall instruments, sea compasses, the vertue of the loadstone in drawing iron, a perspective glasse whereby was shewed manie strange sightes, burning glasses, wildfire woorkes, gunnes, bookes, writing and reading, spring clocks that seeme to goe of themselves, and manie other thinges that wee had, were so straunge unto them, and so farre exceeded their capacities to comprehend the reason and meanes how they should be made and done, that they thought they were rather the works of gods than of men, or at the leastwise they had bin given and taught us of the gods.[41]

The Sioux, Illinois, and Seneca Indians, among whom Father Hennepin journeyed, frequently clapped their hands over their mouths in astonishment at such things as printed books, silver chalices, embroidered chasubles, and iron pots, all of which they designated as "spirits." In the 1630s the natives of southern New England considered a windmill "little less than the world's wonder" for the whisking motion of its long arms and its "sharp teeth biting the corn," and the first plowman little less than a "juggler" or shaman. Being shown the iron coulter and share of the plow, which could "tear up more ground in a day than their clamshells [hoes] could scrape up in a month," they told the plowman "he was almost Abamacho, almost as cunning as the Devil."[42]

In a very short time, the enterprising newcomers discovered how to turn the natives' awe of European technology to private advantage. Columbus's crewmen found that they could make a killing in a trade with the Taínos—over the Admiral's objections—for pieces of broken wine-barrel hoops, earthenware shards, scraps of broken glass, and lace tips. In the next century European colonists on the coasts of Florida and Georgia took advantage of the Indians' eagerness to swap decorative but otherwise useless gold and silver from Spanish shipwrecks for pieces of paper and playing cards. A Calusa man once gave a Spanish soldier 70 ducats of gold for an ace of diamonds. But Captain George Waymouth may have been the most calculating of all. In 1605 he used a magnetized sword to pick up a knife and a needle before a Maine band of potential fur-trading partners. "This we did," he confessed, "to cause them to imagine some great power in us: and for that to love and feare us."[43]

The white man's varied powers were celebrated in the generic names given to him by different native groups. The Narragansetts of Rhode Island called all Europeans "Coatmen" or "swordmen." The Mohawks of New York referred to the Dutch as "Iron-workers" or "Cloth makers," while the Hurons of southern Ontario called the French *Agnonha,* "Iron People." In northern New England the Pocumtucks knew the French as "Knife men," just as the Virginians, and later all white Americans, were known as "Longknives." The strong identification of the European "others" with their metal instruments of death seems sadly appropriate. After all, on the very first day the Taínos met Columbus on the sands of Guanahaní in 1492, the Admiral "showed them swords and they took them by the edge and through ignorance cut themselves."[44]

The Domestication of Difference

The Taíno experience notwithstanding, European encounters with the North American Indians at the very beginning were predominantly peaceful and the natives generally welcomed the newcomers. The white explorers had too much curiosity about, and especially too much need for, the new peoples they had "discovered" to pick gratuitous fights; enough skirmishes would eventually break out through mutual misunderstanding and ham-handed tactics. The Europeans' immediate need was to learn enough about the natives and the land to be able to classify, utilize, and, ultimately, dominate both. In all these efforts they assumed that the American "others" were inferior—culturally and religiously, rather than racially—to themselves. So they began by trying to remake America in the images of the various Europes they had left behind, and to remake America's inhabitants less in their own European likenesses than according to a venerable set of normative stereotypes of aliens and "others."

Despite determined efforts, they foundered on the palpable reality of America. Although the various imperial competitors shared many goals and pursued them over several centuries, they were often stymied in the colonial period by the great number, variety, and determination of native societies living within equally stubborn and varied geographies. But the pattern of thought and activity laid down by these argonauts of empire allows us to glimpse the other side of America's post-Columbian encounters.

Taming the Land

In some ways, the "otherness" of the land was easier to domesticate, at least intellectually, than were the people. Usually before meeting any natives, the Europeans assimilated the land by relating it to familiar scenes at home or abroad, renaming its major features, and claiming it for their sovereigns to forestall competing European claims. The well-traveled Columbus established precedent once again by comparing the green of Antillian trees to those of his adopted Andalusia "in the month of May," and the cultivated fields of Tortuga to "the plain of Cordova." He also thought he recognized mastic like that grown on the Aegean island of Chios, noticed the difference between island palms and those of African Guinea, and believed (wrongly) that the mountains of Hispaniola were loftier than "Tenerife in the Canaries." By contrast, the best way a more sedentary Englishman could describe a large yellow-flowered meadow in South Carolina was "a pasture not inferior to any I have seene in England."[45]

Although the Indians had already endowed many prominent geographical features with names, the first Europeans signaled their imperial intentions by naming or renaming everything in sight. In choosing names they paid homage to their religions, homelands, social superiors, and, not least, their own egos. Catholic explorers were the most eager donors of religious names, such as 'San Salvador,' given "in remembrance of the Divine Majesty, Who had marvellously bestowed all this," said Columbus; "the Indians call it 'Guanahani.'" Other Spaniards dubbed two of their earliest towns 'St. Augustine' and 'Santa Fe.' Cartier baptized the majestic Canadian river 'St. Lawrence,' and wherever Christians came upon bone-covered sites of former epidemics or massacres they dubbed them 'Golgotha.' The hearth-hugging English, of course, were famous for transferring English place-names to the localities of 'New England,' but the French in sixteenth-century Florida also renamed eight rivers after well-known French ones. Flattery, too, had its place in the nominating process, as is proved by the existence of 'Virginia' (after Elizabeth I, the Virgin Queen), 'Montreal' (*mont Royal*, for King Francis I), 'Monterey' (for the viceroy of New Spain), and 'Lake Pontchartrain' (after the French minister of marine in 1699). And self-flattery was never far behind, as 'Lake Champlain,' 'Frobisher Bay,' and 'Pennsylvania' attest.[46]

Claiming the land was hardly more taxing than naming it: the "discoverers" simply stepped off the boat and performed a small number of symbolic acts, thereby accessioning whole islands, regions, and continents for their nation-states. On October 12, 1492, Columbus rowed to the beach at Guanahaní, unfurled the royal standard and two banners of the Green Cross (one for each sovereign), made legal proclamations of possession which his fleet secretary duly recorded and his captains witnessed, and transferred the island to Ferdinand and Isabella. As he continued through the Antilles, he wrote, "my intention was not to pass by any island of which I did not take possession, although if it is taken of one," he assumed, "it may be said that it is taken of all."[47]

European explorers began to rename—and thereby to claim—American places as early as Columbus's arrival on October 12, 1492. This woodcut from the Basel Latin edition of his first letter to Ferdinand and Isabella shows various Caribbean islands with the new names Columbus had given them. From *Carta de Colón* (Basel, 1493).

Even more popular as symbols of possession were large wooden crosses, which also marked convenient harbors and landmarks for countrymen who followed. Simple crosses heralded the claims of Christians but did not specify their nationality unless coats of arms or other telltale insignia were attached. Thus when the Virginia colonists claimed Powhatan's empire for England,

In the 1560s the French sought to lay claim to Florida by erecting tall stone columns on various river banks. In this engraving by Theodor de Bry (after the original painting by eye witness Jacques Le Moyne), the local Timucuans worship one of the pillars as an idol with offerings of food, perfumed oils, and weapons. Other native groups received the columns with suspicion and much less reverence. From Theodor de Bry, *Brevis narratio eorum quae in Florida Americae* (Frankfurt, 1591).

they insured against ambiguity by leaving a cross at the head of the newly renamed James River with the inscription "Jacobus Rex. 1607."[48]

More than one native leader, besides Powhatan, was suspicious of the meaning of these arrogant constructions. When Cartier erected at the entrance of Gaspé Harbor a thirty-foot cross, complete with shield and plaque reading "VIVE LE ROY DE FRANCE" in bold Gothic letters, he got an argument from a Micmac chief. "Pointing to the cross," Cartier recalled, "he made us a long harangue, making the sign of the cross with two of his fingers; and then he pointed to the land all around about, as if he wished to say that all this region belonged to him, and that we ought not to have set up this cross without out his permission."[49]

The French Huguenots who tried to preempt the Spanish in Florida may have gotten a similar message when they planted a white stone pillar on a riverbank. This was one of five man-sized columns they had brought to assert their claims, each inscribed with a royal shield, three fleurs-de-lis, the Queen Mother's initial, and the date '1561.' One of the local chiefs, however, was not amused by their audacity. When Jean Ribault, the French captain, went to visit him with gifts, the chief put on a grave face and only shook his head a little to show that "he was not well pleased" either with the column or the fact that the French had first planted one across the river in the domain of a rival. Before long the disgruntled chief was vindicated. When the French returned three years later to establish a military presence, they were gleefully taken to see the first pillar, which had been protected by the Indians and decorated with "crownes of Bay" and "little baskets of Mill [grain]." Within a year, however, the Spanish demolished the French fort, murdered the garrison, and carried off the offensive column to Havana.[50]

Situational Ethics

Claiming allegedly "virgin" land was one thing, mastering it and turning it to profit was quite another. The Europeans quickly found that the latter was impossible without the active aid of the natives, whom even the most contemptuous invaders realized had strong attachments, if not "legitimate" claims or "natural rights," to the land. The Indians also had unique knowledge of the land and its environmental limits, something European dreamers and schemers often sorely lacked. Before the newcomers could proceed to their larger goals of profiteering and domination, therefore, they had to learn enough about the American "others" to win their confidence and friendship, get them to supplement always-inadequate supplies, and induce them to reveal the sources of America's presumed wealth. Beginning with Columbus, European leaders initially instructed their men to avoid any behavior that would offend the numerically superior natives. "For if any rude and rigorious meanes shuldbe used towardes this people," Ribault predicted, "they would flye hither and thither through the woodes and forestes and abandon there habitations and cuntrye" or else, he did not have to say, they would turn and attack the offending parties.[51]

European Hospitality

So, on the ancient principle of 'When in Rome,' the Europeans tamed their haste for results and bent their initial efforts to reciprocating native hospitality as fully as possible. As they sought to earn reputations for generosity, perhaps the supreme virtue in communal Indian society, they also hoped to impress the natives with their superior technology, intelligence, and spiritual power, all of which they assumed gave them just claim to rule the new land and its people.

European hospitality was not much different from Indian, except that its spirit was more calculating, and the newcomers had no desire to reduce native difference and "inferiority" by incorporating them into their families, which were largely absent in any event. The staples of both welcomes were feasting, entertainment, and gift-giving, the essential lubricant of Indian social relations. For Indians, spending the night in a tarry, creaking ship was apparently considered a treat, perhaps more for the novel food and drink offered than for comfort or company. European-prepared meat, pease, beans, bread, and even ship's biscuits were eaten with gusto. A band of southern New England Indians liked everything Captain Bartholomew Gosnold served them but the mustard, "whereat they made many a sowre face." Alcoholic beverages got a mixed reception. A Timucua chief grew so fond of French wine—or company—that he broke a ban on daytime eating to request a cup in order to drink with Jean Ribault. Yet the Bayogoulas took "very little" of the wine and brandy Iberville offered them, being more stunned by the brandy he set on fire. In 1605 the Abenakis on St. George's River in Maine tasted English *aqua vitae* "but would by no meanes drinke." Sugar candy and raisins were more to their taste.[52]

What caught the attention of the European hosts was not the natives' palate but their unselfish sharing of everything they received. Columbus was the first to notice that when a Haitian cacique left his retinue on deck to go below to join the Admiral at dinner, he took only a small sample of each dish for tasting and "afterward sent the rest to his people, and all ate of it." A century later, Captain Waymouth similarly entertained two Abenakis, who, after eating a modest amount, characteristically "desired pease to carry a shore to their women, which we gave them, with fish and bread," wrote the ship's scribe, "and lent them pewter dishes, which they carefully brought [back] againe."[53]

Once the Indians had been wined and dined, they were serenaded by the European equivalents of native drums, flutes, and rattles. Most expeditions on land and sea carried a complement of martial drummers and trumpeters, who were often pressed into social service to entertain visiting natives. But some ships' crews included bona fide musicians: Sir Humphrey Gilbert had six, John Davis, four. Davis lured several Eskimo groups to trade by playing music and having his crew dance to it on shore. In 1603 some Massachusetts Algonquians were diverted by the "homely Music" of a young guitarist in Martin Pring's crew. After showering the musician with gifts, they danced around him "twentie in a Ring . . . using many Savage gestures [and] singing Io, Ia, Io, Ia, Ia, Io." In Louisiana a century later, the Colapissa villagers who hosted a dozen Frenchmen during one of their periodic supply shortages learned to dance the minuet and *la bourrée* to the fine fiddling of a violinist named Picard. His companions "nearly d[ied] of laughter" over their hosts' capers, but the natives obviously enjoyed themselves and even had the last laugh when Picard could not keep time with the intricate drumming at their traditional dances.[54]

European rituals of hospitality were brought to a close by the giving of gifts to the visiting natives. Fresh from the corrupt courts and countinghouses of Europe, the newcomers tended to see gifts as bribes, necessary palm-crossings to get a job done. In native America, by contrast, gifts were at once "words" in the rich metaphorical language of political councils and sureties for one's word. The potential conflict between these two meanings was largely avoided by the necessity of employing gifts in a native context. Since nothing could be done without them, the Europeans quickly learned that in using them they were bound by the promises made on each occasion. In such a setting, words could not be taken lightly and stark honesty was a necessity, particularly on formal or ceremonial occasions. If the Europeans wanted peace with the natives, reciprocal gift-giving was the only reliable way to secure it.[55]

As in Europe, gifts to leaders usually led to the best results. So it was chiefs and caciques who received an eye-catching drapery from Columbus's bed, red wool caps from Cartier, and "gownes of blewe clothe garnished with yellowe flowers de luce" from Ribault. Since Europe and America were alike in generally adhering to social hierarchy, appropriate gifts were best given to the several ranks. When Cartier was ready to distribute gifts to the Hochelagans, he made the men, women, and children line up separately. "To the headmen he gave hatchets, to the others knives, and to the women, beads and other small trinkets. He then made the children scramble for little rings and tin *agnus Dei,* which afforded them great amusement."[56]

Taking the Americans' Measure

Having earned provisional reputations as "generous men," the explorers could then proceed to two final acts of preparation before attempting to impose their will on the land and the people. The first was to take the measure of the natives, for both intellectual and practical purposes. Attempting to make sense of the natives' novelty was natural to literate people whose culture relied heavily on encyclopedias and other compendia of knowledge to assimilate all that was known about their burgeoning world. And knowing the Americans "others" was the only way to beat them in the competition for their continent.

Like most people, Europeans tended to conceive of the new in terms of the old, to classify novelties according to conventional wisdom. Most explorers, therefore, began to cope with the shiny newness of the natives by putting them in mental pigeonholes constructed from ancient precedent and proximate experience. This had the added advantage of helping the homebound readers of their New World narratives learn by comparison with the known and the familiar.

When Europeans first sought to describe Indians and Indian culture, they slipped their often keen-eyed observations into interpretive slots marked 'Ancients,' 'Africans,' 'wild Irish,' or, the most capacious and indefinite of all, 'Savages.' The people Verrazzano met in Narragansett Bay exhibited the "sweet and gentle . . . manner of the ancients." Arthur Barlowe found the natives of Roanoke "such as lived after the manner of the golden age." But other "ancient" analogies were less flattering to the Indians. When Theodor de Bry republished Harriot's account of Roanoke in 1590, he included many engravings of John White's paintings of "Virginia" Indians and life. After the index, he tucked in a section of five pictures of Picts and Ancient Britons "to showe how . . . the Inhabitants of the great Bretannie have bin in times past as sauvage as those of Virginia." Long-haired, naked, and tattooed from head to toe, a fierce Pict warrior is depicted wearing a deadly curved sword at his belt and holding a shield in one hand and the bloody head of a victim in the other.[57]

Since few other European colonizers had as much experience in Africa as the Portuguese had, the earliest comparisons of American Indians and Africans were limited largely to physical appearance, such as skin color, hair texture, and lip size. These comparisons tended to emphasize contrasts rather than similarities and to favor the Americans, who came closer to European norms of appearance and beauty.[58] The "wild Irish" and their culture, on the other hand, were quite familiar to many English adventurers in North America because the latter had served in Ireland trying to bring it under Elizabeth's royal wing. It was understandable that Captain John Smith likened the Virginians' deerskin robes to "Irish mantels," and Harriot compared their spear-fishing to "the maner as Irish men cast darts [short spears]."[59]

Any other native behavior or social custom that could not be easily classified was assigned to the 'Savage' category, an *omnium gatherum* for temporarily isolating the unfamiliar until it could be defused by myopic familiarity or accepted on its own terms as the stubborn reality of Indian life. In many ways, the first Europeans to meet America's natives were the most open to that reality, before the frustration of their dominating designs permanently warped their vision and judgment.[60]

Taming Tongues

The Europeans' final preparation for New World domination was to learn how to communicate with the Indians. For without the ability to plumb the nuances of their languages, their thoughts and feelings would remain dangerously hidden. The Indians faced the same task: the "other" must become intelligible in order to become predictable and, thereby, controllable. In the beginning the natives enjoyed numerical superiority and could dictate the terms of engagement. A Frenchman who made a grand tour of the Great Lakes in 1669 spoke for all European explorers when he realized early in his journey "how important it was not to engage one's self amongst the tribes of these countries without knowing their language or being sure of one's interpreter." "The lack of an interpreter under our own control," he lamented, "prevented the entire success of our expedition."[61]

Since the crude pantomimes of sign language were clearly not sufficient for reliable discourse, interpreters on both sides had to be trained. This generally entailed a voluntary program of student exchanges, at which the French both in Canada and later in Louisiana proved to be the most adept. Quick-witted children were sent to live with the "others" in order to learn not only their words but the social and cultural realities that lay behind them. It did not tarnish the exchange that the foreign students also served as hostages for the peaceful conduct of their people.[62]

Theodor de Bry's engraving of an ancient Pict warrior served to remind the readers of Thomas Harriot's account of the Roanoke colony that the "Virginia" (actually North Carolina) Indians were not culturally inferior to the colonists' own ancestors. From Harriot, *A briefe and true report of the new found land of Virginia* (London, 1588).

Some interpreters, however, were not volunteers. A few European expeditions that arrived after the initial waves of invasion were fortunate to find countrymen who had been taken captive or saved from shipwrecks and adopted by the Indians and who were already fluent in the regional tongues. Soto's *entrada* would never have left the coast of Florida had he not redeemed Juan Ortiz, a survivor of the Narváez debacle in 1528 who had lived with the natives for twelve years. Fortunately, although he closely resembled the Indians, down to his arm tattoos and breechclout, Ortiz had not forgotten the Spanish he had learned in Seville. When he died somewhere west of the Mississippi in March 1542, the expedition began to unravel, for the only interpreter left was a young Indian slave acquired in northeastern Georgia, where different languages were spoken. "So great a misfortune was the death of . . . Ortiz . . . that to learn from the Indians what he stated in four words, with the youth the whole day was needed; and most of the time he understood just the opposite of what was asked."[63]

The need for interpreters among the early Europeans was so urgent that many ship captains endangered future relations with the natives by kidnapping tribesmen (never women) to take back to Europe for language instruction. Since it was nearly impossible for the Indians to distinguish the temporary "borrowing" of interpreters from the permanent kidnapping of slaves, which Europeans also snatched in alarming numbers, they could be forgiven a certain amount of violence toward the next ships to appear. Columbus inaugurated the sordid practice on his first voyage, but the pairs of interpreters taken by Jacques Cartier and Arthur Barlowe are the more famous because they were safely returned after a year abroad to play key roles in the colonial ventures of Canada and Roanoke, respectively. Chief Donnacona's two sons, Domagaya and especially Taignoagny, did their best to foil French incursions into the St. Lawrence before they were shanghaied a second time, but Manteo and Wanchese from the Outer Banks left a mixed legacy. Wanchese, one of chief Wingina's warriors, was also hostile to European pretensions, but Manteo, a rival Croatoan, was instrumental in securing an English foothold, however briefly, in North Carolina. In 1587 he became the first native convert to the Church of England and was appointed chief of Roanoke Island by the last English governor.[64]

Second Encounters

But the fragile balance of power that characterized the protracted series of first encounters in North America all too quickly and inexorably tipped against the natives. Virtually in the wake of the European explorers sailed three battalions of powerful allies. The first consisted of microbic shock troops which swept unseen through defenseless Indian villages with lethal ruthlessness, reducing dramatically the natives' numerical superiority and exploding forever their mental equilibrium. Missionaries often accompanied these "shock troops" and practiced a new, aggressive faith, armed with self-righteous certitude, a seemingly omniscient culture of print, and the intolerant Truth of Holy Scripture. The third battalion was comprised of humbler clerks and colonial officials who nonetheless wielded with swashbuckling bravado the aggrandizing maps, charters, and long-term policies of Europe's emerging nation-states. The Indians were ultimately no match for these foes and their well-armed, technologically advantaged, and increasingly savvy predecessors. As soon as the invaders achieved a measure of political initiative or military superiority, they sought to realize their dreams of New World wealth, imperial hegemony, and propagation of the gospel, no matter what the cost in native lives, lands, or liberties.

Another casualty of these increasingly tragic encounters was the earliest image each side held of the "other." As the initial honeymoon of contact gave way to conflict and the eruption of irreconcilable differences, naive preconceptions gave way to more realistic notions, at once more complex and less optimistic. In Indian eyes, the strangers in their midst devolved fairly quickly from beneficent "gods" dropped from "the heavens," to dangerously powerful "spirits" or shamans, and finally to all-too-human or even sub-human "enemies" who deserved to be killed before they did irreparable harm.

Ironically, the Europeans' conception underwent a temporary *up*grading during their first encounters with the natives. Having arrived in America with largely negative notions of the "other" (particularly of those outside the cultural magnificence of China and Japan), the invaders were somewhat nonplussed to have their "savage" preconception undermined by the distinctly unsavage, even "civilized," behavior of their native hosts. It was simply difficult for the Europeans to find the hairy, godless, cruel, treacherous cannibals of their myths and fantasies in the smooth-skinned, simple people who appeared to worship them by fêting, feasting, housing, caressing, and showering them with gifts. Their discomfort continued spasmodically as missionaries and other pacific observers captured the benign aspect of native life in pictures and print, giving substance to Europe's self-critical image of the Noble Savage.

But the predestinate European drive for dominion in America ensured that the natives would be forced to defend their countries and cultures with arms, ferocity, and guile, thereby fulfilling the invaders' worst expectations. The history of first encounters, therefore, is a sad reminder that, in spite of the gentle and promising advent of European-Indian relations in many different places and on many different occasions, the intruders could not help but turn their genial hosts into stereotypical "Savages," whose "otherness" was as unfathomable as they were expendable.

TWO

BABEL OF TONGUES

Communicating with the Indians

If I know not the meaning of the voice, I shall be unto him that speaketh
a barbarian, and he that speaketh shall be a barbarian unto me.

I CORINTHIANS 14:10–11

While European ships and the trade winds could bring the people of the "Old
World" face to face with those of the "New," they could not guarantee that the
newcomers would gain more than a wet toehold on the margins of North
America. If the native "others" remained hidden, like Mardi Gras mummers,
behind gaudy face paint, bizarre behavior, and the manifest mime of trade, the
Europeans had no hope of discovering the value of the country or of sizing up—
much less neutralizing or eliminating—their indigenous rivals for it. The key
to the continent was information—reliable, unambiguous, and digestible—
and the quickest and best source of it was the Indians. Rumor simply would not
do in the long run, though it had its motivational uses early on; nor would
guesswork, which was expensive and often dangerous.

Only natives could tell novices where to find assayable gold and silver (not
just the dazzling promise of iron pyrite), how to get around or through the
Appalachians, when and what to plant when Atlantic storms or privateers
claimed supply ships, how to recognize the log-choked mouth of the Mississippi, and where to obtain the plushest beaver pelts. Only natives knew how to
navigate the narrow moccasin trails that crisscrossed the landscape, to draw
maps of the next terra incognita on birchbark, deerskin, or borrowed paper, to
pilot flimsy canoes through dangerous defiles and trackless chains of evergreen
lakes, and to kill enough game en route to keep the travelers alive. Certainly
only natives could teach the strangers to wage effective war against, and to
avoid the lethal ambushes of, other Indians, in short, to think—temporarily
and with malice aforethought—like the enemy in order to win the new high-
stakes game for the continent.

But extracting these vital pieces of information from the natives was no easy
matter. In the face of iconoclastic missionaries and gold-digging prospectors,

the Indians were understandably reticent: why invite sacred customs to be maligned and ridiculed and favorite mountain hunting spoiled?[1] But in less threatening circumstances, the natives were notably forthcoming and eager to share their knowledge. What was needed was a mode of communication, a language, common to both parties.

Finding a common tongue was vastly complicated by the linguistic complexion of Europe and America. Both, as the white man's Bible put it, were Babels, cursed for the overweening pride of Noah's descendants with a profusion and confusion of tongues.[2] Native North America spoke at least 221 mutually unintelligible languages, each fractured into myriad dialects that were themselves confounding even to native ears. East of the Mississippi, four major language families covered most of the map: Algonquian (named after the speech of the Algonquin tribe west of Montreal), Iroquoian (after the five Iroquois nations of New York), Siouan (after the Dakota or Sioux tribes initially found around the western Great Lakes), and Muskogean (after the Creek or Muskogee tribes of Alabama and Georgia).[3] Happily for newcomers, the members of each family shared common parentage and some resemblance. All the Algonquian tongues of eastern Canada, thought the practiced Baron de Lahontan, came as near to Algonquin as Portuguese or Italian did to Spanish. Likewise, the difference between Huron and the other Iroquois languages was "not greater than that between the Norman and the French." Even early in his linguistic acculturation, a French Jesuit found Algonquin and Montagnais (another Algonquian tongue) as close as Provençal and Norman.[4]

But family resemblances did not always make it possible for the speakers of one language to make themselves understood by their conversing cousins. Just as in Europe, dialects and patois muted exchanges between countrymen. Among the Algonquian-speakers of New England, noticed Roger Williams, "the varietie of their Dialects and proper speech within thirtie or fortie miles each of other, is very great." Neighboring tribes, for example, favored different consonants. When the Nipmucks spoke of a *dog*, they said *Alum;* their Quinnipiak brethren in Connecticut said *Arum*.[5] The Carolina backcountry was even more polyglot. To one experienced traveler, "the Difference of Languages, that is found amongst these Heathens, seems altogether strange. For it often appears, that every dozen Miles, you meet with an *Indian* Town, that is quite different from the others you last parted withal." In that part of the country, villages whose residents spoke radically different Iroquoian, Siouan, Muskogean, and even Algonquian tongues might lie within short walks of each other. The peripatetic John Lawson was amazed that the core vocabularies he collected of the Tuscarora, Pamptico, and Woccon tribes—located "not above ten Leagues distant" from each other—differed in literally every word save one.[6] A newly landed European seeking to learn to speak "Indian" clearly had his work cut out for him.

By the same token, native Americans hoping to fathom or tap into the mysterious power of the immigrant strangers were equally nonplussed by the verbal variety behind the newcomers' "European" persona. Even sorting them into "Frenchmen," "Englishmen," and "Spaniards" would not help a great deal. A "French" sailor was likely to speak a northwestern Breton or Norman dialect or the ancient and still-mysterious tongue of the Basques, rather than the "proper" French of Paris and the court. *Troupes de la marine* and *habitants* from the Midi who spoke the soft southern *langue d'oc* had as much trouble parleying with the crew and fellow passengers partial to the northern *langue d'oeil* as they did with new world *sauvages*. As late as the French Revolution, France was still deeply divided by regional patois, which differed almost from parish to parish.[7] English immigrants, largely from East Anglia and the Home Counties, spoke somewhat more congruent tongues, homogenized by London and the King James Bible. Spanish sailors, conquistadors, and settlers from the former Moorish region of Andalusia had some difficulty with the harder sounds of the central tablelands of Castile, but even more with Galician, the ancestor of Portuguese, and Catalan, which is still radically different from nationalized *Español*.

But when Indians and Europeans met for the first time, as they continued to do in many different places over three centuries, it was obvious that they initially would have to communicate not through a common tongue but by some shared syntax of signs, motions, and gestures. Relying on limbs rather than larynx carried a number of serious liabilities and forced each "speaker" upon the resources of his imagination. The first drawback of sign language was that the Indians of North America had no single system of accepted signs, except perhaps on the Plains, and the Europeans had no experience in reading or making signs unless they had traveled or traded in Africa.[8] Since body languages, no less than verbal ones, are culturally variable, the opportunities on both sides for ambiguity and misinterpretation were legion.

A second liability was that signs could not convey abstractions well. Concrete objects and basic human emotions were relatively easy to "talk" about, but concepts of religion, time, and law were less reducible to gesture. Finally, signs, unlike voices, were not "audible" at night or beyond a modest distance, a considerable hazard in unfamiliar territory where the intentions of "others" were equally unknown.

While the new world of mute discourse was fraught with some danger, much frustration, and no little humor, natives and strangers found some room for mutual understanding in signs from the heart and messages from the face, the telltale "mirror of the soul." Unlike the "wild Irish," who camouflaged their eyes behind thick bangs or "glibs," the Indians, while notoriously taciturn among Europeans, did not dissemble their true feelings on their own turf.[9] When they held their hands over their hearts or broke out in toothy grins, the Europeans could take them at their "word" and trust their sincerity.

Unhappily, the reverse was not always possible, because Europeans who had learned to thread their way through the Old World maze of social hierarchy, religious war, and court intrigue were adepts at dissimulation. The two-faced approach was used most by European officers whose task was not to honor native integrity or to safeguard native interests but to accomplish their own imperial goals. Humbler folks and followers, and even some bigwigs in a bind, felt freer to speak with unforked "tongues" at the onset of intercultural relations in a strange land.

When the very first Europeans and obdurate ethnocentrics even later tried to "have speech" with the natives they met, both sides quickly slammed into a wall of incomprehension. Before picking their pride up and dusting it off, they may have resorted to the old tactic of simply speaking their ethnic tongue louder, as if their audience consisted of deaf or disobedient children largely impervious to the voice of right reason. We know that even when Europeans and Indians learned to speak a common language, white men usually spoke too fast and too loudly for native ears, so it is likely that they increased the volume of their initial utterances when confronted with blank stares. Some Indians may have done the same. When Captain George Waymouth's ship approached the Maine coast in 1605, it was intercepted by a canoe whose leader "spake in his language very lowd and very boldly, seeming as though he would know why we were there, and by pointing with his oare [paddle] towards the sea, we conjectured he meant we should be gone."[10]

As soon as it dawned on the participants that dialogue would have to take a nonverbal form, they launched into the search for mutually intelligible signs and gestures to ask questions, return answers, and express feelings. Traders had a relatively easy time of it because the universal context of trade was peace, and the relative value of goods in barter could be established simply by adding or subtracting items, holding up fingers, and nodding or shaking the head. But explorers seeking fabled lands, merchant-adventures chasing gold or the Northwest Passage, and missionaries yearning to bathe savage souls in the "swete and lively liquor of the gospell" faced more daunting obstacles.[11]

Since the Europeans were always outnumbered and in strange surroundings, their first obstacle was to establish the peaceful intent of the natives. This was accomplished fairly quickly through the readable, if novel, nomenclature of native etiquette. The laying down of bows and arrows was perhaps the best sign of the Indians' good intentions, especially if followed by a traditional native greeting involving rubbing, embracing, feeding, smoking, and entertaining.[12]

Thanks largely to the natives' pronounced sense of hospitality, most European newcomers were able to get a foot in the native door without much linguistic effort. But once they gained entry, they were brought up short by their urgent need but excruciating inability to speak with their hosts—to make their purposes and wants known, to convey what they had to offer in return for continued cooperation, and to establish their character as men whose word could be trusted. By the same token, the natives sought to probe the strange tickings of mind behind the foreign faces of their guests, half-hidden behind hair, while assuring those bearers of murderous new weapons of their own benignity and honor.

One way to flatter and reassure the "other" in his own wordless dialect was to imitate his introductory and apparently bona fide behavior. When *La Dauphine* was greeted by twenty canoes of apprehensive natives in Newport harbor, Verrazzano and his crew "reassured them somewhat by imitating their gestures" and throwing them "trinkets." During the next two weeks, the local sachem often visited the ship, "discussing by signs and gestures various fanciful [because unintelligible?] notions" and asking about the ship's equipment. And because he was out of his own element aboard ship, he "imitated our manners," wrote the captain, and "tasted our food" before courteously taking his leave. The French, accordingly, felt free to hobnob with the natives on shore without fear of ambush or betrayal.[13]

Less than sixty years later, not far away in Buzzard's Bay, Gabriel Archer defused a tense situation with some fast and formidable signing. When the local sachem and fifty bowmen advanced hastily toward him and only eight men, he wrote, "I mooved my selfe towards him seven or eight steps, and clapt my hands first on the sides of mine head, then on my breast, and after presented my Musket with a threatening countenance, thereby to signifie unto them, either a choice of Peace or Warre." Perhaps daunted by the Englishman's audacity, the chief returned Archer's "owne signes of Peace" and received a relieved bearhug in reply.[14]

Reassurance was one thing, information-gathering and sharing quite another. When each party's hackles had fallen, it was time for charades. In antic pantomimes that perhaps only children could fully fathom, white and brown folks postured and pranced, wiggled and wagged, gesticulating to noteless scores of imagined song. But unlike charades, this game had few rules to govern play, no spoken words to declare winners and losers, and stakes as high as survival. The work was embarrassing, frustrating, and, more often than the participants would or could admit, wildly ridiculous, but it had to be done if they hoped to actually *speak* the same language in the foreseeable future. Before they could pun, they had to learn to drawl.

On both sides, signing gave rise to prodigious feats of guesswork and wishful thinking, but our evidence, unfortunately, comes from only one side. Columbus was the first but not last European to raise the art of imaginative "listening" to new heights. Transfixed by his dream of reaching the gold-rich provinces of "Catay" and "Cipangu" (China and Japan), the admiral "heard" in the signs of his kidnapped Taino "interpreters" (who, of course, knew no Spanish at first and precious little after three months) mostly what he wanted to hear. As he neared home, Columbus assured his royal sponsors that his interpreters had "soon understood us, and we them, either by speech or signs," a claim totally belied by his daily log.[15]

The self-delusion began as early as his third day in the "Indies." While exploring the eastern part of Guanahaní island, several natives swam to the ship's boat, from which, said the admiral, "we understood that they asked us if we had come from heaven." Two weeks later in a Cuban harbor, local natives allegedly "said by signs that within three days many merchants would come from the interior to buy the things which the Christians brought there, and that they would give news of the king of that land who," as far as Columbus could understand from the signs which they made, "was four days' journey from there, because they had sent many men through the whole land to tell of the admiral"—a flattering but extremely "long-winded" and complex piece of signing. Another gilded bit of news allegedly came from the interpreters on November 12. On "Babeque" (Great Inagua Island), "they said, according to the signs which they made, . . . the people of the place gather gold on the shore at night with candles, and afterwards . . . with a mallet they make bars of it." A month later, Columbus had "heard" enough to convince himself that the Grand Khan of China lived not far away and periodically sent ships to enslave the timorous natives of the islands the Spanish had been visiting. This gave Columbus renewed hope that people speaking an "intelligent" language would soon be found and that he could, at long last, employ his Hebrew-Chaldee-Arabic-speaking interpreter, Luis de Torres.[16]

But it was not to be, on the first or any other of the master sailor's voyages. Geography was the great impediment, of course—Asia was a whole ocean away—but even if the East had been reachable, the initial linguistic barrier was too great to overcome. Columbus had confessed as much to his log in late November. He was confident that "innumerable things of value" could be found in the new lands, but he never discovered what they were because of the shortness of his stays in port, caused largely by his failure to communicate. "I do not know the language," he admitted after six weeks, "and the people of these lands do not understand me, nor do I or anyone I have with me understand them." Moreover, his captive interpreters "I often misunderstand, taking one thing for the contrary, and I have no great confidence in them, because many times they have attempted to escape."[17]

Columbus's many successors in North America had no more cause for smugness in the language department, despite the advantage of hindsight, for neither he nor anyone else left a manual of signing, an anthology of American gestures for tongue-tied invaders. Each explorer had to invent a "silent rhetorick" from scratch, out of scraps of childhood playfulness and the brazen confidence of cultural "superiority." Verrazzano's fifteen-week cruise up the east coast in 1524 allowed the French precious little insight into the inner lives of the native inhabitants. Relying solely on sight rather than speech, the explorers were shocked, for example, to find people in Maine "so barbarous that we could never make any communication with them, however many signs we made to them." Yet this deficiency gave the Christians no pause when it came to ethnography. "Due to the lack of language," they confessed, "we were unable to find out by signs or gestures how much religious faith these people we found possess." So they simply assumed the worst: "We *think* they have neither religion nor laws, that they do not know of a First Cause or Author . . . nor do they even practice any kind of idolatry."[18]

Ten years later, Cartier was equally at sea among the Stadaconans on the Gaspé. Upon spotting the thirty-foot cross the French erected, chief Donnacona pointed to it from his canoe, made a crosslike sign with two fingers, and launched into a "long harangue," sweeping his hand over the surrounding land "as *if* he wished to say that all this region belonged to him, and that we ought not to have set up this cross without his permission." After Cartier explained by signs that the cross was a mere landmark for his eventual return with more substantial trade goods, the Stadaconans "made signs to us that they would not pull down the cross, delivering at the same time several harangues which we did not understand."[19]

The earliest French explorers, in search of temporary trading partners rather than permanent colonies, were positively humble in their interpretation of native signs and sounds compared with the English planters of earliest Virginia. Whether due to national character, inexperience, circumstance, or goals, the Jamestown colonists in 1607 were so confident they could communicate by signs with the inhabitants of the Powhatan (renamed James) River that they placed the most favorable interpretation possible on every native speech they heard—or saw—during their initial exploration to the falls and back. One necessary but not sufficient reason for their confidence was the unusual ability of their Arrohattoc guide Nauirans, whose tribesmen also "would shew us anything we Demaunded, and laboured very much by signes to make us understand their Languadg." After drawing an accurate map of the river with pen and ink upon "being shewn their use," Nauirans successfully mediated the English visit to Powhatan's village near the falls. After only five days out, Gabriel Archer, the trip's scribe, boasted how the Indian "had learned me so much of the Languadg, & was so excellently ingenious in signing out his meaning, that I could make him understand me, and perceive him also wellny [-nigh] in any thing." When some local natives "murmured" at the large cross the English planted near the falls to claim the country as their own, it was Nauirans who signed the allegedly "wise" reply of the friendly Arrohattoc chief who had followed them upriver: "Why should you bee offended with them as long as they hurt you not, nor take any thing away by force, they take but a little waste ground"—an apt description of swampy Jamestown island—"which doth you nor any of us any good."[20]

Nauirans's skill notwithstanding, there is some reason to suspect that the English had fallen prey to wishful thinking. For on May 18, three days before the start of the upriver journey, the Paspahegh chief and a hundred warriors approached the colonists who were in the process of erecting James Fort on his land and signaled two messages. The first—"to lay our Armes away"—was unambiguous and under the circumstances clearly not to be implemented. The second obviously received a thoroughly English interpretation: the chief, they understood, "at length made signes that he would give us as much land as we would desire to take." What the English probably saw was the chief's possessive sweep of arm over his birthright, not unlike Donnacona's. To judge by their fierce attacks in subsequent weeks, the Paspaheghs had most likely issued a strongly "worded" warning against trespass.[21]

The Jamestown English were not alone in thinking they had enjoyed some success in chatting up the natives by signs. On his voyage up the St. Lawrence in 1535, Cartier had the effective help of several signing natives. The chief of Achelacy above modern Quebec City pointed out to the French "clearly by signs and in other ways that the river was extremely dangerous a little higher up" and warned them to be on their guard. At the end of Lac St. Pierre, Cartier asked some Indian fishermen "by signs if this was the way to Hochelaga," their destination on Montreal Island. "They made clear to us that it was," wrote the grateful captain "and that we had still a three days' journey thither," which proved to be correct.[22]

Álvar Núñez Cabeza de Vaca and his fellow survivors of the disastrous Narváez expedition to Florida elicited even more aid as they walked from the East Texas coast to Mexico in the nine years after 1527. Even before leaving Florida, they sent one tenderhearted group of natives into a half-hour howling lamentation by explaining "by signs that our boat had sunk and three of our number had been drowned." By the time they reached the Texas interior, Cabeza de Vaca's party had been reduced to a handful of men and had acquired reputations as shamans and as having facility in six native languages after many months in captivity. "We passed through many and dissimilar tongues," the leader remembered, but "Our Lord granted us favor with the people who spoke them, for they always understood us, and we them. We questioned them, and received their answers by signs, just as if they spoke our language and we theirs."[23]

Few Europeans enjoyed the kind of wholesale success the Cabeza de Vaca party seems to have had. More often, the victories were small, practical, few, and far between. On Bartholomew Gosnold's expedition to Cape Cod in 1602, a gentleman-passenger inquired by signs about the source of the copper from which the natives made drinking cups for trade. An Indian acquaintance answered simply by taking a piece of copper in his hand, making "a hole with his finger in the ground," and pointing to the mainland from which he and his tribesmen had just come. Three years later on the coast of Maine, Captain Waymouth's crew wanted to barter tobacco from the local Indians. But since it was only early June, the natives signed that "it was growen yet but a foot above ground, and [eventually] would be above a yard high, with a leafe as broad as both their hands.[24]

In 1673 the Virginia trader Gabriel Arthur used signs to teach a village of Ohio Shawnees the trading value of beaverskins. When the Shawnees skidded a fat beaver into the compound and proceeded to singe its hair off for roasting, Arthur "made signes to them that those skins were good amongst the white people toward the riseing sun." They in turn wanted to know "by signes" how many skins the English would take for such a knife as Arthur had given to the chief. The trader told them four, and eight for a hatchet, "and made signes that if they would lett him return"—he was a recent captive—"he would bring many things amongst them."[25] And so they did. If Arthur never returned to them with his promised bounty (we have no evidence one way or the other), they may have chalked it up as much to his fumbling fingers as to his forked tongue.

Europeans used sign language to get themselves out of all kinds of sticky situations, not all of which were as potentially life threatening as Arthur's. Indeed, the enlisted men in Iberville's exploring party up the Mississippi in 1700 no doubt regretted their leader's finesse in the American art of gesture and grimace. When the French batteaux pulled up at a friendly Bayogoula village for the night, the chief asked if the strangers would like a warm woman for every man in the company. Apparently Iberville was alarmed by this traditional token of native hospitality and "by showing his hand to them . . . made them understand that their skin—red and tanned—should not come close to that of the French, which was white."[26] The grumbling of the men was not recorded for posterity but is plainly audible even at this remove.

So, too, are the extreme disgruntlement and frustration of those Europeans who were force-fed a steady diet of signs during their initial errands into the wilderness. To hear their complaints is to understand just how inadequate sign language was in eastern America, and how much both sides needed to establish some sort of verbal rapprochement in order to achieve their respective ends. Henri Joutel, the literate but humble chronicler of La Salle's ill-fated colony in Texas in the late 1680s, was anything but a grumbler, yet even he had to give frequent vent to the utter failure of the French survivors to converse intelligibly by signs with the natives they encountered on their slow trek to the Mississippi and eventually to the linguistic familiarity of New France.

Although La Salle had picked up some facility in several Indian tongues on his descent of the Mississippi in 1682, it proved useless when his second expedition two years later overshot the mouth of the great river and grounded in Matagorda Bay on the east coast of Texas. The local natives were initially friendly, "but to no Purpose, for [La Salle] spoke to them in several Languages . . . and made many Signs to them, but still they understood not what he meant." When the French commandeered some of their canoes, however, relations soured and the fragile colony was reduced by attack and forced inland.[27]

In a futile search for the Mississippi, La Salle made several sorties before he was assassinated by some of his men in March 1687. Joutel then was left to live with the Cenis to prepare stores for an all-out search for home. After a week among them, the most useful word he had learned was *Coussica*, "I do not understand you," for most conversation was conducted in signs. Despite the solicitude of the village elders, Joutel spent most of his talks "nodding my Head, tho' very often," he admitted, "I knew not what they meant." When his loneliness without anyone to talk to grew "very irksome," the offer of a young wife brought no consolation. How he must have yearned for some semblance of the diversion that greeted him, in which "all the old Men lifted up their

Right Hands above their Heads, crying out in a most ridiculous Manner." Only a politic regard for his own skin had prevented him from laughing aloud.[28]

A return stay in the Cenis village two months later gave the French, including two Catholic priests, an opportunity to explain the nature of their daily devotions to the inquisitive villagers. "Pointing to Heaven," the French proclaimed that they paid duty to one God, "the only Supreme Sovereign" and Creator of all things. "But this being only by Signs," Joutel confessed, "they did not understand us, and we labour'd in vain." The rest of their journey to the Mississippi was conducted in "dumb Show" only marginally more productive.[29]

La Salle's men had several years' experience in native America before finally realizing that sign language was an impossibly blunt instrument for building a French empire. Colonel Henry Norwood, cast away with other Royalist refugees on the coast of Maryland in 1649 and having no overt interest in empire, had to wait less than two weeks to discover that he was deaf and dumb in the "common dialect of signs and motions" that developed between the English and their native rescuers. Forced to abandon ship on a small island in early January, the English saw no Indians for ten days until a small party visited the secluded women's cabin at night and gave them food. Then the guessing games began. According to the women, the natives had "pointed to the south-east with their hands, which they knew not how to interpret, but did imagine by their several gestures, they would be with them again to morrow." The bookish Norwood concluded that their pointing southeast "was like to be the time they would come, meaning nine o'clock to be their hour, where the sun will be at that time." He was dead wrong: they showed up in midafternoon, as they no doubt had planned. Fortunately, their first communications were encouragingly benevolent: they flashed "most chearful smiles," shook hands all around, and kept intoning "Ny Top" *(nétop),* the common Algonquian word for "friend." Then began the English, particularly Norwood's, descent into befuddlement, for they parleyed in signs, he remembered, "more confounded and unintelligible than any other conversation I ever met withal; as hard to be interpreted as if they had expres'd their thoughts in the *Hebrew* or *Chaldean* tongues."[30]

The next day the Indians returned with an older leader, who tried by signs to pump Norwood for information about his country and the occasion of the English predicament. "I made return to him in many vain words," said the colonel, "and in as many insignificant signs as himself had made to me, and neither of us one jot the wiser. The several nonplus's we both were at in striving to be better understood, afforded so little of edification to either party, that our time was almost spent in vain." Then Norwood remembered a single word from his reading of John Smith's history of Virginia—*werowance,* "chief"— and that word, he thought (probably wrongly), saved their lives because they were immediately ferried by canoe and conducted to the chief of Kickotank, on whose shores they had washed up. En route they were fed royally at the lodge of a "queen," which they left—in a telling phrase—"with all the shews of gratitude that silence of each other's tongues knew how to utter."[31]

Warmly ensconced in the chief's lodge, Norwood was asked by his host, with "many gestures of his body, his arms display'd in various postures," for details of their mishap. "By all which motions," Norwood despaired, "I was not edify'd in the least, nor could imagine what return to make by voice or sign. . . . In fine, I admired their patient sufferance of my dulness to comprehend what they meant, and shew'd myself to be troubled at it." The chief laughed it off and got Norwood to do the same. But the English remained pampered prisoners of silence until one of the chief's councillors scratched a map of the region in the dirt and Norwood recognized "Achomack" on Virginia's Eastern Shore as his destination. Yet even then the English could not move until an English trader and his Indian guide arrived to enlighten the chief in a frontier patois of "broken *Indian*" with "some sprinklings of *English*."[32]

When Norwood reached the "civilized" settlements of Northampton County, he gladly honored the chief's request to have his camblet coat, glittering with gold and silver lace, because, the resolute Royalist quipped, "he was the first king I could call to mind that ever shew'd any inclination to wear my old cloaths." His humor does nothing to conceal from us his profound gratitude to the Kickotank chief for his inexhaustible hospitality and, perhaps equally important, his laughing patience with a stranger's tortured failure to speak or hear by signs.[33]

The essential problem remained: how could the adult speakers of totally foreign languages learn the myriad rules and nuances of each other's tongues fast enough and well enough to begin reliable communication? And if one party sought to dictate the verbal terms of engagement, which would it be? Who would accommodate whom, and how? Human ingenuity being what it is, the new partners-in-contact invented two basic solutions. One was to fashion from shards of a European and one or more Indian languages a *jargon* to facilitate the simpler needs of sporadic trade and treaty. The other, more prevalent option was for one party to create a *pidgin* by reducing its native speech to its simplest elements and suppressing most of the features that made it distinctive and therefore difficult for strangers to learn.

Both solutions were predicated on treating the "others" not as capable adults but as young children just learning to wrap their tongues around polysyllabic words and to tease out of usage the imperfect regularities of grammar and syntax. Pidgins and jargons (which are technically pidgins) were designed specially for neophytes in the difficult art of speaking a new language. If these amateur argots seemed to native linguists like so much "baby talk," the analogy was not inapt.[34]

In addition to simplicity, America's versions of verbal shorthand had three other attractive features. The first was that pidgins were flexible tools capable of growing in sophistication and complexity with the speakers, until they either closely approximated the mature language from which they were chipped or were totally superseded by a rival tongue. The latter was the eventual fate of the four major Indian-based pidgins east of the Mississippi: the Mohawk, Delaware, and Powhatan pidgins succumbed to the mother tongue of the English colonists who swarmed over New York, Pennsylvania, New Jersey, and Virginia; and French supplanted the Mobilian trade language in the Lower Mississippi Valley. The English-based pidgin spoken largely by Indians in colonial New England was "elevated," predictably if slowly, to more standard English, particularly in the anglicized "praying towns" established by Protestant missionaries.

The second feature of the jargons and of any pidgin that served several ethnic groups was their normative neutrality. Since they were no one's proper language, they lent a measure of verbal impartiality and social stability to fragile frontiers where ethnic pride was easily bruised and often inflamed. Accessible and useful to all parties, they were stigmatized by none as inferior or preferential. This quality entailed a third value: Indian groups who used pidgins were able to preserve their proper language and its cultural secrets from the prying ears and mocking mouths of white men.[35]

The oldest pidgin in eastern North America and one of the most durable was born on the hard coasts of the Gulf of St. Lawrence early in the sixteenth century when Basque fishermen and whalers worked, traded, and ate with local Micmacs and Montagnais and possibly visiting Inuits. "Since their languages were completely different," testified a group of Basque fishermen in 1710, "they created a form of lingua franca composed of Basque and two different languages of the Indians, by means of which they could understand each other quite well." When the codfishers greeted their Montagnais helpers each year, they asked them in Basque "*Nola zaude?*" (How are you?), to which the natives replied politely, "*Apaizak hobeto*" (The priests [shamans]are better). The cod, of course, were called *bacaillos* or *bakalaos* even by the local Micmacs, whose own name for them was *apegé*. Four hundred years later, two words of Basque origin are still used by Micmac-speakers: *atlai*, "shirt" (from Basque *atorra*; modern Micmac has no "r") and *elege*, "king" (from Basque *errege*).[36]

When French colonists arrived in Acadia in 1604 and founded Quebec four years later, the language of the coastal tribes, noted one observer, with only small exaggeration, was "half Basque" and had been for a long time. Depending upon how they were treated, natives uttered such Basque phrases as "*Endia chave normandia*" (The French know many things) and "*Maloes mercateria*" (Those from Saint-Malo are unfair traders). They even referred to their own moose as *orignac* (Basque for "deer"), their shamans as *pilotoua* (pilots), and their celebratory feasts as *tabaquia* (shelter, indicating the place where they were held). Although in the 1540s the Indians of the St. Lawrence Gulf palavered with foreign fishermen in "any language," French, English, Gascon, or Basque, by the seventeenth century, a French lawyer said, they traded with the French only in Basque.[37]

This was a slight stretch, because it overlooked the solid substratum of Algonquian words and features that underlay the jargon. According to Marc Lescarbot, a keen-eyed lawyer-historian who spent a year in nascent Acadia, for "convenience" the native Micmacs spoke to the French in a simple, "familiar" version of their own language with which "much Basque is *mixed*," although they also had a fuller, proper tongue "known only to themselves." Around early Quebec it was equally easy to miss the multilingual origins of the jargon used by the Montagnais. In 1633 a Jesuit linguist noticed "a certain jargon . . . which is neither French nor Indian; and yet when the French use it, they think they are speaking the Indian Tongue, and the Indians, in using it, think they are speaking good French." When the Montagnais and French addressed each other, for example, they always used *Ania,* "my brother." But Father Le Jeune already knew that *Nichtais* was Montagnais for "my eldest brother" and *Nichim* for "my youngest," which led him to declare *Ania* "an alien word." It was, predictably, the Basque word for "brother," *anaia,* brought from the Gulf with the rest of the jargon.[38]

In the opening years of the seventeenth century, the "Basque" jargon also drifted down the Maine coast, perhaps into Massachusetts. Micmacs and Etchemins sailing hefty Basque shallops were a frequent sight as they plied the middleman's trade between Maine's native trappers and the Laurentian Gulf's European traders. When Bartholomew Gosnold's ship reached the northern New England coast in mid-May 1602, it was met by eight Indians aboard a "Baske-shallop." The leader wore shoes, stockings, and a black serge seaman's suit; the rest were largely "naked" save for white-painted eyebrows. "It seemed by some words and signes they made," the English surmised, "that some Basks or of S. John de Luz [St.-Jean-de-Luz, a major French Basque port], have fished or traded in this place." The tardy English were right, but they would have been chagrined to learn how long ago those Basque or (as they called them) "Christian" words had entered the working vocabulary of the coast's inhabitants.[39]

The rough equality between the native Americans and the European, particularly Basque, mariners on the Atlantic frontier fostered the growth and maintenance of a bi- or tri-lingual trade jargon for at least a century. Similar conditions and needs gave rise to a near-copy in the Carolinas. Not long after the arrival of the Basques in northern waters, Spain began to explore, claim, and fortify the southern coasts between Florida and Chesapeake Bay. Except for their capital at Santa Elena, however, the Spanish hold on the coast and its natives was exceedingly tenuous. But in maintaining even a minor military and missionary presence, the Spanish had frequent contact with the coastal tribes, with whom they gradually learned to communicate. In 1564 Spanish coastal squadrons were able to track down French interlopers with the help of only native "signs and some intelligible words."[40] During the next century, however, the Spanish and the Indians fashioned a usable jargon for their sporadic interchanges. By the time the English began to make serious inroads in Carolina in the 1660s and 1670s, they were greeted by numerous natives wagging hispanicized tongues.

The crew on William Hilton's exploratory voyage in 1663 quickly learned that *Bonny* meant "good" and *Skerry* its opposite and were so taken with their new vocabulary that they named two landmarks "Mount-Skerry" and "Mount-Bonny." Another native group from Santa Elena greeted the English with what Hilton recognized as "many Spanish words, [such] as, *Cappitan [capitan], Commarado [camarado]*, and *Adeus [adios]*." Seven years later, the first settlers on the newly renamed Ashley River were delighted to be stroked in welcome and greeted with "*Bony Conraro Angles*" (Good friend English). Shortly after, another party laid on them "*Hiddy doddy Comorado Angles Westoe Skorrye*," which was to say, "English very good friends, Westoes"—pugnacious inland enemies—"are nought." Picking up the drift of conversation quickly, the newcomers determined that the natives "hoped by our arrival to be protected from the Westoes."[41]

As the English inundated the Carolina coast, the Spanish-inspired jargon ebbed. Supremely confident of their own cultural superiority and bent on sovereignty, the English settlers, many from the inegalitarian slave society of Barbados, saw no need to perpetuate a bastardized jargon of alien, indeed enemy, tongues. At least on the coast, English would be the lingua franca. For many of the same reasons, the colonists of southern New England sought to replace the indigenous tongues with an English pidgin, scaled down and "juvenilized" for native consumption. In the gruesome wake of plague and smallpox epidemics, the often decimated tribes of the Massachusetts and Plymouth coast were rapidly overwhelmed by the popular success of the Great Migration of the 1630s. In such circumstances, they had little choice but to forge their survival largely in the white man's words, however ridiculous he found them to be on Algonquian tongues.

The first English settlers in New England—as distinguished from fishermen, explorers, and slavers—found conversation with the first Indians they actually met so easy that they must have seen no reason to learn a native tongue. On March 16, 1620, after two-and-a-half months of cold, hard labor building houses and a fort on abandoned Indian land, the Plymouth pilgrims were boldly approached by a nearly naked "savage" who spoke to them in "broken English, which they could well understand but marveled at." Before asking for some beer, an eyewitness said, Samoset "saluted us in English, and bade us welcome, for he had learned some broken English among the Englishmen that came to fish" at Monhegan Island off the coast of his native Maine, from which he had recently come to visit the local Wampanoags. He was so chatty, in fact, that the English spent all afternoon talking with him and could not persuade him to leave the fort for the night.[42]

Far from being a threat to security, Samoset introduced the foreign seekers to another loquacious Indian whose unusual facility in their own tongue would give them a crucial advantage in an uncertain, at times hostile, New World.

Squanto turned out to be a native of the site where Plymouth sat. He had been kidnapped by an English slaver six years earlier, sold in Spain, redeemed, taken to London, where he lived with an officer of the Newfoundland Company, and eventually returned to his birthplace, which in his absence had been depopulated by a shipborne plague in 1616. Understandably, he spoke better English than did Samoset, whose Abenaki accent and fisherman's jargon were not equal to the demands of tricky negotiations between the pushy Pilgrims and a variety of divided Indian polities.[43]

The "broken" English spoken by Samoset and Squanto, liberally spiced with native words and locutions, was to remain the standard language of intercourse between natives and newcomers in southern New England for most of the colonial period. Only missionaries trying to woo native converts were obliged to operate in aboriginal languages. Even in Algonquian mouths, the earliest versions of the pidgin bore little resemblance to the proper native tongues that many Indians continued to speak well into the eighteenth century. Captain Miles Standish discovered the distinction in early March 1623 when he ran into Wituwamat, a caustic character from Massachusetts Bay who was trying to foment a conspiracy against the English on Cape Cod. The Indian made a long speech in an "audacious manner," wrote Edward Winslow, not in the still heavily native pidgin but in a pure Massachusett dialect, "framing it in such sort as the Captain, though he be the best linguist amongst us, could not gather anything from it."[44]

For conversation that sought to include Englishmen, the natives resorted to the increasingly anglicized pidgin. By 1634 an English visitor noticed that although the natives loved anyone who could "utter his mind in their words," they were "not a little proud that they can speak the English tongue, using it as much as their own when they meet with such as can understand it." Indeed, they loved to confound "stranger Indians" with their novel lingo. On occasion, the pidgin even served as a lingua franca between strangers. In 1624 the governor of Maine brought an Abenaki warrior seventy miles to confer with a local native of the same tribe. "They were glad to use broken English to expresse their mind each to other," said a witness, "not being able to understand one another in their Language" because of dialectical differences.[45]

The first thing the Abenakis may have said to each other, as Samoset probably greeted the Pilgrims, was "What cheare *Nétop?*" (How are things, friend?), the general salutation in New English-Indian relations. But since the pressure of English population, land-grabbing, and missionaries soon soured relations, our best examples of pidgin come freighted with fear and hostility. A native memory of their first encounter with a European ship yielded a characteristic line. When the Indians saw this great "walking island" approach, they paddled out to pick strawberries on it. But the ship saluted them with a broadside of "lightning and thunder," which so astonished them that they cried out (as recaptured in 1630s jargon) "What much hoggery, so big walk, and so big speak, and by and by kill." A few years later, the Pequots of southern Connecticut echoed those sentiments when a Massachusetts invasion force coasted along their territory in search of a landing place: "What, Englishmen, what cheer, what cheer, are you hoggery, will you cram us?" An English captain interpreted this to mean "Are you angry, will you kill us, and do you come to fight?"[46]

In a lighter moment forty years later, an English captain, preparing to lead sixty men against three hundred allies of King Philip (Metacomet), plucked off his precious wig and stuffed it into his pants for safekeeping. Having witnessed this bizarre act from a distance, the enemy warriors howled "hideously" and their leader allegedly yelled, "Umh, umh me no stawmerre [understand?] fight Engismon, Engismon got two Hed, Engismon got two Hed; if me cut off un Hed, he got noder, a put on beder as dis." Upon which they fled into the consoling forest.[47]

To English ears, much of the Indian jargon was laughable. The popular trader Christopher Levett obviously relished reporting Abenaki attempts to wield their newfound English words with grace and effect, and he was not a little proud to jabber in broken Algonquian. When two sagamores returned to trade with Levett after a brief flirtation with a rival English captain, they asked if he was angry. He said that he was not, but he warned them that "if they were MATCHETT, that is, naughtie men, and rebellious," he would be MOUCH-ICK HOGGERY, that is very angry, and would CRAM, that is, kill them all." Whereupon they branded the rival trader a "Jacknape," "the most disgraceful word that may be in their conceite," and told Levett that he was, by contrast, a "foure fathom" sagamore, borrowing a metaphor from their wampum strings to indicate his worth. When he explained that he was returning to England to fetch his wife, who would not make the crossing alone, "they bid a pox on her hounds, (a phrase they have learned and doe use when they doe curse) and wished me to beat her," Indian-style. With a more gracious eye to the future, one sagamore predicted "muchicke legamatch, (that is friendship)" between his and Levett's sons "untill TANTO"—an Abenaki deity—"carried them to his wigwam, (that is untill . . . they died)."[48]

In other North American colonies, the initial surge of settlement was nothing like that in New England, and the natives retained the upper hand long enough to concoct the dominant pidgins that would be used by the early colonists. Early Dutch Reformed ministers in New Netherland were particularly stymied by their inability to get past simple trade jargons to more sophisticated concepts of cosmology and religion. Jonas Michaëlius, the first minister in New Amsterdam, thought he knew something about the "savage mind" after brief tours of duty in Brazil and West Africa. To his thinking, the Indians around Manhattan in 1628 were "uncivil and stupid as garden poles, proficient in all wickedness and godlessness, . . . [and] thievish and treacherous as they are tall." Imagine his chagrin, then, when he deduced that the natives designed to "conceal their language from us than to properly communicate it, except in things which happen in daily trade; saying that it is sufficient for us to understand them in that." But the trade jargon—much to his disgust—was nothing but "a made-up, childish language" in which the Indians spoke only "half sentences" made up of "shortened words" that frequently lumped together a dozen or more objects. The Dutch traders who did business in it clearly were fools to think of themselves as "wonderful" linguists, because they badly botched the pronunciation of its "difficult aspirants and many gutteral[s]" and were "wholly in the dark and bewildered when they hear[d] the savages talking among themselves."[49]

If the misanthropic Michaëlius was frustrated by an Algonquian jargon in New Amsterdam, the Reverend Johannes Megapolensis suffered even greater pains in the 1640s learning the Iroquoian Mohawk tongue in order to preach in it. The dominie of Rensselaerwyck's biggest problem was lack of competent instructors. The local Dutch experts knew only "a kind of jargon just sufficient to carry on trade with it" but were ignorant of "the fundamentals of the language." The Mohawks themselves were even less helpful, probably by design. When he asked them for the names of things, he complained, "one tells me the word in the infinitive mood, another in the indicative; one in the first, another in the second person; one in the present, another in the preterit [past]. So I stand oftentimes and look, but do not know how to put it down." The fault, of course, was not his: "As *they* are very stupid," he explained, "I sometimes cannot make them understand what *I* want." To pour salt in his wounds, "they pronounced their words so differently." So Megapolensis asked an eighteen-year veteran of the area for an explanation; the man's best guess was that "they changed their language every two or three years," which seemed a stupid answer even to the ethnocentric evangelist.[50]

At the same time the Dutch founded New Amsterdam and built Fort Orange, however, they had settled briefly on the Delaware River, from 1624 to 1628. There, in pitifully small numbers, they established relations with the powerful and numerous Delaware Indians. Understandably, the natives saw no reason to learn Dutch to be able to communicate with the strangers in their midst. But they did cut their southern Unami dialect down to European size in order to make their own needs and prerogatives known in pidgin form. The resulting Delaware jargon (as it is known) served not only the Dutch, who carried it northward when they moved, but successive colonies of Swedes and English.

In 1683 William Penn characterized the native language of Pennsylvania as "lofty, yet narrow . . .; in Signification full, like Short-hand in writing; one word serveth in the place of three, and the rest are supplied by the Understanding of the Hearer: Imperfect in their Tenses, Wanting in their Moods, Participles, Adverbs, Conjunctions, [and] Interjections." What he described so well was not full and proper Delaware but the jargon used, as an early colonist noted, between natives and "Christians" who traded with them "or when they meet one another in the Woods accidentally, one a looking for his Cattel, and the other a Hunting the Wild Deer, or other Game."[51] Yet the jargon was not entirely useless in other realms. In the 1640s the Swedish minister Johannes Campanius managed to translate Luther's little catechism for children into the Delaware "shorthand." Although it was not published until 1696 in Sweden, it was reimported and saw limited use among the Indians who had inspired it.[52]

The best examples of the Delaware jargon come from a promotional book published in 1698 by Gabriel Thomas, an early Pennsylvanian, and a lengthy word-and-phrase list from the 1680s called "The Indian Interpreter," found in the Salem, New Jersey, land records. Thomas's short dialogue between an Indian hunter and an English woodsman featured practical lines such as "When wilt thou bring me Skins and Venison, with Turkeys?" and "I have good Powder, and very good Shot, with red and blue Machcots [matchcoats]." The native phrases in the "Interpreter" also tended to be "almost grammarless and based chiefly on an English construction," for the convenience of the colonists, but most of the vocabulary was distinctly Delaware, with a spare sprinkling of New England Natick, English, Dutch, and onomatopoetic words. Jargon-speakers called a duck *quing quing*, a lead bullet *alunse* (from *alluns*, the Delaware word for "arrow"), and rum *brandywyne* (a famous Pennsylvania place-name today, thanks to the artistic Wyeths). Sometime in the seventeenth century, the Natick words *squaw* and *papouse* had migrated from eastern Massachusetts to the mid-Atlantic interior. And number and gender, so important in proper Delaware, were ignored in the jargon (except for a distinction between "I" and "we"). As in most pidgins, *me* replaced the first-person singular "I," as in *Me mauholumi* (I will buy it).[53]

Like its New York counterparts, the Delaware jargon eventually was replaced by pidgin English and standard English, but not until the eighteenth century. The Powhatan and Occaneechi pidgins that arose to accommodate and incorporate the English settlers of early Virginia died much faster, the victims of rapid English immigration after the development of saleable tobacco, interracial warfare, and a system of rigid apartheid.[54]

Between 1607 and 1611 Captain John Smith and William Strachey, the first secretary of the Virginia colony, compiled native vocabularies that consisted largely of single terms for trade goods, anatomical parts, natural phenomena, native relationships, numbers, flora, and fauna. One version of Strachey's manuscript was entitled "A Short Dictionary . . . By which, such who shall be Imployed thether may know the readyer how to confer, and how to truck and Trade with the People." Traders would indeed have found it useful, but officials bent on holding conferences with the touchy Powhatans also would have needed a few principles of pidgin grammar, for the list of nearly 750 words contains no guide to sentence construction, perhaps assuming—probably correctly—that English syntax would work most of the time. Smith's much shorter list of 137 words at least gave some examples of pidgin sentences as well as some insight into the psychology of Indian-white relations. One native speaker asked with obvious concern, "In how many daies will there come hether any more English ships?" And we can just hear the gruff captain ordering native messengers to "Bid Pokahontas bring two little Baskets, and I will give her white beads to make her a chaine."[55]

Another pidgin flourished in south-central Virginia to serve the interests of native and English traders who operated between the Tidewater and the Carolina Piedmont. The Occaneechis, who lived on an island in the Roanoke River astride the main north-south route, created a lucrative business as middlemen and brokers. They also fashioned "a sort of general Language ... which is understood by the Chief men of many Nations, as *Latin* is in most parts of Europe, and Lingua Franca quite thro the *Levant*." Their wealth in furs and their key position proved too tempting to the Virginians under rebel Nathaniel Bacon, and they were robbed and eliminated in 1676. But their trade jargon may have persisted in the region well into the eighteenth century. When the Huguenot settler John Fontaine visited Fort Christanna on the Meherrin River in 1716, he jotted down a sample of native words in use by the polyglot remnants of mostly Siouan-speaking tribes, including Occaneechis, who lived around the fort. The vocabulary consisted of almost equal parts Siouan and Algonquian words with a smattering of Iroquoian terms, which probably indicates the character of the original "Occaneechi" pidgin.[56]

The southernmost Indian pidgin enjoyed a much longer life and held sway over a much wider area than did the Powhatan or other southern pidgins. The so-called Mobilian or Chickasaw trade jargon was fashioned in the Lower Mississippi Valley at least by 1700 in response to French explorers and traders from Illinois and the Gulf of Mexico. It soon spread as far as East Texas, the Ohio River, Alabama, and the northwestern Gulf Coast of Florida. Formed on a Western Muskogean lexical base, primarily Choctaw and Chickasaw, it incorporated elements from Alabama and Koasati (Eastern Muskogean tongues) and a very few words from Spanish, French, and Algonquian, and evolved a grammar very different from those of its constituent languages. Since children were never taught the jargon, it remained a secondary contact language that adults learned "by practice rather than by rules" for purposes of trade and diplomacy. It was, testified a French engineer, "a kind of mother tongue which is general for all, and which is understood everywhere. . . . When one knows it, one can travel through all this province [Louisiana] without needing an interpreter."[57]

According to Antoine Le Page du Pratz, an early settler and historian of Louisiana, the Cadodaquioux and the Nachitoches living on the Red River some three hundred miles west of the Mississippi were no strangers to *la langue mobilienne*. Although both spoke their own "peculiar" languages, "there is not a village in either of the nations, nor indeed in any nation of Louisiana, where there are not some who can speak the Chicasaw language, which is called the vulgar [common] tongue, and is the same here as the Lingua Franca is in the Levant."[58]

Nearly as far east of the great river, in Alabama territory, three Frenchmen saved their own necks by their competence in Mobilian. In 1708 two French hunters were sent by their commander to hunt game for the ill-supplied Spanish governor of Passacol (Pensacola). During the chase they were captured by a party of "Alibamons" and asked what they were doing so close to Passacol. The two hunters, "who had a good understanding of the Mobilian tongue in which the Alibamons had addressed them," told them about their hunting assignment. To test the truth of what the Frenchmen said, two chiefs the next day returned their guns and took them hunting. A herd of buffalo appeared, the two natives "in their eagerness fired at once," the hunters shot the natives and returned home with both their and the Indians' scalps.[59]

Three decades later, fluency in Mobilian enabled another Frenchman to escape captivity and possible death. In November 1741, Antoine Bonnefoy was taken from a river convoy bound for Illinois by a war party of Cherokees. After more than five months in captivity, he escaped and made his way to the northernmost Alabama town, Conchabaka, three days' journey from French Fort Toulouse. Since he looked like a Cherokee, the Alabamas were reluctant to allow him in for fear that he was an enemy decoy. But after two hours of questions, which he answered "in French and in Mobillian," the natives were assured of his identity and recent origins. The trouble came when six Carolina traders and fifteen Chickasaw escorts sought his release into their hands. In the council house the English even gladhanded him and, "in the Chicachas language," promised him a good job if he would follow them to Carolina. Choosing the flag over trade, he put them off in Mobilian, "which they understood," and declared his preference for remaining with the Alabama warrior who had first "captured" him, who concurred. The next day, with his "captor's" blessing, he set off for Fort Toulouse and freedom.[60]

In the vast, polyglot Lower Mississippi, Mobilian retained its usefulness as a lingua franca well into the eighteenth century and perhaps even the next. On the proliferating plantations of the whites, the jargon was heard less and less frequently, except in occasional orders to Indian hunters and servants. Inevitably, French—perhaps in pidgin form initially—and American English became the masters' languages of preference. But in the region's innumerable native communities, especially when they fractured, moved, and amalgamated, a common tongue was still needed to bridge Babel's fissures. Mobilian served that need perfectly. And it continued to find uses all over the Southeast, apparently, for only twenty years ago linguists collected more than 150 Mobilian words and phrases in native communities in Louisiana and Texas.[61]

As short-term solutions to the New World's language problem, signs, pidgins, and jargons served their modest purpose. But when the Europeans got down to the serious business of moving inland from their narrow beachheads—opened as often by disease as by words and gifts—they could no longer depend on truncated thoughts, juvenile jabber, and half-baked notions about "savage" culture and institutions. With the exception of the Powhatan chiefdom in tidewater Virginia, the native polities of coastal America were too small, too divided, or too curious to put up much resistance to the explorers, traders, and colonial advance men who scudded in on the flood tides of the sixteenth and seventeenth centuries. Not so the large tribes who dominated the interior, its land, and its resources. The Hurons and Iroquois, Cherokees and Creeks were simply too fit, too proud, and too dangerous to push around or out of the way. If they were to be cajoled into cooperation rather than stampeded into resistance, the invaders had to learn what motivated them and how their social institutions worked. Most of all, they had to learn the characteristic idioms of native thought, for unless they could appeal to the Indians' self-interest—in their own tongues—they hadn't a prayer of converting, conquering, or removing them to open the way for the wagon ruts of progress.

Certainly the vast majority of colonists and officials had no aptitude for or interest in learning to think and speak like Indians. So they searched for reliable surrogates—interpreters whose closeness to native culture gave them an intimate knowledge not only of native tongues but of the mental and moral codes for deciphering native acts, hopes, and fears. An obvious source of experts was, as Columbus discerned, the Indians themselves. Who knew the enemy and his tongue better than the enemy? Early in the colonial process, natives were kidnapped, enticed, or otherwise sent to Europe to pick up enough French, English, or Spanish to be able to translate native words and concepts and to impress their fellow tribesmen with the invaders' homegrown numbers and wonders. In 1534 Cartier purloined two of chief Donnacona's sons from the Gaspé for this purpose and received fair return the following year when they piloted and palavered him up the St. Lawrence. Manteo and Wanchese served the same end fifty years later when they accompanied Ralegh's colonists back to Roanoke. Even earlier in the Chesapeake, a young, possibly York River, Indian was picked up by the Spanish, educated in Mexico, Spain, and Havana, baptized, and returned to Virginia in 1570 as interpreter and guide to a party of Jesuits. Rather than lead his people to the bruited glories of Christian salvation, however, he promptly ran away, took several wives Indian-style, and led the slaughter of the deceived blackrobes.[62]

The earliest Jesuits and Recollects in Canada also were fond of sending native boys, and occasionally girls, to European schools and convents for religious and linguistic acculturation. But their pupils often died en route or in the disease capitals of Europe, reverted to typecast "savagery" on return, or, perhaps most frustrating of all, lost much of their native fluency during the total immersion of their junior years abroad. The Recollects' best hope, Pierre-Antoine Pastedechouen, a Montagnais, was thoroughly ruined by his six years in France. When he returned to Canada in 1626, he certainly knew his French (not to mention Latin) and reveled in Gallic culture, but he had so thoroughly forgotten his own language that he had to be forced to return to his former district around Tadoussac to learn it. Having lost any forest skills he may have had, he earned only contempt from his tribesmen, took to drink, and went through four or five wives before dying of starvation in the woods. The French, who badly needed his skills as an interpreter and missionary language instructor, had to reconsider their options.[63]

One of their solutions was also employed by the English over the next two centuries: sending likely native boys to colonial Indian schools to acquire the invaders' tongue. In the seventeenth century, these stiffly formal institutions proved unequal to the task of endowing aspiring warriors with European minds, manners, and mouths. Both the Recollect and Jesuit *séminaires* (largely for Hurons) folded within five years. The proposed Indian school at Henrico in Virginia came to naught in the Powhatan uprising of 1622. Harvard graduated exactly two Indians, one of whom was killed by native traditionalists, the other by the white man's tuberculosis.[64]

The French learned from their mistakes and never tried again, but the English suffered the selective amnesia of arrogance and periodically dusted off their scheme to anglicize the natives for future deployment as interpreters. In the eighteenth century, a wide variety of New England and Middle Atlantic tribesmen were schooled in English words and ways in Philadelphia, Stockbridge, Massachusetts, New Haven, and Lebanon, Connecticut. Almost the sole accomplishment of Eleazar Wheelock's famous charity school in Lebanon was training a number of Indian boys as interpreters (and schoolmasters) for the frontiers of New York and New England; after a short but bitter run at the business, Wheelock gave up his founding hope of producing native missionaries and settled for the lesser but still important goal.[65]

The basic problem facing Wheelock and all European officials seeking interpreters was that, at bottom, Indians lacked full credibility. While they certainly could be counted on to know what made their brethren tick, they were much less in tune with European modes of thinking and codes of conduct, into which the native views were somehow to be translated. This cultural deficiency was not insurmountable in trade or even day-to-day diplomacy, but in the delicate minuets of treaty-making and in the sacred precincts of religion it was a distinct liability. And as the racial climate in America darkened, no Indian—no matter how fluent, able, or experienced—could ever be fully trusted with the white man's business. The natives' "national" reputation for secrecy, subterfuge, and revenge was too well known to allow the Europeans, the English especially, the luxury of putting their complete faith in native interpreters.

If natives were ultimately unacceptable, then fellow colonists themselves must somehow gain the fluency and understanding of natives. Although their loyalty to their employers could not always be taken for granted, given the normal seductions of party, interest, and greed, at least they began on the right side of the cultural and linguistic divide.

Most European interpreters—and the best—acquired their skills by living among the Indians as teenagers or in their early twenties, when learning is an unstudied and often pleasurable pastime. Their native domicile could be either voluntary or forced, as long as they chose to return to colonial society to earn their living and to own their primary allegiance. The three main groups who followed this course were war captives or adoptees, traders, and boys or young men placed in friendly villages by their parents or colonial officials for total immersion in native words and ways.

Europeans who had been forcibly acculturated by Indians made perhaps the most trustworthy interpreters because, although they might remain sympathetic to their adopted cultures, they were usually happy to be repatriated by their countrymen; their loyalties to their rescuers were reliable. Moreover, their linguistic skills were often pronounced because they had acquired them quickly and in isolation from their natal tongues in order to survive, not from duty or for mere pleasure. Hernando de Soto's *entrada* through the Southeast after 1539 would have become lost even earlier than it did if Soto had not recovered Juan Ortiz from the natives after twelve years of captivity and linguistic immersion.[66]

In the late seventeenth and early eighteenth century, some of the best interpreters were schooled by northeastern tribes after being captured during Euro-Indian conflicts or intercolonial wars. Louis-Thomas Chabert de Joncaire became a formidable agent and interpreter for New France among the Iroquois after he was captured by the Senecas in the 1680s, adopted, and married. He helped broker the major Franco-Iroquois peace treaty of 1701 and fathered (by a French wife) two sons who succeeded him as accomplished interpreters, forest diplomats, and thorns in the sides of British officials.[67] Two of the Joncaires' ablest rivals for Iroquois loyalties were Lawrence Claessen van der Volgen and Jan Baptist van Eps, who worked for the English in New York colony. Both Dutchmen had been captured by French-allied Iroquois in the daring nighttime raid on Schnectady in 1690—Claessen at thirteen, van Eps at seventeen—and raised among the Caughnawagas across the river from Montreal. Having had native tutoring for only three years, van Eps was quickly supplanted as New York's chief interpreter when Claessen returned after ten years of cultural reconditioning.[68]

The three-way contest for New England also bred its share of adept "linguisters." John Gyles was in great demand by English officials for peace negotiations and prisoner exchanges in Maine because he spoke fluent French, Micmac, and Maliseet after nine years of captivity. Taken at the age of nine by a Maliseet war party in 1689, he spent six years with the Indians and another three with a French trader in Acadia before returning to an effective military career on the Maine frontier.[69] Joseph Kellogg and his sister Rebecca were equally effective as hired tongues after they returned from captivity in Canada. At the age of twelve and eight, respectively, they had been seized with the rest of their family from Deerfield, Massachusetts, by a French and Indian war party in 1704. Joseph stayed with the natives only a year but then traveled widely with French traders in Indian country as far as the Mississippi. When he returned to New England, he drew a substantial salary for serving as cap-

tain at Fort Dummer, head of its trading post, sometime teacher at the Hollis
Indian school in Stockbridge, and the best male interpreter in New England.
After twenty-five years among the Caughnawagas, his sister was even better,
but, being a woman, she was seldom used for public diplomacy. Instead, she
employed her "extraordinary" fluency in the Hollis school (which boarded
mostly Iroquois children) and for the Oneida mission of the Reverend Gideon
Hawley at Oquaga, New York.[70]

While the captive experience was invaluable training for potential interpreters, it was not always reliable. Most young captives—literally hundreds—
never returned to their colonial homes at all or were compelled by peace
treaties and prisoner exchanges to do so against their will.[71] A safer way to
produce interpreters was to place "likely lads" in allied Indian villages, usually
in the families of headmen, for at least a year of cultural and linguistic immersion. During their years abroad, the boys served not only as vulnerable sureties
for the good behavior of their colonial sponsors but as unwitting participants
in a venerable native ritual, in which trading partners and allies exchanged
children as tokens of good faith. Only occasionally did the Europeans recip-
rocate by requesting or accepting Indian children; when they did, the political
need for hostages or brown bodies to fill philanthropic Indian schools was
uppermost in their minds, not bowing to "savage" custom.[72]

In the Americas, the French initiated the practice of placing student interpreters in native villages.[73] In the sixteenth century, French sea captains in the
brazilwood trade sent young sailors to native villages along the Brazilian coast
to recruit woodcutters while learning the local languages. Many of these blond
"*truchements de Normandie*" went quite native, going relatively "naked," painting themselves, taking native wives, and even dining on Indian enemies with
their new tribespeople. Protestant French missionaries and rival Portuguese
settlers alike were appalled at the extent of the interpreters' acculturation but
profited immeasurably from their linguistic skills and knowledge of the land
and its peoples.[74]

One of the veterans of the Brazil run was Jacques Cartier of Saint-Malo. On
his third voyage to Canada in 1541, he left with the cooperative chief of
Achelacy "two yong boyes . . . to learne their language." On his previous
reconnaissance of the St. Lawrence six years earlier, the chief had sought to
ally himself with the patently powerful strangers by giving Cartier his own
eight- or nine-year-old daughter, whom Cartier took to France the following
spring. Since Cartier had not returned her to her homeland (she had probably
died of an unfamiliar urban disease), he was taking a calculated risk with the
lives of his two student interpreters. Perhaps the chief had swallowed a version
of the tale Cartier had manufactured for the new chief of Stadacona, that
Donnacona, the former chief, had died in France but that the other four headmen the French had shanghaied upon departing remained there "as great
Lords, and were maried, and would not returne backe into their Countrey."[75]

The French need to prepare their own interpreters was all the more urgent because two of their latest hostages were the same two sons of Donnacona whom Cartier had plucked from the mouth of the river on his first voyage in 1534 and taken to France to learn enough French to serve as his guides and tongues the following year. But the results were mixed: one, Domagaya, was only partially accommodating in French dealings with his wary and politically embroiled father. The other, Taignoagny, used his newfound knowledge of the French to counteract their ploys and policies in his homeland—a scene that would be re-enacted when the English repatriated their two Indian inter- preters at Roanoke a half century later.[76]

After the French resumed their colonizing efforts on the St. Lawrence in 1608, officials soon planted young Frenchmen in the distant villages of all their potential trading partners and allies. Between 1610 and 1629, they sent a dozen to winter *"chez les Sauvages."* Most stayed two or three years, but several served much longer as the eyes, ears, and tongues of the fur trade monopolists and civil governors. Étienne Brûlé lived with the Hurons for eighteen years; Jean Nicollet followed the nomadic Algonquins and Nipissings for ten years; Jean Richer worked the camps of the Montagnais and Algonquins for seven years, half as many as Nicolas Marsolet. When the Recollects and Jesuits launched their different and often rival missions in the same native cantons, they often assailed the morality and loyalty of the acculturated *truchements,* but they usually had no way to get a purchase on the native tongues without their begrudging assistance. Marsolet protected his employer's trading interests by vowing never to teach anyone a word of the native languages he commanded. He relented only to teach an importunate Recollect the Montagnais phrase for "No, I do not understand you." Fortunately for the missionaries, other inter- preters were more forthcoming.[77]

When the French (many of them Canadians) extended their geopolitical reach to Louisiana after 1699, they transferred their effective mode of inter- preter training as well. Since the southern mission was more military than mercantile, the students sent among the Houmas, Bayogoulas, Natchez, and other Mississippi tribes were either cabin boys on naval ships or young cadets in the French army, all under martial command to perform their linguistic duties. In the first three years alone, six boys aged fourteen or fifteen were sent to tribes upriver, while another dozen operated out of the Mobile command post. For strategic reasons, the policy continued throughout the colonial period. Promising or experienced young linguists either were put on the mili- tary payroll as cadets or were selected by the governor, who was ordered by the Minister of Marine to "choose from the number of young cadets . . . those whom he thinks most intelligent in order to learn the Indian languages so that they may be able some day to serve as interpreters and to win the confidence of the Indians." French officials thought that official interpreters of "rank" could command the Indians' respect better than mercenary and dissolute *coureurs de bois* and traders.[78]

The manifest superiority of Indian-trained interpreters was not lost even on English colonizers. Having no opportunity to commandeer natives for language indoctrination in England before they arrived in 1607, as their Roanoke predecessors had done, the Jamestown settlers were obliged to entrust their own boys to the Powhatans to acquire double tongues. After only one month in Virginia, thirteen-year-old Thomas Savage was exchanged for "Emperor" Powhatan's trusty and probably older servant Namontack. Within a short time, Savage was fluent and trusted enough to carry messages from the chief to the Jamestown fort. In 1614 he helped broker the end of armed hostilities between the English and the Powhatans, even though he had angered and perhaps saddened his adopted father by abandoning him four years earlier when the fighting got too hot.[79]

In 1609 Savage was joined by fourteen-year-old Henry Spelman, who initially was given to one of Powhatan's sons and "made very much of." Eventually, he lived in Powhatan's capital and dined at his "Table" with Thomas Savage, until he stole away with a visiting chief from the Potomac, where he lived for a year or more. Other students soon joined them on the native side of the frontier. Captain John Smith left his page Samuel Collier with the Pamunkeys "to learne the Language." By the time he was killed accidentally during the Powhatan uprising in 1622, Collier was considered "very well acquainted with [the Indians'] language and habitation, humors and conditions." Two days before the surprise attack, the Powhatans "sent home to his Master" a young man named Browne, who had lived among them as a language apprentice and apparently had earned enough of their regard to save his life.[80]

Like their French rivals, English officials and merchants continued to educate their own interpreters in native communities throughout the colonial period, not exclusively but often enough to demonstrate their faith in the efficiency and reliability of the method. Up and down the Atlantic seaboard, from post-Conquest Canada to South Carolina, English sons, nephews, and employees were entrusted to native villagers to be raised as complete Indians without forsaking their civic mission or forgetting their natal tongue. Some of the best Indian diplomats in the war-torn eighteenth century—Conrad Weiser and Daniel Claus among them—had their ethnological tutelage at the hands of native experts, thanks to the timely and politically astute sponsorship of English officials and relatives.[81]

The third class of interpreters—traders—also acquired nativized tongues in smoky wigwams and longhouses but usually did so less thoroughly and with less finesse while seeking customers for their beads, guns, and blankets. In pursuit of profits from native deerskins and beaver pelts, most traders regarded native languages pragmatically as relatively crude tools to do a job for their employers or creditors. It is no coincidence that the great majority of Indian-speakers in colonial North America were involved in the Indian trade, either as hired employees—packhorsemen in the Southeast, *engagés* in the Great

Lakes and *pays d'en haut,* truckhouse clerks in New England and Hudson Bay country—or as the "master traders" who put together conglomerates in and ran outfits out of Albany and Philadelphia, Charles Town and Augusta, Montreal and New Orleans. While being able to haggle and attend to the ritual niceties of exchange with their native customers was essential, traders did not require a highly sophisticated vocabulary or a punctilious command of treaty council protocol to make a living. Only when colonial officials were forced to rely on traders as their sole sources of political and military intelligence—and the traders were forced to conduct the colonies' official business in addition to their own—did the traders have to hone their linguistic and cultural skills. Early and prolonged residence in native villages often qualified traders for these demanding tasks of interpreting and explaining the radically different cultures to each other.[82] Often they were assisted by native wives, and not a few were the *métis* products of similar unions themselves.[83]

No matter how adequate the preparation and credentials of the interpreters, they still had to perform their roles consistently and with the utmost accuracy and sensitivity to cultural nuance and norms if the Europeans hoped to obtain their economic, military, and religious ends without bloodshed and undue expense. How well they succeeded is not easy to determine. The quality of interpreters' performances is inherently difficult to judge. Unless critics command the interpreters' double linguistic skills, they can never fully measure the accuracy and spirit of their dialogic translations. Fortunately, in the colonial period several observers, European and Indian, did have these special skills, or at least enough of the second language to detect weaknesses. Together, their judgments give us some understanding of the high art of interpreting and cultural brokering and of how many contemporaries managed to meet its standards.

After verbal dexterity, the main desideratum in any interpretation was trust. Did the interpreter convey faithfully and fully the messages that each side of the cultural conversation intended to send? Or did he, in the privacy of the others' language, tell them what they wanted to hear or what he wanted them to hear? As the mouthpiece for both sides, was he strictly neutral? Or did he allow birth, greed, or party to warp his words? Although the Indians had the most to lose in the contest for North America, especially by using colonial interpreters, as peoples without writing they believed in the inviolability of the spoken word, particularly in public councils and treaties. "As they are honest themselves," Cadwallader Colden noted after long experience in New York Indian affairs, "they naturally think others to be so, until they find themselves abused by them."[84]

They did not have long to wait, at which point they took extra measures to check the performance of the interpreters chosen largely by the colonists from their own ranks. The most telling way was to assign someone they trusted implicitly to monitor the translations as they occurred. After the Pequot War ended in 1637, the Narragansetts of Rhode Island were reluctant to attend any council with the English unless Roger Williams, the exiled Puritan minister who lived among them and was fluent in their tongue, went along. Chief Miantonomo was not confident of the "faithfullnes" of Connecticut's Thomas Stanton "in point of interpretation" nor, in Boston, of interpreters in general, "whom he feares to trust." No doubt he had learned his lesson at a treaty council during the war, when Massachusetts officials "could not well make [the natives] understand the articles perfectly" by one of their own interpreters and had to send a copy to Williams, who everyone agreed "could best interpret them to them." Ten years later, Stanton stood in no better odor. The governor of Connecticut hoped that, at the next meeting of the Commissioners of the United Colonies, an honorable Benedict Arnold might supplement Stanton as interpreter, "wherby all suspitions of mistake may be removed, wherto I doubt wee are very subject in our transactions with Indyans."[85]

A century later, Moravian missionary David Zeisberger, an adopted Onondaga as well as a fluent speaker of Delaware, was entrusted by both tribes to tell them the truth about the colonists' statements in councils. "In what he said they placed full confidence; and when he was absent from treaties held with the white people, they could not be easily reconciled, believing that his presence served as a check upon the interpreters, who (as the Indians were apt to say) would suffer themselves to be bribed—especially when purchases of land were about being made from them." At a council at Onondaga in 1753 to hear a message from the governor of Virginia, the Iroquois politely listened to *métis* Andrew Montour interpret the letter and then asked Zeisberger to translate it again for them, "no doubt," his Moravian companion wrote, "in order to find out whether it agreed with what Andres [Montour] had said." Even though Zeisberger modestly excused himself as being insufficiently qualified, the Moravians "noticed that Andres would not have been much pleased to have him do so."[86]

Six years later, a group of Ohio Indians placed their full confidence in Montour when they asked Pennsylvania authorities that he interpret the written minutes of a conference they had had with Colonel Hugh Mercer at Pittsburgh. "If it be wrong," they suggested mildly, "it might be set right." "We had very bad interpreters."[87] Their problem was common, given the disparity between a rigorously sanctioned oral culture, in which accurate collective memories preserved words verbatim, and the corrasable freedom of a written one, where ink was cheap, hands easy to copy, and sheets of paper virtually indistinguishable. When even white men complained of colonial "faithlessness in Treatys" and testified that they had been "present when an Article of the Peace has run in one sense in the English, and quite contrarie in the Indian, by the Governour's express orders," the natives were understandably anxious to ensure the veracity of their words, agreements, and cessions on the "talking papers" the white men regarded—in their own courts—as enforceable "law."[88]

If only one interpreter (usually a white one) could be engaged to conduct a council meeting or treaty, the natives had three other ways to protect themselves from forked tongues. First, their established council protocol, which Europeans were forced to adopt early in their relationship, mandated that any proposal be recapitulated before offering an answer. Thus repetition opened the interpreter's translations to regular scrutiny on both sides of the fire. Second, by the eighteenth century, growing numbers of settlers, officials, and natives were functionally bilingual, thus enabling more council participants to kibbitz on the official work of the linguisters. Moreover, although many Indians understood English or French, they often refused to speak it in public settings, a habit that allowed them to overhear the opposing side as well as to test the quality of the interpreter's version in "Indian."[89] And, finally, if the natives suspected that their thoughts and words had been misrepresented either orally or in writing, they might, as a Maine Penobscot village did after the Casco Bay treaty in 1727, issue their own written rejoinder and clarification, thus hoisting the scribbling white men on their own petard. The Penobscots' interlocutor, Laurence Sagouarrab, wrote that he wished to broadcast in his "own Tongue" to "you who are spread all over the earth" because of "the diversity and contrariety of the interpretations I receive of the English writing in which the articles of Peace are drawn up." "These writings appear to contain things that are not, so that the Englishman [interpreter] himself disavows them in my presence, when he reads and interprets them to me himself." There followed a long recital of what he (on behalf of his village) did *not* do or say at the conference and a much shorter one of what he did.[90]

Given the vulnerability of their fields, farms, and populations, the colonists, too, had to be concerned with the conduct and quality of their interpreters. According to European lights, Indian notions of "Freedom, property, and independence" were "extravagant" and their brand of warfare terrifyingly effective. A slip of the tongue or an insulting breach of etiquette was often enough to unleash stealthy forces of native revenge on unsuspecting frontier settlements. Unfaithful, corrupt, or simply careless interpreters were well known throughout the colonial period for their ability to cause "frequent mischeifes and mistakes," "disputes and Misunderstandings," "serious mishap[s]," and even bloody wars.[91]

Both the English and the French sought to reduce these risks by professionalizing their interpreter corps. The best linguists were given public or military rank and salaries and expense accounts that allowed them to forgo their usual involvement in the Indian trade.[92] In several English colonies, they were also obliged to swear an oath of fidelity, promising to "faithfully & truly Execute" their office, not to conceal anything they might learn in the course of their duties, and to do all in their power to promote "the good of the province" in Indian affairs.[93] Many official interpreters accumulated long records of service and the competence in conducting delicate negotiations between two different, proud, and often prickly cultures that only practice could bring.

One group of invaders who seldom had access to the best or most obliging interpreters was missionaries, Protestant and Catholic. In many ways, the missionaries' task was more difficult than that of colonial officials, fur traders, and land speculators. In attempting to conquer native souls as well as bodies for the "work of Christ," they had to translate the ancient history and mixed precepts of the Bible for people who knew nothing of Israel, books, sheep, churches, or even candles, much less Heaven, Hell, and Purgatory, and whose languages made it impossible to speak non-possessively of a triune Father-Son-and-Holy-Ghost. Moreover, an interpreter whose own life made a mockery of the morality he propagated, who had no "experimental" (as opposed to doctrinal) knowledge of religion, or who had been raised in the tenets of a rival or, worse yet, no denomination was clearly a liability to devout proselytizers. In the Northeast, missionaries who had yet to master a native dialect seemed to find only mercenary Dutch traders and other "low-lived, ignorant, & commonly Vitious Persons," such as semi-acculturated Indians and former captives, for hire.[94] Such people typically made the kind of mistake Sir William Johnson detected in an interpreter for a Boston missionary, "the best in that Country," who tried to translate "For God is no Respecter of persons" for a native assembly and came out with "God had no Love for such people as them," which cannot have engendered much for him, his employer, or their religion.[95]

For most of the colonial period, the colonists' best interests were served by avoiding conflict with the American natives and cultivating their friendship and cooperation. Discerning the natives' ways and wants was never easy for the confident newcomers from the self-proclaimed center of "civilization," but many people on both sides of the cultural divide made bona fide efforts to clarify and communicate native positions to colonial movers and shakers. Despite seemingly insurmountable differences in thought, values, and language, the two sides managed, for the most part, to understand one another, at least for practical purposes. How, then, do we explain the horrible armed conflicts that periodically shattered the three centuries of colonial coexistence?

Wars broke out not because the colonists failed to understand their Indian neighbors but because they usually did and chose—or their distant European leaders chose—to ignore the natives' needs and wishes. Backed by healthier, proliferating populations of humans and animals, technological superiority, and other forms of social power, Europeans could simply impose their will if the native complaints and concerns they heard through their interpreters and other sensitive observers did not move them to care or caution. Colonial officials who, after decades of determined listening, knew the meaning of the Indians' voice unleashed the dogs of war not upon inscrutable "barbarians" but upon articulate human beings like themselves.

PART II

CONSUMPTION

INTRODUCTION

A search for economic profit drew most Europeans to the New World, following the lead of Columbus who was en route to fabulous and impossibly distant Asian markets when he stumbled upon the more proximate Americas. There they discovered not only large and often eager markets for their manufactures, particularly cloth and metals, but profitable trades in furs, skins, and flora and rich sources of precious metals. Moreover, their native "customers" and trading partners seemed to overvalue the new goods from Europe and to undervalue their own "commodities" (a term and concept they did not recognize). But, in fact, each side thought it was taking advantage of the other and, in some sense, they were, because economic value was, and always is, in the eye of the beholder. But over the course of three centuries, both partners learned, if not always to appreciate or acquire, at least to recognize and honor some of the noneconomic values attached to goods and their exchange by the other.

This education in cultural relativism began immediately, as soon as—or even before—the natives and the newcomers began to fabricate a common language, as I suggest in Chapter Three. "At the Water's Edge" was written for *American Encounter* (the trilogy volume), largely to suggest how eventful and important the sixteenth century was in the formation of Indian-European relations. It was published in *After Columbus* (1988) because the volume seemed to need it for a section on cultural "Confluences."

Chapter Four, "The First Consumer Revolution," originated as a paper for a lecture series on "The Chippendale Wigwam: European and Oriental Styles Invade America" at Mary Washington College in March 1990. It was the bold attempt of the lone ethnohistorian on the program to hold the interest of a decorative-artsy audience in preservation-minded Fredericksburg, Virginia. I even resorted to slides, in good art-historical fashion. It was published with only some of the illustrations in *Beyond 1492* (1992) and remains my sole contribution to the burgeoning literature on the Anglo-American "consumer revolution" of the late seventeenth and eighteenth century.

Chapter Five, "Making Do," focuses on the Southeast in order to sort out the cross-cultural meanings of "luxuries," "conveniences," and "necessities" in that deerskin and slave economy over the course of the eighteenth century. It analyzes the increasing dependence of the region's large native tribes on their French and English neighbors and some of the serious social, economic, and political effects of that dependence. The chapter was first published in *The Indians' New South: Cultural Change in the Colonial Southeast* (1997), a slightly revised version of the Walter Lynwood Fleming Lectures in Southern History I had delivered at Louisiana State University in April 1996.

THREE

AT THE WATER'S EDGE

Trading in the Sixteenth Century

As strange as it may seem, a homely fish brought Western Europeans together with North Americans, perhaps even before Columbus bumped into the West Indies, and bound their two continents in an indissoluble union of fates. For once Europe's mariners were drawn to America's waters, they quickly discovered her native peoples and were drawn into commerce, competition, and conflict.

From the late fifteenth century, fishermen from the Atlantic ports of England, Spain, Portugal, and France headed each spring for the cold waters off Newfoundland in search of the meaty cod. In the form of lightly salted, sundried "poor john," this inexpensive "beef of the sea" was "inexhaustible manna" for Europe's peasants, armies, navies, and urban lower classes.[1] It was also welcome on the tables of Catholics who observed the Church's 57 fast days and 108 days of abstinence, a total of 165 days—five and a half months—in which meat could not be eaten.

The first fishermen to discover the cod-rich waters of the "new found world" may have sailed in the early 1480s from Bristol.[2] But it was an anglicized Venetian, John Cabot, who left the requisite documentary tracks of discovery in 1497. Cabot's reports that the northern seas so swarmed with fish that they could be taken in baskets kindled keen interest in America's offshore resources. By 1517 "an hundred sail" could be found in Newfoundland's summer harbors.[3] The discovery of the Grand Banks in the 1530s only increased the traffic between Europe and America. In the age of the Armada, fishing was definitely big business, the second largest in the European economy. While Spanish gold and silver lit the imaginations of sixteenth-century entrepreneurs, the number of men employed and the tonnage carried by the Newfoundland cod fleet was twice that of the great Spanish flotas. The Gulf of St. Lawrence was a pole of European activity in every way comparable to that of the Caribbean and the Gulf of Mexico.[4]

For forty or fifty years the northern gulf rivaled the southern even in the richness of its cargoes. After 1536 the cod fishermen were joined in America by Basque whalers, who followed Breton pilots to the narrow Strait of Belle Isle between Labrador and Newfoundland. There they chased bowhead and right whales with harpoons in fragile *chalupas*, as they had done for generations off their own Cantabrian coast. When it was shipped to Europe, refined "train oil" was as profitable as liquid gold. For whale oil lit the lamps of Europe, made soap and soup, lubricated everything from frying pans to clocks, and, since the whale was classified as a fish, served as *lard de carême*—Lenten fat—during holy days when meat products were prohibited.

At their peak, two thousand French and Spanish Basques worked out of ports on the northern shore of the Strait, through which the whales funneled each autumn. The twenty-to-thirty ships on which they came each year were not modest fishing barks but large Spanish galleons, heavily armed. In an age of cutthroat piracy, they had to be when even a small ship stowed 55,000 gallons of train oil worth $4–6 million in modern currency. At those rates, the Gulf of Mexico could not afford to look down its nose as its Laurentian cousin.[5]

Basque and other European ships sought to maximize profits by fishing for many markets in American waters. Whalers, the aristocrats of the trade, were not too proud to top their holds with cod. Fishermen would often stop at gulf islands to make train oil from walruses, whose tusks also sold as ivory and whose thick hides made excellent shields for archers and prevented ship's rigging from chafing. All sorts of watermen, even those who plied the banks, put into shore long enough to bargain for Indian furs. While fishing the Strait of Belle Isle in 1542, two Basque crews ate and drank with "very friendly" natives who understood "any language," French, English, Gascon or Basque. They then traded "deer," "wolf," and marten skins for "all kinds of ironware," particularly axes and knives.[6]

By the last quarter of the century, fishing ships often carried a pinnace for coasting in search of furs while the fishing proceeded. Contracts made in several French ports stipulated that vessels departing for "Canada" and the St. Lawrence were to engage in "the fishing of whales and other fish and traffic of merchandise with the Indians."[7] English interest in multipurpose voyages was greatly stimulated by two ships captured in 1591. The *Bonaventure* of Saint-Malo carried the oil, hides, and "teeth" of 1,500 walruses, valued conservatively at £1,430. Its train oil, five carcasses to a hogshead, was so sweet and unfishy that the soap-makers of Bristol, who supplied much of the English cloth industry, took quick notice. "The king of Spaine," declared the mayor of Bristol and the pirate ship's owner, "may burne some of his Olive trees." The French Basque *Catherine de St Vincent* was even more intriguing. Beneath her hatches was found "trayne oyle, Salmon & newland feshe And great Store of Riche Fures," such as beaver, marten, and otter. On other voyages the ship had garnered black fox skins, "the rarest furres that are knowen."[8]

Long before the maritime fur trade began in earnest, the fishermen and whalers had been joined by hundreds of other European sailors on the east coast of North America. Some came to find a Northwest Passage through or around the new continent, hoping to beat European competitors to the known wealth of the East. Others sought to make a living in American waters by plundering the rich cargoes of national rivals, particularly those of Basque whalers and the Spanish bullion fleets that sailed annually through the narrow strait between Florida and the Bahamas. A few even came as tourists to gawk at the bruited wonders of the New World and its strange flora, fauna, and human inhabitants. Somewhat later, when it became known that America was as habitable as profitable, outposts and colonies were planted as factories for entrepreneurs, dumping grounds for convicts and paupers, havens for religious dissenters, and bastions for imperial contenders.[9]

All of these full- or part-time mariners and the American natives eventually met on the watery margin of their respective worlds, and, sometimes deliberately, often inadvertently, pulled each other into human and cultural experiences that were not merely novel but potentially revolutionary. Since the Europeans had initiated contact by thrusting themselves into the natives' world, the onus of change fell heavily on the Indians, who were often required to respond to unwonted and unwanted challenges from the strangers. But the natives were indispensable to most of the European projects on land, as they were not to the cod fishermen, and so they retained considerable cultural autonomy and room for maneuvering. At the same time, the Indians launched the Europeans who stayed in America on a centuries-long rite of passage. By 1600 the process had barely begun, but at the achievement of independence the cultural descendants of the cod fishers, pilgrims, and soldiers of fortune had been ineluctably molded into distinctive American shapes in large part by the impress of their native allies, trading partners, and nemeses.

The earliest explorers of North America were not interested in trade of any sort, at least not in America. Since they were new to the land, they were understandably preoccupied with charting its waters and cataloguing its floral, faunal, and mineral assets to interest investors and crowned heads in future extractive expeditions. They tended to see in the natives only slaves, future interpreters and guides, pawns in the imperial partition of the New World, or walking souvenirs. Columbus set a poor precedent on his first voyage by taking ten West Indians home to Spain, where six were baptized and presented at court as proof of his discovery and Spain's precedence. The following year, however, he took thirty prisoners of war from Hispaniola to sell as slaves in Seville. In the next three years, some 1,400 Indians were shipped to Spanish slave markets.[10]

Not to be outdone, Spain's Portuguese rivals soon got into the act. In 1501 Gaspar Corte-Real sent home to his sovereign about fifty Indian men and women from Newfoundland or the northern coasts. An Italian in Lisbon, after scrutinizing and fingering the human booty, noted that the men, despite their "terribly harsh" tattooed faces, "laugh considerably and manifest the greatest pleasure," probably to disguise their true feelings. "The women," he could not help but notice, "have small breasts and most beautiful bodies, and rather pleasant faces." The Venetian ambassador had his eye on other things. The gypsy-like men, he predicted, "will be excellent for labor and the best slaves that have hitherto been obtained," expressing a southerner's preference for hardy northern natives over the softer Arawaks purloined by Columbus.[11]

The unsavory Iberian appetite for slaves was fed again in 1525 when Estevão Gomes, a Portuguese pilot in the Spanish service, filled two ships with rich furs and fifty-eight Algonquians from New England, "all innocent and half-naked." For a time the port was all atwitter when it was reported that Gomes had returned from his search for a Northwest Passage with a shipload of cloves (*clavos*), presumably from the Spice Islands of the East, rather than a few dozen slaves (*esclavos*), which contravened the king's express orders not to use violence against any natives.[12]

By no means was the penchant for kidnapping confined to southern Europeans, although those taken by the French and the English were fewer and their treatment somewhat better. In 1502 John Amayne's cargo of salt fish included American hawks, an eagle, and three Indians, who were dressed in "beasts' skins" and ate raw meat. Two years later, two of them were seen in Westminster Palace, sartorially passing as Englishmen. Normandy got its first look at "wild" Americans in 1509 when seven Indian men were captured in their bark canoe and conveyed to Rouen. Six of them soon died, but the survivor was carried to King Louis XII for exhibition. We would like to know the native's impression of people who, unlike his own, made a fetish of "bread, wine, [and] money." The year before Gomes plundered New England, Giovanni da Verrazzano, sailing for Francis I, captured an eight-year-old Indian boy somewhere north of the Carolinas, but failed to pick up a feisty young woman who was tall, very beautiful, and exceedingly shrill-voiced when manhandled.[13]

Most of these early captives were taken as curiosities to amuse or impress European officials and courtiers. A few even reached more popular venues. A twenty-year-old Eskimo woman and a seven-year-old child, taken by the French from Labrador in 1566, were exhibited for money at the inns of France, Germany, and the Low Countries. Their landlady in The Hague attempted to introduce the woman to Christianity by showing her a statue of Christ, but the sealskinclad native could only shake her head, lift it up, and put her hands on top of it. The good Dutch woman took this to mean that she had some knowledge of the true Christian God, but that was probably wishful thinking.[14]

The Eskimo man, woman, and baby boy lifted by Martin Frobisher from Baffin Island in 1577 were subject to similar though briefer celebrity in Bristol. Despite a broken rib which eventually punctured a lung and led to his death, the man Calichough entertained the mayor's dinner party by paddling his kayak up and down the Avon and killing a couple of ducks with his bird

A Nuremberg broadside advertising a twenty-year-old Eskimo mother and her seven-year-old daughter, who were kidnapped from Labrador and exhibited around Europe in 1566. Drawn from life, the woodcut accurately depicts the woman's facial tattoos and the cut of her sealskin parka, pants, and buskins. A similar broadside was published in Augsburg in the same year. From a copy of *Warhafftige Contrafey einer wilden Frawen . . . Novaterra gennant* (Nuremberg, 1566) in the Map Library of the British Library, London, by whose courtesy it is reproduced here.

dart. He may even have mounted a horse, backwards, adding humor to the guests' admiration. All three natives sat for portraits, as had their brethren eleven years earlier, whose likenesses circulated from Germany in broadside.[15]

When European thoughts turned to settlement or the fur trade, the kidnapping of Indians took on new purpose. The goal then was to put native tongues to school in a "civilized" language to enable them to interpret for the Europeans when they returned to America. If the Indians were awed by the majesty and power of European cities, courts, and armies, so much the better, particularly if they conveyed that awe to their kinsmen. This is clearly what Jacques Cartier had in mind in 1534 when he kidnapped Taignoagny and Domagaya, sons of the headman of the St. Lawrence Iroquois at modern Quebec City. When he returned the following year, the boys acted as pilots up the tricky St. Lawrence and interpreted the words of Cartier and their father Donnacona. Cartier's motives were more mixed after his winter in Canada when he hoodwinked the chief, his sons, and three tribesmen into sailing to France with him. None of the natives returned to Canada on his final voyage in 1541, but one girl was said to have reached adulthood, and the group was supported at Saint-Malo for at least two years by the king. When the St. Lawrence was finally opened to sea-going fur traders in the 1580s, having been closed by Cartier's callous disregard for native freedom, the French again took two potential interpreters with them when they returned to Saint-Malo.[16] Thus the first extractive industry in colonial North America was kidnapping.

Fortunately, the first true trade with the natives was much less threatening and gave the new partners an opportunity to size each other up in relative safety. After several weeks at sea, virtually all European ships needed to be refurbished with firewood, fresh water, and provisions at early ports of call. Ships taking the southern route stopped in the Azores, Madeiras, Canaries, Cape Verdes, or West Indies en route, but those headed directly west from northern Europe saw only Irish ports before hitting Newfoundland or the coasts of Canada.

Wood and water were usually free for the taking, although Columbus paid the natives of Crooked Island hawk's bells and small glass beads to fill his water casks. Provisions, too, sometimes came at no expense if the natives extended their traditional hospitality to the bearded white strangers. But the mariners quickly learned that reciprocity was the social key to native America and began to reward their hosts with small presents. In 1542 Roberval swapped knives and other "trifles" for generous quantities of red shad with the Stadaconans around Quebec. Seven years later Spanish friars in southern Florida bought fresh fish with shirts because they had no beads, knives, or axes, which the Indians had learned to want. For shirts, knives, and fishhooks, French traders in the Chesapeake in 1560 purchased corn and pumpkins to supplant moldy ship's biscuits, as well as a thousand marten skins. A few years later in the same region, Spanish Jesuits attempting to found a mission on the

York River were forced to "barter for maize with copper and tin" after initially refusing to pay for food as bad precedent.[17]

Just when the North American fur trade began is not documented, although the Vikings who spent three years in "Vinland," probably at L'Anse aux Meadows in northern Newfoundland, around 1010 A.D. have as firm a claim to priority as any. According to Norse sagas, they traded cow's milk and strips of red cloth for bales of sable and other furs with the Skraelings, who turned testy after they were refused metal weapons. In the early modern era, the taciturn Newfoundland fishermen are always accorded first, if brief, respect, but not because they left written evidence of their enterprise. Archaeologists were the first to notice that sixteenth-century Seneca sites in western New York were strewn with ship's bolts, rigging rings, metal tips from belaying pins, and spiral brass earrings worn by Basque sailors. Only later, when they read Nicolas Denys's account of seventeenth-century Acadia, did they realize that fishing crews were notorious for practically selling their ships from under their captains, filling their sea chests with native furs exchanged for "biscuit, lead, quite new lines, sails, and many other things at the expense of the owners."[18]

By the time an Atlantic adventurer first mentions the fur trade, the trade is well under way. When Corte-Real sailed off with fifty natives in 1501, one of them had a piece of a gilt sword made in Italy and another wore a pair of Venetian silver rings in his ears; their heat-hardened javelins may have been tipped with steel.[19] By 1524 the coastal inhabitants of northern New England were so choosey about trade goods that they would accept only knives, fishhooks, and sharp metal. On a march inland Verrazzano saw many natives with what he believed to be "'paternostri' beads of copper in their ears," though some or all of them may have been of native copper. Ten years later, Cartier found Micmacs inviting him to shore to trade by waving furs on sticks. By then, of course, the natives of the Gulf of St. Lawrence had trafficked with European fishermen for at least thirty years, perhaps half a century.[20]

The best evidence that the fur trade predates the earliest known records is that, by the advent of the first chroniclers, the natives had established regular trade protocols for dealing with the strangers, which were undoubtedly modifications of techniques for interacting with native neighbors and trading partners. These protocols consisted of several elements. Unlike native canoes or kayaks, European ships without experience in American waters had to be shown protective harbors and the best approaches to native trading sites or villages. This guidance the natives provided with animated sign or body language, just as the denizens of New York harbor showed Verrazzano's crew the safest place to beach their longboat. In Narragansett Bay natives in canoes guided the *Dauphine* safely to port from a league out to sea.[21] By this time, apparently, the Indians no longer regarded the visitors as capricious and potentially dangerous "gods" or their ships as mysterious "floating islands," as they are often portrayed in retrospective native accounts of their first encounters.

Most of the sixteenth-century trade with the Indians was conducted at seaside from European ships. When the ocean-going traders did not row their own longboats to shore, the Indians paddled their canoes out to the ships to commence trading. In this engraving, based on early written accounts rather than eyewitness, Theodor de Bry depicts Englishmen trading knives and a broad-brimmed hat for furs, feathers, arrows, and shell necklaces (rendered incorrectly as whole shells rather than small wampum beads). From de Bry's *America Pars Decima,* Part XIII (Frankfurt-am-Main, 1634).

To some extent, the white man had already been desacralized by familiarity, and his technology reclassified from miraculous to mundane.[22]

When the Europeans landed safely, each partner sought to assure the other of his peaceful intentions. Occasionally, native suspicions were difficult to allay and the natives would lie concealed out of reach and sight; considering the European penchant for picking up human mementoes, their caution was not misplaced. The only way to win their trust was to leave gifts or trade goods in a conspicuous place. On Prince Edward Island, Cartier "placed a knife and a woollen girdle [sash] on a branch" to reassure a skittish native who had invited the French to land but then had run away. In 1577 Frobisher's desire to entice the natives of Frobisher's Straits into trade "caused knives, & other thinges, to be preferred unto them, whiche they would not take at our handes," wrote a gentleman chronicler, "but beeing layd on the ground, & the partie going away, they came and tooke up, leaving something of theirs to countervaile the same."[23]

Half a century earlier the natives of northern New England had been nearly as reticent. According to Verrazzano, "if we wanted to trade with them ... they would come to the seashore on some rocks where the breakers were most violent, while we remained in the little boat, and they sent us what they wanted to give on a rope, continually shouting to us not to approach the land." After a quick and unceremonious exchange, the Indians "made all the signs of scorn and shame that any brute creature would make, such as showing their buttocks and laughing."[24]

Natives with less caution or fewer bad experiences with European visitors often performed striking ceremonies to celebrate the opening of peaceful relations with their new trading partners. To make an economic truce with John Davis's English crew in 1587, the Inuits of Baffin Island pointed to the sun, cried *Iliaoute* in a loud voice, and struck their chests, which Davis learned to imitate. When Cartier made his way up the St. Lawrence toward Hochelaga on Montreal Island, the Iroquoian headman of Achelacy presented him with two of his children to signify a lasting alliance between his people and the bearers of awesome technological tidings. Since trade always meant peace in native America, socially important hostages were considered the best way to preserve it. The previous year the Micmacs of Chaleur Bay on the Gaspé peninsula had celebrated a successful trading session with Cartier by "dancing and going through many ceremonies, and throwing salt water over their heads with their hands." A large group of women had also danced and rubbed the arms and chests of the Frenchmen in welcome before joining hands and joyfully raising their arms to heaven.[25]

Festivities were effective on both sides. The English, at least, discovered that sales were enhanced by music. On his first voyage in search of a Northwest Passage, Davis opened friendly relations with a band of Inuits by ordering the ship's musicians to play and the crew to dance on shore, which was soon followed by "friendly imbracings and signes of curtesie" all around. The next day the English did a brisk trade for five native kayaks, paddles, clothes, spears, and seal-skins. When Bartholomew Gosnold's trading expedition left southern New England in 1602, the crew threw their caps into the air and made their native partners "the best farewell [they] could" with trumpet and cornet. The following year on Cape Cod, Martin Pring gathered two loads of sassafras from the woods of the local Nausets, who were diverted by the "homely Musicke" of a young man's guitar. After showering the musician with gifts, they danced around him "twentie in a Ring ... using many Savage gestures, singing Io, Ia, Io, Ia, Ia, Io: him that first brake the ring, the rest would knocke and cry out upon." Small wonder that when Sir Humphrey Gilbert set out for the newfound land in 1578 he carried six musicians in addition to the usual martial complement of trumpeters and drummers.[26]

Another vital piece of protocol was the giving of gifts and special deference to native headmen, women, and children. The French particularly learned to deal with Algonquian and Iroquoian groups by going first to their leaders, who stood out by their appearance or the deference of their followers. When the leaders gave their blessing to an exchange, the French gave other small gifts to the women and children present, assuming that the way to a man's heart—and fur cache—was through his family. In the seventeenth century and beyond, Indian women themselves were known to peddle the furs they had so carefully processed after their menfolk had killed the animals. But in the sixteenth century either the women did not get personally involved in the trade, which took place, after all, outside the villages which were their domain, or the male European observers were blind to their role, for no notice was taken of female traders of furs. Presumably, women bartered the produce of their own gardens to sailors seeking relief from weevilly biscuits.

Perhaps because of his previous experiences with the Tupinamba in Brazil, Jacques Cartier seemed to know instinctively that the male hunters he met in Canada had to be courted through their headmen and families. When he arrived in Chaleur Bay in 1534, he sent two crewmen ashore to mollify a band of fur-bearing Micmacs with gifts of knives and iron goods and "a red cap to give to their chief." Shortly, he met three hundred down-at-the-heel Iroquoians from upriver fishing in the Gaspé basin. All the women scattered into the woods, save two or three stalwarts "to whom," Cartier said, "we gave each a comb and a little tin bell." This generosity prompted the men to allow the other twenty women to emerge for gifts; each received a tin ring. When Chief Donnacona and his sons canoed out to the flagship to protest the French erection of a thirty-foot cross at the mouth of the harbor, allegedly as a landmark for future trading ships, Cartier made them come aboard, plied them with food, drink, and "good cheer," and festooned two sons in "shirts and ribbons and in red caps, and put a little brass chain around the neck of each." Thus were Taignoagny and Domagaya selected to spend a junior year abroad learning the words and ways of the French.[27]

When Cartier visited Hochelaga the following year, he was royally greeted with gifts of fish and cornbread. To recompense the natives for their kindness and to seal his status as a generous dignitary, he had the women "all sit down in a row and gave them some tin beads and other trifles; and to some of the men he gave knives." The next day Cartier presented the village headman with two hatchets, two knives, a cross, and a crucifix, "which he made him kiss and then hung it about his neck." After an imposing ceremony of gospel-reading and faith-healing, the captain lined up all the men, women, and children in separate rows. To the other headmen he gave hatchets, to the men knives. The women got beads and other small "trinkets," and the children had to scramble for "little rings and tin *agnus Dei*, which afforded them great amusement." The finale was a blast of trumpets and other musical instruments, "whereat the Indians were much delighted." Cartier's *savoir faire* was rewarded by the headman, who took the crown from his own head and placed it on the captain's. If trade had been the goal of this voyage, Cartier would have become a rich man. But the publication of his *Brief Recit* in 1545 enabled his successors to prosper by showing them the established protocol of American trade and diplomacy.[28]

The last lesson in native protocol the Europeans had to learn was not to haggle over exchange values (in a barter economy, "prices" technically do not exist). There was room for polite negotiation, but only within the bounds of native etiquette. David Ingram, an English mariner who had allegedly walked from the Gulf of Mexico to Cape Breton, advised the America-bound expedition of Sir Humphrey Gilbert in 1572 that "if you will barter wares with [the Indians], then leave the thinge you will sell, on the grounde, and goe from it a pretty waye. Then they come and take it, and sett doune such wares as they will [give] for it in the place. If you thinke it not sufficient, then leave their wares with signes that you like it not. And then they will bringe more untill either they or you be satisfied or will give no more. Or else," he continued, "you may hange your wares on a longe pike or pooles [pole's] end and so putt more or lesse on it till you have agreed on the bargaine and they will hange out their wares on a pooles end in like maner."[29]

In most instances, the natives literally "sold" the clothes off their backs and the boats from under them, expecting only that their European partners would return fair value. If they were disappointed, with one exception they never said so, at least in words or gestures the strangers could understand. Only Cartier's worldly-wise interpreters, Taignoagny and Domagaya, knew enough of European economic values to suspect the fairness of the exchange their tribesmen made with the French. When Cartier swapped various "trinkets" (*menues choses*) for eels and fish during the winter at Stadacona, the French were annoyed to find the interpreters informing the villagers that "what we bartered to them was of no value, and that for what they brought us, they could as easily get hatchets as knives."[30]

Because nearly everything the Europeans had to offer was made of material new to the natives, the natives accepted or expected the same kinds of trade goods for cheap (in European eyes) provisions as for the rarest and richest furs. This sometimes confounded the Europeans' sense of values but more often led them to think that they had taken keen advantage of the gullible natives. High demand at the end of a long, salty voyage made the exchange for fresh food and water seem at least equitable. But in return for pricey furs the mariners gave only what they considered "trifles," because they took for granted the complex processes of manufacture and transportation that underlay their relatively low cost. Étienne Bellenger boasted to an English diplomat that in 1583 he had sowed 40 crowns' worth of "trifles" on the coasts of Acadia and reaped furs that sold in Paris for 440 crowns.[31]

By the same token, the Indians believed themselves the shrewder party because they bartered their own common "trash" for exotic, colorful, and labor-saving items. Since values are always culturally relative, neither partner was wrong. And since the maritime trade was so irregular and haphazard, the trade items on both sides retained their novelty and relative value throughout the sixteenth century. Thus both partners were glad to get what they could and both thought they made out like bandits.

What specifically were these "trifles" and "trash" that seemed so valuable to the other partner? It is customary to think of the North American fur trade largely as a beaver trade, but throughout most of the sixteenth century other furs were more prominent. By the last two decades of the century the beaver hat was gaining popularity in aristocratic circles, but the middling classes had not yet caught the full fever of furry fashion. And until European demand persuaded them to do otherwise, the Indians of the Northeast showed little interest in hunting the elusive beaver. Archaeologists who tally the animal remains on pre-contact Iroquois sites, for example, typically find the bones of only one beaver but numerous whitetail deer, black bears, woodchucks, raccoons, and porcupines.[32] By 1581, when the St. Lawrence was reopened to the French, European hatters were requesting more beavers. In Paris two years later, Richard Hakluyt (the son of a skinner) saw 20,000 crowns' worth of Canadian furs in the shop of the king's skinner, including enough beaver from a recent voyage for six hundred felt hats.[33]

Rather than new fashions in headware, the sixteenth-century fur market revolved around plush pelts of decorative value. Furs were not made into full-bodied winter coats, as in native America, but used only to make muffs for hands and feet and to trim the rich silks and velvets of the upper classes. For ostentatious ruffs, borders, and collars, European gentlefolk preferred a variety of precious "small furs," which could no longer be gotten in sufficient quantity from the Baltic or Russia. While kings and queens affected ermine and sable, nobles and courtiers of other stripes favored fox, otter, lynx, fisher, and particularly marten, the preferred substitute for Siberian sable.[34]

In the 1540s the French sent ships annually down the coast from Chesapeake Bay to South Carolina to trade for martens. On one trip, which excited Spanish jealousy, they picked up 2,000 skins in two days from canoe-borne natives. When Thomas Harriot advertised the "Merchantable commodities" of Virginia forty years later, he promised that the English could harvest "store" of marten furs by the Roanoke natives, although they had produced only two skins while he was there. Monsieur Bellenger had done much better. In his Acadian trove were numerous "Martens enclyning unto Sables," the ultimate compliment.[35]

The French appetite for marten must have been whetted by reports from America. Jean Alphonse, the crack Rochellais pilot who commanded Roberval's fleet to Canada in 1542, let it be known that the natives as far as coastal Maine wore mantles of marten. And one of the *Singularitez de la France antarctique*, wrote André Thevet, the king's cosmographer, was that in winter the Laurentian Indians not only wore large marten coats but wrapped their greasy heads and their unhousebroken babies in "sable martens." "These we

In late medieval Europe, "small furs" from Russia and the Baltic decorated the elegant clothing of the aristocracy and well-to-do, and beaver had not yet replaced wool and velvet in the making of hats. Jan Van Eyck's 1434 portrait of Giovanni Arnolfini and his wife, Italians living in the merchant community of Bruges, captures the sumptuary importance of furs before the discovery of North America produced a vast new supply and fed a new fashion in headwear. From Robert Delort, *Life in the Middle Ages* (New York, 1972).

esteem here for their rarity," he noted with some chagrin, "and thus such furs are reserved for the ornaments of princes and great lords."[36]

Even more desirable were black foxes, which were "of such excellent beauty that they seem to shame the marten." A rare variation on the common red or gray fox, they were found primarily in Canada, the Maritimes, and New-foundland, when they could be found at all. Their shimmering jet-black fur caught the fancy of Europe's lords and ladies no less than the eye of the Hurons, who accounted them "the rarest and most valuable of the three species" of fox in their country. The trick was to afford it: in 1584 one skin brought £100 in London. When French Basques seized an English privateer in Newfoundland in that year, they garnered a sizable fortune in black fox alone; the captain unsuccessfully sued for the return of £1,500 worth, which far outweighed his losses in Caribbean spices and pearls. Well into the next century, even with a burgeoning supply of furs from America, an all-black pelt commanded "several hundred crowns." Those suffering from the courtier's disease may have been willing to pay the price; as Lord Burghley was assured, there was "no soche thinge to Ease a man of the payne of the gowte as thes blacke Foxe Skynes."[37]

Luxury furs were all well and good for the rich, but Europe's poor and mid-dling classes also needed leather of a common sort, which continental cattle-raisers could not fully supply. Workingmen's pants and aprons, shoes for all stations, saddles, saddlebags, tackle, and harness, bookbindings, covered seats and luggage were all made of leather. So the coastal traders of the sixteenth century did not disdain the unfurry skins of larger American animals. King Francis I was pleased to learn that Canada bred "certain animals whose hides as leather are worth ten cruzados each, and for this sum they are sold in France." When John Walker, an English seaman, visited Penobscot Bay in 1580, he discovered in an unattended Etchemin lodge 240 hides of "a kinde of Beaste, much bigger than an Oxe," probably the moose. Each hide was eight-een feet square and sold in France for £2. In Acadia, Étienne Bellenger picked up several of the same "Buff hides reddie dressed [tanned] upon both sides," as well as "Deere skynes dressed well on the inner side, with the hayre on the outside"; both sorts were painted on the skin side with "divers excellent colours, as redd, tawnye, yellowe, and vermillyon." With just a hint of ecolog-ical concern, Harriot assured his English readers that "Deers skinnes dressed after the maner of Chamoes, or undressed, are to be had of the natural inhab-itants [of Virginia] thousands yerely by way of traffike for trifles, and no more waste or spoile of Deere then is and hath bene ordinarily in time before."[38]

Small or large, rare or common, the best furs from the European standpoint were those that had been worn by the natives for a year or two as "matchcoats" or robes. In the winter the Indians wore these garments fur side in, next to their bodies which customarily were rubbed with seal, bear, or raccoon grease as further protection against the cold. The grease and everyday sweat worked their way into the leather, softening it and in effect completing the tanning process begun by the Indian women who fashioned the garments. Beaver pelts especially benefited from this treatment because it wore off the long, lighter-hued "guard hairs" for the European hatters, who wanted only the soft, darker underdown with its microscopically barbed hairs for making felt. Accordingly, the Indians who sold the used beaver coats from their backs commanded the best bargains from traders eager for *castor gras d'hiver*, "greasy winter beaver." Less valuable was *castor sec*, unworn "dry beaver" with thinner, warm-weather fur, extraneous guard hairs, and a stiff, parchment-like hide.

To Europe's sea-going traders, native furs were well worth a cold, danger-ous voyage across the Atlantic. But Indian hunters and trappers put little value on the skins which "cost them almost nothing," except in time (which they had in abundance) and effort (which they knew how to minimize with astute woodlore). Sixteenth-century Canadians undoubtedly felt the same way their early seventeenth-century descendants did as they were courted by European traders of many nations and countless commercial interests. "The Beaver does everything perfectly well," a Montagnais man told a French missionary, "it makes kettles, hatchets, swords, knives, bread: . . . in short, it makes every-thing." The missionary felt obliged to explain to his French readers that the Indian was "making sport of us Europeans, who have such a fondness for the skin of this animal and who fight to see who will give the most to these Bar-barians to get it." France's competitors were seen in no better light. Showing a beautiful knife to the priest, the Indian exclaimed, "The English have no sense; they give us twenty knives like this for one Beaver skin." But even an Englishman had the sense to realize the sharp irony in a cultural situation where "foule hands (in smoakie houses) [had] the first handling of those Fur-res which are after worne upon the hands of Queens and heads of Princes."[39]

In return for these profitable—if odoriferous—furs, the Europeans gave largely what they considered "trinkets," "baubles," or "toys." But the natives saw particularly in metal and cloth goods miracles of technology and spiritual power, for anyone who could make large, unusual, or ingenious objects was regarded as possessing *manitou* (in Algonquian) or an exceptional soul. Unlike the Aztecs and Incas of Latin America, the Woodland Indians had no metal-lurgy, only hand-hammered native copper, and no woven cloth save netlike hemp or grass mantles for summer wear. Accordingly, in tribe after tribe, they dubbed the first Europeans they met "Iron-workers" or "Cloth makers."[40]

The metal goods the natives obtained were of two kinds. The first was tra-ditional or instantly recognizable tools, though made of superior materials, to shorten or improve their work: fishhooks and spears, knives, machetes, and cutting hooks to hack away the semi-tropical undergrowth of the Southeast, spades and hoes for farming, axes, celts, and wedges for cutting firewood and building palisades, scissors, needles, and awls for making leather clothing and moccasins. Rarely found on sixteenth-century native sites or on European lists of trade goods are guns, which quickly would have become useless without European smiths to repair them and residential traders to supply powder and

According to Samuel Champlain, in the early seventeenth century the Canadian Indians in winter wore robes of deer, bear, or beaver "shaped like a cloak, which they wear in the Irish or Egyptian fashion, and sleeves which are tied behind by a cord." Beaver "matchcoats" of this type were especially valued by European fur traders because the skins were supple with grease and smoke and the long guard hairs were worn off, leaving the soft *duvet* used in felting. From Champlain's *Voyages* (Paris, 1620).

shot. Understandably, before the natives saw them in action, European weapons were not particularly attractive. On Columbus's "San Salvador" the Taínos cut themselves by grasping Spanish swords by the blades. And according to Verrazzano, the Indians of Narragansett Bay in 1524 did not yet appreciate metals like iron and steel, "for many times when we showed them some of our arms, they did not admire them, nor ask for them, but merely examined the workmanship."[41]

It was only a matter of time, however, before metal points and blades of all kinds were in great demand. After his first voyage to Canada in 1534, Cartier knew the Iroquoian words for *hatchet, knife,* and *sword;* by the second voyage he had learned a phrase he must have heard often, "Give me a knife." Most eastern tribes loved copper and brass kettles—handles or bodies—for making arrow points and ornaments, not for cooking. The natives around the French Fort Caroline in Florida even broke new knife blades and used the points to tip their arrows. The Inuit near Baffin Island became incontinent thieves in the sight of ordinary nails. In 1587 they purloined two strakes from a new pinnace "onely for the love of the yron in the boords." Like the Beothuks of seventeenth-century Newfoundland, they hammered the nails into durable spear and arrow points.[42]

The Indians' second and major use of metal was decorative. Most tools brought by the Europeans were already in the native workshop; what was new was shiny metal objects that could be used directly or modified as personal ornaments. Buttons were worn, not to fasten clothing, but as jewelry; Frobisher met Inuits who wore copper buttons as decorative headware, which shone against their oily black hair. A major item in the Spanish trade kit was bells of various sizes but primarily "hawk's bells," which in Europe were tied to the legs of pet hawks and falcons. One Florida village even got its hands on a set of English sleigh bells. The inventory for Gilbert's 1583 voyage to Newfoundland included a firkin of Morris bells, largely "to delight the Savage people," wrote a crewman, "whom we intended to winne by all faire meanes possible."[43]

Sheet brass and copper and kettles, old and new, were highly prized because they could be cut and made into traditional objects but would last longer than shell, wood, or bone. Favorite pieces were bracelets, finger rings, gorgets or small breastplates, tubular beads and bangles to sew on clothing or wear as earrings, and incised pendants. One Floridian wore at his ear a small copper plate, "wherwithe they use to scrape and take awaye the sweat from their bodies." Before being buried with it, another made an elongated gorget from an incised copper plate featuring a European man in pantaloons opposite a stag or bull with a prominent penis. Since he was interested in the metal to fashion a traditional ornament, he cut the piece right across both figures, drilled two holes at the top for a thong, and embossed the margin with a punch.[44]

The strong native preference for their own cultural values was also shown by their treatment of Spanish coins, gold, and silver picked up from shipwrecks along the Florida and Georgia coasts. Before drooling Europeans taught them otherwise, the natives put no inordinate value on the "precious" metals, anymore than they did on "precious" furs, and traded them away "for little or nothing" to bauble-bearing French and Spanish soldiers, who sought to gain their friendship while fortifying the coast for their respective sovereigns. John Sparke, an English seaman who visited Fort Caroline in 1565, thought the Indians "had estimation of their golde & silver." But he mistook acquired for traditional values, for the natives habitually flattened, cut, drilled, and incised gold and silver bars, coins, and jewelry to make their own kinds of ornaments. Silver coins were flattened and rolled into heavy tubular beads. Gold coins and discs were beaten into concavo-convex shapes, perforated, and punched around the margin, as were nine copper maravedies bearing the likeness of Charles I of Spain.[45]

While the Indians were understandably drawn to exotic new metals, they were also grateful for more mundane cloth and clothing. In the sixteenth century, wool blankets had not made their conspicuous appearance in trade inventories; the famous striped Hudson's Bay blanket was more than a century in the future. But other types of woven fabrics were major trade items from an early date. When John Cabot set off on his fatal third voyage in 1498, he was accompanied by three or four small Bristol ships freighted with "slight & gross merchandises [such] as coarse cloth, caps, laces, points & other trifles." In 1517 John Rastell, Sir Thomas More's brother-in-law, set out to plant a colony in the New World, armed with "packs of friezes and canvas and coffers of silk and tukes and other mercery ware." One of the first words Cartier learned from the Stadaconans was *Cahoneta*, "Red cloth." By 1584 it was well known in English trading circles that the Indians all around the Gulf of St. Lawrence, because of the sharp cold there, were "greatly delighted with any cappe or garment made of course wollen clothe." Accordingly, Richard Hakluyt predicted that the English would find "greate utteraunce of our clothes, especially of our coursest and basest northerne doosens [dozens] and our Irishe and Welshe fri[e]zes, and rugges."[46]

While the natives of southern New England preferred "red and blue above all colors," as of 1524 they atypically had no interest in cloth of any kind. Within a century Dutch traders from New Netherland had given the Narragansetts a taste for cloth, which the undersupplied pilgrims at Plymouth were not able to capitalize on. Even when Plymouth officials established a trading post on the Kennebec in Maine, they were forced to buy "coats, shirts, rugs, and blankets" from French and English fishermen who carried generous amounts of such items, much as their sixteenth-century predecessors had.[47]

In the warm Southeast, shirts were big sellers because they were colorful, lighter than buckskin, and dried more quickly without losing their softness. In 1549 Spanish friars made several material and spiritual inroads upon native Florida on the strength of a supply of extra shirts. By 1565 René de Laudonniére's starving colonists at Fort Caroline were forced, in a move reminiscent of the Micmacs who doffed their fur mantles for Cartier, "to give away the very

An incised copper plate shows evidence of Indian traditionalism in using novel European trade goods. The plate originally depicted a Spaniard wearing pantaloons facing a stag or bull. Its Indian owner, however, cut it into a traditional gorget, punched two holes from which to suspend it, and embossed it with dots. The item was excavated from a sixteenth-century cemetery in St. Mark's Wildlife Refuge near the Gulf coast of the Florida panhandle. From Hale G. Smith, *The European and the Indian* (Gainesville, 1956), reproduced by courtesy of the Florida Anthropological Society.

shirts from their backs to get one fish" from the local Timucuas. More commonly, the French and the Spanish used clothing to get local chiefs into the habit of alliance or submission. When the French first came to reconnoiter the area around the St. John's River in 1562, they bestowed on the "kings" of both sides of the river and their councillors beautiful "gownes of blewe clothe garnished with yellowe flowers de luce." Two years later, when Fort Caroline was built, Laudonnière sent to remote chiefs who desired the friendship of the French some metal tools and "two whole sutes of apparell." Once the French were eradicated by Spanish arms the following year, Captain Juan Pardo was sent inland from the South Carolina coast to establish a line of six forts on New Spain's northeastern flank. In addition to a variety of metal tools and ornaments, he distributed among friendly headmen fifty pieces of red, green, and "colored" taffeta, "London cloth," satin, silk, and linen.[48]

Measured against valuable furs or invaluable alliances, metal tools and cloth seemed "trifling" expenses to the Europeans, because they counted only the wholesale cost of such items and conveniently forgot the complex operations that produced them. Unlike an Indian trader, who killed his own game, had its fur processed by his wife, and perhaps wore it for a year or two, the European trader handled only the final product of a long skein of economic transactions, whose division of labor, high volume, and efficient distribution ensured him a fairly low price. Like most urban consumers, the sea-going traders of the sixteenth century had no acquaintance with the dirty miners who hacked iron ore from the stubborn bowels of the earth, the carters who carried it to a smelting house, the sooty smelters who refined it in their roaring furnaces, or the blacksmiths who handforged the pig iron into standardized axe heads, knife blades, and celts. For the same reason, the traders were equally unaware of the Cotswold farmers, shearers, carders, spinners, and weavers who transformed sheep's wool into warm Witney blankets or of the poor Irish cottagers whose cold, stiff fingers shuttled gray napped friezes into existence.[49]

Although substantial woven and metal goods were most popular in Indian country, European traders also tried to interest their American partners in smaller and lighter objects of some utilitarian but mostly exotic value. Written and archaeological records of sixteenth-century trade goods contain a number of surprising additions to and omissions from the standard inventories of the next century. We are not particularly surprised to learn that Indians accepted blue and white glass beads (which resembled their own shell beads), ivory or bone combs (like their own bone combs), looking glasses (a novel way to apply one's own face paint or to fix one's hair), or even broken bottles (from which arrowheads could be flaked). But we might wonder how highly they valued the handle of a pewter demitasse spoon, twangy mouth harps, "tablets of glasse, wherein the image of King Charles the ninth was drawen very lively," pieces of paper, or playing cards (a Calusa man gave a Spanish soldier 70 ducats of gold for an ace of diamonds, but he also let half a bar of silver worth 100 ducats go for a pair of scissors).[50]

Upon leaving Kodlunarn Island in 1578, Martin Frobisher built a small house and "garnished it with many kindes of trifles ... thereby to allure & entice the people to some familiaritie against other yeares"—a kind of new world Harrods. The Inuits undoubtedly appreciated the free "Pinnes, Pointes, Laces, [looking] Glasses, [and] Kombes," but whether they regarded "Babes on horsebacke and on foote" and "innumerable other such fansies & toyes" with the childlike awe that was expected of them is unknown, but not likely.[51]

Besides firearms, a few key items did not make a conspicuous appearance until the seventeenth century. No notice is taken of liquor and little notice of clay pipes (whose stems later made good discoidal beads). We do not hear of tobacco until 1597, when a crew of French Basques brought home from Newfoundland, in addition to a load of fish and train oil, "fifty buckskynnes, forty bever skinnes, [and] twenty martins" which they obtained "of the Savadges in trucke for tobacco." Eight years later the *Castor and Pollux* with an Anglo-French crew stopped in the West Indies to pick up tobacco and maize before proceeding up the Atlantic coast to barter for sassafras and ginseng.[52]

Although maritime traders and garrison soldiers conveyed the bulk of European goods to the Indians, many items, particularly metal, reached native users directly when colonial forts and settlements were abandoned or when ships broke up in the relentless surf or on the rocky ledges of the eastern seaboard. It would be difficult to overestimate the number of points, blades, and scrapers that were made from just the nails and hinges left behind at Cartier's fort on the St. Charles, Roberval's miniature city at Cap Rouge, and Roanoke. Cartier specifically gave the Stadaconans the hull of an old ship when he returned to France in 1536 so they could extract and make use of the nails. Roberval left behind three towers and four courts of buildings.[53]

Europeans in Florida were equally generous. When Laudonnière's troops left Florida for the first time in 1563, they bequeathed to the Indians around Charlesfort "all the marchandise that remained," including cutting hooks and shirts. When they pulled out for the last time two years later, Laudonnière planned to fire the fort and all its contents. But he acceded to the wishes of the local chiefs who, he said, "prayed me that I would leave them my house, [and] that I would forbid my souldiers to beate downe the Fort and their lodgings." Within three years the Spanish similarly jettisoned all six of the forts they had built in modern-day North Carolina, South Carolina, and Tennessee, complete with substantial numbers of nails, chisels, knives, and other tools. The nearly 800 pounds of abandoned lead balls, match cord, and powder must have done the natives little good without firearms, and maybe even considerable harm if used carelessly.[54]

As the Pardo expedition suggests, European trade and its cultural effects were not confined to native settlements along the Atlantic coast. Water linkages and long-established trade routes enabled goods obtained on the coast to travel far inland without skipping a paddle beat. In the Southeast, Spanish *entradas* like Hernando de Soto's (1539–43) left vast quantities of European metal, glass, and cloth in their bloody wakes, as well as fast-breeding hogs, deadly microbes, and psychological havoc. Chains and manacles to enslave Indian porters were probably the least attractive artifacts introduced by Soto, but weapons, clothing, and ornaments stripped from Spanish victims may have served as some compensation.[55]

The largest routes to the interior were Chesapeake Bay and the St. Lawrence River. From French, Spanish, and English ships rolling in the mouth of the bay, trade goods traveled in native canoes up its indented reaches to the Susquehanna River, then up that broad river and its East Branch into the heart of Oneida Iroquois country or over small connecting creeks and rivers into the other Iroquois homelands. From there the goods were bartered along traditional trading paths to the Iroquoian-speaking Eries, Neutrals, Petuns, and even Hurons in southern Ontario. But the Hurons and Petuns could more easily obtain European treasure via the "Great Circle Route," which linked Georgian Bay, Lake Nipissing, and Lac St. Jean with the Saguenay, St. Lawrence, and Ottawa rivers in a sweeping clockwise movement of goods.[56]

Within twenty-five years on either side of 1550, each of the Iroquoian nations, from the Susquehannocks on the Susquehanna to the Hurons on Lake Huron, had begun to receive their first European goods indirectly from the traders and fishermen on the Atlantic coast, usually small pieces of copper and brass, nails, awls, knives, axes, and beads. Oddly, the groups one would expect to have received the most obtained almost nothing, if the archaeological record does not deceive. More than 125 sites belonging to the St. Lawrence Iroquois have yielded hundreds of thousands of artifacts, but only a handful of small items of European origin, and none resembling the gifts Cartier presented to the natives in his two voyages up the river. This suggests that in the sixteenth century the Chesapeake-Susquehanna route was more important than the more obvious St. Lawrence for spreading European material culture into the native Northeast. Metal and cloth (which seldom survives archaeologically) were simply shunted along watery paths traditionally used to transport mid-Atlantic marine shell, particularly *Busycon,* to Iroquoian necklace- and bead-makers all across central New York.[57]

In another part of the Northeast, Etchemin and Micmac middlemen, sailing Basque shallops, wearing various items of European clothing, and speaking a half-Basque, half-Indian trade jargon, bartered furs from the coast of Maine for European trade goods in the Gulf of St. Lawrence and at Tadoussac, a major rendezvous for French and Basque traders. When returned to Maine, the goods traveled up the Saco, Androscoggin, Kennebec, and Penobscot rivers to interior tribes, mostly Abenakis, or along the coast to the "Armouchiquois" of Massachusetts, who supplied corn, beans, pumpkins, tobacco, and shell beads to the northern groups who had little or none of their own. Until the seventeenth century, few fishermen or traders seem to have bothered or needed to cruise beyond Nova Scotia and the Bay of Fundy for furs or cod. So enterprising natives turned their familiarity with the sea to account by mediating the coastal trade. The stack of moose hides lifted by John Walker in 1580 from a native hut on Penobscot Bay was undoubtedly awaiting shipment to the gulf by its Etchemin owners.[58]

The sixteenth century in North America was a period of cultural as well as geographical exploration, a time for American natives and European new-comers to feel each other out. Complicating the process was the irregularity of contact. Small garrisons of Spanish soldiers came to Florida to stay and Basque whalers consistently plied the Strait of Belle Isle, but most fishermen came and went, seldom returning to the same spot. Sea-going traders, out to make a quick profit, were even more unreliable. Like the sea itself, the mar-itime trade was unpredictable and often unruly.

The use of native protocol helped to stabilize sensitive and potentially explosive encounters. Among the Inuit phrases John Davis's crew quickly learned to use were "I mean no harme," "Come hither," "Eate some," and "Wil you have this?" At the same time, the natives, although they were on home soil, learned to respect European preferences, persons, and property, and not only because of the strangers' superior firepower. As a French captain put it, "in the end they were constrained to forget their superstitions, and to apply them-selves to our nature, which was somewhat strange unto them at the first." Attracted by European trade goods, they made an effort to ensure a steady flow of them their way. They volunteered to work for the landed immigrants, flensing whales, hunting or growing food, diving for pearls, and digging sas-safras. They imitated European words, phrases, and even tunes, as the Inuits on Baffin Island did for Frobisher in 1578. They drew maps for the strangers and whetted their appetites by filling their ears with rich stories about rich kingdoms just over the horizon. Algonquians on Cape Cod even persuaded an English crew that they made butter and cheese from the milk of tame fallow deer and caribou.[59]

Mutual trust, effort, and necessity often produced not only satisfactory eco-nomic exchanges but delightful personal encounters. Indians and Europeans made music and danced together. They shot off their respective weapons, showed off their respective ingenuity, and played their national games. John Davis's crew had leaping contests with the denizens of Baffin Island, which the English mostly won, but mostly lost at wrestling, even though they had some reputed wrestlers aboard. Later several parties of natives waved the crew ashore to play football, but the English, inured to rough Sunday sport on vil-lage greens, "did cast them downe as soone as they did come to strike the ball," which the "strong and nimble" Inuits did not seem to mind.[60] And as might be predicted of men who had just come off a long, cold voyage, homesick mariners made love with native women, sometimes—to judge from the native protectiveness of their women—with more force than finesse. European crewmen quickly acquired enough fluency to whisper "Kiss me" and "Let us go to bed," as well as the words for *phallus, testicles, vagina,* and *pubic hair.*[61]

Too frequently, however, the cultural interface wore a scowl, largely because European ships carried not only fish hooks and trade goods but large ladings of cultural arrogance. Because they were proselytizing Christians, technologically advanced, and citizens of large nation-states, most European mariners felt they had a right to usurp native territory with a wooden cross or piece of parchment and to steal native people and property. The thirty English gentlemen who left the Inns of Court and Chancery in 1536 to sightsee in Newfoundland certainly carried no brief for America's natives. As soon as one of them spied a boatload of Beothuks approaching, he called the rest above decks to man a longboat "to meete them and to take them." When the natives fled, the tourists went to their campsite and liberated a "bravely" decorated moccasin and a "great warme mitten." Apparently, a side of roast bear on the spit was not to their taste. When native people could not be snatched as souvenirs, Frobisher's men fell back on their vital sled dogs.[62]

Europeans also felt free to contemn native customs not involved with trade. Religious totems they dismissed as "superstitious toyes." Because the Inuits ate raw meat, Frobisher's chronicler thought them "Anthropophagi, or devourers of mans fleshe." When Frobisher kidnapped an old woman, some of his sailors suspected her of being a devil or a witch, so they "plucked off her buskins, to see if she were cloven footed." When she proved to have ten normal toes, they released her, glad not to have to endure her "oughly hewe and deformitie" all the way home. After a happy bartering session, John Davis was urged by his Inuit partners to stand in the smoke of a "sacrificial" fire, which was used throughout eastern America to bless sacred and revered objects. Suspicious of its purpose, he thrust one of the natives into the smoke and ordered his men to "tread out the fire, & to spurne it into the sea . . . to shew them that we did contemne their sorcery." When missionaries came to the New World in the next century, they were no more iconoclastic or contemptuous of native custom.[63]

As provocations like these mounted, the natives "inexplicably" ambushed and killed seamen and stole their property with utter contempt for "civilized" law. Often without knowing the antecedent affront, European crews found themselves being taunted or shot at. Étienne Bellenger lost a pinnace and two crewmen on the coast of Acadia when the crew trusted a party of Micmacs too far. Having kidnapped a man, woman, and child, Frobisher and his men were still incensed by elaborate efforts to lure them to shore. While several of their fellows lay hidden behind rocks, one or two natives alternately waved a white fur, clapped their unarmed hands, laid out food on a rock, and pretended to be disabled. The English finally rang the curtain down on this "counterfeite pageant" by firing a volley at the avengers. These targets just ran away, but by 1564 in Florida and 1593 on Cape Breton, natives had learned to drop to the ground "assoone as ever they saw the harquebuze laide to the cheeke" of a European warrior.[64]

The rising tide of contact, competition, and conflict in the sixteenth century also pitted native against native for access to the Europeans' technology and its attendant spiritual power. Inland tribes sought reliable sources of trade goods, preferably without the undue intervention of coastal tribes. Those groups who were especially well situated on converging watersheds or traditional trade routes may have wished to take advantage of their geographical fortune by supplying tribes even farther from the coast. And many groups worried about the advantages their rivals and neighbors would gain from superior supplies of metal weapons and prestigious goods. For reasons such as these, and undoubtedly others hidden from the prying eyes of historians and archaeologists, three major confederacies sprang up at the end of the sixteenth century. In tidewater Virginia, Powhatan, a keen student of power politics, strong-armed his way from six inherited tribes to an awesome chiefdom of thirty tribes. Five Iroquois "nations" in present-day New York fashioned America's most famous and most powerful confederacy in the interests of legislated peace between members and imposed peace upon neighbors. Perhaps in defensive retaliation, five Huron tribes formed a league in southern Ontario which, like the Powhatan chiefdom, was only completed on the eve of sustained contact with the Europeans in the early seventeenth century. In a very short time, each of these confederations muscled or palavered their way to the center of European attention.[65]

The initial meeting of Indians and Europeans left rich intellectual legacies as well. One was the expansion of known worlds. While the Europeans discovered for themselves a whole "new world," a continent that was not on any of their maps, the Indians were forced to acknowledge the existence of lands beyond the waters surrounding their hemispheric "island on a turtle's back," as their homeland was called in many of their creation myths. Perhaps equally astonishing to both parties was the sudden expansion of humankind. On one fateful day in 1492, Europeans, who believed that yellow Asians and black Africans with themselves comprised the human family of Noah, encountered a race of brown people who were given no space in any of the bibles or encyclopedias of the day. At the same moment, native Americans must have suddenly realized that they, too, stood at the watery edge of a vast, unknown world, only dimly perceived and portentous for being so. Each came face-to-face with a new, ineluctable "other," and the early histories of three continents would be written in large measure by how much of themselves they came to recognize.

FOUR

THE FIRST CONSUMER REVOLUTION

The Seventeenth Century

Most revolutions or events of revolutionary proportions have publicly accepted inaugural dates—July 4, 1776, July 14, 1789, October 12, 1492—which enable us to fill our calendars with commemorative events. But the latest addition to the revolutionary pantheon comes without a birth certificate or scholarly consensus about its credentials and pedigree. I refer to the English "consumer revolution," which claims no kinship to the more famous English revolutions of Tudor government, civil war, or 1688.

It's small wonder that scholars cannot agree about the causes, timing, effects, and long-range importance of this latest revolution because they discovered it only within the last twenty years. Another reason for the lack of consensus owes to its nature: this is one of the first "revolutions" to be discovered by the Early Modern practitioners of the "new" social history, rather than by political historians of a conventional stripe. Given the scope of their questions and the quicksilver quality of their evidence, social historians seldom agree about anything, and the consumer revolution is no exception. Yet the outlines of the phenomenon are becoming clearer with each passing article.

It seems that sometime between 1690 and 1740, first in England and Scotland and soon in England's mainland American colonies, consumers of the gentle and particularly "middling" classes began to purchase an unprecedented number and variety of manufactured goods and to use many of them in conspicuous displays of leisure, social ritual, and status affirmation (or arrogation). Thanks to a pronounced increase in per capita wealth and disposable income, consumers not only upgraded their necessities, such as bedding, eating utensils, and clothing, but chose from a veritable Harrods catalogue of competitively priced luxury goods and amenities, which reached the remotest corners of the land in peddlers' packs and the inventories of myriad country stores.

Often patterned after the latest of the ever-changing fashions of Paris and London and vigorously promoted by window displays, newspaper advertisements, and word-of-mouth, these goods quickly spread from responsive English manufactories across regions and classes in a wide but standardized repertoire. This had the effect of forging strong material bonds between mother country and colonies, even as political fissures were beginning to appear in their union, some the result of mounting debts incurred by colonial shoppers anxious to keep up with the Carters and the Schuylers.[1]

One might legitimately ask, Why is the purchase—even the widespread, cross-class purchase—of satin waistcoats, looking glasses, japaned dressing tables, Wedgwood china, forks, and matching tea services considered "revolutionary?" The experts offer a number of answers. The first is that, unlike the later Industrial Revolution, the consumer revolution was made, less by increased, more efficient, and more competitive productivity on the supply side, than by unprecedented and particular consumer demand, which called forth the supply and inspired many of the technological and organizational advances of the Industrial Revolution. This demand, in turn, was molded by new techniques of mass marketing and the conscious creation of "imaginary necessities." "As wealth and population increased," explained an English visitor to colonial Baltimore, "wants were created, and many considerable demands, in consequence, took place for the various elegancies as well as the necessaries of life."[2]

Enjoying for the first time so many economic choices, consumers, especially women, were empowered by a heady sense of personal independence and the ability to fashion themselves with the material trappings of "gentility." In the American colonies, however, this heavy dependence on the credit extended by English merchants and manufacturers led to fears of economic enslavement. These fears, in turn, exacerbated fears of political tyranny from the Stamp Act on and gave rise to such consumer boycotts as the Association to halt importation of the "effeminating" and enervating "Baubles of Britain." In other words, when the British government injected coercion into its relations with the colonies, the ties of loyalty that bound the colonists to an empire of free-flowing goods quickly came undone. "A constitutional crisis transformed private consumer acts into public political statements" and many Americans "discovered political ideology through a discussion of the meaning of goods."[3]

In sketching the outlines of this eighteenth-century British revolution, I have a strong sense of *déjà vu*. Where have I seen this before? The answer, as might be expected from an ethnohistorian of colonial North America, is in the Indian communities of seventeenth-century North America. Such an answer will undoubtedly be greeted with a certain amount of reasonable skepticism. After all, don't we all know that the American Indians were poor and spiritual people who lived from hand-to-mouth in a precarious environment and put their faith in strange gods and spirits rather than earthly things? Don't we know that their "nomadic" lifestyle and their communal ethic of sharing militated against the senseless acquisition of material comforts? Perhaps unlikelier candidates for a *consumer* revolution could not be found, certainly not fifty or seventy-five years before their "civilized" and admittedly materialistic English counterparts experienced one.

Such skepticism is unwarranted. The Indians of the Eastern Woodlands experienced a consumer revolution every bit as revolutionary as that experienced by their European suppliers, though not identical in every respect, and they did so many years earlier, usually as soon as the commercial colonists founded trading posts, *comptoirs,* and nascent settlements. How, if the natives lived in penury, was this possible? Without gold or silver mines like those in Mexico and Peru, how did native North Americans across the social spectrum (which was not wide in any case) find the purchase price of any European goods, much less goods in sufficient quantity and variety to warrant a "revolutionary" denomination?

The per capita wealth of Indian America, though it cannot be measured in native currencies, increased dramatically from the earliest stages of contact because European traders were willing and eager to pay top pound, franc, and florin for American animal pelts and skins, which the Indians were adept in curing and procuring for their own domestic uses. Three kinds of pelts were the most lucrative for the Indians. Beaver, for which the natives had little use before the trade, became the best seller because its soft, microscopically barbed underfur was in great demand for the manufacture of broad-brimmed felt hats for Europe's gentlemen. A ready market also existed for rare and luxurious "small furs," such as marten, otter, and black fox, which were used to trim the rich gowns of the high-born. And beginning in the last quarter of the seventeenth century, the Indians of the Southeast could sell any number of humbler but larger deerskins, which provided scarce leather for Continental breeches, saddlebags, bookbindings, and workingmen's aprons. The European demand for skins the natives regarded as commonplace was seemingly insatiable and enabled all male hunters of a tribe to participate in the search for income-producing pelts if they wished.

To judge by the traders' export figures, a substantial majority of native hunters did quite well in the new European market. The Mahicans and eastern Iroquois brought about 8,000 beaver and otter skins to the Dutch posts at Fort Orange and New Amsterdam in 1626. By the late 1650s, 46,000 pelts were pouring into Fort Orange alone.[4] The French in Canada were even better supplied by their native partners. In 1614, only six years after the founding of Quebec, 25,000 skins, mostly beaver, were shipped to France's hatters. By the 1620s the Montagnais on the north shore of the St. Lawrence were trading 12–15,000 pelts at Tadoussac every year. In flotillas of 60–70 canoes, some 200 Huron traders from southern Ontario brought 10,000 skins a year to Quebec. Twenty years later, even as their population was cut in half by disease and intertribal warfare, the Hurons produced 30,000 beaver pelts annually.[5] In New England, the Plymouth colony was able to pay off its English creditors only because Abenaki hunters on the Kennebec River in Maine kept them supplied with animal skins: about 8,000 beavers and 1,156 otters between 1631 and 1636 alone. Even then the lion's share of Abenaki pelts went to French traders from Acadia.[6]

To the south, the natives of the interior supplied Charleston's outgoing ships with 54,000 deerskins a year between 1700 and 1715. Between 1740 and 1762 the take was up to 152,000 skins a year. The best hunters were the Muskogees or Creeks of Alabama and Georgia. In 1720 they traded more than 80,000 skins to South Carolina and French Mobile. Forty years later, with a new market in Savannah, they were killing 140,000 deer every season.[7] In the 1750s the Cherokees took 25,000 skins annually from the mountains of North Carolina, Georgia, and Tennessee, an average of 12 deer for each of 2,000 warriors. In the twenty years between 1739 and 1759, Cherokee hunters alone reduced the southeastern deer population by 1.25 million.[8]

Clearly, the natives of eastern America controlled resources that were in great demand in Europe. But did they realize their profit potential? Or did they kill all those animals for a few cheap trinkets and a swot or two of rot-gut rum, leaving themselves no better off than they were before the advent of the white man? British traders in particular knew that the natives, whose simple lives required few necessities, had to be given a sense of personal "Property" if their American business was ever to thrive. For a notion of material accumulation, "though it would not increase their real Necessities, yet it would furnish them with imaginary Wants."[9] By 1679, Indians from Hudson Bay to the Carolinas had discovered that "many Things which they wanted not before because they never had them are by . . . means [of the trade] become necessary both for their use & ornament."[10] They had been, in a stay-at-home European's words, "cosened by a desire of new-fangled novelties."[11]

But had they? To hear both native hunters and knowledgeable Europeans tell it, the Indian was nobody's fool and certainly felt that he made out like a bandit in his dealings with the rubes from the Old World. For ordinary skins "which cost them almost nothing," the Indians received novel trade goods superior to their own artifacts of skin, bone, stone, and wood.[12] A Montagnais hunter once exclaimed that "'The Beaver does everything perfectly well, it makes kettles, hatchets, swords, knives, bread, in short it makes everything.' He was making sport of us Europeans," explained his Jesuit guest, "who have such a fondness for the skin of this animal and who fight to see who will give the most to these Barbarians, to get it." Some while later, the same Indian said to the Frenchman, holding out a very beautiful knife, "'The English have no sense; they give us twenty knives like this for one Beaver skin.'"[13]

While the natives didn't easily understand price fluctuations obedient to Western laws of supply and demand, they were shrewd enough to advance their own bargaining position by playing European competitors against each other, by avoiding superfluities that had no place in their own culture, and by being extremely finicky about the quality and style of goods they would accept. In 1642 Roger Williams noted how the Narragansetts of Rhode Island "will beate all markets and try all places, and runne twenty, thirty, yea, forty mile[s] and more, and lodge in the Woods, to save six pence."[14] Likewise, testified a Recollect priest who knew them well, the Iroquois and natives of the Great Lakes "are rather shrewd and let no one outwit them easily. They examine everything carefully and train themselves to know goods."[15] A Virginia trader in Chesapeake Bay in 1630 complained, to no avail, that his Indian customers were "very long and teadeous" in viewing his array of trade goods and did "tumble it and tosse it and mingle it a hundred times over."[16] Four years later, a trader on the coast of Maine groused to his English boss that "The Indians ar[e] now so well seen Into our tradinge Commodities, that heare is litle to be got by yt." Not only did the competing French and English traders undersell one another in a frenzy to acquire furs, but the Indians refused to buy short English coats, coverlets that were not "soft & warme," or unlined hats without bands.[17] A half-century later, in the mountains of Virginia and North Carolina, William Byrd's Indian customers would have no truck with large white beads (instead of small ones), porous kettles, light (instead of dark) blue blankets, guns with weak locks, or small (instead of large) hoes.[18] "They are not delighted in baubles," Thomas Morton had observed as early as 1632, "but in usefull things."[19] As European trader after trader quickly learned, in native America the customer was always right.

The customer was not only right, he held the upper hand in the struggle over payment. Because his necessities and even his acquired tastes were so few and relatively inelastic, in the establishment of trade the Indians needed the European trader less than he needed them. The sharp competition between company traders, *coureurs de bois*, and government factors for most Indian customers, even those in the *pays d'en haut*, only increased the natives' leverage. So they quickly demanded and received credit from the traders.

In late summer or early fall, the trader advanced the Indians on account the goods, arms, ammunition, and food they needed for the winter hunt. When the hunters returned in the late spring or early summer with their catch, the trader cancelled their debts and, if they had a surplus, furnished them with supplies and luxuries. If the hunters had a poor season, they often escaped the consequences of their growing debts by simply moving to new hunting grounds and striking up business with a new trader, who was only too happy to purchase their pelts and to extend them a line of credit. As a Swedish governor complained of his native trading partners in 1655, "If they buy anything here, they wish to get half on credit, and then pay with difficulty."[20] Traders in Hudson Bay, New France, New England, New Amsterdam, and the Carolinas felt the same crunch early in their relations with the fur-toting natives.

If we are going to declare these new Indian purchases a "consumer revolution," similar to the later English one, we should also analyze in some detail the kind and quantity of trade goods the Indians preferred. We have two major ways to learn about native preferences. One is from the work of archaeologists, whose excavations of Indian villages and burials turn up the broken and discarded material of native life as well as the most treasured possessions buried with the dead. The second way is from the hand of traders' clerks and government officials, who made detailed lists of trade items and diplomatic gifts to be shipped to Indian villages by canoe or packtrain. These two sources can be supplemented to some extent by the findings of underwater archaeologists at the feet of cold northern river rapids, where French canoes overturned with all their bright new cargoes headed for Indian country.[21] These beautifully preserved objects can tell us what in the peddlers' packs may have attracted the Indians, but they do not necessarily tell us whether the natives purchased them or used them in ways that Europeans would expect.

According to all our sources, the *nouveaux-riches* natives bought five kinds of European goods: tools, clothing, decorations, novelties, and occasionally food. Even before they had direct and regular access to European traders, the Indians acquired a variety of utilitarian and decorative items from sea-going traders, abandoned colonial facilities, shipwrecks, or natives who had access to these sources. Many native communities met their first European objects in the sixteenth century, long before the English or the French established lasting colonies in North America. When Gaspar Corte-Real sailed to Newfoundland or a nearby coast in 1501, for example, he met one Indian man clutching a piece of an Italian gilt sword and another sporting a pair of Venetian silver earrings.[22]

The earliest items favored by both native men and women were metal tools to make their work go easier and faster. Since the natives were already fully equipped with the requisite tools to manage their environment, they purchased the same kinds of European implements made of superior materials. Processed metal was brighter, more durable, and held an edge longer than annealed native copper, bone, fired clay, stone, or wood. So the natives sensibly spent their first fur paychecks on iron axes (to save the time involved in burning large trees down), hatchets (to gather firewood and crack enemy skulls), awls (to punch leather and drill shell beads), ice chisels (to break-open beaver lodges), butcher knives (to replace more breakable and costly flint knives), swords (to point spears and arrows with pieces of broken blade), fishhooks (to replace unbarbed bone hooks), wide hoes (to replace deer scapula or short digging sticks), and brass or copper kettles (to replace heavier, thicker, and more fragile clay pots).

We know a good deal about the metal goods the Indians purchased because they survive well in the ground and frequently end up in caring museums. But their numbers are somewhat deceiving, for the best-selling item in native (as in English and colonial) markets from the seventeenth century on was cloth of all kinds.[23] Unfortunately, cloth does not fare well in the ground over centuries unless it happens to be parked next to some copper or brass, whose salts during oxidation preserve vegetable matter. We do have a few archaeological cloth remnants, but most of our knowledge of the Indian appetite and stylistic preferences for cloth comes from lead seals used to certify cloth at its source (which turn up in archaeological contexts) and from the letterbooks and inventories

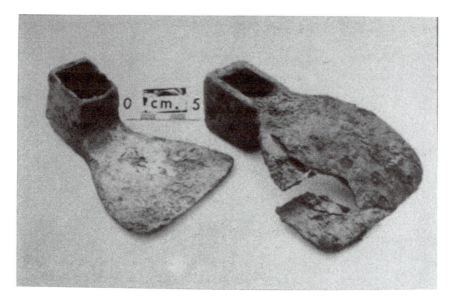

These hoes were excavated from a Narragansett cemetery on Conanicut Island, Jamestown, Rhode Island, by Professor William Simmons in 1966–67. They were buried with an elderly woman as grave offerings between 1620 and 1660. From William Scranton Simmons, *Cautantowwit's House: An Indian Burial Ground on the Island of Conanicut in Narragansett Bay* (Providence: Brown University Press, 1970); it is reproduced with the kind permission of University Press of New England.

of traders. They make it clear why most of the early Indian names for Europeans meant "Cloth makers" or "Coat-men" when they were not called "Iron-Workers" or "Swordmen."[24]

Why would the natives spend their fur proceeds on European cloth when they already had perfectly adaptable fur and skin clothing? Woolen blanketing or duffels was the single biggest seller for several reasons: it was lighter than and as warm as a fur mantle or *matchcoat*, it dried faster and remained softer and suppler than wet skins and was even warm when wet, it came in bright colors which natural berry and root dyes could not duplicate (though most Indians preferred "sad" hues of red and blue), and, with metal knives and scissors, it could quickly be fashioned into leggings, breechclouts, tie-on sleeves, or mantles by women who no longer had to laboriously cure and dress several skins. Another potential advantage was seldom realized because the Indians almost never washed their clothes and literally wore them off their backs.[25] Soap was not in the trader's kit until the more fastidious nineteenth century, and since the dead were always buried in their best clothes, cloth heirlooms and hand-me-downs were rare. With the "bargains" offered by the European traders, the natives found it easier to buy new threads than to slave over a soapy stream.

This Revolutionary-era engraving of Theyanoquin or "King Hendrick" (c. 1680–1755), chief, diplomat, and orator of the Mohawks, demonstrates the native adaptation of European trade cloth. His shirt is linen or calico, and his mantle and breechclout are made of English wool duffels. Hendrick had visited England in 1710 and again in 1740, when he received a blue coat with gold lace and a cocked hat from King George II. The 39 notches on the tree indicate the number of men Hendrick, a Protestant convert, had killed or captured on the warpath against the French and their native allies. From an anonymous engraving, c. 1776, in the Library of Congress, Washington, D.C.

While cloth was in great demand in Indian country, a few items were unpopular. There was almost no market for tight or fitted clothing, for example. Until the genteel eighteenth century, no native man would have been caught dead in a pair of European breeches: they impeded running and other natural functions (southern men, at least, squatted to urinate). Elaborate military-style coats with braid, buttons, and capacious cuffs were worn only by a handful of favored chiefs and head warriors on ceremonial occasions. The only fitted pieces of clothing that sold relatively well were brightly patterned calico shirts, which the men wore open at the neck and flapping in the breeze.

We can be very brief about the food trade because it was rare. In the seventeenth century the native hunters of eastern Canada occasionally bartered a beaver for some durable ship's biscuit or bread when they couldn't find Indian corn among their agricultural neighbors. But prunes and raisins never caught on except as gifts, and sugar, flour, and tea made their way very slowly into native larders, and then only if colonial settlements were close by.[27]

From the earliest indirect contact with Europeans, the Indians sought to enhance their beauty and status with decorations of foreign material or manufacture. Chinese vermilion, sold in tea-bag-sized paper packets, gradually supplanted native red ochre, and verdigris added a brand new color to harlequin faces. As the Portuguese explorer Corte-Real discovered, silver earrings found a male as well as female market. Copper and brass bracelets, tin finger rings (particularly engraved Jesuit rings with religious motifs, initials, and hearts), bangles or jingling cones made from sheet brass, necklaces of Venetian glass beads in both solid colors and stripes, mostly red, white, and blue, corkscrew wire ear dangles, and, in the eighteenth century, German silver brooches, pins, and gorgets custom-made for the Indian trade were among the most popular European jewelry. While several of these items were new in form and function, the natives made more familiar jewelry from thimbles (by attaching a leather thong through a hole cut in the bottom to make jinglers), scraps of kettle or sheet copper (cut into pendants, gorgets, and even sweat scrapers in the Deep South), and gold and silver coins (perforated and worn around the neck as pendants).[28] With jewelry as with most things, the Indians used, adapted, and interpreted Europe's introductions in traditional ways.

This is less but still true of the final category of Indian trade goods, what we must call novelties because they had no native counterparts. Part of the revolutionary character of native consumerism is attributable to the effects some of these material innovations had on native life. Mouth harps, bells, and clothing fasteners (buttons, buckles, and lace points) played only bit parts in transforming Indian culture in the seventeenth and early eighteenth centuries. But guns, alcohol, and even mirrors were center stage.

An arquebus or flintlock was, in one sense, only a noisy bow and arrow. It was also heavier, harder to make and repair, more expensive, less reliable in wet weather, much slower, and incapable of surprise after the first round. Despite the many deficiencies of firearms, however, the Indians rushed to acquire them as soon as they had seen them in action. For guns drove fear into enemy breasts as often as balls, smashed bones and did more internal damage than razor-sharp arrowheads, and heralded the status of their owners in ways that traditional weapons never could. Against traditional wooden slat armor and old-time massed armies, the gun won hands down.[29] One major effect of the advent of firearms, therefore, was the natives' sole reliance on dispersed guerrilla tactics executed behind trees or from ambush. Sir William Johnson,

Among the novelties traded by Europeans to Indians were mouth harps. These examples from a 18th-century Seneca site are missing their flexible brass "twangers," which gave the mouth-held instrument its rhythmic resonance. From the collections of the Rochester Museum and Science Center, Rochester, N.Y., by whose courtesy it is reproduced.

the Superintendent of Indian Affairs for the British northern department, was of the opinion that the authority of chiefs had also declined since the introduction of firearms because, he said, "They no longer fight in close bodies but every Man is his own General."[30]

The effects of alcohol upon Indian society were nearly as destructive. Cadwallader Colden, an expert on the Iroquois, thought that drunkenness among the American tribes "has destroyed greater Numbers, than all their Wars and Diseases put together."[31] He was wrong about the magnitude but right about the seriousness of the problem that the advent of brandy kegs, rundlets of rum, and case bottles of wine posed for native communities. Although—or perhaps because—the Woodland Indians had no previous experience with intoxicating beverages or hallucinogens, they took to liquid spirits with frightening abandon. And they drank only to become fully inebriated, in which state they felt invincible, capable of making antisocial mayhem with a perfect excuse, and perhaps (though the evidence is weak) more susceptible to the dreams in which "guardian spirits" conveyed their sacred secrets for success.[32] When the "water-that-burns" arrived in sufficient quantity in a village, the place was soon turned into the very "image of hell." Drunken "frolics" lasting several days often produced several victims of shootings, stabbings, brawls, burning, biting, and bawdry. Neither resident missionaries nor native leaders were very successful in persuading the traders to halt the profitable flow, although they used

This drawing of a northeastern Indian warrior (Huron?), probably by Jesuit missionary Francesco Bressani, juxtaposes a European gun with the ancient wooden slat armor made obsolete by the advent of firearms. From *Novae Franciae Accurata Delineatio* (1657).

two compelling arguments: the Indians were dying in excessive numbers from drink-related murders (and, we know also, from exposure and increased susceptibility to colds, pneumonia, and other diseases), and the temperance issue "produce[d] all Evil and Contention between man and wife, between the Young Indians and the Sachims."[33] Alcohol was clearly one trade good the natives could well have done without.

By contrast, mirrors seem terribly tame as novelties go. But the first "looking-glasses" and mirror boxes, which reached the remote Senecas of western New York by the 1620s, may have promoted a preoccupation with personal fashion as much as full-length hanging mirrors did among the genteel colonists. Among the Indians, however, "the men, upon the whole, [were] more fond of dressing than the women" and carried their mirrors with them on all their journeys, which the women did not.[34] As a vehicle of vainglory, the mirror was a necessity, especially for young warriors who now had more income to spend on imported face paints, jewelry, and other finery. Before the advent of mirrors, a native coxcomb had to have his face painted "by some woman or girl," which curtailed his independence and let some of the air out of his vanity.[35] With his own mirror, which he wore constantly around his wrist or over his shoulder, he could arrange his hair, refurbish his scalplock, and paint his face to his heart's content in the privacy of his own toilette. One unfoppish Frenchman who knew the Great Lakes tribes well believed that "if they had a mirror before their eyes they would change their appearance every quarter of an hour."[36] But the tell-tale object, like all spiritual power, was capable of bringing bad news as well. During the great smallpox epidemic of 1738, which killed half of the Cherokee population, "a great many" Indians "killed themselves" by shooting, cutting their throats, stabbing, and throwing themselves into fires because they had seen themselves disfigured by the pox in their ubiquitous mirrors and, "being naturally proud," could not stand the literal loss of face.[37]

We can now appreciate the amazing variety of European goods that reached Indian customers in the seventeenth and eighteenth centuries. To constitute a revolution comparable to the later English one, however, these material products had to arrive in native villages in such quantities that tribesmen and women up and down the social scale had their lives altered by the pursuit, purchase, and use of them. There are basically two ways to establish these quantities. The indirect way is to look at the substantial leap in exports from England to the American colonies in the seventeenth century. It is surely no coincidence that exports of woolens and metalwares doubled between the 1660s and 1700, and miscellaneous manufactures, including tableware and sewing accoutrements, increased threefold.[38] Most of those items were the mainstays of the Indian trade, which we know was burgeoning, even as the native population was declining from disease, wars, and dislocation.

The more direct way is to register the changes in Indian villages, either above or below ground, at the time or later. Obviously, we don't have comparable evi-

The effects of the trade mirror on personal grooming and vanity are suggested by this painting of a Flathead Indian "dandy" by a Jesuit missionary in the 1840s. From *Wilderness Kingdom: Indian Life in the Rocky Mountains: 1840–1847. The Journals & Paintings of Nicholas Point, S.J.,* trans. Joseph P. Donnelly, S.J. (New York, 1967). Reproduced with the kind permission of Loyola University Press.

dence for every tribe in every region. But what we do have is strongly sugges-
tive. For example, on both Seneca and Onondaga Iroquois sites from 1600 to
1620, only 10–15 percent of the artifacts found by archaeologists are European
in origin. From sites dated 1650–55, fully 75 percent of the assemblages are
European (and this, remember, grossly underestimates the amount of cloth
used).[39] Small wonder, then, that in 1768 Eleazar Wheelock, the master of an
Indian school in Connecticut, conducted a frustrated search among the eastern
Iroquois nations for a native artifact that was "perfectly Simple, and without the
least Mixture of any foreign Merchandise" to send as a gift to the Earl of Dartmouth, the benefactor of his future college. A "small specimen" was all he could
find because, he apologized, "our Traders have penetrated so far into their
Country." Only "some articles which were defaced by Use" were crafted from
the traditional materials he sought. Perhaps he shouldn't have been so surprised, for two years earlier one of his English missionary-teachers had written
that the Iroquois were "in some measure like those in New England much
degenerated, both as to their Customs, their Dress and their Impliments."[40]

"Degeneration" is the wrong term to describe any cultural change, unless, of
course, we believe that the only bona fide Indian looks and acts like his pre-
Columbian ancestors. But New England's native population, largely converted
to Christianity and settled in "praying towns," had indeed felt the forces of
acculturation in the century since the Reverend John Eliot began to prosely-
tize them. Many lived in English frame houses complete with standard colonial furniture, plowed their fields with horses or oxen, kept cattle, dressed in
English garb, cooked in iron kettles and skillets, and ate off glazed earthenware with spoons and forks. Even those who still lived in wigwams, such as
Phebe and Elizabeth Moheege of Niantic, Connecticut, cooked in an iron pot
suspended from a trammel, drank at a tea table, ate at another table in a chair
(presumably not at the same time), stored their cups and plates in a wall cup-
board and their prized possessions in two wooden chests.[41]

Another symbol of the revolutionary changes in the lives of virtually all
eastern American natives lived just down the road from the Moheeges, across
the Rhode Island line. There in a house or "palace" lived "King George Nini-
gret," the chief of the once-mighty Narragansetts. When Dr. Alexander
Hamilton of Annapolis rode by in 1744, King George owned 20–30,000 acres
of "very fine level land"upon which he had "many tennants" and "a good stock
of horses and other cattle." "This King," Hamilton noted with evident
approval, "lives after the English mode. His subjects have lost their own gov-
erment [*sic*] policy and laws and are servants or vassals to the English here. His
queen goes in a high modish dress in her silks, hoops, stays, and dresses like an
English woman. He educates his children to the belles letters and is himself a
very complaisant mannerly man. We pay'd him a visit, and he treated us with
a glass of good wine."[42]

King George, of course, was atypical of his American brethren in the degree
of his apparent success. He was, after all, a chief. But he was a new kind of

chief, one who sold his tribal lands to white men and pocketed most of the proceeds, rather than consulting the will of his people and distributing the revenues among them. Nor did he share his personal property as a traditional chief would have a century earlier. This Indian looked out for Number One in good capitalist fashion: he gave many thoughts to his own family's future but far fewer to that of his "subjects" who labored menially for his English models and neighbors.[43]

But most Indians in colonial America were unable to ride the crest of change like King George and were caught instead in the undertow and dragged into dependence and debt. In their initial rush to acquire the material marvels of Europe, they gave no thought to the future and hunted out the game that gave them access to foreign markets. When the beaver and white-tail deer disappeared, the natives were left with nothing to sell but their land, their labor, or their military services, which the proliferating colonists were only too glad to buy at bargain rates. Those prices, paid always in desirable trade goods, were low because, with the game diminished, the Indians had little leverage left and had become dangerously dependent on their European suppliers for an ever-growing list of "necessities." In 1705 Robert Beverley noticed that "The *English* have taken away great part of their Country, and consequently made everything less plenty amongst them. They have intro-

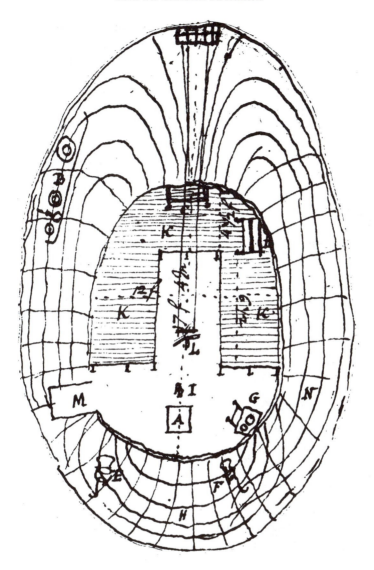

Ezra Stiles, later president of Yale College, drew this plan of Phebe and Elizabeth Moheege's wigwam in Niantic, Connecticut, in 1761. Its acculturated owners had furnished this ancient Indian dwelling with many English colonial items, such as a tea table, chests, a table and chair, and a dresser. Edward G. Schumaker has artistically reconstructed the Moheege's lodge with period furnishings from the Smithsonian Institution's Museum of History and Technology. From William C. Sturtevant, "Two 1761 Wigwams at Niantic, Connecticut," *American Antiquity,* 40:4 (1975), 437–44. Reproduced with the kind permission of the Beinecke Rare Book and Manuscript Library at Yale University and William Sturtevant.

duc'd Drunkenness and Luxury amongst them, which have multiply'd their Wants and put them upon desiring a thousand things they never dreamt of before."[44] These "artificial Wants," as Ben Franklin called them, were so numerous that even the Indians admitted, particularly in the early eighteenth century, that "they could not live without the English" and that they would "always be ruled by them."[45]

Yet, like their colonial neighbors who later formed the Association to rid themselves of foreign debt and debilitating "luxury," many tribesmen in the eighteenth century sought to recapture their autonomous aboriginal past by participating in what anthropologists call "revitalization movements."[46] In 1715 the Yamasees and several Muskogee groups resorted to all-out, purifying war with the South Carolinians because they had accumulated tribal debts of 100,000 deerskins, which, in the face of greatly diminished herds in the increasingly settled coastal region, they had little hope of ever paying off.[47]

But the most famous revitalization took place among the Delawares of western Pennsylvania and the Ohio Valley, where in the early 1760s they were called to action by several messianic prophets. Their message was much the same: if the Indians wished to get to their own heaven and to make life on earth bearable in the meantime, they had to revive their "old" ceremonies and to make several sacrifices. The most onerous but the most purifying was to "learn to live without any trade or connections with the white people, clothing and supporting themselves as their forefathers did."[48]

Such a message was particularly welcome in the camps of the Great Lakes Indians who followed Pontiac into major "rebellion" against the British in 1763. The major cause of their discontent was material: once the French competitors of the British were driven from North America, the British felt free to raise the prices of their trade goods, drastically cut the number of goods (including ammunition) distributed as gifts in the long-standing protocol of diplomacy, and prohibited the sale of liquor, all in a spirit of unmasked contempt for native life and values. No longer able to live without the "Baubles of Britain," Pontiac's warriors decided on a course of action every bit as revolutionary as that followed by the colonists themselves thirteen years later.[49]

FIVE

MAKING DO

Trade in the Eighteenth-Century Southeast

The relative decline of Spanish Florida in the eighteenth century might have seriously reduced native options in the Southeast had the French not moved into the Mississippi delta and valley after 1699. South Carolina continued to throw its weight around in native affairs, particularly as its burgeoning white and black population spread westward into the Piedmont. But the presence of the French in Louisiana, three major Indian uprisings, and the founding of Georgia in 1733 managed to slow if not completely check Carolina's grab for power in the Southeast. Despite the loss of its Franciscan missions to English-allied raiders, Florida remained dangerous as "rebellious" tribes fled South Carolina for sanctuary with and war supplies from the Spanish at St. Augustine and Pensacola.

Because colonial power was, for the most part, evenly distributed and continental diplomats managed to give America long stretches of peace during the course of the eighteenth century, European competition for the Southeast was largely economic and the region's natives were the center of attention, at once the vehicle and the prize. Even the most chauvinistic politicians realized that no southern colony could survive, much less prosper, without the military assistance or armed neutrality of its native neighbors. As late as 1755, Edmond Atkin, soon to be the British superintendent of Indian affairs for the Southern Department, reminded the crown that "the prosperity of our Colonies on the [American] Continent, will stand or fall with our Interest and favour among [the Indians]. While they are our Friends, they are the Cheapest and strongest Barrier for the Protection of our Settlements; when Enemies, they are capable by ravaging in their method of War, in spite of all we can do, to render those Possessions almost useless."[1]

Colonial dependence on the Indians throughout most of the century gave many natives, particularly the distant, larger tribes, substantial (though never unlimited) room for maneuver and a relatively long lease on life, liberty, and land. Although their lives and cultures seemed decidedly impoverished in the eyes of their European neighbors, observers had to acknowledge that "No people in the World understand and pursue their true National Interest, better than the Indians."[2] A French governor made the point less objectively. "All the Indians," he told his superior, "know better than any people in the world how to take advantage of the need one has of them."[3] The natives' ability to play off the competing colonies allowed them to pursue what Edmond Atkin called their "Simple and Plain" national policy, which aimed at "Securing their personal Safety, a Supply of their Wants, and fair Usage."[4]

All of the southern colonies had two main objects: the first was to find, procure, and export products that were in short supply in the mother country; the second was to ensure the colonists' safety as they pursued their economic goals. Indians were essential to the attainment of both ends. In the first several decades of each colony, and even after the profitable export of rice, indigo, tobacco, and naval stores, beaver pelts and particularly deerskins supplied by the Indians were used to offset hefty debit columns in colonial accounts with European suppliers, many of which debts were incurred for large amounts of manufactured trade goods destined for native villages. These trade goods, in turn, secured for the colonies the natives' temporary alliance if not permanent allegiance. In the Southeast there was simply no other way to do so. Unlike in Canada and New England, neither the English nor the French employed enough missionaries or wielded enough spiritual clout to attract Indian allies with nonmaterial means. Governor James Glen of South Carolina recognized the colonists' predicament as clearly as anyone. In 1761 he told readers of his *Description of South Carolina* that "The Concerns of this Country are . . . closely connected and interwoven with *Indian* Affairs, and not only a great Branch of our Trade, but even the Safety of this Province, do . . . much depend upon our continuing in Friendship with the Indians. . . . " "It will be impossible to retain those *Indians* . . . in His Majesty's Interest," he went on, "unless we continue to trade with them."[5] At that juncture, according to Glen's reckoning, one in every eight Carolinians was involved in the Indian trade; their Indian customers made up two-thirds of the colony's inhabitants and supplied some 70,000 deerskins a year. Even after the colonists' separation from England, the half-Scottish Creek leader Alexander McGillivray reminded the Spanish in Florida that "Indians will attach themselves to & Serve them best who Supply their Necessities."[6] South Carolina agent Thomas Nairne had pressed the same point seventy-five years earlier: "They Effect them most who sell best cheap," he counseled. Indians "turn to those who sell them the best pennyworths."[7]

But the natives knew full well—and colonial traders had to learn the hard way again and again—that cost was not everything; "conveniency," quality, and especially "fair Usage" were equally if not more important.[8] English traders usually offered their goods at the lowest prices and paid the most for native deerskins, but they often lost their advantage through an excess of unregulated traders and cutthroat competition involving shady trading practices and abuse of customers. The French, by contrast, seldom had enough or the right sorts of trade goods at competitive prices to satisfy their customers, but they made up for some of these material deficiencies with exemplary conduct. Many English competitors were forced to admit that "No people Carries on ye Indian Trade in So Regular a manner as the French."[9] A Louisiana governor located the key to French policy when he wrote that "good faith in trading [not mere cost] . . . is the essential point and the strongest bond by which we can attach [the natives] to our side."[10]

For all the leverage the southeastern Indians gained from their ability to play the various colonial competitors against one another, the natives could not deflect forever the two heaviest weapons in the European arsenal: the spiraling growth of white and black populations in both the English and French colonies, and the lethal ravages of imported diseases that simultaneously consumed the native population. Peter Wood's careful census of demographical change in the colonial Southeast found that between 1700 and 1790, the Indians lost about 55 percent of their population while white and black numbers grew exponentially. In the older areas of white settlement east of the mountains, in Virginia, North Carolina, and South Carolina, the natives were reduced 95 percent, to some 800 people, while their immigrant competitors proliferated to over 1.3 million. Newly settled Louisiana experienced similar changes. In less than a century, the native population plunged 85 percent to just 4,000 while the total of blacks and whites exceeded 42,000.[11]

The only bright spot—a relatively dim one at that—was the backcountry between the mountains and East Texas. There the native presence was reduced only 48 percent by 1790, to some 48,000, though their white and black neighbors had multiplied from 1,600 to 237,000 in the same period, a five-to-one margin of superiority.[12] Against such odds, the natives of the Southeast had to learn to make do as best they could—to adjust some, often several, aspects of their lives to accommodate and to take advantage of the changing realities of the new South they shared, for better or worse, with Europeans, Africans, and, later, chiaroscuro Americans.

The major source of the Indians' attenuated success in the eighteenth century was the whitetail deer, which seemed to thrive equally well in Alabama canebrakes, Carolina meadows, and Appalachian forests. Thanks to sporadic cattle plagues in Western Europe, England and, less so, France turned increasingly to their American colonies for leather. In our own day of plastics and polyesters, it may be difficult to appreciate the manifold uses of leather in the early modern period. Students of Pope, Hume, and Voltaire will easily acknowledge the ubiquity of leather bookbindings, and mention of leather gloves, belts, and workingmen's aprons will surprise no one. But less familiar, perhaps, are buckskin breeches and coats for gents and proles alike, leather coverings of trunks, coach seats, and containers, leather buckets, leather hats (including one called "the South Carolina hat"), and leather horse tackle.[13] The leather market was big business, and America's natives shared in the action.

In 1764, to take a typical year, the southern colonies together shipped more than 800,000 pounds—400 tons—of deerskin to Europe, most of it from the ports of Charles Town and Savannah. Each skin weighed between one and three pounds. Undressed or "raw" skins obtained in the woods directly from Indian hunters were bought by the skin rather than by weight, the usual measure of the trade. "Half-dressed" skins, the most common, were denuded of flesh and hair by native women and given a quick smoking to prevent decay, but they often turned ripe in steamy warehouses before shipment and had to be beaten in the streets to expel vermin. The best prices went to skins that were "full dressed." After snouts, hooves, tails, and ears were trimmed off, the pelts were carefully smoked over corncob smudges, pounded with stones, and rubbed with deer brains to soften and preserve them. Customarily, these fine leathers ended up as tooled bindings in a gentleman's library, gloves for the opera, or a fancy frock coat.[14]

To obtain the various pelts from native hunters, the competing colonies had to found, finance, and regulate elaborate business organizations that stretched from European manufacturers, suppliers, and shippers to lowly packhorsemen and bilingual traders who operated as far as the Mississippi and often beyond. The headquarters of each organization was usually located in a colonial entrepôt—Charles Town, Augusta, New Orleans—where large merchant partnerships (in the English case) or a monopoly company (for a time in Louisiana) assembled the goods, credit, and personnel to launch expensive packtrains or convoys of pirogues deep into Creek, Chickasaw, Choctaw, or Cherokee country in search of skins.

After the Privy Council struck down South Carolina's public monopoly of the Indian trade in 1719, a hungry assortment of Virginians, Carolinians, and eventually Georgians, mostly undercapitalized and inexperienced, flooded the backcountry.[15] The inevitable result was bankruptcy for most and the concentration of the trade in the hands of relatively few large partnerships or companies. These firms placed trusted employees in major native villages or in convenient forts, where they usually married the daughters of chiefs or other important families to gain sponsors and protective kin. From their key locations, the traders not only fine-tuned the flow of trade goods and finessed the purchase of skins, but they also served their respective governments as ears, eyes, and tongues in the delicate and sometimes deadly game of intercolonial and intertribal politics. If a colonial competitor flooded the market with cheap goods or paid inflated prices for skins, or rumors of war circulated around native campfires, the trader was the first to know and to dispatch a letter, sometimes eccentrically spelled, to the capital with the intelligence.[16]

Although South Carolina and later Georgia instituted sensible systems of licenses, bonds for good behavior, and resident agents and roving commissioners in Indian country, the Indian trade continued to attract characters whose avidity for gain often outran their scruples and common sense. Sometimes the culprits were employees of the larger, more established firms, whose long-term investment in the trade could not countenance behavior guaranteed to alienate native customers and capable of inciting business-destroying war. But more commonly they were small-time adventurers in search of a quick buck (literally), heedless of how they got it. From the perspective of Indians, colonial officials, and seasoned traders alike, both varieties spelled trouble and were variously regarded as "Arab-like" "Horse Pedlars," "abandoned, reprobate, white savages," the "dregs and off-scourings of our colonies," and, least charitably, "monsters in human form, the very scum and out cast of the earth."[17]

The list of allegations against English traders is long, and, if true (as most seem to be), the behavior they describe seriously compromised the usual advantages the English enjoyed in supply, quality, and price. Colonial officials understandably worried when English traders sold goods to the French or Spanish enemy or to unfriendly tribes, such as the Choctaws, who made war on English allies, such as the Chickasaws.[18] They frowned equally on traders who incited intertribal wars in order to secure Indian captives for enslavement and sale (a trade that tapered off in the 1720s but had a long life) or who merely spread rumors of war to increase the sale of guns, ammunition, and war paint.[19] Although some Indian women might not have objected, the merchant-bosses of the Tidewater protested overeager traders who purchased quantities of untrimmed, undressed hides, which lacked the low-cost application of product-enhancing native labor. When Indian superintendent John Stuart negotiated a treaty between the Creek headmen and major Creek merchant-traders in 1767, one provision was that traders could accept only "four undressed skins in the hair" to every 150 pounds of "Indian dressed deerskins" because, he noted, "Trading for skins in the hair leaves room for great imposition of the Indians." He did not have to say that raw skins spoiled and generally brought much reduced prices in Europe.[20] Nor did his readers have to ask what "impositions" were possible. English sharpers had a wide reputation for playing fast and loose with what a Cherokee factor called "fals Stilliards, short Yards, and little Measures."[21]

Another dangerous practice was the overextension of credit to native customers. The credit system was firmly in place in the southern trade, as it was everywhere in North America, but it was subject to abuse, on both sides. Freebooting traders intercepted native hunters in the woods and relieved them of their skins before the Indians could reach the established traders in town who had advanced them supplies for the hunting season. Traders impatient with Indian debtors were known to steal a hunter's wife and children and sell them into slavery to settle his account. Indian tribes that built up impossible debts might decide that a war upon the creditors was the quickest way to clear the books. In 1715 the Yamasees and Creeks, one Carolinian recognized, "at once blott[ed] out all their Debts" by killing 90 of South Carolina's 100 traders.[22] Forty years later, a Carolina agent reported the Cherokees' growing dissatisfaction over the "Debts they owe[d]" and the unhappy choice they had between "paying them and cloathing themselves." They "are now ready," he warned, "to take all Measures . . . to get rid of their Debts," though he believed they had not yet talked of "killing the Traders," an option clearly on his and their minds.[23] Late in the colonial period, large tribal debts, particularly Creek, were settled by alienation of tribal territory to white creditors.[24]

The normal risks of doing business in a cross-cultural context were one thing; contemptible and even dangerous behavior on the part of individual traders was quite another. The low opinion of traders held by many Indians and couth Englishmen alike derived less from the traders' conduct of the trade per se—as slippery as that often was—than from their personal morality in Indian country. In 1715, David Crawley, a Virginian with extensive experience in the South Carolina trade, charged the southern traders with a host of crimes, all of which contributed to the outbreak of the deadly and destructive Yamasee War of that year. He had seen them enter native plantations and villages at will, kill hogs and fowl, and "take what they please without leave" or compensation, such as corn, peas, and watermelons. If the owners grumbled at these brazen robberies, the traders "threaten[ed] to beat and verry often did beat them very cruelly." Before horses were used regularly to convey goods and skins, traders commandeered native porters to carry 70, 80, or even 100-pound packs 300, 400, or 500 miles and "pay[d] very little for it." To add insult to injury, "when [the traders] had sent the [native] men away about their busnes or they were gon ahunting," Crawley had "heard them brag to each other of debauching [the Indians'] wives, sumtime force them," and once had seen it himself "in the day time don."[25]

Equally dangerous though more difficult to diagnose was the behavior of employees like Charles Jordon among the Creeks. In August 1752 "he got drunk and quarreled with the Indians, striped naked, painted himself all over, and r[a]n about [Utchee] Town like a Madman with his Gun in his Hand, telling the Indians that he would now be revenged upon them for all the ill Usage he had received, that he did not care if they did kill him, that his Death would soon be revenged for there was an Army of white People coming up to cutt them all off." Apparently, this was no temporary aberration because the Creek agent had been told that Jordon "has often before endangered both his own Life and every white Man's in the Nation by his mad Actions. . . . Nor is he the only one," the agent continued; "there are several Others that are fitter for Bedlam or New Gate [prison] than to be trusted in an Indian Country where the Lives of many may very much depend upon their Behavior."[26] On the native scale of outrage, traders who made off with Indian horses, mixed too much water in the trade rum, passed off inferior red lead as true vermilion, or allowed their own livestock to dine on Indian gardens scored much lower, though never low enough to be forgiven entirely by people famous for long memories and immense pride.[27]

By means and in manner somewhat different, the French in Louisiana collected about 50,000 deerskins a year—less than a third of South Carolina's best take—from 1720 until their political departure in 1763. They managed to do this in spite of government reluctance and often inability to underwrite the trade, a monopoly company's bankruptcy, lack of adequate settler capital to purchase trade goods from importers too few and too expensive, and relatively low demand and therefore prices for deerskins in France. Only after the crown built several military-trading posts among key Indian tribes, advanced trade goods on reasonable terms to individual settlers and soldiers, and reclaimed responsibility for government and defense in 1731 did the French earn a fighting chance to beat the English at the trading game, even among their closest and most proximate native allies.[28]

Although French traders were not angelic contrasts to their English counterparts—there were too many uninhibited Canadian voyageurs in the colony for that—they did have the sense to realize that alienating their few allies and customers, even if watchful commandants had allowed it, was poor business and poorer diplomacy. So they molded their tongues to tribal languages or the Mobilian trade jargon, the region's lingua franca, learned the patient protocol of the calumet ceremony (which often lasted three days), and adapted themselves to the natives' strong preference for fixed price schedules.[29]

For its part, the government sought to compensate for inadequate and pricey shipments of trade goods with other kinds of largesse. According to their English rivals, the Louisianians gained the affections of their Indian customers primarily with "the Provision of Gunsmiths" gratis and "not so much valuable Presents as a judicious Application of them" in Indian country, in native villages, in annual congresses at Mobile, or at convenient forts. "The French by a constant prudent Practice," noted an envious Edmond Atkin, "make even Trifles productive of the most desirable National Consequences."[30] Careful to avoid the appearance of paying tribute to the tribes, French officials annually conferred guns, ammunition, and fancy outfits on selected leaders, especially "medal chiefs," and warriors who had served the French well, being particular to favor "old Head Men of Note" and orators who would remember the generosity of the French in town house and council. (English gift-givers tended to bypass such ancients in favor of younger hunters who could supply them with deerskins, and to require most recipients to make long treks to disease-ridden Charles Town and Augusta to receive them.)[31] So punctilious were the French in making presents that, on more than one occasion, they were forced to purchase several from their better supplied English competitors.[32]

The final advantage the French enjoyed was their missionaries, who were, according to Edmond Atkin, "almost of as much Consequence as Garrisons.

They have been," he argued, "the means of gaining as much respect from the Indians to the French, as our Traders have caused disrespect to us, by their dissolute Lives and Manners." Governor Bienville noted their uses in 1726 when he told the French Minister of Marine that, "in addition to the knowledge of God that they would impart to them ... nothing is more useful than a missionary to restrain the Indians, to learn all that is happening among them [and] to inform the commandants of the neighboring posts about it, to prevent the quarrels that may arise between the voyageurs and the Indians, and especially to see to it that the former do not sell their goods at too high prices."[33]

If it is now clear that the colonists needed the Indian trade for profit and protection, we have only to establish why the Indians participated so avidly in the colonial trade. Contemporaries thought they knew the answer. As early as 1679, Virginia's John Banister told an English correspondent that "since there has been a way layd open for Trade ... many Things which they wanted not before because they never had them are by that means become necessary both for their use and ornament." At the end of the colonial period, naturalist William Bartram put a heavily moral twist on his explanation when he concluded that the southeastern tribes "wage eternal war against deer and bear, to procure food and cloathing, and other necessaries and conveniencies; which is indeed carried to an unreasonable and perhaps criminal excess, since the white people have dazzled their senses with foreign superfluities."[34]

Both observers were correct to suggest that, before the advent of Europeans and their trade, the Indians were perfectly capable of supplying all of their material needs from the natural resources available in the Southeast. But the order of acculturation they outline—from necessities through conveniences to luxuries—should be exactly reversed. All over North America, natives were given as gifts and then made their first purchases of what traders called "baubles" or "trifles," small goods usually of decorative or aesthetic value, such as hawk's bells, glass beads, finger rings, colored caps, even playing cards and broken pottery shards.[35] None of these things altered the basic ways of native living; they were, in Bartram's word, "superfluities," though nonetheless desirable for their novelty.

The next and final round of purchases simply and sensibly procured a variety of labor-saving "conveniences," tools or clothing or housewares that duplicated perfectly functional native items but were made from technologically or aesthetically superior materials, such as woven cloth, glass, or iron. There was no class of trade goods that we can objectively call "necessities." Only human users transform "conveniences" into "necessities" by changing their psychological need for and dependence upon those goods. The only absolute material necessities of life are food and water; everything else is either a nice convenience or a superfluous luxury.

Among the Indians, cloth and metal tools were quickly recognized as the greatest conveniences and most in demand. In one of the last years of the

A scene from William Bonar's 1757 map of the Creek Nation shows an Indian couple sporting several European trade items. The woman wears a striped duffel blanket and a hair ribbon. The warrior carries a musket, metal-tipped spear, and iron tomahawk and wears garters and a plume in his scalplock. *Reproduced with permission of the Controller of Her Majesty's Stationery Office, courtesy of the British Public Record Office, C0700/Carolina 21.*

Philip von Reck's pencil drawing of a southeastern Indian hunting camp in 1736 shows two trade kettles and at least one gun, used to gather the deerskins stretched and drying on the lean-to poles. *Courtesy of the Royal Library of Denmark, Copenhagen, Manuscript Department, catalog signature Ny kgl. Saml. 565, 4°.*

French regime in Louisiana, the annual list of presents for native allies included 15,800 ells (about 18 × 45 inches each) of limbourg cloth (half red, half blue), 1,020 blankets (worn as substitutes for buffalo or deerskin robes known as "matchcoats"), 806 men's shirts ("as long in the front as in the back" because they were never tucked in), and 200 ells of finer scarlet cloths to make fancy outfits for "medal chiefs" (who, like most Indians, preferred loose breechclouts or "flaps" and detachable leggings to restrictive European-style trousers). And these were only the goods being *given* away. For trade with the Choctaws and six other tribes, the French had ordered 17,000 ells of limbourg, 19,400 blankets, 10,300 men's shirts, and 1,700 women's shirts.[36] Native customers of the English bought even more. So desirable was cloth that some natives were content to purchase second-hand clothing from other Indians who had easier access to the trade. When the Choctaws could not get enough cloth from the French during the naval blockades of the last intercolonial war, fifty of them circumvented French orders not to trade with the English by swapping skins for the "old Cloaths" of the Alabamas, who then obtained new ones from the English traders operating in Creek country.[37] Even shreds and tatters of trade cloth were desirable. Native women bought the lint and litter from traders' packs to make scarlet dye with which to color the duller and less expensive linens and cottons offered by the traders.[38]

The result of these wardrobe changes can be seen in contemporary pictures of natives *en scène*. Thomas Nairne's verbal portrait of Chickasaw women in

Von Reck's 1736 watercolor drawing of "Indiens going a hunting" shows change and persistence in native garb and equipment. The hunter on the left wears a painted leather matchcoat and carries a bow and arrow. The middle figure wears a white woolen trade blanket with red stripes and blue stroud leggings; he carries a metal kettle in his pack, a musket, and "A bottle in which they generally carry rum or brandy." The pipesmoking third man wears traditional leather leggings and moccasins, but his short leather jacket seems to have been tailored to European fashion. *Courtesy of the Royal Library of Denmark, Copenhagen, Manuscript Department, cat. sig. Ny kgl. Saml. 565, 4°.*

1708 requires little imagination. They "look sparkling in the dances," he wrote, "with the Cloaths bought from the English" and were "very loath any different should happen, least they again be reduced to their old wear of painted Buffeloe Calf skins."[39] Several watercolor sketches by Moravian visitor Philip Von Reck all show Georgia Creek costumes in 1736 that reflect the persistence of native styles with the addition of imported materials. Both men and women are wrapped in white trade blankets edged with red stripes, but blankets had not completely replaced intricately painted buffalo robes. Yet virtually everyone wears red or blue stroud cloth leggings, knee-length skirts, or breechclouts. The women also sport flowing red ribbons in their hair, as does a blanketed Creek woman in William Bonar's 1757 drawing that accompanies his wonderful map of the Creek Nation. Leather moccasins were obviously preferred in the forests and swamps of the Southeast, and remained so until a turn in the native economy found a use for heavier soled shoes.[40]

This 1736 watercolor drawing of a Yuchi busk ceremony by Von Reck features native dancers wearing red and blue duffel breechclouts, the gift of Georgia's founder James Oglethorpe. Five trade muskets hang from the cypress-covered lodge. *Courtesy of the Royal Library of Denmark, Copenhagen, Manuscript Department, cat. sig. Ny kgl. Saml. 565, 4°.*

Indian men and women altered their wardrobes not because they wanted to ape their European "betters"—clearly they did not want to and did not consider them superior—but simply because woven cloth had qualities superior to their traditional skin clothing. With scissors, needles, thimbles, and thread obtained in the trade, native women could more easily cut and sew their clothing. Moreover, they no longer had to laboriously tan several cumbersome and smelly skins before beginning the process; fewer raw or half-dressed deerskins could purchase cloth that was not only brighter and more colorful, but always soft, warm, and pliable even after getting wet. If they cared to wash the clothes before they wore out, they could; with skin garments they could not.

Von Reck's and Bonar's drawings also document the importance in native lives of metal trade goods, both weapons and household items. Bonar's Creek warrior wears only a cloth flap, war paint, arm and wrist bracelets, ribbon garters, and a plume in his topknot—all provided by French or English traders. But in addition to a bow, a quiver of arrows, and a metal-tipped spear, he totes an iron tomahawk in his belt and a long musket—upside down and barrel first—over his shoulder. Two of Von Reck's Creek men also carry bows and arrows, but one blanketed hunter has a musket in one hand, a rum bottle

Von Reck's watercolor drawing of the Yuchi chief Senkaitchi and his wife illustrates the inroads made by European trade cloth in 1736, three years after the Georgia colony was founded. The woman wears a white blanket with red stripes, while her husband sports a red duffel breechclout and dark blue leggings beneath a traditional buffalo robe. Facial and body tattoos like the chief's would soon be made with imported gunpowder. *Courtesy of the Royal Library of Denmark, Copenhagen, Manuscript Department, cat. sig. Ny kgl. Saml. 565, 4°.*

in the other, and a trade kettle in his backpack. Two other views of an open hunting lodge show three kettles on or near the fire and a row of five guns hanging muzzles down along one side.[41]

Trade inventories and archaeology suggest that these pictures do not lie. In 1759 the French planned to distribute as presents 2,440 woodcutters' knives, 1,200 clasp knives, 400 pairs of scissors, and 150 brass kettles, "large and medium, no small, larger at the top than at the bottom" to satisfy native preferences. They also sent into Indian country 8,000 pounds of "flat iron for hatchets, pickaxes, and tomahawks," to be hammered into shape by military post blacksmiths or perhaps by the Indians themselves. In trade the southeastern Indians also wanted copious quantities of awls, fire steels (strike-a-lights), hoes, tin pots, sewing supplies, razors, and brass and iron wire.[42] All of these items were mere "conveniences"; they allowed the natives to do the things they had always done with less effort and with gains in efficiency and durability. While the materials were new, the shapes, functions, and meanings of the objects were virtually unaltered.

But the Indians no less than the colonists had a right to acquire new tastes, to form new aesthetic preferences, without our fretting over the decline of

The supreme war chief or captain of the Yuchis, Kipahalgwa, as painted by Von Reck in 1736. An open white shirt, not tucked in for lack of trousers, and red duffel leggings (and probably breechclout) suggest the native adaptation of European trade goods to traditional uses and preferences. The red paint used to color his eyes, noses, and short scalplock was probably already imported vermilion rather than native vegetable dye. *Courtesy of the Royal Library of Denmark, Copenhagen, Manuscript Department, cat. sig. Ny kgl. Saml. 565, 4°.*

some imagined aboriginality. And they exercised it. We should expect no less of cultures that were experiencing a consumer revolution every bit as profound as the one their British colonial neighbors were undergoing simultaneously, particularly since the Indians' revolution had begun at least fifty years earlier than the Brits'.[43] Sooner or later, some daring Creek or Cherokee individualist had the courage or temerity to adopt a new fashion first seen in cosmopolitan Charles Town or New Orleans or in the home or on the person of the native wife of a local trader. If he or she was a respected leader, a chief or warrior or clan mother, the change in fashion would probably spread more rapidly, just as it would in London or Paris if the queen or a noble took the first step. How else can we explain the Creeks' adoption late in the eighteenth century of items of Scottish dress or the wrap-around turban of brightly colored cloth that men affected for many years? They were certainly under no more compulsion to flatter their American neighbors than they were earlier in the century, and no settlers that we know of wore turbans.[44] And how else can we understand the vast array of plain and fancy European cups, jugs, plates, bowls, and serving dishes—creamware, slipware, faience—that the Tunicas, the staunchest French allies, took to the grave in their Mississippi village between 1731 and 1764? Unlike most southeastern tribes, they preferred them to native pottery, they could afford to buy them, and they did so.[45]

The metal tool that enabled the Indians to bring down whitetail deer in sufficient numbers to purchase the other trade goods was, of course, the gun, at 12 to 16 dressed skins the costliest item on the native shopping list. The typical trade gun was lighter, cheaper, and shorter than most European guns. The Indians preferred them to "heavy buccaneer's muskets," said a French official, "because people who are always running through the woods wish nothing except what is very light."[46] In 1759 the French expected to hand out 500 30-caliber trade guns to allies and to trade nearly 4,000 more, in addition to 14 tons of powder, 40,000 flints, and 14,400 gunworms (for extracting wads). The lead for shot came not from Europe but from the famous Galena mines in the Illinois country, which was under Louisiana's aegis.[47]

Since most of the French trade was conducted on or near rivers, the Louisianians were easily able to supply their native customers with munitions. Even the English conceded French superiority in the ammunition trade "by means of their Water Carriage; whereas [English] Traders, being obliged to carry their Goods many hundred Miles upon Horses, [and] consulting their greatest Proffit, only carry but scanty supplies of that heavy Article and of small Value."[48] In 1741 a young French soldier tried to convince his Cherokee captors that, though French guns cost twice as much as English ones, they were better and more durable, and that "a pound of [French] powder had twice as much effect as a pound of the English." Cherokee warriors who received any of the anticipated French supplies on the eve of their 1760 uprising against the English may indeed have felt the extra kick in the special shipment of "powder for war," more potent than that needed to bring down a deer.[49] If, four years earlier, they had also been able to talk Virginia into furnishing them with accurate, long-range rifles like those the French allegedly supplied *their* allies, they would have had firepower at least equal to that of their Carolina enemies. English officials were reluctant to sell the Indians anything but smoothbore muskets because they foresaw that rifles put the Indians "too much upon an Equality with us in Case of a Breach." Most traders probably cared more that they punched larger holes in their whitetailed merchandise.[50]

While guns were, in one sense, only more powerful bows, two other novel and popular trade goods left deep marks upon native society in the eighteenth century, one subtly, one not so. Few observers noticed the quiet revolution wrought by the humble hand mirror, framed in wood or leather and worn around the neck or wrist of every warrior.[51] We who are so used to grooming ourselves in mirrors several times a day will find it difficult perhaps to imagine how people in the past must have felt in discovering their physical identities only through the eyes of others. The advent of portable mirrors enabled Indians for the first time to comb their own hair, apply their own war paint, and decorate their own scalplocks, thereby undamming freshets of vanity and wellsprings of self-regard. Yet the new face in the mirror was not always comforting. During a smallpox epidemic in 1738, a "great many" Cherokees "killed themselves; for being naturally proud," wrote trader James Adair, "they are always peeping into their looking glasses . . . by which means, seeing themselves disfigured, without hope of regaining their former beauty, some shot themselves, others cut their throats, some stabbed themselves . . . many threw themselves with sullen madness into the fire. . . ."[52]

Possessed of equal power to destroy was alcohol—French brandy and English rum. Having, as with the mirror, no counterpart to alcohol in their culture, the Indians had to fashion their own rules for its use, but too often fell prey to its power. Most Indians drank to total inebriation; if every member of the group could not reach that goal, some abstained to ensure an adequate supply for the rest. Because they tended, under its influence, to commit all kinds of antisocial acts, even against their own kinsmen, they decided to blame the liquid or the seller, not the drinker. Despite periodic attempts by native leaders to prohibit its sale in their villages, customers and traders conspired to make it available. Since drunken Indians would "freely sell or part with any thing they have in the World (except their Wives and Children)" but not excepting their prized horses and their own long hair, traders were not reluctant to initiate their sales pitches with firewater. The traders might have earned kudos for "dashing" their liquor with water—one-third was the English "custom"—had they not charged full price for it and taken full advantage of its victims.[53]

Unfortunately, Indian traders as well as European cashed in on the profitably elastic native demand for spirits. Early in the century, the Tuscaroras traveled "several hundred Miles" westward to sell rundlets of watered rum by the mouthful for buckskins. Buyers appeared with bowls and the biggest mouthed friends they could find, but the sellers were only too ready to lambaste anyone who swallowed a drop, by mistake or design. William Bartram found equal humor in a Creek drinking fest in Florida. As bottles were passed freely around the circle, at least one native woman, "with an empty bottle, concealed in her mantle," takes "a good long draught, blushes, drops her pretty face on her bosom, and artfully discharged the rum into her bottle, and by repeating this artifice soon fills it: this she privately conveys to her secret store, and then returns to the jovial game, and so on during the festival; and when the comic farce is over," the woman "retails this precious cordial to them at her own price."[54]

While liquor and sharp trading did their part to separate native hunters from their hard-earned hides, two native customs also created a steady demand for imported merchandise. One was the Busk, the southeastern Green Corn Ceremony, during which the whole tribe assembled to begin a new year. On the first day, they collected "all their worn-out cloaths," housewares, and furniture and burned them in a huge bonfire. On the fourth and final day, they were allowed to don new clothes and reestablish their households with new paraphernalia, all of which the local trader was only too happy to furnish.[55] Similarly, the native habit of burying the dead with all their personal possessions boosted trader sales, particularly as personal accumulation grew in later decades. Kinsmen had to buy their own things in lieu of inheriting them. Only the Cherokees in the 1770s "entirely left off the custom" and bequeathed the deceased's effects to the "nearest of blood." According to James Adair, who had himself traded among them, they did so because of "the reiterated persuasion of the traders." We can only speculate on the cause of the peddlers' sudden and isolated fit of disinterestedness.[56]

For all its magnitude, both economic and geographical, the major effects of the European trade upon native society and culture did not flow from the sheer accumulation of foreign manufactures. The great majority of these items, we have seen, were only pleasing or superior substitutes for functional native-made goods, and their traditional meanings and uses were largely retained. The trade's major impact on the Indians resulted not from the *end* of the trade—the goods themselves—but from the *means* used to acquire them. The catalyst of change was not simply native acquisitiveness, but the Indians' pursuit of the game needed to purchase the new conveniences and luxuries, and their varied interactions with the colonial traders who brought the goods to their world.

If there is any doubt that traditional native values and uses were transferred to the new objects, we have only to look at the myriad European goods that found their way into Indian graves. Many items accompanied their owners just as they had been purchased from the trader's pack, yet even they had obviously been used in ways more consonant with native culture than with European. Copper kettles were placed over the deceased's head as clay pots once were. Gunpowder made excellent (if volatile) tattoos. Coils of brass wire, sold on pencil-like spindles, served not only as trap wire and colonial duct tape, but as squeezable hair pluckers to rid native faces of unsightly and unintelligent beards.[57]

But more than a few grave offerings had been modified to fit traditional styles or functions or cannibalized for materials to fashion familiar objects. Former kettles, even new ones, became copper jewelry, arrowheads, and tinkling cones (for attachment to fringed clothing). Broken gun barrels, heated red hot, exacerbated the torture of war captives or were flattened to make hide scrapers and chisels. A brass milk skimmer was reborn as a gorget and duplicated in brass, down to the hole pattern, by the Indians; going the other way, the owner of a British gorget preferred a less martial crucifix. Like obsidian, glass bottle shards were chipped into scrapers and arrowheads. Used gunflints, some native-made, easily became strike-a-lights. A yellow slip-glazed candleholder was drilled to make a pipe bowl, while the lead seals from bales of English stroud were cut into pendants or melted and poured into carved-stone bullet molds.[58] No matter what form they took or what material they were made from, all of these objects were placed in graves, as personal possessions long had, so that their spirits would accompany the human spirits to the Land of the Dead, which resembled nothing so much as a familiar Indian village in the best of times.[59] Those beliefs and practices did not change in the colonial period, nor for many decades thereafter if at all.

The key to change in the native Southeast, then, lies not in the material end of the trade but in the social and cultural paths the Indians took to it. One of those paths led largely uncontrollable numbers of European and African strangers into the native world. In 1756 a Cherokee delegation to the Creeks indicated what that intrusion meant to them at that historical moment. "The English ha[ve] now a Mind to make Slaves of [us] all," they warned, "for [they] have already filled [our] Nation with English Forts and great Guns, Negroes and Cattle."[60] Their list is telling. While they accommodated traders and their desired wares, colonial forts on native land compromised native sovereignty and independence, threatened the natives' safety, and sheltered unscrupulous traders from the consequences of their actions. African servants might have provided the Indians with valuable object lessons in the loss of freedom, but English officials—not the French—did their best to separate the races lest they form "dangerous connections." For their part, most Indians did not welcome slaves into their villages because the blacks were used mostly to raise food for the traders, which deprived native women of that lucrative business.[61]

When they belonged only to traders, cattle were as unwelcome as slaves because they were unfettered, ate up native gardens, and drove out deer from their fixed territories. But beginning in the 1740s, cows also served the Cherokees as substitutes for diminishing deer and as sources of milk and butter, which they probably sold at the nearest English garrison. The vocabulary gathered by surveyor William De Brahm in the very year of the Cherokee delegation's complaint contains words for *cow, bull, calf, milk,* and *butter,* all derived from *wággaw,* the native rendition of the Spanish *vaca.* Before the end of the century, most southeastern tribes raised cattle or rustled them to compensate for diminished deer herds on diminished tribal lands.[62]

Other European livestock had a similar reception. Along with cattle and chickens, pigs had to overcome the natives' initial belief that natural properties were transfused into humans through the food they ate; "he who feeds on venison," James Adair explained, "is . . . swifter and more sagacious than the man who lives on the flesh of . . . helpless dunghill fowls, the slow-footed tame cattle, or the heavy wallowing swine." "When swine were first brought among [the Creeks]," Adair continued, "they deemed it such a horrid abomination . . . to eat that filthy and impure food, that they excluded the criminal from all religious communion in their circular town-house. . . . Now [in the 1770s] they seldom refuse to eat hogs flesh, when the traders invite them to it." Well before then, in fact, they and other tribes, particularly the Cherokees, were raising them for sale to the colonists and for their own consumption.[63]

Although horses were eaten in desperation (the Creeks and Choctaws called them "big deer"), most native families acquired them to carry their belongings to their hunting grounds and deerskins to the trading post. By the 1770s, Adair said, and probably thirty years before that, "almost every one hath horses, from two to a dozen; which makes a considerable number, through their various nations." Bred from handsome Andalusian stock in Florida and the Southwest, Indian horses allowed hunters to extend their range in search of more and more deer for market. When that extension brought families and tribes into collision with rivals, mounted warfare was often the result. And when the deer population petered out at the end of the century, male and even female horse thieves made a substitute living raiding native and American herds.[64]

The foreseeable depletion of the southeastern deer herds resulted not only from the natives' material desires but from a major change in their hunting ethic. Before deer hunting became big business, Indians killed only as many animals as they needed, they supplicated the master spirit of the species before killing and thanked it after, and they used all parts of the deer for food, clothing, ornaments, and weapons. In their gun-aided haste to harvest ever more skins for the trade, they soon omitted their religious obligations, and, lamented surveyor De Brahm, "they make a great Carnage among the Deers, kill them for the sake of their Skins, and leave their Carcasses [to rot] in the Forrests."[65]

The European competition for native allies and the surrogate war in trade that it fostered wrought many changes in southeastern Indian culture. Epidemic and epizootic diseases made heavy inroads on native populations.[66] Wars became deadlier because of guns and colonial scalp bounties; they became more frequent because of the trade in Indian slaves and America's involvement in European conflicts. Accordingly, civil chiefs lost authority and prestige to their warrior counterparts.[67] Native marriages to white and black traders and soldiers bred a new population of mixed-blood children, who often pushed traditionalists into innovations such as foreign fashions, formal education, personal accumulation, religious conversion, and chattel slavery.[68] Gender relations shifted with new roles in new economies.[69] Traditional crafts and skills were lost with the wholesale advent of goods manufactured abroad.[70] But the most serious change of all was the natives' increasing dependence on their colonial neighbors for economic viability and, by extension, their loss of political autonomy.

As early as 1681, the Lords Proprietor of South Carolina had an economic plan to dominate the Indians of their colony and beyond. "Furnishing a bold and warlike people with Armes and Ammunition and other things usefull to them," they informed their governor and council, "[would tie] them to soe strict a dependance upon us . . . that whenever that nation that we sett up shall misbehave . . . toward us, we shall be able whenever we please by abstaineing from supplying them with Ammunition . . . to ruine them."[71] That, of course, is exactly what happened, even though the English could not foresee that the arrival of the French would allow the natives of the Southeast to prolong their parole for several decades.

But sooner or later, the Indians themselves recognized that their new involvement in a global economy made them prisoners as well as players. At a conference in Charles Town in 1753, Skiagunsta of the Lower Cherokees told Governor Glen that "[I] have always told my People to be well with the English for they cannot expect any Supply from any where else, nor can they live independent of the English. What are we red People?" he asked. "The Cloaths we wear, we cannot make ourselves, they are made [for] us. We use their Amunition with which we kill Dear. We cannot make our Guns, they are made [for] us. Every necessary Thing in Life we must have from the White People."[72] The implications of that dependence were clearly seen by the "Tattoed Serpent," a Natchez war chief. "Why did the French come into our country?" he once asked a French neighbor. "Before they came, did we not live better than we do [now]? . . . In what respect, then, had we occasion for them: Was it for their guns? The bows and arrows which we used were sufficient to make us live well. Was it for their white, blue, and red blankets? We can do well enough with buffalo skins which are warmer. . . . In fine, before the arrival of the French, we lived like men who can be satisfied with what they have; whereas at this day we are like slaves, who are not suffered to do as they please."[73]

In 1764, British Indian superintendent John Stuart summed up the Indians' historical plight all too well. "The Original great tye between the Indians and Europeans was Mutual conveniency. [But] A modern Indian," he knew, "cannot subsist without Europeans. . . . So that what was only Conveniency at first is now become Necessity and the Original tye Strengthened."[74] A mutual bond had led to a kind of bondage for the natives, though in reality they were no more—or less—imprisoned by the capitalist world-system than were their European partners and rivals. But the native situation was indeed different, on two counts. First, the Indians' new world *felt* worse to them because their dependence—not just upon nature but now too upon anonymous strangers—was so new; the colonists could not remember a time when they were truly self-sufficient. And, second, when the "Mutual conveniency" that brought them together melted away after the American Revolution, the new Americans soon had no economic or political need for the Indian people (as distinguished from their land), while the Indians could never again live free of the American economy.

Before the colonists' declaration of independence, southern leaders were agreed that "it can never be our Interest to extirpate [the Indians], or to force them from their Lands" because "their Ground would be soon taken up by runaway *Negroes* from our Settlements, whose Numbers would daily increase, and quickly become more formidable Enemies than Indians can ever be. . . . "[75] Removing the 48,000 natives who inhabited and dominated the southern backcountry was simply not feasible in 1770 or in 1790. But within forty years, white America found it both necessary and convenient to do just that.

PART III

CONVERSIONS

INTRODUCTION

Although I have published three histories of what most people would recognize (at least from their titles) as education, all of my work, including seven books on Indian-European relations, has been driven by a sustained interest in education, past and present. But education is defined not only as the function of schools and colleges, but as the whole deliberate process by which a society *enculturates* its young and other newcomers (such as immigrants) to its distinctive values and lifeways. While writing my second book, *The School upon a Hill: Education and Society in Colonial New England* (1974), I also discovered that I was equally fascinated by what anthropologists call (or used to call) *acculturation*, the changes that all cultures undergo, adaptively and reactively, when they interact. The last chapter of that book sought to assess what kinds of education the New England colonists received at the hands of their Indian neighbors and enemies. These tandem interests led directly to my first book of essays, *The European and the Indian* (1981), and to the first volume in my Oxford trilogy, *The Invasion Within: The Contest of Cultures in Colonial North America* (1985), both of which deal with various kinds of cultural conversion and other forms of educational change.

In the early stages of writing *The Invasion Within*, I was invited to contribute a paper on religious processes to a Yale University conference on comparative frontiers in North America and South Africa. Chapter Six, a partial summary of the book-in-progress, was the result. Delivered originally in May 1979, it describes in detail just what the French and English missionaries found lacking in their respective Indian neophytes and how they proposed to remedy those deficiencies through both cultural and religious means. It does not, as the fuller book does, address the difficult question of how the natives, both those eager and reluctant to adapt or adopt the new religion, perceived or received its strange messages and rituals, a topic that recent scholarship has rightly complicated and begun to untangle adroitly.* The version that appeared in *The European and the Indian* (1981) and appears here was first

---

*See, for example, Charles L. Cohen, "Conversion among Puritans and Amerindians: A Theological and Cultural Perspective," in Francis J. Bremer, ed., *Puritanism: Transatlantic Perspectives on a Seventeenth-Century Anglo-American Faith* (Boston, 1993), 233–256; Jane T. Merritt, "Dreaming of the Savior's Blood: Moravians and the

published in *The Frontier in History: North American and Southern African Comparisons*, edited by Howard Lamar and Leonard Thompson (1981).

Colonial attempts to "civilize" the Indians before converting them took several forms. Perhaps the most quixotic means were schools and colleges, cold, informal institutions that had no counterparts in native society. Chapter Seven documents the signal failure of the Reverend Eleazar Wheelock to educate native students for Christian missions at his schools in Connecticut and New Hampshire and at Dartmouth College, which he founded allegedly for that purpose. It was first delivered in October 1977 as a paper at the Conference on Iroquois Research in honor of William N. Fenton, the dean of Iroquois studies and a Dartmouth alumnus, and a year later at Dartmouth, several of whose assembled alumni fundraisers did not welcome its disinterested iconoclasm. It was published in *The European and the Indian* (1981) and in the Fenton festschrift, *Extending the Rafters: Interdisciplinary Approaches to Iroquoian Studies*, edited by Michael K. Foster, Jack Campisi, and Marianne Mithun (1984).

The contrast between Indian and European methods of converting, *re*-educating, their cultural rivals struck me forcefully at the very outset of my ethnohistorical studies. In April 1972, at the annual meeting of the Organization of American Historians, I delivered a paper on "The White Indians of Colonial America" to analyze the alarmingly effective process by which Indian groups all over eastern North America converted hundreds of their colonial captives to native ways of life. The sharp contrast between the Indians' ability to persuade white children and many adults to trade "civility" for "savagery" (in loaded colonial terms) and the poor colonial record in "civilizing" Indian youngsters (never adults) continues to intrigue readers and should inform any discussion of early America's cultural formation.

Chapter Eight was first published in the January 1975 issue of the *William and Mary Quarterly* and reappeared in slightly altered form in *The Invasion Within* (1985). After it was first published, Alden Vaughan and Daniel Richter suggested that my admittedly unscientific estimate of the percentage of colonial captives who "went native" was too high.** Yet their own more careful counting of known New England captives comes to virtually the same number if their substantial category of captives about whom nothing is known after capture (probably because they were folded fully and quietly into native life) is added to the number of captives who were documented as staying with their adopted native families, at least until they were repatriated, often forcibly. The numbers, in any event, are much less important than the educational process behind them.

Indian Great Awakening in Pennsylvania," *William and Mary Quarterly*, 3rd ser. 54 (Oct. 1997), 723–746; Kenneth Mills, "Bad Christians in Colonial Peru," *Colonial Latin American Review*, 5:2 (Dec. 1996), 183–218; Christopher Bilodean, "Christianity and the Illinois Indians, 1666–1730," *William and Mary Quarterly* (forthcoming)

**"Crossing the Cultural Divide: Indians and New Englanders, 1605–1763," *Proceedings of the American Antiquarian Society*, 90, pt. 1 (April 1980), 23–99, esp. Appendix B.

SIX

THE INVASION WITHIN

The Contest of Cultures

The invasion of North America by European men, machines, and microbes was primarily an aggressive attempt to subdue the newfound land and its inhabitants, and to turn them to European profit. Because it was not totally unlike that of Europe, the land itself could be brought to terms by the increasingly effective methods of Western technology and capitalist economy. The American natives, however, posed a more serious problem. While they shared certain characteristics with the rest of mankind known to Europe, their cultures were so strange, so numerous, and so diverse that the invaders found it impossible to predict their behavior. If the Europeans hoped to harness, or at least neutralize, the numerically superior natives, they could ill afford to tolerate behavior that was as unpredictable as it was potentially dangerous.

Fortunately, not all natives were inscrutable at all times. European traders quickly discovered that the Indians were no strangers to an economy of barter and exchange. Even without the medium of mutually intelligible languages, Europeans exchanged Indian furs, skins, and food for manufactured goods with the aid of elemental sign languages or trade jargons. Where language was lacking, the familiar behavior of trade communicated the Indians' intentions and terms. Military officers who sought native allies against less receptive natives—or who were sought as allies by native factions—recognized with equal ease the normative behavior of military allies. If their Indian partners seldom conducted war with the martial discipline of Europe, they at least shared a common enemy and a common understanding of strategic alliance.

But traders and soldiers were soon greatly outnumbered, especially in the English colonies, by invaders whose goals were much less compatible with the life-styles of the eastern woodland Indians. When European farmers and townsmen arrived in the New World, they brought no interest in any aspect of Indian culture or behavior. To these colonists—who quickly established the distinctive character of the European invasion—the native possessors of the soil stood as living impediments to agricultural "civilization," little different from stony mountains, unfordable rivers, and implacable swamps. Since it was highly unlikely that the Indians would vanish into thin air or exile themselves to some arid corner of the continent, the best these invaders could hope for was their pacification and resettlement away from the plowed paths of prosperity. In any event, they had to be rendered predictable to make America safe for Europeans.

As if heaven-sent, a small but determined cadre of invaders offered the ultimate answer to the settlers' prayers. Christian missionaries, who had come to America in the earliest phases of invasion, espoused a set of spiritual goals that colored but ultimately lent themselves to the more material ends of their countrymen. From the birth of European interest in the New World, religious men had ensured that the public goals of exploration and colonization included a prominent place for the conversion of the natives to Christianity. But the Christianity envisioned was not a disembodied spiritual construct but a distinct cultural product of Western Europe. Conversion was tantamount to a complete transformation of cultural identity. To convert the Indians of America was to replace their native characters with European personae, to transmogrify their behavior by substituting predictable European modes of thinking and feeling for unpredictable native modes. By seeking to control the Indians' thoughts and motives, the missionaries sought to control—or at least anticipate—their actions, which could at any time spell life or death for the proliferating but scattered settlements on the farming frontier. Unwittingly or not, they lent powerful support to the European assault upon America by launching their own subversive invasion within.

From its inception, the invasion of North America was launched on waves of pious intent. Nearly all the colonial charters granted by the French and English monarchs in the sixteenth and seventeenth centuries assign the wish to extend the Christian Church and to save savage souls as a principal, if not the principal, motive for colonization.[1] Even patently economic ventures such as the Virginia, Newfoundland, and Susquehannah companies, as one colonist put it, "pretended, and I hope intended" to hold pagan salvation dearer than pounds sterling.[2]

Obviously the mere desire to convert the American natives was insufficient to accomplish the task. The missionaries also had to believe that the Indians were educable. For unless they were potentially convertible, they could never become Christian converts, a thought no missionary could entertain for long and remain in his calling. From their map-strewn studies in London and Oxford the cousins Hakluyt described the Indians as people "though simple and rude in manners, . . . yet of nature gentle and tractable."[3] Richard Eburne, a fellow promoter, agreed. His *Plain Pathway to Plantations* was lined with "exceeding[ly] tractable" natives, who were not only "industrious and ingenious to learn of us and practice with us most arts and sciences" but "very ready to leave their old and blind idolatries and to learn of us the right service and worship of the true God."[4] Since none of these men had ever made the American voyage to take personal measure of the natives' capacity, they were drawing on the Christian humanist's faith in the reforming power of education as well as the optimism of early explorers for their assessments. In 1609, as the Virginia Company was outfitting its third fleet for western waters, the Reverend Robert Gray gave classical expression to that belief when he told potential investors, "It is not the nature of men, but the education of men, which make[s] them barbarous and uncivill." "Chaunge the education of men," he predicted, "and you shall see that their nature"—corrupted at the source by Adam's sin—"will be greatly rectified and corrected."[5] According to Paul Le Jeune, the Jesuit superior of Quebec, it was optimism such as this that caused "a great many people in France [to] imagine that all we have to do is to open our mouths and utter four words, and behold, a Savage is converted."[6]

While the Indians were felt to be ultimately redeemable, there was one crucial hitch: they were still in a state of "savagery" or "barbarism," which every civilized person knew to be an "infinite distance from Christianity."[7] They were much too "degenerate" for religion to flourish or for the Word to work its magic. The heart of the matter was that they could not be trusted with the holy church ordinances "whilst they lived so unfixed, confused, and ungoverned a life."[8] The missionary prospectus was thus drawn for the next century and a half. All the European missionary societies, Protestant and Catholic, began and with few exceptions ended their American efforts with the belief that it was necessary to "civilize Savages before they can be converted to Christianity, & that in order to make them Christians, they must first be made Men."[9] The English Protestants never questioned this assumption until a few were forced to in the 1760s by a growing record of crushed hopes and unflattering self-comparisons with the Canadian Jesuits, most of whom after extensive field experience had ceased to practice what they had once preached by the middle decades of the previous century.[10] With scarcely a dissenting voice in all those years, the missionaries of North America clearly felt it their responsibility to give the Indians "Civilitie for their bodies" before "Christianitie for their soules," for while the second made them *"happy,"* the first made them *"men."*[11]

In implying that the Indians were not yet "men" the Europeans meant one of three things. The first meaning was that the natives were the children of the human race, their passions still largely unrestrained by reason. The second meaning also emphasized their passions, but gave them a much less charitable interpretation. Rather than innocent children, the Indians in this view were little better than animals, incapable of reason and enslaved by the most brutal passions. The third and by far most prevalent meaning, however, was simply that the Indians had not mastered the "Arts of civil Life & Humanity."[12] While civilized Europeans, even the lower classes, could be assumed to have acquired at least the rudiments of these arts through education or social osmosis, the Indians were thought to lack them totally. Consequently, the missionaries' perceived duty was to *"root out* their vicious habits" and "national vices," and to replace them with a "civil, orderly & Christian way of living."[13] As the Recollect friars proposed upon coming to Canada in 1615, the Indians were to be "regulated by French laws and modes of living" in order to render them capable of understanding the "profound mysteries" of Christianity, "for all that concerns human and civil life is a mystery for our Indians in their present state, and it will require more expense and toil to render them men than it has required to make whole nations Christian."[14]

Whenever plans were drawn for "humanizing" the American natives, the English missionaries chose a peculiar phrase that speaks volumes about their religious attitudes and cultural preconceptions. Time and again, from the sixteenth century to the American Revolution, it was said that the first goal of the English was to "*reduce*" the Indians from savagery to "civility."[15] The phrase is puzzling because we would expect a people with a superior self-image to attempt to *raise* their inferiors, rather than *reduce* them, to their level. To my knowledge, only two missionaries during the whole colonial period ever expressed their goal as one of elevation—both only once and both well into the eighteenth century—and even their aberrance was wholly out of character.[16] Why did they speak as if Indian culture needed a kind of *de*grading before measuring *down* to English civility?

The answer lies in the nature of the wholesale changes in Indian culture required by the English—and the French Recollects, Sulpicians, and early Jesuits as well—to render the natives worthy of religious conversion. From the European perspective, the Indians were deficient in three essential qualities: Order, Industry, and Manners. This meant in essence that they were non-Europeans, the polar opposite of what they should be and should want to be. So with characteristic confidence the missionaries proceeded in the heady decades after settlement to prescribe a veritable pharmacopoeia of remedies for their savage condition. Their diagnosis of the natives' deficiencies helps to explain why cultural health could be restored only by "*reducing* them to civility."

The immediate concern of the Europeans was to remove the Indians from their "disordred riotous rowtes and companies, to a wel governed common wealth," from what they took to be civil anarchy to the rule of European law. For of all "humane Artes," the missionaries knew, "Political government is the chiefest."[17] To men accustomed to kings and queens, administrative bureaucracies, standing armies, police, courts, and all the punitive technology of justice known to "civilized" states, the Indians seemed to suffer from unbenign neglect. If they were acknowledged to have any government at all, it was usually the capricious tyranny of an absolute theocrat, such as Powhatan in Virginia or Uncas in Connecticut. More prevalent was the view that the "common rules of order in the administration of justice"—the rules followed in Parliament or the Estates General—were not observed in Indian society. Indeed, so subtle and covert were the workings of Indian justice that the colonists were "astonished to find that such societies can remain united" at all.[18] Cast in such a light, these "wild people" obviously needed the Europeans to "bring them to

Political life, both in Ecclesiastical society and in Civil, for which," the missionaries assured themselves, "they earnestly long and enquire."[19]

Another disturbing symptom of native disorder was their "scattered and wild course of life."[20] "Towns they have none," wrote an English visitor with England in mind, "being alwayes removing from one place to another for conveniency of food."[21] The predominantly hunting tribes of Canada and Maine were the least fixed because survival depended on following the non-herding big game animals in small family groups and living off the stingy land. Even their more sedentary southern neighbors spent only five or six months congregated around their corn fields in villages ranging in size from a few families to a thousand inhabitants. And then they too broke up and moved more than once in search of fish, shellfish, berries, nuts, game, maple sap, "warme and thicke woodie bottomes" to escape the winter winds, more wood for their fires, or simply relief from the fearless fleas of summer.[22]

It was obviously disconcerting to Europeans accustomed to finding towns in the same place year after year to discover a village of a hundred wigwams gone "within a day or two" for parts and reasons unknown.[23] Not only were such a people physically uncontrollable but, perhaps worse, they were unpredictable, and surprise was the last thing the invaders wanted in the New World. Equally upsetting was the discovery that the natives, in all their basest "savagery," dared to break God-graven class lines by usurping the privileges of the European aristocracy. Forever tweaking the nose of authority, Thomas Morton of Merrymount all but visibly rubbed his hands over his observation that when the Indians "are minded to remoove," they "remoove for their pleasures . . . after the manner of the gentry of Civilized nations."[24] The same impish glee cannot describe the pious Edward Johnson of Massachusetts, who nonetheless volunteered that the Indians' wigwams bore an uncanny resemblance to gentlemen's "Summer-houses in England."[25] To have viewed the Indians as America's noblemen, commuting conspicuously between winter "castle" and summer cottage-by-the-sea, would clearly not have served. Better that their movements be seen as the vagrant shiftings of dissolute barbarians. For then, in the name of European civility and the Christian religion, such flagrant "disorder" and "chaos" could be "reduced" and the Indians brought under control.

The natives were considered deficient not only in civil order but in industry as well. In one of his first meetings with the Massachusetts, John Eliot told them that they and the English were already "all one save in two things," the first being that the English were Christians and they were not. The second difference was somewhat less obvious but to English minds nearly as important: "we labour and work in building, planting, clothing our selves, &c. and they doe not."[26] The key word in Eliot's comparison was "labour." To the idealistic missionaries, many of whom had pursued the life of learning because their constitutions were "unsuited to labour," it did not mean simply to "work" (as Eliot's additional use of that word implies), for even the Indians could be said to "work" by expending energy and thought upon various tasks. Rather it meant to work *laboriously* in the sense of severe, painful, or compulsory *toil,* the kind that a plowman knows as he walks behind a pair of huge oxen in the late-spring heat.[27] In that sense, of course, the Indians had never known work, a deficiency exacerbated by what all Europeans diagnosed as a congenital "national vice"—idleness.

In the midst of their back-breaking efforts to hew villages and farms from the American forests, the first settlers were struck by the contrast with their native neighbors. "They are not industrious," observed the Reverend Robert Cushman at second hand, "neither have art, science, skill or faculty to use either the land or the commodities of it, but all spoils, rots, and is marred for want of manuring, gathering, ordering"—that word again—"etc."[28] Nearly two centuries later, when the white frontier had shifted into western New York, the Reverend John Thornton Kirkland, a missionary and the son of a missionary, assured the members of the Massachusetts Historical Society that the situation had not changed in all that time. The Oneida, Stockbridge, and Brotherton Indians, he wrote from personal observation in 1795, "have none of the spirit, industry, and perseverance necessary in those who subdue a wilderness. . . . They seem to have an insurmountable aversion to labour; and though they discover some energy in the chace, wholly want it in husbandry and the arts of life."[29] So tempting was the native way of life that many Indian converts apostatized because, as the English admitted, "they can live with less labour, and more pleasure and plenty, as Indians, than they can with us."[30] In fact, one of the reasons given by colonists who either ran away to the Indians or refused to return from captivity was that amongst the Indians they enjoyed the "most perfect freedom, the ease of living, [and] the absence of those cares and corroding solicitudes which so often prevail with us."[31]

When the colonists found idleness endemic to Indian culture, the cultural norm by which they judged applied to only half the native population—the male half. For upon closer examination it appeared to European observers, almost all of whom were male, that, while Indian men were indeed epitomes of slothful indulgence, the work done by Indian women came respectably, even pitiably, close to the missionaries' ideal of "labour." Since such behavior ran counter to their civilized expectations, there was double cause for raised eyebrows. According to the Reverend Francis Higginson, one of the "discommodities" of *New-Englands Plantation* was that Indian "Men for the most part live idlely, they doe nothing but hunt and fish" while "Their wives set theire corne and doe all their other worke."[32] The reason for this unequal division of labor was, as most colonists saw it, the refusal of the chauvinistic Indian men "to be seene in any woman like exercise" for fear it "would compromise their dignity too much."[33] "Such [was] the pride of these lazy lords of the wilderness" that European settlers who did not treat their women similarly were blamed "for their folly in spoyling good working creatures."[34]

Bred like all people to an ethnocentric world-view, the European invaders saw what they expected to see in Indian life. Initially jarred by the half-correct observation that native men were not responsible for the agricultural livelihood of their society, the colonists never recovered their visual focus enough to notice that what was normal behavior in Europe did not always obtain in America, that Indian men played a role in their economy every bit as important as European farmers did in theirs, and that Indian women did not view their social position in the light cast by the male observers from another culture.

On their face the European criticisms of Indian "industry" were serious enough, but a number of less overt grievances reveal even more about the cultural preconceptions of the colonists and therefore about the remedial prescriptions that could be expected from the missionaries. The first group of objections, assailing the nature of Indian farming, were stated typically in the form of deficiencies. Not only was native farming done largely by women but it did not employ the deep-cutting plow harnessed to animal power, fences to enclose the fields, or—particularly symbolic—fertilizer in the form of tame animal manure.

Thomas Harriot, one of the Roanoke colonists in 1585, observed that the natives "never enrich the soil with refuse, dung, or any other thing, nor do they plough or dig it as we do in England." Nevertheless, their corn reached prodigious heights and "the yield is so great that little labor is needed in comparison with what is necessary in England."[35] Happily for the Massachusetts Bay Company, John Winthrop decided that the New England natives "inclose noe Land, neither have any setled habytation, nor any tame Cattle to improve the Land by," and so were devoid of any legal claim to their territory.[36] Although the Indians could watch a European plow "teare up more ground in a day, than their Clamme shels [hoes] could scape up in a month," they preferred their own methods throughout the colonial period.[37] To those colonists who swore by the work ethic recognized today as having been shared by Protestants and Catholics alike, there was nothing more galling than to discover that wild "savages" reaped the proverbial fruits of the earth without working up a European-style sweat.

Another criticism of Indian farming was implied by the fact that no more equipment was required than a crude hoe and a few handmade baskets. This meant that the natives' technology was as portable as their housing, which rendered them still more difficult to bring to "order." Without horses, barns, carts, harrows, plows, halters, collars, and harnesses—in other words, without a substantial material investment in the capitalist way of life—the Indians could not be securely anchored to one plot of ground where they could always be found (and disciplined if they got out of line).[38] In addition, without an involvement in the encircling web of credit that husbandry entailed, the Indians could at any time pull up stakes and head for the hinterland, out of the reach of scriptural and European law.

Trying to persuade the Indians, even the most Christian, to invest in the heavy technology of farming was a task of no little difficulty because it raised their deeply engrained suspicions of anything that threatened their independence and offended their sense of utility. The English, keen entrepreneurs that they were, understood that the civilized citizen was "attached to his country by property, by artificial wants which render that property necessary to his comfortable subsistence."[39] So one of the first tasks of those who would attach the Indians to the English political interest was to "multipl[y] their Wants, and put them upon desiring a thousand things, they never dreamt of before."[40] Thus "their wants will be encreased," reasoned "The Planter" in an eighteenth-century Philadelphia newspaper, "while on us they must in a manner wholly depend to have them supplied."[41] For a society of men uniquely responsive to the marketplace, it was a strategy with promise. But it failed to reckon with the alien psychology of the native Americans, for whom wealth was communal and sharing a sovereign duty. Moreover, "they care for little, because they want but little," William Penn tried to explain to his English partners. "In this they are sufficiently revenged on us. . . . We sweat and toil to live; their pleasure feeds them, I mean, their Hunting, Fishing and Fowling."[42]

Penn's characterization of Indian hunting as "pleasure" introduces a second group of English objections to the Indian division of labor. It was bad enough that women should manage the Indian fields without the aid of either their menfolk or the labor-inducing technology of the English, but almost worse was that those truant warriors misspent their days sporting in the woods or the water. Like the founder of Pennsylvania, colonists up and down the eastern seaboard felt that Indian hunting and fishing were more pleasant pastimes than real work. While they could sometimes appreciate that the native men took "extreame paines" in those pursuits, they could not forgive them for expending their energies in places other than plowed fields or fragrant cow-barns.[43]

A southern gentleman put his finger on the true cause of English concern when he noted, after an extensive survey of the Indian country between Virginia and North Carolina, that native men "are quite idle, or at most employ'd only in the *Gentlemanly* Diversions of Hunting and Fishing."[44] By this William Byrd II, the English-bred scion of one of the wealthiest families in Virginia, indicated that the Indians' greatest offense was the usurpation of aristocratic privilege, the disorderly jumping of class lines. For in England the only people who hunted were members of the upper classes, who did not kill to eat, or poachers who did and risked their ears—or necks—in the attempt. Forests were not public property but belonged to the nobility who regarded them as private game preserves. Guns were expensive and their ownership was generally forbidden by law.

These were the assumptions that the colonists carried to America, where the forests seemed to belong to no man, where guns became a household fixture, where hunting was often a necessity, and where English class lines failed to replicate themselves. In spite of all the social and environmental changes that should have engendered a different outlook toward hunting (and in some instances did toward their own), the colonists who did not rely on Indian hunters for marketable furs and skins continued to view the economic activities of Indian men with Old World eyes. Regarded as the social inferiors of all Englishmen, the Indians were harshly judged by semi-feudal standards that simply made no sense in the New World, much less in an alien culture.

The English had other, seldom articulated, misgivings about Indian hunting that lay just beneath the surface of their vocal disdain. These revolved around the fearful fact that in native society hunting and warfare were but two aspects of the same activity. Not only was warfare conducted according to hunting patterns, but hunting was a sort of ritualized warfare, carried on under strong religious sanctions. The education for one was the training for both. The English—and French—knew only too well that the practice of stealing through the woods to get near the game unnoticed served the warrior equally well in laying ambush upon unsuspecting enemies. Whether intended or not, the English reduction of Indian hunting to a harmless "diversion" served to disarm—at least mentally—a disturbing and dangerous alternative.

Disorder and idleness were structural weaknesses inherent in native society as a whole, but on a personal level, where most Europeans and Indians met, the natives were also seen as woefully deficient. As surely as their government and economy needed reform, their manners cried out for civilizing treatment. Nothing less than total assimilation to European ways would fulfill the uncompromising criteria of "civility," nothing less than renunciation of the last vestige of their former life. For a "Christian" and a "savage" were incompatible characters in the invaders' cosmology, and only a willing departure from all she had known, all he had been, could prepare an Indian for a life of Christ. In European eyes, no native characteristic was too small to reform, no habit too harmless to reduce.

One of the first objects of reform was the Indians' names. To European ears, inured to the peculiar accents of home and the sea, the Algonquian, Iroquoian, and Muskogean languages of the eastern woodlands struck a discordant note. Words, including names, were often long and seemingly undifferentiated, full of throaty glottals and short of defining labials. Understandably, the colonists wished to abbreviate, translate, or Europeanize the names of those natives with whom they had any commerce, especially those selected for conversion. Perhaps the easiest way to bestow intelligible European names was to intercept the native child at birth before an Indian name could be given. In "praying towns" and villages with a resident missionary, this was done most readily at the baptism of the child. On such religious occasions biblical names naturally found favor with the ministers, though just as often Indian parents preferred common French or English names.

Baptisms were not the only occasions for conferring European names, nor were children the only recipients. The eastern tribes shared a custom of renaming in which an individual could give himself or be given a new name when-

ever changed circumstances, personal fortune, or mere whim warranted.[45]
One of the occasions that might call for a new name was the realization that
the friendship of the colonists could be an advantage in trade, politics, or religion. If assuming a short European name would make it easier to deal with the
increasingly dominant invaders, many natives were willing to make the
change, especially if around their own fires they were still known by their
Indian names or relationships.

European persistence and Indian preference soon led to a pandoran variety
of native names in the areas touched by settlement. Some were quaintly
medieval (William of Sudbury), others reminiscent of black slaves who lost
their family surnames for a racial tag (Joseph Indian, Miriam Negro, Charles
Slave or Panis). Many were either legitimate translations of Indian names
(Cornplanter, Blacksnake) or fabricated "Indian" names given by the colonists
(Pipe, White-Eyes). Most were simply compromises between utility and history, a union of European given names and native surnames (Pierre Chihwa-
tenha) or translations of surnames (Mercy Fish, Merry Porridge). All, however, forced the natives to compromise their personal identity for the
convenience and ideology of the white invaders.

If the intimacy of a personal name could be violated, it is small wonder that
the missionaries did not hesitate to pass harsh judgment upon native sexual
mores. The most visible cause for concern was the Indians' state of undress,
especially in the summer when visits from the colonists were most frequent.
Children went completely naked until puberty, men sported only skimpy
breechclouts, and women, as one colonial admirer testified, "commonly go
naked as far as the Navel downward, and upward to the middle of the Thigh,
by which means they have the advantage of discovering their fine Limbs and
compleat Shape."[46] In European eyes a direct relation existed between such
tempting nudity and the Indians' libidinous behavior. Young people took to
sexual exploration early in their teens and found nothing shameful about their
bodies or their amorous potential; they were certainly strangers to the invaders'
concept of "fornication." Although adultery was widely prohibited by tribal
law, their parents appeared more universally guilty because the Christians did
not recognize the validity of Indian divorce, which easily ensued upon the
transfer of one spouse's affections and belongings to the lodge of another. By
the same token, native polygamy seemed to be rampant when in fact very few
tribesmen took more than one wife and they were usually visible sachems or
men of importance whose obligations of hospitality required more female
hands than two.

The intrusive lengths to which the Europeans would go to "civilize" the
American natives has perhaps no better measure than the English missionaries' attempts to proscribe "the old Ceremony of the Maide walking alone and
living apart so many dayes."[47] This referred to the widespread native belief that
a menstruating woman possessed spiritual powers, capable of poisoning food
with her touch, scaring game with her scent, or injuring a man's health with

her glance. In nearly all hunting and most horticultural tribes, women "in their courses" withdrew to a small hut in the woods (*wetuomémese* in Narragansett) for the duration, where they lived alone, cooked their own meals with special utensils, and lowered their eyes when a tribesman came near. At the end of a woman's period "she washeth herself, and all that she hath touched or used, and is again received to her husband's bed or family."[48] Despite the intriguing similarity of menstrual seclusion to ancient Jewish custom, the missionaries wanted not only to move the Indians away from a hunting economy, where the menstrual taboo was strongest, but to undercut the whole belief system upon which it was founded. But before they could re-educate the natives in personal hygiene, physiology, and metaphysics, they simply ruled that the Indian woman's time-honored way of dealing with her natural processes was taboo and subject to the scrutiny of foreign men. What the modern woman's movement once called "vaginal politics" was clearly not unknown to the Anglo-Protestants who led the invasion within.

However exemplary the Indians' daily—or nocturnal—behavior, one look told the colonists that the natives needed to be clothed in more than modesty. In the eyes of the invaders, native dress was a phantasmagoria of animal pelts, bird feathers, and reptile skins, of colors and textures as wild as the people themselves. Beautifully tanned leathers were thrown together with bird-wing headdresses, mantles of animal heads, feet, and tails, snakeskin belts, smoky fur robes, and swan's-down ear decorations. Any exposed skin might be covered with totemic tattoos, shell jewelry, bear grease, or lurid paintings. In all seasons frail-looking, soft-soled moccasins were worn without stockings—if at all—while men donned buttock-revealing leather leggings as pants against the cold and underbrush. Clearly such uncouth garb would have to be replaced by fashions *à la mode* in Boston and Quebec. For if an Indian could be persuaded to change his whole life-style, so that he looked as well as lived and acted like a European, the chances were considered good that he would eventually think European thoughts and believe Christian truths. He would, in effect, cease to be an Indian, the conversion process would be complete, and the colonial "Indian problem" would be solved. The trick, however, was to get the half-naked forest dwellers to look like European colonists. In some respects this proved to be the easiest task of all, but in the end the Europeans enjoyed only partial success. For in the seemingly indifferent matter of personal appearance they encountered the paramount symbol of Indian identity and the rock upon which most white efforts to "reduce" it were broken.

Several obstacles stood in the way of an abrupt change of habit by the Indians. The largest was that the great majority of woodland Indians had small use for fitted clothes designed for brierless farms and open fields. As many colonists discovered to their loss, woven cloth garments were quickly shredded by the rough life of the woods. Moreover, European clothes, if they were to present a civilized appearance, had to be washed, ironed, bought in multiples to reduce wear, stored, and frequently replaced, none of which the Indians

were willing or able to do. "Therefore they had rather goe naked," a New Englishman noted, "than be lousie, and bring their bodies out of their old tune,
making them more tender by a new acquired habit."[49] Fitted trousers were
particularly abhorrent, especially in the South where native men squatted to
urinate.[50] The most clothing that the majority of Indians could be induced to
buy was a stroud breechclout, a shirt, which they proceeded to wear unwashed
until it distintegrated, and a large woolen blanket, which served at once as
overcoat, raincoat, blanket, and nightshirt. The heavy European serges, baize,
and fustians, cut into fitted garments that restricted movement and ventila-
tion, found little favor in the native markets of North America—until the missionaries gave their proselytes new reason to buy them.

That reason was the European belief that a European appearance visibly
segregated Indian converts from their recalcitrant "pagan" brothers and provided a sign in times of frontier unrest by which "friend Indians" could be readily distinguished from enemies. For the first few decades of settlement this reasoning made some sense. But as the native resistance to foreign cloth
weakened, more tribesmen adopted various articles of European dress for their
decorative value or because the loss of game made traditional garb impossible.
When the woods became such a sartorial hodgepodge, native intentions and
allegiances were much more difficult to discern. But even then, the infallible
mark of a Protestant "praying Indian" was his English appearance: short hair,
cobbled shoes, and working-class suit. So important was European clothing as
a badge of "civility" that an Indian's degree of acculturation could almost be
read in his appearance. The more he wished to emulate the invaders and to
become one with them, the more Europeanized his dress became and the more
pains he took to put aside his native costume. In the eastern woodlands you
could often tell a convert by his cover.

But in New England, dress alone was not an infallible guide to the Indian's
political allegiance, much less to his religious convictions, unless it was accompanied by an equally decisive *un*covering—short hair. For nothing symbolized
the Indian's identity—his independence, his sense of superiority, his pride—
more effectively than his long hair. A willingness to cut his long black hair signaled his desire to kill the Indian in himself and to assume a new persona
modeled upon the meek, submissive Christ of the white man's Black Book.
Since this was the missionaries' ultimate goal, they wasted no time in persuading their native proselytes to submit to the barber's shears.

When the ministers succeeded, the loss was dramatic. Eastern native hair-
styles were infinite and various, many of which would "torture the wits of a
curious Barber to imitate."[51] Whether they chose roaches, pigtails, tonsures,
scalplocks, baldness, or ingenious combinations thereof, most native men
affected some form of long hair and a studied fancy that to many English
observers betrayed "the sparkes of natural pride," a vanity that did not seem
present in their clothing, houses, or material possessions.[52] As such, their hair
drew unexpectedly cutting remarks from the missionaries.

The Puritan abhorrence of long hair was rooted, like many of their values, in Scripture, but it took on political shading during the English civil wars when the long hair and powdered wigs of "Cavaliers" seemed to run riot in pulpit, court, and quadrangle. The English battle was soon refought in New England, where the "roundheads" were led by missionary John Eliot, the vocal minister of the Roxbury congregation. With zeal surprising in a matter of acknowledged "indifferency," he and his short-haired colleagues proceeded to prod their congregations, university, and governments into outlawing "proud fashions" and "the wearing of long haire after the manner of Ruffians," "wild-Irish," and, not least, "barbarous Indians."[53]

Whether the wearer was English or Indian, the principal sin of long hair was pride. And seventeenth-century Englishmen did not need reminding that pride was the original sin of their spiritual parents, Adam and Eve. In the innumerable laws, proclamations, and warnings that resulted from the colonial establishment's dismay over long hair, overweening pride was the "badge" of those who refused to cover themselves with Christian "humility, sobriety, modesty, [and] shamefastness."[54]

If the Indians had inadvertently or casually worn their hair long, they would still have offended the Protestants' fine sensitivity to personal pride and vanity, but not as grievously as they obviously did. For long hair aptly symbolized the Indians' deeper affront to Anglo-Christianity, which was their characteristic pride and independence. Whenever the European invaders took measure of the native Americans, these two qualities found the page with great frequency. Secular men on the frontier might appreciate and even emulate the Indians, but good Christians, especially ministers, could only be chagrined that some of God's creatures were not duly "mortified and humbled" before their creator. As God's servants on earth, the missionaries felt a strong obligation to ensure that the Indians, "the dregs and refuse of Adams lost posterity," were drawn from their "sinful liberty" into "Subjection to Jehovah."[55]

Setting the pace for those who followed, Eliot's goals were "to convince, bridle, restrain, and civilize" the Indians "and also to humble them." In describing their religious goals, the missionaries most commonly used the metaphor of placing such "heady Creatures" in the "yoke of Christ" and teaching them to "bridle" their savage instincts.[56] In other words, becoming a Christian was comparable to assuming the posture and character of tame cattle—docile, obedient, submissive. Or, in another popular metaphor, their goal was to "reduce" the Indians' proud independence and godless self-reliance to the total dependence of a "weaned child."[57] Since it was total, this dependence was at once political, social, and religious. In short, the Indians would become "civilized." The "savage" would give way to the "civil man" by repressing his native instincts, habits, and desires and quietly taking the political bit in his teeth and the religious yoke upon his neck.

Thus, the meaning of the puzzling phrase, "to reduce them to civility," becomes clear. As long hair symbolized pride for the English, so too did the long-haired Indian. In the Christian cosmology, the proud Indian—wandering, lawless, and unpredictable—occupied the higher place: he was puffed up with self-importance, inflated with a false sense of superiority, and unrestrained by law, labor, or religion, not unlike the Devil whom he was thought to worship. It was therefore an affront to God—and, of course, his Christian soldiers—that the Indians remained in such an unnatural and undesirable state.

What should also be clear is the sincerity of the religious goals of European colonization. If we interpret "conversion" as the invaders did, not as modern theologians do, there can be no doubt that the conversion of the natives was indeed a primary goal—logically and chronologically primary. For given the almost unanimous belief that "savages" had to be "civilized" before they could be "Christianized," the initial problem all the European colonies faced—the natives' dangerous unpredictability—was soluble by "reducing them to civility." If in the process the conquerors were served as much as Christ, who could gainsay their fortune? Certainly not the missionaries, who were keenly aware that "until Christians are the absolute masters of the Indians, missionaries will have scant success without a very special grace of God, a miracle which He does not perform for every people."[58]

The broad consensus about the goals of the Christian missions in North America, emerging from a common Western European experience and ideology, entailed a limited range of conversion methods upon the French and English invaders. Since the "civilizing" and religious conversion of the Indians was essentially an educational task, a process of *re*-education in effect, the colonists turned naturally to the major social and educational institutions of their cultures for models and methods. The institution that promised to work the greatest number of changes in native culture was the town, the European symbol of "civility" (from the Latin *civis*, citizen) and locus of law and order. The town was expected to fix, restrain, and order Indian life, to direct its licentious energies into productive and predictable channels. "*Reserves*" in New France and "praying towns" in New England and elsewhere gave the missionaries some hope of segregating their neophytes and converts from the corrupting example of imperfect colonists and the seductive "paganism" of their native neighbors. Moreover, they were calculated to severely cramp the Indians' mobile style by encouraging them to substitute agriculture for hunting, to build heavy, European-style houses, to surround themselves with the cumbersome trappings of European technology, and to remake their civil polity in the European image. Not the least of their attractions for the colonists was that congregations of natives would greatly reduce the manpower and therefore economic needs of the missions and provide non-European frontier buffers against enemy war parties.

It took only small experience in America for the missionaries to conclude that "if some one could stop the wanderings of the Indians, and give authority to one of them to rule the others, we would see them converted and civilized in a short time."[59] The need, of course, was to give them an economy overnight that would make their seasonal moves unnecessary, for only then could they stay among their fellow converts the year round to receive instruction from a resident priest or pastor and to nurture their new faith. Father Le Jeune was not wrong to observe that "it is the same thing in an Indian to wish to become sedentary, and to wish to believe in God."[60] But his successor as superior of the Canadian missions, Barthelemy Vimont, had a point too when he regretted that the Jesuits had "greater trouble in keeping our Christians than in acquiring them. . . . The land that we clear, the houses that we build for them, and the other aid, spiritual and material, that we endeavor to give them, keep them stationary for a while, but not permanently."[61] If the new townsmen could be fed until they became agriculturally self-sufficient, the praying town had a good chance of fostering substantial changes in the native life-style, the most important of which was the imposition of new forms of government, discipline, and morality.

The fundamental weakness of Indian life, the missionaries felt, was the natives' belief that they ought "by right of birth, to enjoy the liberty of Wild ass colts, rendering no homage to any one whomsoever, except when they like."[62] Since "they are born, live, and die in a liberty without restraint, they do not know what is meant by bridle or bit."[63] Consequently, no aspect of their "reduction to civility" was more essential than persuading or forcing them to place their necks in "the yoke of the law of God," which, translated, meant European-style autocracy, law, and compulsion. When the Jesuit *reserve* of Sillery was settled after 1637, its Algonquin and Montagnais inhabitants felt the need for a civilized form of government to regulate their civil and religious affairs. For the first time in their experience, the men elected by majority vote rather than consensus three magistrates, two moral overseers, and a "Captain of prayers" to assist the hereditary sachem. Four of the winners were "Christians," as was their leader. To prove that the traditional rule of suasion was being replaced by coercion, the new officers borrowed the use of Quebec's dungeon until they could build their own prison to punish (mostly female) breakers of their new adamantine code of morality. "Pagans" who dared to resist their authority were imprisoned, chained, whipped, and starved until they learned to obey "a peremptory command" and to submit humbly to "any act of severity or justice." Even the death penalty was seriously considered as a "perpetual" deterrent to moral turpitude.[64]

For most neophytes, French or English, the "yoke of Christ" must have felt anything but "mild and easy," as the missionaries hoped it would.[65] It was virtually impossible not to run afoul of the law when the law proscribed every aspect of traditional life, great and small. In the twenty-four years after 1650, John Eliot gathered some 1100 Massachusett and Nipmuc Indians into fourteen praying towns. Plymouth's missionaries sponsored eight more towns for 500 persons, and the Mayhews on Martha's Vineyard established still others.

Most of the New England towns strongly resembled the seven major Jesuit *reserves* in their puritanical leadership and strict prescription of European ways. Faithful converts who were elected or appointed by the missionaries to office promptly drafted long legal codes to govern the towns, which usually consisted at first of unstable mixtures of zealous converts and resistant traditionalists. Concord's rules passed in 1647 were typical. Fines up to twenty shillings or whippings were meted out for infractions ranging from fighting, "powwowing" (resorting to traditional medicine men), gaming, "fornication," and lice-biting to sporting long hair (male) or bare breasts (female), body-greasing, polygamy, mourning with "a great noyse by howling," and menstrual seclusion. (Adultery, witchcraft, and worshipping any deity but the Christian God were punishable by death under colony law, to which the Indians were already subject.) Predictably, the townsmen were expected not only to give up their former habits but to replace them with English ways. Three laws enjoined them to "observe the Lords-Day," to "fall upon some better course to improve their time than formerly," and, most significant, to "labour after humility, and not be proud."[66]

By compelling the natives to avoid idleness, the praying town laws sought to edge them into a European economy, to transform them from "lazy savages" into "*bons habitants*" and "laborious" husbandmen. Skilled trades for the Indians were seldom considered and, when they were, were quickly put aside for fear of providing unnecessary competition for colonial workers. Farming and a variety of marginal home industries, such as the manufacture of brooms, pails, and baskets, berrying, and hunting and fishing for hire, were as far as the praying Indians climbed up the ladder of economic success. But by anchoring their converts to the soil, the missionaries accomplished two important ends, one for themselves and one for the colonists. As Eliot explained, "a fixed condition of life" enabled the natives to be more trusted with the church ordinances because "if any should through temptations, fall under [church] Censure, he could easily run away (as some have done) and would be tempted so to do, unless he were fixed in an Habitation, and had some means of livelihood to lose, and leave behind him."[67] And, as a colonial English soldier happily observed, the colonists had it "more in our power to Distress them" if they shook off the civilized bridle or yoke "as we can revenge ourselves on their fixed habitations, & growing corn."[68] Once again, the missionaries served Christ and conquest without qualm or contradiction.

Being the scholastic products of book learning themselves, the ministers and officials who designed the American missions inevitably turned to formal institutions of education for help in "reducing" the Indians to "civility," hoping thereby to reform their mental as well as physical habits as early as possible. Throughout the colonial period, the missionaries tried to reach Indian children and adults at the same time, to trap native culture, as it were, in a squeeze between generations. Both the Recollects and Jesuits established French-style "seminaries" for Indian children during the first years of their missions, but within five years each had folded for lack of funds, students, and success.[69] They then turned their energies toward native *reserves* near the major centers of French population along the St. Lawrence and to religious missions to remote Indian villages all over New France. The English, by contrast, were initially frustrated in their attempts to convert native adults, so their emphasis shifted perceptibly toward the young. This was a logical emphasis because from the beginning the English hoped to train native preachers, teachers, and interpreters to assume the task of converting their brethren to "civilized" Christianity. The only feasible way to train this cadre of native agents was to catch Indian children early in their development, before the hereditary stain of "savagism" became indelible, and "bring them up English."

The instruments the missionaries chose for this task were traditional English schools and colleges, adapted not one whit to the special needs of Indian students fresh from the forest. Until the eighteenth century, most of them were boarding schools located in English territory, far from the contagion of traditional habits, indulgent parents, and distracting friends. The missionaries agreed with the Jesuits that "the consciousness of being three hundred leagues distant from their own country makes these young men more tractable."[70] Under the nervous eyes and guns of the colonists, the students might have taken an extra stab at docility had they known that their teachers viewed them as "hostages" for the safety of the English in their country and along their borders; chiefs' sons were especially welcome as students for this reason.[71] When they arrived at school, they were effectively quarantined from all contaminating female contact for the duration of their studies, as if they were undergoing a special, long-term puberty rite. In the male world of the missionaries, boys were considered the prime candidates for conversion because it was assumed that they would return to their tribes, assume office by (newly acquired) merit, and lead their "pagan" brethren to "civility." (Girls, when they were noticed at all, were educated separately in the two Rs, religion, and "housewifery" to make them suitable partners for French colonists or Christian Indians.)

The master of such a male school was, of course, a patriarchal figure—serious, pedantic, and strict. Although—or because—Indian parents were "too fond" to "tolerate the chastisement of their children" at home, the missionaries in their colonial strongholds proceeded to institute a birchen government calculated to "humble them, and reform their manners." Schoolmasters such as the Reverend Eleazar Wheelock felt free to administer punishment as they pleased, confident that "Evils so obstinate as those we may reasonably expect to find common in the Children of Savages, will require that which is severe."[72]

As in most classrooms, the medium of instruction and discipline was probably louder and clearer than the message of the curriculum, which was unfailingly traditional: religious catechism, English grammar, arithmetic, Latin, and Greek. When the frustration or boredom of their inactive lives erupted in highjinks, the birch rod covered their skin with welts they had never seen at home. By the eighteenth century the contrast between English schooling and Jesuit proselyting was blatantly obvious, especially to the Indians. In 1772 the Onondaga council rejected Wheelock's offer to educate their children with a sharp reproof. "Brother," they said, "you must learn of the French ministers if you would understand, & know how to treat Indians. They don't speak roughly; nor do they for every little mistake take up a club & flog them."[73]

By the fall of Canada in 1760, the English missions had seldom ventured beyond the safety of well-populated and well-fortified colonial settlements. Their praying towns were surrounded by the proliferating towns and farms of southern New England, as were the great majority of their Indian schools. Only a handful of missionaries had ever ventured into Indian country as far as Maine, New York, or the Ohio country, and then with conspicuous lack of success. This timidity was due to three considerations: their ideological insistence on "reducing the Indians to civility" before trying to convert them to Christianity, the belief of many land-hungry farmers and speculators that "the way of conquering them is much more easie than of civilizing them by faire meanes," and a major ecclesiastical deficiency.[74] Until the opening years of the eighteenth century, the English Protestant churches—with the exception of the Church of England, which showed little interest in Indians at the time— were hampered in their missionary endeavors by an ecclesiastical polity that restricted the ministry to those specifically called by an individual congregation of the elect. A minister without a congregation, no matter how holy or how learned he was, was simply a man without the ministry. He could not administer the sacraments of baptism or communion—the only two recognized—or gather a formal church. Furthermore, despite evangelical assertions to the contrary, the minister was effectively prevented from winning new souls to Christ by being tied to the needs and wishes of his small flock. Unless the unregenerate happened to wander into his congregation on the Sabbath—and understood English—the minister was not likely to encounter many potential converts. "By [Puritan] principles," an Anglican visitor criticized, "no Nation can or could ever be converted."[75]

By contrast, the Jesuits were organized hierarchically in an international order, freed from parish work to attack heresy and paganism wherever it flourished. From the middle of the seventeenth century, when they gave up the idea of Frenchifying the Indians, the Jesuits took their missions into the remote corners of New France, west to Lake Superior, north to Hudson Bay, south to Louisiana. In these places they attempted to insinuate Christianity into the natives' lives with methods learned less in the scholastic classrooms of France than in the inhabited forests of America.

The priest's first step was to gain admission to the target village. An ideal way was to talk a leading man or sachem into adopting him, which gave him an extensive set of readymade relatives, food, shelter, and some measure of physical protection. Then, by his exemplary behavior, the priest made every effort to show the villagers that he was no threat to their continued existence.

Without an apparent interest in guns, women, beaver skins, or land, he sought to convince them that he had left his refined and comfortable life in Europe solely to help them reach God and eternal happiness. He especially sought the favor of the children, who had great power over their parents' affections, not least because he could easily learn the language from them while teaching them their first words of French.

While ingratiating himself by learning their language, the Jesuit began to practice his order's worldwide technique of acculturating themselves to the natives' way of life to win their trust for the task ahead. Unlike the Dominicans and Franciscans within their own church and the Puritans and Anglicans without, the Jesuits articulated and practiced a brand of cultural relativism, without, however, succumbing to ethical neutrality. While they, like all missionaries, sought to replace the Indians' cosmology and religion with their own, they were more willing than their Christian counterparts to adopt the external life-style of the Indians until their goal could be realized. Rather than immediately condemn and destroy what they found, they carefully studied native beliefs and practices and tried to reshape and reorient them in order to establish a common ground on which to begin conversion.[76] As Father Vimont put it in 1642, "to make a Christian out of a Barbarian is not the work of a day. . . . A great step is gained when one has learned to know those with whom he has to deal; has penetrated their thoughts; has adapted himself to their language, their customs, and their manner of living; and, when necessary, has been a Barbarian with them, in order to win them over to Jesus Christ."[77] In large measure, whatever success the Jesuits enjoyed was gained not by expecting less of their converts, as the English accused, but by accepting more.

As the priest learned to adjust his ways to those of the Indians, he also began to promulgate his Christian message by appealing to all their senses. In native hands he put attractive silver and brass medals, rings, crucifixes, and rosaries as mnemonic devices to recall his oral message, not unlike their own wampum belts, medicine sticks, and condolence canes. To their noses he introduced the mysterious fragrances of incense. To their lips he lifted holy wafers. To their eyes he offered huge wooden crosses, candle-lit altars rich with silk and silver, long brocaded chasubles, and pictorial images of the major acts in the drama of Christianity. And into their ears he poured sonorous hymns and chants, tinkling bells, and an endless stream of Indian words, haltingly, even laughably, pronounced at first, but soon fluent and cadenced in native measures. Here his long training in logic, rhetoric, and disputation stood him in good stead, once he grasped the novel motivations, interests, and fears of his listeners. Believing that "in order to convert these peoples, one must begin by touching their hearts, before he can convince their minds," the priest sought to manage their dispositions by an adroit use of flattery, bribery, ridicule, insult, "mildness and force, threats and prayers, labors and tears."[78]

If the priest was at all effective, he would soon succeed in fomenting a serious factional split between "Christians" and "Pagans" at all levels of village society, a division he would quietly work to widen in hopes of placing his converts in all the positions of civil leadership. By administering the sacraments, especially baptism, only to the deserving after considerable instruction and lasting personal reform, he protected the hard-won reputation of his flock and the holy ordinances from familiar contempt.

But his most important goal was to supplant the village shaman, his chief opposition for the minds of the people. By his possession of printed truths (which initially impressed the members of that oral culture), a scientific understanding of nature (whereby a magnet or compass could be used to attract a following away from a divination rite), and an unrelenting questioning of the habitual (which no cultural practice can long survive), the missionary sought to erode the shaman's prestige and to establish his own in its place. If the fortuitous administration of a cordial, the lancet, or baptismal water happened to rescue a native from the grave, his stock as a functional replacement for the medico-religious shaman would rise dramatically. When the priest saw his converts at the head of village government and himself accepted as the resident shaman, he could consider his mission at least a partial success. While he had not "civilized" his hosts, he had Christianized them without destroying their usefulness to the French as hunters, trappers, and military allies. His only remaining task, as Father Vimont warned, was to keep his Christians in the Faith, a task that a village church would greatly lighten.

While the Jesuits enjoyed several advantages over their English rivals, by no means did they enjoy universal or permanent success in converting the Indians even to Christianity. At the end of two centuries of effort, both the French and the English were forced to admit that they had largely failed to convert the native Americans to European religion and culture.[79] The reasons are not difficult to find. In fact, they are so plentiful and so overwhelming that we should rather wonder how they achieved as much success as they did. The usual explanations, those most commonly given by contemporaries in a spirit of half-hearted expiation, pointed to the regrettable but inevitable results of contact with European cultures: disease (to which the Indians had no immunities), war (fomented by European trade competition and exacerbated by European firearms), alcohol (for whose use the natives had no cultural sanctions), and the immoral example of false Christians (who, instead of raising the Indians' sights, "reduced them to civility"). Cotton Mather spoke for many when he confessed that the Europeans had "very much *Injured* the *Indians . . .* by *Teaching* of them, *Our Vice.* We that should have learn'd them to *Pray,* have learn'd them to *Sin.*"[80]

While no one would deny that these external forces did much to undermine the conversion process, the traits within Indian culture that resisted change should be emphasized, as should the defects of the missions themselves. The first and most serious obstacle was native religion.[81] Several of the first explorers and some of their less perceptive colonial followers thought that the Indians had no religion, just as they appeared to have no laws or government ("*ni foi, ni loi, ni roi*"). Shortly, however, a closer look enabled settlers and missionaries to grant the natives a modicum of religious beliefs and observances, but these were seen only as "superstitions" because of their non-Christian character. But one man's superstition is another man's religion, and Indian religion, for all its novelty, was at once bona fide and culturally pervasive, capable of explaining, predicting, and controlling the world in emotionally and intellectually satisfying ways. Like all peoples known to ethnology, the various native groups of the Northeast each possessed a religion in that they performed "a set of rituals, rationalized by myth, which mobilize[d] supernatural powers for the purpose of achieving or preventing transformations of state in man or nature."[82] Despite their linguistic and cultural differences, they shared enough beliefs and practices to allow generalization, and, to some extent, comparison with Christianity. For the Indians were not as far from the Christian invaders in religious belief as they seemed to be in practice (or ritual), which partially explains the successes of the missions as well as their failures.

Behind all native religion lay a cosmology, a hierarchy of states of being and a science of the principles of their interaction. The most populous tier consisted of supernatural beings known as "spirits" or "souls," who were continuous "selves" capable of changing form. Though they were invisible, they were audible to men, with whom they could interact directly (such as by shaking a tent) and by whom they were manipulable in the right circumstances. Possessing will and consciousness, they knew the future as well as the past because of their continuity. Human souls, for instance, could separate temporarily from the corporeal body in sleep, travel to other realms of experience, and return to inform or instruct the person in dreams. Consequently, dreams were regarded by many missionaries as the heart of native religion, for the Indians believed that the supernatural guidance of their lives came from these "secret desires of the soul," which had to be fulfilled if they were to enjoy health, happiness, and success.[83] In death the soul left the body permanently to travel to an afterlife, which was probably vaguely conceived before the Christians began to preach of Heaven and Hell, but which seemed to be an ethereal version of the happiest life they had known on earth, replete with good hunting, abundant fruits, and fine weather. For the long journey to this spirit village in the Southwest, the soul, which had assumed a visible, anthropomorphic ghostly shape, needed food and proper equipment. So the deceased was buried with small pots of food and the tools of his or her calling, the souls of which items would separate from the physical artifacts and accompany the traveler's soul. Although the missionaries managed to alter some small aspects of Indian burial, they seldom persuaded even their converts to deprive the dead of their grave goods.[84]

Just as angels differed in power and character from the Christian God, so Indian spirits and souls differed from the more powerful "guardian spirits," who enjoyed the ultimate power of metamorphosis, and the "Master Spirit." According to native belief, every plant and animal species had a "boss" or "owner" spirit whose experience encompassed all the individuals of the species.

Many Indian myths were narratives of the "self" adventures of these spirits. More importantly, a young man—less commonly a young woman—who sought a supernatural talisman of success underwent a vision quest alone in the woods in hopes of receiving instruction from a guardian spirit. If he was successful, the being he saw became his personal helpmate for the rest of his life, during the course of which it would give additional counsel, usually when ritually called upon in time of need. So important was the possession of a guardian spirit or "manitou," wrote a Moravian missionary late in the eighteenth century, that an Indian without one "considers himself forsaken, has nothing upon which he may lean, has no hope of any assistance and is small in his own eyes. On the other hand those who have been thus favored possess a high and proud spirit."[85] The missionary's task was to humble the favored Indian's pride by giving him the meek spirit of Jesus Christ as a new guardian.

The ultimate being in the Indian pantheon, just as in the Christian, was an all-powerful, all-knowing "Master Spirit" or "Creator," who was the source of all good but was seldom or never seen. More frequently encountered, especially after the advent of the Hell-bearing Europeans, was an evil god, a *matchemanitou*, who purveyed devilry and death if not appeased. Much to the chagrin of the missionaries, most of the Indians' religious worship seemed to center on attempts to deflect the maleficences of this deity instead of praising the benefactions of the Creator.

The Indians mobilized the supernatural in their world by a number of religious observances and rituals. Just as in the Christian churches, some of these rituals, such as personal prayer, could be performed by any individual, but many were efficacious only when administered in a communal context by a specially qualified priest or shaman, known to the Europeans as a "powwow," "juggler," or "sorcerer." The native priest was almost always a male religious specialist who through apprenticeship and visions had acquired extraordinary spiritual power. Unlike his Christian counterparts, however, he possessed *personal* supernatural power that allowed him to manipulate the spiritual cosmology on his tribesmen's behalf; he was not a mere intermediary whose only strength lay in explanation and supplication. But because all spiritual power in the native universe was double-edged, capable of both good and evil, the shaman was as feared as he was revered. For while he could induce trances that made him impervious to pain, influence the weather, predict the future, and interpret dreams for the villagers, he could also cause as well as cure witchcraft, the magical intrusion of a small item into the body or the capture of a soul in dream by any person with spiritual "power," which caused illness and eventually death. Bewitchment was the most feared calamity in Indian life because the assailant and the cause were unknown unless discovered by a shaman whose personal power was greater than that of the witch. Because persons exhibiting strange behavior were usually suspected of malicious intentions, the Catholic missionaries who lived with no women, read the hieroglyphical pages of a black book, dipped water on the foreheads of native people, fondled crosses and beads, and mumbled incomprehensible incantations always stood the chance of being branded as witches and shunned if not killed.

By the same token, the Indian shaman was the missionaries' number one enemy because he seemed to hold their potential converts in the devil's thraldom through errant superstition, hocus-pocus, and fear. If he happened to be a sachem as well, as occurred from time to time in New England, the missionary faced a formidable task. For such a man controlled the political and social as well as the expressive and emotional resources of the community. If he could be discredited and supplanted, the missionary might have relatively smooth sailing. But while his opposition persisted, large-scale conversion to a Christian alternative stood little chance of success. So adamant was the resistance of these spiritual leaders that more than one missionary must have entertained the sentiment of an early Virginia minister, who insisted that "till their Priests and Ancients have their throats cut, there is no hope to bring them to conversion."[86]

The second obstacle to the success of the missions was the Indian languages. Although the colonial French and English encountered only four of the major language groups of North America, each tribe—sometimes each village—spoke a distinct dialect that might be largely unintelligible to their neighbors. Unlike the traders and trappers who also pursued their callings in Indian country, the missionaries were denied the company of those female "sleeping dictionaries" who so quickly formed the strangers' tongues to native vocabularies, syntax, and accents. For the clerics, said one of their best linguists, "practice is the only master that is able to teach us."[87] To European ears, the languages themselves were mixtures of great richness and disconcerting poverty. They were rich in proper nouns for concrete objects, in metaphorical expressions of "real beauty," and in a variety of ways to signify the same object or action in various states or relations. But they were poor in abstract words, universals, and of course words from another world. It thus appeared to the Jesuits that "neither the Gospel nor holy Scripture has been composed for them." Even mundane parables to symbolize the Christian mysteries were nearly untranslatable for lack of vocabulary: the natives simply had no words for salt, sin, gold, prison, candle, king, shepherd, or flock. "Their ignorance of the things of the earth," lamented the worldly priests, "seem to close for them the way to heaven."[88] This was an obstacle that neither culture completely overcame.

Another serious obstacle, especially to the French missions, was native marriage. The Catholic priests, of course, regarded monogamous marriage as one of the seven sacraments and divorce as anathema. The Indians, on the other hand, had always exercised, as Father Vimont put it, "a complete brutal liberty, changing wives when they pleased—taking only one or several, according to their inclination." Understandably, "conjugal continence and the indissolubility of marriage, seemed to them the most serious obstacles in the progress of the Gospel."[89] When the Indians understood the marital implications of baptism, many pulled up short of the "yoke of single marriage" that the French wished to impose. As late as 1644 Father Vimont was still complaining that "of all the Christian laws which we propound to them, there is not one that seems so hard to them as that which forbids polygamy, and does not allow them to break the bonds of lawful marriage. . . . It is this that prevents most of the infidels from accepting the Faith, and has caused some to lose it who had already embraced it."[90]

The Christian way of life offered many other stumbling blocks for the Indians. Lenten fasting at the end of winter scarcity (even though the Sorbonne declared the beaver to be a fish for religious purposes); discriminating between people after death when in life they had been equals; pretending that Christians professed the one true faith when missionaries from many denominations hawked their spiritual wares; confining people in the "yoke of God" on the Sabbath when the struggle for life required a full week; being obsessed by death and the afterlife, especially by the palpable threat of eternal torture by fire; asserting that baptism conferred everlasting life when it was often followed by death—all these practices and more seemed unreasonable to a people who had been raised in a religious tradition that was better adapted to the natural and social world in which they lived.[91]

When the missionaries overstepped the native bounds of courtesy and pressed them to change their thinking, the Indians made two characteristic responses, both of which constituted serious obstacles to their conversion. If during a theological debate with the missionary a native leader was not convinced of the wisdom of the Christian position, he would close it with a subtle plea for toleration. "All your arguments," warned Pierre Biard from experience with the Micmacs, "and you can bring on a thousand of them if you wish, are annihilated by this single shaft which they always have at hand, *Aoti Chabaya* (they say), 'That is the Indian way of doing it. You can have your way and we will have ours; every one values his own wares.'"[92] "If we reply that what they say is not true, they answer that they have not disputed what we have told them and that it is rude to interrupt a man when he is speaking and tell him he is lying."[93] Sometimes the rejection could be quite pointed. The Iroquois at Shamokin minced no words in spurning the offer of the Reverend David Brainerd in 1745 to settle among them for two years, build a church, and call them together every Sunday "as the whites do." "We are Indians," they announced, "and don't wish to be transformed into white men. The English are our Brethren, but we never promised to become what they are. As little as we desire the preacher to become Indian, so little ought he to desire the Indians to become preachers."[94] The preacher left the next day.

The Indians could have raised many objections to Christianity—and often did when pushed far enough—but usually only sachems, speakers, or shamans chose to lock minds with the Europeans on their own dialectical turf. Most simply deployed the ultimate Indian weapon against aggressive Europeans, a weapon that has frustrated the best-laid plans of white men for four centuries.

Louis Hennepin, a Recollect priest who worked the Great Lakes and Illinois country, explained why "a savage must not be regarded as convinced as soon as he seems to approve the statements made him."

> Complete indifference to everything is a form of politeness with these Indians; they would consider a man ill bred if he did not agree to everything or if he contradicted arguments in council. Even though the most absurd and stupid things are said, they will always answer "*Niaova*—that is excellent, my brother; you are right." They believe, however, only what they privately choose to believe.[95]

On the receiving end of such treatment, not every missionary agreed that it sprang from "mere Civility." Claude Allouez chalked it up to "dissimulation," "a certain spirit of acquiescence," and "stubbornness and obstinacy."[96] After researching the history of the Canadian missions, Pierre de Charlevoix said it stemmed "sometimes from mere complacency, sometimes from some interested motive, more frequently from indolence and sloth."[97] Whatever its origins—and Hennepin was closer to the truth than his Jesuit counterparts—more European missionaries than one must have asked in frustration, "What can one do with those who in word give agreement and assent to everything, but in reality give none?"[98]

While the Indians deployed their secret weapon in the heat of cultural combat, they were seldom if ever the aggressors. For the path of least resistance was an extension of the basic Indian toleration of other religions and the correspondent wish to pursue their own. "The *French* in general take us for Beasts," Adario, the semi-fictional Huron sachem, told his friend Lahontan, "the Jesuits brand us for impious, foolish, and ignorant Vagabonds. And to be even with you, we have the same thoughts of you; but with this difference, that *we* pity you without offering invectives."[99] Nor did the contrast end there, as Joseph Le Caron saw as early as 1624. "No one must come here in hopes of suffering martyrdom . . . ," he counseled his Recollect brethren, "for we are not in a country where savages put Christians to death on account of their religion. They leave every one in his own belief."[100] It was true, as every missionary knew. But being Christians they persisted in their attempts to change the Indians.

Yet the missionaries' mediocre showing was due not only to Indian resistance—which took many forms, including the show of arms—but to the missions themselves. The poorest record belonged to the few tardy missionaries who attempted to preach the English gospel deep in Indian country, where the long arm of English law did not reach even in the eighteenth century. Unlike their Jesuit competitors who came early, stayed long, and strove to understand native ways before altering them, they persuaded none and alienated many with their ethnocentric ineptitude.[101] Only their brothers who worked among the remnant groups of New England enjoyed anything like success.

The English missionaries' performance was closely rivaled by that of the Indian schools, which were also few in number and short-lived. If consumption or smallpox did not carry the native students off prematurely, the racism of their English fellows and masters, the sedentary life of study, corporal punishment, homesickness, and an irrelevant curriculum soon drove them off. Perhaps those who graduated suffered the cruelest irony when they discovered that their polite education earned them no place in English society, where merit faced a color bar, and alienated them from their own. As an Iroquois council allegedly observed in rejecting an offer to send more of their sons to William and Mary, "after they returned to their Friends, they were absolutely good for nothing, being neither acquainted with the true methods of killing deer, catching Beaver or surprizing an enemy."[102] The major difficulty for Indian students was that they came to school too late and left too early, and received no social integration, racial tolerance, or love from the English. The passage from Indian to English culture was simply too long and too hard, and the English did little to make it any easier. The contrast with the Indian way of turning white captives into bona fide Indians could not have been starker.[103]

And yet during the colonial period many Indians did become Christians, both genuine and nominal, and adopted in some degree European ways. In New England alone, 91 praying towns were established before the Revolution, and 133 natives had qualified as teachers, catechists, or preachers to Indian congregations.[104] Many Algonquian and Iroquoian people were also persuaded that the Catholic, Anglican, Moravian, or Congregational faiths spoke more to their spiritual and cultural condition than did traditional religions.[105] How do we explain the existence and variety of these conversions while at the same time accounting for those Indian groups who remained stubbornly traditional?

Any explanation must begin with the continuous, longterm changes in native religion that occurred before the arrival of Columbus and his successors. As archaeology, folklore, and historical linguistics prove without question, no aspect of pre-Columbian Indian culture was static. Therefore we should resist the temptation to judge post-contact changes as either happy or tragic deviations from a noble norm of savage innocence. Purposeful change and adjustment was the only norm.

The first discernible changes occurred very early in the pre-contact period when native groups borrowed particular beliefs, myths, culture heroes, religious artifacts, ceremonies, and even whole cults from other groups, some at considerable distances via long-established trade routes. Through this continuous process of borrowing and transfer, tribes in contiguous culture areas, such as the northeastern woodlands, came to share a large number of religious traits.

The next round of changes took place in response to the bruited arrival of the Europeans in the period of proto- or indirect contact. Before they actually met any Europeans, many tribes encountered often fabulous stories of white "gods" or "spirits," some of the products of their awesome technology, and their selectively lethal diseases. When the invaders finally appeared in Indian villages, thereby inaugurating the period of direct contact, the crisis of intellect precipitated by rampant sickness and death, novel forms of magic, and the unknown was only exacerbated by the need to account for the existence of strange bearded men with white skins and barbarous tongues who were obviously not, like themselves, "original people."[106]

The Indians responded to this general crisis in a variety of ways, depending largely on their geographical and political distance from colonial authority, their economic independence, the health of their population and the succession of leadership, their strength relative to neighbors who may have become allied with the invaders, and their intellectual and emotional flexibility and morale, which was the product of their recent past experience.

Tribes who still enjoyed relatively healthy populations, stable social structures, and political and economic independence could choose to deal with the Christian missionary in at least four ways. They could, as many groups in New England did, direct a steady stream of searching questions at him about the consistency of his theology.[107] Or they could question its applicability to their culture by unleashing their polite but frustrating "secret weapon" of outer agreement and inner disagreement. On the other hand, if the proselytizer annoyed them enough, they could simply ignore him until he despaired and went home, or if he persisted, they could chase him away with arms or kill him as a troublemaker and witch. Whatever course of action they chose, the result was the persistence of traditional religion and the unimpaired authority of the native priest.

Sooner or later, all the eastern tribes began to lose their aboriginal sovereignty and strength. As colonial settlements drew closer, disease tore at the native social fabric, leaving gaps in the web of kinship, political succession, technological expertise, and corporate memory. Trade goods from the shops and factories of Europe became desirable luxuries, then necessities. Entangling alliances forced the tribes into the periodic embrace of the colonial governments when they could no longer play them off against each other. And missionaries were emboldened to plunge into native cantons in search of converts. In these dangerous though not yet fatal circumstances, the native community split into factions as different individuals and interest groups variously perceived the nature of the problems facing them and the best solutions. A dissident minority always had the option of voting with its feet, as was common in pre-Columbian times, by moving to either a more traditional village or a Christian praying town or *reserve*. More frequently, a faction stayed to fight for the political and social control of the community and its future religious and cultural direction.

Those who saw an urgent need to adjust to post-European conditions without surrendering their ethnic and cultural identity could exercise two options— if both existed. The first was to join a revitalization movement led by a native prophet or charismatic figure who warned the Indians to reaffirm their ancient beliefs and resume their ancient ways before the Europeans captured their spirits as well as their furs. Many of these leaders, such as the eighteenth-century

Delaware Prophet and Handsome Lake in the early nineteenth century, incorporated Christian elements in their religions while clearly rejecting Christianity itself. Many others, however, were intolerant of any foreign intrusions, seeking to restore their culture to an imagined pre-contact purity.[108]

A second option was also to revitalize native culture but through the selective use of Christianity rather than nativism. Tribes who escaped the worst maladies of European contact had little need of the full "civilized" cure offered by the Christian doctors. To have taken it would have brought on premature cultural suicide. But the complete prescription did contain some useful ingredients, such as political and military alliance, guaranteed land, economic aid, and trade advantages. If to obtain them the Indians had to swallow the bitter pill of religious conversion, the sacrifice was small enough, considering that Christianity might truly satisfy some new intellectual or emotional hunger. If there was none to be satisfied, the convert could simply, in time-honored Indian fashion, add the power of the Christian God to that of his own deities and proceed to syncretize the beliefs and practices of the new religion with the deep structures of her traditional faith. By accepting the Christian priest as the functional equivalent of a native shaman and by giving traditional meanings to Christian rites, dogmas, and deities, the Indians ensured the survival of native culture by taking on the protective coloration of the invaders' culture. Obviously, this brand of Christianity often lay very lightly on the surface of their lives, its acceptance largely expedient to ensure their independence and group identity. But many Indians found in Christianity genuine sources of spiritual strength that helped them cope with their rapidly changing world. As John Smith noticed very early, "all things that were able to do them hurt beyond their prevention, they adore with their kinde of divine worship."[109]

Several tribes who responded even more positively to the mission offerings were the coastal Algonquians of southern New England. So seriously were they crippled by a plague in 1616–18 and so thoroughly overrun by the colonial juggernaut in the following two decades that only John Eliot's complete system of moral rearmament, social reconstruction, and religious revitalization was capable of saving them from ethnic annihilation. Lacking any viable options, large numbers of them, led in many cases by traditional leaders of the "blood," converted to Christianity and the English way of life that accompanied it. Even though their conversion entailed wholesale cultural changes, it preserved their ethnic identity as particular Indian groups on familiar pieces of land that carried their inner history. At the cost of a certain amount of material and spiritual continuity with the past, their acceptance of Christianity—however sincere—allowed them not only to survive in the present but gave them a long lease on life when many of their colonial landlords threatened to foreclose all future options. Ironically, the acute English sense of cultural superiority—which was colored by racism before the eighteenth century—helped the Indians to maintain the crucial ethnic core at the heart of their newly acquired Christian personae. In colonial eyes, they were still Indians and always would be, no matter how "civilized" or Christianized they became. Despite the assimilative goal of the missions, the English had serious limitations as agents of social reconstruction. They were far better at "rooting out" than transplanting.

On any frontier, acculturation is a two-way process, especially in the early stages of contact. But in colonial North America the direction of religious change—unlike changes in other aspects of culture—was decidedly unilinear, largely because Indian religion was pragmatically incorporative and tolerant of other faiths, and Christianity was aggressively evangelical and exclusive. Indian religious culture was forever on the defensive, trying to minimize the adjustments necessary to group survival and independence; Christianity sought to cajole or strong-arm the natives into spiritual submission. Any changes in colonial religion were minor and self-generated, and not due to native pressure to convert to a False Face or Midéwiwin society. At most, the Indian presence sporadically brought out the evangelical inheritance of some of the colonial denominations and moved them marginally away from their own narrow brand of tribalism.

To be on the defensive, however, does not imply the total loss of initiative. The Indians were incredibly tenacious of their culture and life-style, but their traditionalism was neither blind nor passive. As the history of the missions clearly shows, the native peoples of the Northeast were remarkably resourceful in adjusting to new conditions, especially in using elements of European religious culture for their own purposes. According to the social and political circumstances in which they found themselves after contact, they accepted the missionaries' offerings in just the amounts necessary to maintain their own cultural identity. They may have made individual or short-term miscalculations of self-interest, white strength, and policy direction—no group is capable of a perfect functionalism—but in general they took what they needed for resistance and accepted only as much as would ensure survival. Because of their creative adaptability and the defects of the mission programs, many Indian people were never fully "washed white in the blood of the lamb." Although their outer lives could be partially "reduced to civility," their inner resources were equal to the invasion within. As long as native people continued to think of themselves as "original people," the religious frontiers of North America remained open.

SEVEN

DR. WHEELOCK'S LITTLE RED SCHOOL

Oh, E-le-a-zar Whee-lock was a ver-y pi-ous man;
He went in-to the wil-der-ness to teach the In-di-an.

RICHARD HOVEY, "ELEAZAR WHEELOCK"

To generations of Dartmouth men—and women—who have sung his praises, Eleazar Wheelock was the pious founder not only of their beautiful alma mater but of a venerable tradition of educational benevolence. Popular legend and collegial folklore tell us that Dartmouth was hewn out of the New Hampshire forest as an "Indian college" to convert the natives to Christianity and civilization. Although the Indian symbol of the college's origins came under attack in the 1970s and has been replaced by a color, the legend itself remains healthy. The stoic warrior who emblazoned Dartmouth sweat-shirts and beer mugs and braved frosty autumn afternoons bare-chested to cheer the football team is all but dead, the victim of a new generation of unstereotypical Indian students. But the college motto designed by Wheelock still features an aboriginal "voice crying in the wilderness" for the white man's brand of salvation.

Not surprisingly, the man who did the most to link Dartmouth with the Indians in our historical imagination was Wheelock himself. An indefatigable publicist and politician, he assured his friends and tried to persuade his enemies that his college in Hanover was nothing more than a noble continuation of his Indian school in Lebanon, Connecticut. To disarm the skeptical, he carefully worded the college charter to certify that Dartmouth was intended "for the education & instruction of Youth of the Indian Tribes in this Land in reading, writing & all parts of Learning which shall appear necessary and expedient for civilizing & christianizing Children of Pagans as well as in all liberal Arts and Sciences . . . ," to which he added, as if an afterthought, "and also of English Youth and any others."[1] The New Hampshire legislature, at least, was sufficiently convinced of the Doctor's sincerity to incorporate the college in 1769.

Nor has posterity questioned the official version of Dartmouth's founding, if numerous American histories are any index. Dartmouth usually appears in general textbooks in two places. The most frequent reference is to the Dartmouth College Case in 1819 when alumnus Daniel Webster argued successfully before the Supreme Court that the state of New Hampshire had no right to revoke the college charter and place Dartmouth under state jurisdiction. Few textbooks omit this landmark decision because it established judicial precedent for the protection of private corporations from the power of the state. The other place where Dartmouth appears is the section devoted to the "Great Awakening," that revival of puritanical religious feeling associated with Jonathan Edwards and George Whitefield that began in New England during the late 1730s and soon spread to the Middle Atlantic colonies. In this context Dartmouth always appears in the company of Brown and Princeton as a product of the denominational "College Enthusiasm," a "New Light" (as the revivalists were called) challenge to the spiritual torpor of Yale and especially Harvard. Invariably, the new college in Hanover is described as a direct "outgrowth" of Wheelock's Indian school in Connecticut. Even specialized studies of the Great Awakening perpetuate the legend of the "Indian School at Lebanon [which] was later moved to New Hampshire where it became Dartmouth College."[2]

The "Indian college" tradition has survived largely because it fails to distinguish between Wheelock's (actually Moor's) Indian Charity School and Dartmouth College. The Doctor *did* found and maintain a well-known school for Indians in Connecticut for some fifteen years. He *did* found a college in New Hampshire in 1769 that claimed to have Indian education as its primary focus. And he *did* move the Indian school to Hanover in 1770 to prepare boys for admission to Dartmouth. But the college and the school were always distinct, though Wheelock did little to discourage, and sometimes more than a little to foster, their identification. Only by untangling the histories of these two institutions can we establish Wheelock's true motives in founding Dartmouth and the aptness of the Indian as the college symbol.

According to his own recollection, Eleazar Wheelock was no Johnny-come-lately to Indian affairs. He told an Iroquois council in 1765 that he had had the Indians upon his heart "ever since I was a boy"—he had been born in Windham, Connecticut, in 1711—and that he had prayed daily for their temporal and spiritual salvation for the past thirty years.[3] But not until the Great Awakening did providence bring him his first native student.

After earning a bachelor's degree at Yale, Wheelock had been licensed to preach in 1734 and the following year was called to the pulpit of the Second Congregational Church in Lebanon. When the Great Awakening of religious fervor broke over New England in 1740, Wheelock was its warmest supporter in Connecticut. He traveled extensively, preached persuasively, and served as the chief intelligencer of revival news. But the religious establishment of the colony, the so-called "Old Lights," did not appreciate his itineracy, the neglect of his own parish, or his promulgation of "a meer *passionate* Religion." So in

1743 he was deprived of his church salary (though not his office) by the General Assembly act "for regulating abuses and correcting disorders in ecclesiastical affairs."[4]

Although Wheelock owned considerable farmland, the loss of his salary prompted him to take a few English boys into his house for college preparation. They were soon joined by Samson Occom, a young Mohegan Indian from New London, Connecticut, who came to Wheelock with the hope of improving his self-taught literacy in three or four weeks of tuition. As a leading "New Light," Wheelock saw an opportunity to extend the divine hand to New England's non-white pagans, and invited the twenty-year-old Indian to join his small group of students. Occom stayed nearly five years, in which time he became a devoted Christian, an affecting public speaker, and a partial convert to the English way of life. Despite his unusual accomplishments, however, there was no place for a man of his color in English society. He returned to a wigwam and spent the next twelve years in poverty, teaching and preaching to the Montauk Indians on Long Island, binding books, and carving spoons, pails, and gunstocks for his white neighbors, most of whom were his spiritual and intellectual inferiors.[5]

If Occom's postgraduate career did not speak well for the conceptual clarity of Wheelock's later design, the Doctor was unaware of it. In late 1754 he took two Delaware Indian boys under his wing, which prompted a charitable neighbor, Colonel Joshua More, to endow the fledgling school with several buildings and two acres of land. By the summer of 1761 "Moor's Charity School" had accepted ten Indian students from the "remnant" tribes of the northeastern seaboard. But with the fall of Canada a wide door was opened to the relatively uncontaminated "back nations" of America, and Wheelock entered it with a driving vision of tawny souls blanched by the Bible.

General James Wolfe's victory on the Plains of Abraham was well timed, for Wheelock was becoming increasingly disenchanted with the "little Tribes" of New England. Schools set among them, he felt, had always failed because the natives placed no value on the white man's "Learning," led an unsettled, impoverished existence, lacked any social or familial authority, and resented the English masters who tried to impose a "good and necessary Government" over their children.[6] Most damning of all in Wheelock's eyes was their stubborn ingratitude for the inestimable benefits offered by Protestant saints such as himself. It was simply foolish to waste God's time and the public's money on ingrates while there were "such Vast Numbers intirely without Means of Knowledge and"—he was assured by friends—"continually suing and pleading for Missionaries and Schoolmasters to be sent among them."[7] Turning his back on too-familiar local tribes, Wheelock was quickly captured by the unknown challenge of the Six Nations.

He did not have long to wait before confronting the challenge he had so blindly and blithely accepted. On August 1, 1761, three Mohawk boys sent by Sir William Johnson, the British superintendent of Indian affairs, arrived in

Samson Occom (1723–1792), the first Indian pupil of the Reverend Eleazar Wheelock, founder of Moor's Indian Charity School in Lebanon, Connecticut, and later of Dartmouth College. From a 1768 mezzotint. Courtesy of the Dartmouth College Library.

Lebanon with "great Caution and Fear." Each brought a horse, "prepared to return in haste, if there should be occasion."[8] One, Joseph Brant, understood a little English and, being the son of a "Family of Distinction," was "considerably cloathed."[9] But his teenaged companions, Negyes and Center, were nearly naked and "very lousey."[10] Neither could "speak a Word of English."[11] Center was visibly ill, his "blood spoiled" according to the local physician, so he was sent home to die. But not before swallowing the bitter pill of white prejudice. "I was very sorry," Wheelock wrote Johnson, "for the Jealousies which the [English] Schollars conceived concerning the Nature of Center's Disorder while I was gone to Boston, and that there was that said or done which gave him a Disgust."[12] Negyes, too, was soon lost to the cause, for when he accompanied Center home he was "captivated by a young Female and married."[13]

Less than four months later two Mohawk boys arrived to take their places, "direct from the wigwams." One had learned "4 or 5 letters in the Alphabet, the other knew not one, nor could either of them Speak a Word of English." Excepting "two old Blankets & Indian Stockins," their clothing "was not worth Sixpence." And as Wheelock had come to expect of such "poor little Naked Creatures," "they were very lousey, which occasioned considerable Trouble." Yet they were hardly typical schoolboys. Johannes had "carried a Gun" in the army that captured Montreal the previous year—at the age of twelve.[14]

A scant two weeks after their arrival, Wheelock penned a *cri de coeur* that might well stand as the motto of Moor's Charity School: "Few conceive aright of the Difficulty of Educating an Indian and turning him into an Englishman but those who undertake the Trial of it."[15] To the Reverend George Whitefield, who had the good sense not to try, he explained his predicament:

> They would soon kill themselves with Eating and Sloth, if constant care were not exercised for them at least the first year. They are used to set upon the Ground, and it is as natural for them as a seat to our Children. They are not wont to have any Cloaths but what they wear, nor will without much Pains be brought to take care of any. They are used to a Sordid Manner of Dress, and love it as well as our Children to be clean. They are not used to any Regular Government, the sad consequences of which you may a little guess at. They are used to live from Hand to Mouth (as we speak) and have no care for Futurity. They have never been used to the Furniture of an English House, and dont know but that a Wine-glass is as strong as an Hand Iron. Our Language when they seem to have got it is not their Mother Tongue and they cannot receive nor communicate in that as in their own ... And they are as unpolished and uncultivated within as without.[16]

Predictably, time and experience brought little relief, and Wheelock's list of headaches only grew. Before he moved the school to Hanover in 1770, he tried to turn some 67 native children—49 boys and 18 girls—into English men and women.[17] Many came from the New England tribes with a helpful modicum of English language, dress, and religion, but the largest number—thirty— were Iroquois, tough adolescents like Johannes and Negyes with an ingrained suspicion of the English and their schemes for "reducing" them to "civility." In his *Narrative* of the school to 1771, Wheelock boasted that he had produced forty "good readers, and writers," all sufficiently masters of English grammar and arithmetic and some advanced in Latin and Greek, who had behaved well in school and left with "fair and unblemished characters." But he also admitted that "I don't hear of more than half who have preserved their characters unstain'd either by a course of intemperance or uncleanness, or both; and some who on account of their parts, and learning, bid the fairest for usefulness, are sunk down into as low, savage, and brutish a manner of living as they were in before any endeavours were used with them to raise them up."[18] Six of the best were already dead.

If these twenty apostates are added to the twenty-seven matriculants who dropped out prematurely (most of whom were Iroquois), Moor's Charity School—on its own accounting—enjoyed a success rate in the *short* run of something less than thirty percent. Perhaps this figure fell within the range of Wheelock's expectations after his introduction to the Iroquois. In 1763 he told his public benefactors that "if one half of the Indian boys thus educated shall prove good and useful men, there will be no reason to regret our toil and expence for the whole . . . and if but one in ten does so, we shall have no cause to think much of the expence."[19] In all likelihood the public had somewhat higher hopes for their benefactions, as well they might at an annual cost of £16 to 20 per boy, the equivalent, some critics said, of that for an English boy at Harvard College.[20]

A satisfactory explanation for this inauspicious record is hard to find. Colonial critics suggested that the native students came too late and left too early, that the curriculum was inappropriate, and that the goal of civilizing the Indians before Christianizing them was unnecessary if not impossible in the first place. Wheelock's characteristic response was to lament the heartbreaking "Behavior of some I have taken unwearied pains for" and to turn his energies toward a less frustrating project.[21] Rather than redefine his objectives, he merely sought more malleable subjects. But of all people, the Indians—his students and their parents—had the best insights into the cause of Wheelock's failure, a failure magnified by the boundless ambition and unblinking certitude of his goals.

Like those of his Puritan predecessors, Wheelock's missionary goals were essentially two: to save the Indians from themselves and to save the English from the Indians. The best way to accomplish both was, as he stated so facilely, to turn the Indians into Englishmen. In religious terms one of the primary goals of nearly all the American colonies was the "enlargement of Christian Religion" and the "propagating of the gospel" (Protestant version) to the western hemisphere.[22] In Massachusetts, where Wheelock's great-grandfather landed in 1637, the settlers were enjoined in the royal charter to live such exemplary lives that their "orderlie conversation maie wynn and incite the natives of the country to the knowledge and obedience of the onlie true God and Savior of mankinde, and the Christian fayth."[23] The key word was obedience, as it was to be in all the English dealings with the natives. Unlike the king's patent, most of the colonial plans for Indian missions spoke of *re*ducing rather than *se*ducing Indians to "Civil Societie and Christian Religion."[24] The reason was simple—if you subscribed to the English cosmology. In English eyes the Indians were "savages," beings closer to "brutes" than to true "men," whose unbridled impulses needed to be tamed by God's chosen people.[25]

From such premises it was obvious to "the most sensible Writers" of Wheelock's day that "it is necessary to civilize Savages before they can be converted to Christianity."[26] With fitting medical metaphor, the Doctor said that his educational goal was to "cure the Natives . . . of their Savage Temper" and to "purge all the Indian out" of his students.[27] Even a casual acquaintance with eighteenth-century medical practices will convey the full rigor of the treatment implied. Yet the medicine, however caustic, was administered in the patients' best interests. Without a strong purgative to rid the Indians of their "savage" disorders, their body politic would not absorb the "civilized" antidote to the white man's contaminants—alcohol and land greed. Only a settled agricultural life like that of the English colonists could guarantee the Indians' subsistence "when their Resources from the Wilderness fail, (as they certainly must do, when, and so fast, as the English extend their Settlements among them)."[28] And time was running out, especially for the obstinate Iroquois. "They evidently appear to be in, and very far gone already by, a quick consumption," wrote Wheelock in 1771, "they are wasting like a morning dew . . . before the rising sun."[29]

If the "savages" could be saved from themselves, the English would also be saved from the "savages"—and could turn a pretty penny in the bargain. For anglicized Indians would no longer threaten the English frontiers, which could then be greatly extended westward. Wheelock and his colleagues were convinced that missions and schools for the Indians were far more effective and far less expensive instruments of colonial policy than guns, armies, and gifts. If the missions had worked as well in practice as they did on paper, they would have been right. "Nothing can be more Agreeable to our Christian Character than to send the Gospel to the benighted Pagans," a like-minded friend wrote Wheelock, "Nothing more Conducive to our Civil Interests than to bring them to a Subjection to the Religion of Jesus."[30] "Civilizing the Indians" was tantamount to "reducing them to Peace and good Order," according to the mission litany, and only by "being civilized, and taught the Knowledge of the only true GOD and SAVIOR" could they be made "good Members of Society, and peaceable and quiet Neighbours."[31] But either way the English stood to gain. "For if [the Indians] receive the gospel," admitted Wheelock, "they will soon betake themselves to agriculture for their support, and so will need but a very small part, comparatively, of the lands which they now claim . . . ; and if they will not receive the gospel, they will, as they have done, waste away before it. . . . "[32]

Wheelock's way of winning the Indians to Christian civility was to induce native children, usually aged eleven to fourteen, to come to his school in Connecticut, far removed from the "pernicious Influence of their Parents Example."[33] There he proceeded to inure them to "Decency and Cleanliness" in the form of soap and water, English clothes, and, of course, the critical difference between handirons and wineglasses.[34] In an atmosphere of beetle-browed piety, they were initiated into the arcana of the Westminster Assembly's *Shorter Catechism*, the English alphabet and grammar, arithmetic, and, in still more abstruse languages, the pastoral classics of ancient Greece and Rome. Since they were designed to return to their own villages as preachers, teachers, and interpreters of the English way, they were encouraged to retain their native languages and to teach them as well to their fellow students—Indians from other tribes and English boys preparing for Indian missions. Their spare time was "improved" by learning a trade, such as blacksmithing, from a local master or "husbandry" from the hands on Wheelock's farm. Native girls were apprenticed to local women to learn "the Female Part, as House-wives, School-mistresses, [and] Tayloresses" whereby they, as the helpmates of the native missionaries, would prevent "their turning savage in their Manner of Living, for want of those who may do those Offices for them."[35] Over all, Wheelock sought to spread a benevolent but firm patriarchalism, to treat them as "My [own] Children" and to make them feel at home as "in a Father's House."[36] What the Indians, especially the Iroquois, soon discovered, however, was that English children were treated much differently from children in the longhouse.

One of the reasons, perhaps the main reason, Wheelock preferred to locate his school among the English was that he knew the Indians' "great Fondness for their Children" was incompatible with the birchen "Government" necessary to "humble them, and reform their Manners."[37] "Here," he admitted, "I can correct, & punish them as I please, . . . but there, it will not be born."[38] When in 1772 the Onondaga council rejected for the last time Wheelock's offer to educate their children, they condemned ten years of hard usage of Iroquois children at the hands of his self-fulfilling prophecy. Grabbing Wheelock's high-handed son Ralph by the shoulder and shaking him, the council speaker replied with unaccustomed anger: "Brother, do you think we are altogether ignorant of your methods of instruction? . . . We understand not only your speech, but your *manner* of teaching Indian[s]. . . . Brother, take care," he warned, "you were too hasty, & strong in your manner of speaking, before the children & boys have any knowledge of your language." And then in a verbal slap that must have stung the Wheelocks' Protestant souls to the quick, he concluded: "Brother, you must learn of the French ministers if you would understand, & know how to treat Indians. They don't speak roughly, nor do they for every little mistake take up a club & flog them."[39]

The sting of the rod was perhaps the sharpest indignity the Indians suffered, but it was not the only one nor the worst. The school's work program, aimed at teaching the boys in play time to farm, seemed to the boys little more than an elaborate ruse for getting the master's chores done at no expense. Wheelock hoped that part-time farm work would "effectually remove the deep prejudices, so universally in the minds of the Indians, against their men's cultivating lands."[40] Instead, it seemed to confirm them and to create new ones against the Doctor for taking advantage of his students. Long was Wheelock's list of Indian students who were "reluctant to exercise [themselves] in, or learn any thing about Husbandry."[41] Only slightly shorter was the roster of complaining students and parents. John Daniel, a Narragansett parent, told Wheelock that "I always tho't Your School was free to the Natives; not to learn them how to Farm it, but to advance in Christian Knowledge, which wear the Chief motive that caus'd me to send my Son Charles to you; not that I'm anything against his Labouring some for You, when Business lies heavy on you," he allowed, "but to work two Years to learn to Farm it, is what I don't consent to. . . . "[42] The Onondaga council simply made it clear that they expected their children to be treated "as *children* at your house, & not *servants!*"[43] But the last word came from Daniel Simon, a Narragansett and later Dartmouth's first Indian graduate (1777): "if we poor Indians Shall work as much as to pay for our learning," he told Wheelock, "we Can go some other place as good as here for learning."[44]

When Hezekiah Calvin, a Delaware and one of Wheelock's former school-masters to the Iroquois, opted out of the Doctor's "Design" in 1768, he let it be known around New England that the inmates of Moor's School were not one big happy family. A Rhode Island correspondent told Wheelock that Calvin had "given the School a bad Charracter," complaining (among other things) that "you use the Indians very hard in keeping of them to work, & not allowing them a proper Privelidge in the School, that you . . . Diot & Cloath them with that that's mean, . . . That Mary [Secutor, a Narragansett] ask'd for a small peice of Cloth to make a p[ai]r of Slippers, which you would not allow her, [saying] twas to[o] good for Indians &c . . . [and] That you wont give no more of the Indians more learning than to Read, & Write—[alleging] 'twill make them Impudent; for which they are all about to leave you."[45]

Regardless of the accuracy of these criticisms, many of the Indians and their tribesmen *felt* them to be true. What was not in doubt, however, was that the Indian students were surrounded on every side by overt prejudice that often exceeded cultural arrogance and fell clearly into the category of racism. Wheelock instinctively knew that native students could never be mixed with English (except those special few who were preparing for Indian missions), "for it hath been found by some few Instances of *Indians* educated elsewhere, that the *English* Students have been apt to look upon them with an Air of *disdain*, which these Sons of *ranging* Liberty cannot so well brook."[46] For this reason even Yale, his alma mater, was inappropriate for his Indian graduates; too many sons of Eli would "disdain in their Hearts to be Associates and Companions with an Indian. And what the Consequences of such Contempt of them will be is not hard to guess."[47]

The problem could also be found closer to home. Wheelock had great difficulty in apprenticing his Indian boys because "their fellow Prentices viz. English Boys will dispise them & treat them as Slaves."[48] In 1765 David

Fowler, an older Montauk student, received such an "injury" and "provocations" from the Lebanon townies in a sleighing incident that his mentor was somewhat surprised that his new "Christian forebearance" overcame his native spirit of revenge.[49] Even a young minister turned down Wheelock's offer of an Indian mission because, he said, "[I] should be prodigiously apt to batter some of their Noses, or else Skulk and run for it."[50]

The pestilence of racism, however, infected all of New England, especially during the Seven Years' War and the Indian "rebellion" that concluded it. Wheelock could not raise funds for the school because his potential donors in the colonial legislatures and churches "breath[ed] forth nothing towards [the Indians] but Slaughter & destruction."[51] A collection plate passed in Windsor, Connecticut, in 1763 returned empty save for "a Bullet & Flynt," symbolizing an attitude that survived in Wheelock's own colony long after the frontier hostilities had ceased.[52] Four years later the table conversation of several gentlemen in Middletown was reported to Wheelock, and it could not have pleased—or much surprised—him. They spoke frankly of the hopelessness of converting Indians by anything but "Powder & Ball." On the basis of a wide acquaintance with "human nature," at least as he knew it in New England, one of them declared the Doctor's scheme "absurd & fruitlis" because of "the ireconsilable avertion, that white people must ever have to black. . . . So long as the Indians are dispised by the English we may never expect success in Christianizing of them." For their own parts, the gentlemen confessed that "they could never respect an Indian, Christian or no Christian, so as to put him on a level with white people on any account, especially to eat at the same Table, no—not with Mr [Samson] Ocham himself, be he ever so much a Christian or ever so Learned."[53] As the cultural competition of the seventeenth century gave way to the racial antipathies of the eighteenth, popular support in America for "Grand Designs" such as Wheelock's evaporated.

There was a slim chance that the Indian students could have withstood the corrosive currents of popular prejudice that swirled about them if Wheelock had shown some sensitivity to their cultural dilemma and sustained his originally high sense of their purpose. Unfortunately he did not, for his cultural and theological assumptions were as ethnocentric and racist as those of his neighbors, and the Indians were quickly reduced to a secondary role in their own salvation. If he was not before, the Great Awakening turned Wheelock into a seventeenth-century religious Puritan. For the misnamed "New Lights" of the revival, the religious premises of the old covenant theology acquired renewed relevance. Basic to that theology was a dim view of human nature, which had been corrupted at the source by Adam's fall, and a belief that the original sin, pride, must be constantly crushed in man to allow God's omnipotent will full sway. That in Wheelock's eyes the Indians were the proudest people on earth did nothing to make their life in Moor's School an easy one.

Of all the sins committed by his Indian students, none so angered Wheelock as "Insufferable pride," which he felt to be the foundation of their "Contempt of all Authority," particularly his own.[54] When Jacob Woolley, a twenty-year-old Delaware, got drunk, threw a clench-fisted tantrum, cursed God, and tried to throw his bed out the window, Wheelock judged him not culturally disoriented or personally frustrated but simply guilty of "Pride of Heart," and administered several stripes to "humble & tame him."[55] When he ran away to the Mohegans five months later, Wheelock presented him with an "Indian Blanket" because he had renounced his "polite education" and "herded with Indians (little better than Savages)." A clerical correspondent agreed that this was a "mortification" more "humbling" than blows or stripes, and added his hope to Wheelock's that "God will yet humble him."[56] In such an atmosphere it was inevitable that Wheelock's need to dominate absolutely would collide with the sons of the Mohawks, who were, he complained, "proud and high in their own Esteem above any other Tribe, having long been reckon[e]d at the head of the Nations."[57] In 1767 he rusticated two Mohawk youths, though, understandably, not without some misgivings. "Great William," the natural son of Sir William Johnson by an Indian woman, had been "too proud, & litigious to consist with the Health & well being" of the school. His traveling companion, who had been at the school only a few months, was "so lifted up with his having been in the Wars, and sent to Hell one or two of the poor Savages with his own hand, that [Wheelock's] House was scarcely good enough for him to live in, or any of the School honourable enough to speak to him. . . . There is," the Doctor told Sir William, "& shall be Government in this School."[58]

At the root of Wheelock's unhappy relations with his Indian students was a racial attitude that placed Indians on a level with blacks—on the lowest shelf of humanity. Like many of his contemporaries, Wheelock frequently referred to his "Black" children, especially his "black son" Samson Occom, and to the "Black Tribes" on the frontier who needed his help, a verbal preference that was not lost on his students.[59] Just the way they wrote to him, even as adults, betrays how they must have been treated and taught to think of themselves in his presence. Joseph Johnson must have been taught well. On one occasion he referred to himself as "a Despicable Lump of polluted Clay, as is inclosed in this tawny skin of mine," on another as "your Ignorant Pupil, and good for nothing Black Indian." "If I was an Englishman, & was thus Respected by you," he wrote, "I should be very thankful, but much more doth it now become me, being an Indian, to be humble & very thankfull in very deed." Though Johnson was a Mohegan, he sought temporary relief from his educated self-abasement among the Oneidas in 1768 when "he turn'd pagan for about a week—painted, sung, danc'd, drank & whor'd it, with some of the savage Indians he could find."[60] Hezekiah Calvin, the Delaware drop-out, may have chosen an even apter symbol of protest: he is last seen in prison for "forging a pass for a Negro."[61] As an owner of black slaves for much of his life, Wheelock was perfectly capable of distinguishing the two races; that he did not suggests an unconscious reduction of the people he was consciously trying to elevate and a deep ambivalence about his "Grand Design."

Wheelock's innate distrust of the Indians worked to the surface during the course of the 1760s. Originally he felt that Indian missionaries were superior to Englishmen and gave a dozen reasons in his first *Narrative* (1763). Yet as early as 1760 he was planning to take "poor & promising [English] Youth" into the school "in case of a failure of Indians."[62] By the time the first Iroquois arrived he was no longer talking privately of Indians as schoolmasters, interpreters, *and* missionaries—only of the first two. He was obviously lowering his sights. In 1762 he had his revised plans confirmed by the Boston Board of the Scottish Society that funded much of his work. "If the Design is to Educate only a few that shall be qualified, to be Missionaries, Schoolmasters &c," they wrote, "We Apprehend Indians will not be so proper for these Purposes, as Persons Selected from Among the English."[63] After several frustrating years with his Iroquois students, the Doctor needed only an excuse to complete his institutional shift to white missionaries.

In the winter of 1769 the Oneidas provided one by abruptly withdrawing their six children. They gave Wheelock an innocuous reason, but he suspected two others: that "an ugly fellow" had spread "Slanders" that "their Children were not well treated" at school, and that, having heard a rumor of an impending Indian war with the colonies, they were "not willing their children should be with the English [as hostages] at such a time."[64] Whatever their reasons, Wheelock considered their action providential; he sent the other Iroquois students home and prepared to move to Hanover to found a college for English missionaries. God, he told his English benefactors, had convinced him that "Indians may not have the lead in the Affair, 'till they are made new Creatures." Their "Sloth," "want of Stability," and "doleful Apostacy" disqualified them.[65]

In the future, after the Indian school was transplanted in less fertile New Hampshire soil, Wheelock would prefer native students from the "praying towns" or Indian *reserves* of Canada—St. Francis, Lorette, Caughnawaga— who were descended from adopted English captives, even though most had been raised as Catholics. "Though they were born among the *Indians*," he wrote, "and have been exposed to partake of their national Vices . . . ; yet they appear to be as sprightly, active, enterprising, benevolent towards all, and sensible of Kindnesses done them, as English Children commonly are."[66] His racial preference was unmistakable, as was his characteristic feeling that the "other" Indians, just over the horizon, were always more susceptible to his designs. These Anglo-Indians, he vowed, were "by far the most promising set of Youths, I have ever yet had from the Indian Country."[67] How quickly he had forgotten his words to Sir William Johnson only a few years before: "The Boys I have from your parts behave very well, better than any I have had from any other Quarter, and it seems to me they are really a much better Breed."[68] Apparently the Doctor wished to begin his experiment in cultural transmogrification with subjects who resembled as nearly as possible his desired results. With the unpromising methods and attitudes he employed, that was perhaps the only way to ensure success.

Wheelock's self-confessed failure to produce a cadre of native missionaries made in his own image met with a timely remedy in 1767 upon the return of Samson Occom and the Reverend Nathaniel Whitaker from a fund-raising tour of England and Scotland. Sent by Wheelock to procure donations for his Indian school, the pair raised more than £12,000 during their two-year sojourn.[69] This enormous windfall enabled Wheelock to sever all ties with the missionary societies upon which he had long depended and to begin a serious search for a way to subordinate his involvement in the unrewarding "Indian business" to a project that gave more scope to his energy, political acumen, and need to dominate. He found such an outlet in Dartmouth, a liberal arts *college* intended primarily for English missionaries that borrowed the name of the *school's* ranking English benefactor, the Earl of Dartmouth.

But the idea of founding such a college was not new to Wheelock; the British donations only made it possible for the first time. As early as 1761 Wheelock had begun to cast his eye around the Northeast for a college site. His heart was initially set on the rich farmlands of Iroquois country, "near the Bowells of the Pagan Settlements," where he thought fifteen to twenty square miles would suffice to plant a model Christian community, including a school for Indians and a college for English missionaries.[70] When it became clear that the Iroquois and their Anglican protector, Sir William Johnson, would never countenance an invasion of grasping, grim-lipped New England Congregationalists, Wheelock considered other sites in Ohio, New York, Pennsylvania, and most of the New England colonies before accepting Hanover's offer of land and capital. In that day as in ours, colleges were economic boons to their towns, and Dartmouth simply went to the highest bidder. Wheelock now had the makings of an institution equal to his ambitions and the opportunity to delegate his waning interest in the schooling of Indians. Moor's Charity School continued to admit Indians after the move to New Hampshire, but with increasing admixtures of English students. The dilution of its original purpose and the lengthening shadow of the college finally closed its doors in 1829.

The subordination of the Indians in Wheelock's new design for Dartmouth College was symbolized nowhere better than in his first draft of its charter. Dartmouth was being founded, Wheelock wrote, to educate "Youths of *the English* and also of the Indian Tribes in this Land in reading, writing & all . . . liberal Arts and Sciences." Then he remembered that several thousand British benefactors had given thousands of pounds to a charity school primarily for Indians, not white colonists, and he scratched out the reference to English youth and added it at the end of the passage as if to indicate their subordinate position in his design.[71] In its revised form the charter became New Hampshire law, and Doctor—now President—Wheelock proceeded to exhaust his ample treasury—over the protests of his English trustees—on a liberal arts college that graduated only three Indians in the eighteenth century and eight in the nineteenth.[72]

Eleazar Wheelock (1711–1779), the minister of Lebanon, Connecticut, founded Moor's Charity School for Indians in 1754 and in 1769, after repeated frustrations in the "Indian business," Dartmouth College for young English men. The rich carpet and appointments of his college study aptly symbolize the Doctor's turn from the small rewards of Indian education. Courtesy of the Dartmouth College Library.

But not everyone was fooled by the Doctor's legerdemain, least of all his "black Son," Samson Occom. With the frank shrewdness he had shown all his troubled life in his dealings with the English, Occom told his mentor, "your having so many White Scholars and so few or no Indian Scholars, gives me great Discouragement. . . . I am very jealous that instead of your Semenary

Becoming alma Mater, she will be too alba mater [white mother] to Suckle the Tawnees, for She is already adorned up too much like the Popish Virgin Mary." In short, he accused, "your present Plan is not calculated to benefit the poor Indians."[73]

President Wheelock did not have to be told.

EIGHT

THE WHITE INDIANS

The English, like their French rivals, began their colonizing ventures in North America with a sincere interest in converting the Indians to Christianity and civilization. Nearly all the colonial charters granted by the English monarchs in the seventeenth century assigned the wish to extend the Christian Church and to redeem savage souls as a principal, if not *the* principal, motive for colonization.[1] This desire was grounded in a set of complementary beliefs about "savagism" and "civilization." First, the English held that the Indians, however benighted, were capable of conversion. "It is not the nature of men," they believed, "but the education of men, which make them barbarous and uncivill."[2] Moreover, the English were confident that the Indians would want to be converted once they were exposed to the superior quality of English life. The strength of these beliefs was reflected in Cotton Mather's astonishment as late as 1721 that

> Tho' they saw a People Arrive among them, who were Clothed in *Habits* of much more Comfort and Splendour, than what there was to be seen in the *Rough Skins* with which they hardly covered themselves; and who had *Houses full of Good Things,* vastly out-shining their squalid and dark *Wigwams;* And they saw this People Replenishing their *Fields,* with *Trees* and with *Grains,* and useful *Animals,* which until now they had been wholly Strangers to; yet they did not seem touch'd in the least, with any *Ambition* to come at such Desirable Circumstances, or with any *Curiosity* to enquire after the *Religion* that was attended with them.[3]

The second article of the English faith followed from their fundamental belief in the superiority of civilization, namely, that no civilized person in possession of his faculties or free from undue restraint would choose to become an Indian. "For, easy and unconstrained as the savage life is," wrote the Reverend William Smith of Philadelphia, "certainly it could never be put in competition with the blessings of improved life and the light of religion, by any persons who have had the happiness of enjoying, and the capacity of discerning, them."[4]

And yet, by the close of the colonial period, very few if any Indians had been transformed into civilized Englishmen. Most of the Indians who were educated by the English—some contemporaries thought *all* of them—returned to Indian society at the first opportunity to resume their Indian identities. On the other hand, large numbers of Englishmen had chosen to become Indians—by running away from colonial society to join Indian society, by not trying to escape after being captured, or by electing to remain with their Indian captors when treaties of peace periodically afforded them the opportunity to return home.[5]

Perhaps the first colonist to recognize the disparity between the English dream and the American reality was Cadwallader Colden, surveyor-general and member of the king's council of New York. In his *History of the Five Indian Nations of Canada*, published in London in 1747, Colden described the Albany peace treaty between the French and the Iroquois in 1699, when "few of [the French captives] could be persuaded to return" to Canada. Lest his readers attribute this unusual behavior to "the Hardships they had endured in their own Country, under a tyrannical Government and a barren Soil," he quickly added that "the *English* had as much Difficulty to persuade the People, that had been taken Prisoners by the *French Indians*, to leave the *Indian* Manner of living, though no People enjoy more Liberty, and live in greater Plenty, than the common Inhabitants of *New-York* do." Colden, clearly amazed, elaborated:

> No Arguments, no Intreaties, nor Tears of their Friends and Relations, could persuade many of them to leave their new *Indian* Friends and Acquaintance[s]; several of them that were by the Caressings of their Relations persuaded to come Home, in a little Time grew tired of our Manner of living, and run away again to the *Indians*, and ended their Days with them. On the other Hand, *Indian* Children have been carefully educated among the *English*, cloathed and taught, yet, I think, there is not one Instance, that any of these, after they had Liberty to go among their own People, and were come to Age, would remain with the *English*, but returned to their own Nations, and became as fond of the *Indian* Manner of Life as those that knew nothing of a civilized Manner of living. What I now tell of Christian Prisoners among *Indians* [he concluded his history], relates not only to what happened at the Conclusion of this War, but has been found true on many other Occasions.[6]

Colden was not alone. Six years later Benjamin Franklin wondered how it was that

> When an Indian Child has been brought up among us, taught our language and habituated to our Customs, yet if he goes to see his relations and make one Indian Ramble with them, there is no perswading him ever to return. [But] when white persons of either sex have been taken prisoners young by the Indians, and lived a while among them, tho' ransomed by their Friends, and treated with all imaginable tenderness to prevail with them to stay among the English, yet in a Short time

Colonel Henry Bouquet defeated the "Ohio Indians" at Bushy Run in 1763. The following year he demanded the return of all white captives and any children they had had by Indian spouses. Most of the captives, especially young children who had become totally assimilated, returned to English society with great reluctance. From [William Smith, D.D.], *An Historical Account of the Expedition against the Ohio Indians, in the Year MDCCLXIV* ... (Philadelphia, 1765; reprinted London, 1766), engraving by Benjamin West.

they become disgusted with our manner of life, and the care and pains that are necessary to support it, and take the first good Opportunity of escaping again into the Woods, from whence there is no reclaiming them.[7]

In short, "thousands of Europeans are Indians," as Hector de Crèvecoeur put it, "and we have no examples of even one of those Aborigines having from choice become Europeans!"[8]

The English captives who foiled their countrymen's civilized assumptions by becoming Indians differed little from the general colonial population when they were captured. They were ordinary men, women, and children of yeoman stock, Protestants by faith, a variety of nationalities by birth, English by law, different from their countrymen only in their willingness to risk personal insecurity for the economic opportunities of the frontier.[9] There was no discernible characteristic or pattern of characteristics that differentiated them from their captive neighbors who eventually rejected Indian life—with one exception. Most of the colonists captured by the Indians and adopted into Indian families were children of both sexes and young women, often the mothers of the captive children. They were, as one captivity narrative observed, the "weak and defenceless."[10]

The pattern of taking women and children for adoption was consistent throughout the colonial period, but during the first century and one-half of Indian-white conflict, primarily in New England, it coexisted with a larger pattern of captivity that included all white colonists, men as well as women and children. The Canadian Indians who raided New England tended to take captives more for their ransom value than for adoption. When Mrs. James Johnson gave birth to a daughter on the trail to Canada, for example, her captor looked into her makeshift lean-to and "clapped his hands with joy, crying two monies for me, two monies for me." Although the New England legislatures occasionally tried to forbid the use of public moneys for "the Ransoming of Captives," thereby prolonging the Indians' "diabolical kidnapping mode of warfare," ransoms were constantly paid from both public and private funds. These payments became larger as inflation and the Indians' savvy increased. Thus when John and Tamsen Tibbetts redeemed two of their children from the Canadian Indians in 1729, it cost them £105 10s. (1,270 livres). "Being verry Poore," many families in similar situations could ill afford to pay such high premiums even "if they should sell all they have in the world."[11]

When the long peace in the Middle Atlantic colonies collapsed in 1753, the Indians of Pennsylvania, southern New York, and the Ohio country had no Quebec or Montreal in which to sell their human chattels to compassionate French families or anxious English relatives.[12] For this and other reasons they captured English settlers largely to replace members of their own families who had died, often from English musketballs or imported diseases.[13] Consequently, women and children—the "weak and defenceless"—were the prime targets of Indian raids.

According to the pattern of warfare in the Pennsylvania theater, the Indians usually stopped at a French fort with their prisoners before proceeding to their own villages. A young French soldier captured by the English reported that at Fort Duquesne there were "a great number of English Prisoners," the older of whom "they are constantly sending . . . away to Montreal" as prisoners of war, "but that the Indians keep many of the Prisoners amongst them, chiefly young People whom they adopt and bring up in their own way." His intelligence was corroborated by Barbara Leininger and Marie LeRoy, who had been members of a party of two adults and eight children captured in 1755 and taken to Fort Duquesne. There they saw "many other Women and Children, they think an hundred who were carried away from the several provinces of P[ennsylvania] M[aryland] and V[irginia]." When the girls escaped from captivity three years later, they wrote a narrative in German chiefly to acquaint "the inhabitants of this country . . . with the names and circumstances of those prisoners whom we met, at the various places where we were, in the course of our captivity." Of the fifty-two prisoners they had seen, thirty-four were children and fourteen were women, including six mothers with children of their own.[14]

The close of hostilities in Pennsylvania came in 1764 after Col. Henry Bouquet defeated the Indians near Bushy Run and imposed peace. By the articles of agreement reached in October, the Delawares, Shawnees, and Senecas were to deliver up "all the Prisoners in [their] Possession, without any Exception, Englishmen, Frenchmen, Women, and Children, whether adopted in your Tribes, married, or living amongst you, under any Denomination, or Pretence whatever." In the weeks that followed, Bouquet's troops, including "the Relations of [some of] the People [the Indians] have Massacred, or taken Prisoners," encamped on the Muskingum in the heart of the Ohio country to collect the captives. After as many as nine years with the Indians, during which time many children had grown up, 81 "men" and 126 "women and children" were returned. At the same time, a list was prepared of 88 prisoners who still remained in Shawnee towns to the west: 70 were classified as "women and children." Six months later, 44 of these prisoners were delivered up to Fort Pitt. When they were captured, all but 4 had been less than sixteen years old, while 37 had been less than eleven years old.[15]

The Indians obviously chose their captives carefully so as to maximize the chances of acculturating them to Indian life. To judge by the results, their methods were hard to fault. Even when the English held the upper hand militarily, they were often embarrassed by the Indians' educational power. On November 12, 1764, at his camp on the Muskingum, Bouquet lectured the Shawnees who had not delivered all their captives: "As you are now going to Collect all our *Flesh,* and *Blood,* . . . I desire that you will use them with Tenderness, and look upon them as Brothers, and no longer as Captives." The utter gratuitousness of his remark was reflected—no doubt purposely—in the Shawnee speech when the Indians delivered their captives the following spring at Fort Pitt. "Father— Here is your *Flesh,* and *Blood* . . . they have been all tied to us by Adoption, although we now deliver them up to you. We will always look upon them as Relations, whenever the *Great Spirit* is pleased that we may visit them . . . Father—we have taken as much Care of these Prisoners, as if they were [our] own Flesh, and blood; they are become unacquainted with your Customs, and manners, and therefore, Father we request you will use them tender, and kindly, which will be a means of inducing them to live contentedly with you."[16]

The Indians spoke the truth and the English knew it. Three days after his speech to the Shawnees, Bouquet had advised Lt.-Gov. Francis Fauquier of Virginia that the returning captives "ought to be treated by their Relations with Tenderness and Humanity, till Time and Reason make them forget their unnatural Attachments, but unless they are closely watch'd," he admitted, "they will certainly return to the Barbarians."[17] And indeed they would have, for during a half-century of conflict captives had been returned who, like many of the Ohio prisoners, responded only to Indian names, spoke only Indian dialects, felt comfortable only in Indian clothes, and in general regarded their white saviors as barbarians and their deliverance as captivity. Had they not been compelled to return to English society by militarily enforced peace treaties, the ranks of the white Indians would have been greatly enlarged.

From the moment the Indians surrendered their English prisoners, the colonists faced a series of difficult problems. The first was the problem of getting the prisoners to remain with the English. When Bouquet sent the first group of restored captives to Fort Pitt, he ordered his officers there that "they are to be closely watched and well Secured" because "most of them, particularly those who have been a long time among the Indians, will take the first Opportunity to run away." The young children especially were "so completely savage that they were brought to the camp tied hand and foot." Fourteen-year-old John McCullough, who had lived with the Indians for "eight years, four months, and sixteen days" (by his parents' reckoning), had his legs tied "under the horses belly" and his arms tied behind his back with his father's garters, but to no avail. He escaped under the cover of night and returned to his Indian family for a year before he was finally carried to Fort Pitt under "strong guard." "Having been accustomed to look upon the Indians as the only connexions they had, having been tenderly treated by them, and speaking their language," explained the Reverend William Smith, the historian of Bouquet's expedition, "it is no wonder that [the children] considered their new state in the light of a captivity, and parted from the savages with tears."[18]

Children were not the only reluctant freedmen. "Several women eloped in the night, and ran off to join their Indian friends." Among them undoubtedly were some of the English women who had married Indian men and borne them children, and then had been forced by the English victory either to return with their mixed-blood children to a country of strangers, full of prejudice against Indians, or to risk escaping under English guns to their husbands and adopted culture. For Bouquet had "reduced the Shawanese and Delawares etc. to the most Humiliating Terms of Peace," boasted Gen. Thomas Gage. "He has Obliged them to deliver up even their Own Children born of white women." But even the victorious soldier could understand the dilemma into which these women had been pushed. When Bouquet was informed that the English wife of an Indian chief had eloped in the night with her husband and children, he "requested that no pursuit should be made, as she was happier with her Chief than she would be if restored to her home."[19]

Although most of the returned captives did not try to escape, the emotional torment caused by the separation from their adopted families deeply impressed the colonists. The Indians "delivered up their beloved captives with the utmost reluctance; shed torrents of tears over them, recommending them to the care and protection of the commanding officer." One young woman "cryed and roared when asked to come and begged to Stay a little longer." "Some, who could not make their escape, clung to their savage acquaintance at parting, and continued many days in bitter lamentations, even refusing sustenance." Children "cried as if they should die when they were presented to us." With only small exaggeration an observer on the Muskingum could report that "every captive left the Indians with regret."[20]

Another problem encountered by the English was the difficulty of communicating with the returned captives, a great many of whom had replaced their knowledge of English with an Algonquian or Iroquoian dialect and their baptismal names with Indian or hybrid ones.[21] This immediately raised another problem—that of restoring the captives to their relatives. Sir William Johnson, the superintendent of Indian affairs, "thought it best to advertise them [in the newspapers] immediately, but I believe it will be very difficult to find the Freinds of some of them, as they are ignorant of their own Names, or former places of abode, nay cant speak a word of any language but Indian." The only recourse the English had in such instances was to describe them "more particularly . . . as to their features, Complexion etc. That by the Publication of Such descriptions their Relations, parents or friends may hereafter know and Claim them."[22]

But if several colonial observers were right, a description of the captives' physiognomy was of little help after they had been with the Indians for any length of time. Peter Kalm's foreign eye found it difficult to distinguish European captives from their captors, "except by their color, which is somewhat whiter than that of the Indians," but many colonists could see little or no difference. To his Maine neighbors twelve-year-old John Durell "ever after [his two-year captivity] appeared more like an Indian than a white man." So did John Tarbell. After thirty years among the Indians in Canada, he made a visit to his relatives in Groton "in his Indian dress and with his Indian complexion (for by means of grease and paints but little difference could be discerned)." When O. M. Spencer returned after only eight months with the Shawnees, he was greeted with a newspaper allusion "to [his] looks and manners, as slightly resembling the Indians" and by a gaggle of visitors who exclaimed "in an under tone, 'How much he looks like an Indian!'" Such evidence reinforced the environmentalism of the time, which held that white men "who have incorporated themselves with any of [the Indian] tribes" soon acquire "a great resemblance to the savages, not only in their manners, but in their colour and the expression of the countenance."[23]

The final English problem was perhaps the most embarrassing in its manifestations, and certainly was so in its implications. For many Indians who had adopted white captives, the return of their "own Flesh, and Blood" to the English was unendurable. At the earliest opportunity, after bitter memories of the wars had faded on both sides, they journeyed through the English settlements to visit their estranged children, just as the Shawnee speaker had promised Bouquet they would. Jonathan Hoyt's Indian father visited him so often in Deerfield, sometimes bringing his captive sister, that Hoyt had to petition the Massachusetts General Court for reimbursement for their support. In

1760 Sir William Johnson reported that a Canadian Indian "has been since down to Schenectady to visit one Newkirk of that place, who was some years a Prisoner in his House, and sent home about a year ago with this Indians Sister, who came with her Brother now purely to see Said Newkirk whom she calls her Son and is verry fond of."[24]

Obviously the feelings were mutual. Elizabeth Gilbert, adopted at the age of twelve, "always retained an affection toward John Huston, her Indian father (as she called him), for she remembered his kindness to her when in captivity." Even an adult who had spent less than six months with the Indians honored the chief who had adopted him. In 1799, eleven years after Thomas Ridout's release, his friend and father, Kakinathucca, "accompanied by three more Shawanese chiefs, came to pay me a visit at my house in York town (Toronto). He regarded myself and family with peculiar pleasure, and my wife and children contemplated with great satisfaction the noble and good qualities of this worthy Indian." The bond of affection that had grown in the Indian villages was clearly not an attachment that the English could dismiss as "unnatural."[25]

Children who had been raised by Indian parents from infancy could be excused perhaps for their unwillingness to return, but the adults who displayed a similar reluctance, especially the women who had married Indian men and borne them children, drew another reaction. "For the honour of humanity," wrote William Smith, "we would suppose those persons to have been of the lowest rank, either bred up in ignorance and distressing penury, or who had lived so long with the Indians as to forget all their former connections. For, easy and unconstrained as the savage life is, certainly it could never be put in competition with the blessings of improved life and the light of religion, by any persons who have had the happiness of enjoying, and the capacity of discerning, them." If Smith was struck by the contrast between the visible impact of Indian education and his own cultural assumptions, he never said so.[26]

To find a satisfactory explanation for the extraordinary drawing power of Indian culture, we should begin where the colonists themselves first came under its sway—on the trail to Indian country. For although the Indians were known for their patience, they wasted no time in beginning the educational process that would transform their hostile or fearful white captives into affectionate Indian relatives.

Perhaps the first transaction after the Indians had selected their prisoners and hurried them into cover was to replace their hard-heeled shoes with the footwear of the forest—moccasins. These were universally approved by the prisoners, who admitted that they traveled with "abundant more ease" than before. And on more than one occasion the knee-deep snows of northern New England forced the Indians to make snowshoes for their prisoners in order to maintain their pace of twenty-five to thirty miles a day. Such an introduction to the superbly adapted technology of the Indians alone would not convert the English, but it was a beginning.[27]

The lack of substantial food supplies forced the captives to accommodate their stomachs as best they could to Indian trail fare, which ranged from nuts, berries, roots, and parched corn to beaver guts, horseflank, and semi-raw venison and moose, eaten without the customary English accompaniments of bread or salt. When there was nothing to eat, the Indians would "gird up their loins with a string," a technique that at least one captive found "very useful" when applied to himself. Although their food was often "unsavory" and in short supply, the Indians always shared it equally with the captives, who, being hungry, "relished [it] very well."[28]

Sometimes the lessons learned from the Indians were unexpectedly vital. When Stephen Williams, an eleven-year-old captive from Deerfield, found himself separated from his party on the way to Canada, he hallooed for his Indian master. When the boy was found, the Indian threatened to kill him because, as Williams remembered five years later, "the Indians will never allow anybody to Hollow in the woods. Their manner is to make a noise like wolves or any other wild creatures, when they call to one another." The reason, of course, was that they did not wish to be discovered by their enemies. To the young neophyte Indian this was a lesson in survival not soon forgotten.[29]

Two other lessons were equally unexpected but instrumental in preparing the captives for even greater surprises when they reached the Indian settlements. Both served to undermine the English horror of the Indians as bloodthirsty fiends who defile "any Woman they take alive" before "putting her to Death." Many redeemed prisoners made a point of insisting that, although they had been completely powerless in captivity, the Indians had never affronted them sexually. Thomas Ridout testified that "during the whole of the time I was with the Indians I never once witnessed an indecent or improper action amongst any of the Indians, whether young or old." Even William Smith admitted that "from every enquiry that has been made, it appears—that no woman thus saved is preserved from base motives, or need fear the violation of her honour." If there had been the least exception, we can be sure that this champion of civilization would have made the most of it.[30]

One reason for the Indians' lack of sexual interest in their female captives was perhaps aesthetic, for the New England Indians, at least, esteemed black the color of beauty.[31] A more fundamental reason derived from the main purpose of taking captives, which was to secure new members for their families and clans. Under the Indians' strong incest taboos, no warrior would attempt to violate his future sister or cousin. "Were he to indulge himself with a captive taken in war, and much more were he to offer violence in order to gratify his lust, he would incur indelible disgrace." Indeed, the taboo seems to have extended to the whole tribe. As George Croghan testified after long acquaintance with the Indians, "they have No [J]uri[s]diction or Laws butt that of Nature yett I have known more than onest thire Councils, order men to be putt to Death for Committing Rapes, wh[ich] is a Crime they Despise." Since murder was a crime to be revenged by the victim's family in its own way and time, rape was the only capital offense punished by the tribe as a whole.[32]

Equally powerful in prohibiting sexual affronts was a religious ethic of strict warrior continence, the breaking of which was thought to bring misfortune or death. "The Indians will not cohabit with women while they are out at war," noted James Adair, a trader among the southeastern tribes for thirty years, "they religiously abstain from every kind of intercourse even with their own wives, for the space of three days and nights before they go to war, and so after they return home, because they are to sanctify themselves."[33] When William Fleming and his wife were taken from their bed in 1755, the Indians told him "he need not be afraid of their abusing his wife, for they would not do it, for fear of offending their God (pointing their hands toward heaven) for the man that affronts his God will surely be killed when he goes to war." Giving the woman a plundered shift and petticoat, the natives turned their backs while she dressed to emphasize the point.[34]

Captive testimony also chipped away at the stereotype of the Indians' cruelty. When Mrs. Isabella M'Coy was taken from Epsom, New Hampshire, in 1747, her neighbors later remembered that "she did indeed find the journey [to Canada] fatiguing, and her fare scanty and precarious. But in her treatment from the Indians, she experienced a very agreeable disappointment. The kindness she received from them was far greater than she had expected from those who were so often distinguished for their cruelties." More frequent still was recognition of the Indians' kindness to children. Thomas Hutchinson told a common story of how "some of the children who were taken at Deerfield, they drew upon slays; at other times they have been known to carry them in their arms or upon their backs to Canada. This tenderness," he noted, "has occasioned the beginning of an affection, which in a few years has been so riveted, that the parents of the children, who have gone to Canada to seek them, could by no means prevail upon them to leave the Indians and return home." The affections of a four-year-old Pennsylvania boy, who became Old White Chief among the Iroquois, seem to have taken even less time to become "rivetted." "The last I remember of my mother," he recalled in 1836, "she was running, carrying me in her arms. Suddenly she fell to the ground on her face, and I was taken from her. Overwhelmed with fright, I knew nothing more until I opened my eyes to find myself in the lap of an Indian woman. Looking kindly down into my face she smiled on me, and gave me some dried deer's meat and maple sugar. From that hour I believe she loved me as a mother. I am sure I returned to her the affection of a son."[35]

When the returning war parties approached the first Indian village, the educational process took on a new complexion. As one captive explained, "whenever the warriors return from an excursion against an enemy, their return to the tribe or village must be designated by war-like ceremonial; the captives or spoils, which may happen to crown their valor, must be conducted in a triumphant form, and decorated to every possible advantage." Accordingly, the

cheek, chin, and forehead of every captive were painted with traditional dashes
of vermilion mixed with bear's grease. Belts of wampum were hung around
their necks, Indian clothes were substituted for English, and the men and boys
had their hair plucked or shaved in Indian fashion. The physical transformation was so effective, said a twenty-six-year-old soldier, "that I began to think
I was an Indian." Younger captives were less aware of the small distance
between role-playing and real acceptance of the Indian life-style. When her
captor dressed Frances Slocum, not yet five years old, in "beautiful wampum
beads," she remembered at the end of a long and happy life as an Indian that
he "made me look, as I thought, very fine. I was much pleased with the beautiful wampum."[36]

The prisoners were then introduced to a "new school" of song and dance.
"Little did we expect," remarked an English woman, "that the accomplishment
of dancing would ever be taught us, by the savages. But the war dance must
now be held; and every prisoner that could move must take its awkward steps.
The figure consisted of circular motion round the fire; each sang his own
music, and the best dancer was the one most violent in motion." To prepare for
the event each captive had rehearsed a short Indian song on the trail. Mrs.
Johnson recalled many years later that her song was "danna witchee natchep-
ung; my son's was nar wiscumpton." Nehemiah How could not master the
Indian pronunciation, so he was allowed to sing in English "I don't know
where I go." In view of the Indians' strong sense of ceremonial propriety, it is
small wonder that one captive thought that they "Seem[e]d to be Very much
a mind I Should git it perfect."[37]

Upon entering the village the Indians let forth with some distinctive music
of their own. "When we came near the main Body of the Enemy," wrote
Thomas Brown, a captive soldier from Fort William Henry, "the *Indians* made
a Live-Shout, as they call it when they bring in a Prisoner alive (different from
the Shout they make when they bring in Scalps, which they call a Dead-
Shout)." According to another soldier, "their Voices are so sharp, shrill, loud
and deep, that when they join together after one has made his Cry, it makes a
most dreadful and horrible Noise, that stupifies the very Senses," a noise that
naturally frightened many captives until they learned that it was not their
death knell.[38]

They had good reason to think that their end was near when the whole village turned out to form a gauntlet from the entrance to the center of the village and their captors ordered them to run through it. With ax handles, tomahawks, hoop poles, clubs, and switches the Indians flogged the racing captives
as if to beat the whiteness out of them. In most villages, significantly, "it was
only the more elderly People both Male and Female wh[ic]h rece[iv]ed this
Useage—the young prisoners of Both Sexes Escaped without it" or were rescued from any serious harm by one or more villagers, perhaps indicating the
Indian perception of the captives' various educability. When ten-year-old John
Brickell was knocked down by the blows of his Seneca captors, "a very big

Indian came up, and threw the company off me, and took me by the arm, and led me along through the lines with such rapidity that I scarcely touched the ground, and was not once struck after he took me."[39]

The purpose of the gauntlet was the subject of some difference of opinion. A French soldier who had spent several years among the northeastern Indians believed that a prisoner "so unfortunate as to fall in the course of the baston-nade must get up quickly and keep on, or he will be beaten to death on the spot." On the other hand, Pierre de Charlevoix, the learned traveler and his-torian of Canada, wrote that "even when they seem to strike at random, and to be actuated only by fury, they take care never to touch any part where a blow might prove mortal." Both Frenchmen were primarily describing the Indians' treatment of other Indians and white men. Barbara Leininger and Marie LeRoy drew a somewhat different conclusion from their own treatment. Their welcome at the Indian village of Kittanning, they said, "consisted of three blows each, on the back. They were, however, administered with great mercy. Indeed, we concluded that we were beaten merely in order to keep up an ancient usage, and not with the intention of injuring us."[40]

William Walton came closest to revealing the Indians' intentions in his account of the Gilbert family's captivity. The Indians usually beat the captives with "great Severity," he said, "by way of Revenge for their Relations who have been slain." Since the object of taking captives was to satisfy the Indian fami-lies who had lost relatives, the gauntlet served as the first of three initiation rites into Indian society, a purgative ceremony by which the bereaved Indians could exorcise their anger and anguish, and the captives could begin their cul-tural transformation.[41]

If the first rite tried to beat the whiteness out of the captives, the second tried to wash it out. James Smith's experience was typical.

> The old chief, holding me by the hand, made a long speech, very loud, and when he had done he handed me to three squaws, who led me by the hand down the bank into the river until the water was up to our middle. The squaws then made signs to me to plunge myself into the water, but I did not understand them. I thought that the result of the council was that I should be drowned, and that these young ladies were to be the executioners. They all laid violent hold of me, and I for some time opposed them with all my might, which occasioned loud laughter by the multitude that were on the bank of the river. At length one of the squaws made out to speak a little English (for I believe they began to be afraid of me) and said, "No hurt you.' On this I gave myself up to their ladyships, who were as good as their word; for though they plunged me under water and washed and rubbed me severely, yet I could not say they hurt me much.[42]

More than one captive had to receive similar assurance, but their worst fears were being laid to rest.

Symbolically purged of their whiteness by their Indian baptism, the initiates were dressed in new Indian clothes and decorated with feathers, jewelry, and paint. Then, with great solemnity, the village gathered around the council fire, where after a "profound silence" one of the chiefs spoke. Even a hostile captive, Zadock Steele, had to admit that although he could not understand the language spoken, he could "plainly discover a great share of native eloquence." The chief's speech, he said, was "of considerable length, and its effect obviously manifested weight of argument, solemnity of thought, and at least human sensibility." But even this the twenty-two-year-old New Englander could not appreciate on its own terms, for in the next breath he denigrated the ceremony as "an assemblage of barbarism, assuming the appearance of civilization."[43]

A more charitable account was given by James Smith, who through an interpreter was addressed in the following words:

> My son, you are now flesh of our flesh and bone of our bone. By the ceremony that was performed this day, every drop of white blood was washed out of your veins. You are taken into the Caughnewaga [French Mohawk] nation and initiated into a war-like tribe. You are adopted into a great family and now received with great seriousness and solemnity in the room and place of a great man. After what has passed this day you are now one of us by an old strong law and custom. My son, you have now nothing to fear. We are now under the same obligations to love, support and defend you that we are to love and to defend one another. Therefore you are to consider yourself as one of our people.[44]

"At this time," admitted the eighteen-year-old Smith, "I did not believe this fine speech, especially that of the white blood being washed out of me; but since that time I have found that there was much sincerity in said speech; for from that day I never knew them to make any distinction between me and themselves in any respect whatever until I left them . . . we all shared one fate." It is a chord that sounds through nearly every captivity narrative: "They treated me . . . in every way as one of themselves."[45]

When the adoption ceremony had ended, the captive was taken to the wigwam of his new family, who greeted him with a "most dismal howling, crying bitterly, and wringing their hands in all agonies of grief for a deceased relative." "The higher in favour the adopted Prisoners [were] to be placed, the greater Lamentation [was] made over them." After a threnodic memorial to the lost member, which may have "added to the Terror of the Captives," who "imagined it to be no other than a Prelude to inevitable Destruction," the mood suddenly shifted, "I never saw . . . such hug[g]ing and kissing from the women and crying for joy," exclaimed one young recipient. Then an interpreter introduced each member of the new family—in one case "from brother to seventh cousins"—and "they came to me one after another," said another captive, "and shook me by the hand, in token that they considered me to stand in the same relationship to them as the one in whose stead I was placed."[46]

Most young captives assumed the places of Indian sons and daughters, but occasionally the match was not exact. Mary Jemison replaced a brother who had been killed in "Washington's war," while twenty-six-year-old Titus King assumed the unlikely role of a grandfather. Although their sex and age may not always have corresponded, the adopted captives succeeded to all the deceased's rights and obligations—the same dignities, honors, and often the same names. "But the one adopted," reported a French soldier, "must be prudent and wise in his conduct, if he wants to make himself as well liked as the man he is replacing. This seldom fails to occur, because he is continually reminded of the dead man's conduct and good deeds."[47]

So literal could the replacement become at times that no amount of exemplary conduct could alter the captive's reception. Thomas Peart, a twenty-three-year-old Pennsylvanian, was adopted as an uncle in an Iroquois family, but "the old Man, whose Place [he] was to fill, had never been considered by his Family as possessed of any Merit." Accordingly, Peart's dress, although in the Indian style, was "in a meaner Manner, as they did not hold him high in Esteem after his Adoption." Since his heart was not in becoming an Indian anyway, and "observing that they treated him just as they had done the old worthless Indian . . . he therefore concluded he would only fill his Predecessor's Station, and used no Endeavours to please them."[48]

When the prisoners had been introduced to all their new relatives and neighbors, the Indians proceeded to shower them with gifts. Luke Swetland, taken from Pennsylvania during the Revolution, was unusually fêted with "three hats, five blankets, near twenty pipes, six razors, six knives, several spoons, gun and ammunition, fireworks, several Indian pockets [pouches], one Indian razor, awls, needles, goose quills, paper and many other things of small value"—enough to make him the complete Indian warrior. Most captives, however, settled for a new shirt or dress, a pair of decorated moccasins, and abundant promises of future kindness, which later prompted the captives to acknowledge once again that the Indians were "a[s] good as their word." "All the family was as kind to me," related Thomas Gist, "as if I had realy been the nearest of relation they had in the world." The two women who adopted Mary Jemison were no less loving. "I was ever considered and treated by them as a real sister," she said near the end of a long life with them, "the same as though I had been born of their mother."[49]

Treatment such as this—and it was almost universal—left an indelible mark on every captive, whether or not they eventually returned to English society. Although captives like Mrs. Johnson found their adoption an "unnatural situation," they had to defend the humanity of the practice. "Those who have profited by refinement and education," she argued, "ought to abate part of the prejudice, which prompts them to look with an eye of censure on this untutored race. . . . Do they ever adopt an enemy," she asked, "and salute him by the tender name of brother?" It is not difficult to imagine what effect such feelings must have had in younger people less habituated to English culture, especially those who had lost their own parents.[50]

The formalities, purgations, and initiations were now completed. Only one thing remained for the Indians: by their daily example and instruction to "make an Indian of you," as the Delawares told John Brickell. This required a steady union of two things: the willingness and gratitude of the captives, and the consistent love and trust of the Indians. By the extraordinary ceremonies through which they had passed, most captives had had their worst fears allayed. From a state of apprehension or even terror they had suddenly emerged with their persons intact and a solemn invitation to begin a new life, as full of love, challenge, and satisfaction as any they had known. For "when [the Indians] once determine to give life, they give every thing with it, which, in their apprehension, belongs to it." The sudden release from anxiety into a realm of affirmative possibility must have disposed many captives to accept the Indian way of life.[51]

According to the adopted colonists who recounted the stories of their new lives, Indian life was more than capable of claiming their respect and allegiance, even if they eventually returned to English society. The first indication that the Indians were serious in their professions of equality came when the adopted captives were given freedom of movement within and without the Indian villages. Naturally, the degree of freedom and its timing depended on the captive's willingness to enter into the spirit of Indian life.

Despite his adult years, Thomas Ridout had earned his captor's trust by the third night of their march to the Shawnee villages. Having tied his prisoner with a rope to himself the first two nights, the Indian "never afterwards used this precaution, leaving me at perfect liberty, and frequently during the nights that were frosty and cold," Ridout recalled, "I found his hand over me to examine whether or not I was covered." As soon as seventeen-year-old John Leeth, an Indian trader's clerk, reached his new family's village, "my father gave me and his two [Indian] sons our freedom, with a rifle, two pounds of powder, four pounds of lead, a blanket, shirt, match-coat, pair of leggings, etc. to each, as our freedom dues; and told us to shift for ourselves." Eleven-year-old Benjamin Gilbert, "considered as the [Indian] King's Successor," was of course "entirely freed from Restraint, so that he even began to be delighted with his Manner of Life." Even Zadock Steele, a somewhat reluctant Indian at twenty-two, was "allowed the privilege of visiting any part of the village, in the day time, and was received with marks of fraternal affection, and treated with all the civility an Indian is capable to bestow."[52]

The presence of other white prisoners complicated the trust relationship somewhat. Captives who were previously known to each other, especially from the same family, were not always allowed to converse "much together, as [the Indians] imagined they would remember their former Situation, and become less contented with their present Manner of Life." Benjamin Peart, for example, was allowed the frequent company of "Two white Men who had been taken Prisoners, the one from Susquehanna, the other from Minisinks, both in Pennsylvania," even though he was a Pennsylvanian himself. But when he met his captive wife and infant son by chance at Fort Niagara, the Indians "separated them again the same Day, and took [his] Wife about Four Miles Distance."[53]

Captives who were strangers were permitted not only to visit frequently but occasionally to live together. When Thomas Gist suddenly moved from his adopted aunt's house back to her brother's, she "imajined I was affronted," he wrote, and "came and asked me the reason why I had left her, or what injury she or any of the family had done me that I should leave her without so much as leting her know of it. I told her it was the company of my fellow prisoners that drew me to the town. She said that it was not so far but I mite have walked to see them every two or three days, and ask some of them to come and see me those days that I did not chuse to go abroad, and that all such persons as I thought proper to bring to the house should be as welcom[e] as one of the family, and made many promises how kind she would be if I would return. However," boasted the twenty-four-year-old Gist, "I was obstinate and would not." It is not surprising that captives who enjoyed such autonomy were also trusted under the same roof. John Brickell remarked that three white prisoners, "Patton, Johnston, and Mrs. Baker [of Kentucky] had all lived with me in the same house among the Indians, and we were as intimate as brothers and sisters."[54]

Once the captives had earned the basic trust of their Indian families, nothing in Indian life was denied them. When they reached the appropriate age, the Indians offered to find them suitable marriage partners. Understandably, some of the older captives balked at this, sensing that it was calculated to bind them with marital ties to a culture they were otherwise hesitant to accept. When Joseph Gilbert, a forty-one-year-old father and husband, was adopted into a leading family, his new relatives informed him that "if he would marry amongst them, he should enjoy the Privileges which they enjoyed; but this Proposal he was not disposed to comply with, . . . as he was not over anxious to conceal his Dislike to them." Elizabeth Peart, his twenty-year-old married sister, was equally reluctant. During her adoption ceremony "they obliged her to sit down with a young Man an Indian, and the eldest Chieftain of the Family repeating a Jargon of Words to her unintelligible, but which she considered as some form amongst them of Marriage," she was visited with "the most violent agitations, as she was determined, at all events, to oppose any step of this Nature." Marie LeRoy's honor was even more dearly bought. When "it was at length determined by the [Indians] that [she] should marry one of the natives, who had been selected for her," she told a fellow captive that "she would sooner be shot than have him for her husband." Whether her revulsion was directed toward the act itself or toward the particular suitor was not said.[55]

The distinction is pertinent because the weight of evidence suggests that marriage was not compulsory for the captives, and common sense tells us that any form of compulsion would have defeated the Indians' purpose in trying to persuade the captives to adopt their way of life. Mary Jemison, at the time a captive for two years, was unusual in implying that she was forced to marry an Indian. "Not long after the Delawares came to live with us, at Wiishto," she recalled, "my sisters told me that I must go and live with one of them, whose name was She-nin-jee. Not daring to cross them, or disobey their commands, with a great degree of reluctance I went; and Sheninjee and I were married

Frances Slocum (1773–1847) was captured at the age of five and raised by the Delawares. Sometime in her late teens she married a Delaware and, when he deserted her, a Miami war chief. By the latter she had two sons (who died young) and two daughters. In 1839 her Pennsylvania relatives discovered her in Indiana. Two years later they had her portrait painted by George Winter, a young English artist traveling in America. One daughter would not show her face, having the widespread Indian fear of lifelike images. From *The Journals and Indian Paintings of George Winter, 1837–1839* (Indianapolis: Indiana Historical Society, 1948); reproduced by courtesy of Mrs. Evelyn Ball.

according to Indian custom." Considering the tenderness and kindness with which most captives reported they were treated, it is likely that she was less compelled in reality than in her perception and memory of it.[56]

For even hostile witnesses could not bring themselves to charge that force was ever used to promote marriages. The Puritan minister John Williams said only that "great *essays* [were] made to get [captives] married" among the Canadian Indians by whom he was captured. Elizabeth Hanson and her husband "could by no means obtain from their hands" their sixteen-year-old daughter, "for the squaw, to whom she was given, had a son whom she intended my daughter should in time *be prevailed with to marry*." Mrs. Hanson was probably less concerned that her daughter would be forced to marry an Indian than that she might "in time" want to, for as she acknowledged from her personal experience, "the Indians are very civil towards their captive women, not offering any incivility by any indecent carriage." An observer of the return of the white prisoners to Bouquet spoke for his contemporaries when he reported—with an almost audible sigh of relief—that "there had not been a solitary instance among them of any woman having her delicacy injured by being compelled to marry. They had been left liberty of choice, and those who chose to remain single were not sufferers on that account."[57]

Not only were younger captives and consenting adults under no compulsion, either actual or perceived, to marry, but they enjoyed as wide a latitude of choice as any Indian. When Thomas Gist returned to his Indian aunt's lodge, she was so happy that she "dress'd me as fine as she could, and . . . told me if I wanted a wife she would get a pretty young girl for me." It was in the same spirit of exuberant generosity that Oliver Spencer's adopted mother rewarded his first hunting exploit. "She heard all the particulars of the affair with great satisfaction," he remembered, "and frequently saying, 'Enee, wessah' (this is right, that is good), said I would one day become a great hunter, and placing her forefingers together (by which sign the Indians represent marriage) and then pointing to Sotonegoo" (a thirteen-year-old girl whom Spencer described as "rather homely, but cheerful and good natured, with bright, laughing eyes") "told me that when I should become a man I should have her for a wife." Sotonegoo cannot have been averse to the idea, for when Spencer was redeemed shortly afterward she "sobbed loudly as [he] took her hand, and for the moment deeply affected, bade her farewell."[58]

So free from compulsion were the captives that several married fellow white prisoners. In 1715 the priest of the Jesuit mission at Sault-au-Récollet "married Ignace shoetak8anni [Joseph Rising, aged twenty-one] and Elizabeth T8atog8ach [Abigail Nims, aged fifteen], both English, who wish to remain with the Christian Indians, not only renouncing their nation, but even wishing to live *en sauvages*." But from the Indians' standpoint, and perhaps from their own, captives such as John Leeth and Thomas Armstrong may have had the best of all possible marriages. After some years with the Indians, Leeth "was married to a young woman, seventeen or eighteen years of age; also a prisoner to the Indians; who had been taken by them when about twenty months old." Armstrong, an adopted Seneca, also married a "full blooded white woman, who like himself had been a captive among the Indians, from infancy, but who unlike him, had not acquired a knowledge of one word of the English language, being essentially Indian in all save blood."[59] Their commitment to each other deepened their commitment to the Indian culture of which they had become equal members.

The captives' social equality was also demonstrated by their being asked to share in the affairs of war and peace, matters of supreme importance to Indian society. When the Senecas who had adopted Thomas Peart decided to "make a War Excursion," they asked him to go with them. But since he was in no mood—and no physical condition—to play the Indian, "he determinately refused them, and was therefore left at Home with the Family." The young

Englishman who became Old White Chief was far more eager to defend his new culture, but his origins somewhat limited his military activity. "When I grew to manhood," he recalled, "I went with them [his Iroquois kinsmen] on the warpath against the neighboring tribes, but never against the white settlers, lest by some unlucky accident I might be recognized and claimed by former friends." Other captives—many of them famous renegades—were less cautious. Charlevoix noticed in his travels in Canada that adopted captives "frequently enter into the spirit of the nation, of which they are become members, in such a manner, that they make no difficulty of going to war against their own countrymen." It was behavior such as this that prompted Sir William Johnson to praise Bouquet after his expedition to the Ohio for compelling the Indians to give up every white person, even the "Children born of White Women. That mixed Race," he wrote, referring to first-generation captives as well, "forgetting their Ancestry on one side are found to be the most Inveterate of any, and would greatly Augment their numbers."[60]

It is ironic that the most famous renegade of all should have introduced ten-year-old Oliver Spencer to the ultimate opportunity for an adopted captive. When he had been a captive for less than three weeks, Spencer met Simon Girty, "the very picture of a villain," at a Shawnee village below his own. After various boasts and enquiries, wrote Spencer, "he ended by telling me that I would never see home; but if I should 'turn out to be a good hunter and a brave warrior I might one day be a chief.'" Girty's prediction may not have been meant to tease a small boy with impossible delusions of grandeur, for the Indians of the Northeast readily admitted white captives to their highest councils and offices.[61]

Just after Thomas Ridout was captured on the Ohio, he was surprised to meet an English-speaking "white man, about twenty-two years of age, who had been taken prisoner when a lad and had been adopted, and now was a chief among the Shawanese." He need not have been surprised, for there were many more like him. John Tarbell, the man who visited his Groton relatives in Indian dress, was not only "one of the wealthiest" of the Caughnawagas but "the eldest chief and chief speaker of the tribe." Timothy Rice, formerly of Westborough, Massachusetts, was also made one of the clan chiefs at Caughnawaga, partly by inheritance from his Indian father but largely for "his own Super[io]r Talents" and "war-like Spirit for which he was much celebrated."[62]

Perhaps the most telling evidence of the Indians' receptivity to adopted white leadership comes from Old White Chief, an adopted Iroquois.

I was made a chief at an early age [he recalled in 1836] and as my sons grew to manhood they also were made chiefs. . . . After my youngest son was made chief I could see, as I thought, that some of the Indians were jealous of the distinction I enjoyed and it gave me uneasiness. This was the first time I ever entertained the thought of leaving my Indian friends. I felt sure that it was displeasing to the Indians to have three of my sons, as well as myself, promoted to the office of chief.

My wife was well pleased to leave with me, and my sons said, "Father, we will go wherever you will lead us."

I then broke the subject to some of my Indian relatives, who were very much disturbed at my decision. They immediately called the chiefs and warriors together and laid the plan before them. They gravely deliberated upon the subject for some hours, and then a large majority decided that they would not consent to our leaving. They said, "We cannot give up our son and brother" (meaning myself) "nor our nephews" (meaning my children). "They have lived on our game and grown strong and powerful among us. They are good and true men. We cannot do without them. We cannot give them to the pale faces. We shall grow weak if they leave us. We will give them the best we have left. Let them choose where they will live. No one shall disturb them. We need their wisdom and their strength to help us. If they are in high places, let them be there. We know they will honor us."[63]

"We yielded to their importunity," said the old chief, and "I have never had any reason to regret my decision." In public office as in every sphere of Indian life, the English captives found that the color of their skin was unimportant; only their talent and their inclination of heart mattered.

Understandably, neither their skill nor their loyalty was left to chance. From the moment the captives, especially the young ones, came under their charge, the Indians made a concerted effort to inculcate in them Indian habits of mind and body. If the captives could be taught to think, act, and react like Indians, they would effectively cease to be English and would assume an Indian identity.[64] This was the Indians' goal, toward which they bent every effort in the weeks and months that followed their formal adoption of the white captives.

The educational character of Indian society was recognized by even the most inveterately English captives. Titus King, a twenty-six-year-old New England soldier, spent a year with the Canadian Indians at St. Francis trying—unsuccessfully—to undo their education of "Eight or ten young [English] Children." What "an awfull School this [is] for Children," he wrote. "When We See how Quick they will Fall in with the Indians ways, nothing Seems to be more takeing in Six months time they Forsake Father and mother Forgit their own Land Refuess to Speak there own toungue and Seemin[g]ly be Holley Swollowed up with the Indians." The older the person, of course, the longer it took to become fully Indianized. Mary Jemison, captured at the age of fifteen, took three or four years to forget her natural parents and the home she had once loved. "If I had been taken in infancy," she said, "I should have been contented in my situation." Some captives, commonly those over fifteen or sixteen years old, never made the transition from English to Indian. Twenty-four-year-old Thomas Gist, soldier and son of a famous scout and Indian agent, accommodated himself to his adoption and Indian life for just one year and then made plans to escape. "All curiosity with regard to acting the part of an Indian," he related, "which I could do very well, being th[o]rougherly satisfied, I was determined to be what I really was."[65]

Children, however, took little time to "fall in with the Indians ways." Titus King mentioned six months. The Reverend John Williams witnessed the effects of eight or nine months when he stopped at St. Francis in February 1704. There, he said, "we found several poor children, who had been taken from the eastward [Maine] the summer before; a sight very affecting, they being in habit very much like Indians, and in manners very much symbolizing with them." When young Joseph Noble visited his captive sister in Montreal, "he still belonged to the St. François tribe of Indians, and was dressed remarkably fine, having forty or fifty broaches in his shirt, clasps on his arm, and a great variety of knots and bells about his clothing. He brought his little sister . . . a young fawn, a basket of cranberries, and a lump of sap sugar." Sometime later he was purchased from the Indians by a French gentleman who promptly "dressed him in the French style; but he never appeared so bold and majestic, so spirited and vivacious, as when arrayed in his Indian habit and associating with his Indian friends."[66]

The key to any culture is its language, and the young captives were quick to learn the Indian dialects of their new families. Their retentive memories and flair for imitation made them ready students, while the Indian languages, at once oral, concrete, and mythopoeic, lightened the task. In less than six months ten-year-old Oliver Spencer had "acquired a sufficient knowledge of the Shawnee tongue to understand all ordinary conversation and, indeed, the greater part of all that I heard (accompanied, as their conversation and speeches were, with the most significant gestures)," which enabled him to listen "with much pleasure and sometimes with deep interest" to his Indian mother tell of battles, heroes, and history in the long winter evenings. When Jemima Howe was allowed to visit her four-year-old son at a neighboring Indian village in Canada, he greeted her "in the Indian tongue" with "Mother, are you come?" He too had been a captive for only six months.[67]

The early weeks of captivity could be disquieting if there were no English-speaking Indians or prisoners in the village to lend the comfort of a familiar language while the captives struggled to acquire a strange one. If a captive's family left for their winter hunting camp before he could learn their language, he might find himself, like Thomas Gist, "without any com[p]any that could unders[t]and one word that I spake." "Thus I continued, near five months," he wrote, "sometimes reading, other times singing, never melancholy but when alone. . . . About the first of April (1759) I prevailed on the family to return to town, and by the last of the month all the Indians and prisoners returned, when I once more had the pleasure to talk to people that understood what I said."[68]

Younger captives probably missed the familiarity of English less than the adult Gist. Certainly they never lacked eager teachers. Mary Jemison recalled that her Seneca sisters were "diligent in teaching me their language; and to their great satisfaction I soon learned so that I could understand it readily, and speak it fluently." Even Gist was the recipient of enthusiastic, if informal, instruction from a native speaker. One of his adopted cousins, who was about five or six years old and his "favorite in the family," was always "chattering some thing" with him. "From him," said Gist affectionately, "I learn'd more than from all the rest, and he learn'd English as fast as [I] did Indian."[69]

As in any school, language was only one of many subjects of instruction. Since the Indians generally assumed that whites were physically inferior to themselves, captive boys were often prepared for the hardy life of hunters and warriors by a rigorous program of physical training. John McCullough, aged eight, was put through the traditional Indian course by his adoptive uncle. "In the beginning of winter," McCullough recalled, "he used to raise me by day light every morning, and make me sit down in the creek up to my chin in the cold water, in order to make me hardy as he said, whilst he would sit on the bank smoking his pipe until he thought I had been long enough in the water, he would then bid me to dive. After I came out of the water he would order me not to go near the fire until I would be dry. I was kept at that till the water was frozen over, he would then break the ice for me and send me in as before." As shocking as it may have been to his system, such treatment did nothing to turn him against Indian life. Indeed, he was transparently proud that he had borne up under the strenuous regimen "with the firmness of an Indian." Becoming an Indian was as much a challenge and an adventure for the young colonists as it was a "sore trial," and many of them responded to it with alacrity and zest. Of children their age we should not expect any less.[70]

The captives were taught not only to speak and to endure as Indians but to act as Indians in the daily social and economic life of the community. Naturally, boys were taught the part of men and girls the part of women, and according to most colonial sources—written, it should be noted, predominantly by men—the boys enjoyed the better fate. An Ohio pioneer remembered that the prisoners from his party were "put into different families, the women to hard drudging and the boys to run wild with the young Indians, to amuse themselves with bow and arrow, dabble in the water, or obey any other notion their wild natures might dictate." William Walton, the author of the Gilbert family captivity narrative, also felt that the "Labour and Drudgery" in an Indian family fell to "the Share of the Women." He described fourteen-year-old Abner Gilbert as living a "dronish Indian life, idle and poor, having no other Employ than the gathering of Hickory-Nuts; and although young," Walton insisted, "his Situation was very irksome." Just how irksome the boy found his freedom from colonial farm chores was revealed when the ingenuous Walton related that "Abner, having no useful Employ, amused himself with catching fish in the Lake. . . . Not being of an impatient Disposition," said Walton soberly, "he bore his Captivity without repining."[71]

While most captive boys had "nothing to do, but cut a little wood for the fire," draw water for cooking and drinking, and "shoot Blackbirds that came to eat up the corn," they enjoyed "some leisure" for "hunting and other innocent devertions in the woods." Women and girls, on the other hand, shared the burdens—onerous ones in English eyes—of their Indian counterparts. But Mary Jemison, who had been taught English ways for fifteen years before becoming an Indian, felt that the Indian women's labor "was not severe," their tasks "probably not harder than that [*sic*] of white women," and their cares "certainly . . . not half as numerous, nor as great." The work of one year was "exactly similar, in almost every respect, to that of the others, without that endless variety that is to be observed in the common labor of the white people . . . In the summer season, we planted, tended and harvested our corn, and generally had all our children with us; but had no master to oversee or drive us, so that we could work as leisurely as we pleased. . . . In the season of hunting, it was our business, in addition to our cooking, to bring home the game that was taken by the [men], dress it, and carefully preserve the eatable meat, and prepare or dress the skins." "Spinning, weaving, sewing, stocking knitting," and like domestic tasks of colonial women were generally unknown. Unless Jemison was correct, it would be virtually impossible to understand why so many women and girls chose to become Indians. A life of unremitting drudgery, as the English saw it, could certainly hold no attraction for civilized women fresh from frontier farms and villages.[72]

The final and most difficult step in the captives' transition from English to Indian was to acquire the ability to think as Indians, to share unconsciously the values, beliefs, and standards of Indian culture. From an English perspective, this should have been nearly an impossible task for civilized people because they perceived Indian culture as immoral and irreligious and totally antithetical to the civilized life they had known, however briefly. "Certainly," William Smith assumed, "it could never be put in competition with the blessings of improved life and the light of religion."[73] But many captives soon discovered that the English had no monopoly on virtue and that in many ways the Indians were morally superior to the English, more Christian than the Christians.

As early as 1643 Roger Williams had written a book to suggest such a thing, but he could be dismissed as a misguided visionary who let the Narragansetts go to his head. It was more difficult to dismiss someone like John Brickell, who had lived with the Indians for four and one-half years and had no ax to grind with established religion. "The Delawares are the best people to train up children I ever was with," he wrote. "Their leisure hours are, in a great measure, spent in training up their children to observe what they believe to be right. . . . [A]s a nation they may be considered fit examples for many of us Christians to follow. They certainly follow what they are taught to believe right more closely, and I might say more honestly, in general, than we Christians do the divine precepts of our Redeemer. . . . I know I am influenced to good, even at this day," he concluded, "more from what I learned among them, than what I learned among people of my own color." After many decades with them, Mary Jemison insisted that "the moral character of the Indians was . . . uncontaminated. Their fidelity was perfect, and became proverbial; they were strictly honest; they despised deception and falsehood; and chastity was held in high veneration." Even the Tory historian Peter Oliver, who was no friend to the Indians, admitted that "they have a Religion of their own, which, to the eternal Disgrace of many Nations who boast of Politeness, is more influential on their Conduct than that of those who hold them in so great Contempt." To the acute discomfort of the colonists, more than one captive maintained that the Indians were a "far more moral race than the whites."[74]

In the principled school of Indian life the captives experienced a decisive shift in their cultural and personal identities, a shift that often fostered a considerable degree of what might be called "conversion zeal." A French officer reported that "those Prisoners whom the Indians keep with them . . . are often more brutish, boisterous in their Behaviour and loose in their Manners than the Indians," and thought that "they affect that kind of Behaviour thro' Fear of and to recommend themselves to the Indians." Matthew Bunn, a nineteen-year-old soldier, was the object of such behavior when he was enslaved—not adopted—by the Maumee in 1791. "After I had eaten," he related, "they brought me a little prisoner boy, that had been taken about two years before, on the river called Monongahela, though he delighted more in the ways of the savages than in the ways of Christians; he used me worse than any of the Indians, for he would tell me to do this, that, and the other, and if I did not do it, or made any resistance, the Indians would threaten to kill me, and he would kick and cuff me about in such a manner, that I hardly dared to say my soul was my own." What Bunn experienced was the attempt of the new converts to pattern their behavior after their young Indian counterparts, who, a Puritan minister observed, "are as much to be dreaded by captives as those of maturer years, and in many cases much more so; for, unlike cultivated people, they have no restraints upon their mischievous and savage propensities, which they indulge in cruelties."[75]

Although fear undoubtedly accounted for some of the converts' initial behavior, desire to win the approval of their new relatives also played a part. "I had lived in my new habitation about a week," recalled Oliver Spencer, "and having given up all hope of escaping . . . began to regard it as my future home. . . . I strove to be cheerful, and by my ready obedience to ingratiate myself with Cooh-coo-cheeh [his Indian mistress], for whose kindness I felt grateful." A year after James Smith had been adopted, a number of prisoners were brought in by his new kinsmen and a gauntlet formed to welcome them. Smith "went and told them how they were to act" and then "fell into one of the ranks with the Indians, shouting and yelling like them." One middle-aged man's turn came, and "as they were not very severe on him," confessed the new Indian, "as he passed me I hit him with a piece of pumpkin—which pleased the Indians much." If their zeal to emulate the Indians sometimes exceeded their mercy, the captives had nonetheless fulfilled their new families' expectations: they had begun to act as Indians in spirit as well as body. Only time would be necessary to transform their conscious efforts into unconscious habits and complete their cultural conversion.[76]

"By what power does it come to pass," asked Crèvecoeur, "that children who have been adopted when young among these people, . . . and even grown persons . . . can never be prevailed on to re-adopt European manners?"[77] Given the malleability of youth, we should not be surprised that children underwent a rather sudden and permanent transition from English to Indian—although we might be pressed to explain why so few Indian children made the transition in the opposite direction. But the adult colonists who became Indians cannot be explained as easily, for the simple reason that they, unlike many of the children, were fully conscious of their cultural identities while they were being subjected to the Indians' assiduous attempts to convert them. Consequently, their cultural metamorphosis involved a large degree of personal choice.

The great majority of white Indians left no explanations for their choice. Forgetting their original language and their past, they simply disappeared into their adopted society. But those captives who returned to write narratives of their experiences left several clues to the motives of those who chose to stay behind. They stayed because they found Indian life to possess a strong sense of community, abundant love, and uncommon integrity—values that the English colonists also honored, if less successfully. But Indian life was attractive for other values—for social equality, mobility, adventure, and, as two adult converts acknowledged, "the most perfect freedom, the ease of living, [and] the absence of those cares and corroding solicitudes which so often prevail with us." As we have learned in the last thirty years, these were values that were not being realized in the older, increasingly crowded, fragmented, and contentious communities of the Atlantic seaboard, or even in the newer frontier settlements.[78] By contrast, as Crèvecoeur said, there must have been in the Indians' "social bond something singularly captivating."[79] Whatever it was, its power had no better measure than the large number of English colonists who became, contrary to the civilized assumptions of their countrymen, white Indians.

PART IV

CLASHES

INTRODUCTION

When European colonists could not achieve their goals through peaceful palaver, diplomacy, trade, intermarriage, or conversion, they often resorted to violence, or provoked the natives to violence by long—and sometimes short—trains of abuses and usurpations (in the language of their own Declaration of Independence from Britain), to which they could then respond "defensively" with righteous force. Sooner or later, the Europeans' organizational and technological superiority, burgeoning populations, and international rivalries brought new causes and modes of war to North America.

In the case of the Spanish, flushed with success in South and Central America, violence followed closely on the heels of the earliest explorers. Chapter Nine describes "The Spanish Incursion" into the sixteenth-century Southeast, particularly the social and cultural changes forced upon the native peoples in the path of Hernando de Soto's failed but ferocious *entrada*. The damage wrought by Spanish horses and Toledo swords was not less than the disruption caused by the long-term billeting of the army in native villages, the commandeering of hundreds of male porters and female camp followers, and the lethal legacies of new diseases. The chapter was first published in *The Indians' New South* (1997).

For the Powhatans of Virginia, the English invasion of 1607 bore a strong resemblance to the hard tactics of the Spanish and their results. Although the English employees of the Virginia Company of London intended to settle peacefully to promote commerce, they chose perhaps the single worst site on the East Coast, located in the midst of a jealous and powerful native chiefdom and initially devoid of profitable commodities or trade opportunities. In 1995 I described the scenario and results of this all-but-inevitable clash between two proud "empires" in an illustrated booklet in Colonial Williamsburg's "Foundations of America" series and, earlier with endnotes, in *After Columbus* (1988). The full version appears here as Chapter Ten.

When colonists, particularly English but also Dutch and French, were flummoxed by their inability to counter the terrifying guerilla warfare of their Indian enemies, their governments often offered cash bounties to soldiers and volunteers who could produce enemy scalps—of men, women, and children—

after taking the war into the Indians' own camps. In the 1960s and 1970s, the era of the Indian rights movement, it was widely believed by natives and their political allies that Europeans had invented scalping and spread it to the "innocent" Indians through the nefarious use of scalp bounties. William Sturtevant and I debunked that plausible but inaccurate rumor in an article entitled "The Unkindest Cut; or Who Invented Scalping?" in the *William and Mary Quarterly* (July 1980).

But I continued to be interested in the moral implications of scalping and scalp bounties for both Indians, who had practiced hair-raising all over the continent for hundreds of years before Columbus, and colonists, who learned it in America and had to make room for it in their cultural and religious mores. Chapter Eleven was published in *The European and the Indian* (1981) under the title "Scalping: The Ethnohistory of a Moral Question." Surrounding it were several articles and chapters in which I argued that historians, like other humanists, not only have an obligation to make moral or normative judgments about their subjects, they have no choice in the matter if they use language, which is invariably loaded with "mental depth charges" whose cognitive shrapnel shower our understanding with fragments of accumulated meaning, value, and association.* As I try to show in Chapter Eleven, the historian's moral opportunities and obligations are only multiplied when he or she approaches the contact between cultures, each with its own moral imperatives.

After Columbus (1988), chs. 1–2; *Beyond 1492* (1992), ch. 10; "The Moral Implications of 1492," *The Historian,* 56 (Autumn 1993), 17–28.

NINE

THE SPANISH INCURSION

When Spanish adventurers made their way into the Southeast after 1513, they entered a native world at once promisingly strange and dangerously familiar. The earliest explorers who sailed north out of the decreasingly profitable Caribbean discovered native societies resembling the pugnacious chiefdoms of Hispaniola and Puerto Rico and not the less organized, more biddable villagers of the Bahamas. This discovery was dismaying because the Caribbean chiefdoms, situated in tropical, often mountainous terrain and led by astute and powerful *caciques,* foiled Spanish grabs for power and gold longer and more effectively than would the more populous Aztecs and Incas, at a punishing cost in Spanish blood and treasure.[1] Likewise, the conquistadors who came later, flushed with success and wealth from Mexico or Peru, were disappointed not to find the large, complex, hierarchical, urbanized populations they had conquered relatively easily at Tenochtitlan and Cajamarca. Nor did either group of invaders find the veins or stores of precious metals that made their previous conquests so profitable. But native rumors, wishful thinking, and obliging geographical theories that planted gold and silver in tropical and semitropical zones—wherever the Spanish happened to land—kept the search alive, even in the face of daunting native opposition and unremitting empty-handedness. Before an official change of plans in the 1560s, their quixotic search for treasure led the Spanish into a native quagmire and a series of deadly and costly failures.

The native societies and polities of the Southeast were well configured to frustrate if not halt the Spanish irruption. Aided by environments and climates inhospitable to the invaders from the dry tablelands and cordilleras of central, western, and southern Spain, the southeastern Indians were organized largely into chiefdoms ruled by chiefs and paramount chiefs whose political power was enhanced by the religious reverence of their subjects. Thanks to the advent of maize horticulture from Mesoamerica after 900 A.D., the southeastern populations had grown appreciably, as had the concentration of settlements around the fields that produced food surpluses for the first time. With the surge in population came specialized divisions of labor, ascribed rather than earned social ranking, and intergroup warfare for political prestige and control of the best farmlands along rivers.

Also from the west came religious cults that exalted political leaders and priests and elevated their houses to the top of earthen platform mounds or around large ceremonial plazas. When these leaders died, they were buried in elite charnel houses or in mounds with elaborate grave goods and sometimes with a number of sacrificed wives and servants to accompany their souls to the land of the dead. In life they were equally distinguishable by their rich wardrobes, transportation on shaded litters, and possession of cult objects such as copper axes, wooden bird effigies with gemstone eyes, or carved shell gorgets in coiled rattlesnake motifs.

The southeastern chiefdoms, which comprised what is known as the Mississippian cultural tradition from *ca.* 1000 to *ca.* 1700 A.D., posed major military problems for invaders because they were essentially alliances of tribal provinces under chiefs who ruled independently or who owed material tribute and military assistance to paramount chiefs. Virtually every village, province, and chiefdom was on a war footing. In societies where every hunter was a well-trained warrior, formidable armies could be quickly mobilized, in small numbers or large, for ambush or conquest warfare. For invading Spanish *entradas* dependent on native food supplies, the ample buffer zones between chiefdoms represented deserts of starvation. The palisades, ditches, and moats around the largest towns, which contained between 200 and 500 houses, proved equally difficult to cross.

Yet, as the Spanish soon discovered, native chiefdoms such as Coosa, Calusa, and Cofitachequi were fundamentally unstable. Tributary provinces jockeyed for position within the chiefdom or strove to break away, either to fashion their own chiefdom or to join another that allowed more autonomy and exacted less tribute. Natural disasters, lost battles, or the death of key leaders could easily cause succession or other political crises. Successful raids and battles upset the delicate balance of prestige and power by capturing numbers of women and children as servants and field hands, destroying temples, charnel houses, and elite lodgings, and desecrating sacred objects, including the corpses of high-ranking ancestors with whom the defeated or retreating leaders felt close kinship.[2]

The earliest Spanish invaders, of course, were ignorant of these obstacles, and later ones seem not to have learned much if anything from the hard experiences of their predecessors. In one sense, the native conditions found in the huge region the Spanish claimed as "La Florida" initially were not a great impediment. Even before Juan Ponce de León put Florida on the European map, unlicensed Spanish entrepreneurs from the Caribbean made their secret way to the peninsula and its keys to pluck Indians from the shore for enslavement in Hispaniola, where the native population was rapidly being depleted by disease, overwork, and cruelty. Some of these victims must have escaped and returned home, perhaps in the company of local Indians also seeking to escape Spanish hands. When Ponce de León explored the west coast of Florida in June 1513, he met an Indian representing cacique Carlos "who understood the Spaniards" and was believed to have come from "La Española, or from another island inhabited by Spaniards." Although Ponce de León purloined a couple of natives to act as guides and future interpreters, his initial goal was only to locate the fabled island of Bimini, which promised riches and perhaps "that celebrated fountain, which the Indians said turned men from old men [into] youths."[3] Other escapees like Carlos's man must have given lively seminars in their coastal villages on the temper of the hairy Castilians they had met and the kind of treatment any Indians could expect if the Spanish should appear on their shores. The attacks and attempted thefts Ponce de León's three ships suffered on both the Atlantic and Gulf coasts may have been instigated by this kind of native intelligence. That Spanish voyages made repeated and large-scale attempts to capture Indian slaves from as far north as South Carolina immediately after Ponce de León's discovery only confirmed the warnings of lucky survivors, of whom there were always too few.[4]

Another group of early Spanish visitors was also largely unconcerned about the size or military prowess of native chiefdoms because they had sheer survival on their minds. After the conquest of Mexico in 1521 and the establishment of regular traffic across the Gulf of Mexico to Hispaniola and through the Keys and Bahama Channel to Spain itself, Spanish ships were frequently caught in storms and driven aground on the Florida coasts. The survivors of these wrecks—largely Spanish but also African slaves, Central American Indians, and native Mexicans—found themselves in the hands of coastal chiefs as slaves and adoptees, and they had much to learn of native locutions, methods, and mores in order to stay alive. Once in rough native hands, castaways found that the relative strength of their captors' polities made little difference to their dire predicament.

Spaniards who brushed the coast briefly or washed ashore as human jetsam obviously had less opportunity to test the full power of southeastern chiefdoms or to alter native culture in major ways than did the gold-seekers who made forays into the interior and the projected colonies that soon followed Ponce de León's discovery and Pedro de Quejo's careful reconnaissance of the Atlantic coast in 1525. Having made a shady fortune in Indian slaves in Santo Domingo, Lucas Vázquez de Ayllón took six ships and 500 Spanish recruits in 1526 to settle a fortified town in a fabled "land of Chicora" near Winyah Bay, South Carolina. With the loss of a large supply ship, the abrupt departure of his Indian interpreters, and the lack of native settlements or fertile farmland to exploit, Ayllón moved the colony south to Sapelo Sound. Within two months, 150 survivors had been driven by disease, mutiny, starvation, rebellious black slaves, and angered Indians back to the Antilles. After their harrowing experience in La Florida, they should have been able to empathize with the 60 South Carolina natives who were inveigled aboard two of Ayllón's ships and shanghaied to Santo Domingo five years earlier. One of the ships was lost at sea. "The Indians in the other died shortly afterwards of sorrow and hunger," wrote a contemporary historian of the Indies, "for they would not eat what the Spaniards gave them." Instead, they preferred "dogs, asses and other beasts which they found dead and stinking behind the fence and on the dungheaps." Those who survived these miseries were allocated as slave labor to Spanish households, goldmines, and fields in Hispaniola.[5]

Pánfilo de Narváez, the one-eyed veteran of Cuban conquests, had no better luck in his attempt to colonize Florida in 1528. His *entrada* of 400 failed to find the habitable embrace of Tampa Bay, got separated from its supply ships, and was constantly misled by native guides away from the populous, well-fed Apalachee towns of the Panhandle until they despaired and retreated to the sea. After killing the last of their horses, 250 survivors crowded aboard five makeshift rafts and set off for Mexico. Only a handful, including the expedition's treasurer and second-in-command, Álvar Núñez Cabeza de Vaca, reached their destination to tell the tale of their misfortunes and painful encounters with the Floridians.[6]

When Cabeza de Vaca reached Spain in 1537, he led people to understand that La Florida, despite his own horrific experiences there, was "the richest country in the world." Similar rumors enabled Hernando de Soto, newly rich from his part in the conquest of Peru, to recruit several hundred conquistadors for an *entrada* "to conquer, pacify, and populate" the pagan land of La Florida.[7] After four hapless years careering around the Southeast, as far north as Tennessee and North Carolina and across the Mississippi into Arkansas and Texas, Soto's army of 700 Spaniards and black slaves, 220 horses, assorted war dogs, and a proliferating drove of pigs was reduced to 311 human survivors who reached Mexico in a small fleet of jerry-built brigantines. Soto had engaged most of the largest and most powerful chiefdoms in the region, sometimes imposing his will and hungry troops on them, often suffering their guile, arrows, and formidable resistance. He certainly failed to find gold or silver or to reduce the landscape to peace; like Ayllón and Narváez, Soto drew his last breath and presumably lost his soul in native America.

A few more Spanish attempts to find riches or security in the southeastern interior were equally fruitless and ended equally badly before the crown shifted its geopolitical priorities in the 1560s. When French Huguenots under Jean Ribault and René de Laudonnière planted stone pillars of possession, forts, and a small colony in La Florida after 1562, Spain realized that its first obligation was to rid its North American claims of foreign interlopers, to safeguard the routes of its treasure fleets around the Florida peninsula, and coincidentally to bring the local Indian tribes and chiefdoms to acknowledge Spanish sovereignty. This was the large task of Pedro Menéndez de Avilés, commander of Spain's Caribbean fleet and newly created *adelantado* of La Florida. After liquidating the French "heretics" in 1565, Menéndez proceeded to build a garrison town at St. Augustine, to establish his capital at Santa Elena on Parris Island, South Carolina, to redeem several European captives from the Indians while befriending or cowing many of the coastal tribes, and to sponsor the first Catholic missionaries in native villages, particularly among the Georgia Guales, the Calusas of southwestern Florida, and the Timucuas of northeast Florida.[8] When English Protestants sent by Walter Ralegh planted a fragile colony on Roanoke Island in the 1580s, hoping to establish a secure base from which to launch privateers against the Spanish flotas, or treasure fleets, the Spanish took alarmed note of their presence. Fortunately, English ineptitude as bad as any shown by the conquistadors in Florida, the same hurricanes that sank many Spanish ships and plans, and the threat to England of the great Spanish Armada killed the colony before the Spanish could.[9]

No matter how numerous or powerful the Spanish were, no matter how long they stayed or how far they penetrated into Indian country, native contact with any Spaniards or other Europeans was potentially momentous, capable of altering Indian lives and culture irrevocably and often for the worse. The brevity of slaving voyages to the South Carolina and Georgia barrier islands, for example, did nothing to mitigate the damage they did to the native lives they touched, directly and indirectly. Two expeditions sponsored by Ayllón and partners suggest the magnitude of the losses to native groups. Sometime between 1514 and 1516, Captain Pedro de Salazar took from a South Carolina "Island of Giants" some 500 Indians, who appeared to the Spanish crew much taller than the natives of the Bahamas and Caribbean. Despite their robustness, two-thirds of the captives died at sea, mostly from starvation. Upon landing in Hispaniola, the weak survivors were "tattooed" or branded and divided among the voyage's backers and other buyers, but most of them died before the Spanish could extract enough labor to justify the high prices they paid for them. Their treatment at Spanish hands contrasted sharply with the hospitality and openhandedness they had shown possibly the first white men in their midst.[10] The loss of hundreds of kinsmen must have shredded the social fabric of the relatively small settlements along the coast, seriously endangering their subsistence, defenses, historical memory, and social continuity. For the survivors left behind, the "social death" of relatives and loved ones was not only a deep personal affliction, but served to breed distrust, fear, and hatred of future newcomers, particularly those who came from the sea in strange, giant canoes. Having learned the hard way that Spanish weapons could kill and maim at a distance, they prepared schemes of ambush and what the victims would call "treachery" in order to defend themselves against any future attempts to steal and enslave them.

Unfortunately, the lessons learned by one group did not necessarily get passed to all the others, even along the same coast. In 1521 Captain Quejo and crew spent three weeks making peaceful overtures to a South Carolina river tribe and allegedly, as Quejo later testified in court, "trying to decide whether to take Indians or not." Lulled by appearances, the natives quickly regretted their credulity when the Spanish sailed off with sixty tribesmen for sale in the slave marts of Santo Domingo.[11]

Yet some groups were unambiguously forewarned about the Spanish disregard for native life and liberty. Tribes or villages from which the Spanish kidnapped likely lads they intended to train as guides and interpreters for future expeditions usually got the message without difficulty. If the Indians had second thoughts when the Spanish returned with their sons, who now sported new looks, clothes, names, tongues, and shiny gifts, the young men themselves quickly dispelled them by running away from their captors and stiffening their people's resistance with cautionary tales and horror stories about Hispanic behavior and values. One of the few survivors of Ayllón's slaving voyage of 1521 was a young boy renamed Francisco, who returned to his home on Winyah Bay with Ayllón's colony five years later. Having learned Castilian well, "el Chicorano" (as he was nicknamed) had been educated and converted by Ayllón, taken to Spain, and treated "as if [Ayllón] had procreated him." Having filled his new father's ears with tall tales of the large, excellent pearls in his homeland and gotten him to bankroll an expedition to those parts, Francisco deserted the Spanish within days, never to be seen again by Spaniards but undoubtedly heard by his native kin and neighbors, who helped ensure the demise of the colony with arrows.[12]

In 1570 a young Virginian who had been taken by the Spanish from the York or James River ten years before exacted revenge even more directly when he was returned home to interpret for eight Jesuit missionaries. Although to all appearances he had been thoroughly hispanicized by Menéndez in Mexico City and Havana, sponsored in baptism by the viceroy of New Spain (whose name he took), and presented to the king in Spain, Don Luis de Velasco quickly ran away to his own people, reassumed native dress, took several Indian wives, and led a lethal attack on the mission with hatchets the priests had traded for corn.[13]

Other challenges to and changes in native life also came from the sea, often after pyrotechnical southern storms. As unlikely as it might seem, the flotsam of Spanish shipwrecks was also capable of affecting native culture in often unpredictable ways. The first novelties to wash up were material goods: ship parts, cargo, and the personal belongings of passengers and crew. When Narváez's *entrada* arrived in Tampa Bay in 1528, they found the local natives in possession of pieces of linen and woolen cloth, shoes, canvas, iron, and "bunches of feathers like those of New Spain," perhaps the beautiful quetzal feather fans or shields that so impressed Albrecht Dürer when he viewed some of Cortés's Aztec booty in Brussels in 1520. More mundane but more significant were several shipping crates "like those used for merchandising in Castile," each of which contained "a dead man covered with painted deerskins." Upon closer inspection the bodies proved to be European, presumably from the wrecked ship. Yet the expedition's Franciscan friars regarded these burial treatments as "some form of idolatry and burned the crates and corpses" to exorcise the evil spirits. This was unfortunate because the natives had obviously treated the dead strangers with high respect: the apparently undesecrated corpses were carefully wrapped in valuable painted skins and consigned to equally valuable wooden containers made with techniques largely unknown to the Floridians.[14]

Salvage of another sort often led Spanish explorers to fatally erroneous conclusions and sent them on wild goose chases. Many ships that foundered off the Florida coasts were laden with gold and silver jewelry and ingots taken from Indian troves in Mexico, Tierra Firme, and Peru. The Floridians eagerly collected these metals from the wrecks, not because they appreciated their monetary value in European terms—they did not—but because of their color, brilliance, and possibly weight and their uses as media for their own artistic forms. Gold jewelry made in naturalistic shapes by the natives of South and Central America apparently was respected by the Florida natives for its artistic novelty because many pieces were buried unmodified in mounds with their elite owners. Beautiful lizards, jaguars, eagles, scorpions, and human effigies cast in gold may have inspired local Indians to emulate either the shapes or the casting techniques of the artifacts that washed up on their beaches.[15]

The Floridians' reworking of salvaged gold and silver led Spanish conquistadors and sailors to conclude that Florida was a land rich in precious metals, ripe for the picking. Whenever the Spanish landed among coastal Indians, the natives invariably possessed caches of gold and silver rods, beads, pendants, and other forms of jewelry that they had worked by hammering, abrading, drilling, casting, and incising salvaged coins and bullion. Silver rods were routinely cut, drilled, and rounded or melted down and cast into barrel-shaped beads. Silver *reales* were hammered flat, drilled, and incised to make cult effigy pendants worn from the neck exactly like those traditionally made of shell. Thin sheets of gold were cut and rolled into beads for stringing or tinkling cones for fringed clothing.[16]

The Spaniards, of course, fairly salivated over these riches and did their best to wheedle or wangle them from native hands. The trick was to do so without appearing to place too high a value on the metals for fear the Indians would inflate their own modest valuation of them. This was no easy task when common soldiers and sailors realized that some caciques commanded "as much as a million dollars, or over, in bars of silver, in gold, and in articles of jewelry made by the hands of Mexican Indians." Even the caciques of land-poor Ais and Jeaga on the east-central coast of the peninsula were rich from the sea. Spanish prisoners reported that they often saw their captors head for the local beaches after a storm and return with "great wealth, in bars of silver and gold, and bags of reals."[17] When Adelantado Menéndez journeyed in 1566 to the powerful Calusa chiefdom of "King Carlos" on the southwestern coast to redeem shipwreck victims, Carlos gave him a silver bar worth 200 ducats, but Menéndez refused to barter for any more "so that the Indians should not think that he came in search of gold." His men, however, made out like happy bandits, exchanging some 3,500 ducats' worth for what they regarded as "baubles." "For a playing card . . . an ace of diamonds, one [Indian] gave a soldier a piece of gold worth 70 ducats; and for a pair of scissors, half a bar of silver worth 100 ducats." The soldiers got rich so quickly that "they began to gamble," like their new Indian partners "holding the money of little account." To the Indians, the rarity and novelty of a colorful playing card printed on paper and of sharp metal scissors were far more valuable than the shiny metals that they seemed to be able to obtain in abundance with little effort.[18]

Of even greater value to the Indians were the novel humans they salvaged from the surf, who could be enslaved or adopted into their families and households. Since the Spanish flotas contained black Africans and light-skinned Spaniards as well as more familiar brown-skinned Indian people from Central and South America, the Floridians' world view had to expand to incorporate and account for these strangers and the geographies and cultures from which they came. This is never a small undertaking because it involves a major adjustment of a people's ethnocentric sense of uniqueness at the navel of the universe. If it does not reduce their sense of superiority, it certainly complicates it by introducing disturbing intimations of cultural relativism.

While the Indians always had the upper hand, absorbing shipwreck victims and educating them for useful roles in native society could not happen overnight, particularly with older prisoners. Nor was acculturation a one-way process, for the captives had strongly held ways of speaking and thinking, relating and doing things, that were asserted or at least much in evidence as their captors attempted to replace them with native versions. Some of these cultural habits must have rubbed off on the Indians. We know that Spanish clothes had some cachet in native circles, perhaps more for ceremonial occasions than everyday wear and for the elite than commoners, because they were eagerly salvaged by and divided among coastal tribes.[19]

Language, too, was a valuable item of exchange, especially as the Spanish presence and assertion of sovereignty grew after Menéndez's appointment. Interpreters who could negotiate in both languages were as useful to the Indians as to the conquistadors. Cacique Carlos even found that a small amount of linguistic accommodation could turn Spanish captives into more willing tribesmen. Hernando d'Escalante Fontaneda, who had learned four native languages while a prisoner of the Calusas from the age of thirteen to thirty, and a "free negro" interpreter similarly acculturated once persuaded Carlos that new shipwreck victims who simply could not understand their captors' peremptory commands to dance and sing or to climb to the lookout were not unwilling to cooperate and did not deserve to be killed for their "rebellion." Whereupon Carlos told his subjects that "when they should find Christians thus cast away, and seize them, they must require them to do nothing without giving notice, that one might go to them who should understand their language."[20] For one of the most powerful chiefs in all of Florida, this was a noteworthy concession to another culture and a new way to view his suddenly expanding world.

Perhaps the most permanent change in Indian life resulted from the biological amalgamation of the castaways and their native captors. Spanish men and women who found themselves after a time in need of support, companionship, and love married Indian spouses and often produced *mestizo* offspring. So genuine were these attachments that Spanish women, when redeemed by Spanish colonial officials, sometimes elected to return to their native homes, husbands, and children rather than rejoin a Spanish society they had long since ceased to know. Mestizo children not only looked like the products of two increasingly intersecting peoples but often served as mediators and brokers for the two cultures they straddled, a role of great importance as European power made itself felt over wider swaths of the native Southeast.[21]

Although slave raids and shipwrecks were sporadic and unannounced, Spanish *entradas* into the interior were large, noisy, and soon predictable in their methods. The biggest and baddest was Soto's, which blundered and plundered its way through the Southeast for nearly four years. The effects of Juan Pardo's more focused fort-building expeditions into the mountains of North Carolina and Tennessee between 1566 and 1568 were much more benign.[22] The bloated settlement attempt of Tristán de Luna in 1559–61 simply came unstuck from the beginning and suffered from, more than it hurt, the natives.[23] Yet all Spanish (and French) thrusts into the Southeast bore consequences for its native peoples and cultures. Some changes were temporary and relatively superficial; others were serious and often did permanent damage.

The *modus operandi* of a typical *entrada* was predicated on obtaining native bearers, guides, and interpreters for the journey, clearing the way of military obstacles, and locating native food to supplement always short supplies, often frustratingly lost at the last moment in American ports to hurricanes, as Ayllón's and Luna's were. After the first, most expeditions brought their own native interpreters, who had been taken on previous voyages and taught Castilian toward their return. Ayllón had Francisco—briefly—and Luna brought a Coosa woman who had been taken to Mexico by Soto's men sixteen years earlier.[24] When Soto's two *lenguas* (literally, tongues) ran off as soon as they were returned home, he was extremely lucky to stumble upon Juan Ortiz, a thirty-year-old survivor of the Narváez debacle who had learned at least two Timucuan languages while in captivity. So relieved was Soto to find Ortiz that he gave him a black velvet suit to cover his tattooed "nakedness," "some good arms and a beautiful horse." After twelve years with the Indians, even this well-bred Sevillan had some difficulty not only with a surfeit of strange clothes but in resurrecting his native language. "He had even forgotten how to pronounce the name of his own country," one soldier recalled, calling Sevilla "Xivilla," and was forced to make a cross with his hand and bow when he could not remember how to announce that he was a Christian to stop the lance of a Spanish horseman. "He was among us more than four days," recalled another, "before he could join one word with another, since upon saying one word in Spanish, he would say another four or five in the language of the Indians, until finally he was again able to speak our language well." He soon proved invaluable as the *entrada's* mouthpiece. When he died in the late winter of 1542, Soto was forced to use the inexpert services of a young Indian man seized in Cofi-tachequi two years earlier. "To learn from the Indians what [Ortiz] stated in four words, with the youth the whole day was needed; and most of the time he understood just the opposite of what was asked. . . . "[25]

The elite troops of Spanish *entradas* were haughty *hidalgos* whose gentle status allowed them to forgo working with their hands, so they invariably brought along a few, mostly African, servants to carry their baggage and do other menial chores. But once ordinary soldiers reached America's native provinces, they, too, felt entitled to lord it over the "pagan" Indians by taking slaves of their own. This desire, coupled with that of the army's general need to transport substantial food supplies, arms, and ammunition, led to Soto's impressment of hundreds of native bearers, or, as they were called in Mexico and Hispaniola, *tamemes,* as he moved from chiefdom to chiefdom.[26] As he came to the head town of each chiefdom, he sought to take the cacique and some of his principal headmen hostage. This was meant to ensure the docility of their warriors and the collection of ample corn and sometimes meat or fish to sustain the army during its uninvited stay and until it could reach the next destination in another chiefdom. Usually the porters were released in the next chiefdom, even though their entry into enemy territory was potentially lethal. At the end of Soto's expedition, many soldiers complained that now-Governor Luis de Moscoso abandoned "five hundred *head* of Indians, male and female" at the mouth of the Mississippi, thinking it "inhuman . . . in payment of the great service they had performed, to take them away in order to abandon them outside their lands to become captives of others." Many of these tamemes, including boys and girls, had been with the *entrada* so long that they "spoke and understood Spanish" and had become Christians of some sort.[27]

Because most porters were adult or at least healthy young males, whose martial prowess and knowledge of the landscape made them risky servants, Soto had most of them put in iron collars and chains to prevent escape. Although the southeastern tribes regularly took captives in small numbers from rival chiefdoms to use as slave labor and often cut nerves and tendons in one foot to hobble them, the loss of as many as 400 to 800 males for potentially long periods opened their towns and villages to enemy attack, deprived families of hunting, fishing, trading, craftsmanship, and perhaps planting or harvesting, and truncated the group's social memory and political structure.[28] If hunger overtook the *entrada* as it moved in an inclement season or through a buffer zone between chiefdoms or a population that hid its food, the native porters suffered the most because they were always fed and covered last and least. In the Soto *entrada's* final march back to the Mississippi, "almost all the Indians of service died" from exposure, starvation, and disease. Like all armies, Soto's moved on its stomach, quartering for weeks at a time in major towns to recover from punishing reprisals or to wait out winter cold or spring floods. Even a short stay could clean out a town's *barbacoas,* the raised cribs where the chief stored his tributary produce against a public emergency and seed corn for the next planting. "Forced by necessity," the Indians of Aminoya even volunteered to serve Soto's army in hopes that "they might give them some of the ears of maize they had taken from them" on a previous pass through their territory. "Those who came to the town [from hiding] were so weak and enfeebled that they had no flesh on their bones; and many near the town died of pure hunger and weakness."[29]

The Spanish had other needs that required the forced participation of native women, usually thirty or so at a time. Some women, in even larger numbers, were captured to serve as hostages to neutralize their chiefs and warrior husbands. An occasional woman was drafted as a guide or interpreter.[30] And the rival caciques of powerful Pacaha and Casqui tried to outdo each other in offering close relatives to Soto to cement their temporary alliance in marriage. The lord of Casqui offered up one of his daughters, "a pretty girl," whereas Pacaha's leader upped the ante by sacrificing one of his wives, "fresh and [allegedly] very virginal," one or two of his sisters, "tall of body and plump in figure," and possibly "another principal Indian woman." Not to be outdone, Casqui later exchanged two women with two Spaniards for a shirt apiece.[31] Whether this kind of female barter was more the result of callous male chauvinism or a politic attempt to fend off even worse arrogations by the ruthless Spaniards is hard to tell.

But no one had any doubts about why the larger groups of women were requested with frequency. According to Soto's secretary on the expedition, the Spanish wanted the women not only as porters and cooks but in order "to make use of them and for their lewdness and lust," and "they baptized them more for their carnal intercourse than to instruct them in the faith."[32] The *entrada's* long and short stays in Indian towns clearly led to sexual relations with native women, some of whom complied for gifts, some from a traditional sense of hospitality, and some undoubtedly by force. Just how the natives in general regarded these liaisons is difficult to judge at this distance. If the natives resembled other Eastern Woodland peoples in the next two centuries, they were, initially at least, not racially prejudiced toward the newcomers and may even have been impressed by the spiritual power they seemed to possess by virtue of their advanced technological skills.[33]

They were certainly receptive to Spanish and African deserters who fled the entrada at various junctures, many of whom were enamored of native women they had met while quartered in the women's towns or on the march. En route to Guaxule in the North Carolina mountains, three black slaves were seduced from the march "by the attraction of [Indian] women." Two were persuaded to return, but the third joined forces with the niece of the cacica of Cofitachequi, who also escaped. An eyewitness testified that the couple definitely "held communication as husband and wife" and planned to return to Cofitachequi 250 rough leagues away. Toward the end of the expedition, the "bastard son of a gentleman of Seville" also deserted to the Indians "in fear lest [some of his Spanish colleagues] seize from him as a gaming obligation an Indian woman

whom he had as a mistress and whom he took away with him."[34] To judge by
their treatment in one of the most powerful chiefdoms, Spanish deserters did
not have to fear for their lives. A gentleman soldier from Salamanca and a
black slave who slipped away in Ulibahali lived for eleven or twelve years
among the Coosans and were still remembered in 1560—eight or nine years
after their deaths—when Luna's expedition arrived in Coosa.[35] Presumably,
they left behind mestizo and mulatto children, as their fellow invaders and
deserters must have done throughout the Southeast in the sixteenth century.

Spanish *entradas* and European settlements left their mark on native life in
three other ways. Largely benign was the gift, theft, or loss of a veritable cor-
nucopia of material objects and artifacts. When Laudonnière and the French
twice withdrew from Florida in 1563 and 1564, they purposely left behind a
boat and refrained from burning their fort to save its metalware and leftover
supplies for their Timucuan allies.[36] Indian porters walked away from Soto's
columns with parcels of Spanish clothing and supplies as well as iron chains
and collars which they soon filed off and found new uses for. Soto occasionally and Pardo always distributed small gifts to their native hosts and helpers,
such as tubular blue Nueva Cadiz beads, hawk's bells, hand mirrors, silver-
colored feathers, chisels, knives, wedges, axes, pieces of brightly colored cloth,
enameled buttons, leather shoes, and fiber sandals. On his way back to Santa
Elena, Pardo even gave some of the coastal chiefs beautifully painted skin
mantles and breechclouts that he had obtained from mountain tribes, thereby
fostering an intertribal trade that already dealt in such items as Gulf Coast
conch shells, which Pardo also gave—perhaps unwittingly—to one important
mountain chief.[37]

The impact these goods had on native habits or artistic conventions is hard
to assess. Most new materials, such as cloth and metal, were usually given traditional forms and uses. Many objects were monopolized by the native elite
and interred with them in mounds or charnal houses. A few European artifacts may have inspired native imitations in local media, as they did increasingly during the next two centuries. In the temple at Cofitachequi, Soto found
glass beads and rosaries and Biscayan axes retrieved from Ayllón's ill-fated
colony on the South Carolina coast. Some items of skin clothing seemed to
have been made by natives after instruction by Ayllón's colonists. Apparently,
the Cofitachequans had fashioned "breeches and buskins, and black gaiters
with laces of white hide, and with fringes or edging of colored hide, as if they
had been made in Spain."[38]

Nearly as widespread but far more malign were the military effects of the
Spanish *entradas*, particularly Soto's. Although they were on foreign and often
dangerous ground, the Spanish enjoyed several advantages in motive and
materiel. The all-consuming search for precious metals and other instant
wealth spurred the Spanish soldiers, from the lowest to the highest, through
long and tedious hardships. The Spaniards' pronounced ethnocentrism and
assumption of religious superiority, fostered by eight hundred years of recon-

quest of the Iberian peninsula from the Moors and inflated by unlikely victories over the overwhelming native forces of Mexico and Peru, gave them a leg up on Indians who did not fight for religion or to impose their beliefs and values on others. Even after four years of profitless suffering and losses, Luis Moscoso could rally Soto's tired troops with the old battle cry of the *Reconquista*, "Come on, men, Santiago, Santiago, and at them!"[39]

Primed with arrogant fervor, the Spanish wielded a large arsenal of offensive weapons. Ships had the capacity—if not always the good fortune—to supply and resupply *entradas* from the ports of Spain, Mexico, and the Antilles. The novel size and speed of Spanish horses frightened the natives, scattered them in pitched battles, and chased them down on relatively dry ground.[40] If horses could not follow them in bogs and brush, trained war dogs could. No Indian could outrun or escape the jaws of an Irish greyhound or mastiff, and the Spaniards spread even greater fear of the dogs by periodically throwing Indians to them, which led to the coining of a special Spanish word for the atrocity, *aperrear*.[41] Fifteen-foot lances were initially effective in running down Indians on horseback, but the pikes and halberds of foot soldiers quickly proved cumbersome in the southeastern forests, whose warriors seldom attacked head on. More efficient and lethal were crossbows, arquebuses, and particularly double-edged Toledo swords. The Spanish were fierce and expert swordsmen who did not hesitate to slash and hack at exposed native limbs. Twenty percent of the Indian skeletons at the King site in northwest Georgia bore deep gashes and gouges from Soto's swords.[42] At other points along the *entrada*'s route, commoners and caciques alike were slashed in the head and back and had their arms, hands, and noses cut off.[43] When the inhabitants of the large Tascaloosa town of Mabila suddenly attacked Soto's forces in October 1540, the Spanish did not end their revenge until they had killed 2,500 men, women, and children. Not long after, Soto "ordered that no male Indian's life should be spared" when he sicked his troops on Nilco, a town of five or six thousand, in a preemptive strike to terrorize the region.[44]

Because the natives were no match for the well-armed ferocity of Soto's numerous troops and their horses in a showdown, they sought to neutralize the Spanish threat by deflecting, coopting, or avoiding the invaders. At considerable personal risk, Indian guides commandeered by Soto led the entrada away from their chiefdom's major towns and food supplies into barren or enemy territory.[45] If the Spanish wanted to stay put, local caciques allied themselves with the intruders in order to direct Spanish swords against rival provinces and chiefdoms, which invariably upset the delicate balance of Mississippian prestige and power.[46] Having Soto's troops quartered in one's town was a large price to pay, but it was still smaller than being ravaged by angry Spaniards or by a Spanish alliance with a rival chiefdom. And if none of these ploys worked, the Indians simply abandoned their towns and fields to avoid contact, sometimes torching both to deny the invaders any succor or satisfaction.[47] The only place where the Indians could deliver punishing blows to the

Spanish was on the Mississippi, where the conquistadors' swords, horses, and heavy armor did them no good and native canoes literally ran circles around the Spaniards' clumsy, exposed brigantines.[48]

Although Soto's *entrada* made its escape from the Southeast, as did Ayllón's, Narváez's, Luna's, and Pardo's, the unvictorious Spanish bequeathed a legacy of death and disintegration that had little to do with swords or guns. The forces of occupation left behind by every European ship, settlement, and *entrada*, no matter how briefly they remained in La Florida, were biological. A few were relatively benign. Many of Soto's imported pigs escaped and multiplied prodigiously to become the famous razorback hogs of the southern mast forests, for which many Indian groups acquired a decided taste.[49] Pedro de Quejo's voyage to Winyah Bay in 1525 may have introduced European plants to the native Southeast. According to court testimony, Quejo gave the Indians seeds for various Spanish plants that his employer Ayllón hoped they would cultivate before he planted his proposed colony among them the following year. Even without Quejo's careful instructions in how to grow them, the seeds may have taken on a life of their own.[50]

Certainly other imported plants—and animals—did well in and on the humid soils of the Southeast. Inland natives were often growing peach trees and watermelons before they were contracted directly by Spanish explorers. By the seventeenth century, mission Indians added garbanzos, figs, and hazelnuts to a mixed diet that already included wheat, which was initially grown to make communion wafers for the resident friars. The Indians never took to sheep or goats and only slowly to cattle—the pastoral Spaniards' favorite animals—but carefree chickens and pigs gained instant favor as complements to, if never complete substitutes for, wild game and fish.[51] It is not difficult to imagine the proliferation and hybridization of species throughout Spanish and native Florida of the 600 chickens, 550 pigs, 492 pumpkin squashes, 505 loads of cassava, and 854 *fanegas* of corn that Menéndez imported from Havana in 1566.[52] No one bothered to record the silent arrival of rats and weeds, but they, too, came in the holds of European ships and created a niche for themselves in native fields and villages.

Equally quiet but far more dangerous were those microscopic messengers of death, epidemic diseases. Isolated from the microbial history of Europe, Asia, and Africa by the reflooding of the Bering Strait, America's natives had developed no immunities to serious infectious diseases because they virtually had none.[53] When explorers stepped off ships from the disease capitals of Europe, they brought lethal strains of influenza, typhus, diphtheria, bubonic plague, and smallpox as well as so-called "childhood diseases" such as measles, mumps, and chicken pox. All of these and more throve in the "virgin soil" disease environments of the native Southeast and proceeded to cut down its peoples with merciless efficiency.[54] When Soto's *entrada* reached the main town of Cofitachequi, over a hundred miles from the South Carolina coast, the Spaniards noticed that several surrounding towns were uninhabited and "choked with vegetation" because the province had suffered a "great pestilence" within the last year or two. Survivors had fled to the woods and planted no crops. In one town the conquistadors found "four long houses full of bodies of those who died from the plague that had raged there." In all likelihood, death had made its slow but steady way, on one human host after another, from Ayllón's squalid colony at Sapelo Sound over the course of ten or eleven years.[55] More rapid was the unfamiliar contagion that felled the seventy-four natives who were laid out at the same time in the Tatham mound in west-central Florida in the wake of Soto's entrada. The presence of only two sword cuts on the skeletons is stark testimony to what must have been the terrifying lethality of the conquerors' invisible allies.[56]

Disease and Soto's destructiveness brought many of the Mississippian chiefdoms to their knees and by the beginning of the seventeenth century had seriously depopulated and decentralized the native Southeast. As the populations of the chiefdoms dropped, often precipitously in the areas visited by Soto, towns were abandoned for lack of viability and their inhabitants moved to less damaged ones, thereby reducing the areal extent of each chiefdom. Most towns, even those replenished with polyglot refugees, covered much less ground than before. Several main towns, particularly in northwest Georgia and eastern Tennessee, moved south into central and southern Alabama, where in the next century they formed the Creek confederacy. Other groups moved into less accessible upland regions between rivers, and those who remained in the valleys built more dispersed, elongated settlements without defensive palisades.

Along with their populations and warrior counts, the political hierarchies of the chiefdoms collapsed. The authority of chiefs declined, as did the ascribed status of the elites, part-time craft specialization, and elaborate funeral rites and differential grave offerings for the elite. Tributary payments and obligations gave way to local autonomy. Paramount chiefs disappeared and tribal chiefs ruled more by persuasion than by force or religious charisma. Mound centers were abandoned and no new mounds were built because chiefs no longer had the coercive power to command labor for large-scale public projects. And the religious cults that had sustained the whole Mississippian hierarchy lost their explanatory power and adherents.[57]

Although the southeastern interior fared poorly, many of the coastal Florida groups retained much of their former strength and belligerence toward the Spanish. Less ravaged by disease because of their dispersed settlements, they successfully resisted Spanish missionaries and attempts to render them obedient to a distant monarch for many decades. Since neither corn nor cattle prospered in the southern two-thirds of the peninsula, particularly along the coasts, the natives held on to their age-old diets of fish and game, traditional lifeways, and familiar forms of government and religion far longer than their Timucua and Apalachee neighbors in the north who allowed Catholic missions into their midst.[58]

Yet for the Southeast as a whole, the Spanish advent offered little redemption; according to some farsighted natives, the foreigners' continued presence promised even less. In 1541, six leaders from an Indian town near the Mississippi visited Soto's camp. "They were come," they said, "to see what people [the Spanish] were" because "they had learned from their ancestors that a white race would inevitably subdue them."[59] Whether the Spanish interpreters or chronicler put words in their mouths or not, the elders' prophecy would certainly *not* come to pass in the Southeast in the sixteenth, seventeenth, *or* eighteenth century.

TEN

The Rise and Fall of the Powhatan Empire

Today, "empire" is not a word most Americans associate with their nation or its past. Because we do not wish to see ourselves or our ancestors as "imperialists," we have, from the very beginning, regarded America as a "virgin land," a wide-open continent largely devoid of human inhabitants and free for the taking. In doing so, we have seriously misread our history.

For in the first decade of the seventeenth century, what became the United States began in Virginia as a fierce clash of empires. The invaders were English, a mixture of experienced soldiers, desperate servants, and hopeful settlers, all unwitting makers of the first British Empire. The American empire they sought to conquer was not Spanish, Dutch, or French, as we might expect, but an unusual Indian mini-state headed by a powerful "emperor."

By mid-century the English were firmly planted in Virginia, but only at a tremendous cost in human life, both English and native. The Powhatan empire (as it is called after its native leader) lay in ruins as royal Virginia began her steady rise to become the largest and wealthiest English colony on the continent and, in due course, the political birthplace of the nation.

Tsenacommacoh: Seat of Empire

Powhatan's empire lay in the tidewater region of Virginia, bounded on the north by the Potomac River, on the south by the Great Dismal Swamp, and on the west by the falls of the major tidal rivers that sliced the area into long peninsulas. It was also defined by its native enemies: Iroquoian-speakers on its northern and southern flanks, Siouan-speakers in the hills to the west.

Powhatan's empire-building began on modest foundations sometime in the last quarter of the sixteenth century, when he inherited six tribes on the upper James and middle York rivers. In 1597 he conquered the Kecoughtans, a large and prosperous tribe at the mouth of the James. By 1608 he had forged some thirty tribes into a monarchy with himself as paramount chief or *wero-wance*. With the exception of the Chesapeakes at Cape Henry and the semi-independent Chickahominies on the river to which they gave their name, all of the tribes between the James and Piankatank rivers were under Powhatan's thumb, obedient to the relatives and trusted councillors he intruded as local chiefs. Even tribes on the Eastern Shore across Chesapeake Bay and on the Potomac paid him tribute to remain free from his imperial embrace.[1]

A native monarchy such as Powhatan's was highly unusual north of the Aztecs in Mexico. Eastern Woodland tribes were known to confederate loosely to reduce conflict between themselves and for defense against common enemies; the five-nation Huron and Iroquois confederacies in southern Ontario and New York are the best known. But most Indians on the Atlantic coast were notorious individualists, who tolerated only minimal interference in their lives. Villages of a few hundred people were the largest polities they recognized, and the authority of their elected or hereditary chiefs depended solely on their powers of persuasion. Coercion was out of the question where jails, police, and standing armies were absent and personal revenge was the guiding principle of native law.

How Powhatan (pronounced Pō'-ĕ-tan) managed to fashion a monarchy from such unlikely material we do not know. His ruthless use of armed might, "subtle understanding," and "politique carriage" obviously had much to do with his success.[2] And we can only guess at his reasons for doing so. The most plausible reason is that he feared the loss of his exposed inheritance. His own birthplace and two-thirds of his tribal patrimony lay near the falls of the upper James, a short paddle from traditional Monacan and Manahoacan enemies to the west. His York River tribes lay exposed to a new and even more dangerous threat, as events in his young manhood had shown.

Threat from the East

Throughout the sixteenth century, Spanish, French, and English ships put into Chesapeake Bay in search of fresh water, firewood, and trade. Three kinds of exchange took place between the sailors and the coastal inhabitants. The first was inadvertent—the introduction of European diseases to native populations without experience of or immunities to them. Epidemics of smallpox, influenza, plague, and even relatively benign childhood diseases such as measles scythed through Indian villages with lethal efficiency. In 1608 Powhatan told the English, with some exaggeration, that he had seen "the death of all my people thrice, and not one living of those 3 generations, but my selfe."[3]

The first epidemic may have resulted from another exchange made in 1561, when a young York River Indian, the nephew of the local chief and probably a relative of Powhatan, was kidnapped by a Spanish crew. (European explorers

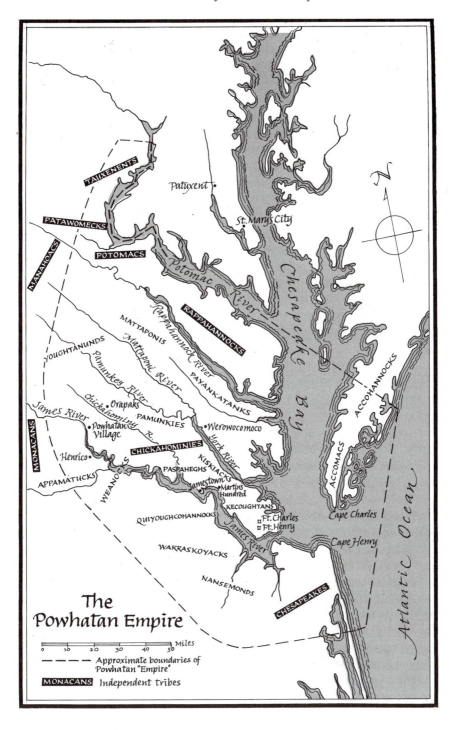

TAUXENENTS

PATAWOMECKS

MANAHOACS

POTOMACS

Patuxent

St. Mary's City

Potomac River

Chesapeake Bay

N

MATTAPONIS

Rappahannock River

RAPPAHANNOCKS

YOUGHTANUNDS

Mattaponi River

PAYANKATANKS

Pamunkey River

ACCOHANNOCKS

Chickahominy R.

Orapaks

PAMUNKIES

Werowocomoco

MONACANS

James River

Powhatan Village

CHICKAHOMINIES

Henrico

York River

KISKIACKS

ACCOMACS

PASPAHEGHS

APPAMATUCKS

WEANOCKS

Jamestown

Martins Hundred

KECOUGHTANS

Cape Charles

QUIYOUGHCOHANNOCKS

Ft. Charles

Ft. Henry

James River

Cape Henry

WARRASKOYACKS

Atlantic Ocean

NANSEMONDS

CHESAPEAKES

The
Powhatan Empire

Miles

0 10 20 30 40 50

— — — Approximate boundaries of
Powhatan "Empire"

MONACANS Independent tribes

had an incurable itch for human souvenirs.) After education in Hispanic ways and Catholic religion in Spain and Havana, he was baptized Don Luis de Velasco. Nine years later he led a small party of Jesuit missionaries back to the York, which he had advertised in his new tongue as a land of milk and honey. But the priests found only "famine and death," which had ravaged the population for six years. Don Luis soon ran off to his own people, took several wives native-style, and led an attack on the mission. With hatchets the priests had traded for corn, the "renegade" and his tribesmen killed all of the Spaniards but a boy. The following year, 1572, a Spanish fleet exacted terrible revenge by killing many natives and hanging the chief from the yardarm of their flagship.[4]

The third kind of exchange was more benign in the transaction but equally alarming in its implications for the inland tribes. The Europeans traded metal tools, cloth, and small luxuries they regarded as "toys" or "baubles" for native furs, pearls, and food. The land-bound Powhatans envied their coastal neighbors who were given shiny copper pieces for mere corn, and feared those who obtained iron tools which could be cut and hammered into deadly weapons.[5]

For any or all of these reasons—to build a viable population, to protect it from European invaders, and to monopolize access to the seaborne trade— Powhatan may have dared to dream of empire. Although his inherited tribes were too far and too weak to have wiped out Sir Walter Ralegh's colony at Roanoke in the 1580s, the last two reasons undoubtedly prompted him in 1606 or 1607 to assassinate the Roanoke survivors who were sheltered by tribes south of the James. That the Englishmen had taught his native rivals how to beat copper from local mines and to build two-story stone houses gave Powhatan only more cause for envy.[6]

The Emperor

We know very little about the young man who built this novel empire, but from English descriptions of the aging ruler we begin to understand the measure and secret of his success. When the English first met him in 1607, he was in his sixties. Despite his age and the hard times he had seen, he was a tall, well-proportioned man, sinewy, active, and hardy. Lank gray hair hung to his broad shoulders, framing a round face, somewhat sad and "sower." Wisps of gray beard—usually plucked by the Indians—protruded from his upper lip and chin. Unlike the monarchs of Europe, Powhatan dressed like a commoner, in deerskin breechclout, moccasins, and raccoon cape or mantle, which he made himself. Met in the woods alone, he would not have struck the English as extraordinary.

When the English met him, however, he was never alone and never ordinary. For he never deigned to visit the English in their settlements; the colonists always paid court to him at his native capital. There, surrounded by his bodyguard of forty tall bowmen, the finest of his hundred wives, and his chief councillors, priests, and orators, he sat on an elevated throne "with such

When Captain John Smith first saw the "Emperor" Powhatan in the winter of 1607, the Indian's regal bearing was cause for special note. After his military experiences in eastern and western Europe, Smith was not easily impressed; but Powhatan, seated on his raised "throne" in a longhouse, drew Smith's admiration for his dignified demeanor and his astute statecraft. From an engraved map of Virginia by Smith and William Hole in Smith's *Generall Historie of Virginia* (London, 1624).

a Majestie as I cannot expresse," marveled Captain John Smith, who was not easily impressed, "nor yet have often seene, either in Pagan or Christian."[7] From that fur-lined eminence he dispensed orders to his thirty-three "kings" and two "queens" and summary justice to his people.

While Indian law was custom, Powhatan's will was also law. Out of fear and respect, his people esteemed him "not only as a king but as halfe a God."[8] His werowances knew accurately their respective territories, but they held them all from Powhatan, to whom they paid tribute amounting to 80 percent of all furs, copper, pearls, game, and corn. The valuables he promptly stored in a treasure house half as long as a football field, attended only by priests and guarded at its four corners by fierce carved images.[9] By redistributing most of the food to the taxpayers, the emperor, like the federal government, earned their gratitude and allegiance. By the same token, his justice was terrible and swift. Petty offenders were beaten bloody with cudgels; serious offenders were thrown into pits of hot coals, brained on altar stones, or tortured and butchered with razor-sharp shells and reeds. Understandably, subjects went out of their way to avoid his displeasure.

Tassantasses: The English Strangers

When the first three English ships tacked into the James in April 1607, of course, their hundred and four passengers had no knowledge of Powhatan or his empire. Blissfully unaware of his 14,000 subjects and 3,200 warriors, they were unafraid of his terrible majesty. Their minds were on other things. They, too, had dreamed of empire, and in Virginia they sought to make their dreams come true.

All through the reign of Queen Elizabeth, the "Virgin Queen" for whom Ralegh had named the region, the Protestant English had coveted the fabulous wealth extracted from the New World by the Spanish, their Catholic archrivals in Europe. Surely, gold and silver like that of the Incas and Aztecs could be found in the temperate zones of North America. If not, English privateers could lie on the southern coast to pounce on the Spanish bullion fleets as they navigated the narrow Strait of Florida and the Bahama Channel.

Gold-digging and piracy were incentives for some, but most investors in colonial enterprise had other, equally quixotic, goals. One was to discover, at long last, a Northwest Passage through the inconvenient American continent to the legendary riches of the Orient and East Indies. Chesapeake Bay and its large rivers flowing from the northwest fired many imaginations.

Another goal was to convert the American "savages" to Christianity and a European brand of "civility." The best way to do this, it was thought, was to establish faithful replicas of Old World society in the New and a "good and sociable traffique" with the natives. The godly lives of the settlers and the goodly lines of their wares would quickly seduce the natives from their "anarchy" and "Devil-worship" to "the true knowledge of God, and the Obedience to us."[10] In that day, politics and religion were old bedfellows.

Since full-scale colonies were expensive and long-term projects, Virginia's initial investors thought more of planting a commercial outpost in the midst of the native population. From a secure base on a major route to the interior, company employees could trade English cloth and iron goods for American minerals, furs, and rare natural products. In time, they could even expect to export citrus, olives, wines, and silk, which normally came from hostile Spain and Portugal.

The Virginia Company

For the first seventeen years in Virginia, most of the English colonists were governed by and worked for the Virginia Company of London, a joint-stock enterprise of gentry and merchant investors. While King James I gave them a royal charter and a royally appointed council oversaw their affairs for the first three years, the company was a private venture whose commercial goals took precedence over national concerns. The main object of the colony was to produce a return on the stockholders' investments; it not only had to pay its own way but to turn a profit. If it could not do so in a reasonable time, the colony would have to be abandoned as a business venture or, as eventually happened, taken over by the crown.

The corporate search for profits molded the early character of the colony and deeply affected its relations with the Powhatans. As the first ships left England, the London Council instructed its colonial officers to "have Great Care not to Offend the naturals" (the Indians) as the colonists moved over the countryside in search of rich minerals and the passage to the "East India Sea." They were also ordered to trade with the Indians for corn before the natives realized the English meant to settle among them, in the event that the English seed corn did not prosper in the first year.[11] But what was intended as a temporary measure quickly became a way of life, because the food supplies sent from England were never adequate and the majority of colonists were singularly ill-suited for the task of colonization.

In the first flush of commercial zeal, the company recruited too many "big wigs" and too few "horny hands." Of the initial 295 settlers, 92 were tender-fingered gentlemen, accompanied by seven tailors, two goldsmiths, two refiners, a jeweler, a perfumer, and a pipe-maker; only two blacksmiths, three masons, four carpenters, and forty-four ordinary laborers were sent to build and sustain the colony.[12] Conspicuously underrepresented were husbandmen to feed the adventurers, and soldiers equally handy with pickaxe and musket. When supplies sent from London spoiled in transit, were eaten by rats in storage, or were wasted by ships' crews that dallied too long in Virginia ports, the colonists were forced to beg, borrow, or steal food from the Powhatans, who often had little enough for winter consumption and spring seed.

First Encounters

Food was not yet a problem in May 1607 when the English moored their three ships to the trees on Jamestown Island and began to build a triangular fort and living quarters. While the fort was under construction, Captain Christopher

Newport, a one-armed former privateer, took two dozen men to explore the river and its native habitations.[13] Armed with a map drawn by an Indian guide, the party sailed upriver as far as the falls near modern-day Richmond. Along the way they exchanged gifts and courtesies with Powhatan's local werowances, who were easily identified by their red-dyed deer hair "crowns." Near the falls they met Powhatan himself for the first time, who warned the English not to proceed any farther lest they be set upon by his enemies, the Monacans. (In fact, he was probably more worried that the gun-toting strangers would be drawn into alliance with the Monacans.) The two leaders then concluded a military pact against the Monacans and a revenge pact against the Chesapeakes, who had attacked the English when they first landed in late April. To seal their new league of friendship, Powhatan gave his own fur mantle to Newport, who reciprocated with glass beads, hawk's bells, pocket knives, and scissors. Then the parties toasted their union with draughts of English beer, brandy, and sack, which gave more than one Indian leader a powerful bellyache.

The Englishmen's "hot drinks" were to prove less painful to the Powhatans than two other foreign introductions. The first was the surreptitious English claim to the whole "River of Powhatan," which they promptly renamed the James in honor of their own king. This was done in the presence of only one Indian on an island at the falls by planting a wooden cross inscribed "Jacobus Rex. 1607" and giving a "great shout." When their native guide Nauirans looked suspicious, Newport explained with a straight face that the two arms of the cross signified Powhatan and himself, the joint where they met was their league of amity, and the shout the reverence they paid to Powhatan. When Nauirans later conveyed the English version of this presumptuous ceremony to Powhatan, he too was taken in, at least temporarily.[14]

The English were not totally disingenuous with the Indians because they thought their "discovery" of the river gave their sovereign "the most right unto it" against the competing claims of other *Christian* kings, particularly the Spanish.[15] When they thought at all of native rights to Virginia, they saw them as temporary "natural" impediments to the superior "civil" claims of "civilized" people. The waters of the James, of course, belonged to the society whose naval technology could dominate its course.

Although the English were badly outnumbered, they lost no time in trying to persuade the Powhatans that, even if the European version of "international" law did not support their American claims, might made right. Perhaps the tribe that needed the most persuasion was the Paspahegh, in whose territory Jamestown was located. Although the intruders understood no Algonquian dialect, they claimed that the Paspahegh werowance had *by signs* given them as much land as they desired. But the chief and a hundred bowmen had left the negotiations "in great anger" and thereafter did their best to rid the land of the interlopers by hook or crook. When forty bowmen appeared at the fort two days later, the English sought to impress them with shows of military power. The plan literally misfired when a soldier asked an Indian to shoot an arrow at a wooden English shield, which a pistol could not pierce. When the bowman sent his shaft a foot through the shield, the English hurried to cover their chagrin by putting up a steel shield. The second arrow shattered on impact, causing the bowman to bite another arrow in rage and stomp off.[16]

Body armor—mail, breast-plate, and morion—was even more daunting to lightly-clad warriors wielding hand-held weapons. With or without armor, however, the English sought to impose their will in Virginia largely with firearms. As they returned from the falls, Newport's party was eager to demonstrate their guns to the local natives, who through pantomime had made them realize the cruel ferocity and speed of native warfare. The "thunder" and smoke of English matchlocks was, of course, terrifying; several Indians who were visiting the English shallop leaped overboard when a soldier discharged his weapon.[17] Time would soon show how lethal lead balls were and how horribly they shattered bones and tore tissue even when they were not, quite unlike stone-tipped arrows. Until the Powhatans could obtain their own guns, their only recourse was to stay well hidden behind trees, to drop flat at the report or flash of a musket, or to have their shamans conjure rain, with which to extinguish English matches and soak their powder.

Testing Time

Newport's party returned from their peaceful river mission to find the Jamestown fort recovering from a hot attack by several hundred Paspaheghs, who were driven off largely by bar shot fired from the ships' guns. The honeymoon was clearly over. For the next two years the English and the Powhatans felt each other out, probing for weaknesses and ways to use the other without provoking a final break. Force and fear would play key roles in the drama of contact, but so would economic necessity, social compromise, and political accommodation.

Powhatan's policy toward the intruders was double-edged. On the one hand, he had as best he could to limit their land acquisitions, constrict their military movements, and persuade them to keep their noses out of his political tents, tasks which carried the risk of confrontation and warfare. On the other hand, he needed to cultivate their friendship in order to maintain a steady supply of desirable trade goods and to secure their armed services against his traditional enemies west of the fall line and reluctant members of his confederacy who might try to bolt. This meant that enough Englishmen would have to be kept alive to ensure the continued arrival of the company ships but not enough to overrun his lands and seduce his subjects. The result was a policy that vacillated between killing and kindness, depending on the moods and needs of Powhatan and his local werowances as well as those of the English settlers and their London sponsors.

Because the tribes nearest Jamestown were pressed the hardest by the hungry English presence, their responses were understandably the least friendly. They sent a steady stream of armed spies to keep an eye on the fort, to steal metal tools and weapons, and to kill any English stragglers they could find. Despite their apparent ferocity, they also received English runaways who fled to them for food, freedom, or shelter. The English were initially surprised when these renegades were returned unharmed during interludes of peace, grateful at least that their neighbors were "no Canyballs."[18]

But other tribes and these tribes at other times pursued a policy of wary welcome. When several of his confederates murmured at the first English planting in their country, the werowance of Powhatan's town near the falls asked, "Why should you bee offended with them as long as they hurt you not, nor take any thing away by force? They take but a little waste ground"—an apt description of Jamestown Island—"which doth you nor any of us any good."[19] Out of kindness or cunning, other tribes supplied the inept settlers with corn, bread, fish, and meat, sometimes gratis, often for copper, hatchets, and precious blue glass beads. They also taught them how to plant corn and other vegetables Indian-style, by hilling rather than wholesale plowing, and to build fish weirs and tackle. When English food was in extremely short supply one summer, the natives even took several groups of colonists into their scattered settlements, where fastidious stomachs quickly learned to relish "Salvage trash."[20]

The proud Powhatans did not fail to detect the least trace of contempt in English attitudes such as this, nor did they disguise their own scorn for people who could not feed themselves. Powhatan reminded an English trading party that strong-arm tactics would only cause the productive natives to "hide our provisions and flie to the woodes, whereby you must famish." When seventeen colonists deserted to the Kecoughtans in search of food, they were all killed and their mouths stuffed with bread, to symbolize the natives' contempt for such weakness.[21]

For Powhatan's own part, that "subtell owlde foxe" played a deft game of keeping the English off balance and dependent on his good will.[22] At times the English believed that he had ordered his confederates to starve them out by refusing to trade food or by secretly moving their settlements out of reach. On another occasion he invited the English to move their settlement from Paspahegh country to his own, where he said he could guarantee their "safety" and feed them generously. Whenever English parties visited his towns, he tried to persuade them as friends and allies to lay down their arms, saying that their guns frightened his women and children or that the burning matches for the muskets made them sick. More than once he tried to ambush the visitors, with no little success. As we all know, he captured Captain John Smith, but he also inveigled thirty-four traders into his people's lodges in twos and threes before they were captured, tortured, and killed.

Yet at other times the "Emperor" appeared to be the colonists' firm friend. He ordered the Paspaheghs to cease their harassment of the fort and to provide it with food. He treated his captive John Smith well and sent him home with guides, servants, and a load of bread. In exchange for an English student-interpreter, he sent Namontack, his symbolic "son," with Captain Newport to England to celebrate the alliance of the two empires (and perhaps, as Smith suggested, "to know our strength and Countries condition").[23] He sent his real and favorite daughter Pocahontas to Jamestown to heal a temporary breach and to ask for the return of Indian prisoners. In an apparent gesture toward "civility," he asked the English to build him an English-style frame house and to provide him with a grindstone, a cock, and a hen. He may even have promised that he and his sons would "abandon their religion and believe in the God of the English," which led a credulous Irish visitor to boast that "it seems easy to convert them because they are so friendly."[24]

English Policy Toward the Powhatans

By the same token, English policy toward the Powhatans was framed in unequal measure by colonial ideology, native unpredictability, and cruel necessity. The colonists were presented with two imperatives. The first was the company's order not to offend the natives while discovering commodities for profitable export. The second was the more serious need to survive in the face of inadequate supplies and an inscrutable and often hostile native population. Local conditions in Virginia only exaggerated the incompatibility of these demands. Not only did Jamestown have too few farmers, but those it might have had were diverted from timely labor by a feverish search for nonexistent gold. Infected by "gilded refiners with their golden promises," the colonists could talk, dream, or work at nothing but "dig gold, wash gold, refine gold, load gold."[25] Weak, self-aggrandizing, factionalized leadership allowed fields to go unplanted, fish uncaught, and shelter unbuilt as company ships dumped more people into the colony. Some of the newcomers' carelessness led to the burning of the whole town and much of its palisade in the winter of 1608.

But the worst problem was the frightful mortality of the colonists, who arrived weakened by long voyages only to find little or no housing, pitiful food allowances, and a pestilential location. Despite the company warning not to settle in any "low and moist place," the colonists had chosen Jamestown Island, an unprepossessing tangle of bogs and marshes. It was located half-way up the James where the fresh water from upriver met the salt water tides of Chesapeake Bay, producing a stagnant zone that was seldom flushed of impurities. This water not only rolled by the doors of the fort but seeped into the island's water table, where it was drunk from shallow wells. Consequently, Jamestown became a giant morgue for Virginia adventurers, particularly in the summer, because the turbid water harbored the organisms that cause dysentery and typhoid as well as enough salt to cause salt poisoning. Wracked by "Swellings, Fluxes, [and] Burning Fevers," plagued by the constant threat of starvation, and confined to close quarters by aggressive Indians, the colonists lapsed into apathy and listlessness and perished in alarming numbers. When the first supply ship arrived in January 1608, just thirty-eight of the initial 104 colonists were barely alive. Hundreds more died in the ensuing years, far fewer from Powhatan arrows than from their own heedlessness.[26]

For all these reasons the English needed to befriend and make peace with Powhatan. So they went out of their way to please him with gifts, follow his trading protocol, and assist him in his feuds with the Monacans. Upon his release from captivity, John Smith with Captain Newport presented the old chief "a sute of red cloath, a white Greyhound, and a Hatte." In acceding to his wish for a "great Gunne," they even offered to send him four demi-culverins by his servants, "being sure that none could carrie them" or procure the requisite powder and shot.[27] On a sincerer note, Newport bent to Powhatan's demand that trade be conducted not in a "pedling manner," item for item, but after seeing "all our Hatchets and Copper together, for which he would give us corne."[28] Not until Smith saw that Powhatan had developed a sudden craving for blue glass beads did the English get what they considered a square deal. The following September, Newport and 120 soldiers made good on his promise to visit the Monacans, but the trip proved an empty gesture. Newport returned with none of the women and children captives Powhatan had wanted to adopt, nor had he slain any men, probably because his eyes were firmly fixed on gold mines, Lost Colonists, and the South Sea.

The desire of the English to gratify the "Emperor" and to enlist him more fully in their own imperial cause is perfectly symbolized by Newport's attempt to "crown" him as a tributary to King James in September 1608. At Werowocomoco, Powhatan's capital on the north bank of the York, Newport presented the chief an English basin, ewer, and bed (which he proudly stored in his treasure house) and draped him in a scarlet cloak. "But a fowle trouble there was to make him kneele to receave his [copper] crowne," Smith reported, "he neither knowing the majestie, nor meaning of a Crowne, nor bending of the knee . . . At last by leaning hard on his shoulders, he a little stooped, and Newport put the Crowne on his head." Then the boats fired a volley in his honor, which startled the old man into "a horrible fear." To conclude this comic scene, Powhatan gave his old moccasins and mantle to Newport to repay his kindness.[29]

The Reign of Captain Smith

John Smith was not amused. Having dealt with the Powhatans at close range while Newport was scuttling back and forth across the Atlantic, he was certain that "this stately kinde of soliciting made [Powhatan] so much overvalue himself" that he was contemptuous of the English rather than impressed or grateful. Smith also put no faith in the Indians' word, believing them to be "inconstant in everie thing, but what feare constraineth them to keepe."[30] Accordingly, after he was elected president of the colony in the fall of 1608, he instituted a "get-tough" policy with both the mismanaged colonists and the natives. To begin to solve the food crisis at home, he put everyone to work, some to fish, some to plant, others to cut cedar clapboards for export. Palisades were repaired and houses built. Perhaps most important, he built a blockhouse to stymie the illegal Indian trade, which the settlers were underwriting to their private advantage rather than the company's with tools, swords, pikes, and even guns stolen from the company store.

To "suppresse the insolencie of those proud Savages," Smith trained nearly a hundred soldiers in the language, customs, and fighting-style of the Powhatans.[31] With these commandoes he proceeded to serve notice on the natives that he would not be trifled with. When the Paspaheghs and Chickahominies sent their warriors against him or refused to trade, he pursued them with such vehemence and did such damage to their houses, boats, and weirs that they quickly sued for peace and loaded his barges with corn. To secure the return of stolen weapons and tools he did not scruple to torture Indian prisoners or, worse yet from their standpoint, shackle them in a dungeon.

His field commanders were equally ruthless. When two English emissaries sent to purchase an island from the Nansemonds were tortured and killed, troops under Captains John Martin and George Percy "Beate the Salvages outt of the Island, burned their howses, Ransaked their Temples, Tooke downe the Corp[s]es of the deade kings from of[f] their Toambes, and caryed away their pearles, Copper and braceletts, wherewith they doe decor[at]e their kings funeralles." When Captain Francis West and three dozen men were sent to the Potomac to trade for corn, they loaded their pinnace but "used some harshe and Crewell dealinge by cutteinge of[f] towe of the Salvages heads and other extremetyes."[32]

Smith saved Powhatan and his younger brother and successor Opechancanough (pronounced Ō-pĕ-chań-cǎ-nō) for himself. In the winter of 1608–9 he and thirty-eight men visited the Pamunkeys on the York in search of corn. At Werowocomoco Powhatan and Smith engaged in some spirited verbal sparring before the English, with cocked matches, forced a phalanx of warriors to drop their weapons and load the boats with corn. Before Smith left, Powhatan scolded him for his pugnacious approach but confessed that "it is better to eate good meate, lie well, and sleep quietly with my women & children, laugh and be merrie with you, have copper, hatchets, or what I want, being your friend: then bee forced to flie from al[l], to lie cold in the woods, feed upon acorns, roots, and such trash, and be so hunted by you, that I can neither rest, eat, nor sleepe."[33]

That Smith's new policy was practical if not pretty was shown two days later when the English party reached Opechancanough's town of Pamunkey. After trading for a partial load, Smith and fifteen soldiers suddenly found themselves surrounded by several hundred warriors. In the course of challenging

Opechancanough to hand-to-hand combat, "conquerer take all," Smith grabbed the taller Indian by his scalplock and held a cocked pistol to his "trembling" breast. With customary bravado, Smith warned the surprised Pamunkeys that if they shed "one drop of blood" of any of his men, he would not cease revenge until he had eradicated the whole nation. Reminding them that it was they and their chief who had captured him the year before, he concluded, "You promised to fraught my ship ere I departed, and so you shall, or I meane to load her with your dead carkases." The rest of the day went swimmingly, but Opechancanough never forgot his rough handling at the hands of the brash invaders. As Smith well knew, "they seldome forget an injury."[34]

When Smith returned to England in the fall of 1609, having been seriously burned by an exploding powder bag, the colonists reverted to their old tricks and entered a horrible winter of famine and death. While Smith was no saint, the colony had prospered briefly under his forceful command. It was he, for example, who had the good sense to send many colonists away from the lethal waters of Jamestown to live with the natives in the summer of 1609. Perhaps his greatest legacy was an Indian policy that respected the natives' military audacity and economic shrewdness while meeting them head-on with daring and determination. As he had once told Powhatan, "I have but one God, I honour but one king; and I live not here as your subject, but as your friend."[35] Like this little captain with the Napoleonic personality, the imperial representatives who succeeded him would not be bullied by Powhatan or his empire.

The Starving Time

The shuffle of officers that followed Smith's departure left the colony bereft of strong leadership as it entered an infamous half-year known as "the starving time." With his chief nemesis gone, Powhatan again sent his warriors against the intruders and sought to starve them out. In the night he "cut off some of our boats; he drave away all the deer into the farther part of the country; he and his people destroyed our hogs (to the number of about six hundred); he sent none of his Indians to trade with us but laid secret ambushes in the woods." "Now for corne, provision, and contribution from the Salvages," the colonists had "nothing but mortal wounds with clubs and arrowes." Even with foreknowledge of the bloody uses to which they would be put, the settlers scrambled to sell the Indians "swords, arrowes, peeces [guns], or anything" to obtain a little corn or fish. After six months, only sixty cadaverous survivors remained from the nearly five hundred souls left by Smith. The rest had perished for "want of providence, industrie, and government," unwitting victims—as were the grain-poor Indians—of the driest seven-year episode in the past 770 years. Driven to extremes by the "sharpe pricke of hunger," they fed upon anything that moved and several things that did not—horses, dogs, cats, rats, snakes, roots, old shoe leather, and even corpses. Some of the poorer sort

His men badly outnumbered by Pamunkey warriors, Captain John Smith grabs Opechancanough by his scalplock (the physical manifestation of the soul and considered sacred), holds a pistol to his chest, and threatens to load a barge with carcasses if the Indians do not produce the corn they had promised to trade. An engraving by Robert Vaughan from Smith's *Generall Historie of Virginia* (London, 1624).

excavated recent Indian graves and stewed up the remains with roots and herbs. Another man "murdered his wyfe, Ripped the childe outt of her woambe and threw itt into the River, and after chopped the Mother in pieces and salted her for his foode." He managed to digest part of his grisly fare before the better-fed authorities discovered his crime and executed him.[36]

The English threat to the Powhatan empire nearly extinguished itself in that desperate winter of 1609–10. Many of those who did not die from disease or starvation ran away to the Indians, feeling that a slim chance of survival was better than none at all. By the time two small pinnaces arrived in May bearing reinforcements under Sir Thomas Gates, the new governor whose supply ship had been wrecked on Bermuda, the colony's will to persevere was gone. So in early June the whole colony tumbled into four pinnaces and turned tail for home. Fortunately, they did not put torch to the fort as they left, because before they could get out of the James they met three well-furnished ships under Lord de la Warr, the newly appointed captain-general, with three hundred men. Much to Powhatan's chagrin, Jamestown was not only repopulated and enlarged but the colony was placed under tough military discipline and began to send out permanent tentacles of fortified settlement up and down the James. In leaders like Gates and Sir Thomas Dale, soldiers cut from John Smith's cloth and fresh from command experience in Ireland and the Netherlands, Powhatan met his match for the second time.

The Military Regime

In issuing orders to its colonial officers under the new charter of 1609, the Virginia Company had already foreseen the necessity of striking a more bellicose pose to ensure the colony's survival and prosperity. The Indians were now considered critical not only to survival but to prosperity as well. The first order of external business was thus to reduce the Powhatan empire from independent to tributary status. Since Powhatan obviously "loved not our neighbourhood" and could not be trusted, the company deemed it essential, if he could not be made prisoner, to make his werowances "acknowledge no other lord but Kinge James" and to free them all from his "tirrany." Rather than the 80 percent duties levied by the emperor, each chief would deliver to the English "so many measures of corne at every harvest, soe many basketts of dye, so many dozens of skins, [and] so many of his people to worke weekely" in clearing ground for planting, in return for protection from their enemies. If they refused to cooperate and fled into the woods, the colonists were to seize half their harvests and their leading families, the young males of which they would educate in Christian civility for future leadership roles in the brave new English world. To speed the conversion of the whole empire, which was considered "the most pious and noble end of this plantation," the native priests and shamans were to be surprised, imprisoned, and perhaps put to death, so great was their "continuall tirrany" over the credulous laity. If the colonists needed any help in these tasks, they were to make alliances with Powhatan's traditional enemies.[37]

After organizing the colonists into work-train bands of fifty men each and laying down the martial law to govern them, the officers bent to their initial military task—revenge. Not unlike their native adversaries, they pursued it with all the callous cruelty that war can breed. Spies caught around the fort were either executed as "a Terrour to the Reste" or had a hand cut off and were sent home with it as a warning. To revenge the deaths of the seventeen food-seeking runaways at the hands of the Kecoughtans the previous year, Gates sent a taborer ashore to lure the Indians with his playing and dancing. When they assembled around the entertainer, Gates and his troops ambushed them and seized their village and fertile fields. Two forts were erected to command the area and to serve as healthy points of disembarkation for new settlers.[38]

In August seventy men under Captain Percy, led by an Indian prisoner in a hand-lock, assaulted the Paspahegh town, killing sixteen and capturing the chief's wife and children. After burning the natives' houses and cutting down their corn (which was not unneeded in Jamestown), the soldiers groused that any natives were spared. So a military council met and decided to put the children to death, "which was effected by Throweinge them overboard and shoteinge owtt their Braynes in the water." With great difficulty Percy managed to prevent his men from burning the "Queen" at the stake until she could more humanely be put to the sword. On the way home the expedition stopped at Chickahominy to cut down the inhabitants' corn and burn their houses, temples, and religious "idols."[39]

Such scenes were repeated up and down the river all fall and the following summer after the arrival of nearly six hundred men and "a great store of Armour," munitions, cattle, and provisions. The Nansemonds were Sir Thomas Dale's first target. The Indians were nonplussed by his hundred men in armor, who did not fall as they had in other conflicts. So their conjurers began a series of "exorcismes, conjuracyons and charmes, throweinge fyer upp into the skyes, Runneinge up and downe with Rattles, and makeinge many dyabolicall gestures" in hopes of producing a rainstorm to extinguish the English matches. (They did not yet know the power of rust.) The English destroyed their village and crops, killed many, and captured some anyway.[40] In the late summer Dale took three hundred men to fortify and inhabit the falls on a permanent basis. They built Henrico on a defensible neck of land and paled it like an English town in colonial Ireland. Several other paled plantations were laid out nearby, including some five miles away on a large neck of land taken from the Appamatucks the following winter. When some of Dale's lazy men ran off to the Indians, those he captured felt the full force of martial law "to terrefy the reste." "Some he apointed to be hanged, Some burned, Some to be broken upon wheles, others to be staked, and some to be shott."[41]

Powhatan dealt with these and other invasions of his territory in two ways. First, in the interest of safety, he moved his capital from Werowocomoco, only twelve or fifteen miles overland from Jamestown, to Orapaks at the head of the Chickahominy River. Second, from his new seat he dispatched war parties to harass the English at the falls. Their arrows claimed a few soldiers, including Lord de la Warr's nephew, and they captured at least two prisoners, but the colonial juggernaut could not be stopped. So the warriors resorted to flinging "a kind of angry song" at the English, which concluded with a petition to their *Okis* or deities to plague the English and their posterity.[42] The leader of these forces was Nemattanow, whom the colonists called "Jack-of-the-Feathers" because he appeared in the field "all covered over with feathers and Swans wings fastened unto his showlders as thowghte he meante to flye." For the next eleven years this clever and courageous war captain would persuade his followers that he was impervious to English shot and secretly led the Powhatans in a revitalization movement to rid themselves and their lands of the proliferating Tassantasses.[43]

Virginia's Nonpareil

The English and the Powhatans continued to skirmish until 1614, when an uneasy peace settled over the tidewater for the first time in seven years. The unwitting though not unwilling agent of this cease-fire was Pocahontas, the "Little Wanton" who as an eleven-year-old used to cartwheel naked through the fort with the ships' boys. In April 1613, while visiting the Potomacs, she was enticed on board Captain Samuel Argall's trading ship and detained as a hostage for her father's return of English weapons, tools, and runaways. Powhatan sent no reply for three months, and then returned only seven men with seven broken muskets. The English felt that he could do much better, so they sent his daughter to Henrico for instruction from the Reverend Alexander Whitaker. Pocahontas took so well to the English way of life that she renounced her native "idolatry," converted to Christianity, and was baptized Rebecca. As everyone knows, she also took to John Rolfe, a twenty-eight-year-old widower who had just begun to introduce sweet West Indian tobacco to the colonial economy. After an abortive visit to her father, during which she accused him of loving a bunch of old swords, guns, and axes better than her, she married Rolfe in the Jamestown church in April 1614, witnessed by her uncle and two brothers. Powhatan sent the newly-weds two dressed deerskins and inquired warmly "how they lived, loved and liked."[44]

A year later she gave Powhatan a half-English grandson, and in 1616 sailed to England with her family and ten tribesmen to visit the royalty of her adopted empire. There she had a moody reunion with John Smith, whom she chastised for never sending her word of his health or whereabouts. As the young girl who had saved his neck more than once, at the risk of being a traitor to her own people, she rightly felt that he owed her that simple courtesy. With the bluff embarrassment of a bachelor soldier, Smith took his leave for the West Country and recommended the Indian princess to Queen Anne, "seeing this Kingdome may rightly have a Kingdome by her meanes."[45]

One of Pocahontas's native companions was Uttamatomakkin, a Powhatan councillor who had been sent to count the English population on a notched tally stick. "He was quickly wearie of that taske," Smith observed. The Indian was less impressed by his theology lessons from English divines and his audience with King James. "You gave Powhatan a white Dog," he complained to Smith, "but your King gave me nothing, and I am better than your white Dog."[46] Another young native was taken under the wing of George Thorpe, a gentleman member of the Virginia Company. Thorpe's three-year relationship with the boy soon prompted him to adventure his purse and person in Virginia as the leading exponent of Indian conversion.

Pocahontas's capture, marriage, and premature death in March 1617, as she was sailing down the Thames on her way home, took its toll on her aging father, now more than seventy. He had been at war most of his adult life and now longed for peace. So he transferred the scepter to his younger brother Opechancanough and retired to an easy life of progresses around his empire, "taking his pleasure in good friendship" with the colonists, though at a respectful distance.[47] Having lost one daughter to the intruders, he declined to marry another to Sir Thomas Dale, who had a wife in England but sought to confirm the new peace by having the English symbolically become "one people" with the natives.[48] Powhatan did not live to see that alien dream fulfilled. He died in 1618, four years too early to witness, not the melding of two peoples, but the blazing resurgence of his imperial creation.

The Tawny Weed

Ironically, Powhatan's son-in-law contributed not a little to that fateful clash in 1622. Rolfe's successful experiments with tobacco milder than the bitter native variety gave the struggling colony an economic lease on life. The craze for "drinking" tobacco had already erupted in Europe, so dramatically that the puritanical King James felt compelled to issue an anonymous *Counterblaste to Tobacco* in 1604. He attributed the origin of smoking to "the barbarous and beastly maners of the wilde, godlesse, and slavish Indians" and thoroughly condemned it as "a custome lothsome to the eye, hateful to the Nose, harmefull to the braine, [and] dangerous to the Lungs."[49] The subjects of his American colony were not the least contrite, particularly when their hogsheads of cured leaf were bringing three shillings a pound on the London wharves. By 1617 "the market-place, and streets, and all other spare places were set with the crop, and the Colonie dispersed all about, planting Tobacco."[50] The colonists had to be reminded by authorities to plant enough grain crops to feed themselves, but many were deaf to such edicts. As more than 3,000 immigrants poured into the colony between 1619 and 1622, often with inadequate supplies, corn had to be traded from the Indians, once again, to fill the gap.

The boom mentality in Virginia put increasing pressure on the Powhatans for more land. After 1616 the company began to make land grants to its stockholders and to its servants at the end of their contracts, and the following year encouraged associations of private investors to sponsor settlers by granting large "hundreds" or "particular plantations" to them along the James and its tributaries. The rules governing these grants dictated that the colony would become dangerously distended, without adequate protection from concerted attack by land or sea. But in the relatively quiet years under Samuel Argall, Sir George Yeardley, and Sir Francis Wyatt, safety did not seem as important as the profits to be made from smoke.

Unfortunately, tobacco was a soil-depleting crop; three years were about as many as the sandy loams of the tidewater could give before their nutrients petered out. In the labor-expensive economy of Virginia, the best answer to worn-out fields was a move to new ground. And the best new grounds belonged to the Powhatans—their already-cleared village sites and fields.

There were several ways to acquire native land, all of which the English used at one time or another. One was to take it in "just wars," which the English deemed all their actions against the Indians. Another was to purchase it from a local werowance for trade goods mutually agreed upon. A third way was to claim lands depopulated by disease, famine, or migration. Fourth, when the English established economic hegemony on the James, the loss of wild game and the constriction of native croplands drove some local chiefs to mortgage their lands to the colony in exchange for English wheat or even seed corn. When they could not repay their debts, like other chiefs who could not pay their annual tribute, the English foreclosed and took the land. And finally, in 1621, for reasons not entirely clear, Opechancanough "gave the English leave to seate themselves any where on his Rivers where the Natives are not actually seated."[51] Through all these means, the colony acquired enough land before 1622 to grant forty-odd "particular plantations," some of which contained as many as eighty thousand acres.

The Cultural Offensive

Not content to squeeze the Powhatans out of their land, the colonists also sought to remake their culture to English specifications. The chief architect of this policy was George Thorpe, who came to Berkeley Plantation in 1620 as a member of the governor's council. Thorpe enjoyed a small legacy of good will and a larger one of ambitious plans. In 1616 the king had ordered his bishops to collect funds in their parishes for the education of American natives, and in two years some £1,500 was sent to the Virginia Company to administer. In the meantime private donors contributed hundreds of pounds to the same cause. In 1619 the company set aside ten thousand acres at Henrico and another thousand in Charles City for the generation of funds to build an Indian college and feeder school. Thorpe was appointed deputy over the hundred tenants sent by the company to work the college lands. Funds were also invested in an ironworks in hopes of subsidizing native students, and each major settlement in Virginia was ordered to educate a likely Indian lad toward admission to the college when it was built.[52]

But the colonial governors discovered that the Powhatans were extremely reluctant to part with their children, knowing they could be used as hostages for the good behavior of the tribe. Opechancanough was even more reluctant to put them in English hands after hearing Uttamatomakkin's disparaging report of "England, English people, and particularly his best friend Thomas Dale."[53] Three solutions to this personnel problem suggested themselves to Governor Yeardley. One was simply to "purchase" children from their parents with gifts of trade goods. Another was to capture students in raids on enemy tribes. In 1619 Jack-of-the-Feathers proposed that eight or ten English soldiers accompany a Powhatan war party above the falls to revenge the murder of some Powhatan women by a Siouan tribe. In addition to providing the English with moccasins and carrying their armor until it was needed, the Indians offered to "share all the booty of male and female children" and corn and to "divide the Conquered land into two equall parts." The governor's council embraced the offer because it was not a major investment of manpower and the captive children might in time "furnishe the intended Collidge." When the projected raid failed to materialize, Opechancanough agreed the following year to place whole families in the colonial settlements for education in English ways, provided the company would build them houses, lay out corn fields for their use, and provide them with a few head of cattle and some European clothing.[54]

For his part Thorpe promoted the idea of the Indian college and the conversion of his native neighbors with persistence and an excess of good will. When English mastiffs frightened the Indians, he caused some of the dogs to be killed in their presence, and would have gelded the rest to make them less fierce if he had had the chance. When any of his college tenants did the Indians "the least displeasure," he punished the workers "severely." He lavished gifts of clothes and household items upon the natives, thinking "nothing too deare [expensive] for them." For Opechancanough he built "a faire house after the English fashion," complete with lock and key, which the chief so admired that he would lock and unlock the door "a hundred times a day." Thus "insinuating himselfe into this Kings favour for his religious purpose," as John Smith put it, "he conferred oft with him about Religion . . . and this Pagan confessed to him [that] our God was better then theirs, and seemed to be much pleased with that Discourse, and of his company."[55]

But Thorpe did not have a smooth road to evangelical success, nor was Opechancanough's conversion anything but apparent. For the Indians could not miss the sad fact that, as Thorpe lamented, "there is scarce any man amongest us that doth soe much as affoorde them a good thought in his hart and most men with theire mouthes give them nothinge but maledictions and bitter execrations." "If there bee wronge on any side," he concluded, "it is on ours who are not soe charitable to them as Christians ought to bee."[56] Typical of these un-Christian sentiments were those of the Reverend Jonas Stockham, who in 1621 complained that the Indians "devoured" the gifts bestowed on them, "and so they would the givers if they could," and returned nothing but "derision and ridiculous answers" to the English attempts to convert them

with kindness. This man of the cloth, like many of his countrymen, was persuaded that "till their Priests and Ancients have their throats cut, there is no
hope to bring them to conversion."[57]

The Powhatans' reluctance to be converted in any but superficial ways
stemmed from fierce cultural pride, which was being fanned by Nemattanow's
feathered pursuit of revitalization, and from their realization that Thorpe's
educational program was nothing but the company's old imperial goal in a new
guise. As William Strachey, the colony secretary, expressed it in 1612, English
policy toward the Indians was "by degrees [to] chaung their barbarous natures,
make them ashamed the sooner of their savadge nakednes, informe them of the
true god, and of the waie to their salvation, and fynally teach them obedience
to the kings Majestie and to his Governours in those parts."[58] For the Indians,
of course, this was tantamount to cultural suicide, a step they would not take
lightly or prematurely. Indeed, they never took it but chose a much more radical solution for dealing with the suffocating presence of the Tassantasses.

The Empire Strikes Back

On March 22, 1622, according to a brilliant plan, the Powhatans rose in concert against the 1,240 colonists scattered up and down the James, killing 347
men, women, and children. To show their contempt for their victims, they fell
upon the dead again, "defacing, dragging, and mangling the dead carkasses
into many pieces, and carrying some parts away in derision." Among the fatal-
ities was George Thorpe, their professed friend and protector.[59]

The key to the Powhatan success was complete surprise. They rose without
warning as if at a predetermined signal, and they did not have far to go. They
were sitting at breakfast, bending over trading counters, and standing with the
colonists at work in the fields, enjoying their "daily familiarity," when they
seized the nearest axe, knife, or hoe and struck deep into their unsuspecting
foes. In the days preceding they had guided Englishmen safely through the
woods, borrowed boats, and come unarmed to houses to trade game, fish, and
furs. None of this was the least unusual, for the colonists' houses were "generally set open to the Savages, who were alwaies friendly entertained at the tables
of the English, and commonly lodged in their bed-chambers."[60]

Why they struck when they did was no mystery to contemporaries. Edward
Waterhouse, a Company spokesman, attributed the general cause of the uprising to "the dayly feare that possest them, that in time we by our growing continually upon them, would dispossesse them of this Country." As if to give
weight to their reason, he went on to argue that one of the many hidden benefits to be gained from the bloody event was native real estate. "Now their
cleared grounds in all their villages," he beamed, "(which are situate in the
fruitfullest places of the land) shall be inhabited by us, whereas heretofore the
grubbing of woods was the greatest labour."[61]

Theodor de Bry's rendering of the Powhatan uprising of March 22, 1622. Seizing tools and weapons from their unsuspecting hosts, the Indians slew 347 English men, women, and children in a concerted attack. Many more colonists died later of starvation, exposure, and disease. The buildings reflect contemporary German architecture in de Bry's Frankfurt-am-Main rather than American reality. As in the illustrations for Smith's works, the Indians tower over their hapless victims; in reality they may have been only slightly taller. From de Bry's *America Pars Decima,* Part XIII (1634).

But the timing of the event from a military standpoint was all wrong. Food supplies were low, corn had not even been planted, and the trees were still bare of protective foliage. Only an extraordinary event forced Opechancanough to launch his attack in March—the murder of Nemattanow. Two weeks before the "massacre," Jack-of-the-Feathers had killed a planter as he accompanied him to trade at Pamunkey. When he foolishly returned to the planter's house wearing the victim's cap, two young servants shot him. Before he expired, however, he asked the boys for two favors, which they could never guess were calculated to serve the Powhatan quest for spiritual power: "the one was, that they would not make it knowne hee was slaine with a bullet; the other, to bury him amongst the English." Understandably, he did not want his followers to discover that the magic ointment they wore was not immortal proof against English lead.[62]

To the edgy English, Opechancanough quickly sent word that the death of Nemattanow, "beinge but one man, should be noe occasione of the breach of the peace, and that the Skye should sooner falle then Peace be broken, one his parte."[63] But he had been seriously plotting the destruction of the colonists for at least a year. In the summer of 1621 he had tried to buy a quantity of poison from a tribe on the Eastern Shore for use on the settlers. Significantly, the assault was timed to coincide with a religious ceremony for "the taking upp of Powhatans bones." For some reason it was postponed—until the sudden death of his chief war captain and spiritual catalyst.[64]

For nearly a month after the attack, the survivors reeled in stunned lethargy as the natives picked off stragglers and destroyed herds of cattle. While the settlers made their way to five or six fortified settlements, Governor Wyatt and his officers decided that total, unrelenting war was the only permanent solution to the natives' "perfidious treachery," a decision that was soon seconded by the London council. The goal was to wreak "a sharp revenge uppon the bloody miscreantes, even to . . . the rooting them out from being longer a people uppon the face of the Earth." Since the Indians were "swift as Roebucks," the only ways to beat them were "by force, by surprise, by famine in burning their Corne, by destroying and burning their Boats, Canoes, and Houses, by breaking their fishing Weares, by assailing them in their huntings, . . . by pursuing and chasing them with our horses, and blood-Hounds to draw after them, and Mastives to seaze them, . . . by driving them (when they flye) upon their enemies, who are round about them, and by animating and abetting their enemies against them."[65]

For the next several years the colonists stalked the Powhatans as they had once been stalked. They, too, sought to give their enemies a false sense of security by letting their corn ripen before pouncing and putting it and their villages to the sword. In one raid they cut down enough corn to feed four thousand people for a year. Likewise, they entertained Opechancanough's peace overtures only long enough to redeem English prisoners before setting on his settlements again. At a parley in May 1623, the English killed nearly two hundred natives by having them toast the peace with poisoned sack and another fifty by luring them into an ambush; the latter provided the colonists with their first scalps, whose collection and uses Powhatan had taught them several years before.[66]

Despite severe domestic problems, the colonists managed to exact a fearsome price from the Powhatans for their audacity. At the end of the winter campaigns of 1622–23, the Indians themselves confessed that the English had slain more of them in one year than had been killed since the beginning of the colony. In a two-day battle in July 1624, sixty Englishmen cut down eight hundred Pamunkeys on their home ground. Apparently, the "old cast[-off] Armes" from the Tower of London that the colonists used, while "of no use for moderne Service," were perfectly "serviceable against that naked people."[67]

Of course, the war continued to claim colonial victims. The most important was the Virginia Company itself, which the king dissolved in May 1624 for its hapless handling of the colony and its dangerous neighbors. Henceforth Virginia was a royal colony, whose governor was appointed by the crown. From the Powhatans' perspective, it made little difference who governed the colony. Their major concern was to preserve their independence and the land base that made it possible. By 1632, however, it was clear that further resistance was impossible, so Opechancanough sued for peace. Many colonists still felt that "it is infinitely better to have no heathen among us, who at best were but as thornes in our sides, then to be at peace and league with them." But the attractions of new lands and quiet prosperity persuaded the English to accept the chief's capitulation, while still regarding him and his people as "irreconcilable enemies."[68] The Powhatans withdrew to the dark corners of the colony to lick their wounds, sharpen their resentment, and dream of a day when they might be free of the English.

The Empire in Eclipse

Such a day had come, they hoped, on April 18, 1644, when they rose again without warning, killing nearly five hundred colonists. But this time the English were too thick on the ground to be seriously affected. With a reduced death rate and royal supervision of immigration, the colony had grown to perhaps ten thousand. The cause of the Powhatans' desperation was that English plantations were no longer confined to the James but had spread up all the rivers that veined the tidewater region, effectively pushing Opechancanough against the western wall of his diminished empire. At the same time, the colonists had shifted most of their trade around the Powhatans to the Potomac-Susquehanna region of the Chesapeake and to the Occaneechis on the Roanoke River. When the English civil war broke out, therefore, Opechancanough decided that, with factionalism in the colony and the unlikelihood of aid from England, the colonists would be easy prey to his warriors.

The war sputtered on for nearly two years, but the English survivors felt confident enough to return to their plantations within six months. Indeed, only planters on the Southside of the James and high up the other rivers had been seriously discommoded; the populous core of settlements on the James-York peninsula had not been afflicted. When Governor William Berkeley captured Opechancanough in the late summer of 1646, the once-powerful emperor was "now grown so decrepit, that he was not able to walk alone; but was carried about by his Men" on a litter. "His Flesh was all macerated, his Sinews slacken'd, and his Eye-lids became so heavy, that he could not see, but as they were lifted up by his Servants."[69]

Berkeley brought his prisoner to Jamestown and clapped him in jail, where crowds of curiosity-seekers came to peer at him. Rising with difficulty on his cot, the Indian "call'd in High Indignation for the Governour" and "scornfully told him, That had it been his Fortune to take Sir William Berkeley Prisoner, he should not meanly have exposed him as a Show to the People." Berkeley, indeed, had planned to take Opechancanough to England to present King Charles with a "Royal Captive." But within a fortnight of his capture, "one of the Soldiers, resenting the Calamities the Colony had suffer'd by this Prince's Means, basely shot him thro' the back."[70]

By October, when a punitive treaty was imposed upon Opechancanough's malleable successor, the Powhatans were "so rowted, slayne and dispersed, that they are no longer a nation." The aggressive empire fashioned by Powhatan lay in ruins, completely supplanted by the imperial energy of the Tassantasses. The haunting prophecy of a Powhatan priest, that "bearded men should come & take away their Country," had at last come to pass.[71]

ELEVEN

THE MORAL DILEMMAS
OF SCALPING

The specter of scalping haunted the colonists of North America, and it continues to bedevil the thinking of America's historians and their readers. The bloody possibility of having one's scalp ripped off to a heart-rending cry of exaltation by a hideously painted, half-naked warrior was understandably terrifying to the colonists whose brand of warfare had not prepared them for such a fate. Despite the perspective of time, the strange horribleness of scalping still fascinates students of history for whom the possibility is much more remote. But to judge by some of their moral and historical observations, it also confounds them. Not only have they contributed importantly to the myth that European colonists taught the Indians how to scalp by offering them bounties for enemy hair, but they have generally assumed moral postures toward the issue that add little or nothing to our understanding of scalping's impact on early American culture. This essay is an attempt to probe a small but significant feature of the process that helped to Americanize the English colonists by exploring some of the moral, psychological, and social meanings that scalping and scalp bounties held for them.

The myth of the European invention of scalping is only one indication that modern Americans feel guilty about many aspects of Indian-white relations in America, especially during the colonial period. But no more so than did many colonists for numerous offenses, such as making a god of land, dispossessing the Indians of theirs through force, fraud, or unfair exchange, killing rather than converting the natives by giving them the vices, not the virtues, of English society, losing the battle of souls to the Catholic missionaries of New France, and admiring, even preferring, the freedom of Indian society to the civilized constraints of their own. Guilt led to the fabrication of myths to disguise the reality of their deeds and feelings and to the projection of negative traits dimly or fearfully perceived in themselves onto their Indian adversaries.

As the accusations of their historical heirs suggest, many colonists also felt guilty about their adoption of certain "barbarous" methods of warfare, especially scalping of the dead. But rather than admitting that by adopting them they had been "reduced to savagery" or had deviated seriously from "civilized" Christian standards, they projected their guilt onto the Indians by insisting that the (mythically) "unprovoked" assaults of savages demanded a savage response. Since guerrilla warfare tends to force the enemy to retaliate in kind, the practice of scalping and the use of scalp bounties by the English may have been only a necessary adaptation of Indian means to English ends, of "savage" tactics to "civilized" (and therefore ultimately "redeeming") strategies, the most important of which was the elimination of the "Indian menace" on the ever-elastic English frontiers. But we should also consider the possibility that for at least some colonists scalping and the attitudes it engendered toward alien people left an ugly scar on their individual psyches and to that extent on the collective mentality of their society.

Obviously, the act of scalping, whether by Indians or Europeans, was morally loaded for contemporaries and carries considerable moral freight in modern discussions of Indian-white relations. How can we, as ethnohistorians, approach moral questions in the past without succumbing to either fruitless outrage or ethnocentric favoritism? Like all historians, we are first obligated to judge each society by its own standards and values, not those of today. We can compare individual choices of action with those made by other people in the same or similar circumstances or with other choices possible for *that* society at *that* time because "we hold people responsible only to the degree that we think them free to choose their course."[1] Second, we must strive to be scrupulously fair to all parties, which is possible only after immersing ourselves so deeply in the historical sources of each society that we are as much or more at home in their time and place than in our own.

When two or more societies and value systems collide, however, ethnohistorians face a problem of judgment that most historians who deal with one society seldom face. Sheer success or results are inappropriate standards because pragmatic "winners" are sometimes moral "losers" on any but the grossest scale. While the normative character of our everyday language will inevitably force us to make value judgments about the actions we describe, we can reduce the dangers of moral absolutism and presentism by letting the conflicting societies judge each other.[2] This technique will not only stress the relativity of cultural values but maintain a strict impartiality toward the conflicts of the past. If the sources for one society are slim, a sensitive application of imagination and empathy to a mastery of the available sources can often establish a culturally valid standard of judgment by which to redress the balance. To the same end, a light use of irony or gentle iconoclasm can effectively prick the pretensions and self-promotions of a dominant society blessed with an advantage of records. If more comment or moral criticism is called for by the complexity, abnormality, or enormity of the conflict situation, the ethnohistorian can use the standards of other contemporary societies, preferably neighbors who found themselves in similar circumstances. Beyond this kind of concrete, contextual treatment, most ethnohistorians will not need or want to go. Personal preference will dictate whether they proceed to apply "quasi-universal" moral standards in a "new cultural context, . . . free from the interpretations and assumptions under which [the original actions were] performed or observed by the participants."[3]

The moral attitudes struck by modern historians over scalping in the colonial period stand in marked contrast to an ethnohistorical approach. One surprising response has been to deny the existence of any moral problem at all, for the colonists or for us. In a section coyly entitled "On the Gentle Art of Scalping," a biographer of Sir William Johnson, the British superintendent of Indian affairs for the northern colonies, claimed that "scalping was then so common that no practical man, like Johnson, would have dreamed of eliminating it from the code of his red allies. . . . A scalp was just a scalp, no more— simply proof that the scalper had done his duty. . . ."[4] In a similar vein, an authority on Pennsylvania's scalp bounties asserted that "colonial Americans were not sensitive about the trade in scalps" and by the 1750s had "grimly accepted the ethics of scalp buying."[5] Even more nonchalant was an historian of the Revolution who held that the scalping done by American riflemen on the frontier was "a natural act," a simple matter "of course and of reprisal."[6]

The more typical response of historians has been to recognize the moral implications of scalping but to interpret the colonists' involvement in two different ways. The more equable interpretation, while admitting that scalp bounties fostered "inhumanity," "callous[ness]," and an "upsurge of brutality," carefully pinned the blame on the "intense heat" and "brutalizing influence of wilderness warfare," not on "sadist savages" or their bloody-minded French instigators, as an older history had done.[7] The other interpretation sought (often unconsciously) to elevate the Indians by degrading the colonists. In a history of the fall of Canada, the great-grandson of a Mohawk woman cited a few random, largely spurious, colonial scalp bounties before commenting, "Christian races, not savage ones, were the inspirations behind these horrible deeds in that bloody dawn of our history when the United States was about to be born."[8] Two historians of New England, though they differed strenuously on most issues, made common cause unwittingly when trying to explain scalping. One, normally a defender of the Puritans, was at pains to show that Indian scalp-taking had English analogues in drawing and quartering and "the displaying of heads on London Bridge and other prominent landmarks." "The seventeenth century," he insisted, "had its share of barbarity on both sides of the Atlantic."[9] The other historian, no friend of the Puritans, thought that scalping in native New England was adopted "as a convenient way to collect provincial bounties for heads without having to lug about the awkward impedimenta attached to the scalps." "If savagery was ferocity," he charged, "Europeans were at least as savage as Indians . . . Indians never achieved the advanced stage of civilization represented by the rack or the Iron Maiden."[10]

If we wish to capture the meaning of scalping for the competing societies of colonial America, we will have to move beyond attempts to rank them on a pejorative scale of "savagery." The "Americanization" of colonial warfare denotes a value-free process of acculturation, the logical starting point of which is the native uses of and attitudes toward scalping. Although the advent of the Europeans and their scalp bounties introduced some changes in Indian scalping, native customs were surprisingly durable throughout the colonial period. In fact, when seeking Indian allies for scalping raids against French or Indian enemies, the English were forced to adapt themselves to native ways, not vice versa. As in many other areas of warfare, native pipers continued to call their own tunes, no matter who paid them.

The Eastern Woodland Indians took scalps as "visible proofs of their valour," without which "they are afraid that their relations of the combat and the account they give of their individual prowess might be doubted or disbelieved."[11] In those oral societies, a man's word was the touchstone of his integrity and worth as a reliable member of his face-to-face community. But since the honors of war were so eagerly sought and so highly valued, the temptations to exaggerate or even fabricate one's martial achievements were considerable. Having to produce the scalp of the enemy helped to reduce those temptations, as did two other customs. Only the individual scalplock from an enemy's crown was to be lifted, and the scalps were to be publicly displayed on cabin, post, or palisade "until every body has examined and declared them not to have been taken unwarrantably from their Friends; but bravely from their Enemies."[12] A Moravian missionary once asked a Delaware warrior why, if he believed that scalplocks were generous invitations to "take off each other's scalps in war with greater facility," the Indians did not grow hair on the whole head. The Indian patiently replied, "My friend! a human being has but one head, and one scalp from that head is sufficient to shew that it has been in my power. Were we to preserve a whole head of hair as the white people do, *several* scalps might be made out of it, which would be *unfair.* Besides, the coward might thus without danger share in the trophies of the brave warrior, and dispute with him the honour of victory."[13]

Scalps were not mere trophies or booty of war, however. The whorl of hair on the crown and especially male scalplocks, braided and decorated with jewelry, paint, and feathers, represented the person's "soul" or living spirit. To lose that hair to an enemy was to lose control over one's life, to become socially and spiritually "dead," whether biological death resulted or not. The crucial distinction was the transference of power and identity into the victor's hands. "When the Indians relate their victories," observed John Heckewelder, "they don't say that they have taken so many '*scalps,*' but so many '*heads,*' in which they include as well those whom they have scalped, but left alive (which is sometimes the case), and their prisoners, as those whom they have killed."[14] Accordingly, when the Iroquois painted pictographs of their exploits on trees or marked the handles of their tomahawks, human figures signified prisoners, bodies without heads, scalps.[15]

Once a warrior possessed his enemy's scalp, he did with it as he wished. Sometimes he wore or displayed it with pride, perhaps on a thong at his side. Rarely, he sacrificed it to a war god in thanksgiving for his success or offered it to another tribe as an inducement to join him on the warpath. But most commonly he adopted it in the room of a living captive to replace a clan member who had died or gave it to another family or allied tribe for the same purpose, perhaps to satisfy a request for such a replacement. Whatever its fate, the scalp was regarded as a living "spirit" not to be trifled with. When the southeastern tribes exposed their enemies' scalps in the squares before their townhouses, "no Woman, Girl, or Boy" could be prevailed upon to go near them at night for "they say, among the Scalps wander the Spirits of the killed."[16]

When the English began to offer their Indian allies bounties for enemy Indian and later French hair, native traditions of scalping underwent a number of adjustments, most of them relatively minor. Iroquois war parties hired by Massachusetts in 1723 to bring the Maine Indian "rebels" into line had their autonomy (and pay) somewhat abridged by the English need for cost accounting. To prevent any garrison from mistaking the Iroquois for hostiles and "for avoiding any doubt or disputes that may arise about the Scalps that may be brought in by any of their parties," two Englishmen were ordered to join each party of ten Indians. Upon their return, the whites were to "certify upon Oath that a Scalp for which a Premium is Demanded is the Scalp of an Enemy Indian with their Age and Sex Slain in Fight and also to receive an Equal Proportion of the Scalp money with them." When the premiums stood at £100 for the scalp of every male over the age of twelve and £50 for that of any other "Killed in fight," fiscal responsibility demanded the exercise of due caution, particularly when a pagan warrior's oath was considered worthless.[17] In the military heat of the Seven Years' War, several colonies were willing to substitute "sufficient satisfaction" for an Indian's oath that he had produced a legitimate scalp for reward.[18]

Another alteration may have stemmed from sporadic English attempts to humanize frontier warfare, ultimately to their own advantage. In early-eighteenth-century Carolina, the Indians' cruelty to Spanish prisoners knew no bounds "if the *English* [were] not near to prevent it." To revenge Spanish murders and enslavement, explained John Lawson, the natives scalped their prisoners alive, "Notwithstanding the *English* have us'd all their Endeavours" to prevent it, and the Spanish governor of Florida banned scalping and scalp dances among his own Indian tributaries in 1701.[19] Perhaps British regulars, unacquainted with American morality, impinged most heavily on the Indians' customs, but even this came late in the colonial period. When "Gentleman Johnny" Burgoyne treated with the Iroquois in 1777 to enlist them against the colonial rebels, he told them that he and his officers took it upon themselves

to regulate your passions when they overbear, [and] to point out when it is nobler
to spare than to revenge. . . . Aged men, women, children and prisoners, must be

held sacred from the knife or hatchet, even in the time of actual conflict. You shall receive compensation for the prisoners you take [he warned them] but you shall be called to account for scalps. In conformity and indulgence of your customs . . . you shall be allowed to take the scalps of the dead, when killed by your fire and in fair opposition; but on no account, or pretence, or subtilty, or prevarication, are they to be taken from the wounded, or even dying; and still less pardonable, if possible, will it be held, to kill men in that condition, on purpose. . . . [20]

Just how successful Burgoyne was likely to have been in deflecting the Iroquois from their ancient customs can be gauged from the previous actions of others much wiser in the ways of the forest than he. William Johnson, an adopted Iroquois, knew his brethren and the limiting conditions of their warfare well enough to allow them to produce for reward scalps of all ages and sexes. The members of the New York Assembly also knew their native neighbors. When the governor's Council sought to exclude rewards for "Scalping or taking poor women or Children Prisiners" from the scalp act of 1747, the Assembly assured Governor Clinton (who assured Johnson) that "the Money shall be paid when it so happens, If ye Indians insist upon it."[21] Some of the Canadian kinsmen of the Iroquois were among the Indians who would not join the French in attacking Quebec in February 1760 "until they were assured that they should be rewarded with the scalps of all the killed and wounded."[22]

Johnson's deep knowledge of Iroquois culture allowed him to enlist his native kinsmen in yet another way without seriously affecting their scalping traditions. As an adopted kinsman married to Molly Brant, an influential Mohawk clan matron, and as the king's superintendent of Indian affairs, Johnson was able to assume the traditional authority of a clan matron in requesting kinsmen to capture an enemy prisoner or scalp to replace a deceased "relative," English or Iroquois. In the summer of 1756, Warraghiyagey (as Johnson was known to the Iroquois) requested a party of Onondagas to bring him a prisoner or scalp to replace his and their friend Tyanogo, Capt. Benjamin Stoddert, who had been killed at Lake George. The following year, Johnson "gave a War Belt to a Mohock named Zacharius in order to go to War & get a Scalp or Prisoner to give in the Room of Anias a Jenundadie who died of the small Pox in the Mohock Castle [village]."[23] While it did little to change the essential operations of Iroquois scalping, Johnson's subtle usurpation of the clan matrons' role in instigating wars of revenge was another attempt on his part to reduce their political authority in what he thought should be exclusively councils of men. Beyond the Iroquois, however, Johnson's unusual influence did not extend and most tribes remained free from direct English control.

Yet the white man's bounties also worked upon the native scalping ethic indirectly—and perhaps more powerfully because, strictly speaking, the changes came from within native society. The first change was the transition from a military adventure wholly dominated by the search for personal prestige, tribal honor, and familial revenge to one partially subordinated to the commercial constraints and military needs of white foreigners. Once the Indians had been drawn into the English web of trade, the purchasing power to be gained by killing Indians hostile to the economic and political interests of English suppliers could not be rejected lightly. The more dependent on English clothing, food, and guns the Indians became, the more susceptible their traditional warfare became to commercialization. Indeed, when an Indian leader asked to receive scalp bounties for his military assistance, as did King Hendrick of the Mohawks in 1747 and Teedyuscung of the Delawares ten years later, he effectively certified his dependence on the colonial economy, though not necessarily the surrender of his political autonomy.[24] It comes as no surprise that in the eighteenth century Indian scalp-takers preferred payment in goods rather than currency, and that William Johnson spent ten times more feasting his Iroquois scalping parties and supporting their families during their absence than he did redeeming the scalps they brought him.[25]

Johnson was a major anomaly among colonial officials in adjusting English military needs to the traditions of Indian warfare, but even he contributed to an alteration of the natives' use of enemy scalps. Although he distributed redeemed scalps in acceptably Indian ways, he nonetheless, early in his career as an agent of the colony of New York, *purchased* scalps from their native owners and disposed of them as he, not they, saw fit. The colonial legislatures placed even higher demands on Indian warriors who traditionally displayed their trophies in public. Under the English bounty system, a warrior could not be paid for his services until he had surrendered his enemy's scalp to a colonial official, who then in the honest company of a legislative or judicial committee burned the hairy token or buried it in a secret spot; the last thing the impecunious legislatures wanted was to be duped into paying two large bounties for one small scalp.[26] Only the behavior of the Salem, Massachusetts, selectmen would have made much sense to the Indians. Until 1785, when the town courthouse was torn down, scalps redeemed from local scalp-hunters were hung along its walls for all to see.[27]

The magnitude of the changes entailed upon native warriors by involvement in the English brand of commercial warfare can be glimpsed in two contrasting incidents, one showing the tenacity of native custom, the other the potentially disruptive effects of change. The first took place in an Iroquois encampment in the early years of the American Revolution. Thomas Anburey, a lieutenant in Burgoyne's army, saw several hooped scalps hanging upon poles before the Indians' wigwams, one of which had "remarkably fine long hair." A fellow officer in search of a distinctive American souvenir offered to purchase it, but its Indian owner "seemed highly offended, nor would he part with this barbarous trophy, although he was offered so strong a temptation as a bottle of rum."[28] It is possible that the Indian found the price insultingly low, but more likely he was unwilling to part with a symbol of his prowess and courage at any price, even though Burgoyne was offering no "compensation" for scalps.

The second incident revealed more directly the confusion caused by the impingement of the new commercial ethic upon older native traditions. In May 1757 representatives from Gov. Horatio Sharpe of Maryland met with a group of Cherokees under Warhatchie, chief of the southern towns, at Fort Frederick on the colony's western frontier. The colonists had brought a few presents to induce the Cherokees to continue their incursions upon the Delawares and Shawnees who were raiding the colony's exposed flanks, but, the Indians were told, additional presents would not be forthcoming until prisoners and scalps were handed over to the Maryland authorities as directed by the provincial scalp law of 1756. "With some warmth," Warhatchie replied that merely showing the scalps was sufficient because "it was the Indians Custom to preserve as Trophies the Hair of the Enemies that they killed in Battle and to carry them home to their own People, and in short that if they were not to have the Goods that had been talked of unless they would purchase them with their Prisoners or Scalps they would return home naked as they came thence and that they would think no more of going to War if they were not allowed to keep what they set the highest value on as it procured them most Honour among their own People." Captain Pearis, the colony's Cherokee interpreter, tried to persuade them in private to give up some of the scalps to be destroyed according to the provincial law, but Warhatchie remained obstinate. A second chief, however, promised to send Sharpe the scalps as a "present," though he made it clear that he could not see them destroyed "in such a manner as the Act Directs, lest he should be charged by his own People with selling them." With this compromise, the officials sent for an additional £200 worth of presents—the bounty price of four scalps—and divided them among the natives. Even Warhatchie relented and sent a batch of "Hair" to Sharpe as a gift. But handing over their two prisoners was out of the question; they were destined for adoption as Cherokees.[29]

Governor Sharpe was obviously pleased with the results of his use of Indian mercenaries. Not only did the danger to his frontiers abate, but

> when [the Cherokees] received my Present for the Scalps [he told Lord Baltimore], they gave the Soldiers that were with them a Share, & gave no room to complain of their Behaviour unless their Refusing to give up the Prisoners & to suffer their Scalps to be destroyed . . . can be called criminal. For my part I think they should be indulged in their own Customs as much as possible, & as the Evidence of the Officer & Men that will always go out with them is enough to prevent the Frauds that the Assembly were sollicitous to provide against, I shall endeavour to get that part of the Act which forbids the Agents to pay for any Enemy's Scalps till they are actually burnt repealed at the next Session.[30]

But Edmond Atkin, a South Carolina trader-merchant and the newly appointed superintendent of Indian affairs for the southern colonies, had a different view of the situation. Following William Johnson's expert lead, Atkin thought that Indian allies should be rewarded "in proportion to their Services, . . . without Regard to the Number of Scalps" they produced. Part of his reasoning stemmed from his knowledge of Warhatchie's exploits, which smacked, he said, of "Impudence, Selfishness, and avaric[e]." Apparently the Cherokees had not relinquished all their scalps to the Maryland authorities and had carried them to Winchester to collect the Virginia bounty of £10. When Atkin's appearance in Winchester foiled their "scheme," most of Warhatchie's party—without the chief—stole off "privately" to try their luck at Fort Loudon in Pennsylvania. Atkin managed to warn the fort in time, but allowed the Indians part of the Pennsylvania present anyway, which was transported to Winchester for distribution at his hands. Surely this man who grew wealthy in the Carolina Indian trade knew that the English seldom had honored their 1730 treaty with the Cherokees in which the Indians promised to fight the colonists' enemies for being "furnished with all Manner of Goods that they wanted, by the Carolina Traders." If a sense of guilt as well as equity obliged Atkin to feel that the Cherokees "ought undoubtedly to receive a reasonable Reward for their Time and Trouble, while taken from their Hunts to assist us," and to distribute additional gifts, the Indians had good cause to feel that their reward from one colony was *not* reasonable, especially when they were virtually forced to surrender their trophies of war.[31] William Johnson agreed with them. To the Lords of Trade he complained that the government of Virginia—and by implication his southern counterpart, Atkin—treated the Cherokees, a vital link in the English chain of defense against the encircling French, with "an ill-timed frugality which greatly disgusted them."[32]

By the Seven Years' War, troublesome episodes such as this contributed to the feeling among several colonial officials that Indians should not be eligible for the provincial scalp bounties. Not only did native customs clash with the pragmatic requirements of colonial bureaucracy, but once the Indians were inured to the new commercial ethic of warfare they were prone to other, more serious misdemeanors. One form of cheating was the subdivision of scalps. When a French and Indian war party attacked Fort Lydius on the upper Hudson in the summer of 1757, they killed eleven English soldiers and wounded four. "The Indians, however, brought back thirty-two scalps," noted Montcalm's aide-de-camp; "they know how to make two or even three out of one."[33] The Cherokees employed by the English on the Pennsylvania and Virginia frontiers in the same summer were even more adept at multiplying their honors. Edmond Atkin knew that among the many scalps "hanging exposed in publick" at the army camp in Winchester were a friendly Chickasaw's scalp made into two and the scalps of five Frenchmen cut into twenty. He was doubtless right that the provincial scalp bounties "open a Door to great Fraud & Imposition upon the Colonies or the Donors themselves."[34] On the other hand, *caveat emptor* should have occurred to the English when they agreed to buy hair without telltale scalplocks and attracted needy native sellers to their military markets.

As Atkin's notice of the Chickasaw's murder suggests, opposition to scalp bounties for Indians had another source: "it is encouraging to the utmost *pri-*

vate Scalping, whereby the most innocent & helpless Persons, even Women &
Children, are properly murdered. . . . They are so many Temptations to some
Indians to kill others that are our Friends," which might easily engulf the colonial frontiers in a general Indian war.[35] Even more to the point was the danger to Englishmen. When the Pennsylvania Council asked Conrad Weiser,
Johnson's shrewd deputy, for his opinion in September 1757 about Indian eli-
gibility for the rewards offered by the 1756 scalp act, he advised them to
"Allow as much for Prisoners as you please, rather more than was intended"
but that "no Encouragements should be given to the Indians for Scalps, for
fear we must then pay for our own Scalps, and those of our Fellow Subjects, as
will certainly be the case."[36] Weiser's fears were well grounded in the absence
of a foolproof method for distinguishing a French scalp from an English one.
From long experience among the Cherokees, Lt. Henry Timberlake knew that
"they were pretty hospitable to all white strangers, till the Europeans encouraged them to scalp; but the great reward offered [by the colonial governments]
has led them often since to commit as great barbarities on us, as they formerly
only treated their most inveterate enemies with."[37] Self-interest, if not Christian compunction, dictated that scalp bounties be confined to Englishmen,
particularly "poor white Men, who have been used to the Woods" and "driven
from their own Habitations in the back settlements, by the War."[38]

Although colonial officials eventually developed misgivings about English
scalping, scalp bounties enjoyed great popularity, especially among frontiersmen, whenever the colonies felt their backs to the wall from Indian or French
attacks. The earliest bounties were offered to encourage native allies to kill Indians hostile to the interests of the European governments, the accepted specie
of proof being heads. In 1637 the English in Connecticut paid their Mohegan
allies for Pequot heads, and in 1641 the Dutch in New Amsterdam paid ten
fathoms of wampum for each Raritan head brought in.[39] When King Philip's
War erupted in 1675, the Narragansetts of Rhode Island were offered one
"Coat (that is, two Yards of Trucking Cloth, worth five Shillings per Yard here)"
for every enemy "Head-Skin."[40] But the New English quickly found that
Indian allies were neither numerous nor trustworthy enough to solve their military problem, so it was felt necessary to give colonial soldiers a mercenary
incentive to pursue Philip's mobile forces. With the tide of events quickly turning to flood, the governments of Connecticut and Massachusetts offered their
own men thirty shillings for every enemy "Head." As Col. Benjamin Church,
Philip's final nemesis, remarked, "Methinks it's scanty reward and poor encouragement; though it was better than what had been some time before."[41]

With the outbreak of the intercolonial wars in 1689, the frontier inhabitants
of first New England and then most of the other colonies had another guerrilla force to contend with. By the late seventeenth century, scalping was so
familiar to all European transplants that the French did not scruple to enlist
its terrors against their more numerous Protestant neighbors. While the
English took and maintained the lead in promoting the white scalping of Indi-

ans, to the French goes the distinction of having first encouraged the Indian scalping of whites. In 1688, even before the official declaration of war in Europe, the governor of Canada offered ten beaver skins to the Indians of northern New England for every enemy scalp, Christian or Indian. Not to be outdone, the English regained the palm in 1696 when the New York Council "*Resolved for the future,* that Six pounds shall be given to each Christian or Indian as a Reward who shall kill a french man or indian Enemy."[42] Thereafter, until the Seven Years' War when different motives prompted each to reassess their practices, the French and English governments periodically fostered the scalping of European and Indian enemies by offering bounties or other economic incentives.

Although the New England colonies resorted to scalp bounties in the first three wars with the French and Indians, the popular enthusiasm and official rationale for them appear no more clearly than in Pennsylvania during the Seven Years' War. Pennsylvania had extensive northern and western frontiers bordering on the territory of still-powerful Indian tribes—Delaware, Shawnee, and Iroquois. Only precipitous mountains, with their inaccessible trails and myriad hiding places, separated the land-hungry English from most of the Indians' fertile lands in the Ohio country and along the upper Susquehanna. With the French also ensconced in the Ohio valley from Fort Duquesne northward, war parties of French and Indians had small difficulty in laying waste the province's frontier settlements and killing, scalping, or capturing their inhabitants, which they began to do in earnest in the spring of 1756 following Gen. Edward Braddock's stunning defeat the previous summer. Within a few months, their lightning strikes had thrown the backcountry of Maryland, Virginia, and Carolina as well into total chaos. "All these provinces are laid waste for forty leagues [*ca.* 125 miles] from the foot of the mountains, in the direction of the sea," Governor Vaudreuil informed the French minister of marine in August. "The number of prisoners in these territories since last April [1756], is estimated at about three thousand—men, women and children, in addition to thirteen hundred horses carried off to the River Oyo [Ohio], or the Beautiful River; the houses and barns that have been burnt, and the oxen and cows which have been killed wherever found, have not been counted."[43] The only way to stop this devastation, the English thought, was to seize the offensive from their enemies and force them into a defensive posture, for which their inferior civil and military populations, fragile economies, and weak fortifications were ill-equipped. And the quickest way to mount such an offensive with woodsmen experienced in guerrilla warfare was the scalp bounty.

The most vocal demand for a bounty came from the ravaged settlements themselves, where vengeful inhabitants sought to drop their reliance on distant forts and defense-minded provincial troops and form their own volunteer war parties, financed largely by the bounties on enemy hair. No sooner had Braddock's survivors dragged themselves home than the western tribes, emboldened by their sudden success on the Monongahela, launched a blitzkrieg on the exposed Pennsylvania settlements. When Conrad Weiser met with the recent victims of Bethel, Tulpenhacon, and Heidelberg townships on November 19, 1755, he heard loud threats to all Indians "without Destinction" and even to himself as an Indian lover. Although an impromptu war council of officers, gentlemen, and freeholders raised a militia company and established pay scales, "the People . . . cried out that so much for an Indian Scalp they would have (be they Friends or Enemies) from the Governor." Impatient of action by the Quaker-dominated eastern establishment, they forced Weiser and some other freeholders to "promise them a Reward of four Pistoles for every Enemy Indian man they should kill" until the legislature could act. As for that, Weiser told Lieutenant (and acting) Governor Robert Hunter Morris, "They want to force us to make a Law, that they should have a Reward for every Indian which they kill; They demanded such a Law of us, with their Guns Cocked, pointing it [*sic*] towards us."[44] Perhaps the precedent of Maryland and Virginia, who had passed scalp laws in July and August respectively, added insult to injury. To all appearances, a Paxton prophecy had come true: "We must bid up for Scalps and keep the Woods full of our People hunting them," John Harris had warned less than three weeks before, "or they will ruin our Province."[45]

Though tardily, bid them up the government did. In January the governor guaranteed forty pieces of eight for every Indian scalp lifted by a militia company. By April the legislature had raised £1000 for military operations and appointed a board of commissioners to oversee the distribution of scalp and prisoner bounties; $130 went to the taker of the scalp of any male Indian ten years or older. On April 24, Morris explained his strategy to William Johnson, a strategy substantially shared by Virginia and Maryland. "I have been constrained to yield to the importunate Demands of the enraged People (not being able otherwise to afford them a sufficient Protection for want of Arms, Amunition and an equal and compulsory Militia Law)" to declare war on the Delawares and to offer "large rewards for Prisoners and Scalps," he wrote, "hoping that this woud engage such of our Inhabitants as had any courage left, as well as all others in the Neighbouring Provinces, to hunt, pursue and attack them in their own Country and by these means keep them at home for the Defence of their own Towns and prevent the total desertion of the back Counties. . . . " Although a scalp bounty was "loudly called for on my Return from New York, in December last, and since importunately and frequently repeated," Morris felt he had to wait on Johnson's and the Iroquois attempts to control the Delawares through diplomacy. "I own," he continued, "had I had the least notion that they coud be stopt in the midst of their furious Career, I woud not have gratified the People but despairing of this, you will agree with me no other method is so likely as this to bring a force into the Enemys Country and drive them from their lurking places and from their Towns."[46]

The persistent English faith in the offensive potential of scalp bounties, however, was seldom rewarded with lasting military success, especially against the countless small raids characteristic of the early stages of the Seven Years' War. Just as Massachusetts' use of Iroquois mercenaries failed to solve her northern frontier problem in the early eighteenth century—salvation could not come from *Maqua ex machina* (in Richard Johnson's apt phrase)—so were irregular scalping parties incapable of stemming the French and Indian tide along the Middle Atlantic frontiers in mid-century.[47] The real source of trouble were the French forts that supported, supplied, and sent out the predominantly Indian war parties, and only disciplined British troops in impressive numbers, aided by artillery and the European art of siege warfare, could hope to neutralize them. English scalping parties could at best make the Indians think twice before leaving their own villages; at worst they could find themselves outfoxed by superior woodsmen and wind up as hairy hoops in those same villages. Governor Morris predicted accurately that bounties "indeed may induce men to go out in company, but the cutting off one or two small partys will put a stop to that kind of war."[48]

A larger impediment to their success was the ingrained defensiveness of the colonists—despite their initial encroachments on Indian and what the French believed to be French land—and the need of farmers to stay at home in the very months when Indian men, freed by their horticultural women, took to the warpath.[49] "Our people are nothing but a set of farmers and planters, used only to the axe and hoe," groaned one colonial strategist. "The most we do is to defend our selves at Home," lamented a Massachusetts minister in 1750, "but they are for an offensive War." When sixty enemies were killed near Fort Massachusetts, only three scalps were taken, "which shows us that our Men will not venture out after the Enemy on any Scalping Act whatsoever," not even "if they should be much greater than ever they have been."[50]

The "Love of Money" that colonial officials hoped would incite their people to "risque their lives in the service and defence of the country" was a motivating force clearly inadequate to seize the initiative from offense-minded enemies.[51] The list of complaints that the bounty acts were "ineffectual" was long.[52] Perhaps the most eloquent testimony to their military failure came from the actions of the Maryland legislature in 1765. Nine years after the province set aside £4000—one-tenth of the total war chest—to encourage "Parties of active Men not only to go in Quest of [hostile Indians] on our Borders, but even to Attack and Annoy them in their own Settlements," a committee of the lower house set fire to nearly half of it. Virginia's burgesses did not wait as long to admit that their scalp law did "not . . . answer the purposes thereby intended."[53] They scuttled it in 1758 when it became obvious that the character of warfare in America was taking a decisively European turn.

Yet when Indian hostilities erupted in Pontiac's uprising and in the Revolution, the colonists renewed their tarnished faith in scalp bounties, "the only effectual Weapon against the Savages," hoping against hope that their efficacy would outweigh their "abuses" and "Inconveniences."[54] The colonists' ardent faith in scalping parties must have lain less in their lethal efficiency than in the boost they gave to morale and the outlet to revenge. Since the first revolutionary scalp bounties followed the last of the Seven Years' War proclamations by no more than twenty years, the American officials who promoted them could not have been unaware of their mixed record as offensive weapons. But their popularity whenever frontier settlements suffered from guerrilla raids, whether French, British, or Indian, strongly suggests that bounties were one of the few ways available to colonial leaders to translate the colonists' hurt and anger into offensive zeal against the proper enemy, thereby deflecting it away from themselves. Whether many enemy scalps were actually produced mattered less than filling the woods with audacious, vengeful gunmen who plied the military trade—however irregularly—at a fraction of the cost of maintaining British or provincial troops. For most of these hunters, perhaps, the dangerous, difficult search for revenge probably served to maintain their general mental health by sublimating or exhausting the initially warping excesses of hatred and frustration that drove them. As many bounty hunters discovered to their peril, it was "ill fighting with a wild Beast in his own Den." And "who," many asked, "can catch a fleeing Indian?"[55]

If scalping did not prove to be the colonists' military salvation, it may have contributed to their moral damnation by encouraging an act that contravened their own cultural norms for the conduct of warfare and generalized Christian standards for the treatment of the dead. Just as the changes in traditional Indian scalping must be assessed in their own cultural terms, so must the moral dimensions of English scalping. Moreover, it is necessary to determine the proportion of colonial society that accepted the new ethic of scalping, implicitly or explicitly, for it is manifestly unfair—and historically inaccurate—to ask the innocent and powerless to share equally the moral burdens of society's movers and shakers, however numerous they were. By definition, aberrant behavior, such as scalping by the English colonists, is seldom the work of a whole society, though the attitudes and emotions that give rise to it may be shared by large segments of the society.

There is good reason to think that scalping was familiar and largely acceptable to a substantial portion of the colonial population. To frontier inhabitants, of course, bounties, scalps, and even survivors of scalping were bitter fixtures of life during the war years and vivid memories, frequently renewed in tale and boast, even in peacetime. To judge by the vociferous demand for bounties from the frontiers whenever the Indians turned hostile, few generations could have avoided their emotional impact. But scalping's legacy reached far beyond the frontier into the safer towns and cities of the colonies, even into the highest niches of polite society and to the mother country. Scalp bounties were widely proclaimed through broadsides, newspapers, and military chains of command. Colonial newspapers in wartime were filled with stories of scalping by and of the English, providing material for an already knowledgeable oral culture of news distribution. Graphic descriptions of the victims of Indian attacks, particularly pregnant women and little children, served to kindle the righteous anger of potential bounty hunters, and accounts of colonial successes enticed them into the field. When three New Jersey children were killed in 1756, for example, it was considered (exceptionally) newsworthy by the Philadelphia and New York papers that "none of them were Scalped," though one child's throat was (predictably) "cut quite across" and all were (poignantly) "found Dead with Flowers in their Hands."[56] Even in the fragile interstices of peace, the provocations for English scalping were never far from the colonial consciousness. In 1755 a Philadelphia newspaper noted the appearance of a Mohawk chief and some warriors "among the Ladies on their Assembly Night, where they danced the Scalping Dance with all its Horrors, and almost terrified the Company out of their Wits."[57] Given the "savage" addiction to "treachery," it mattered little that the Mohawks were allies.

If stories about scalps were a pallid substitute for the objects themselves, they could be seen and admired even in civilized circles far from their rough origins. Any inhabitant of Salem, Massachusetts (and no doubt other towns as well) could wander into the town courthouse to view the dusty hair-pieces tacked to the walls. As today, scalps could also be seen in museums. When Gov. Thomas Penn was given the scalp of a notorious Delaware chief in 1758, he "thought of sending it to the British Museum with a plate engraved giving an account of the action" at Kittanning where it was taken.[58] In 1782 a locally lifted scalp was displayed in Pierre-Eugène du Simitière's "American Museum" in Philadelphia.[59] Like soldiers in many wars, America's warriors, particularly British officers, had a habit of collecting souvenirs of their service in the colonial wilds. Gen. George Townshend, Wolfe's successor at Quebec, almost paid dearly for the collection of "scalps & some Indian arms & utensils" he took back to England. After a fashionable dinner party at Townshend's in January 1760, an Indian boy whom the general had given to Lord George Sackville as an American memento "got to the box & found a scalp which he knew by the hair belong'd to one of his own nation. He grew into a sudden fury (tho' but eleven years old) & catching up one of the scalping-knives made at his master with intention to murther him, who in his surprise hardly knew how to avoid him, & by laying open his breast, making signs, & with a few words of French Jargon, that the boy understood, at last with much difficulty pacified him."[60]

More memorable for the colonists was the sight of fresh scalps paraded through the streets of colonial towns such as Albany, Dover, Boston, and New York by strutting English woodsmen or befeathered native allies. Capt. John Lovewell's "brave company," entering Boston in 1725 "in triumph" with ten hooped trophies on poles (Indian-style), could not have failed to stir the blood and admiration of spectators. Only Lovewell's and a Lieutenant Farwell's wearing of wigs made from enemy Indian scalps, which they did to the scriptural disapproval—more of the wigs than the scalps—of a single eccentric minister, may have won more plaudits for patriotic daring.[61]

Although scalping was considered a male occupation, women, even refined urban ladies, were not ignorant of or necessarily squeamish about it. The story of Hannah Dustin's capture and escape with ten of her captors' scalps, which gained in the telling, was a forceful reminder that the enemies of colonial men were the enemies of all English settlers.[62] The Mohawk scalp dance at the Philadelphia Assembly served the same purpose, as did the frank correspondence between an army officer and a young demoiselle who may have seen the dance four years earlier.[63] Even more telling was Archibald Kennedy's *Serious Advice to the Inhabitants of the Northern-Colonies* in 1755. After hearing the impassioned laments of a roomful of New York ladies that they could not go to war to revenge Braddock's defeat, Kennedy seriously proposed that the young women of the North "enter into an Association, not to admit any Youth of the Age of Eighteen to the smallest Share of their good Graces, until such Time as they had either laid a *French* Scalp, *bona Fide* taken, at their Feet," certifiably served in one campaign, or "shewed a Wound received in Front, in the Defence of their Country."[64] Apparently, the sight of a bloody French scalp— or an Indian's—at their satined feet would not have sent well-bred colonial girls into a faint or pious outrage. By the mid-eighteenth century, it seems safe to say, scalping was as Anglo-American as shillings and succotash.

But by no means was there a colonial consensus that scalping by Englishmen was either necessary or desirable, and calls for the abolition or strict limitation of scalp bounties were frequent if not loud. English culture had a strong conscience that never stopped protesting the colonists' deviation from "civilized" Christian norms, even when arguments from necessity were deafening. The first Massachusetts act of 1694 to encourage volunteers against the Indians offered bounties "for every [hostile] Indian, great or small, which they shall kill, or take and bring in prisoner." In 1704 the act was renewed, but the General Court amended it in the direction of "Christian practice" by establishing a scale of rewards graduated by age and sex and giving no rewards for the scalps of children under ten years. Subsequently, in Massachusetts as well as most of the other colonies, twelve years was the most common age for distinguishing "adult" enemies from children. On two occasions, however, heavily attacked Pennsylvania reverted to ten years, while relatively secure New Jersey and Connecticut could afford to allow Indian boys to reach the age of fifteen and sixteen respectively before putting a high price on their heads.[65]

While some colonists were concerned about the effects of the bounties on Indian lives, others worried about the effects on their own countrymen. As chairman of a committee on volunteers during the 1712 session of the Massachusetts General Court, Samuel Sewall tried to prevent the bounty hunters from turning their bloody work into a "Trade" at the expense of the government. Forced to give in to frontier pressure for "12s 6d Wages [a week] and Subsistence" for the volunteers in addition to the scalp bounty, he tried to degrade the volunteers' special status by ensuring that "stand[ing] forces, Marching and in Garrison might have the same Encouragement as to Scalp Money," which at that time stood at £100. All the talk of mercenary warfare clearly made the judge uneasy, and he concluded that "if persons would not be spirited by love of their wives, Children, Parents, [and] Religion, twas a bad Omen."[66]

Some years later, in Pennsylvania, the Reverend Thomas Barton was nagged by a similar concern. In 1763 the former military chaplain wrote that "the general cry and wish is for what they call a Scalp Act. . . . Vast numbers of Young Fellows who would not chuse to enlist as Soldiers, would be prompted by Revenge, Duty, Ambition & the Prospect of the Reward, to carry Fire & Sword into the Heart of the Indian Country. And indeed, if this Method could be reconcil'd with *Revelation* and the *Humanity* of the English Nation, it is the only one that appears likely to put a final stop to those Barbarians." As more than one reluctant advocate of scalping argued, "necessity pleads an Excuse for following so inhuman an Example, as the shortest way . . . to put an End to such Barbarities."[67]

The most popular excuse was the need for revenge upon the French and/or their Indian allies. "We should deal exactly with them as they do by us, destroy and scalp as they do," argued a New York official. Even a strong opponent of scalping allowed that "Reprisals of the same Kind" were justified by "the Laws of Nations, and indeed by all Laws divine and human."[68] Following an earlier governor's lead in blaming the "Barbarous . . . Scalping [of] the Dead" on French bounties, the Massachusetts lower house passed a scalp act in 1747 to be "aveng'd and retaliated" on the Canadians for warring in a "Way and Manner abhor'd by christian and civilized Nations, and justifiable from the Principles of Self-Preservation only." In the same spirit Gen. Jeffrey Amherst in June 1759 ordered his troops to preserve enemy women and children from harm, but threatened to "revenge" the murder or scalping of any English woman or child by killing—and presumably scalping—two enemy men "whenever he has occasion." A month later, General Wolfe, "strictly forb[ade] the inhuman practice of scalping, except when the enemy are [male] Indians, or Canadians dressed like Indian," revealing thereby the standard limitation on even the most sensitive English conscience.[69] As Christians and white Europeans, the French might receive civilized treatment, even when they did not deserve it, but America's savages remained forever beyond the pale.

A few critics, however, remained adamantly opposed to English scalping under any circumstances. The Reverend Hugh Graham thought that bounties even on Indian scalps were "a Blot on Britain's Escutcheon." In 1779 Congress and General Washington were reluctant to give rewards for British scalps for fear "it may be improved by our Enemies to a national Reproach."[70] Gov. Jonathan Law of Connecticut worried less about the fickle eddies of public opinion than about moral absolutes. "As for the giving Premiums for humane Scalps or any other Creatures not equally mischievous to a Wolf," he told Governor Shirley of Massachusetts in 1747, "I must look upon to be unchristian, inhumane and barbarous with as great an Odium and Abhorrence as the good Marquis [Charles de la Boische de Beauharnois, governor of Canada] or any other Gentleman do[e]s or can doe." But in some ways the silent reproach of the British troops under Colonel Henry Bouquet was the most damning. After their surprising victory over the Indians at Bushy Run in August 1763, Bouquet told his commander, "Our brave men disdained So much to touch the dead body of a Vanquished Enemy that Scarce a Scalp Was taken Except by the [American] Rangers and Pack Horses Drivers," most of whom, "Stupified by Fear," had hidden in the bushes during the battle.[71]

Perhaps such uncompromising stances were possible only for those relatively new and unattached to America, such as Bouquet's troops, or safely distant from the danger of French and Indian war parties, as was Governor Law. Colonists within reach of an enemy scalping knife enjoyed small philosophical distance from the vengeful hatred of war, which helps to explain the proposals of a New Yorker who sought earnestly to abolish scalping, especially of "poor Women and innocent Children," as barbarous and unchristian. Finding no way out of the vicious American cycle of revenge, he recommended to an Albany council of war that, rather than punishing Indian enemies in kind, the English should sacrifice three Indian "Right-Hands or Thumbs" for every "Mother of Children scalped or murdered, or otherwise abused; for every other Female two; [and] for every old Man, or such as are incapable of bearing Arms, or making any Resistance, two." If Frenchmen accompanied war parties that harmed English innocents, "let their Eyes, or the Eyes of those destined for Reprisals, by a gentle Puncture, pay for it, as well as their Hands, (or why not Castration?) and let them return, as live Monuments, and Examples of Cowardice and Cruelty. This will," he predicted, "strike a greater Terror than Death itself."[72] As the endless parade up Tyburn showed, death familiar lost its sting; mutilation did not.

Colonial Englishmen could not escape the judgment of their own religion and culture when they scalped declared enemies out of revenge and necessity. Still less could they do so when they scalped innocents in peacetime and committed other atrocities of the spirit and the flesh. The contorting animosities of war were not easily forgotten in peace. If a provincial officer was "justly incens[e]d" at Indian raids and "determined to scalp all I lay my Hands on with unrelenting Rage," how much more prone were his less disciplined backcountry troopers, who may have lost friends and family to the scalping knife, to forget the constraints of Europeanized warfare after a brief stint in the local militia and to blur the distinction between war and peace.[73] The uneasy period after the Seven Years' War was particularly rife with opportunities for the tardy exercise of vengeance, especially when former soldiers began to seep illegally into the fertile Ohio valley, and Maryland continued to offer scalp money until the fall of 1765. Well after Pontiac's uprising had been put down in the west and peace restored on the Pennsylvania frontiers, Colonel Bouquet discovered that "one of the Maryland Volunteers, had killed a Shawnee Indian near Fort Pitt & produced a Scalp for the reward; And that Some of the Frontier People were out in the Woods Endeavoring to fall upon some straggling Indians to get their Scalps." And the killing continued, right up to the Revolution when bounties again made it legal. When a British Indian Department officer met with the head warriors of several western nations at Fort Pitt in 1768, they complained that "the English are certainly determined [to ma]ke War on us, or otherwise they would not Scalp our [peop]le—the Scalping those Indians is worse than murdering [them]," declared the officer.[74]

Some atrocities were caused not by an understandable search for revenge but by simple greed. In 1756 four New Jersey men combined to murder a family of loyal Indians, long-time residents of the area, and to pass their scalps in Philadelphia as having been lifted in Pennsylvania. Armed with "Guns, Cutlasses and an Ax," they attacked the wigwam about midnight on April 12. The husband, George, escaped unharmed, but his wife Kate died when one of the men "cut her Head all to Pieces" with the axe and another fired a "Brace of Balls" into her stomach. An eleven-year-old girl was "much bruised about the Head, stabbed in the Shoulders and her Right-hand almost cut off at the Wrist." Her twelve-month-old twin siblings were "cut and gashed in [a] frightful Manner." In the end, none was scalped because George raised an alarm that led to the bounty hunters' arrest. So strong was the temptation to pervert the bounties in this way that when Pennsylvania offered $150 for the return of any English captive of the Indians, the government needed to spell out that it would pay "nothing for their Scalps."[75]

The frontier's craving for scalp money and revenge gave rise to several practices that would have been regarded by traditional Indians as dishonorable to both the warrior and his enemy. One was double-scalping, not to cheat the provincial paymaster (although some men were not above that) but to secure another remunerative trophy when the first had been lost in flight. In 1725, for example, an eighteen-year-old soldier who had been captured by two Indians and carried into the Maine woods managed at night to knock them both on the head and scalp them. But in fording a river on the way home, he lost one scalp and a gun. He eventually collected the bounties on both scalps, however, because when he returned to his garrison a dozen men accompanied him to the place where he had slain his captor and "skin'd another off his head." The young soldier's victim had been dead only a day when he was scalped a second time; a scouting party from Fort Massachusetts took a full week to find one of their Indian victims and scalp him, this in early July which can be very warm in the Hoosic Valley. In a somewhat related vein, Massachusetts once paid £30 to a Northfield man who had spent fourteen months in a Quebec prison with a scalp he had taken just before his capture. The knowledge of how he managed to conceal an Indian scalp from his Indian captors and his French jailers all that time is, unfortunately, one of history's small casualties.[76]

A rather larger casualty, though no one seems to have noticed it at the time, was the morality of a New Jersey patrol alerted in 1758 by a young boy who had wheeled and shot a pursuing Delaware warrior on the Sussex road. Armed with guns and dogs, the local scout went to the scene of action where the dogs picked up a bloody trail. A short search led them to a "great heap of brush" where the Indian was found buried "close under a Log" with his "two Blankets, Tomahawk, Pipe and Tobacco Pouch by his Side." Since he was clearly not deserving of Christian respect, they "took off his Scalp," purloined the grave goods, and marched off to Perth Amboy to collect the provincial bounty.[77] That the incident was reported by the Pennsylvania and New Jersey newspapers without comment or murmur speaks eloquently to the blinding acceptance of the scalp bounty and its morality in eighteenth-century America.

What is not explicable—much less excusable—by any discernible English or American standard is the behavior of Col. George Rogers Clark at the taking of the British Fort Sackville at Vincennes in 1779. During a temporary truce, a detachment of Clark's men captured fifteen or sixteen Indians and whites returning to the fort and brought them bound to the street opposite the fort. Sitting in a ring on the ground, the Indians were serially tomahawked by the Americans as they sang their death songs. Then one of the French soldiers in the scout, Francis Maisonville, was set in a chair "and by Col'l Clarkes order," testified Col. Henry Hamilton, the British commander who watched from the fort, "a man came with a scalping knife, who hesitating to proceed to this excess of barbarity on a defenceless wretch, Colonel Clarke with an imprecation told him to proceed . . . When a piece of the scalp had been raised the man stopped his hand, he was again ordered to proceed, and as the executor of Col. Clarke's will, was in the act of raising the skin," a brother of the victim who had joined the American cause prevailed on Clark to desist. Maisonville never recovered from this traumatic encounter with American frontier justice: he lost his reason during a long confinement in Williamsburg and committed suicide. According to Hamilton, who may have exaggerated but certainly did not invent the details of this affair, when Clark came to the fort to talk of its surrender, "yet reeking with the blood of those unhappy victims," he spoke "with rapture of his late achievement, while he washed of[f] the blood from his hands stain'd in this inhuman sacrifice."[78]

During the American Revolution each side spread propaganda about the other's use of Indian mercenaries, scalp bounties, and atrocities. While exaggerated for effect, most of these stories were plausible because the English in America had seen nearly every imaginable variation on the act of scalping, committed either by Indians or by colonists. But George Rogers Clark's exploits in the streets of Vincennes added a chilling new chapter to scalping's long and bloody history.

In war as in peace, English colonial society judged itself by two standards, one narrowly religious, the other broadly cultural. Thomas Barton referred to them as "*Revelation* and the *Humanity* of the English Nation." By the second standard and without too much tergiversation, scalping and the use of scalp bounties could be judged acceptable—or at least not wholly objectionable—because they were necessary to the survival and prosperity of the English way of life in America. Scalping, after all, was a new cultural custom, whose method and much of whose morality derived from indigenous sources. The colonists scalped and encouraged others to scalp primarily because their Indian and later French enemies scalped them, and vengeance, like many other Old Testament traits, was deeply engrained in the Protestant English character. As scalping was resorted to with greater frequency and intensity, it developed an institutional status that could accommodate a number of operational and moral variations on the traditional Indian theme. Englishmen could, for example, legitimately scalp not only Indian and French men but also Indian women and children. The scalps could be taken not only upon felling the enemy but up to several days after, when the corpse had obviously reached a state of semi-putrefaction. Scalps could even be torn from buried enemies without overstepping the bounds of acceptable behavior. Of course, some Englishmen objected unreservedly to both scalping and scalp bounties, but they voiced a minority opinion that was all but drowned out by the advocates of the new ethic.

But "Revelation" was a much less flexible measure of social morality. In pure form, it played no favorites and tolerated no change. Its adamantine strictures applied with hard impartiality to all men and all nations. The rub, however, was that the English, even the ministerial custodians of Scripture, were incapable of living a pure text. Since it was obvious that scalping simply would not pass the test of Christian behavior exemplified by the life of Christ, "Revelation" had to be bent to fit the needs of the day. Not unexpectedly, there were many clerics ready to bend it.

The famous ambush of Capt. John Lovewell's volunteer band at Pigwacket (Fryeburg), Maine, on a Sabbath morning in May 1725 was launched as Jonathan Frye, the expedition's young Harvard-trained chaplain, had finished scalping a lone Indian hunter. In the heat of the day-long fight that ensued, Frye scalped another fallen adversary before he was himself wounded and left to die. The Reverend Thomas Smith of Falmouth (Portland) took no such personal risk. Rather, he was one of a group of gentlemen who hired a squad of hardy parishioners to go on a "Scout or Cruse for the killing and captivating of the Indian enemy." In return for supplying the bounty hunters with "Ammunition and Provision," the investors received "one full third Part of fourteen fifteens of the Province Bounty for every Captive or Scalp, and of every Thing else they shall or may recover or obtain." In his journal for June 18, 1757, the minister recorded, "along with pious thoughts, 'I receive 165 pounds 3-3 . . . my part of scalp money.'"[79]

When ministers not only looked the other way but shared in the profits from Indian deaths, the moral barometer of America dipped dangerously low. At the bottom, however, lay the American Revolution, in which Englishmen scalped Englishmen in the name of liberty. Scalping and other techniques of Indian warfare, placed in the hands of a larger European population, eventually sealed the Indians' fate in North America, but not before wreaking upon the white man a subtle form of moral vengeance.

PART V

CONSEQUENCES

INTRODUCTION

Previous chapters have documented a variety of cultural interactions between American natives and European newcomers. It remains only to take stock of their larger meanings and longer-term consequences for both groups.

Chapter Twelve serves to frame the question of mutual impact by looking briefly and broadly at the evolution of the eastern half of the continent over three centuries. In 1990, at a conference in Princeton sponsored by the New Jersey Historical Commission, I was invited to address "the general nature of North American society resulting from an amalgamation of Western European, Native American, and West African societies," all in forty-five minutes. Given my time limit and audience, I felt obliged to restrict my focus to British North America—what became the future United States—and only to glance at New Spain and New France for notable contrasts. Since "coverage" of three hundred years of complicated social history was impossible, I tried to suggest the nature and magnitude of change between 1492 and 1790 by juxtaposing two snapshots of North America, taken at each end of the period, and by hinting at some of the causes of difference. A somewhat longer version of Chapter Twelve was published as "The Columbian Mosaic in Colonial America" in *Beyond 1492* (1992) and, in a differently abbreviated, unfootnoted version, in the September/October 1991 issue of *Humanities* [NEH].

The colonial impact on the natives of eastern North America has preoccupied me as it has previous generations of ethnohistorians. Most of the previous chapters describe and analyze the repercussions of those changes for native society and culture. In May 1978 I presented a preliminary essay on "The English Colonial Impact on Indian Culture" at a conference at the Newberry Library in Chicago; an expanded version was published in *The European and the Indian* (1981). It documented what anthropologists have long argued, that the *way* members of a culture use or adapt another culture's artifacts (ideas, material objects, institutions, language) is more diagnostic of cultural change or acculturation than *what* they adapt. Adaptation, in other words, is less often a sign of capitulation than of capitalization. Even Indians who have given up the buckskins, wigwams, and shamans of their ancestors have not surrendered their Indian identities, their instinct for autonomy, or even their ancient sense of superiority to the powerful strangers in their midst.

In October 1992, the Quincentenary year, I was given an opportunity to restate those conclusions at a conference on "Transatlantic Encounters" at Vanderbilt University. But for the session on "Native Americans: Vision of the Vanquished," with its reference to Nathan Wachtel's seminal book on colonial Peru, I sought to emphasize not the colonial impress per se but how the natives in various settings coped with or resisted it. In arguing for native agency I was by no means "blaming the victims" for their fate, but rather celebrating the resilience and ingenuity of native peoples who often found themselves between a colonial rock and a hard place. Chapter Thirteen was published in *Beyond 1492* (1992) and appears here with only minor changes.

In the final chapter I try my hand at probing "The Indian Impact on English Colonial Culture," a topic I first essayed at the May 1980 colloquium of the Institute of Early American History and Culture and then in *The European and the Indian* (1981). It parts company from a number of earlier articles and recent books on acculturation by focusing only on the English mainland colonies (large enough topic), not all the Americas or even the whole United States before and after independence, and by assessing the *ways* in which Anglo-American culture used or adapted the Indian artifacts and traits previous authors have so lovingly enumerated. While most of these (predominantly anthropological) authors would not automatically assume that a contemporary Indian driving a Toyota 4 × 4 was or considered him- or herself no longer an Indian, they fail to exercise the same caution when treating the white frontiersmen and colonists who selectively adopted Indian ways and means. They also tend to ignore what I call "reactive" changes spurred by the ubiquitous presence of Indians as military foes and cultural foils. These largely negative reactions to the native challenge, I argue, made a deeper imprint on colonial culture as a whole than did the "adaptive" changes made by adopting temporarily Indian means to perdurable English ends.

An alternative way to address the issue is counterfactually: what would colonial America have looked like if the Indians had never existed? That question prompted me to write "Colonial America without the Indians," which was published in the *Journal of American History* (March 1987) and in *After Columbus* (1988). It extends the analysis to include the French and Spanish colonies but is considerably shorter and less detailed than Chapter Fourteen. Both, however, show that colonial America would simply not be recognizable without the presence and impact of its Indian peoples and cultures.

TWELVE

THE COLUMBIAN MOSAIC

After the revolution, the new United States were a source of great curiosity to citizens of the Old World. Not only had the American upstarts pulled off the biggest small-r republican coup in recent memory, they had beaten the greatest empire in the modern world in the process. Who were these brash new giant-killers? What kind of societies had they fashioned in the American wilderness? How did they manage to wrest their new country from its aboriginal inhabitants? Where did their wealth—and audacity—come from? What manner of folks were they and how did they differ from their European cousins?

To find the answers to these and similar questions, a veritable host of European travelers and sightseers struck off on tours of America in the 1780s and '90s, usually in a north-south direction. Men of every major nation in Europe made the grand tour from New England to South Carolina, often in the company of countrymen or servants. Sometimes they combined their trips with other business—military, scientific, political, or mercantile. But each visitor sought to encompass the regional and human diversity of the former colonies, as if their letters and journals would give Europe its only true and accurate portrait of the new nation.

In their uneven progress through the land, the visitors, like all tourists, tended to generalize from the small range of details they had seen with their own eyes and from the accumulated lore of new, often chance, acquaintances. When, for instance, Francisco de Miranda, the gifted Venezuelan revolutionary, toured Connecticut in 1783, he inferred from tombstones in a Norwich churchyard that "this place is highly salutary, for the age dates are quite high, and among them I counted more than twelve between eighty and ninety years of life."[1] Similarly, Louis-Philippe, the future king of France, noticed that in the Shenandoah Valley of Virginia, the young people reached "notable heights." Most of them, he said, "seem taller than their elders" and are "increasing still."[2] These and other observations on the bounty of American farms suggested that the great white middling population, at least, was experiencing exceptional health and an enviable amount of prosperity. The most prosperous colony of all, Pennsylvania, had had on the eve of revolution a population of 350,000, some 275,000 of whom Moreau de St. Méry estimated to have been "Foreigners, all bought" as indentured servants or redemptioners. Twenty years later, they, too, were enjoying the salubrity of the state's economy and climate and reproducing like rabbits.[3]

But for everyone who prospered, there were many who suffered, usually those of a darker complexion. Johann David Schoepf, a learned scientist stationed in America with the Hessian troops until 1783, noted that even German and Irish indentured servants were unwilling to be sold in Carolina and Virginia because "they are too proud to work with and among the negroes who . . . are almost the only working people" in those states. "Any [white] man whatever, if he can afford so much as 2–3 negroes, becomes ashamed of work and goes about in idleness, supported by his slaves." Most visitors choked on the blatant disparity between a republic founded on the philosophical freedom of man and the actual bondage of men who happened not to be white. Schoepf could not decide to laugh or cry over a North Carolina slave sale where the auctioneer talked up the slaves' qualities while the "merchandise" sassily downgraded themselves from the platform "because they knew well that the dearer their cost, the more work will be required of them."[4] Having fled the excesses of the French Revolution in 1793, the West Indian-born Moreau de St. Méry was appalled that white American children "beat little slaves and if grown-up slaves try to interfere, adult whites beat them in turn."[5] Virtually every visitor agreed that slaves were treated more harshly in the South than in the North. The Italian naturalist Luigi Castiglioni heard a South Carolina planter "justify his vicious behavior toward negroes" by declaring "without blushing that they were a kind of animal closer to monkeys than to man."[6]

By contrast with the imported Africans and Europeans, the most American group of all received hardly any notice from the travelers unless they happened to venture into the still-dangerous "back-country." For in the settled portions of the new states, native Americans were in very short supply, restricted largely to tiny reservations. In his discussion of the racial composition of Philadelphia, Moreau de St. Méry felt no need to speak of Indians, he said, because "they inhabit only such places as are set apart for them; and if they appear in cities . . . it is always for some political reason."[7] In South Carolina the Catawbas called twelve square miles home, while in spacious New York, said Chateaubriand, "the remains of the [once-mighty] five Iroquois nations [are] enclaved in the English and American possessions."[8] When a young Oneida Iroquois returned to Boston in 1788 after three years of French education, testified a fellow passenger, Brissot de Warville, "he caused as much surprise as he had in Paris, for Indians are never seen there. They have been gone from Massachusetts for so long that people have forgotten what one looks like."[9] The outlook for their western cousins was no brighter, according to the French general, the marquis de Chastellux. In 1780 he had predicted with uncanny but sad accuracy that "a necessary consequence of a peace, if favorable to Congress, will be their total destruction, or at least their exclusion from all the country this side of the [Great] lakes."[10]

For all their perspicacity, acquired knowledge, and luck, those traveling ethnographers invariably missed the big picture of New America. Like all tourists, they suffered from the myopia of personal experience. How could it have been otherwise? They were virtually all white, male, foreign, insulated by wealth, class, or connections, and traveling low to the ground. While they could read about the conventional histories of some of their destinations, before or after leaving, and could pick up assorted facts and gossip en route, they were essentially prisoners of their own eyes and expectations. Since they were short of time, they took only one road, usually well worn, through a region, leaving 99 percent of its byways and precincts unexplored. Understandably, they gravitated to towns and great houses, where they could obtain bugless bedding, clean laundry, credit, and a soupçon of society, but in the process they missed much of the country, in both senses.

One source they might have used to trace the social profile of the new America, had it been available to them, was the first Federal census of 1790. In addition to the uncounted and undercounted, the new United States of nearly 900,000 square miles was populated by almost 4 million people, black and white. A few over 3 million were white, three-quarters of a million—19 percent—were black. Ninety-five percent of these folks still lived in the country; only 24 towns could count more than 2500 inhabitants. More than a third of America's households contained seven or more persons, though the average was not quite six. Predictably, the white population was predominantly British in origin: nearly 80 percent had English, Scottish, or Irish surnames.[11]

But one group was conspicuous by its absence from the census figures: according to the new U.S. Constitution, Indians who were "not taxed" were excluded from the count, and that meant virtually all Indians, who were either too poor or too inaccessible to fall prey to the tax collector. Therefore, the social portrait the census paints is strictly chiaroscuro; we don't really know how much burnt umber ought to be added to America's features. In one large region, however, we have a good idea. Historian Peter Wood's detailed demography of the colonial Southeast shows that Indians in 1790 numbered about 56,000, or 3 percent of the population. More than a third of all southerners were black, more than a million were white.[12] But that was the South, and the complexion of other regions was much paler. In Massachusetts, for instance, the black population was only 5000, less than 1 1/2 percent of the total; Indians numbered only a few hundred.[13] In 1790, tourists and census-takers alike saw mostly white faces in the new Republic.

Whatever the regional proportions, newly independent America was a triracial, multicultural society. It was a "mosaic" rather than a "melting pot," a huge, constantly changing, imperfect amalgamation of biologies, histories, and anthropologies. Perhaps the best way to view such a restless and complex organism is to look at it over time by twisting the eyepiece of an historical kaleidoscope. For each twist in time will tumble the multicolored human fragments in space, throwing them into strikingly new patterns of American density and destiny.

We might well call America a *Columbian* mosaic because it was the Italian admiral who effectively bound together all of the world's continents with the shipping lanes of one continuous ocean sea. When Columbus bumped into America en route to Asia after a maritime apprenticeship in Europe and Africa, he made it likely—indeed, inevitable—that the peoples of the world's insular continents would no longer live in splendid isolation but would soon become a single "global village," due largely to European colonialism, technology, and communications. Although he never set foot on the North American continent, he was personally responsible for introducing Europeans to America, and Americans—albeit in chains—to Europe. It was left to Nicolás de Ovando, his successor as governor of the Indies, to introduce African slaves in 1502, just as Columbus set sail on his fourth and final voyage.[14] The paternity of triracial America is not in doubt; the only question is, how did the new American mosaic of 1790 come about?

The short answer is that Europeans emigrated in great numbers to the Americas and, when they got there, reproduced themselves with unprecedented success. But a somewhat fuller explanation must take account of regional and national variations.

The first emigrants, of course, were Spanish, not merely the infamous conquistadors, whose bloody feats greatly belied their small numbers, but Catholic priests and missionaries, paper-pushing clerks and officials who manned the far-flung bureaucracy of empire, and ordinary settlers: peasants, artisans, merchants, and not a few hidalgos, largely from the cities and towns of central and southwestern Spain. Since permission to emigrate was royally regulated, "undesirables" such as Moors, Jews, gypsies, and those condemned by the Inquisition reached the New World only in small, furtive numbers. In the sixteenth century perhaps 240,000 Spaniards slipped into American ports. They were joined by 450,000 more in the next century. The great majority were young men; only in the late sixteenth century did the proportion of women reach one-third. This meant that many men had to marry, or at least cohabit with, Indian women, which in turn gave rise to a large *mestizo* or mixed population. The relative unhealthiness of Latin America's subtropical islands and coasts also contributed to a slow and modest increase in Spanish population. When the mature population finally doubled by 1628, it had taken more than fifty years and only half the increase was due to biology; the other half was contributed by emigrants from home.[15]

In sharp contrast to the Spanish were the French in Canada, which Voltaire dismissed as "a few acres of snow." In a century and a half, Mother France sent only 30,000 emigrants to the Laurentian colony, the majority of them against their will. Only a few hundred paid their own way, many of them merchants eager to cash in on the fur and import trade. The rest were reluctant *engagés* (indentured servants), soldiers, convicts (primarily salt smugglers), and *filles du roi* or "King's girls," sent to supply the colony's superabundant, shorthanded, and lonely bachelors with wives. Not until 1710 were the Canadian genders balanced. But even in the seventeenth century, Canadiennes married young and produced often, doubling the population at least every thirty years. Fortunately for their Indian hosts and English neighbors, this high rate of natural increase was wasted on a minuscule base population. When Wolfe climbed to the Plains of Abraham in 1759, New France had only 75,000 Frenchmen, a deficit of colonial population on the order of 30 to 1.[16]

The biggest source of white faces in North America was Great Britain. In the seventeenth century she sent more than 150,000 of her sons and daughters to the mainland colonies and at least 350,000 more in the next. In 1690, white folks numbered around 194,000; a hundred years later they teemed at 3 million-plus.[17] Emigration obviously accounted for some of this astounding growth. In the eighteenth century, 150,000 Scotch-Irish, 100,000 Germans (many of them "redemptioners" from the Palatinate), 50,000 British convicts, and 2000–3000 Sephardic Jews made their way to English lands of opportunity.[18] But the proliferation of pale faces was predominantly a function of natural increase by which the colonial population doubled every twenty-five years, to that time the highest rate of increase known to demographers. After an initial period of "gate mortality," when food shortages, new diseases, and climatic "seasoning" might exact a high toll, white couples in most of the English colonies began to produce an average of four children who lived to become parents themselves.[19]

The reasons for their success were mainly two: in the words of Ben Franklin, "marriages in *America* are more general, and more generally early, than in *Europe*."[20] Colonial women married at the age of 21 or 22, about four or five years sooner than their European sisters, and they remarried quickly if their helpmates died, both in part because men tended to outnumber women. When their children were born (at the normal European rate), fewer died in infancy and childhood (before the ages of one and ten, respectively) and fewer mothers died in childbed. Women continued to have babies every two years, in the absence of Catholic prohibitions (as in Latin America and Canada) and birth control (except that partially provided by breast-feeding). But American mothers were healthier and lived longer than European mothers, thanks to sparser settlements, larger farms, more fertile land, fuller larders of nutritious food, and less virulent diseases. They therefore produced larger, taller, and healthier families, who in turn did the same.[21]

The results of all this fecundity were impressive to imperial administrators, catastrophic for the Indians. The Powhatans of Virginia could not have been too alarmed by the initial wave of English settlers and soldiers because 80 percent of them died of their own ineptitude and disease. But by 1640 the pale-faced population had recovered from the deadly uprising of 1622 to reach some 10,000, largely through persistent supplies from England. By 1680 the contest for the colony had been decisively won by the tobacco-planting English, who now outnumbered the natives about 20 to 1.[22]

Massachusetts, the other pole of archetypal Anglo-America, grew even faster. From only 9000 Puritans in 1640, the commonwealth of the cod spurted to 150,000 within a century, owing largely to unpuritanical bedroom behavior; Boston alone housed over 15,000 people.[23] But the fastest growing region, both by emigration and nature, was eighteenth-century Pennsylvania. Between 1690 and 1790, "the best poor man's country" (as its fans liked to describe it) saw its white population increase 38-fold. On the eve of independence, Philadelphia was the largest and most diverse city in North America, filled with religious denominations, ethnic groups, and social strata of every imaginable stripe. The Iroquois and Delaware chiefs who came to be wooed to neutrality or the rebel cause in the imminent war cannot have failed to be daunted by its 25,000 crowded inhabitants.[24]

Yet numbers alone do not allow us to draw a bead on the early American story. We must not only know *how many* Europeans emigrated to—or invaded—Indian America but *why*. For without an understanding of their motives, we cannot treat them as moral agents with choices to make or hold them accountable for the foreseen and foreseeable consequences of their actions. The one thing we can be sure of is that they came for a wide and usually mixed variety of reasons. At the beginning of the "Great Migration" to Massachusetts, even a Puritan promoter harbored no illusions about the exclusivity or purity of the migrants' motives. "As it were absurd to conceive they have all one motive," wrote John White in *The Planter's Plea*, "so were it more ridiculous to imagine they have all one scope. . . . It may be private interests may prevail with some. One brother may draw over another, a son the father, and perhaps some man his inward acquaintance. . . . Necessity may press some, novelty draw on others, hopes of gain in time to come may prevail with a third sort."[25]

For many, but by no means all, settlers of New England, religion played a key role in their decision to uproot their families and move to America. But religious motives did not always guarantee the health, sovereignty, or well-being of the American natives. Believers who wished simply to practice their own faiths without persecution, real or imagined, may be let off the hook, unless, of course, like the Puritans, their own intolerance and desire for a state monopoly led them to proscribe the natives' worship of their own gods. On the other hand, French nuns and missionaries were sent to Canada by visions of transforming the "pagan" wilderness into a "new Jerusalem," where nomadic native souls "washed white in the blood of the [paschal] lamb" would join good French Catholics to form "one [sedentary] people." New English missionaries not only reduced the native landbase by resettling the Indians in smaller, anglicized "praying towns" but inadvertently increased their neophytes' risk of contagious disease. In other words, good intentions alone are not sufficient to exempt historical actors from criticism, and history, unlike the law, has no statute of limitations.[26]

Other motives are equally hard to condemn wholesale. Can we blame ordinary European farmers, craftsmen, and merchants for wanting to forge a better life for their families, even if they wound up on land that once belonged to America's native inhabitants? The vast majority of immigrants hardly, if ever, *saw* the original owners, much less cheated or forced them from their land. Even male freeholders seldom knew about the backroom chicanery of their elected representatives who speculated with ill-gotten Indian lands. Much less could the voters control the machinations of imperial officials and army officers who wheeled and dealed for the same sorts of native property. If we blame ordinary colonists for wanting lower taxes, less crowding, more land, higher wages, healthier climates, more and better food, and family harmony, we will have to include ourselves in the blame—and most of the human race, for that matter. Collective guilt of such magnitude doesn't seem very productive.

On the other hand, immigrants were not only drawn to America but pushed out of Europe. Many shipped out because they were trying to run away from something: death sentences, debtor's prison, bishop's courts, oppressive seigneurial dues, recruiting sergeants. We may have little sympathy for those who chose to evade their civil responsibilities and the law, but what about the scrupulous avoiders of sin and immorality, who ran from drinking, gambling, and wanton women as if from the plague? Should we cut no slack for poor henpecked husbands who fled from shrews and harridans, or young women who could not wait an extra four or five years to marry and start a family? How hardened do we have to become to withhold our empathy from young servants who escaped abusive masters or young lovers kept apart by flinty or tight-fisted patriarchs?

If we want to take a hardnosed stance on the spoiling, illegitimate, or immoral character of white immigration, we would do better to focus on those who came solely to highjack America's wealth to Europe, often with the help, witting or unwitting, of its native owners and trustees, or those who carried war and destruction to Indian country, directly or indirectly in pursuit of geopolitical objectives of a European sort. Obviously it is easier to pillory the designers, and to some extent the agents, of military and economic imperialism than it is the run-of-the-mill emigrant who carried no conscious intent to defraud, harm, or dispossess anyone. Oppressive Spanish mine owners, freebooting pirates, absentee owners of West Indian sugar plantations, and fork-tongued traders who swindled Indians of their furs and skins with watered rum and false measures undoubtedly deserve our censure, mostly because they contravened the moral standards of their own day, less, perhaps, because those standards resemble our own.

At the same time, we should recognize that to condemn every aggressive military, religious, or economic action in the past is to question some of the fundaments of Western society, past *and present.* If everything associated with mercantilism, capitalism, evangelical religion, and armed force is beyond the moral pale, we may find it difficult, if not impossible, to approach our past—or the histories of most of the world's cultures—with the requisite empathy, understanding, and disinterestedness.

Another topic that requires an abundance of all three qualities but allows ample room for moral judgment is slavery. Nineteen percent of the human shards in the social mosaic of the new United States were black, the result of a legal, culturally sanctioned, but heinous trade in African slaves.[27] The slave trade was already ancient by the time America was brought into the European orbit in 1492. But the discovery of gold, the development of sugar plantations, and the founding of cities in Spanish and Portuguese America created a vast new market for the human chattels brought from the African interior by rival African kings, merchants, and war chiefs.[28]

Before independence, the Spanish alone transported 1.5 million blacks to their colonies, perhaps 200,000 before 1650. In the Caribbean the blacks replaced Indian laborers, who died in massive numbers from oppression, dislocation, and imported diseases. By the seventeenth century, the native populations of Mexico and coastal Peru were also seriously depleted, so black slaves were substituted as panners of gold (they died too easily in the cold damp of the mines), cutters of sugar cane, sailors, shipwrights, and particularly domestic servants in urban households. They did their work so well that by the eighteenth century the majority of blacks were free, especially the women and children of the cities who were manumitted by their owners at death or by purchase.[29]

In Canada the French preferred Indian slaves from the eastern Plains and Great Lakes called *panis* (after the Pawnees of modern-day Nebraska). In 125 years they imported only 1,132 Africans (fewer than ten a year), mostly as household servants in Quebec and Montreal. Since they were expensive and relatively rare, their lot was not onerous and, contrary to expectations, they adjusted to the Canadian winters with little difficulty.[30]

But their brethren in French Louisiana had a much harder row to hoe, to judge from the mortality rates. Between 1719 and 1735, royal and company administrators imported some 7000 Africans, mostly "Bambaras," or acculturated slave soldiers, from Senegal. Yet in 1735 only 3400 remained to be counted. The same loss of life must have occurred during the next fifty years: over 20,000 arrived but the black population in 1785 was only 16,500. Even immigration could not keep pace with Louisiana's morbid climate and the physical demands of plantation labor.[31]

The English demand for black labor grew much more slowly than did the Spanish, largely because the supply of indentured servants from the British Isles was adequate until the late seventeenth century. With the renewal of tobacco prices in Europe and the development of rice culture in South Carolina, however, English planters in the tidewater and the piedmont alike had a need for hands that could not be fully met with white workmen, who in any event often proved troublesome to the colonial elite upon gaining their freedom. So the planters turned primarily to "seasoned" slaves from the West Indies to fill the gap. Thanks to an increase in the African traffic in colonial and British bottoms, the price of a strong male slave remained a bargain when amortized over a lifetime. But after 1720, demand for acculturated West Indian slaves outstripped the supply and 80 percent of the slaves for English plantations came directly from Africa.[32]

Black talent and energy were never equally distributed in time or space. In 1690, for example, both Maryland and Connecticut had white populations of 21,000, but the New England colony had only 200 blacks to Maryland's nearly 2200. With double the white inhabitants, Virginia had more than four times the number of Maryland's blacks. Overall, the English mainland colonies could count fewer than 17,000 blacks, or 8 percent of the intrusive population. A hundred years later, more than three-quarters of a million blacks had moved into Indian America with their white masters.[33]

After 1680 the proliferation of black faces was especially noticeable in the South from the Chesapeake to South Carolina. In 1680, Virginia's social complexion had been only 7 percent black; by 1720 it was 30 percent. The proportion of blacks in South Carolina went from 17 to 70 percent in the same forty years, making it the only mainland colony with a black majority. And that was just the beginning: between 1730 and 1770, Anglo-America imported between 4000 and 7000 Africans every year. Strangely enough, even this influx did not amount to much on an international scale: only 4.5 percent of the 10 million slaves who survived capture and the horrendous "Middle Passage" to the New World were landed in the English mainland colonies. The vast majority went to the Caribbean, where their chances for living long were very slim, and to Latin America, where they were somewhat better. Although the condition of perpetual bondage was never easy, life on English farms and plantations—for economic more than humanitarian reasons—was tolerable enough to allow the black population to increase naturally as well as by constant infusions of new or "outlandish" Africans.[34]

Despite the uninvited presence of some four million Europeans and Africans, it could be argued—and was—that America in 1790 had plenty of elbow room for both natives and strangers. Even if the natives had been at full, pre-Columbian strength, some said, a slight change in their economy would have freed up enough land for all the newcomers without any noticeable pinch. By giving up the wild, nomadic life of the hunter for the taming, sedentary life of the farmer, the Indians (by which was meant male Indians) would require only a fraction of their former real estate and would be happy to swap the residue to their white neighbors for the more valuable blessings of civilization, such as Christianity, short hair, and long pants. And if for some perverse reason they did not like the sound of foreign neighbors, they could always move west, beyond the Mississippi where the white man would never think of moving.[35]

But of course the natives were *not* at full strength in 1790 and their room for maneuvering was greatly circumscribed by nearly three hundred years of cultural crowding and numerical decline. In the South, where they were at their strongest, they had suffered a 72 percent drop in population since 1685, while the white settlers had multiplied 21 times and the blacks nearly 18 times. The hardest hit were the natives of eastern South Carolina, who went from 10,000 to 300 in a century, a loss of 97 percent. The Natchez and other Indians of the lower Mississippi were not far behind at 90 percent: at 4000 they were actually experiencing a slight rebound from a nadir of 3600 in 1760, but they had irretrievably lost 38,000 relatives since the seventeenth century. The Choctaws and Chickasaws, who had been able to play off the Louisiana French and the Carolina English before 1763, had lost only half their people, but the Cherokees, located closer to the English colonies, suffered a 75 percent decline.[36] The story in New England, Pennsylvania, and Virginia was no different: everywhere, the original inhabitants had been reduced to a fragile fraction of their former selves and an even smaller minority of the states' new citizens. How had this come about?

Contemporaries who wishfully asserted that eastern America was big enough for everyone made one large, erroneous assumption about the Indian economy: they assumed that the natives were primarily hunters who chased wild game over the whole map. In fact, the Indians in the huge area claimed by the kings of England subsisted primarily on vegetables—corn, beans, and squash—cultivated by the women in the most fertile soils available. Among these three-season fields they lived in semipermanent towns and villages ranging from several hundred to a couple of thousand inhabitants. Although the women provided 50–75 percent of the annual diet, native men did have to range far and wide for the rest. Until the men could be persuaded by white reason or necessity to obtain their protein from domestic cattle and pigs rather than fish and game, the natives were forced to guard their extensive hunting and fishing grounds as jealously as they defended their villages and fields.

The advent of European farmers in search of those same cleared and fertile fields put them on a predestinate collision course with the Indians. Initially, there was no question of sharing the best soils because in most areas the native population pressed hard against the carrying capacity of the environment and fully occupied most of the prime farm land. The issue that was to be decided over the next three centuries was whether one intrusive group of farmers (and land speculators) would replace another, indigenous group of farmers. How this was in fact done varied from colony to colony. But in general the English (and their reluctant black helpers) prevailed by out-reproducing the natives and bringing about their precipitous decline as independent peoples.

The Indians could not reproduce themselves because their mortality rates far outstripped their birth rates. The single greatest cause of native deaths was epidemic diseases imported from Europe without malice aforethought.[37] Throughout the colonies from the beginning of contact, Old World pathogens served as the shock troops of the European invasion, softening up the enemy before the battalions of busy farmers waded ashore. From the English stand-point, these were "preparative Stroakes" of divine providence. As a South Car-olina governor put it so succinctly, "the Hand of God was eminently seen in thin[n]ing the Indians, to make room for the English."[38] And thin them He—or the diseases—did.

Smallpox was the worst scourge. In 1699 it typically swept away a whole nation in coastal South Carolina, "all [but] 5 or 6 which ran away and left their dead unburied, lying upon the ground for the vultures to devour."[39] Forty years later the Cherokees were cut in half by a contagion which had been "conveyed into Charlestown by the Guinea-men," as James Adair called African slaves, "and soon after among them, by . . . infected goods" carried on packtrain by English traders. The Cherokee medicine men attributed the epidemic to a polluting outbreak of "unlawful copulation" by young marrieds who "violated their ancient laws of marriage in every thicket" and bean-plot "in the night dews." A "great many" of those who survived the onslaught horribly killed themselves, not out of shame for their sacrilegious actions, but because they literally could not bear to live with the pock-marked faces they saw in their recently acquired hand mirrors.[40]

The second major horseman of the Indian apocalypse was war and the dis-location, starvation, and exposure that accompanied it. Most of the Anglo-Indian wars were named after the Indians involved: the "Powhatan Upris-ing"—or "Massacre"—of 1622, the "Pequot War" of 1637, "King Philip's War" of 1675 (named for the Wampanoag chief Metacomet who was dubbed King Philip by the English), the "Tuscarora War" of 1711, the "Yamasee War" of 1715, the ever-popular "French and Indian War" of 1754–63, and "Pontiac's Rebellion" of 1763. This should not surprise us because the victors have always written the histories and blamed the losers for instigating war in the first place. But in every "Indian" war in colonial America, the warring Indians invariably *reacted* to European provocations, usurpations, or desecrations, arrogations much more specific and serious than mere trespassing on Indian soil. Because quickly outnumbered by the prolific and technologically superior newcomers, the warring tribes or confederacy had to have their collective back to the wall or their stoical patience exhausted before they would risk armed conflict.

Their caution and forbearance were well placed, for once the aggressing colonists felt the sting of attack, they became in their own minds aggrieved victims with holy vengeance for their cause. Their retaliations were usually savage, if not particularly swift: their lack of defensive preparation was predi-cated on their disbelief that anyone could doubt their innocence. So the Indi-ans suffered doubly. To take but one example, of some 11,600 natives in south-ern New England in 1675, King Philip's War claimed almost 7900 victims, or 68 percent of the belligerent population, in little more than a year: perhaps 1250 died in battle, 625 later died of wounds, 3000 succumbed to exposure and disease, 1000 were sold as slaves and transported out of the country, and 2000 became permanent refugees from their native land.[41]

In every English colony, native people found themselves regarded as environmental impediments to colonial "improvement," not unlike awkwardly placed swamps or undiscriminating wolves. If the crowding of the English did not kill them through war or contagion, the colonists developed an arsenal of tactics to wrest the land from them or to dispirit them enough to move "voluntarily." One way was to incite "civil" war between rival tribes and to reward one side for producing Indian slaves, who were then sold to the West Indies, often for more biddable black slaves.[42] Another was to play on the reasonable native regard for European trade goods, particularly cloth, metal tools, guns, and addictive alcohol. By extending credit, the English traders got the Indians into deep debt, which could not be settled without selling real estate or hunting the local fur-bearing fauna to extinction.[43]

But for effortless cunning, the third ploy took the cake. English farmers simply released their corn-loving cattle and swine into the natives' unfenced fields. The Indian plea on this score to the Maryland legislature in 1666 speaks eloquently for the plight of most coastal Algonquians in the seventeenth century. "Your hogs & Cattle injure Us, You come too near Us to live & drive Us from place to place," Mattagund complained matter of factly. "We can fly no farther; let us know where to live & how to be secured for the future from the Hogs & Cattle."[44]

But of course the honorable assemblymen of Maryland had nothing to say. Like their successors in the national Congress of 1790, they sat on their hands as Indian America was slowly but inexorably transmuted into a lopsided mosaic—predominantly white and significantly black, with only a fading margin and a few shrinking islands of native brown.

THIRTEEN

NATIVE REACTIONS TO THE INVASION OF AMERICA

In 1492 Columbus inaugurated what we in this historical generation are choosing to call the "Columbian Encounter" between the cultures and peoples of *two* old worlds—the Americas and the rest of the world known to Western Europeans. The term "encounter" is largely apt because it suggests that the so-called discovery was mutual: the American natives discovered, laid fresh eyes on, the swarthy Spanish sailors as surely and as importantly as the sailors discovered them for the first time.

But "encounter" is not a perfect fit: it is slightly misleading because it implies true parity of initiation and participation. Certainly the natives were involved up to their necks in America's rapidly evolving history from the moment Columbus and his crew stepped off the boats, not just in relatively segregated "Indian affairs," where we would expect to find them, but in many, perhaps most, aspects of colonial life for literally hundreds of years, where historians and ethnohistorians are increasingly discovering them (and where native people knew them to be all along). But the interaction between Indians and Europeans (and their unwilling African partners) occurred almost exclusively in the Americas, not in the other "Old World." And the Indians spent most of the conquest and colonial periods reacting and responding *to* the European strangers and invaders. Thus, the American Encounter was largely initiated by the Europeans but took place locally, on the Indians' turf, which forced the natives primarily into a defensive mode.

Although the Indians were put on the defensive by the European incursion, they remained so only in a general sense. In the three hundred years after 1492, they had plenty of room and ability to respond to the European challenge, not as Pavlovian automata acting in a few predictable ways, but as infinitely various, creative shapers of their own destinies. Like the actions of their new rivals, native responses were fashioned from experience, expectations, and situational calculations of self-interest and odds of success. They also varied according to native interest groups, to the perceived nature, power, and stance of the European challengers, and to the timing or stage of contact. Except in the scenarios of generalizing historians, the American encounters were never between generic "Indians" and "Europeans" but always between segments or factions of native groups (which we call "tribes" for convenience) and similar, equally interested subgroups of European nationalities. Both sets of factions were grounded in differences of age, gender, social status, kinship, history, and perception of the problem and its potential solution.

In the fluid conditions of contact, the American natives understandably sought to maintain the *status quo ante* as much and as long as possible. In the face of new challenges from a people and a world they had never before known or even imagined, the various Indian groups worked mightily and often cleverly to maximize their political sovereignty, cultural autonomy, territorial integrity, power of self-identification, and physical mobility. In one way or another, of course, the European colonists over time sought to or effectively did minimize the natives' freedoms in order to reduce the natives' "otherness" to familiarity, predictability, and control.[1] To counter this offensive, the natives resorted to five basic strategies, which were not always sequential or mutually exclusive: initially, they tried to *incorporate* the newcomers; when that failed, they tried at various times to *beat* them, to *join* them, to *copy* enough of their ways to beat them at their own game, and to *avoid* them altogether.

In the inaugural stage of exploration, natives and newcomers enjoyed a relatively short "honeymoon," a peaceful period of feeling each other out. Because the technologically stronger Europeans were greatly outnumbered and found themselves in the dangerous unknown of someone else's country, they kept their weapons sheathed and put on their most accommodating behavior until they could get the lay of the land and probe the weaknesses of its peoples. But they were extremely wary the whole time because they brought to America prefabricated images of the "savage," occasionally noble but mostly ignoble, from their experiences in Africa and Asia and from their reading of ancient, biblical, and Renaissance travel literature.[2] They expected the worst and, in their ignorance or ham-handedness, often provoked the natives into fulfilling their expectations.

Likewise, the Indians based their initial behavior upon their own preconceptions and expectations. But unlike the Europeans, the natives expected novel strangers to be either equal or superior to themselves, either powerful and potentially dangerous "persons," animated by living "souls" like their own, or "gods," "spirits" from the heavens whose powers were of a higher order.[3] The strangers' skin color was less noticeable than their hairiness; to the smooth-skinned natives, European beards and tufted chests and limbs were simply uncouth, signs of unintelligence and unmanliness.[4] It was largely the items the newcomers wore, carried, and made that marked them as "spirits" of extraordinary ability and power. European cloth, metal, glass, and especially objects that seemed to "speak," such as clocks, books, and guns, all impressed the Indians as worthy of respect if not worship, as were their makers.[5]

In order to harness or at least neutralize these unusual powers, the natives tried to incorporate the Europeans as honorary Indians or "true men," just as they adopted native strangers and even enemies captured in battle. They greeted them in friendly fashion by clapping them on their chests, rubbing their arms, or painting their faces. They seated them on their best mats or furs and feasted them on their tastiest dishes. They showered them with presents, offered them the calumet pipe or wampum belt of peace, and made long speeches of welcome and adoption. They then bestowed Indian names upon them, the ultimate sign of acceptance. On occasion, they offered their young women as partners for the night or forever.[6]

But even native groups who did not immediately offer the strangers full acceptance extended help, advice, and friendship. When European ships skirted the Atlantic or the Gulf coast after several weeks at sea, Indians usually guided them to safe anchorages, helped their crews collect firewood, food, and fresh water, and opened a small trade, sometimes giving the lonely sailors sexual favors or decorated fur pouches for hometown girls in exchange for durable (if weevilly) hardtack, rum, or movable pieces of ship's equipment. Natives often rained loaves of cornbread or freshly caught fish into the visitors' longboats; one crew of rowers in North Carolina also found themselves crowded with two tall, beautiful young women, the "gift" of native leaders who sought to win the strangers' alliance through marriage, American-style.[7]

Communication quickly became a problem, once the antic pantomime of sign language ventured beyond simple counting and exchange of visible objects. As the numerically dominant party on their home ground, the natives sought to make the gibbering newcomers learn the language of the country. Assuming that the hairy incompetents were the equivalent of Indian children, the natives quickly devised simplified pidgin languages for them, featuring elemental vocabularies and truncated grammars and syntax. A few European words might be thrown in to designate newly introduced objects, but the linguistic base remained American. When the explorers caught on as fast as Indian toddlers, they prided themselves on their linguistic skills and unwittingly bequeathed the childish pidgins to future generations as full-blown adult languages.[8]

Spanish and English explorers, however, were usually too ethnocentric to do in Rome as the Romans did, so they sought to turn the linguistic tables by making the natives learn their national languages or regional dialects instead. Some Indians were eager and able to put their tongues to a new school and quickly became indispensable as interpreters and brokers between the two cultures. A few young adventurers must have volunteered to sail away with the departing ships in order to see the touted miracles of the strangers' "new world" and to participate in the earliest American exchange programs for language immersion. But when volunteers could not be found, the Europeans did not hesitate to shanghai candidates for a year or more before returning them to America to serve as bilingual guides and go-betweens.[9]

Those who were well treated and did not suffer unduly from the curiosity or contempt of their European hosts sometimes returned to be helpful to the invaders; Manteo at Roanoke and Squanto in Plymouth exercised considerable influence among their countrymen by virtue of their command of the English language and apparent possession of the secrets of English power.[10] Others, however, quickly reverted to native ways and used their new skills against their teachers. Domagaya and Taignoagny, the two sons of chief Donnacona who were kidnapped by Jacques Cartier in 1534, taught their kinsmen at Stadacona (present-day Quebec City) to offer much lower prices for French knives and hatchets, presumably because they had seen how cheaply they could be made in Brittany.[11] And when an Indian renamed Don Luis was returned to his native Virginia in 1571 after several years of involuntary education in Spanish hands, he immediately ran away, took several wives Indian-style, and led the killing of the Jesuit missionaries sent to pacify his tribesmen.[12]

Don Luis's behavior marks a transition from the wary but peaceful human explorations of initial contact to the often hostile reaction of natives upon what might be called "second contact." Second contacts are easily confused with truly first contacts because they are the initial encounters described in several famous documents by European colonizers. But, in fact, we know from other sources and even the same documents that the natives had been provoked into bellicosity by previous European insults or injuries. When, for example, the English landed at Cape Henry in Virginia in 1607, Chesapeake warriors crept up on all fours "like Bears, with their Bowes in their mouthes" and charged the newcomers "very desperately in the faces," wounding a captain and a sailor with arrows "very dangerous[ly]."[13] In the winter of 1620 the Plymouth Pilgrims had a similar "First Encounter," for which they (re-)named the Cape Cod location where it occurred. Apparently for no reason, a number of Wampanoag warriors suddenly emerged from the woods and let fly several volleys of arrows at an English exploring party. The English expected the worst from the American "savages," but we can easily see that the Indians' response was not some atavistic bloodlust vented upon innocent white men. They had had plenty of contact with and provocation from Europeans before the Pilgrims stumbled into their midst. Some of the arrows they shot were tipped with European brass. Only six years earlier, Thomas Hunt of Virginia, the leader of a fishing party left behind when Captain John Smith sailed back to England, had, under the pretense of trade, kidnapped twenty-seven natives from the Cape and sold them as slaves in Spain. And to add insult to injury, the curious Pilgrims had rifled temporarily abandoned houses, corn caches, and graves of the local Indians while looking for a suitable site for settlement.[14] It is small wonder that the natives were not prone to regard the latest wave of bearded seafarers simply as peace-loving pilgrims seeking religious toleration, as our textbooks have led generations of American schoolchildren to regard the Pilgrims.

The advent of large-scale parties of permanent settlers drastically recast the Indian-European equation, demanding from the increasingly beleaguered natives a set of responses as creative as they were crucial. The first major challenge posed by European settlers was inadvertent and only indirectly personal, namely, the importation of epidemic diseases that killed with added virulence in the "virgin soil" populations of the Americas. Ancient European scourges such as smallpox, diphtheria, and influenza and childhood diseases such as measles and mumps alike snuffed out the lives of astonishing numbers of defenseless Indian adults and children, leaving wide rents in the social fabric of native life. The biggest killer, smallpox, was capable of striking down 50–90 percent of an Indian village or tribe, partly because everyone fell sick at the same time, leaving no one to provide fires, food, and especially water for the fever-ravaged victims, partly because the natives initially had no immunities from previous exposure to the disease.[15] And native responses to the diseases, which were spread largely by human touch and breath, only increased their deadly reach and exacerbated their effects. It was native custom to crowd around the bunk of an ailing relative to lend comfort and a sense of solidarity; in the new disease environment, such behavior was as far from quarantine as it was possible to get. Moreover, the preferred native cure for most ailments was a stint in a steaming sweatlodge, followed by a naked plunge into the nearest snowbank or body of cold water. Particularly for the deadly fevers of smallpox, this was the worst course the Indians could have taken. Only when compassionate colonists in the eighteenth century persuaded them to forsake this traditional remedy did native mortality rates deaccelerate to some extent.[16]

Although the natives remained helpless before the onslaught of foreign microbes all through the colonial period, they did respond flexibly to the demographic devastation wrought by them. As disease left yawning gaps in their social structures, technological repertoires, and communal memories, the Indians made three adaptations to cope with their losses. First, many tribes, the Iroquois nations of New York in particular, resorted increasingly to warfare with both native and colonial enemies to replenish their lodges. In traditional "mourning wars," native clans that suffered losses from disease or battle sent their menfolk on the warpath to capture prisoners as replacements. Once captured and brought home, prisoners were treated well, ritually separated from their former allegiances, and adopted fully and faithfully into the suffering clan in the precise place of the deceased. This process served the dual purpose of healing the losses of the grieving group while removing kith and kin from the ranks of the enemy.[17]

Two other strategies were also variations on age-old schemes. One was to intermarry with black Africans and white Europeans. This practice did not differ much from inter-tribal marriages resulting from the adoption of native prisoners. To the culturally "colorblind" Indians, taking spouses of a different hue was a much less "racial" act than it appeared to the increasingly race-conscious colonists. Nor was it confined to one sex, as intermarriage and sexual relations tended to be in patriarchal colonial societies. Indian women felt as free to move in with European traders, hunters, and soldiers as Indian men did to take captive or runaway Europeans to wife.[18]

Like the first and second, the third strategy was a sensible response not only to epidemic mortality but to all forms of depopulation and dislocation caused by colonization. When tribal or village populations approached unviable levels, the survivors sought cultural and military refuge with more populous neighbors or with linguistically related kin even at a distance. The handful of Patuxets who survived a deadly sea-borne plague just before the Pilgrims arrived abandoned their village site overlooking Plymouth Harbor and threw in their lot with their Narragansett and other inland neighbors, who had been relatively unscathed.[19] After the Tuscaroras rose up against the encroaching North Carolinians in 1711 and were beaten back by larger and better-armed English forces, the Iroquoian-speaking natives slowly made their way to western New York, where they were adopted in 1722 by the Iroquois confederacy and given their own homeland in which to live, plant, and hunt.[20] And in the first half of the eighteenth century, the amalgamated Catawba Nation earned a place as one of the four "most considerable" Indian peoples in the Southeast, more than filling the vacuum created by the removal of the Tuscaroras. Along the gentle Catawba River in the Carolina piedmont, the nation was formed by the confluence of a host of small, Siouan-speaking tribes—Sugaree, Esaw, Shutaree, Cheraw, Pedee, Nassaw, Weyaline—who were buffeted by disease, war, dislocation, and pressure from English settlers and northern Iroquois enemies. The Catawbas chose not to become emasculated Settlement or "Parched Corn" Indians, like some of the coastal tribes, but to remain masters of their own fate in their own territory. Even when ripped by further epidemics, the nation's attractiveness to southeastern remnant groups ensured their autonomy nearly until the nineteenth century.[21]

Geographical relocation was a prominent native response to colonization all over North America. But it was not, contrary to popular opinion, then and now, easy for the semi-sedentary—not nomadic—natives to pull up stakes and leave their ancestral homelands. Nor was the direction of movement always predictable. Many groups, such as the Western Abenakis in northern New England and the Powhatans in Virginia after the 1622 uprising, responded to the European incursion by quietly drifting away from the new settlements and their corn-loving cattle and melting into the forgotten corners of the land.[22] To maintain the hunting and gathering facets of their economies, native groups in the East had to put wide swaths of woodland between themselves and the spreading fields and unfettered herds of the colonists.

But some colonial establishments were not as intrusive as English farms and towns, and several native groups actually moved toward them to take advantage of their economic, military, or religious services. French trading posts and settlements in Canada and Louisiana were the most obvious beneficiaries of native relocations. After the founding of Quebec in 1608, nomadic hunters north of the St. Lawrence shifted their summer encampments along the river closer to the new town in order to receive presents and preferential rates from the French traders there.[23] Beginning in the 1640s, natives from all over the Northeast moved to the vicinity of Montreal and Quebec to occupy *reserves* where missionary Catholicism, sedentary farming, and marginally frenchified living prevailed. Only *reserve* Indians who converted to Christianity were allowed to buy guns, with which they often defended the underpopulated French outpost of empire from the grasp of its Dutch and particularly English neighbors until 1760.[24]

Native movements on the St. Lawrence were nothing compared with the French-sponsored resettlements in Louisiana, which resembled a high-speed chess game. The other European player in the early eighteenth century was the frail Spanish garrison at Pensacola. Because the Spanish were militarily weak and poorly provisioned, they could not give adequate protection or guarantee a steady supply of trade goods to their Indian neighbors and allies. When the French arrived in 1699, therefore, several small tribes moved to the new French capital at Mobile, around which French officers allotted them tribal domains. One such tribe was the Tawasas, who arrived in 1705. "They had deserted the Spaniards . . . ," wrote André Pénicaut, a literate ship's carpenter and chronicler, "because they had been daily exposed to raids of the Alibamon [Indians], and the Spanish had not stood by them." But they were certainly no drag on the French economy, for they were "good hunters," Pénicaut testified, "and every day they brought us much game of all kinds." They also brought a "great deal of corn" to plant the fields they were allotted. Some Apalachees who came the same year were regarded as "excellent Catholics" to boot; they had been well catechized by Spanish priests at Pensacola and were easily put under the wing of a French missionary.[25]

As soon as the French moved up the Mississippi, local native villages leapt into a merry minuet, to an old French tune. In 1709 the Houmas "departed their settlement" and went to live on the west bank of the Mississippi near the river of the Chitimachas, while the Tunicas shifted to the Houmas' old site, closer to the French. A few years later, the pugnacious Chitimachas made peace with the French and were persuaded to "leave their homes on the river where they were and . . . settle on the bank of the Missicipy . . . in a place that was marked off for them." Their move in turn "caused other native [*sauvage*] nations to make several changes of dwelling place," most of them to the banks of the river that served as the French life-line to the rich Illinois country and upper Great Lakes. "All these nations are highly industrious," noted an appreciative Frenchman, "and all are quite helpful in furnishing food to the French, to the troops as well as to the people on the concessions."[26] He did not have to say that the natives also furnished the deerskin staple of the French trade and the crucial military difference between life and death.[27]

Virtually everywhere the Europeans went, disease, depopulation, and dislocation followed close on their heels. As favorite hunting and planting grounds were lost and traditional economic activities constricted, native individuals and tribes adjusted to the best of their abilities to the new order. For tribes blessed with access to the fur- and skin-bearing animals craved by colonial traders, initial efforts were directed toward harvesting those supposedly inexhaustible resources with just enough energy to supply their everyday needs, leaving intact their cultural and political autonomy. But these needs increasingly included imported European objects, made of superior materials or available in preferable colors and styles, such as woven cloth, glass beads, metal tools, ceramic tableware, and guns and ammunition. Over time, even the most abstemious natives became dependent on European manufacturers and distributors and the credit system that oiled the nascent "world system" in which they were all enmeshed.[28] They also depleted their animal resources in their accelerating quest to supply colonial demand and their own, newly awakened wants and needs.[29]

The advent of this predicament typically drew three related responses from the Indians. The first was to accelerate their search for rival Europeans as economic and political partners. By playing off at least two of their French, English, Dutch, and Spanish competitors, native tribes tried to augment their leverage as allies and customers, on the principle that two fighting foxes might ignore the vulnerable henhouse. If a tribe was not located conveniently between two European colonies or outposts, they might move to such a place, invite a colonial post or garrison to locate near them to complete the desired triangle, or carry their furs and skins long distances to another supplier to show their more proximate partner their independence. Since virtually all colonies needed Indian neutrality or allies to succeed, the natives were usually assured of success in obtaining better prices, more gifts, and some increase in services, justice, and respect for their sovereignty. Only after the English drove the French from Canada and Louisiana and the Spanish relinquished Florida did the Indians find themselves between a rock and hard place.[30]

A second Indian response to increased debt and scarcity of marketable game was to sell land to eager English farmers, cattlemen, and governments. Between 1650 and 1670, the natives of the upper Connecticut River valley were largely forced by mounting debts at John Pynchon's stores, reduced colonial markets for surplus native food, and the overhunting of fur-bearing animals to sell major portions of their tribal estates along the river. But this remedy was not universally approved by the natives because they, like their English competitors, were riven by political factions. They knew, as Peter Thomas has reminded us, that "Indian leaders were no less guilty than some English of pursuing self-aggrandizement at the ultimate expense of other members of their own society."[31] At a similar though later stage of development, the western Massachusetts Indians who had been settled by the English in a reserve town at Stockbridge on the Housatonic River chose to sell the land surrounding the town proper to satisfy English creditors. In 1765 these creditors persuaded the Massachusetts General Court to allow the natives to reduce their debts—accumulated largely in purchasing farm and household equipment to make them more like their English neighbors—by alienating land. Within three years, the English had acquired sixty-five native plots, usually at greatly discounted prices; by 1788 the Stockbridges had moved to Oneida territory in New York for a clean start.[32]

The Cherokees and Muskogees or Creeks resorted to similar tactics to unburden themselves of trading debts. In 1771 the Cherokees ceded sixty square miles of prime farmland on the Savannah River to a group of English traders who had advanced them considerable sums on credit both before and after the Cherokee-English war of 1760–61. Although the British superintendent of Indian affairs was disconcerted that the deal was closed behind his back, he acknowledged the justice of compensating the traders because they had lost all their goods and skins at the sudden outbreak of war, and after it had entrusted the destitute Cherokees for all their purchases, including high-priced woolens. But the fly in the ointment was the Creeks, who claimed the ceded land as their own by right of conquest in the war, when they fought beside the English. Understandably, they wished to use the contested land to erase their own trading debts, which had mounted even though they were "good hunters" and owned "the most extensive hunting-ground of any nation" in the Southeast.[33]

The Creeks and Cherokees were unusual in still having large territories at their disposal well into the eighteenth century and in being able to lop off sizable chunks of unessential land to appease their creditors. Until the 1760s they also felt only modest pressure from South Carolina and Georgia settlers, cattlemen, and government officials, who needed their friendship, labor, and trade more than their land. But smaller, less insulated groups closer to European settlements felt the pressure to sell much earlier and more forcefully. If we may generalize from the behavior of the Delawares in northern New Jersey, these natives alienated their real estate in ways that prolonged their tenure on ancestral lands far longer than anyone could reasonably expect, given the growing hegemony of the colonists. The Delawares retained their autonomy for a century and a half by selling land slowly and methodically and by extracting as many concessions from the buyers as possible. "At no time were lands sold in a scattered or random fashion." Only parcels that abutted already alienated tracts were sold by native proprietors. In order to ingratiate themselves with their more powerful colonial neighbors and to forestall more drastic forms of aggrandizement, the natives sold cheaply. Low sale prices helped them retain use of the land until the colonists actually fenced, plowed, and built upon it. By deeds of sale, Indians all over the English colonies were permitted to hunt, trap, fish, plant, cut wood, or gather natural resources for the foreseeable future.[34] And finally, native sellers were sometimes quite choosey about their buyers, preferring honest, peace-loving, non-speculative neighbors such as Quakers, Labadists, and members of other minority groups seeking their own fruits of toleration.[35]

When the constriction of their land base and traditional sources of livelihood began to pinch the natives, they turned to a third strategy to ensure a future: they went to work in the colonial economy, usually on its margins but occasionally in major industries. Most of these jobs were part-time and compatible with traditional skills and occupations. The fur and skin trades required not only expert Indian hunters and trappers but guides, packhorsemen, canoemen, interpreters, and sometimes factors.[36] Government officers in New England and elsewhere relied on swift Indian messengers and couriers.[37] Particularly in the early eighteenth century, white southern planters and slave-dealers needed native hunters and trackers to capture Indian slaves from Spanish missions in Florida and to return African runaways.[38] Virtually every colonial army needed the keen eyes and ears of native scouts and flankers and the daunting ferocity of guerrilla warriors.[39] On Long Island, Cape Cod, and Nantucket, experienced natives earned good salaries on English whaling vessels, especially as harpooners.[40] Early explorers in New England and later entrepreneurs in Canada and New York relied on the practiced native eye for fugitive sassafras and ginseng, which enjoyed short boom periods on European markets.[41] And colonial tables were often supplied by Indian hunters, who occasionally passed off sides of the colonists' own cattle as "venison" or "moose" and tough eagle meat as tender turkey.[42] The only role that native men found totally distasteful and inconsonant with their dignity was that of farm laborer. In the Eastern Woodlands, particularly in patrilineal New England, Indian men were not accustomed to the backbreaking drudgery of planting, weeding, chopping, and harvesting, which was women's work, nor the repetitive round of chores required on a colonial farm. They were certainly not used to having their independence curtailed, which many experienced for the first time when they sold themselves as indentured servants to make ends meet.[43]

But these were jobs filled mostly by men. Native women were equally industrious in adjusting to the new economic order. They, too, hired out their services as farm and household servants, but more often they opted for work that guaranteed better pay and more freedom. They grew crops to feed European garrisons, where some of them had white or black husbands on duty.[44] They handcrafted baskets, brooms, birchbark containers, porcupine-quill-decorated pouches, multi-colored reed mats and hangings, and finger-woven wool sashes for urban and country customers. They married colonial traders, taught them their language and cultural protocols, and finessed their access to the native hierarchy. Other "trading girls" only leased their charms for short periods and ample amounts of trade goods.[45] Perhaps the most resourceful entrepreneurs of all were the women who controlled the alcohol trade among their tribesmen. Iroquois and Creek women obtained much of the rum and brandy from colonial suppliers and conveyed it in wooden rundlets and kegs to their villages, sometimes stopping to top off less-than-full containers with water. These may have been the same women who, when offered swigs of the fiery liquids by generous party-throwers, surreptitiously spit the contents into a bottle hidden beneath their blankets for later resale to the men.[46]

Becoming a part of the colonial economy was one step away from auton-

Indians assisted European whalers in North Atlantic waters from the 16th century. Many natives were excellent harpooners, like Queequeg in Herman Melville's *Moby-Dick*. From Theodor de Bry, *Americae*, Part IX (Frankfurt, 1602).

omy. Still, other Indians chose to move even farther by becoming Christian converts and cultural neophytes in European "praying towns," missions, or *reserves*. In Spanish Florida and Georgia, French Canada, and Puritan New England, native individuals and families, and sometimes whole villages and tribes, placed themselves under the spiritual and cultural guidance of Christian missionaries, who eagerly worked to exorcise their traditional "paganism," convert them to "one, holy, and apostolic faith," and acculturate them to an idealized brand of domesticated agriculture and behavior known as "civility." Frequently, commitment to the new cultural programs entailed movement away from ancestral villages and homelands and amalgamation with members of other tribes, even ancient or recent enemies. Enlisting invariably put white foreigners over them in positions of highest authority, although native leaders might still play familiar roles in secular affairs.[47] At the same time and for many of the same reasons, some Indian parents placed their children under the cultural tutelage of white schoolmasters, usually far from home. Although colonial officials frankly regarded the native children as "hostages" for the good behavior of their tribal adults, Indian leaders willingly sent their sons— seldom their daughters—to learn the white men's ways.[48]

From certain modern perspectives, Indians who turned to European schools and praying towns seem to have been committing cultural suicide. In submitting themselves to European institutions, values, and authorities, they appear to have abandoned their struggle for autonomy and opted to live under the heavy colonial thumb. A few individuals may indeed have acted out of cowardice or weakness, but the majority of Indian neophytes turned to the invaders' cultures and religions for empowerment, knowledge, and skills with which to sustain native identities and values in other guises. They threw in their lot with the blackrobes for three major reasons.

First, villages and tribes that reconstituted themselves in praying towns, particularly in New England and Florida, had been so badly crippled by disease, dislocation, and depopulation that their only other alternatives were to amalgamate with other groups in a similar condition or to place themselves at the mercy of ancient enemies, neither of which seemed calculated to promote a long or happy life. They were in such danger of extinction as distinct peoples that only the distasteful but powerful remedy offered by the colonists held out any hope of long-term survival. So they swallowed the bitter prescriptions that sought to turn them into tawny replicas of "civilized" European farmers and housewives, knowing that beneath their new fitted clothes and short hair they would still be "true people" (as they identified themselves in tribal name).[49] They would still enjoy communal property (guaranteed to some extent by colonial law) and native leaders chosen from traditional ranks of authority. In time of need, they might count on military and material assistance from their colonial sponsors. And despite the missionary idealization of farming as the only "civilized" way of life, they could in fact pursue most aspects of their tradition economies, at least part-time. In other words, accepting the circumscribed life of "praying Indians" gave them the time and protective coloration to adjust to the worst stresses of living in a dangerous new world.[50]

Individual Indians sought in the invaders' religions and customs two other ways to cope with that world. One was to acquire some of the white men's "power" or *manitou* (as Algonquian-speakers called it) by learning to call upon their god through prayer. Although the missionaries warned that their God was supreme, all-sufficient, and intolerant of rivals, many converts reasonably added Him to their traditional pantheons in hopes of increasing their spiritual odds. For them, Christianity and its cultural attendants offered answers to serious and disturbing questions posed by the strange and sudden advent of white and black people, epidemic diseases, enlarged cosmologies and geographies, and technological wonders. The people who sailed into and shattered the natives' old world seemed most able to reassemble the old and the new pieces with some coherence and meaning.[51]

Secondly, native neophytes sought practical as well as intellectual skills for contending with their new world. While colonial schoolmasters aimed ultimately at giving their pupils the cultural luxury of Latin and Greek, native parents sent their beloved children primarily to learn to read, write, and count—

skills that would protect their people from fraudulent deeds, inflated debts, and selectively enforced laws. If they and their praying elders also learned to manage a colonial-style farm and household, to sew, knit, weave, cobble, hammer, and saw, and to manipulate the machinery of colonial courts, so much the better.[52]

While the praying Indians were forging survival tactics in the midst of the enemy, other, more fortunate tribes armed themselves at home for the inevitable assaults upon their independence, lands, and ways of life. Of course, even in the most embattled tribes, factional divisions prevented united responses. Some parties wanted to sell out fast and relocate to avoid colonial aggression; others complained loudly and often to colonial governors and imperial officials about the criminal activities and trespassing of white hunters, traders, and cattlemen on Indian land. Most tribes made concerted efforts to play the competing European powers against each other, yet strong factions invariably pulled for each competitor as well as for strict neutrality in what they considered white men's wars. Members of pro-colonial factions sometimes risked transatlantic journeys to the dazzling courts of Europe in order to plead for more aid, effort, or justice.[53]

Sooner or later, the strongest tribes with seductive acreage felt they had to defend their domains with force: the Powhatans in 1622 and 1644, the Pequots in 1636–37, the Wampanoags and Narragansetts in 1675, the Tuscaroras in 1711, the Yamasees and Creeks in 1715, the Cherokees in 1760, and the Ottawas and other Great Lakes tribes in 1764, to mention but a few. Typically, they did not fight alone. They either made peace with a former rival or two to coordinate action against the interlopers or to buy space for their own, or, more rarely, they concocted larger pan-Indian alliances to eradicate the foreign menace. In 1770 the British superintendent of Indian affairs warned the governor of Virginia that "at this very time there are in the Creek nation deputies from the Shawnese, Delawares, and other Northern tribes, accompanied by some Cherokees, endeavouring to form a general confederacy on the principle of defending their lands from our daily encroachments."[54]

The natives of southern New England had perceived a similar threat as early as 1641. In the summer of that year, a Narragansett chief from Rhode Island had secretly approached the Montauks on Long Island with plans for a coordinated attack upon all the English settlements of the region. To the Montauks he argued:

> So are we all Indians as the English are, and say brother to one another; so must we be one as they are, otherwise we shall be all gone shortly, for you know our fathers had plenty of deer and skins, our plains were full of deer, as also our woods, and of turkies, and our coves full of fish and fowl. But these English having gotten our land, they with scythes cut down the grass, and with axes fell the trees; their cows and horses eat the grass, and their hogs spoil our clam banks, and we shall all be starved.

Therefore, he concluded, forty-one days hence they should "fall on and kill men, women, and children, but no cows, for they will serve to eat till our deer be increased again."[55]

As colonial goods and values infiltrated native life, and settlers, farms, and cattle chewed up tribal lands, many Indians found themselves on the brink of despair. When none of the options we have been discussing seemed feasible, these natives faced two final alternatives. One was to lose themselves in alcoholic stupor, to forget the frightening prospect around them in the amnesia of drunkenness.[56] The other option arose largely in the late eighteenth century, when a new breed of native prophets began to preach salvation through the purification and revitalization of Indian culture. Neolin among the Delawares and Great Lakes tribes and later Handsome Lake among the Iroquois sought to infuse native culture with new life by persuading the Indians to purge themselves of all dependence on whites, particularly by ridding themselves of trade goods and alcohol. If they returned to the "old ways" of their pre-Columbian ancestors, the invaders would be powerless to harm them and the path to the Spirit World would be open and bright.[57]

Fortunately, very few natives enjoyed regular access to, or commanded the resources to purchase, sufficient fire-water to wash away their troubles effectively. But unfortunately, alcohol was more plentiful than prophets or hope, and too many troubled Indians found relief only in the bottom of a bottle. At the end of the colonial period, the native population of Eastern America was a small fraction of what it had been before 1492, and their landbase was comparably constricted.[58]

It would be all too easy in the current climate of opinion to attribute the native predicament wholly to Columbus or to the European explorers and colonists who followed him to America, who were certainly responsible for a good share of it. While that might be emotionally satisfying, it would not advance our moral understanding of the past or prepare us—Indians and non-Indians alike—to face the future with equanimity, courage, and imagination. Because it would reduce the Indians to passive victims and deny them an active role in the making of history, theirs and ours together. If we wish to rectify the colonists' worst mistake—their failure to regard the natives as not only humanly *different* from but *equal* to themselves—we must acknowledge that the Indians, in large measure, fashioned their own new world.[59] Within certain cultural and physical constraints, which were always changing, partly by their own actions, they chose their own directions and fates. They had plenty of options, as I have tried to show, and when those ran out, they invented more, like other creative cultures who have found themselves in a bind. Perhaps the best measure of their inventive strength is that, after five hundred years of stiff competition, nearly two million Americans are proud to call themselves "Natives."[60]

FOURTEEN

THE INDIAN IMPACT ON ENGLISH COLONIAL CULTURE

As the cultural heirs of the English "winners," historians of colonial America have been relatively alert to signs of the European impact upon Indian culture, perhaps as a way of explaining the "inevitable" triumph of a "superior" way of life. But they have been far less ready to recognize the surge of cultural influence in the opposite direction. Even ethnohistorians, who learn early that acculturation is a two-way street, have concentrated so intently upon the native side of the frontier that they have largely ignored the important reciprocal changes wrought upon colonial culture. Thus both groups of historians have been unable to convince their colleagues, students, or the general public that the Indians are anything but an exotic if melancholy footnote to American history.[1]

Where historians have not deigned to tread, others have rushed in. Since the last quarter of the nineteenth century, several articles and chapters have treated "The Contributions of the American Indian to Civilization" or "Americanizing the White Man."[2] But most of them are either derivative, unhistorical, or downright foolish. They all suffer from at least one of four major problems. First, with one antiquated exception, they take as their subject all of American history and culture, with no differentiation of sections, classes, demography, or chronology. Second, "Indian" culture is similarly overgeneralized; no allowance is made for tribal, culture area, or even chronological differences. Third, they focus on isolated *materials* or *traits* rather than on cultural *complexes* (how items were used, valued, and integrated by the Indians) or on cultural *creativity* (how they were used, perceived, and adapted by the colonists). And finally, the conclusions of some and the implications of all lack common sense. To suggest, even indirectly, that "what is distinctive about America is Indian, through and through" or that Americans are simply Europeans with "Indian souls"[3] is blithely to ignore the "wholly other" nature of English colonial society—its aggressive capitalism; exploitative attitudes toward natural resources; social hierarchy; patriarchalism; nuclear kinship system; religious intolerance; literacy and print communication; linear sense of time; imperialism based on "directed contact" and conquest; superiority complex based on religion, technology, social evolution, and ultimately race; and desire to replicate the major features of the mother society as completely and quickly as possible.

One way to avoid these pitfalls is to limit our study to the first two centuries of American history when the English and the eastern woodland Indians, both relatively homogeneous cultures, commingled and competed for the continent east of the Appalachians. By paying attention to the nature, timing, and extent of the changes induced in colonial culture by the Indian presence, we should be able to assess with some historical accuracy and realism the "Indianization" of American culture in its formative and perhaps most pliable phase. If the Indian impact was not great in the period of closest and most sustained contact, it is likely to have been even smaller in subsequent periods when the frontier constituted an ever-diminishing proportion of America's human and physical geography.

Although the scholarly study of what came to be known as "transculturation" did not begin until the late nineteenth century, the "Indianization" of English culture was recognized throughout the colonial period. Contemporary descriptions took three basic forms. The most common descriptions—which have unduly dominated the historical literature since—lamented the "barbarism" or "savagery" of the colonists who lived in horrid isolation on the frontiers, far from "civilized" settlements. They spoke to the generalized fear of backsliding that is characteristic of all colonial societies founded in the midst of native peoples. The image of "the Indian" in these descriptions was an entirely negative reflection of English metropolitan ideals, seen largely by their clerical and political custodians.[4]

The Puritan ministers of New England were the most vocal critics of scattered frontier settlements, where many "were contented to live without, yea, desirous to shake off all Yoake of Government, both sacred and civil."[5] "There hath been in many professors" of the Puritan faith, scolded the Boston synod in 1679, "an insatiable desire after Land, and worldly Accommodations, yea, so as to forsake Churches and Ordinances, and to live like Heathen, only that so they might have Elbow-room enough in the world."[6] By moving into the shadowed corners of the land, the settlers bade defiance "not only to Religion, but to Civility itself" and exposed their children to the danger of degenerating into "heathenish ignorance and barbarisme."[7] Particularly lamentable was the decline of family government and the sinful indulgence of masters and parents toward their children and servants. "In this respect," observed Increase Mather, "Christians in this Land, have become too like unto the Indians."[8] The cultural consequences of this "*Criolian* Degeneracy" were predictably ghastly. In the "more Pagan [out-]Skirts of *New-England,*" shuddered his son Cotton, "Satan *terribly* makes a *prey* of you, and *Leads you Captive to do his Will.*"[9]

But the New England frontier was not the only hotbed of heathenism in America. In the eyes of an Indian missionary from New England, "the whites on the extensive frontiers of [eighteenth-century] Virginia, are generally white Savages, and subsist by hunting, and live like Indians."[10] When the itinerant Anglican minister, Charles Woodmason, preached his way through the Carolina backcountry in the late 1760s, he was as shocked by the "Indianization" of the settlers as any Puritan would have been. The living and behavior of the settlers, predominantly Scots-Irish, were "as rude or more so than the Savages." Bred of unalloyed "Indolence and Laziness," they lived in log cabins "like Hogs," their dirty children ran "half naked" and their women hardly less so. "The Indians are better Cloathed and Lodged," thought Woodmason. Not surprisingly, "many hundreds live in Concubinage—swopping their Wives as Cattel, and living in a State of Nature, more irregular and unchastely than the Indians." When Woodmason attempted to reduce them to good order through religion, they were "as rude in their Manners as the Common Savages, . . . firing, hooping, and hallowing like Indians" to interrupt his services. When the county sheriff brought a party of Catawba Indian deputies to quell the disturbances, the natives behaved "more quiet and decent than the lawless Crew" of whites. But there was "no bringing of this Tribe into any Order. They are the lowest Pack of Wretches my Eyes ever saw," swore the minister, "or that I have met with in these Woods—As Wild as the very Deer."[11]

The second group of descriptions of "Indianized" colonists were generally more neutral in tone. These characterized the English traders who spent much or all of the year in Indian villages where, for the sake of ingratiating themselves with their customers, they adopted their dress, technology, language, protocol, and other customs, especially sexual ones. Unlike the representatives of the large trading companies of the late eighteenth and nineteenth century, these traders tended to be individual entrepreneurs who owed any pejorative assessment to their character as traders rather than to their adoption of Indian life. John Long, a company trader of considerable experience in both Canada and the northern English colonies, observed that the companies used to "purchase convicts and hire men of infamous character to carry up their goods among the Indians, many of whom ran away from their masters to join the savages."[12] From his long experience in the South Carolina Indian trade, Edmond Atkin knew the village traders to be "generally the loosest kind of People, . . . whose Behaviour, being for the most part the most worthless of Men, is more easy to be conceived than described."[13] James Adair, a southern trader of liberal education, concurred. "Many of the present traders," he wrote about 1769, "are abandoned, reprobate, white savages," not because they were "Indianized" but rather because they infected the Indians with the worst kinds of English "obscenity and blasphemy."[14]

Far more common were accounts of the traders' ready acceptance of native mores. Perhaps because the traders were among the few Englishmen to intermarry with the Indians, early observers—often other traders—dwelt in loving detail on these cross-cultural unions. John Lawson, for example, spilt much ink over the "trading girls" among the Carolina Indians, whose special haircuts showed that they were "design'd to get Money by their Natural Parts." The hairstyle, Lawson dryly noted, was intended to "prevent Mistakes," a distinct possibility in villages frequented by the Indian traders. On the other hand, many traders took Indian wives "whereby they soon learn the *Indian* Tongue, keep a Friendship with the Savages; and, besides the Satisfaction of a She-Bed-Fellow, they find these *Indian* Girls very serviceable to them, on Account of dressing their Victuals, and instructing 'em in the Affairs and Customs of the Country. Moreover," Lawson continued, "such a Man gets a great Trade with the Savages; for when a Person that lives amongst them, is reserv'd from the Conversation of their Women, 'tis impossible for him ever to accomplish his Designs amongst that People."[15]

Sometimes the unions did not last, and the trader returned to the English settlements, leaving his offspring "like bulls or boars to be provided for at random by their mothers."[16] Perhaps as often, the traders with native wives "have been so allur'd with that careless sort of Life, as to be constant to their *Indian* Wife, and her Relations, so long as they liv'd, without ever desiring to return again amongst the English, although they had very fair Opportunities of Advantages amongst their Countrymen." John Lawson knew several men of this sort.[17]

In other parts of the country, traders became "Indians" only temporarily in order to prepare themselves for higher careers in commerce. According to Anne Grant, the young boys of eighteenth-century Albany were apt to "contract a love of savage liberty which might, and in some instances did, degenerate into licentious and idle habits" by spending every free hour tramping the woods with gun, fishing pole, and axe.[18] When marriage seemed imminent, the boy received a small stake from his father, a Negro boy, and a dugout canoe, into which he piled his jerked beef and Indian corn staples and his trade goods. He began to smoke, dressed himself in "a habit little differing from that of the aborigines," and launched his career as an Indian trader. From the profits of their first venture, the young Albanians often launched themselves on larger careers in New York or on the Atlantic trade routes.[19]

Far more distressing to colonial observers was the third group of "white Indians" on the colonial frontier. These were the relatively small but significant number of colonists who had chosen quite literally to become Indians by running away from colonial society, by not trying to escape after being captured, or by electing to remain with their Indian captors when treaties of peace periodically afforded them the opportunity to return home. In English eyes, the first group, comprised of army deserters, runaway slaves, outlaws, and more generally "renegades," were nothing more than traitors to king, church, and country. Typical of this breed of reckless men were Joshua Tift and William Baker. In 1637 Roger Williams reported that Baker, formerly a Plymouth trader on the Connecticut River, was being pursued by the English authorities for "uncleanes with an Indian squaw, who is now with child by him," and was living with the Mohegans, amongst whom he had "gotten another squaw." The following year Williams learned that this man who "can speake much Indian . . . is turned Indian in nakednes & cutting of haire, & after many whoredomes, is there maried." Such a "fire brand," the minister warned, had best be extinguished before he and surviving Pequots, both bent on revenge, "fire whole townes."[20]

Joshua Tift was considered an even more incendiary character. When he was captured among the Wampanoags by the English in King Philip's War, he was condemned to die the death of a "Traytor" by hanging and quartering. According to the Reverend William Hubbard, his crimes clearly merited such severity for he had "divested himself of Nature itself, as well as Religion." Tift was a "Renegado English-man of *Providence,* that upon some discontent amongst his neighbours, had turned *Indian,* . . . conformed himself [in dress] to them amongst whom he lived . . . , married one of the *Indian Squaws,* [and] renounced his Religion, Nation and natural Parents all at once, fighting against them. . . . As to his Religion he was found as ignorant as an Heathen, which no doubt," Hubbard noted piously, "caused the fewer tears to be shed at his Funeral."[21] It was the potential danger of "renegades" like Baker and Tift that prompted the Connecticut legislature in 1642 to threaten with fines, corporal punishment, and three years imprisonment those "diverse persons [who] departe from amongst us, and take up their aboade with the Indians, in a prophane course of life."[22]

Far more numerous were the colonists—men, women, and children—who had been captured by Indians in wartime and adopted into their families as permanent replacements for lost relatives. In a widely popular literature of captivity narratives, written for public consumption or only family record, the "Indianization" of hundreds, perhaps "thousands," of Englishmen was described in ways that must have set contemporary teeth on edge while planting the troublesome question of how it was accomplished without force, coercion, or bribery. The results were plain to see: captives who had replaced their own language with an Algonquian or Iroquoian dialect; who dressed, moved, and even looked like their new relatives; who had married Indians and had children by them; who became chiefs and respected leaders in their adopted societies; who presumably thought much like Indians; and who strenuously resisted their forced return to white society. It was this conspicuous group of converts to "savagery" who most demanded explanation.[23]

Unfortunately, contemporaries gave explanations much less frequently than they tried to explain *away* the fact that for many Englishmen Indian life held conscious and legitimate attractions. One escape was to resort to the uniquely American adage, "It is very easy to make an Indian out of a white man, but you cannot make a white man out of an Indian."[24] Another was to cast aspersions on the character or sanity of the converts. "For the honour of humanity," wrote the Reverend William Smith in 1765, "we would suppose those persons to have been of the lowest rank, either bred up in ignorance and distressing penury, or who had lived so long with the Indians as to forget all their former connections."[25]

When the colonists did try to explain the conversion of their own, they generally resorted to some form of environmentalism. The earliest and least convincing expression of this theory attributed the strange behavioral changes in the colonists to the influence of the American climate. In 1724 Cotton Mather sent two illustrations of this theory to a team of English physicians interested in climatic power.

> One very observable quality of our Indians has always been this, that they have no family government among them; . . . Their children are the most humored, cockered, indulged things in the world. . . . Now 'tis observable that tho' the first English planters of this country had usually a government and a discipline in their families that had a sufficient severity in it, yet, as if the climate had taught us to Indianize, the relaxation of it is now such that it seems almost wholly laid aside, and a foolish indulgence to children is become an epidemical miscarriage of the country. . . .

By the same token, Mather regretted the growing Indian-like laziness of the colonists, who seemed to be powerless in the grip of the American climate.[26]

Later in the eighteenth century, however, a more sophisticated version of environmentalism dominated attempts to account for the "Indianization" of the colonists. According to this explanation, mankind was divided into three great classes: "The savage lives by fishing and hunting, the barbarian by pasturage, and the civilized man by agriculture." Each class is formed not by one influence, such as climate, but by many, such as "government, . . . mode of husbandry, customs, and peculiarity of circumstances." Thus "the arts of civilization may be expected, in a considerable degree, to correct the effects of the climate."[27]

While it might bear a faint resemblance to a later concept of culture, the early national view of the "stages of society" was hardly value-free. Particularly when asked to explain the transition of men from one stage to another, contemporaries fell back on characterizations that smacked of the perdurable contrast between "savagism" and "civilization." To explain why "civilized" Englishmen frequently chose the life of "savage" Indians, Samuel Stanhope Smith postulated that man was placed on earth at the creation in a civilized state, and that "savage life seems to have arisen only from idle, or restless spirits, who, shunning the fatigues of labor, or spurning the restraints and subordinations of civil society, sought, at once, liberty, and the pleasures of the chace, in wild, uncultivated regions remote from their original habitations." As everyone knew, "once hunters, farewell to the plough." "Men who have once abandoned themselves to the restless and adventurous life of the hunter," Alexis de Tocqueville noted, "feel an insurmountable disgust for the constant and regular labor that tillage requires." "Such is the charm of [the Indians'] wandering and independent state," Smith told his sedentary students at Princeton, "the pleasure of alternately pursuing their game, and reposing in indolence, that many of the citizens of the United States are found voluntarily to renounce all the conveniences of civilization to mingle with the savages in the wilderness, giving the preference to their idle and vagrant habits of life." When contemporaries wished to account for the totally "Indianized" colonists who had chosen native life, this was the kind of argument they summoned. It was simply a law of nature that "all men naturally wish for ease, and to avoid the shackles of restraint."[28]

Those who made a full transition to "savagery" were at least explicable by the prevailing theory. But those who got stuck somewhere between stages, such as frontiersmen, had to run a gauntlet of abuse. Hector de Crèvecoeur described the colonists who chose to live out of the reach of the law and the church as "off-casts," the "impure part" of society, a "mongrel breed," and "the most vicious of our people." "Our bad people are those who are half cultivators and half hunters," he observed, "and the worst of them are those who have degenerated altogether into the hunting state. As old ploughmen and new men of the woods, as Europeans and new made Indians, they contract the vices of both," without, apparently, any of their virtues. Like that of the Indian, the hunter's time was divided between "the toil of the chase, the idleness of repose, or the indulgence of inebriation." Consequently, their characters were cast in the same mold: "ferocious," "gloomy," "unsociable," "profligate," "indolent," "licentious," "erratic," "irreligious," "lawless," and "wild."[29]

Thus, for contemporaries, the "Indianized" colonists played no role in the formation of English colonial culture because their transformation—their degeneration—placed them outside the pale of "civilized" society, outside history itself. Regarded as social deviants who lived on the dark margins of the English frontier or as mental or moral misfits who reverted to "savagery," they were simply not counted as bona fide members of English society, and so their cultural impact could not be weighed. But we are better able to distinguish between climatic mutation and acculturation, to see that English frontiersmen were forced to borrow from their native neighbors and rivals if they wished to master their new environment, and to realize that the Indian impact on colonial culture extended far beyond the frontier into the thoughts, values, and feelings of virtually every Englishman in America. While the colonists who chose to become Indians did remove themselves from English culture, and our focus, their less fully "Indianized" brethren who remained on the English side of the frontier require some attention to establish the exact nature of their cultural adaptations, the reasons for them, and the ways they were used and regarded.

It is significant that all the colonists who were regarded by contemporaries as "white Indians" lived on the wooded frontiers of English settlement, often closer to the villages of their Indian neighbors than to the larger towns and cities of the Atlantic seaboard. With few exceptions, frontier farms encroached upon Indian hunting territories, as did those restless souls who abhorred a plow as much as did any warrior and made their living by the gun. Frontiersmen were primarily woodsmen to whom survival was of greater moment than economic security or prosperity. Limited in their life choices, they chose to live off the bounty of the American forests rather than to lose their independence as tenants, servants, or apprentices.

But especially in the early stages of settlement, much of their forest environment was new, strange, and even dangerous—except to the natives who had learned to live with it over centuries. It was therefore as natural as it was necessary for the colonists to borrow some of the Indians' time-tested skills, techniques, and technology for coping with the frontier environment, which included the Indians themselves. Contrary to metropolitan colonial opinion, this cultural exchange did not turn the frontiersmen into Indians, just as Indians who selectively adopted English habits and articles did not turn into Englishmen. Indian *means* were simply borrowed and adapted to English *ends*. The frontiersmen did not regard themselves as Indians nor did they appreciably alter their basic attitudes toward the native means they employed. If those means were regarded favorably, or at least no longer negatively, it was not because they were Indian but because they *worked* to effect the English conquest of the American environment. Moreover, they were not borrowed in cultural context, as parts of larger, integrated complexes. They were taken piecemeal, while the native values, functions, and structures that surrounded them were ignored. The English goal was mastery of the New World, and to men in a hurry, the end often justifies the means, however alien those means might at first sight seem.

In the beginning the American frontier was on the Atlantic coast and along the banks of the rivers that sliced into the interior. For explorers and settlers newly arrived from England, one of the first orders of business was to familiarize themselves with the new land and its plants, animals, and birds. Some were well known from European experience or from a growing travel literature about other parts of the rapidly expanding world. But many were indigenous only to North America and so had to be named, classified, and related to the known. In such circumstances, it was natural for the English to rely upon the substantial knowledge of the coastal Algonquians for their identification and instruction in their uses.

Equally pressing was the need to communicate with the natives in order to understand their values, motives, and behavior, to be able to predict how they might react in various circumstances to the English presence. On the frontier, where the Indians were equal if not superior in force and numbers, traders needed to understand their economic institutions and motivations, military officers their alliances and modes of warfare, missionaries their religions, political leaders their governments, laws, and protocol, and ordinary farmers and town-founders their systems of land tenure and concepts of property. Again, the likeliest and best teachers were the Indians themselves, provided some means of communication could be found.

Three possibilities existed, all of which were tried at various times. Before sustained contact, explorers and traders managed to converse in hand signs, pidgin trade jargons consisting of word elements from both languages or a third (such as French), and the often burlesque antics of pantomime.[30] These, however, soon proved inadequate for both partners. An alternative, the one most popular with the English, was to have the Indians learn to speak English. Communication in a "civilized" tongue would, it was thought, reduce the potential for misunderstanding and at the same time help to reduce the "savage" mind to "civilized" modes of thought, which was the ultimate solution to the natives' unpredictability. Because of the practical advantages to be gained from a working knowledge of the invaders' tongue, a number of Indians did learn to speak it, only the most famous of whom were Squanto and Samoset. But a third possibility was more popular with the natives, and that was to have the strangers learn to converse in an indigenous dialect. Despite a good deal of ethnocentric resistance to such a course, the English frontiersmen were often forced to it by demographic and political realities.

The colonists made some effort to encourage professional interpreters to learn the nuances of the major Indian languages, initially (in Virginia) by sending young boys to live with the Indians, later (in New England) by placing apt students in schools with Indian children, who were expected to teach them their native dialects in return for an English education.[31] But most of the frontiersmen who acquired any linguistic skills gained them from living in or near Indian villages and from frequent conversations with native speakers. In this way Edward Winslow, Plymouth's emissary to Massasoit, and Capt. John Smith, Powhatan's nemesis, became capable speakers and Roger Williams, John Eliot, and Thomas Mayhew, missionaries to the New England tribes, gained fluency. Those who followed them and required less than full command of the languages could resort to a number of word lists, phrase books, dictionaries, and grammars, such as Williams's *A Key into the Language of America* (London, 1643).[32]

What Williams systematized and analyzed, other colonists picked up in verbal fragments, sometimes from unsystematic word and phrase lists appended to historical or ethnographic descriptions, such as John Smith's *A Map of Virginia* (Oxford, 1612), which was sent to the colony by the Virginia Company the year following the disastrous Powhatan uprising of 1622.[33] Undoubtedly it was a copy of Smith that John Powell, a young servant in Virginia's Northern Neck, was reading in 1638 "in the field . . . to learne to speake the Indyan tongue" when another servant "desired to buy it of him and would have given him pipes for it," perhaps because he was planning to run off to "the Dutch plantation" to "live like gentlemen" and had to pass through Indian territory to reach it.[34] It was certainly Smith's writings that helped Colonel Norwood win the aid of a Maryland tribe when his party was shipwrecked near the Eastern Shore in 1649. After several frustrating attempts to register their distress and destination to a passing group of natives by signs, Norwood remembered from a distant reading of Smith's travels that the word *werowance*, which one of the Indians kept repeating, meant "king." "That word, spoken by me, with strong emphasis," explained the castaway colonel, "together with the motions of my body, speaking my desire of going to [their chief]," effected the rescue of the group. "This one word was all the Indian I could speak," he admitted, "which (like a little armour well plac'd) contributed to the saving of our lives." The rescue party, however, also contributed to the peaceful denouement by "discover[ing] their faces with the most chearful smiles, without any kind of arms, or appearance of evil design, . . . shaking hands with every one they met," and repeating *"Ny Top"* (*netop*), which was "soon interpreted to signify my friend."[35]

Both Algonquian words entered the mainstream of Anglo-American speech, as did scores of others. Long after the Indian frontier was pushed beyond the majority of colonial settlements and most settlers had little if any personal contact with the natives, Indian names of places, wildlife, and native artifacts, social relations, and institutions lingered on English tongues to enrich and acculturate the imported language. When the colonists met in the woods the *moose, racoon, opossum, musquash* (muskrat), *skunk, chipmunk,* and *moonack* (woodchuck), they recognized them by their pure or anglicized Algonquian names, just as they did numerous species of American fish—*scuppaug, pauhagen,* or *menhaden* (sea herring), *chogset* (blue perch), *cisco* (lake herring), *muskelunge* (pike), and *quasky* (blue-back trout). As they slogged through marshy *muskeg, pocosin* (Virginia), and *pokeloken* (Maine), pestered by *musketoes,* they spotted stands of *tamarack, hickory, chincapin* (chestnut), and *pecan.* Along the seashore they found *mananosay* (Chesapeake soft-shelled clams), *pooquaw* or *quahog* (Long Island Sound hard-shelled clams), and other shellfish used by the Indians to make *wampum* (New England), *sewan* (New York), and *roanoke* (Virginia). Having been initiated by the natives into American food-ways, they grew *maize, squantersquash* (New England), *cashaw* and *maycock* (Virginia pumpkin and squash) and learned to extract the tuberous *neshannock* (Pennsylvania white potato) and *tuckahoe* (a southern fungus root). From the corn, parched and ground, they made a variety of Indian dishes such as *hominy, pone, nocake, sagamite,* and *succotash.* In North Carolina they drank a grape beverage called *scuppernong.* Farther north they smoked *kinnikinnick,* tobacco mixed with sumac and willow leaves, or *sagakomi,* a bear-berry substitute for tobacco, perhaps around Indian fires in *wigwams* with *sanops* (ordinary men), *squaws, papooses, powwows* (shamans), *sachems, werowances, cockarouses* (Virginia elders or chiefs), *sagamores* (northern New England chiefs), and other important *mugwumps* (leaders or great men). Because the Indians were such good hosts, the colonists called their own picnics, outings, and dances after the native *squantums, tuckernucks,* and *canticos.* In Connecticut's Mohegan country, anything so "delightful or pleasant" was remembered as *wauregan.*[36]

Although the colonists used a substantial number of Indian words on and beyond the frontier, they used them in distinctive ways which minimized their normative impact on colonial culture. First, they borrowed Indian words only when English words did not exist, as they did words from Dutch, Spanish, or French. New England's 5000 place-names and the numerous names of wildlife indigenous to North America are typical loans of this kind.[37] But to ears inured to the peculiar accents and cadences of English shires and towns, the Algonquian dialects were simply jarring and confusing. As Edward Eggleston put it with inimitable verbosity in 1900, "the general repulsion to the use of aboriginal words was no doubt increased by the polysyllabic prolixity of the agglutinated vocables that gave stateliness to the intervals of utterance with which a savage broke the monotony of his native taciturnity."[38] Therefore, the words borrowed were often tailored to fit English mouths. Southern New England's *askutasquash* was shortened to its suffix, for example, as was the Virginia dish *rockahominy*. Few colonists were comfortable with *pawscohicora*, so the tree quickly became known as *hickory*. *Wampumpeak* was unnecessarily long to English thinking; *wampum* gained currency in some parts of the Northeast, *peak* in others. The Jamestown colonists could not pronounce *cawcawwassough* correctly (much less spell it), so they anglicized it to *cockarouse*.[39]

As is only too apparent from those already given, many Indian words were used only for a season, as long as the objects and concepts to which they referred survived and remained relevant to the colonial experience or until the colonists could supplant them with newly coined English words. Few of us still trip the light fantastic at *canticos,* roast *chincapins* on an open fire, or on February 2 consult the furtive *moonack* about the end of winter. Finally and most important, the colonists looked to the Indians only for individual words, not syntax, grammar, or special patterns of thought and meaning. The loan words were simply incorporated into English modes of ideation and speech, with little or no alteration of the basic contour of English values. Even phrases like "happy hunting ground," "go on the warpath," and "bury the hatchet" were usually poor translations interpreted in pejorative English ways, carrying little cultural freight from their native contexts. As with so many other aspects of native culture, Indian words were tools used to subdue the continent, no more and no less.

From the time the first colonists rowed ashore, they began to borrow items of native material culture, as often by imitation, perhaps, as from verbal instruction. One of their first requirements in the New World was shelter, for "they had now no friends to welcome them nor inns to entertain or refresh their weatherbeaten bodies; no houses or much less towns to repair to, to seek for succour."[40] Some colonists accepted the hospitality of the natives and took temporary refuge in their wigwams, those snug flexed-bough domes covered with bark or reed mats.[41] Others simply built their own wigwams, substituting on occasion a daub-and-wattle chimney at one end for the central smokehole of the American houses. The materials were cheap and plentiful, and the design simplicity itself, as many New England adventurers happily discovered.

When Christopher Levett landed upon the Maine coast in 1623 to reconnoiter the Council of New England's domain, he built a "Wigwam, or house, in one houres space." "It had no frame" of sawn timbers, he told his English readers, who would not easily understand, "but was without forme or fashion, only a few poles set up together, and covered with our boates sailes which kept forth but a little winde, and less raigne and snow."[42] Settlers of the nascent Massachusetts Bay towns of Watertown, Boston, Salem, Woburn, and Marblehead seem to have had similar problems because they, too, could not duplicate the natives' watertight construction. Some covered their wigwams with thatch, as they would have at home, which kept off "the short showers from their Lodgings, but the long raines penetrate[d] through, to their great disturbance in the night season."[43] A more serious problem was fire. Wooden chimneys and thatched roofs were a volatile combination, which prompted the Massachusetts authorities to outlaw them in 1631. But the wigwam design itself lived on wherever English immigrants needed time and perhaps money to build more substantial frame houses.[44]

And yet the wigwam had no lasting effect on colonial culture. Not only was its use confined largely to New England, but it was considered only a stopgap measure, primarily by the poor who could not employ others to build permanent housing for them with some expedition or in advance of their arrival. The average settler built a conventional English frame house of clapboard and shingles as fast as possible in an effort to replicate the familiar surroundings of home. Playing Indian in a crude, cramped wigwam held no romance for him, especially with a cold rain dripping down his neck. He was only too thankful that well before 1652 "the Lord hath been pleased to turn all the wigwams, huts, and hovels the English dwelt in at their first coming, into orderly, fair and well-built houses."[45]

If the Indians did little to put a roof over the colonist's head, they did a great deal more to fill his belly. Since America was 3000 sea miles from the metropolitan sources of supply, the settlers needed to become economically self-sufficient as soon as possible. This need was all the more pressing when the ships that brought the colonists left them with insufficient supplies to stretch to the first harvest, or sold them at usurious rates. The gap was filled, as every American schoolchild knows, by the coastal Algonquians who readily shared their own food and showed the ignorant newcomers how to grow, catch, and gather the distinctive foods of their new environment.

In 1609 two Powhatan prisoners, Kemps and Tassore, taught the Jamestown colonists "how to order and plant" their first 30 or 40 acres of corn, that "Salvage trash" that many idlers "so scornfully repine[d] at" until Captain Smith billeted them among the neighboring Indians. There, necessity taught them "how to gather and use their fruits as well as themselves," a palatable lesson that soon soured relations with the Powhatans.[46] When the factionalized white militants, still riven by idleness and disease, decided that even Indian food was preferable to starvation, they forced the natives, often at gunpoint, to contribute their precious supplies of corn. It mattered little to them that the drought-plagued tribesmen themselves might starve, have insufficient seed for the next planting, or be unable to render unto Powhatan their customary tribute-in-kind. Abuses such as this prompted the Powhatans to rise up in 1622 in an attempt to expel the invaders, but too late. While still numerically inferior, the acquisitive colonists had become firmly wedded to a profitable economy based on tobacco—another Indian crop—and looked to the outbreak of war with singular relish. As one leader wrote after the attack which killed some 350 colonists, the English,

> who hitherto have had possession of no more ground then their waste and our purchase . . . may now by right of Warre, and law of Nations, invade the Country . . . whereby wee shall enjoy their cultivated places, turning the laborious Mattocke into the victorious Sword (wherein there is more both ease, benefit, and glory) and possessing the fruits of others labours. Now their cleared grounds in all their villages (which are situate in the fruitfullest places of the land) shall be inhabited by us, whereas heretofore the grubbing of woods was the greatest labour.[47]

The first colonists in New England had no need to resort to such tactics because the deadly plague of 1616–18 had swept most of the native planters off their cleared fields around Plymouth and Massachusetts Bay, leaving the land free for the settlers' taking. But, as elsewhere along the Atlantic coast, Indian know-how was needed to bring them to fruition. Landing on Cape Cod in the dead of winter, the urbanized Pilgrims knew enough about farming to recognize that the caches of multi-colored Indian corn they disinterred constituted their best hope for spring planting. So they took it with the intention of repaying the natives when their crops should prosper. Fortunately, twenty acres of Indian corn did prosper because the six acres sown in English barley and pease "came not to good." The Indian who stood between the colonists and starvation was, of course, Squanto, who showed them "both the manner how to set [the Indian corn], and after how to dress and tend it."[48] Equipped only with hoes, the farmers were taught to plant four or five seeds in hills about five or six feet apart rather than to broadcast seed carelessly over a fully plowed field, as they would have done at home. When the stalks of corn began to mature, beans were planted in the same hills. The nitrogen-fixing beans slowed the depletion of the soil while the cornstalks supported the bean tendrils during growth. Still later, Indian squashes and pumpkins were planted between the hills, further maximizing the use of the land.

Another valuable lesson Squanto taught them was to set two or three herring or alewives in each hill as fertilizer because, he said, the former Indian fields being used at Plymouth were "old." (He might well have added that New England soils were not rich even in pristine condition.) Naturally, the Pilgrims assumed that, since an Indian had showed them this trick, the use of fish fertilizer was consistent native practice, an assumption that subsequent generations have extended to eastern Indians in general.[49] In truth, only the coastal Algonquians of southern New England—who were near an annual supply of alewives—appear to have used fish to fertilize their own fields, but only those with poor soil or worn out. The use of well-spaced hills and the chemistry of bean-and-corn agriculture depleted the soil less rapidly than European practices, and when it was nearly exhausted, it was easier to clear new fields by girdling trees and firing the underbrush than it was to carry numerous loads of fish from distant streams and shores to merely postpone the inevitable. Besides, fields left fallow for a time could always be reclaimed with minimal clearing or burning.[50]

Succeeding generations of New England farmers were less concerned about the provenience of fish fertilizer and other techniques of Indian agriculture than they were about its labor-saving, economic, and culinary potential. That corn breads, puddings, and other dishes—most of them prepared according to native recipes—were nutritious and edible was quickly discovered. But so too was the fact that traditional Indian farming required a good deal of back-breaking hoeing. Since English men had somewhat taller backs to break and smaller reservoirs of time and patience than the Indian women who did the farming in Algonquian societies, the colonists quickly adapted native agriculture to their own familiar uses. Tree girdling and burning to clear the fields were popular enough with the newcomers as were the use of hills, fish fertilizer, and interstitial planting of squash and such. But to avoid laborious hoeing, the English formed hills by cross-plowing the fields at six-feet intervals and reduced the frequency of weeding by plowing between the original furrows once in mid-summer.[51] Moreover, as soon as necessity allowed, the settlers began to supplant corn with traditional English grains, reserving the American food largely for the "baser sort" among themselves, cattle fodder (stalks and ears), export to the West Indies and other colonies, and trade with northern tribes for more profitable furs. After the first few decades of settlement, most colonial farms devoted no more than half their fields to Indian corn, and even these were increasingly plowed and manured in conventional English fashion.[52]

Corn, beans, and squash were not the only American products to succor the stomachs and pocketbooks of English frontiersmen. Early voyages to the New World were financed by the sale of sassafras in London, while later colonists were enriched by the marketing of ginseng. Maple sugar sweetened many a colonial dish when the expense or unavailability of refined cane sugar required. Potatoes and wild rice were added easily to English diets, as were clams, lobsters, and other exotic foods from the sea. But perhaps the most common additions to the frontier menu were fish and game predominantly taken and prepared by Indian methods. In the absence of lines, seines, and hooks, the colonists imitated the Indians by fishing with sapling weirs, spears, arrows, scoop-nets, and jacklights. (Few Englishmen tried to rope and ride the giant sturgeon to exhaustion as some of the southern Indians did.)[53] When caught, the fish were commonly split and baked on planks, Indian-style, before an open fire or smoked over it.

In the ways of the forest, of course, the Indians were past masters, and any colonist who wished to survive, much less prosper, there apprenticed himself to them with alacrity. Frontier boys at an early age learned, like their native counterparts, to imitate bird and animal calls, to shoot the bow and arrow, to stalk, to set snare and dead-fall traps, and to scent beaver traps with castoreum. With age and experience, the best frontiersmen became adept at setting life-like decoys, ferreting out hibernating bears, tracking, skinning, jerking thinly sliced meat over a slow fire, chasing down molting wildfowl with a club, tanning skins with the fat and brains of the animal, and preserving fresh game by packing it inside and out with snow.[54] In pursuit of game, the colonists quickly adopted the springy snowshoe which allowed winter travel at speeds, one expert thought, greater than those possible on dry land; the toboggan for transporting supplies out and game back; and the bark or dugout canoe—light and maneuverable on shallow or rapid waters. But occasionally more than technology was borrowed; Indian values, too, sometimes played a small role in helping the English adapt to their new environment. The forest laws of Connecticut's Indians "were esteemed so just, and their equity appeared in such a glaring light," noted a minister in 1729, "that our English hunters have governed themselves by them in their fishery and hunting, and determined controversies by these old customs."[55]

As many English tenderfeet discovered to their great sorrow, life in the American wilderness could be hazardous to one's health if proper care was not taken. Again, the Indians had much to offer the colonists by way of prevention and cure. Because lying on the damp ground bred colds and rheumatism in woodsmen of all races, the English learned to emulate the healthy natives by lying with their feet to the fire when "abroad in the woods" and even "at home." If a person failed to hear the rattlesnake's warning and was bitten, the Indians could usually prevent death by applying a variety of "snake roots" to the wound. Similarly, they could heal arrow wounds with herbal or bark poultices. So many frontier teas, poultices, and decoctions were made to native prescription that "Indian doctors" did a brisk business in many settlements, loath to anger their gods by revealing to the white men the ancient secrets imparted to them alone. Most of the cures were bona fide. At least 170 indigenous drugs listed in the official *Pharmacopeia of the United States* were discovered and used by the Indians north of Mexico, the great majority in the eastern woodlands.[56] Among them were abortifacients and drugs to promote temporary sterility and to ease childbirth, which may have been of some interest to colonists unstereotypically concerned not to have large families. In 1769 a Connecticut physician requested a missionary among the Oneidas to "make Enquiry, what Medicines the Indian Parturient Women take antecedent to Delivery which occasions so easy a Travail—they have given some of our [English] Captives Medicines which have had very Extraordinary Effects to Ease their Travail Pains."[57] Given the characteristic Indian jealousy of their trade secrets, it is unlikely that he received an answer.

Frontier life was as hard on clothes as it was on bodies, so many English-men wisely adopted elements of native garb, partly of necessity, partly to reduce wear and tear, and partly to blend less obtrusively into the landscape they shared with the Indians and the animals they hunted. The first to go were the bright colors seen in most English clothes, even those of the much maligned Puritans. Colonial woodsmen quickly found that for stalking wild game or enemies—or being stalked—red coats, blue trousers, and yellow waistcoats were signal failures. Far better were the forest's natural dull shades of brown and green. Another early change was the substitution of moccasins for hard-heeled cobbled shoes. Indian war parties headed for white settle-ments always carried extra pairs of moccasins for their captives to wear on the long journey home, a change of footwear the captives usually welcomed, as did the "white Indians" who remained on the English side of the frontier. Moc-casins were superior in the woods because they were cheap to make, easy to repair, quickly winterized by stuffing them with deer's hair, dry leaves, or grass, and as silent as the deer from whose skin they were made. Their chief draw-back was that, despite natural oils, they were not waterproof. "In wet weather," one frontiersman noted, "it was usually said that wearing them was 'A decent way of going barefooted.'"[58] But they could be wrung out and dried more quickly than heavier leather shoes, as the frontier minister Roger Williams "often proved."[59]

Somewhat less popular than moccasins were *mitasses,* or long, fitted deer-skin leggings, and breechclouts, which in most parts of colonial America were not widely worn on the frontiers until the eighteenth-century wars with the French and Indians. In Indian encampments or isolated hunting camps, such dress on an Englishman would not have seemed out of place. But in more "civ-ilized" settlements even in the back-country, it must have raised many a female's consciousness. Like their native counterparts, strapping young colonists in leggings and breechclouts exposed "the upper part of the thighs and part of the hips." "Instead of being abashed by this nudity," lamented a frontier minister, the English warriors were actually "proud" to appear in pub-lic in their Indian outfits. When they sauntered into his church services, he quipped, their appearance "did not add much to the [religious] devotion of the young ladies."[60]

The final item of frontier clothing thought to have been borrowed from the Indians was the hunting shirt, which gained great symbolic importance for colonists in the early stages of the Revolution. But, in fact, the hunting shirt was strictly a colonial invention, which had no native counterpart. The closest item in the Indians' wardrobe was a print or calico trade shirt worn open at the neck, not tucked in, and often decorated with trade silver pins. The hunting shirt may initially have been made of buckskin, but the colonists learned as quickly as the Indians had that wet buckskin "sticks to the skin, and is very uncomfortable, requires time to dry, with caution to keep it to its shape."[61] By the eighteenth century, therefore, linsey-woolsey, coarse linen, or canvas had become the dominant material for the shirt, which was simply "a kind of loose frock, reaching half way down the thighs, with large sleeves, open before, and so wide as to lap over a foot or more when belted." Often attached was a large cape or hood, "sometimes handsomely fringed with a ravelled piece of cloth of a different colour," and invariably the belt held a tomahawk on the right and on the left a scalping knife in a leather sheath. Clad in moccasins, leggings, war paint, and hunting shirt, the English warrior was distinguishable from his American archetype only to a discerning eye.[62] Which was precisely the symbolic identification the rifle companies from Virginia's backcounties wanted to make when they turned out in such dress in the spring of 1775 to oppose the king's redcoats.[63] Throughout the colonial period, whenever the colonists asserted their social or cultural distinction from the mother country, they commonly identified themselves as "Indians" to suggest their lack of sophistication and untutored virtue.[64] When the perpetrators of the Boston Tea Party donned "Mohawk" disguises and the Virginia "shirtmen" arrayed themselves *au sauvage*, however, more than literary metaphor was intended. These native Americans also sought to announce their fierce determination to defend their natural rights to a king whose memory of the obduracy of "savage" warfare needed only a slight jogging.

The "Indianized" Virginians and other colonial militiamen who emerged during the Revolution were not novelties in colonial America, for English warfare had been forced to acculturate from the earliest encounters with the Indians in the seventeenth century. Until the Seven Years' War, when France finally realized that the English meant not merely to contain French expansion but to obliterate totally the French presence in North America, warfare in America consisted largely of frontier skirmishes, raids, and ambushes conducted on Indian principles. With the exception of a few European naval attacks upon coastal towns, the military assaults thrown at the English colonies invariably came from the Indian side of the frontier, spearheaded largely by Indian warriors even when led or accompanied by Frenchmen. As the English pushed the Indian frontiers steadily back in the older colonies and created them in new colonies, the natives seldom had long to wait for sufficient provocation to seek revenge. In having to respond frequently to Indian attack, the English colonists readily adopted several aspects of native warfare that they hoped would help them beat the enemy at his own deadly game.

Some of the most permanent adoptions were technological, especially in the northeastern colonies where sustained encounters with the Indians occurred during King Philip's War in 1675–76 and the four intercolonial wars after 1689. Since Indian warfare consisted primarily of cat-and-mouse raids of stealth and surprise, the only way the English could effectively retaliate was to learn to play the cat: to overtake the raiders in the woods, to lay their own ambushes on likely warpaths leading to the English settlements, or to catch Indian villages unawares with their own "commandoes." The one indispensable piece of equipment for these tasks was the moccasin. English scouts would not think of setting off without several pairs, nor would rangers and light infantry trained in the eighteenth century by one of the American-experienced British officers, such as Lord George Howe, John Forbes, or Henry Bouquet. Without "Indian shoes," the officers warned the colonial legislatures, "they can't perform their duty."[65] Moccasins were also the accepted footwear for Indian-style snowshoes, which enabled the militia of the northern colonies to forestall enemy raids and to carry fire into the heart of enemy territory in the winter, which before contact the conventions of both Indian and continental warfare had accounted a time of informal truce. Thanks largely to snowshoes, a season "which before was dreaded as most hazardous" frequently became the time of "greatest safety," even along the exposed frontiers of New England.[66]

Whatever good fortune the colonists enjoyed—and it seldom lasted long—was due also to a number of other adaptations to the necessities of Indian warfare. In the American forests, war conducted with long or even half pikes, heavy matchlocks with rests, carriage cannon, brightly colored uniforms, ponderous supply trains, and female camp followers was quickly reduced to "a meer Farce" by the French and Indians who, "being lightly cloathed and armed," lamented one colonial reformer, "are sometimes in our Front, sometimes in our Rear, and often on all Sides of us, Hussar Fashion, taking the Advantage of every Tree and Bush."[67] Although regular British troops did not adapt their equipment or tactics to the Indian enemy appreciably until the Seven Years' War, their officers were prepared to do so by considerable experience with guerrilla warfare in Austria, Flanders, and the Scottish Highlands during the 1740s and 1750s.[68] Many colonial militia, especially rangers on frontier patrol, responded with greater alacrity to the need for light, camouflaged clothing (including deerskin breeches and hunting shirts or light jackets), short muskets with browned barrels to prevent telltale glints in the sun, small packs to carry personal blankets and field provisions (sometimes Indian *nocake* or parched corn meal), tomahawks, and scalping knives—a reduction of perhaps 25 to 35 pounds from the standard issue of the British soldier.[69]

Because European military discipline was considered by many "of little use" in the American woods, colonial soldiers altered their tactics as well as their uniforms.[70] When the English fought their first battles with the Indians, they beat up the drum, flew the colors, and marched in massed ranks into the nearest open field to engage the enemy—who, of course, thought the whole display sheer madness and remained concealed in the woods. Prolonged exposure to this frustratingly "uncivilized" enemy and frequent lessons from native allies in King Philip's and subsequent wars forced numbers of colonial commanders to the realization that "in this country," as General John Forbes admitted in 1758, "wee must comply and learn the Art of Warr, from Ennemy Indians or anything else who have seen the Country and Warr carried on in itt."[71] After Braddock's defeat in 1755, even regular army officers had to concede that massed fire was ineffective against scattered, concealed targets unless it was combined with disciplined movement: bayonet charges, flanking actions, and tactical retreats. Large deployments of regular troops eventually carried the day in North America, but not until the troops learned to reach their destination without serious damage.[72] In Indian country, travel was extremely hazardous, so the colonists took a page from the native manual of war and marched out in thin "Indian file," separated by several paces and covered on all sides by scouts, flankers, and perhaps dogs. Superfluous noise and smoking were prohibited. To avoid ambush, return was never made on the same trail, and river banks were well secured before crossing. When attacked, the commander cried "Tree all!" and the men scattered for cover, from which they would not all fire at once to avoid an assault during reloading. Finally, maneuvers appropriate to American conditions would be executed to draw the covert enemy into error or a more open engagement, where disciplined English fire could take its toll.[73]

In war as in peace, English frontiersmen "Indianized" themselves only as much as was necessary to give them the upper hand in their struggle with America and its native peoples. Their goal was not to become Indian, nor did their selective and piecemeal adaptations of native techniques and technology make them so. While it may be true in a physiological sense that "you are what you eat," in no sense could it be said that the colonists' consumption of Indian corn rendered them cultural Indians. While superficially "clothes makes the man," the adoption of Indian moccasins and forest garb did not necessarily turn the English frontiersmen into Indians, any more than a modern Boy Scout Indian dance team qualifies for an arts grant from the Bureau of Indian Affairs. And while the brutal imperatives of Indian warfare often forced English soldiers to fight guerrilla-style, they did not become Indian in their goals or values.

To have become truly Indian, the colonists would have had to think like Indians, to value the same things that the Indians valued, and, most important, to identify themselves as Indians and their future with native society. A significant number of Englishmen did make this complete transition from one culture to another; these were the "white Indians" who melted into historical anonymity behind the Indian frontier. But those colonists who remained on the frontiers of English society chose to remain Englishmen and to pursue English goals by largely English means. Their adaptation of selected facets of native material culture did little or nothing to alter their self-identities as "civilized" Englishmen nor their goal of mastering the American environment and its denizens, no matter how fallen from cultural grace their colonial superiors found them. If there were any doubts about their ultimate allegiance to the English way of life, their sacrifice of lives and martial vengeance whenever the Indians made war on the frontier settlements should have proven them groundless. If the intensity of their commitment to king, church, and cashbox was less than that of their seaboard brethren, they still regarded themselves as white Christian Englishmen, an identity that distinguished them sharply from their Indian friends and enemies.

While the colonists borrowed consciously and directly from Indian culture only on the frontier, English colonial culture as a whole received a substantial but indirect impress from the Indians by being forced to confront the novel "otherness" of native culture and to cope with its unpredictability, pride, and retaliatory violence. Having the Indians as sometime adversaries and full-time contraries helped not only to reinforce the continuity of vital English traits and institutions but to Americanize all levels of colonial society more fully than the material adaptations of the frontiersmen. These *reactive changes* were, in large measure, responsible for transforming colonial Englishmen into native Americans in feeling, allegiance, and identity, a change without which, John Adams reminded us, the American Revolution would have been impossible.[74] While the growing political opposition to the British ministry during the 1760s and 1770s eventually led the colonies to coordinated armed resistance and a united declaration of independence, the whole colonial experience of trying to solve a related series of "Indian problems" had much to do with giving the colonists an identity indissolubly linked to America and their apprenticeship in political and military cooperation.

One of the earliest changes induced by the realities of Anglo-Indian relations was the reordering of colonial priorities. According to the early English promotional literature and the royal charters of the majority of colonies, the primary goal in settling the New World was the conversion of the natives to Christian "civility," followed by the enhancement of overseas trade with the natives and the extension of the English empire at the expense of her European rivals.[75] However, the early English encounters with the Indians of Roanoke, Virginia, Connecticut, Cape Cod, and Maine made it obvious that the order of these goals was the product of armchair explorers and missionaries who had never met the indians on their own ground. Not only were the natives far from eager to receive the blessings of Christ, as some wishful thinkers had promised they would be, but they maintained a tenacious sense of superiority to English cultural values, even as they admired and adapted some of their material culture. Moreover, in asserting this unexpected superiority, the natives often resisted the intruders with armed force, rendering the exposed English beachheads and settlements highly unsafe in wartime and potentially unsafe at all times.

Due largely to these depressing and often deadly developments, the operative English goals rather quickly shifted to give paramount importance to the pacification of the natives, sometimes by Bible and blanket, more often by statute and sword. More than any other factor, this change forced to the forefront the major thrust behind English colonization in North America—the establishment of an Anglo-Protestant empire as a bulwark against the imperial designs of Catholic Spain and France. Conversion remained an important goal, but it was reduced to instrumental status in the hierarchy of colonial objectives. Reducing the "savages" to "civility" consumed more time and therefore assumed more importance than simply converting them to Christianity.

As the Catholicized Indians of Canada demonstrated after 1689, mere conversion was no guarantee of English safety, for it did little to dampen the natives' ardor for war or to sublimate their ferocious conduct of it. Only a complete change of cultural identity, it was thought, could ensure that an Indian convert would never slip from praying to preying. As events proved, the English were not wrong in their thinking, but the reluctance of most Indians to commit cultural suicide elevated even higher the imperatives of empire while lowering those of religion.

Although conversion of the natives suffered some demotion in the operative scheme of colonial values, the idealism of the original goal retained its power in New England and helped to evangelize its "tribal" Protestant churches.[76] Even before the English settlements began to spread beyond the lands depopulated by the plague of 1616–18, the need to acquire more land and to forestall any native opposition to its acquisition called for the establishment of praying towns among the neighboring Indians. If the Indians could be persuaded to exchange the life of the hunter and warrior for that of the farmer, they would require much less land for their livelihood, and their military prowess would be greatly weakened. At the same time, the churches of Massachusetts were being reminded of the religious goal of their colonial charter by Anglican and Parliamentary critics at home and by the noisy success of the Canadian Jesuits who were teaching their neophytes to bear crosses against the Devil but would soon teach them to bear arms against heretics. Thus goaded into action (as well as by tensions inherent in Puritan theology), New England Congregationalism slowly discarded its defensive, genealogical shell and began to evangelize the black, white, and particularly tawny peoples of the region who were not fortunate enough to have been born to "elect" parents.[77] The missionary thrust of John Eliot and the Mayhews, the New England Company, the Commissioners of the United Colonies, and later the Mathers, Judge Samuel Sewall, and many others forcibly reminded the English that God was no longer the exclusive deity of a small white clan but in his majesty and grace was capable and desirous of serving many tribes. To accommodate this renewed vision of the evangelical church, the Protestant churches of New England and the Middle Atlantic colonies created in the early decades of the eighteenth century an ecclesiastical niche for roving missionaries who did not have to be called by a congregation to exercise their sacramental office. This change, in turn, gave a healthy push to the aggressive denominationalism that altered the religious landscape of eighteenth-century America. The denominational competition for white souls after 1740 coincided with and in some instances followed a similar competition for key Indian missions.[78]

Despite the efforts of many zealous individuals and charitable societies, the great majority of eastern woodland Indians were "reduced" not to civility by religion but in numbers and morale by disease, alcohol, warfare, unfair trading practices, loss of land, and prejudice. As countless Englishmen acknowledged throughout the colonial period, the sad fact was that English missionary efforts were sporadic, often half-hearted, and powerless to counteract the negative example of nominal christians who failed to practice what they preached. "They met with Enemies when we came amongst them," lamented a North Carolinian in 1709, "for they are no nearer Christianity now, than they were at the first Discovery, to all Appearance."[79] "We that should have learn'd them to *Pray,* have learn'd them to *Sin,*" admitted a New England minister, while a Pennsylvania missionary of long experience was confident that "our vices have destroyed them more than our swords."[80] Honest laments such as these exacerbated the feelings of declension and failure that gnawed at the souls of second- and third-generation Christians and cast the self-proclaimed righteousness of the English colonists in doubt as they strove to claim God's special grace in their successive battles with the Indians, the French, and the king. Judged by the purity of their earliest religious goal, the English record in Indian relations made it impossible for men of conscience to deny that either the colonies were basely born or they grew up in bastardly fashion.

The stubborn persistence of Indian culture also provided a deeply disturbing counterpoint to the English missionary efforts and was therefore instrumental in shaping colonial culture in two additional ways. First, the generalized European fear of barbarism that worried colonial planners and leaders was given specific shape and meaning by the Indian embodiment of the "heathenism" that seemed so contagious to English frontiersmen and by the greater danger of Englishmen converting to an Indian way of life in captivity or, worse still, voluntarily as "apostates" and "renegades." When Cotton Mather warned New England that in "Ungospellized Plantations" on the frontier "Satan *terribly* makes a *prey* of you, and *Leads you Captive to do his Will,*" his audience knew that Satan wore moccasins, breechclout, and warpaint.[81]

Second, and more generally, the Indians contributed crucially to the English definition of themselves in America by symbolizing the "savage" baseness that would dominate human nature if man did not—paradoxically—"reduce" it to "civility" through government, religion, and the capitalistic work ethic. "The Indian became important for the English mind, not for what he was in and of himself," Roy Harvey Pearce reminded us long ago, "but rather for what he showed civilized men they were not and must not be."[82] Because the early settlers were "especially inclined to discover attributes in savages which they found first but could not speak of in themselves," they defined themselves "less by the vitality of their affirmations than by the violence of their abjurations."[83] Even the faithful descriptions of native culture by keen observers such as Roger Williams and Daniel Gookin were prefaced by self-reflexive editorials. Wrote Gookin of the New England Algonquians in 1674, "Here we may see, as in a mirror, or looking glass, the woful, miserable, and deplorable estate, that sin hath reduced mankind unto naturally, and especially such as live without means of cultivating and civilizing, as these poor, brutish barbarians have done for many ages."[84] While all peoples to some extent define themselves by contrast with other peoples, the English colonists forged their particular American identity more on an Indian anvil than upon other European colonists or Africans. If that identity was ambivalent and paradoxical, the colonists' persistent (though declining) faith in the salvation of savages and the obdurate character of Indian culture were in no small part responsible.[85]

For the whole spectrum of colonial society, urban and rural, the Indians as ungrateful objects of religious charity and as cultural contraries were not as frustrating, alarming, or influential as the Indian enemy. As masters of an unconventional warfare of terror, they seared the collective memories, imaginations, and even subconscious of the colonists, leaving a deep but blurred intaglio of fear and envy, hatred and respect. Having the American natives as frequent and deadly adversaries—and even as allies—did more not to "Indianize" but to "Americanize" the English colonists than any other human factor and had two contradictory results. When native warfare frustrated and humbled the English military machine, its successes cast into serious doubt the colonists' vaunted sense of superiority as God's chosen people, especially when the only recourse seemed to be the hiring of equally "savage" mercenaries.[86] At the same time, victorious Indians seemed so insufferably insolent—a projection of the Christians' original sin—that the colonists redoubled their efforts to claim divine grace and achieve spiritual and social regeneration through violence.[87] One of the pathetic ironies of early America is that in attempting to exterminate the wounding pride of their Indian enemies, the colonists inflated their own pride to sinful proportions.

The Indians' brand of unannounced, "skulking," bushwhacking warfare, involving the "indiscriminate slaughter of all ranks, ages and sexes," atrocious mutilation, and captivity for torture or permanent adoption, gave rise to several colonial reactions.[88] The first reaction to the offensive war of the Indians (which was in reality retaliation for previous wrongs, real or perceived) was a well-founded increase in fear and paranoia. Since the Indians might attack at any time of day and in any season, "one is never sure either that they are there or that they are not[,] hence we have to beware of them all the time."[89] Few colonial frontiersmen and farmers did not know personally a victim of a silent arrow, a concealed musket, or the scalping knife, knowledge that could not help but raise a morbid curiosity about one's own or loved ones' chances for survival. And the fear cut deep. When the Reverend Ebenezer Parkman of Westborough, Massachusetts, left an Indian couple to hoe his cornfields in 1726, his wife, who was recovering from childbirth complications, became "very much affrighted with the Indians, and full of fear of what they might do." Though the Indians could not have shown greater peace and good temper, explained the minister, "the Weakness of her Body brought strange apprehensions in the mind."[90] Similar apprehensions overwhelmed young Mercy Short in 1692 when she was assaulted by a devil "not of a Negro, but of a Tawney, or an Indian colour." Her "Captivity to Spectres" closely resembled the actual captivity she had suffered two years earlier because her tormentor was always accompanied by "some French canadians, and some Indian Sagamores," a party that a Salem witch confessed had accompanied her to sabbats "to concert the methods of ruining New England."[91] Even from the comparative safety of Princeton, New Jersey, in 1755 a young mother told a friend in Boston, "You cant conceive . . . what a tender Mother undergoes for her children at such a day as this, to think of bring[ing] up Children to be *dashed against the stones by our barbarous enemies*—or which is worse, to be inslaved by them, and obliged to turn *Papist.*"[92] When the Indians were on the warpath—and even when they were not—they were never far from the colonists' thoughts.

The second reaction to the Indian offensive was the development of a defensive "fortress mentality," which in turn reinforced the colonists' sense of being a chosen if momentarily abandoned people. As the Israelites had suffered oppression and attack in another wilderness, the English felt themselves beseiged by Satan's minions in the form of pagan Indians and papistical Frenchmen. A common response to this predicament, made largely though by no means exclusively by the New English, was to search their communal soul for private and public sins that might have driven God to withdraw his special protection and to allow the forces of anti-Christ to scourge them. "O our *sins*, our *sins*," cried the daughter of Jonathan Edwards at the news of Braddock's defeat, "they are grown up to the very heavens, and call aloud for Vengence, the Vengance that the Lord has sent."[93] Significantly, the Lord's whip in the English jeremiads most frequently assumed the form of an Indian attack, not the aggression of other Europeans, slave rebellion, pestilence, or drought. The prescribed remedy for spiritual backsliding was to eschew anything that smacked of Indianization—"*Criolian* Degeneracy" as Cotton Mather called it—and to drive the Devil out of the land, even if the land happened to be his in the first place. By killing satanic Indians, the colonists sought to regain God's favor and to fulfill his providential promise in America. Although they did not feel that they had fully done so until the reduction of Canada in 1760 removed both enemies at once, the nature of the military effort expended in that holy quest further distinguished colonial culture from that of its English progenitor.

Most of the American colonists had never seen battle in Europe, but even professional soldiers were sickened by the atrocities committed by the Indians on their victims, alive and dead, young and old, male and female. European warriors were as resourceful as the Indians in killing their enemies, but most could not match—or understand—the natives' postmortem desecration of the human body. Even an enemy in embryo was considered potentially dangerous and "torn from [the murdered mother's] pregnant womb and elevated on a stick or pole, as a trophy of victory and an object of hor[r]or, to the survivors of the slain."[94] Of the niceties of torture most Englishmen were also ignorant until they watched the Indians at work or discovered the charred remains of one of their victims.

Being thus forced to confront such a heinous enemy, the colonists were frequently torn from their "civilized" moorings and swept into the kind of "savage" conduct they deplored in their enemies, motivated conspicuously by cold-blooded vengeance. In their mounting fury, especially in the eighteenth century, they fell to the slaughter and torture (except by fire) of Indian prisoners, even women and children, encouraged in part by government bounties that paid only a fraction more for living prisoners than for their scalps.[95] During King Philip's War, the colonial militia looked largely to surrogates to sate their appetite for revenge. A wounded Indian prisoner narrowly escaped torture only to be "knock'd on the Head" by native allies before an assembly of English troops and their general. In another theater of the war, a female prisoner was ordered "to be torn in pieces by dogs." Two years later, in the fishing village of Marblehead, a group of women emerging from church set upon two Indian prisoners from Maine and with their bare hands literally tore them apart. An eyewitness reported that "we found [the Indians] with their heads off and gone, and their flesh in a manner pulled from their bones."[96]

But with the expansion and prolongation of Indian warfare during the four wars for empire, the soldiers themselves set to work with savage determination, often inspired by the invocations of their ministers. "Our holy Religion teaches us to bear *personal* Injuries without *private* Revenge," Samuel Davies lectured a Virginia company in 1755, "But *national* Insults, and Indignities ought to excite the *public* Resentment."[97] At the beginning of the first "French and Indian" war, Cotton Mather had been less ambiguous. The Indians of Maine, he reminded an audience of soldiers, "have horribly Murdered some scores of your dear Country-men, whose Blood cries in your Ears, while you are going to fight, *Vengeance, Dear Country-men! Vengeance upon our Murderers.*"[98] But many colonists, particularly the swelling ranks of those who had lost friends and relatives in Indian raids, needed no sermons to act, even in peacetime. Throughout the eighteenth century, some of their worst atrocities upon Indian victims departed sufficiently from acceptable conduct to be noticed by the colonial establishment, but most of them were unobjectionable according to the standards of the day. A visitor from England might record in his diary in 1760 that "Some People have an Indian's Skin for a Tobacco Pouch," but an officer in Sullivan's campaign against the Iroquois in 1779 could note matter-of-factly that he was given a pair of boot tops made from the freshly skinned legs of two enemies.[99]

Although the colonists were never able to realize their ambitions, they did from time to time desire to commit the worst atrocity of all—genocide. This urge was the product not only of the frustrating encounter with Indian warfare but of the extreme ethnocentrism and racism of a people laboring under the illusion that they were chosen by God to wash America "white in the blood of the Lamb." Perhaps the first secular expression of genocidal intent was recorded in Virginia after the Powhatan uprising of 1622, but predictably New England gave the expression a scriptural twist. In 1640 the governments of

New Haven and Connecticut "declared their dislike of such as would have the Indians rooted out, as being of the cursed race of Ham," indicating that those who had called for—and nearly gotten—the total extirpation of the Pequots three years earlier were still not satisfied.[100] As the soldier-poet Roger Wolcott saw it from the security of the eighteenth century, the Mystic Fort fight with the Pequots was Armageddon, different even from the capture of French Louisbourg in 1745 at which he was second in command:[101]

> Fate has determined that this very day
> Shall try the title of America:
>
> . . .
>
> If this day's work by us be once well done,
> America is for the English won:
> But if we faint or fail in this design,
> The numerous nations will as one combine
>
> . . .
>
> and with violence
> Destroy the English and their settlements.

Although the sentiment if not the phrase "The only good Indian is a dead one" flourished longest on the colonial frontiers, seaboard adherents to its philosophy were not in short supply. In 1711, for example, the Virginia House of Burgesses cast aside the governor's inexpensive proposal to calm the Indian frontier by a regulated trade and educational missions and voted with a "violent disposition" a £20,000 war bill "for exterpating all Indians without distinction of Friends or Enemys."[102] When General Jeffrey Amherst allowed smallpox blankets to be sent among his native adversaries during Pontiac's uprising, the British high command had become infected with the deadliest strain of colonial hatred which had been gestating for over a century and a half.[103]

For all their best—and worst—efforts, the English colonists could not make the Indians disappear either by converting them or by burying them. The costs, both moral and financial were simply too great. But in trying to overcome the stubborn resistance of the Indians, the political and social history of the colonies was altered in significant ways. Since the Indians would not hold still for conventional English warfare, the cost of fighting them was very high. Untrained militiamen were simply not equal to the task, so frontier defenses of rangers and cavalry patrolling between chains of forts had to be mounted.[104] These new expenses were borne largely by the colonial legislatures, which in general gained parity with, if not superiority to, the royal governors during the eighteenth century. The legislatures themselves were frequently riven by the factionalism of seaboard representatives who did not accede to frontier demands for more protection, economic relief, and equal representation. The Quakers lost their political grip on Pennsylvania, for instance, primarily because their pacifism and legislative economies failed to protect the westerners from the Indian raids of the Seven Years' War.

It soon became obvious that the colonies could not cope with their Indian problems alone. Powhatan's uprising gave the Virginia Company the *coup de grâce* and King Charles I tucked the colony under his wing. Later in the century Massachusetts's inability to defend her northern borders from French and Indian incursions led to her and New Hampshire's incorporation in the imperial system as royal colonies. In the final showdown with the French in the Seven Years' War, of course, the colonies were heavily dependent on British troops whose support contributed to a soaring national debt at home. When English taxpayers refused to underwrite American defense costs alone after the war and Parliament tried to assess the colonial beneficiaries, these levies and the manner in which they were obtained formed the backbone of the colonial grievances against the mother country that led to open rebellion in 1776.

It is both fitting and ironic that the symbol chosen by revolutionary cartoonists to represent the American colonies was the Indian, whose love of liberty and fierce independence had done so much to Americanize the shape and content of English colonial culture.[105] It is fitting because the Indians by their long and determined opposition helped to meld thirteen disparate colonies into one (albeit fragile) nation, different from England largely by virtue of having shared that common history of conflict on and over Indian soil. It is ironic because after nearly two centuries of trying to take the Indians' lives and lands, the colonists appropriated not only the native identity but the very characteristics that thwarted the colonists' ultimate arrogations.

NOTES

Prologue

1. *Ethnohistory,* 4–12 (1954–1965).

2. Ibid., 13:1–2 (Winter-Spring 1966).

3. Ibid., 18:1 (Winter 1971).

4. Ibid., 29:1–4 (1982).

5. Ibid., 31:1 (1984)–33:2 (1986).

6. See James Axtell, "Ethnohistory: An Historian's Viewpoint," *Ethnohistory,* 26:1 (Winter 1979), 1–13, esp. 9, n. 3; repr. in Axtell, *The European and the Indian: Essays in the Ethnohistory of Colonial North America* (New York, 1981), ch. 1.

7. Ibid., 2.

8. Ibid.

9. Charles Horton Cooley, *Life and the Student* (New York, 1927), 201–2.

10. L. P. Hartley, *The Go-Between* (New York, 1954), 3.

11. Nancy Oestreich Lurie, "Ethnohistory: An Ethnological Point of View," *Ethnohistory,* 8 (1961), 78–92, esp. 83.

12. See, for example, Hayden White, *Tropics of Discourse: Essays in Cultural Criticism* (Baltimore, 1978); White, *The Content of the Form: Narrative Discourse and Historical Representation* (Baltimore, 1987); Michel de Certeau, *The Writing of History,* trans. Tom Conley (New York, 1988); Greg Dening, "A Poetic for Histories: Transformations that Present the Past," in Aletta Biersack, ed., *Clio in Oceania: Toward a Historical Anthropology* (Washington, D.C., 1991), 347–80; Patrick Williams and Laura Chrisman, eds., *Colonial Discourse and Post-colonial Theory: A Reader* (New York, 1994); Benita Parry, "Problems in Current Theories of Colonial Discourse," *Oxford Literary Review,* 9 (1987), 27–58; Edward Said, "Representing the Colonized: Anthropology's Interlocutors," *Critical Inquiry,* 15 (1989), 205–25; Rolena Adorno and Walter D. Mignolo, eds., *Colonial Discourse,* in *Dispositio,* 14:36–38 (1989); René Jara and Nicholas Spadaccini, eds., *1492–1992: Re/Discovering Colonial Writing,* in *Hispanic Issues* 4 (1989); Patricia Seed, "Colonial and Post-colonial Discourse," *Latin American Research Review,* 26:3 (1991), 181–200.

13. William N. Fenton, *American Indian and White Relations to 1830: Needs and Opportunities for Study* (Chapel Hill, 1957), 21–22; Fenton, "Field Work, Museum Studies, and Ethnohistorical Research," *Ethnohistory*, 13 (1966), 71–85, esp. 75.

14. Walter J. Ong, *Orality and Literacy: The Technologizing of the Word* (London, 1982); Eric A. Havelock, *The Muse Learns to Write: Reflections on Orality and Literacy from Antiquity to the Present* (New Haven, 1986); Brian Swann, *Smoothing the Ground: Essays on Native American Oral Literatures* (Berkeley, 1983); Arnold Krupat and Swann, *Recovering the Word: Essays on Native American Literature* (Berkeley, 1987); Krupat, *Ethnocriticism: Ethnography, History, Literature* (Berkeley, 1992); William S. Simmons, *Spirit of the New England Tribes: Indian History and Folklore, 1620–1984* (Hanover, N.H., 1986).

15. Gordon M. Day, "Rogers' Raid in Indian Tradition," *Historical New Hampshire*, 17 (June 1962), 3–17; Day, "Oral Tradition as Complement," *Ethnohistory*, 19:2 (Spring 1972), 99–109.

16. For the colonial period, see the contributions of William C. Sturtevant to *The American Drawings of John White, 1577–1590*, ed. Paul Hulton and David Beers Quinn, 2 vols. (London and Chapel Hill, 1964); Sturtevant, "First Visual Images of Native America," in Fredi Chiappelli, ed., *First Images of America: The Impact of the New World on the Old*, 2 vols. (Berkeley, 1976), 1:417–54; Bernadette Bucher, *Icon and Conquest: A Structural Analysis of the Illustrations of de Bry's Great Voyages*, trans. Basia Miller Gulati (Chicago, 1981); Christian F. Feest, "The Virginia Indian in Pictures, 1612–1624," *Smithsonian Journal of History*, 2 (Spring 1967), 1–30; John C. Ewers, "An Anthropologist Looks at Early Pictures of North American Indians," *New York Historical Society Quarterly*, 33 (October 1949), 222–34. On nineteenth-century photographers, see Christopher M. Lyman, *The Vanishing Race and Other Illusions: Photographs of Indians by Edward S. Curtis* (New York, 1982), and Joanna Cohan Scherer, *Indians: The Great Photographs that Reveal North American Indian Life, 1847–1929, from the Unique Collection of the Smithsonian Institution* (New York, 1973).

17. Robert C. Wheeler et al., *Voices from the Rapids: An Underwater Search for Fur Trade Artifacts, 1960–73* (St. Paul, 1975).

18. C. C. Willoughby, "Mohawk (Caughnawaga) Halter for Leading Captives," *American Anthropologist*, 40 (1938), 49–50.

19. J. B. Harley, "Maps, Knowledge, and Power," in Denis Cosgrove and Stephen Daniels, eds., *The Iconography of Landscape: Essays on the Symbolic Representation, Design and Use of Past Environments* (Cambridge, 1988), 277–312; Harley, "Silences and Secrecy: The Hidden Agenda of Cartography in Early Modern Europe," *Imago Mundi*, 40 (1988), 57–76; Harley, *Maps and the Columbian Encounter: An Interpretive Guide to the Traveling Exhibition* (Milwaukee: Golda Meir Library, University of Wisconsin, 1990); Harley, "New England Cartography and the Native Americans," in Emerson W. Baker et al., eds., *American Beginnings: Exploration, Culture, and Cartography in the Land of Norumbega* (Lincoln, 1994), ch. 13; Gregory H. Nobles, "Straight Lines and Stability: Mapping the Political Order of the Anglo-American Frontier," *Journal of American History*, 80:1 (June 1993), 9–35; G. N. G. Clarke, "Taking Possession: The Cartouche as Cultural Text in Eighteenth-century American Maps," *Word and Image*, 4:2 (April–June 1988), 455–74.

20. Louis De Vorsey, Jr., "Amerindian Contributions to the Mapping of North America: A Preliminary View," *Imago Mundi*, 30 (1978), 71–78; De Vorsey, "Silent

Witnesses: Native American Maps," *Georgia Review,* 46:4 (Winter 1992), 709–26; G. Malcolm Lewis, "The Indigenous Maps and Mapping of North American Indians," *Map Collector,* 9 (1979), 145–67; Lewis, "Indian Maps," in Carol M. Judd and Arthur J. Rays, eds., *Old Trails and New Directions: Papers of the Third North American Fur Trade Conference* (Toronto, 1980), 9–23; Lewis, "Misinterpretation of Amerindian Information as a Source of Error on Euro-American Maps," *Annals of the Association of American Geographers,* 77 (1987), 542–63; Lewis, ed., *Cartographic Encounters: Perspectives on Native American Mapmaking and Map Use* (Chicago, 1998); Gregory A. Waselkov, "Indian Maps of the Colonial Southeast," in Peter H. Wood, Waselkov, and M. Thomas Hatley, eds., *Powhatan's Mantle: Indians in the Colonial Southeast* (Lincoln, 1989), 292–343.

21. Richard White, "Native Americans and the Environment," in W. R. Swagerty, ed., *Scholars and the Indian Experience: Critical Reviews of Recent Writing in the Social Sciences* (Bloomington, 1984), 179–204; White, "Indian Peoples and the Natural World: Asking the Right Questions," in Donald L. Fixico, ed., *Rethinking American Indian History* (Albuquerque, 1997), ch. 5; Shepard Krech III, *The Ecological Indian: Myth and History* (New York, 1999); William Cronon, *Changes in the Land: Indians, Colonists, and the Ecology of New England* (New York, 1983); Carolyn Merchant, *Ecological Revolutions: Nature, Gender, and Science in New England* (Chapel Hill, 1989); Timothy H. Silver, *A New Face on the Countryside: Indians, Colonists, and Slaves in South Atlantic Forests, 1500–1800* (New York, 1990); Gary C. Goodwin, *Cherokees in Transition: A Study of Changing Culture and Environment Prior to 1775,* University of Chicago, Department of Geography, Research Paper No. 181 (Chicago, 1977).

22. James Axtell, ed., *The Indian Peoples of Eastern America: A Documentary History of the Sexes* (New York, 1981); Mona Etienne and Eleanor Leacock, eds., *Women and Colonization: Anthropological Perspectives* (New York, 1980); Rayna Green, *Native American Women: A Contextual Bibliography* (Bloomington, 1983); Walter L. Williams, *The Spirit and the Flesh: Sexual Diversity in American Indian Culture* (Boston, 1986); Deborah Welch, "American Indian Women: Reaching Beyond the Myth," in Colin G. Calloway, ed., *New Directions in American Indian History* (Norman, 1988), 31–48; Gretchen M. Bataille and Kathleen M. Sands, *American Indian Women: A Guide to Research* (New York, 1991); Nancy Shoemaker, ed., *Negotiators of Change: Historical Perspectives on Native American Women* (New York, 1995); Theda Perdue, "Writing the Ethnohistory of Native Women," in Fixico, *Rethinking American Indian History,* ch. 4.

23. Shepard Krech III, "The State of Ethnohistory," *Annual Review of Anthropology,* 20 (1991), 345–75, esp. 363–64.

24. James H. Merrell, "Some Thoughts on Colonial Historians and American Indians," *William and Mary Quarterly,* 3d ser. 46 (January 1989), 94–119, esp. 113–15.

25. Ibid., 115, n. 96.

26. Bruce G. Trigger, "Indian and White History: Two Worlds or One?" in Michael K. Foster, Jack Campisi, and Marianne Mithun, eds., *Extending the Rafters: Interdisciplinary Approaches to Iroquoian Studies* (Albany, N.Y., 1984), 17–33, esp. 21.

27. Trigger, *Natives and Newcomers: Canada's "Heroic Age" Reconsidered* (Kingston and Montreal, 1985); Axtell, "Colonial America without the Indians: Counterfactual Reflections," *Journal of American History,* 73 (March 1987), 981–96, repr. in Axtell, *After Columbus: Essays in the Ethnohistory of Colonial North America* (New York, 1988), ch. 11. See also Chapter 13 below.

28. H. C. Porter, "Reflections on the Ethnohistory of Early Colonial North America," *Journal of American Studies*, 16:2 (August 1982), 243–54, esp. 246, 250. For a counterattack by an English-born historian of early native America, see Colin G. Calloway, "In Defense of Ethnohistory," *Journal of American Studies*, 17:1 (April 1983), 95–100. My review of *The Inconstant Savage* appeared in the *Journal of American History*, 66 (March 1980), 902–3. Calloway cites the other reviews on 99, n. 13.

29. Krech, "State of Ethnohistory," 363, 364.

30. Francis L. K. Hsu, "Rethinking the Concept 'Primitive,'" *Current Anthropology*, 5:3 (June 1964), 169–78.

31. Trigger, "Ethnohistory: Problems and Prospects," *Ethnohistory*, 29:1 (1982), 1–19, esp. 11.

32. Krech, "State of Ethnohistory," 350.

33. (New York, 1987), 15, 135, 194, 197, 207.

34. Ibid., 116, 117.

35. Ibid., 126.

Chapter One

1. Philip L. Barbour, ed., *The Jamestown Voyages Under the First Charter, 1606–1609*, Hakluyt Society Publications, 2d ser. 136–37 (Cambridge, 1969), 1:133–34. See James Axtell, "Europeans, Indians, and the Age of Discovery in American History Textbooks," *American Historical Review*, 92:3 (June 1987), 621–32; for more recent treatments, see below Chapter 8.

2. Charles Horton Cooley, *Life and the Student* (New York, 1927), 201–2.

3. Donald M. Frame, ed. and trans., *The Complete Works of Montaigne* (Stanford, 1948), 80, 152; Corinthians I, 14:10–11.

4. Richard Bernheimer, *Wild Men in the Middle Ages: A Study in Art, Sentiment, and Demonology* (Cambridge, Mass., 1952); John Block Friedman, *The Monstrous Races in Medieval Art and Thought* (Cambridge, Mass., 1981); Olive Patricia Dickason, *The Myth of the Savage and the Beginnings of French Colonization in the Americas* (Edmonton, 1984).

5. James Axtell, *The Invasion Within: The Contest of Cultures in Colonial North America* (New York, 1985), ch. 1.

6. David B. Quinn, ed., *New American World: A Documentary History of North America to 1612*, 5 vols. (New York, 1979), 1:428, 2:127; David B. Quinn, *North America from Earliest Discovery to First Settlements: The Norse Voyages to 1612*, New American Nation Series (New York, 1977), 196.

7. Edmund Berkeley and Dorothy Smith Berkeley, eds., *The Reverend John Clayton: A Parson with a Scientific Mind: His Scientific Writings and Other Related Papers* (Charlottesville, 1963), 39; William Strachey, *The Historie of Travell into Virginia Britania (1612)*, ed. Louis B. Wright and Virginia Freund, Hak. Soc. Pubs., 2d ser. 103 (London, 1953), 104–5.

8. Thomas Shepard, *The Clear Sun-shine of the Gospel Breaking Forth upon the Indians in New-England* (London, 1648), in *Collections of the Massachusetts Historical Soci-*

ety, 3d ser. 4 (1834), 44. See also William S. Simmons, *Spirit of the New England Tribes: Indian History and Folklore, 1620–1984* (Hanover, N.H., 1986), 68.

9. Reuben Gold Thwaites, ed., *The Jesuit Relations and Allied Documents,* 73 vols. (Cleveland, 1896–1901), 5:119–21.

10. Father Chrestien Le Clercq, *New Relation of Gaspesia* [Paris, 1691], ed. and trans. William F. Ganong (Toronto: Champlain Society, 1910), 109.

11. Ella Elizabeth Clark, ed., *Indian Legends of Canada* (Toronto, 1960), 150–51.

12. John Heckewelder, *History, Manners, and Customs of the Indian Nations Who Once Inhabited Pennsylvania and the Neighbouring States* [1818], ed. William G. Reichel (Philadelphia, 1876), 71–75.

13. L. A. Vigneras, ed., *The Journal of Christopher Columbus,* trans. Cecil Jane (New York, 1960), 196; also Oliver Dunn and James E. Kelley, Jr., ed. and trans., *The Diario of Christopher Columbus's First Voyage to America, 1492–1493* (Norman, Okla., 1989), 137, 235.

14. Quinn, *New American World,* 2:41, 46, 47, 51. For a definitive text, see Rolena Adorno and Patrick Charles Pautz, *Álvar Núñez Cabeza de Vaca: His Account, His Life, and the Expedition of Pánfilo de Narváez,* 3 vols. (Lincoln, 1999).

15. *Ibid.,* 2:112, 130, 139, 141. See also Lawrence A. Clayton, Vernon James Knight, Jr., and Edward C. Moore, eds., *The De Soto Chronicles: The Expedition of Hernando de Soto to North America in 1539–1543,* 2 vols. (Tuscaloosa, 1993).

16. David B. Quinn and Alison M. Quinn, eds., *Virginia Voyages from Hakluyt* (London, 1973), 69–73; Louise Phelps Kellogg, ed., *Early Narratives of the Northwest, 1634–1699,* Original Narratives of Early American History [ONEAH] (New York, 1917), 74–75; Ruth Lapham Butler, ed. and trans., *Journal of Paul Du Ru . . . Missionary Priest to Louisiana* (Chicago, 1934), 5–6.

17. Dunn and Kelley, *Columbus's Diario,* 137; Quinn, *New American World,* 2:45.

18. Kellogg, *Early Narratives of the Northwest,* 75, 107, 108, 240, 242.

19. Alexander S. Salley, Jr., ed., *Narratives of Early Carolina, 1650–1708,* ONEAH (New York, 1911), 132; Clarence W. Alvord and Lee Bidgood, eds., *The First Exploration of the Trans-Allegheny Region by the Virginians, 1650–1674* (Cleveland, 1912), 212–13.

20. Dunn and Kelley, *Columbus's Diario,* 267; Quinn, *New American World,* 2:322; H. P. Biggar, ed. and trans., *The Voyages of Jacques Cartier,* Publications of the Public Archives of Canada 11 (Ottawa, 1924), 147, also 172; Kellogg, *Early Narratives of the Northwest,* 85.

21. Quinn, *New American World,* 2:42, 45.

22. Biggar, *Voyages of Cartier,* 56, 62, 162; Quinn, *Virginia Voyages from Hakluyt,* 4; Quinn, *New American World,* 4:235, 236, 240, 242.

23. Salley, *Narratives of Early Carolina,* 91, 117, 132; Richebourg Gaillard McWilliams, ed. and trans., *Fleur de Lys and Calumet: Being the Pénicaut Narrative of French Adventure in Louisiana* (Baton Rouge, 1953), 5; *Iberville's Gulf Journals,* ed. and trans. Richebourg Gaillard McWilliams (University, Ala., 1981), 46; Jay Higginbotham, ed. and trans., *The Journal of Sauvole* (Mobile, 1969), 31; Kellogg, *Early Narratives of the Northwest,* 85, 115.

24. Kellogg, *Early Narratives of the Northwest,* 242.

25. McWilliams, *Fleur de Lys and Calumet,* 5, 24, 57; *Iberville's Gulf Journals,* 46. See also Ian W. Brown, "The Calumet Ceremony in the Southeast and Its Archaeological Manifestations," *American Antiquity,* 54 (1989), 311–31.

26. Kellogg, *Early Narratives of the Northwest,* 85, 129; Butler, *Journal of Du Ru,* 18; Walter James Hoffman, "The Menomini Indians," Bureau of American Ethnology, *14th Annual Report* (Washington, D.C., 1896), pt. 1:214–16; Quinn, *New American World,* 1:240.

27. Dunn and Kelley, *Columbus's Diario,* 295, 297; Biggar, *Voyages of Cartier,* 164.

28. Biggar, *Voyages of Cartier,* 132–33, 143–44, 188.

29. *Iberville's Gulf Journals,* 86n. 141, 112, 113.

30. Buckingham Smith, ed. and trans., *Memoir of Dº. d'Escalente Fontaneda Respecting Florida* [c. 1575] (Miami, 1944), 17–19, 24; Quinn, *New American World,* 2:339; James Axtell, "The White Indians of Colonial America," in *The European and the Indian: Essays in the Ethnohistory of Colonial North America* (New York, 1981), ch. 7.

31. Quinn, *New American World,* 2:132.

32. Salley, *Narratives of Early Carolina,* 51, 105.

33. McWilliams, *Fleur de Lys and Calumet,* 24.

34. Quinn, *Virginia Voyages from Hakluyt,* 9–10; Lawrence C. Wroth, *The Voyages of Giovanni da Verrazzano, 1524–1528* (New Haven, 1970), 134, 135; McWilliams, *Fleur de Lys and Calumet,* 4.

35. McWilliams, *Fleur de Lys and Calumet,* 4, 112; Kellogg, *Early Narratives of the Northwest,* 75.

36. Biggar, *Voyages of Cartier,* 165; Quinn, *New American World,* 2:31–32, 38, 40, 47, 130 (Soto).

37. Quinn, *Virginia Voyages from Hakluyt,* 36, 71–72, 73.

38. Vigneras, *Journal of Columbus,* 196; Quinn, *Virginia Voyages from Hakluyt,* 10; Higginbotham, *Journal of Sauvole,* 40–41.

39. Wroth, *Voyages of Verrazzano,* 137.

40. Biggar, *Voyages of Cartier,* 134–35; Kellogg, *Early Narratives of the Northwest,* 46, 50, 73, 75, 77, 243; *Father Louis Hennepin's Description of Louisiana* [Paris, 1683], ed. and trans. Marion E. Cross (Minneapolis, 1938), 98.

41. Quinn, *Virginia Voyages from Hakluyt,* 70.

42. *Hennepin's Description of Louisiana,* 82, 96, 98, 105, 108–9, 130; William Wood, *New England's Prospect* [London, 1634], ed. Alden T. Vaughan (Amherst, Mass., 1977), 96.

43. Vigneras, *Journal of Columbus,* 196; Quinn, *New American World,* 2:331, 482, 4:236, 250; David B. Quinn and Alison M. Quinn, eds., *The English New England Voyages, 1602–1608,* Hak. Soc. Pubs., 2d ser. 161 (London, 1983), 274.

44. James Axtell, *After Columbus: Essays in the Ethnohistory of Colonial North America* (New York, 1988), 270n.22; Dunn and Kelley, *Columbus's Diario,* 67.

45. Dunn and Kelley, *Columbus's Diario,* 93, 117, 227, 251; Vigneras, *Journal of Columbus,* 201; Salley, *Narratives of Early Carolina,* 91.

46. Vigneras, *Journal of Columbus*, 191; Quinn, *New American World*, 2:392–93, 5:438; Biggar, *Voyages of Cartier*, 155; Arthur J. Krim, "Acculturation of the New England Landscape: Native and English Toponomy of Eastern Massachusetts," in Peter Benes, ed., *New England Prospect: Maps, Place Names, and the Historical Landscape*, The Dublin Seminar for New England Folklife: Annual Proceedings 1980 (Boston, 1983), 69–88; Quinn, *New American World*, 2:292, 296. See also George R. Stewart, *Names on the Land: A Historical Account of Place-Naming in the United States* (New York, 1945).

47. Dunn and Kelley, *Columbus's Diario*, 63, 79; Vigneras, *Journal of Columbus*, 191.

48. Barbour, *Jamestown Voyages*, 1:88.

49. Biggar, *Voyages of Cartier*, 64–65.

50. Quinn, *New American World*, 2:295, 309, 314, 316, 321. Patricia Seed's deeply flawed *Ceremonies of Possession in Europe's Conquest of the New World, 1492–1640* (Cambridge, 1995) should be read with Arthur S. Keller, Oliver J. Lissitzyn, and Frederick J. Mann, *Creation of Rights of Sovereignty through Symbolic Acts, 1400–1800* (New York, 1938), which she does not cite.

51. *Ibid.*, 2:291.

52. Quinn, *English New England Voyages*, 154, 272; Quinn, *New American World*, 2:289; *Iberville's Gulf Journals*, 46.

53. Dunn and Kelley, *Columbus's Diario*, 243; Quinn, *English New England Voyages*, 275, also 272, 279, 283–84.

54. Quinn, *New American World*, 3:190, 4:29, 235; Quinn, *English New England Voyages*, 220; McWilliams, *Fleur de Lys and Calumet*, 106–7, 109–10, 115.

55. Wilbur R. Jacobs, *Wilderness Politics and Indian Gifts: The Northern Colonial Frontier, 1748–1763* (Stanford, 1950); Cornelius J. Jaenen. "The Role of Presents in French-Amerindian Trade," in Duncan Cameron, ed., *Explorations in Canadian Economic History: Essays in Honour of Irene M. Spry* (Ottawa, 1985), 231–50.

56. Dunn and Kelley, *Columbus's Diario*, 243; Biggar, *Voyages of Cartier*, 53, 166; Quinn, *New American World*, 2:288.

57. Wroth, *Voyages of Verrazzano*, 138; Quinn, *Virginia Voyages from Hakluyt*, 8; Thomas Hariot, *A briefe and true report of the newfound land of Virginia* (Frankfurt, 1590); original painting in Paul Hulton, ed., *America 1585: The Complete Drawings of John White* (Chapel Hill, 1984), pl. 65.

58. Vigneras, *Journal of Columbus*, 200; Strachey, *Historie of Travell in Virginia*, 71; Albert Cook Myers, ed., *Narratives of Early Pennsylvania, West New Jersey, and Delaware, 1630–1707*, ONEAH (New York, 1912), 230; see also Winthrop D. Jordan, *White Over Black: American Attitudes Toward the Negro, 1550–1812* (Chapel Hill, 1968), 14, 22, 27.

59. Philip L. Barbour, ed., *The Complete Works of Captain John Smith (1580–1631)*, 3 vols. (Chapel Hill, 1986), 2:115; Quinn, *Virginia Voyages from Hakluyt*, 64. See also David Beers Quinn, *The Elizabethans and the Irish* (Ithaca, N.Y., 1966); Nicholas P. Canny, *The Elizabethan Conquest of Ireland: A Pattern Established, 1565–76* (New York, 1976); James P. Myers, Jr., ed., *Elizabethan Ireland: A Selection of Writings by Elizabethan Writers on Ireland* (Hamden, Conn., 1983).

60. H. C. Porter, *The Inconstant Savage: England and the North American Indian, 1500–1660* (London, 1979); Karen Ordahl Kupperman, *Settling with the Indians: The*

Meeting of English and Indian Cultures in America, 1580–1640 (Totowa, N.J., 1980); Bernard W. Sheehan, *Savagism and Civility: Indians and Englishmen in Colonial Virginia* (Cambridge, 1980); Dickason, *Myth of the Savage.*

61. Kellogg, *Early Narratives of the Northwest,* 185.

62. Philippe Jacquin, *Les Indiens blancs: Français et Indiens en Amérique du Nord (XVIe–XVIIe siècle)* (Paris, 1987), ch. 3; James M. Crawford, *The Mobilian Trade Language* (Knoxville, Tenn., 1978), 30–32.

63. Quinn, *New American World,* 2:104, 137.

64. Dunn and Kelley, *Columbus's Diario,* 207; Vigneras, *Journal of Columbus,* 196; Biggar, *Voyages of Cartier,* 65–67, 225–27; Quinn, *Virginia Voyages from Hakluyt,* 12, 102; David Beers Quinn, *Set Fair for Roanoke: Voyages and Colonies, 1584–1606* (Chapel Hill, 1985), 232–36.

Chapter Two

1. John Lawson, A *New Voyage to Carolina,* ed. Hugh Talmage Lefler (Chapel Hill, 1967 [1709]), 214, 219, 239.

2. Genesis 11:1–9

3. Harold E. Driver, *Indians of North America,* 2d rev. ed. (Chicago, 1969), ch. 3.

4. Baron de Lahontan, *New Voyages to North America,* ed. Reuben Gold Thwaites, 2 vols. (New York, 1970 [1703]), 1:47, 2:733–34; Thwaites, ed., *The Jesuit Relations and Allied Documents* (hereafter cited as *JR*), 73 vols. (Cleveland, 1896–1901), 5:115 (Paul Le Jeune, 1633)

5. Roger Williams, *A Key into the Language of America* (London, 1643), A2v-3r, 104–105.

6. Lawson, *New Voyage to Carolina,* 233, 239.

7. Fernand Braudel, *The Identity of France,* Vol. 1, *History and Environment,* trans. Siân Reynolds (New York, 1988), 85–96; Robert Mandrou, *Introduction to Modern France, 1500–1640: An Essay in Historical Psychology,* trans. R.E. Hallmark (New York, 1977), 62–65; Patrice L-R. Higonnet, "The Politics of Linguistic Terrorism and Grammatical Hegemony during the French Revolution," *Social History,* 5 (1980), 41–69.

8. W.P. Clark, *The Indian Sign Language* (Philadelphia, 1885; repr. Lincoln, 1982); Garrick Mallery, *Sign Language among North American Indians* (Washington, D.C., 1881; repr. The Hague, 1972); D. Jean Umiker-Sebeok and Thomas A. Sebeok, eds., *Aboriginal Sign Languages of the Americas and Australia,* 2 vols. (New York, 1978).

9. David Beers Quinn, *The Elizabethans and the Irish* (Ithaca, 1966), 92, 126, 151, 169.

10. David B. Quinn and Alison M. Quinn, eds., *English New England Voyages, 1602–1608,* Hakluyt Society Publications, 2d ser. 161 (London, 1983), 267.

11. Richard Hakluyt the Younger, "Discourse of Western Planting" (1584), in E.G.R. Taylor, ed., *The Original Writings and Correspondence of the Two Richard Hakluyts,* Hakluyt Society Publications., 2d ser. 76–77 (London, 1935), 215 (continuous pagination).

12. See above, Chapter 1, pp. 24–27.

13. Lawrence C. Wroth, *The Voyages of Giovanni da Verrazzano, 1524–1528* (New Haven, 1970), 138–39.

14. Quinn and Quinn, ed., *English New England Voyages,* 134 (1602).

15. *The Journal of Christopher Columbus,* trans. Cecil Jane, ed. L. A. Vigneras (New York, 1960), 196.

16. Ibid., 27, 50, 51, 57.

17. Ibid., 76.

18. Henry Norwood, *"A Voyage to Virginia. By Colonel Norwood"* [1649], in Peter Force, comp., *Tracts and Other Papers Relating Principally to the Origin, Settlement, and Progress of the Colonies in North America . . .* , 4 vols. (Washington, D.C., 1836–1847), vol. 3, no. 10, p. 38; Wroth, *Voyages of Verrazzano,* 140, 141 (my emphasis).

19. Biggar, ed., *Voyages of Cartier,* 65, 67 (my emphasis). For a similarly guilty interpretation of Indian speech by a seagoing European trader, see Quinn and Quinn, ed., *English New England Voyages,* 267.

20. Philip L. Barbour, ed., *The Jamestown Voyages Under the First Charter, 1606–1609,* Hakluyt Society Publications., 2d ser. 136–37 (Cambridge, 1969), 90, 94, 141 (continuous pagination).

21. Barbour, ed., *Jamestown Voyages,* 139.

22. Biggar, ed., *Voyages of Cartier,* 143, 147.

23. David B. Quinn, ed., *New American World: A Documentary History of North America to 1612,* 5 vols. (New York, 1979), 2: 29, 51.

24. Quinn and Quinn, ed., *English New England Voyages,* 156, 280.

25. Clarence W. Alvord and Lee Bidgood, eds., *The First Explorations of the Trans-Allegheny Region by the Virginians, 1650–1674* (Cleveland, 1912), 222–23.

26. Richebourg Gaillard McWilliams, ed., *Iberville's Gulf Journals* (University, Ala., 1981), 24.

27. *Henri Joutel's Journal of La Salle's Last Voyage, 1684–7,* ed. Henry Reed Stiles (Albany, N.Y., 1906), 71. A reprint edition published in 1962 by Corinth Books is a photo-duplicate of the Stiles edition, but because it lacks Stiles's historical introduction, its pagination begins thirty-two pages earlier.

28. *Joutel's Journal,* 139, 140, 148.

29. *Joutel's Journal,* 156–57, 168.

30. Norwood, *"Voyage to Virginia"* in Force, *Tracts,* vol. 3, no. 10, pp. 29, 39.

31. Ibid., 30, 35.

32. Ibid., 36, 39, 43.

33. Ibid., 44.

34. Robert A. Hall, *Pidgin and Creole Languages* (Ithaca, 1966); Dell Hymes, ed., *Pidginization and Creolization of Languages* (Cambridge, 1971); Emanuel J. Drechsel, "'Ha, Now Me Stomany That': A Summary of Pidginization and Creolization of North American Indian Languages," *International Journal of the Sociology of Language,* 7 (1976), 63–81; Albert Valdman, ed., *Pidgin and Creole Linguistics* (Bloomington,

Ind., 1979); Michael Silverstein, "Dynamics of Linguistic Contact," in *Handbook of North American Indians,* vol. 17, *Language,* ed. Ives Goddard (Washington, D.C., 1996), 117–36; Silverstein, "Encountering Language and Languages of Encounter in North American Ethnohistory," *Journal of Linguistic Anthropology,* 6 (Dec. 1996), 126–44.

35. Emanuel J. Drechsel, "Towards an Ethnohistory of Speaking, The Case of Mobilian Jargon: An American Indian Pidgin of the Lower Mississippi Valley," *Ethnohistory,* 30 (1983), 165–76 at 168.

36. Francisque Michel, *Le pays Basque* (Paris, 1857), 159, quoted in Peter Bakker, "Two Basque Loanwords in Micmac," *International Journal of American Linguistics,* 55 (1989), 258–61 at 259; René Bélanger, *Les Basques dans l'Estuaire du Saint-Laurent, 1535–1635* (Montreal, 1971), 86 (quoting a Basque chronicle of 1625); Marc Lescarbot, *The History of New France,* ed. and trans. W.L. Grant, intro. H.P. Biggar, 3 vols. (Toronto: Champlain Society, 1911 [1609]), 2:24.

37. Lescarbot, *History of New France,* 2:24; Peter Bakker, "Basque Pidgin Vocabulary in European-Algonquian Trade Contacts," in *Papers of the Nineteenth Algonquian Conference,* ed. William Cowan (Ottawa: Carleton University, 1988), 7–15 at 10–11; H.P. Biggar, ed. and trans., *A Collection of Documents Relating to Jacques Cartier and the Sieur de Roberval,* Publications of the Public Archives of Canada [hereafter PAC] 14 (Ottawa, 1930), 453–54; Pierre de Lancre, *Tableau de l'inconstance des mauvais anges et démons* (Paris, 1613), quoted in Bakker, "Basque Pidgin Vocabulary," 9.

38. Lescarbot, *History of New France,* 3:125 (my emphasis); *JR* 5:113, 115 (Paul Le Jeune, 1633). See also Peter Bakker, "A Basque Nautical Pidgin, a Missing Link in the History of FU?," *Journal of Pidgin and Creole Languages,* 2 (1987), 1–30; Bakker, "The Language of the Coast Tribes is Half Basque: a Basque-Amerindian Pidgin in Use between Europeans and Native Americans in North America, ca. 1540–ca. 1640," *Anthropological Linguistics,* 31 (1989), 117–47.

39. Quinn and Quinn, ed., *English New England Voyages,* 117, 145–46. See Bruce J. Bourque and Ruth Holmes Whitehead, "Tarrentines and the Introduction of European Trade Goods in the Gulf of Maine," *Ethnohistory,* 32 (1985), 327–41, and Laurier Turgeon, "La traite Française dans le Saint-Laurent au XVIe siecle," *Saguenayensia,* 27 (1985), 190–92.

40. Quinn, ed., *New American World,* 2:311–13.

41. Alexander S. Salley, Jr., ed., *Narratives of Early Carolina, 1650–1708,* Original Narratives of Early American History (New York, 1911), 39, 50–51, 117, 119.

42. William Bradford, *Of Plymouth Plantation, 1620–1647,* ed. Samuel Eliot Morison (New York, 1952), 79; *A Journal of the Pilgrims at Plymouth: Mourt's Relation,* ed. Dwight B. Heath (New York, 1963 [1622]), 51.

43. Bradford, *Of Plymouth Plantation,* 80; *Mourt's Relation,* 55: Neal Salisbury, "Squanto: Last of the Patuxets," in David G. Sweet and Gary B. Nash, eds., *Struggle and Survival in Colonial America* (Berkeley, 1981), 228–46.

44. Edward Winslow, *Good News from New England* (London, 1624), repr. in Edward Arber, ed., *The Story of the Pilgrim Fathers, 1606–1623* (London and Boston, 1897), 544–45.

45. William Wood, *New England's Prospect,* ed. Alden T. Vaughan (Amherst, Mass., 1977 [1634]), 110; Christopher Levett, *A Voyage into New England* (London,

1628), repr. in *Forerunners and Competitors of the Pilgrims and Puritans*, ed. Charles H. Levermore, 2 vols. (Brooklyn, N.Y., 1912), 2:629.

46. Williams, *Key into the Language*, 2; Wood, *New England's Prospect*, 95–96; Captain John Underhill, *Newes from America* (London, 1638), reprinted in Charles Orr, ed., *History of the Pequot War* (Cleveland, 1897), 7.

47. Charles H. Lincoln, ed., *Narratives of the Indian Wars, 1675–1699*, ONEAH (New York, 1913), 39.

48. Levett, *Voyage into New England*, 2:622–24. For more on the New England pidgin, see Douglas Leechman and Robert A. Hall, "American Indian Pidgin English: Attestations and Grammatical Peculiarities," *American Speech*, 30 (1955), 163–71; Ives Goddard, "Some Early Examples of American Indian Pidgin English from New England," *Int. J. of Amer. Linguistics*, 43 (1977), 37–41; Goddard, "A Further Note on Pidgin English," ibid., 44 (1978), 73.

49. J. Franklin Jameson, ed., *Narratives of New Netherland, 1609–1664*, ONEAH (New York, 1909), 126–27, 128.

50. Ibid., 172–73 (my emphasis). See also Lois M. Feister, "Linguistic Communication between the Dutch and Indians in New Netherland, 1609–1664," *Ethnohistory*, 20 (1973), 25–38.

51. Albert Cook Myers, ed., *Narratives of Early Pennsylvania, West New Jersey, and Delaware, 1630–1707*, ONEAH (New York, 1912), 230 (Penn), 342 (Gabriel Thomas, 1698).

52. *Martin Luther's Little Catechism Translated into Algonquian Indian by Johannes Campanius*, notes by Isak Collijn, New Sweden Tercentenary Publications (New York, 1937).

53. Myers, ed., *Narratives of Early Pennsylvania*, 342–43; J. Dyneley Prince, "An Ancient New Jersey Indian Jargon," *American Anthropologist*, n.s. 14 (1912), 508–24; Ives Goddard, "The Delaware Jargon," in Carol E. Hoffecker et al., eds., *New Sweden in America* (Newark, Del., 1995), ch. 1 (thanks to Dr. Goddard for an advance copy of his essay). See also his "The Ethnohistorical Implications of Early Delaware Linguistic Materials," *Man in the Northeast*, 1 (1971), 14–26.

54. See below, Chapter 10, and Axtell, *After Columbus: Essays in the Ethnohistory of Colonial North America* (New York, 1988), ch. 10.

55. John Smith, *A Map of Virginia* (Oxford, 1612), in Philip L. Barbour, ed., *The Complete Works of Captain John Smith (1980–1631)*, 3 vols. (Chapel Hill, 1986), 1:136–39; William Strachey, *The Historie of Travell into Virginia Britania (1612)*, ed. Louis B. Wright and Virginia Freund, Hakluyt Society Publications., 2d ser. 53 (London, 1953), 174–207 at 174. For linguistic analyses of these word-lists that fail to recognize their pidginization, see Barbour, "The Earliest Reconnaissance of the Chesapeake Bay Area: Captain John Smith's Map and Indian Vocabulary," pt. 2, *Virginia Magazine of History and Biography*, 80 (1972), 21–51, and Frank T. Siebert, Jr., "Resurrecting Virginia Algonquian from the Dead: The Reconstituted and Historical Phonology of Powhatan," in James B. Crawford, ed., *Studies in Southeastern Indian Languages* (Athens, Ga., 1975), 285–453.

56. Robert Beverley, *The History and Present State of Virginia*, ed. Louis B. Wright (Chapel Hill, 1947 [1705]), 19; Wilcomb E. Washburn, *The Governor and the Rebel: A History of Bacon's Rebellion in Virginia* (Chapel Hill, 1957), ch. 3; *The Journal of John*

Fontaine: An Irish Huguenot Son in Spain and Virginia, 1710–1719, ed. Edward Porter Alexander (Williamsburg, 1972), 12–13.

57. Antoine Simon Le Page du Pratz, *Histoire de la Louisiana*, 3 vols. (Paris, 1758), 2:323; Louis François Benjamin Dumont de Montigny, *Mémoires historiques sur la Louisiane*, 2 vols. (Paris, 1753), 1:181–82.

58. M. Le Page du Pratz, *The History of Louisiana* (London, 1774), 318.

59. Richebourg Gaillard McWilliams, ed., *Fleur de Lys and Calumet: Being the Pénicaut Narrative of French Adventure in Louisiana* (Baton Rouge, 1953), 126–27.

60. "Journal of Antoine Bonnefoy's Captivity among the Cherokee Indians, 1741–1742," in Newton D. Mereness, ed., *Travels in the American Colonies* (New York, 1961), 253–55.

61. James M. Crawford, *The Mobilian Trade Language* (Knoxville, 1978); Mary R. Haas, "What Is Mobilian?" in Crawford, ed., *Studies in Southeastern Indian Languages*, 257–63; Emanuel J. Drechsel, "An Integrated Vocabulary of Mobilian Jargon, a Native American Pidgin of the Mississippi Valley," *Anthropological Linguistics*, 38 (Summer 1996), 248–354; Drechsel, *Mobilian Jargon: Linguistic and Sociohistorical Aspects of a Native American Pidgin*, Oxford Studies in Language Contact (Oxford, 1997).

62. H.P. Biggar, ed. and trans., *The Voyages of Cartier*, Publications of the PAC, 11 (Ottawa, 1924) 66–67, 102–3, 106, 120–24, 127–28; David B. Quinn and Alison M. Quinn, eds., *Virginia Voyages from Hakluyt* (London, 1973), 12, 32, 99, 101, 109; Clifford M. Lewis and Albert J. Loomie, *The Spanish Jesuit Mission in Virginia, 1570–72* (Chapel Hill, 1953), 15–18, 36–55, 89, 92, 108–12. See also Lynn Guitar, "Franciscano Chicorano: A North American Indian in King Charles I's Court," *Terrae Incognitae*, 29 (1997), 1–9, for another runaway interpreter.

63. James Axtell, *The Invasion Within: The Contest of Cultures in Colonial North America* (New York, 1985), 56.

64. Ibid., ch. 8; Margaret Connell Szasz, *Indian Education in the American Colonies, 1607–1783* (Albuquerque, N.M., 1989); Samuel Eliot Morison, *Harvard College in the Seventeenth Century*, 2 vols. (Cambridge, Mass., 1936), 1:ch. 17.

65. See below, Chapter 7, and Axtell, *The Invasion Within*, 204–15.

66. Quinn, ed., *New American World*, 2:104, 137; Lawrence A. Clayton, Vernon James Knight, Jr., and Edward C. Moore, eds., *The De Soto Chronicles: The Expedition of Hernando de Soto to North America in 1539–1543*, 2 vols. (Tuscaloosa, 1993), 1:59–62, 76, 130. For Spanish interpreters in other parts of the Americas, see Francisco de Solano, "El intérprete: uno de los ejes de la aculturación," *Estudios sobre la política indigenista española en América. Terceras Jornadas Americanistas de la Universidad de Valladolid* (1975), 265–78; Solano, ed., *Documentos sobre política lingüística en Hispanoamérica (1492–1800)*, Coleccion tierra nueva e cielo nuevo 32 (Madrid, 1991); Emma Martinell Gifre, *Aspectos lingüísticos de descubrimiento y de la conquista* (Madrid, 1988), 60–99; Carroll L. Riley, "Early Spanish-Indian Communication in the Greater Southwest," *New Mexico Historical Review*, 46 (1971), 285–314.

67. *Dictionary of Canadian Biography* [hereafter *DCB*], 2:125–27; 3:101–102; 4:137–38.

68. Nancy L. Hagedorn, "Brokers of Understanding: Interpreters as Agents of Cultural Exchange in Colonial New York," *New York History*, 76 (Oct. 1995), 379–408 at

383–85. On the Potomac, Henry Fleet served as interpreter for Virginians and Mary-landers after living four years with the Nacotchtanks, who had seized him from a canoe brigade in 1623. J. Frederick Fausz, "Middlemen in Peace and War: Virginia's Earliest Indian Interpreters, 1608–1632," *Virginia Magazine of History and Biography*, 95 (Jan. 1987), 41–64 at 60.

69. Richard VanDerBeets, ed., *Held Captive by Indians: Selected Narratives, 1642–1836* (Knoxville, 1973), 91–129; *DCB*, 3:272–73. Stuart Trueman, *The Ordeal of John Gyles* (Toronto, 1966) is semi-fictional. Gyles's written English was never equal to his speech.

70. Hagedorn, "Brokers of Understanding," 393–94. For the Hollis school, see James Axtell, "The Rise and Fall of the Stockbridge Indian Schools," *Massachusetts Review*, 27 (Summer 1986), 367–78.

71. See below, Chapter 8, and Axtell, *The Invasion Within*, ch. 11. See also Alden T. Vaughan and Daniel K. Richter, "Crossing the Cultural Divide: Indians and New Englanders, 1605–1763," *Proceedings of the American Antiquarian Society*, 90 (April 1980), 23–99.

72. Axtell, *The Invasion Within*, 55–59, 179–217; Szasz, *Indian Education in the American Colonies*.

73. In the fifteenth century, Portuguese explorers employed a progression of local slaves educated in Portugal to traverse the linguistic Babel of coastal Africa. For his final approach to India, however, Vasco Da Gama shipped out ten Portuguese *degrada-dos* (convicts) to scout unknown shores and to acquire local languages. Jeanne Hein, "Portuguese Communication with Africans on the Searoute to India," *Terrae Incogni-tae*, 25 (1993), 41–51.

74. Jean de Léry, *History of a Voyage to the Land of Brazil*, ed. and trans. Janet What-ley (Berkeley, 1990), xix, 43, 128, 153, 170; John Hemming, *Red Gold: The Conquest of the Brazilian Indians, 1500–1760* (Cambridge, Mass., 1978), 8–13.

75. Biggar, ed., *Voyages of Cartier*, 143–44, 252, 257.

76. Ibid., 66–67, 120, 128, 129, 133, 187–88, 212–13, 227, 249. To lure the suspi-cious Stadaconans into his grasp, Cartier assured the two brothers that his master, King Francis I, "had forbidden him to carry off to France any man or woman but only two or three boys to learn the language," a plausible lie (idem, 224).

77. Marcel Trudel, *Histoire de la Nouvelle-France*, II, *Le Comptoir, 1604–1627* (Montreal, 1966), 390–91; Trudel, "Discours du President: Les premiers balbu-tiements du bilinguisme, 1524–1634," Canadian Historical Association, *Report 1964*, 1–8; Benjamin Sulte, "Les interprètes du temps de Champlain," *Transactions of the Royal Society of Canada* (1882), 47–56; Philippe Jacquin, *Les Indiens blancs: Francais et Indiens en Amérique du Nord (XVIᵉ-XVIIIᵉ siècle)* (Paris, 1987), 37–67 at 45; *DCB*, 1:130–31, 341, 493–95, 516–18; H.P. Biggar, ed. and trans., *The Works of Samuel de Champlain*, 6 vols. (Toronto, 1922–1936), 2:138–42, 188, 201, 205–206, 307; 5:100–101, 108, 132; F. Gabriel Sagard Théodat, *Histoire du Canada*, 4 vols. (Paris, 1865 [1636]), 2:334 (quotation), 335–36.

78. Patricia Galloway, "Talking with Indians: Interpreters and Diplomacy in French Louisiana," in Winthrop D. Jordan and Sheila L. Skemp, eds., *Race and Fam-ily in the Colonial South* (Jackson, Miss., 1987), 109–29, 161–64; Dunbar Rowland, Albert Godfrey Sanders, and Patricia Kay Galloway, ed. and trans., *Mississippi Provin-*

cial Archives: French Dominion, 5 vols. (Jackson and Baton Rouge, 1927–1984), 3:128–29, 585–86 (quotation); 4:100; McWilliams, ed., *Fleur de Lys and Calumet,* 25, 30, 67–68, 73, 78, 79: McWilliams, ed., *Iberville's Gulf Journals,* 137, 176–77.

79. Fausz, "Middlemen in Peace and War," 41–64; Martha Bennett Stiles, "Hostage to the Indians," *Virginia Cavalcade,* 12 (Summer 1962), 5–11.

80. Henry Spelman, "Relation of Virginea," in Capt. John Smith, *Works, 1608–1631,* ed. Edward Arber (Birmingham, Eng., 1884), ci–civ; Barbour, ed., *Complete Works of Captain John Smith,* 2:193, 294, 315; Susan Myra Kingsbury, ed., *The Records of the Virginia Company of London,* 4 vols. (Washington, D.C., 1906–35), 3:129.

81. See, for example, Paul A.W. Wallace, *Conrad Weiser (1696–1760): Friend of Colonist and Mohawk* (Philadelphia, 1945), 17–18, 24–25, 326, 330–31, 332, 337–39; William H. Beauchamp, *The Life of Conrad Weiser as It Relates to His Services as Official Interpreter between New York and Pennsylvania* (Syracuse, 1925); Milton W. Hamilton, *Sir William Johnson: Colonial American, 1715–1763* (Port Washington, N.Y. 1976), 82–84; Salley, ed., *Narratives of Early Carolina,* 104–105; *John Long's Voyages and Travels in the Years 1768–1788,* ed. Milo Milton Quaife, Lakeside Classics (Chicago, 1922), 8, 45–46; Fausz, "Middlemen in Peace and War," 62.

82. See, for example, Hagedorn, "Brokers of Understanding," 386–88; Nicholas B. Wainwright, *George Croghan, Wilderness Diplomat* (Chapel Hill, 1959); Wallace, *Conrad Weiser;* Hamilton, *Sir William Johnson;* Dunbar, Sanders, and Galloway, *Mississippi Provincial Archives,* 4:100; Wilbur R. Jacobs, ed., *The Appalachian Indian Frontier: The Edmund Atkin Report and Plan of 1755* (Lincoln, 1967 [1954]), 12, 29, 81; Feister, "Linguistic Communication between the Dutch and Indians," 35–36; Peter Wraxall, *An Abridgement of Indian Affairs . . . in the Colony of New York [1678–1751],* ed. Charles Howard McIlwain, Harvard Historical Studies, no. 21 (Cambridge, Mass., 1915), 155; William L. McDowell, Jr., ed., *Documents Relating to Indian Affairs, 1750–1765,* 2 vols., Colonial Records of South Carolina, series 2 (Columbia, 1958–70), 1:23, 75, 148; 2:55, 192–93, 196–97, 334–35, 437, 485 (hereafter cited as *S. C. Indian Records*); Eirlys M. Barker, "Much Blood and Treasure: South Carolina's Indian Traders, 1670–1775" (Ph.D.diss., College of William and Mary, Dept. of History, 1993); Francis Jennings, "Jacob Young: Indian Trader and Interpreter," in Sweet and Nash, eds., *Struggle and Survival in Colonial America,* 347–61.

83. Hagedorn, "Brokers of Understanding," 381, 382, 388; James Sullivan et al., eds., *The Papers of Sir William Johnson,* 14 vols. (Albany, 1921–65), 13:631; Howard Lewin, "A Frontier Diplomat: Andrew Montour," *Pennsylvania History,* 33 (April 1966), 153–86; Nancy L. Hagedorn, "'Faithful, Knowing, and Prudent': Andrew Montour as Interpreter and Cultural Broker, 1740–1772," in Margaret Connell Szasz, ed., *Between Indian and White Worlds: The Cultural Broker* (Norman, 1994), 44–60, 308–12; James H. Merrell, "'The Cast of His Countenance': Reading Andrew Montour," in Ronald Hoffman, Mechal Sobel, and Fredricka J. Teute, eds., *Through a Glass Darkly: Reflections on Personal Identity in Early America* (Chapel Hill, 1997), 13–39; *DCB,* 3:147–48 (Elizabeth Couc?); Raphael Semmes, *Captains and Mariners of Early Maryland* (Baltimore, 1937), 539–60, 724–26, 803–804 at 550, 552; Milo Milton Quaife, ed., *The Siege of Detroit in 1763,* Lakeside Classics (Chicago, 1958), 18–19n., 50n., 88n.

84. *The Letters and Papers of Cadwallader Colden,* 9 vols., *Collections of the New York Historical Society,* vols. 50–56, 67–68 (New York, 1917–1935), 9:106 (1751).

85. *Collections of the Massachusetts Historical Society,* 4th ser. 6 (1863), 224 (1638), 263 (1640), 335 (1647); *[John] Winthrop's Journal "History of New England," 1630–1649,* ed. James Kendall Hosmer, 2 vols., ONEAH (New York, 1908), 1:193 (21 Oct. 1636). Williams published his *Key into the Language of America,* a sophisticated guide to Narragansett language and culture, in 1643. See the critical edition by John J. Teunissen and Evelyn J. Hinz (Detroit, 1973).

86. Paul A.W. Wallace, ed., *Thirty Thousand Miles with John Heckewelder* (Pittsburgh, 1958), 86; William M.. Beauchamp, ed., *Moravian Journals Relating to Central New York, 1745–66* (Syracuse, 1916), 175. In 1754 Conrad Weiser was asked to play the same role at a meeting with the Iroquois in Albany. He declined to be the principal interpreter for Pennsylvania, allegedly because he was out of practice, but he allowed that his understanding of the spoken language was unimpaired and he would "Use his Endeavour that whatever is said by the Indians be truly interpreted to the Gentlemen" (*Minutes of the Provincial Council of Pennsylvania,* ed. Samuel Hazard, 16 vols. [Philadelphia and Harrisburg, 1838–53], 6:49 [June 2, 1754]).

87. Minutes of conference with Indian messengers, Philadelphia, Feb. 8, 1759, Historical Society of Pennsylvania, Penn MSS., Official Correspondence, vol. 3 (reproduced in *Iroquois Indians: A Documentary History of the Diplomacy of the Six Nations and Their League,* ed. Francis Jennings et al., microfilm [Woodbridge, Conn., 1984], reel 23, 1759, Feb.8–9). Thanks to Nancy Hagedorn for this and other references. See her "'A Friend to Go between Them': Interpreters Among the Iroquois, 1664–1775" (Ph.D. diss., College of William and Mary, Dept. of History, 1995); "'A Friend to Go between Them': The Interpreter as Cultural Broker during Anglo-Iroquois Councils, 1740–70," *Ethnohistory,* 35 (Winter 1988), 60–80; and "'A Great Deal Depends upon the Interpreters': Anglo-Iroquois Relations and Imperial Diplomacy in the Colonial Northeast, 1664–1774," International Seminar on the History of the Atlantic World, 1500–1800, Harvard University, *Working Paper* no. 97–23 (Cambridge, Mass., 1997), 1–43.

88. W. Noel Sainsbury et al., eds., *Calendar of State Papers, Colonial Series: America and the West Indies* (London, 1860–), 28:233–35 (no. 521, July 15,1715).

89. Hagedorn, "'A Great Deal Depends upon the Interpreters,'" 20–21.

90. E.B. O'Callaghan and Berthold Fernow, eds., *Documents Relative to the Colonial History of the State of New-York,* 15 vols. (Albany, 1856–87), 9:966–67 (Aug.4,1727) (hereafter cited as *NYCD*).

91. Sullivan, ed., *Papers of William Johnson,* 3:915 (Oct. 24, 1762); E.B. O'Callaghan, ed., *Documentary History of the State of New York,* 4 vols. (Albany, 1846–51), 2:946 (Aug. 21, 1769); *Virginia Magazine of History and Biography,* 14 (1906), 294 (1677); Sagard, *Histoire du Canada,* 2:444.

92. The traders who resided among the several Creek and Cherokee towns and served as sworn interpreters for South Carolina were the major exceptions.

93. Minutes of the [New York] Indian Commissioners, Jan. 6, 1739, quoted in Hagedorn, "'A Great Deal Depends upon the Interpreters,'" 21. See also Semmes, *Captains and Mariners of Early Maryland,* 544; Wraxall, *An Abridgement of Indian Affairs,* 212; Jacobs, ed., *The Appalachian Indian Frontier,* 12, 81; McDowell, ed., *S. C. Indian Records,* 1:290, 298; 2:336–37.

94. Eleazar Wheelock to George Whitefield, July 4, 1761, Papers of Eleazar Wheelock, Dartmouth College Library, Hanover, N.H. (microfilm), no. 761404. Two

prominent exceptions who assisted roving missionaries in western Pennsylvania and the Ohio country were Joseph Peepy and Moses Tatamy, both Delaware converts. See the favorable accounts in *Diary of David McClure . . . 1748–1820*, ed. Franklin B. Dexter (New York, 1899), 46–47, 72, 81, 86; and *David Brainerd: His Life and Diary*, ed. Jonathan Edwards (Chicago, 1949 [1817]), 208–12, 247–48, 324–25.

95. *NYCD*, 7:970 (Sept. 22, 1767).

Chapter Three

1. Nicolas Denys, *The Description and Natural History of the Coasts of North America (Acadia)* [Paris, 1672], ed. and trans. William F. Ganong (Toronto: Champlain Society, 1908), 257.

2. David Beers Quinn, *England and the Discovery of America, 1481–1620* (New York, 1974), ch. 1.

3. David B. Quinn, ed., *New American World: A Documentary History of North America to 1612*, 5 vols. (New York, 1979), 1:171.

4. Laurier Turgeon, "Pour redécouvrir notre 16e siècle: les pêches à Terre-Neuve d'après les archives notariales de Bordeaux," *Revue d'historie de l'Amérique française*, [hereafter *RHAF*], 39 (1986), 523–49 at 528; Monique Bois, "Tabellionage de Rouen: Meubles—1ère et 2ème séries: selection de documents concernant l'histoire du Canada," Public Archives of Canada, Manuscript Report (Sept. 1984), 7, 10.

5. René Bélanger, *Les Basques dan l'estuaire du Saint-Laurent, 1535–1635* (Montreal, 1971); Selma Barkham, "The Spanish Province of Terra Nova," *Canadian Archivist*, 2 (1974), 73–83; Barkham, "Guipuzcoan Shipping in 1571 with Particular Reference to the Decline of the Transatlantic Fishing Industry," in William A. Douglass, Richard W. Etulain, and William H. Jacobsen, Jr., eds., *Anglo-American Contributions to Basque Studies: Essays in Honor of Jon Bilbao* (Reno, 1977), 73–81; Barkham, "The Basques: filling a gap in our history between Jacques Cartier and Champlain," *Canadian Geographical Journal*, 96 (1978), 8–19; Barkham, "A Note on the Strait of Belle Isle during the Period of Basque Contact with Indians and Inuit," *Études/Inuit/Studies*, 4 (1980), 51–58; Barkham, "The Documentary Evidence for Basque Whaling Ships in the Strait of Belle Isle," in G. M. Story, ed., *Early European Settlement and Exploitation in Atlantic Canada: Selected Papers* (St. John's, Newf., 1982), 53–95; Barkham, "The Basque Whaling Establishments in Labrador, 1536–1632: A Summary," *Arctic*, 37 (1984), 515–19; "16th-Century Basque Whalers in America," *National Geographic*, 168 (July 1985), 40–71; Laurier Turgeon, "French Fishers, Fur Traders, and Amerindians during The Sixteenth Century: History and Archaeology," *William and Mary Quarterly*, 3rd Ser. 55:4 (Oct. 1998), 585–610; James A. Tuck and Robert Grenier, *Red Bay, Labrador: World Whaling Capital A. D. 1550–1600* (St. John's, Newf., 1989).

6. H. P. Biggar, ed., *A Collection of Documents Relating to Jacques Cartier and the Sieur de Roberval*, Publications of the Public Archives of Canada [hereafter PAC] 14 (Ottawa, 1930), 453–54, 462.

7. Turgeon, "Pour redécouvrir notre 16e siècle," *RHAF*, 39 (1986), 534–35, 537–39.

8. Quinn, *New American World*, 4:46, 60–61; Quinn, *England and the Discovery of America*, 316–21.

9. David B. Quinn, *North America from Earliest Discovery to First Settlements: The Norse Voyages to 1612* (New York, 1977).

10. Salvador de Madariaga, *Christopher Columbus* (London, 1949), 216–17, 288, 296, 310; Bartolomé de Las Casas, *History of the Indies,* ed. and trans. Andrée Collard (New York, 1971), 37, 56; Olive Patricia Dickason, *The Myth of the Savage and the Beginnings of French Colonialism in the Americas* (Edmonton, 1984), 205–6.

11. Quinn, *New American World,* 1:148–51.

12. Quinn, *New American World,* 1:273–75.

13. Quinn, *New American World,* 1:110, 157, 283.

14. David B. Quinn, *Sources for the Ethnography of Northeastern North America to 1611,* National Museum of Man, Mercury Series, Canadian Ethnology Service Paper 76 (Ottawa, 1981), 35; Quinn, "La Femme et l'enfant inuit de Nuremberg, 1566," *Recherches amérindiennes au Québec,* 11 (1981), 311–13.

15. Neal Cheshire, Tony Waldron, Alison Quinn, and David Quinn, "Frobisher's Eskimos in England," *Archivaria,* 10 (1980), 23–50; Quinn, *New American World,* 4:216–18.

16. H. P. Biggar, *The Voyages of Jacques Cartier,* Pubs. of the PAC, 11 (Ottawa, 1924), 66–67, 224–27; Quinn, *Sources,* 24–25; Dickason, *Myth of the Savage,* 210–11.

17. *The Journal of Christopher Columbus,* trans. Cecil Jane, ed. L. A. Vigneras (New York, 1960), 40; Biggar, *Voyages of Cartier,* 267; Quinn, *New American World,* 1:217–18, 2:195, 559–60.

18. Erik Wahlgren, *The Vikings and America* (London, 1986), chs. 7–9; Quinn, *North America,* 10–11, 14; John Witthoft, "Archaeology as a Key to the Colonial Fur Trade," *Minnesota History,* 40 (1966), 204–5; Denys, *Description of Acadia,* 445.

19. Quinn, *New American World,* 1:151. Quinn's translations of Damião de Góis in *New American World,* 1:152 ("they wound as if they were overlaid with steel") and *Sources,* 11 ("tipped with steel") seem to be contradictory.

20. Quinn, *New American World,* 1:287; Biggar, *Voyages of Cartier,* 49.

21. Quinn, *New American World,* 1:284, 285. It is somewhat difficult, though not impossible, to reconcile this kind of pragmatic behavior with the later Delaware legend of the first meeting with Dutch ships in the Hudson. According to John Heckewelder, the Moravian missionary to the Delawares in the eighteenth century, the surprised Indians took Hudson's ship for "a remarkably large house in which the Mannitto (the Great or Supreme Being) himself was present" and its captain, dressed in "a red coat all glittering with gold lace," for the selfsame Mannitto. Since the crew of Verrazzano's longboat and ship never disembarked at New York because of a sudden squall, the natives may have retained no strong memory of their arrival nearly a century before Hudson. Verrazzano did say that he arrived to "loud cries of wonderment" (Rev. John Heckewelder, *History, Manners, and Customs of the Indian Nations Who Once Inhabited Pennsylvania and the Neighbouring States,* ed. Rev. William C. Reichel [Philadelphia, 1876], 71–75).

22. James Axtell, *The Invasion Within: The Contest of Cultures in Colonial North America* (New York, 1985), ch. 1; George R. Hamell, "Trading in Metaphors: The Magic of Beads," in Charles F. Hayes III, ed., *Proceedings of the 1982 Glass Trade Bead Conference,* Rochester Museum & Science Center, Research Records 16 (Rochester, N.Y., 1983), 17–20.

23. Biggar, *Voyages of Cartier,* 42; Quinn, *New American World,* 4:209–10. Beothuks were to behave the same way toward the English colonists of Newfoundland early in the next century. See Gillian T. Cell, ed., *Newfoundland Discovered: English Attempts at Colonisation, 1610–1630,* Hakluyt Society Publications, 2d ser. 160 (London, 1982), 71, 76, 85–86; also Quinn, *New American World,* 4:153, 156, 163, and Ingebord Marshall, *A History and Ethnography of the Beothuk* (Montreal and Kingston, 1996), chs. 1–2.

24. Quinn, *New American World,* 1:287.

25. Quinn, *New American World,* 4:235, 240, 242; Biggar, *Voyages of Cartier,* 53, 56, 62, 143.

26. Quinn, *New American World,* 3:190, 4:29, 235; David B. Quinn and Alison M. Quinn, eds., *The English New England Voyages, 1602–1608,* Hakluyt Soc. Pubs., 2d ser. 161 (London, 1983), 157, 220.

27. Biggar, *Voyages of Cartier,* 53, 60–62, 64–67.

28. Biggar, *Voyages of Cartier,* 151–53, 162–66.

29. David Beers Quinn, ed., *The Voyages and Colonising Enterprises of Sir Humphrey Gilbert,* Hakluyt Soc. Pubs., 2d ser. 83–84 (London, 1940), 297 (continuous pagination).

30. Biggar, *Voyages of Cartier,* 187.

31. Quinn, *New American World,* 3:78–79.

32. James A. Tuck, *Onondaga Iroquois Prehistory* (Syracuse, 1971), 44, 70, 118, 135, 146; William A. Ritchie and Robert E. Funk, *Aboriginal Settlement Patterns in the Northeast,* New York State Museum and Science Service, Memoir 20 (Albany, 1973), 269, 290, 329.

33. Axtell, *The Invasion Within,* 30.

34. Robert Delort, "Les fourrures en France au XVIe et au début du XVIIe siècle," paper delivered at the 5th North American Fur Trade Conference, Montreal, May 31, 1985.

35. Quinn, *New American World,* 1:217–18, 3:142, 4:307.

36. Quinn, *Sources,* 28; Roger Schlesinger and Arthur P. Stabler, ed. and trans., *André Thevet's North America: A Sixteenth-Century View* (Kingston and Montreal, 1986), 11, 12, 13.

37. Marc Lescarbot, *The History of New France* [Paris, 1609], ed. and trans. W. L. Grant, intro. H. P. Biggar, 3 vols. (Toronto: Champlain Society, 1907–14), 3:7; Father Gabriel Sagard, *The Long Journey to the Country of the Hurons* [Paris, 1632], ed. George M. Wrong, trans. H. H. Langton (Toronto: Champlain Society, 1939), 222; Quinn, *New American World,* 4:46, 61. See also Cell, *Newfoundland Discovered,* 88; Denys, *Description of Acadia,* 384; and Reuben Gold Thwaites, ed., *The Jesuit Relations and Allied Documents,* 73 vols. (Cleveland, 1896–1901), 69:127 (hereafter cited as *JR*).

38. Biggar, *Cartier and Roberval,* 78; Quinn, *Voyages of Gilbert,* 464; Quinn, *New American World,* 3:78, 142, 214, 4:307.

39. Denys, *Description of Acadia,* 441; *JR* 6:297–99; Roger Williams, *A Key into the Language of America* (London, 1643), 166.

40. James Axtell, *The European and the Indian: Essays in the Ethnohistory of Colonial North America* (New York, 1981), 370 n.28.

41. *Journal of Columbus,* 24; Quinn, *New American World,* 1:285.

42. Biggar, *Voyages of Cartier,* 80–81, 243; Quinn, *New American World,* 2:366, 4:214, 248; Ralph Pastore, "Beothuk Acquisition and Use of European Goods," paper delivered at 1983 meeting of Canadian Archaeological Association, Halifax, N.S.; Pastore, "Fishermen, Furriers, and Beothuks: The Economy of Extinction," *Man in the Northeast,* 33 (Spring 1987), 47–62.

43. Quinn, *Sources,* 41; Quinn, *New American World,* 2:290 (scraper), 3:206, 4:29 (Morris bells); Jeffrey P. Brain, "Artifacts of the Adelantado," *Conference on Historic Site Archeology Papers* 8 (1975), 129–38; Hale G. Smith, *The European and the Indian: European-Indian Contacts in Georgia and Florida,* Florida Anthropological Society Publications 4 (Gainesville, 1956), 30–31, 38 (sleigh bells).

44. Quinn, *New American World,* 2:290; Smith, *European and Indian,* frontispiece, 32.

45. Quinn, *New American World,* 2:368, 482; Smith, *European and Indian,* 17, 23, 32, 35 (silver beads); Charles Pearson, "Evidence of Early Spanish Contact on the Georgia Coast," *Historical Archaeology,* 11 (1977), 74–83 (copper coins).

46. Quinn, *New American World,* 1:102, 162, 3:83; Biggar, *Voyages of Cartier,* 80–81. "Points" were the metal tips of laces; "dozens" were coarse wool kerseys (*OED*).

47. Quinn, *New American World,* 1:285; William Bradford, *Of Plymouth Plantation, 1620–1647,* ed. Samuel Eliot Morison (New York, 1952), 202, 220.

48. Quinn, *New American World,* 1:193–96, 218, 2:288–89, 334, 341, 345; Chester B. DePratter and Marvin T. Smith, "Sixteenth Century European Trade in the Southeastern United States: Evidence from the Juan Pardo Expeditions (1566–1568)," in Henry F. Dobyns, ed., *Spanish Colonial Frontier Research,* Spanish Borderlands Research 1 (Albuquerque: Center for Anthropological Studies, 1980), 71–72.

49. Carolyn Gilman, *Where Two Worlds Meet: The Great Lakes Fur Trade* (St. Paul: Minnesota Historical Society, 1982) illustrates the intersecting commercial journeys of a European axe and an Indian fur. See also Alexandra van Dongen et al., '*One Man's Trash Is Another Man's Treasure': The Metamorphosis of the European Utensil in the New World* (Rotterdam, 1995).

50. Quinn, *New American World,* 2:331 (tablets), 482 (card), 4:236 (paper), 250 (cards). The spoon handle is in the material assemblage from the Adams site, a Seneca village occupied c. 1555–1575 (Rochester Museum & Science Center, Rochester, N.Y.).

51. Quinn, *New American World,* 4:224.

52. Smith, *European and Indian,* 33, 37 (pipes); Quinn, *New American World,* 4:120, 5:123.

53. Biggar, *Voyages of Cartier,* 223; Quinn, *New American World,* 1:338.

54. Quinn, *New American World,* 2:306, 353; DePratter and Smith, "Sixteenth Century European Trade," in Dobyns, *Spanish Colonial Frontier Research,* 73.

55. Quinn, *North America,* ch. 9; Quinn, *New American World,* 2:97–188.

56. Sagard, *Long Journey to the Hurons,* 86–87; Bruce G. Trigger, *Natives and Newcomers: Canada's 'Heroic Age' Reconsidered* (Kingston and Montreal, 1985), 150.

57. James F. Pendergast, The Introduction of European Goods on the Atlantic Coast and the Iroquoian Protohistoric Era (MS, 1985); "The Significance of Some

Marine Shell Excavated on Iroquoian Archaeological Sites in Ontario," in Charles F. Hayes III, ed., *Proceedings of the 1986 Shell Bead Conference: Selected Papers,* Rochester Museum and Science Center, Research Records No. 20 (Rochester, N.Y., 1989). 97–112. Thanks to the author for both of these important reports.

58. Bruce J. Bourque and Ruth Holmes Whitehead, "Tarrentines and the Introduction of European Trade Goods in the Gulf of Maine," *Ethnohistory,* 32 (1985), 327–41; Quinn, *New American World,* 3:214; Quinn, *Voyages of Gilbert,* 464.

59. Quinn, *New American World,* 2:298 (French), 4:241 (Davis); Quinn, *Sources,* 41 (Florida); Quinn, *English New England Voyages,* 303.

60. Quinn, *New American World,* 1:285, 4:240, 246.

61. Quinn, *New American World,* 4:241; Biggar, *Voyages of Cartier,* 241–46.

62. Quinn, *New American World,* 1:207, 4:211, 220.

63. Quinn, *New American World,* 4:211, 214, 240, 243.

64. Quinn, *New American World,* 2:349, 4:62 (gun), 212, 307.

65. Christian F. Feest, "Powhatan: A Study in Political Organization," *Wiener Völkerkundliche Mitteilungen,* 13 (1966), 69–83; Helen C. Rountree and E. Randolph Turner III, "On The Fringe of the Southeast: The Powhatan Paramount Chiefdom in Virginia," in Charles Hudson and Carmen Chaves Tesser, eds., *The Forgotten Centuries: Indians and Europeans in the American South, 1521–1704* (Athens, Ga., 1994), 355–72; Elisabeth Tooker, "The League of the Iroquois: Its History, Politics, and Ritual," in William C. Sturtevent, gen. ed., *Handbook of North American Indians,* 15: *Northeast,* ed. Bruce G. Trigger (Washington, D.C.: Smithsonian Institution, 1978), 418–22; Trigger, *The Children of Aataentsic: A History of the Huron People to 1660,* 2 vols. (Montreal, 1976), 1:156–63.

Chapter Four

1. For the British phase of the revolution, see Neil McKendrick, John Brewer, and J. H. Plumb, eds., *The Birth of a Consumer Society: The Commercialization of Eighteenth-Century England* (Bloomington, Ind., 1982); Lorna Weatherill, *Consumer Behaviour and Material Culture in Britain, 1660–1760* (London, 1988); Joan Thirsk, *Economic Policy and Projects: The Development of a Consumer Society in Early Modern England* (Oxford, 1978); Eric Jones, "The Fashion Manipulators: Consumer Tastes and British Industries, 1660–1800," in Louis P. Cain and Paul J. Uselding, eds., *Business Enterprise and Economic Change: Essays in Honor of Harold F. Williamson* (Kent, Ohio, 1973), 198–226; Carole Shammas, *The Pre-industrial Consumer in England and America* (Oxford, 1990).

On the American side, see Shammas, *ibid.;* T. H. Breen, "An Empire of Goods: The Anglicization of Colonial America, 1690–1776," *Journal of British Studies,* 25 (Oct. 1986), 467–99; Breen, "'Baubles of Britain': The American and Consumer Revolutions of the Eighteenth Century," *Past and Present,* no. 119 (1988), 73–104; Breen, "The Meaning of Things: Interpreting the Consumer Economy in the Eighteenth Century" (William Andrews Clark Memorial Library Lectures: The Birth of Consumer Societies, 1988–89); Gloria L. Main and Jackson T. Main, "Economic Growth and the Standard of Living in Southern New England, 1640–1774," *Journal of Economic His-

tory, 48:1 (March 1988), 27–46; Lois Green Carr and Lorena S. Walsh, "The Standard of Living in the Colonial Chesapeake," *William and Mary Quarterly,* 3d ser. 45:1 (Jan. 1988), 135–59; Carr and Walsh, "Consumer Behavior in the Colonial Chesapeake," in Cary Carson, Ronald Hoffman, and Peter J. Albert, eds., *Of Consuming Interests: The Style of Life in the Eighteenth Century* (Charlottesville, 1992); Cary Carson, "The Consumer Revolution in Colonial British America: Why Demand?," *ibid.,* 483–697.

2. William Eddis, *Letters from America,* ed. Aubrey C. Land (Cambridge, Mass., 1969), 51–52.

3. Breen, "'Baubles of Britain'," 88, 90.

4. Allen W. Trelease, *Indian Affairs in Colonial New York: The Seventeenth Century* (Ithaca, N.Y., 1960), 131; José António Brandão, *"Your Fyre Shall Burn No More": Iroquois Policy Toward New France and Its Native Allies to 1701* (Lincoln, 1997), 86–88.

5. Marcel Trudel, *Histoire de la Nouvelle-France. II: Le comptoir, 1604–1627* (Montreal, 1966), 207; Bruce G. Trigger, *The Children of Aataentsic: A History of the Huron People to 1660,* 2 vols. (Montreal, 1976), 286, 336–37, 603–5 (continuous pagination); Conrad Heidenreich, *Huronia: A History and Geography of the Huron Indians, 1600–1650* (Toronto, 1971), 280.

6. William Bradford, *Of Plymouth Plantation, 1620–1647,* ed. Samuel Eliot Morison (New York, 1952), 286–89; Ruth A. McIntyre, *Debts Hopeful and Desperate: Financing the Plymouth Colony* (Plymouth, Mass.: Plimoth Plantation, 1963).

7. Verner W. Crane, *The Southern Frontier, 1670–1732* (Ann Arbor, 1956, 1929), 111, 330 (table 4); Joel W. Martin, "The Creek Indian Deerskin Trade, 1670–1805" (manuscript), table 1.

8. Gary C. Goodwin, *Cherokees in Transition: A Study of Changing Culture and Environment Prior to 1775,* U. of Chicago, Dept. of Geography, Research Paper No. 181 (Chicago, 1977), 98.

9. John Hardman, Liverpool merchant, 1749, quoted in E. E. Rich, "The Indian Traders," *The Beaver,* outfit 301 (Winter 1970), 5–20 at 18.

10. Joseph and Nesta Ewan, eds., *John Banister and His Natural History of Virginia, 1678–92* (Urbana, Ill., 1970), 42.

11. *The Essayes of Michael Lord of Montaigne,* trans. John Florio, 3 vols., Everyman ed. (London and Toronto, 1910), 1:170 ("Of cannibals").

12. Nicolas Denys, *The Description and Natural History of the Coasts of North America (Acadia),* ed. and trans. William F. Ganong (Toronto: The Champlain Society, 1908), 441.

13. Reuben Gold Thwaites, ed., *The Jesuit Relations and Allied Documents,* 73 vols. (Cleveland, 1896–1901), 6:297, 299.

14. Roger Williams, *A Key into the Language of America* (London, 1643), 163.

15. *Father Louis Hennepin's Description of Louisiana,* ed. and trans. Marion E. Cross (Minneapolis, 1938), 167.

16. Quoted in Albright G. Zimmerman, "European Trade Relations in the 17th and 18th Centuries," in Herbert C. Kraft, ed., *A Delaware Indian Symposium,* Pennsylvania Historical and Museum Commission, Anthropological Series No. 4 (Harrisburg, 1974), 57–70 at 66.

17. James Phinney Baxter, ed., *Documentary History of the State of Maine. III: The Trelawny Papers* (Portland, Me., 1884), 25–26, 29.

18. Marion Tinling, ed., *The Correspondence of the Three William Byrds of Westover, Virginia, 1684–1776*, Virginia Historical Society Documents 12–13 (Charlottesville, 1977), 29, 30, 57, 60, 64, 66.

19. Thomas Morton, *New English Canaan* (London, 1632), in Peter Force, comp., *Tracts and Other Papers, Relating Principally to the Origin, Settlement, and Progress of the Colonies in North America*, 4 vols. (Washington, D.C., 1836–47), vol. 2, no. 5, p. 40.

20. Governor Johan Rising, June 14, 1655, in Albert Cook Myers, ed., *Narratives of Early Pennsylvania, West New Jersey, and Delaware, 1630–1707*, Original Narratives of Early American History (New York, 1912), 157. See also Toby Morantz, "'So Evil a Practice': A Look at the Debt System in the James Bay Fur Trade," in Rosemary E. Ommer, ed., *Merchant Credit and Labour Strategies in Historical Perspective* (Fredericton, N.B., 1990), 203–22.

21. Robert C. Wheeler *et al.*, eds., *Voices from the Rapids: An Underwater Search for Fur Trade Artifacts, 1960–73*, Minnesota Historical Archaeological Series No. 3 (Minneapolis: Minnesota Historical Society, 1975).

22. See above, Chapter 3, esp. p. 85, and Axtell, *After Columbus: Essays in the Ethnohistory of Colonial North America* (New York, 1988), ch. 9, esp. p. 154.

23. Kenneth E. Kidd, "The Cloth Trade and the Indians of the Northeast during the Seventeenth and Eighteenth Centuries," Royal Ontario Museum, Division of Art and Archaeology, *Annual* (Toronto, 1961), 48–56; Louise Dechêne, *Habitants et marchands de Montréal au XVIIe siècle* (Paris, 1974), 507 (graphique 11); Peter A. Thomas, "Cultural Change on the Southern New England Frontier, 1630–1665," in William W. Fitzhugh, ed., *Cultures in Contact: The Impact of European Contacts on Native American Cultural Institutions, A.D. 1000–1800* (Washington, D.C., 1985), 146; Joel W. Martin, *Sacred Revolt: The Muskogees' Struggle for a New World* (Boston, 1991), 57–58; Dean L. Anderson, "The Flow of European Trade Goods into the Western Great Lakes Region, 1715–1760," in Jennifer S. H. Brown, W. J. Eccles, and Donald P. Heldman, eds., *The Fur Trade Revisited: Selected Papers of the Sixth North American Fur Trade Conference, Mackinac Island, Michigan, 1991* (East Lansing/Mackinac Island, 1994), 93–115; Linda Welters, Margaret T. Ordoñez, Kathryn Tarleton, and Joyce Smith, "European Textiles from Seventeenth-Century New England Cemeteries," in Lu Ann DeCunzo and Bernard L. Herman, eds., *Historical Archaeology and the Study of American Culture* (Winterthur, Del. and Knoxville, 1996), 193–232.

24. Axtell, *After Columbus*, 135.

25. *Peter Kalm's Travels in North America: The English Version of 1770*, ed. Adolph B. Benson, 2 vols. (New York, 1966), 520 (continuous pagination); William Wood, *New England's Prospect* [London, 1634], ed. Alden T. Vaughan (Amherst, Mass., 1977), 84; Stanley Pargellis, ed., "The Indians in Virginia . . . 1689," *William and Mary Quarterly*, 3d ser. 16 (1959), 230.

26. James Axtell, *The European and the Indian: Essays in the Ethnohistory of Colonial North America* (New York, 1981), 58.

27. Trigger, *Children of Aataentsic*, 358–59; Bruce G. Trigger, *Natives and Newcomers: Canada's "Heroic Age" Reconsidered* (Kingston and Montreal, 1985), 138, 204, 238;

Paul A. Robinson, Marc A. Kelley, and Patricia E. Rubertone, "Preliminary Biocultural Interpretations from a Seventeenth-Century Narragansett Indian Cemetery in Rhode Island," in Fitzhugh, *Cultures in Contact,* 119.

28. Axtell, *After Columbus,* ch. 9.

29. Brian J. Given, "The Iroquois Wars and Native Arms," in Bruce Alden Cox, ed., *Native People, Native Lands: Canadian Indians, Inuit and Métis,* Carleton Library Series No. 142 (Ottawa, 1988), 3–13; Axtell, *The European and the Indian,* 259–63; Thomas Abler, "European Technology and the Art of War in Iroquoia," in Diana Claire Tkaczak and Brian C. Vivian, eds., *Cultures in Conflict: Current Archaeological Perspectives,* Proceedings of the Twentieth Annual Conference of the Archaeological Association of the U. of Calgary (Calgary, 1989), 273–82.

30. James Sullivan *et al.,* eds., *The Papers of Sir William Johnson,* 14 vols. (Albany, N.Y., 1921–62), 12:952 (Johnson to Arthur Lee, March 28, 1772).

31. Cadwallader Colden, *The History of the Five Indian Nations of Canada* (London, 1747), 13–14.

32. Axtell, *The European and the Indian,* 257–59. There are only two sources for the much-cited connection between inebriation and the dream or vision quest, and neither provides direct evidence that the natives themselves took to alcohol as a short cut to visions: Edmund S. Carpenter, "Alcohol in the Iroquois Dream Quest," *American Journal of Psychiatry,* 116:8 (Aug. 1959), 148–51, and André Vachon, "L'eau-de-vie dans la société indienne," Canadian Historical Association, *Report* (1960), 23. R. C. Dailey, "The Role of Alcohol Among North American Indian Tribes as Reported in The Jesuit Relations," *Anthropologica,* 10 (1968), 48–50, Maia Conrad, "From Visions to Violence: Iroquoian Alcohol Use in the Seventeenth Century" (paper presented at the annual meeting of the American Society for Ethnohistory, Chicago, Nov. 5, 1989), and Peter C. Mancall, *Deadly Medicine: Indians and Alcohol in Early America* (Ithaca, 1995), 74–75 are more circumspect about the lack of direct evidence.

33. "[François Vachon de] Belmont's History of Brandy," ed. and trans. Joseph P. Donnelly, *Mid-America,* 34 (1952), 60.

34. Kalm, *Travels in North America,* 520–21.

35. Thwaites, *Jesuit Relations,* 44:283.

36. Nicholas Perrot, "Memoir on the Manners, Customs, and Religion of the Savages of North America," in Emma Helen Blair, ed. and trans., *The Indian Tribes of the Upper Mississippi Valley and Region of the Great Lakes,* 2 vols. (Cleveland, 1911), 1:142.

37. [James] *Adair's History of the American Indians* [London, 1775], ed. Samuel Cole Williams (New York, 1966), 245.

38. Ralph Davis, "English Foreign Trade, 1660–1700," *Economic History Review,* 2d ser. 7:2 (Dec. 1954), 150–66.

39. James W. Bradley, *Evolution of the Onondaga Iroquois: Accommodating Change, 1500–1655* (Syracuse, N.Y., 1987), 130; Charles F. Wray, "The Volume of Dutch Trade Goods Received by the Seneca Iroquois, 1600–1687 A.D.," *New Netherland Studies,* Bulletin KNOB, 84:2/3 (June 1985), 100–112.

40. Papers of Eleazar Wheelock, Dartmouth College Library, Hanover, N.H., catalogued in *A Guide to the Microfilm Edition of the Papers of Eleazar Wheelock* (Hanover,

N.H.: Dartmouth College Library, 1971), 766554 (Theophilus Chamberlain to Wheelock, Oct. 4, 1766), 768672 (Wheelock to Dartmouth, Dec. 22, 1768). See also *Travels of William Bartram* [Philadelphia, 1791], ed. Mark Van Doren (New York, 1955), 401: "As to the mechanic arts or manufactures, at present [the Indians of the Southeast] have scarcely any thing worth observation, since they are supplied with necessaries, conveniences, and even superfluities by the white traders."

41. William C. Sturtevant, "Two 1761 Wigwams at Niantic, Connecticut," *American Antiquity*, 40:4 (Oct. 1975), 437–44; Kathleen J. Bragdon, "The Material Culture of the Christian Indians of New England, 1650–1775," in Mary C. Beaudry, ed., *Documentary Archaeology and the New World* (Cambridge, 1988), 126–31; Daniel Mandell, "'To Live More Like My Christian English Neighbors': Indian Natick in the Eighteenth Century," *William and Mary Quarterly*, 3d ser. 48 (Oct. 1991), 552–79.

42. Carl Bridenbaugh, ed., *Gentleman's Progress: The Itinerarium of Dr. Alexander Hamilton, 1744* (Chapel Hill, 1948), 98.

43. John A. Sainsbury, "Indian Labor in Early Rhode Island," *New England Quarterly*, 48 (1975), 378–93.

44. Robert Beverley, *The History and Present State of Virginia* [London, 1705], ed. Louis B. Wright (Charlottesville, 1968), 233.

45. Albert Henry Smyth, ed., *The Writings of Benjamin Franklin* (New York, 1907), 10:97; John Phillip Reid, *A Better Kind of Hatchet: Law, Trade, and Diplomacy in the Cherokee Nation During the Early Years of European Contact* (University Park, Pa., 1976), 194–95.

46. Anthony F. C. Wallace, "Revitalization Movements: Some Theoretical Considerations for Their Comparative Study," *American Anthropologist*, 58 (1956), 264–81.

47. Richard L. Haan, "The 'Trade Do's Not Flourish as Formerly': The Ecological Origins of the Yamassee War of 1715," *Ethnohistory*, 28:4 (Fall 1981), 341–58.

48. Howard H. Peckham, *Pontiac and the Indian Uprising* (New York, 1970, 1947); Charles E. Hunter, "The Delaware Nativist Revival of the Mid-Eighteenth Century," *Ethnohistory*, 18:1 (Winter 1971), 39–49; Anthony F. C. Wallace, *The Death and Rebirth of the Seneca* (New York, 1969), 114–22; Alfred A. Cave, "The Delaware Prophet Neolin: A Reappraisal," *Ethnohistory* 46:2 (Spring 1999), 265–90. Gregory Evans Dowd, "The French King Wakes Up in Detroit: 'Pontiac's War' in Rumor and History," *Ethnohistory*, 37:3 (Summer 1990), 254–78 at 259–61, reminds us that Neolin, the major Delaware prophet, made a partial exception for the gift-giving French.

49. Peckham, *Pontiac and the Indian Uprising*, 101–2; Michael McConnell, *A Country Between: The Upper Ohio Valley and Its Peoples, 1724–1774* (Lincoln, 1992), ch. 9; Gregory Evans Dowd. *A Spirited Resistance: The North American Indian Struggle for Unity, 1745–1815* (Baltimore, 1992), chs. 1–2.

Chapter Five

1. Wilbur R. Jacobs, ed., *The Appalachian Indian Frontier: The Edmond Atkin Report and Plan of 1755* (Columbia, S.C., 1954; Lincoln, 1967), 3–4 (hereafter cited as *Atkin Report*).

2. *Atkin Report*, 38.

3. Dunbar Rowland, A. G. Sanders, and Patricia Kay Galloway, ed. and trans., *Mississippi Provincial Archives: French Dominion, 1701–1763*, 5 vols. (Jackson, Miss. and Baton Rouge, 1927–1984), 3:234, Bienville to Maurepas, August 26, 1734 (hereafter cited as *MPAFD*).

4. *Atkin Report*, 39.

5. [James Glen,] *A Description of South Carolina* (London, 1761), 59, 63, facsimile reprint in Chapman J. Milling, ed., *Colonial South Carolina: Two Contemporary Descriptions* (Columbia, S.C., 1951), 67, 71.

6. John W. Caughey, *McGillivray of the Creeks* (Norman, 1938), 65.

7. [Thomas] *Nairne's Muskhogean Journals: The 1708 Expedition to the Mississippi River*, ed. Alexander Moore (Jackson, Miss. 1988), 56, 75.

8. *Atkin Report*, 13, 39; Journal of the [South Carolina] Commons House of Assembly, March 24, 1736, quoted in John Phillip Reid, *A Better Kind of Hatchet: Law, Trade, and Diplomacy in the Cherokee Nation During the Early Years of European Contact* (University Park, Pa., 1976), 149; John Stuart, Report to the Lord Commissioners of Trade and Plantations, March 9, 1764, quoted in Kathryn E. Holland Braund, *Deerskins & Duffels: The Creek Indian Trade with Anglo-America, 1685–1815* (Lincoln, 1993), 26.

9. George Croghan, 1749, quoted in Gregory A. Waselkov, "French Colonial Trade in the Upper Creek Country," in John A. Walthall and Thomas E. Emerson, eds., *Calumet & Fleur-de-Lys: Archaeology of Indian and French Contact in the Midcontinent* (Washington, D.C. 1992), 35.

10. *MPAFD*, 3:670–71, Bienville to Maurepas, April 20, 1734.

11. Peter H. Wood, "The Changing Population of the Colonial South: An Overview by Race and Region, 1685–1790," in Wood, Gregory A. Waselkov, and M. Thomas Hatley, eds., *Powhatan's Mantle: Indians in the Colonial Southeast* (Lincoln, 1989), 35–103, esp. tables I (pp. 38–39) and 3 (p. 90).

12. *Ibid.*, 90, table 3. I have excluded Wood's figures for East Texas in each case because that region was not settled by Europeans early in the eighteenth century nor was it heavily involved in trade with the rest of the colonial Southeast.

13. Braund, *Deerskins & Duffels*, 88.

14. *Ibid.*, 68–69, 88–89.

15. Verner W. Crane, *The Southern Frontier, 1670–1732* (Ann Arbor, 1956 [1929]), ch. 8; Reid, *A Better Kind of Hatchet*, chs. 13–15.

16. Eirlys Mair Barker, "'Much Blood and Treasure': South Carolina's Indian Traders, 1670–1755" (Ph.D. diss., College of William and Mary, Dept. of History, 1993); Braund, *Deerskins & Duffels*, chs. 3, 5–6; Reid, *A Better Kind of Hatchet*, chs. 9, 12, 15.

17. [James] *Adair's History of the American Indians* [London, 1775], ed. Samuel Cole Williams (New York, 1966), 306, 394, 444; *Atkin Report*, 36; Bernard Romans, *A Concise Natural History of East and West Florida* [facsimile of 1775 edition] (Gainesville, 1962), 60.

18. *Atkin Report*, 12, 15, 17, 23, 25.

19. Reid, *A Better Kind of Hatchet,* 42–43, 143–44; Braund, *Deerskins & Duffels,* 191; William L. McDowell, Jr., ed., *Documents Relating to Indian Affairs, 1750–1765,* Colonial Records of South Carolina, Series 2, 2 vols. (Columbia, S.C. 1958–70), 2:355 (hereafter cited as *S.C. Indian Records*).

20. *Atkin Report,* 35; Braund, *Deerskins & Duffels,* 89, 191, 192; Reid, *A Better Kind of Hatchet,* 170–71. A shift in European preferences in the late 1760s temporarily encouraged the importation of undressed hides.

21. *S.C. Indian Records,* 2:41–42, 334.

22. Crane, *Southern Frontier,* ch. 7, p. 167 (quotation); Reid, *A Better Kind of Hatchet,* 52–54; *S.C. Indian Records,* 2:355.

23. *S.C. Indian Records,* 2:45.

24. Braund, *Deerskins & Duffels,* 54, 148, 150–51.

25. *Calendar of State Papers, Colonial Series, America and West Indies, Preserved in the Public Record Office,* vol. 28, ed. Cecil Headlam (London, 1928), 247–48, no. 540, Crawley to William Byrd, July 30, 1715; Braund, *Deerskins & Duffels,* 107, 192; [Dr. George Milligen-Johnston,] *A Short Description of the Province of South-Carolina* [1763] (London, 1770), 78, in Milling, ed., *Colonial South Carolina,* 188.

26. *S.C. Indian Records,* 1:283.

27. *Ibid.,* 2:267, 334; Braund, *Deerskins & Duffels,* 146, 152; Reid, *A Better Kind of Hatchet,* 137, 143, 191–92.

28. Paul Chrisler Phillips, *The Fur Trade,* 2 vols. (Norman, 1961), 1:361–76, 448–51, 464–83, 536–40, 569–73; Daniel H. Usner, Jr., "The Deerskin Trade in French Louisiana," *Proceedings of the Tenth Meeting of the French Colonial Historical Society, April 12–14, 1984,* ed. Philip P. Boucher (Lanham, Md., 1985), 75–93; N. M. Miller Surrey, *The Commerce of Louisiana During the French Regime, 1699–1763,* Columbia University Studies in the Social Sciences 167 (New York: 1916; 1968), ch. 19.

29. James M. Crawford, *The Mobilian Trade Language* (Knoxville; 1978); Emanuel J. Drechsel, *Mobilian Jargon: Linguistic and Sociohistorical Aspects of a Native American Pidgin,* Oxford Studies in Language Contact (Oxford, 1997); Ian W. Brown, "The Calumet Ceremony in the Southeast and Its Archaeological Manifestations," *American Antiquity,* 54 (1989), 311–31; *MPAFD,* 3:565–66, King to Bienville and Salmon, February 2, 1732.

30. *Atkin Report,* 9–10, 63. The cost to the crown of presents was not inconsiderable. In 1713, Indian presents had cost only 4,000 livres; by 1744, they had exploded to 73,617 livres (*MPAFD,* 2:147; Phillips, *The Fur Trade,* 1:473). See *MPAFD,* 5:228–30 for a list of presents ordered in 1758–59.

31. *Atkin Report,* 10–11, 29; *MPAFD,* 1:193, 2:249–50, 4:46, 159n.8; Gregory A. Waselkov, Brian M. Wood, and Joseph M. Herbert, *Colonization and Conquest: The 1980 Archaeological Excavations at Fort Toulouse and Fort Jackson, Alabama,* Auburn University Archaeological Monograph 4 (Montgomery, Ala., 1982), 93–99.

32. *Atkin Report,* 6, 12, 15, 17, 23, 25.

33. *Ibid.,* 12–13; *MPAFD,* 3:515.

34. Joseph and Nesta Ewan, *John Banister and His Natural History of Virginia, 1678–1692* (Urbana, 1970), 41–42; *Travels of William Bartram,* ed. Mark Van Doren (New York, 1955), 184, 401.

35. See above, Chapter 3, and Axtell, "At the Water's Edge: Trading in the Sixteenth Century," *After Columbus: Essays in the Ethnohistory of Colonial North America* (New York, 1988), ch. 9.

36. *MPAFD*, 5:228–32 (1758–59). In 1731, Choctaws suffering from disease blamed English traders for planting bad medicine made from sugar cane in the limbourg they traded to the Choctaws via the Chickasaws (*MPAFD*, 4:58–59, Régis du Roullet to Périer, February 21, 1731).

37. *S. C. Indian Records*, 2:423 (December 26, 1757).

38. Braund, *Deerskins & Duffels*, 123.

39. *Nairne's Muskhogean Journals*, 57.

40. Braund, *Deerskins & Duffels*, illus. 1, 6–7, 9–12 (following p. 108); *Von Reck's Voyage: Drawings and Journals of Philip Georg Friedrich von Reck*, ed. Kristian Hvidt (Savannah, 1980), 107, 111, 115, 118, 127, 129.

41. Braund, *Deerskins & Duffels*, illus. 1, 6–7, 9, 11; *Von Reck's Voyage*, 117, 119, 127.

42. *MPAFD*, 5:228–32; [William Gerard] *De Brahm's Report of the General Survey in the Southern District of North America* [1765–66], ed. Louis DeVorsey, Jr., Tricentennial Edition, No. 3 (Columbia, S.C., 1971), 107; *S.C. Indian Records*, 2:567–68, 576–79.

43. See above, Chapter 4, and Axtell, "The First Consumer Revolution," *Beyond 1492: Encounters in Colonial North America* (New York: Oxford University Press, 1992), ch. 5.

44. Dorothy Downs, "British Influences on Creek and Seminole Men's Clothing, 1733–1858," *Florida Anthropologist*, 33 (1980), 46–65; Braund, *Deerskins & Duffels*, 124–25.

45. Jeffrey P. Brain, *Tunica Treasure*, Papers of the Peabody Museum of Archaeology and Ethnology 71 (Cambridge, Mass., and Salem, Mass., 1979); Brain, *Tunica Archaeology*, Papers of the Peabody Mus. of Arch. and Ethnol. 78 (Cambridge, Mass.; 1988), 327. The Creeks around Fort Toulouse made traditional pottery and colono ware for the use of the French soldiers and settlers there (Waselkov, "French Colonial Trade in the Upper Creek Country," 44). On the Creek preference for their own pottery, see Carol Mason, "Eighteenth Century Culture Change Among the Lower Creeks," *Florida Anthropologist*, 16 (Sept. 1963), 65–80 at 69.

46. *MPAFD*, 1:349 (1737). See also *MPAFD*, 2:613; *De Brahm's Report*, 107, "Guns (very slight)."

47. *MPAFD*, 5:228–32.

48. *Atkin Report*, 11, 12, 52, 57–58 (quotation), 64. See also Newton D. Mereness, ed., *Travels in the American Colonies* (New York, 1961), 290 (De Beauchamps, 1746); *MPAFD*, 4:209.

49. Mereness, ed., *Travels in the American Colonies*, 250 (Antoine Bonnefoy, 1741–42); *MPAFD*, 5:232.

50. David H. Corkran, *The Cherokee Frontier: Conflict and Survival, 1740–62* (Norman, 1962), 69 (1756); *S.C. Indian Records*, 2:296; Braund, *Deerskins & Duffels*, 122, 190.

51. *MPAFD*, 5:229–31; *Jean-Bernard Bossu's Travels in the Interior of North America*,

1751–1762, ed. and trans. Seymour Feiler (Norman, 1962), 116; *Von Reck's Voyage*, 47–48.

52. *Adair's History*, 245; M. Le Page du Pratz, *The History of Louisiana* [Paris, 1758] (London, 1774), ed. Joseph G. Tregle, Jr., Louisiana Bicentennial Reprint Series (Baton Rouge, 1975), 305–306. On the psychological importance of mirrors, see Michelle Perrot, ed., *A History of Private Life. Vol. 4: From the Fires of Revolution to the Great War*, trans. Arthur Goldhammer (Cambridge, Mass., 1990), 460 (Alain Corbin); James W. Fernandez, "Reflections on Looking into Mirrors," *Semiotica*, 30:1–2 (1980), 27–39; Benjamin Goldberg, *The Mirror and Man* (Charlottesville, 1985).

53. John Lawson, *A New Voyage to Carolina* [London, 1709], ed. Hugh Talmage Lefler (Chapel Hill, 1967), 210, 212, 232; Braund, *Deerskins & Duffels*, 125–27, 146; John Brickell, *The Natural History of North-Carolina* [Dublin, 1737] (New York, 1969), 292–93; *De Brahm's Report*, 108; W. L. McDowell, ed., *Journals of the Commissioners of the Indian Trade, September 20, 1710–August 29, 1718*, Col. Recs. of S.C., Ser. 2 (Columbia; S.C., 1955), 104. On native prohibition efforts, see Peter C. Mancall, *Deadly Medicine: Indians and Alcohol in Early America* (Ithaca, 1995), ch. 5. Archaeologists have found liquor bottles on many Indian sites. See, for example, Brain, *Tunica Treasure*, 85–93; George I. Quimby, *The Bayou Goula Site, Iberville Parish, Louisiana*, Fieldiana: Anthropology, 47:2 (Chicago: Chicago Natural History Museum, 1957), 135–36; Vernon James Knight, Jr., *Tukabatchee: Archaeological Investigations at an Historic Creek Town, Elmore County, Alabama, 1984*, Report of Investigations 45, Office of Archaeological Research, Alabama State Museum of Natural History, University of Alabama (Tuscaloosa, 1985), 123, 126; Kurt C. Russ and Jefferson Chapman, *Archaeological Investigations at the Eighteenth Century Overhill Cherokee Town of Mialoquo (40MR3)*, Report of Investigations, No. 37, Dept. of Anthropology, University of Tennessee, and Tennessee Valley Authority Publications in Anthropology, No. 36 (Knoxville, 1983), 100, 102; Gerald F. Schroedl, ed., *Overhill Cherokee Archaeology at Chota-Tanasee*, Report of Investigations, No. 38, Dept. of Anthrop., U. of Tenn., and TVA Pubs. in Anthrop., No. 42 (Knoxville, 1986), 418–19.

54. Lawson, *New Voyage to Carolina*, 232–33; *Travels of William Bartram*, 214–15.

55. *Von Reck's Voyage*, 48–49; *Travels of William Bartram*, 399; Louis Le Clerc de Milford, *Memoir; or, A Cursory Glance at My Different Travels & My Sojourn in the Creek Nation*, ed. John Francis McDermott, trans. Geraldine de Courcy (Chicago, 1956), 152.

56. *Lieut. Henry Timberlake's Memoirs, 1756–1765*, ed. Samuel Cole Williams (Johnson City, Tenn., 1927), 90–91; *Adair's History*, 187; Braund, *Deerskins & Duffels*, 130; Alexander Longe, "A Small Postscript of the Ways and Manners of the Indians called Cherokees [1725]," ed. David H. Corkran, *Southern Indian Studies*, 21 (Oct. 1969), 3–49 at 26.

57. Brain, *Tunica Archaeology*, 327 (kettles); *De Brahm's Report*, 109 (tattoos); *Adair's History*, 7; Schroedl, *Chota-Tanasee*, 441, fig. 8.11.h, 444 (hair pluckers).

58. Brain, *Tunica Archaeology*, 192, fig. 156k, l; Knight, *Tukabatchee*, 134–35, pl. 5:5c; Schroedl, *Chota-Tanasee*, 441, fig. 8.11.a-b (kettles); Richebourg Gaillard McWilliams, ed. and trans., *Fleur de Lys and Calumet: Being the Pénicaut Narrative of French Adventure in Louisiana* (Baton Rouge, 1953), 99–100; Schroedl, *Chota Tanasee*, 443, fig. 8.12.d (gun barrels); Brain, *Tunica Treasure*, 186, 196 (skimmer); Schroedl,

Chota-Tanasee, 442 (gorget); Brain, *Tunica Archaeology,* 193, fig. 156w; Lawson, *New Voyage to Carolina,* 63; Robert S. Neitzel, *The Grand Village of the Natchez Revisited: Excavations at the Fatherland Site, Adams County, Mississippi, 1972,* Archaeological Report, No. 12, Miss. Dept. of Archives and History (Jackson, 1983), pl. xxix.f (bottle glass); Brain, *Tunica Archaeology,* 100, fig. 78l, m; Russ and Chapman, *Mialoquo,* 125 (gun flints); William W. Baden, *Tomotley: An Eighteenth Century Cherokee Village,* Report of Investigations, No. 36, Dept. of Anthrop., U. of Tenn., and TVA Pubs. in Anthrop., No. 35 (Knoxville, 1983), 185, fig. II.4.d, 196 (candleholder), 186, fig. II.5.f, 194; Schroedl, *Chota-Tanasee,* 425 (bale seals).

59. Charles Hudson, *The Southeastern Indians* (Knoxville, 1976), 327–36; James Axtell, "Last Rights: The Acculturation of Native Funerals in Colonial North America," *The European and the Indian: Essays in the Ethnohistory of Colonial North America* (New York, 1981), ch. 5.

60. *S.C. Indian Records,* 2:152 (July 31, 1756).

61. Braund, *Deerskins & Duffels,* 75, 192 (John Stuart, Creek treaty, 1767); *S.C. Indian Records,* 2:357.

62. Braund, *Deerskins & Duffels,* 72, 75–76; *Adair's History,* 138, 242; *De Brahm's Report,* 122; Robert D. Newman, "The Acceptance of European Domestic Animals by the 18th Century Cherokee," *Tennessee Anthropologist,* 4:1 (1979), 101–107.

63. *Adair's History,* 139–40, 241, 242; *S.C. Indian Records,* 2:264 (Dec. 8, 1756).

64. *Adair's History,* 139, 242; Braund, *Deerskins & Duffels,* 67, 76–77; Schroedl, *Chota-Tanasee,* 481; James Taylor Carson, "Horses and the Economy and Culture of the Choctaw Indians, 1690–1840," *Ethnohistory,* 42:3 (Summer 1995), 495–513.

65. *De Brahm's Report,* 110–11n.; [Mark] *Catesby's Birds of Colonial America* [London, 1731–43], ed. Alan Feduccia, Fred W. Morrison Series in Southern Studies (Chapel Hill, 1985), 147; Charles M. Hudson, Jr., "Why the Southeastern Indians Slaughtered Deer," in Shepard Krech III, ed., *Indians, Animals, and the Fur Trade: A Critique of KEEPERS OF THE GAME* (Athens, Ga., 1981), ch. 7.

66. George R. Milner, "Epidemic Disease in the Postcontact Southeast: A Reappraisal," *Mid-Continental Journal of Archaeology,* 5:1 (1980), 39–56; Ann F. Ramenofsky, *Vectors of Death: The Archaeology of European Contact* (Albuquerque, 1987); Peter H. Wood, "The Impact of Smallpox on the Native Population of the 18th Century South," *New York State Journal of Medicine,* 87 (Jan. 1987), 30–36; Calvin Martin, "Wildlife Diseases as a Factor in the Depopulation of the North American Indian," *Western Historical Quarterly,* 7:1 (Jan. 1976), 47–62.

67. Ian K. Steele, *Warpaths: Invasions of North America* (New York, 1994), chs. 2–3, 7–8; James Axtell, "Scalping: The Ethnohistory of a Moral Question," *The European and the Indian,* ch. 8; Almon Wheeler Lauber, *Indian Slavery in Colonial Times Within the Present Limits of the United States* (Williamstown, Mass., 1979 [1913]); William Robert Snell, "Indian Slavery in Colonial South Carolina, 1671–1795" (Ph.D. diss., University of Alabama, Dept. of History, 1972); *Nairne's Muskhogean Journals,* 38, 41 (war chiefs).

68. Jack D. Forbes, *Africans and Native Americans: The Language of Race and the Evolution of Red-Black Peoples* (2d ed., Urbana and Chicago, 1993); Alexander Spoehr, *Changing Kinship Systems: A Study in the Acculturation of the Creeks, Cherokee, and Choctaw,* Anthropological Series 33:4, Field Museum of Natural History (Chicago,

1947); Alan Gallay, "Indian-Black Relations on the Southern Colonial Frontier" (Paper presented at the annual meeting of the Organization of American Historians, Washington, D.C., March 1990); Kenneth Wiggins Porter, *The Negro on the American Frontier* (New York, 1971), 7–137, 154–81; Theda Perdue, *Slavery and the Evolution of Cherokee Society, 1540–1866* (Knoxville, 1979); Eirlys Barker, "Networking in the Colonial Southeast: Indian Traders and Carolina Customers" (Paper presented at the Colloquium on Indians of the Americas, College of William and Mary, February 1996); Braund, *Deerskins & Duffels,* 78, 83–85, 107–108.

69. Theda Perdue, *Cherokee Women: Gender and Culture Change, 1700–1835* (Lincoln, 1998); Raymond D. Fogelson, "On the 'Petticoat Government' of the Eighteenth-Century Cherokee," in David K. Jordan and Marc J. Swartz, eds., *Personality and the Cultural Construction of Society* (Tuscaloosa, 1990), 161–81; Kathryn E. Holland Braund, "Guardians of Tradition and Handmaidens to Change: Women's Roles in Creek Economic and Social Life during the Eighteenth Century," *American Indian Quarterly,* 14:3 (Summer 1990), 239–58; Thomas Hatley, "Cherokee Women Farmers Hold Their Ground," in Robert D. Mitchell, ed., *Appalachian Frontiers: Settlement, Society, and Development in the Preindustrial Era* (Lexington; Ky., 1991), 37–51, 289–93.

70. Braund, *Deerskins & Duffels,* ch. 7; *William Byrd's Histories of the Dividing Line Betwixt Virginia and North Carolina* [London, 1728], ed. William K. Boyd (New York, 1967), 116 (April 7, 1728); K. G. Davies, ed., *Documents of the American Revolution, 1770–1783,* 20 vols. (Dublin, 1972–79), 8:91 (April 14, 1774); *Travels of William Bartram,* 401.

71. A. S. Salley, indexer, *Records in the British Public Record Office Relating to South Carolina, 1663–[1710],* 5 vols. (Atlanta and Columbia, 1928–47), 1:116, 118 (March 7, 1680/81).

72. *S.C. Indian Records,* 1:453 (July 3, 1753).

73. Du Pratz, *History of Louisiana,* 44–45.

74. Quoted in Braund, *Deerskins & Duffels,* 26, 30.

75. Milling, ed., *Colonial South Carolina,* 185.

Chapter Six

1. See, for example, *Edits, ordonnances royaux, déclarations et arrêts du conseil d'état du roi concernant le Canada,* 3 vols. (Québec, 1854–56), 1:3, 5–6, 3:11; Merrill Jensen, ed., *American Colonial Documents to 1776,* in David C. Douglas, ed., *English Historical Documents,* 12 vols. (New York, 1955), 9:65, 82, 85, 93.

2. Charles Orr, ed., *History of the Pequot War* (Cleveland, 1897), 110–11; Mary Francis Farnham, ed., *The Farnham Papers, 1603–1688, Documentary History of the State of Maine, Collections of the Maine Historical Society,* 2d ser. 7 (1901), 8–9; Peter Force, ed., *Tracts and Other Papers Relating Principally to the Origin, Settlement, and Progress of the Colonies in North America,* 4 vols. (Washington, D. C., 1836–47), vol. 3, no. 1, p. 5; Samuel Purchas, *Hakluytus Posthumus or Purchas His Pilgrimes* [London, 1625], 20 vols. (Glasgow, 1903–5), 19:406–9; Julian P. Boyd and Robert J. Taylor, eds.,

The Susquehannah Company Papers, 11 vols. (Wilkes-Barre, Pa., and Ithaca, 1930–71), 1:255.

3. E. G. R. Taylor, ed., *The Original Writings and Correspondence of the Two Richard Hakluyts,* Hakluyt Society Publications, 2d ser. 76–77 (London, 1935), 76:164–65; see also 77:223, 339.

4. Richard Eburne, *A Plain Pathway to Plantations* [London, 1624], ed. Louis B. Wright (Ithaca, 1962), 55–56.

5. Robert Gray, *A Good Speed to Virginia* (London, 1609), fols. C1v-C2r. See also Reuben Gold Thwaites, ed., *The Jesuit Relations and Allied Documents,* 73 vols. (Cleveland, 1896–1901), 5:33, 6:229–31, 19:39 (hereafter cited as *JR*), and *Father Louis Hennepin's Description of Louisiana* [Paris, 1683], ed. Marion E. Cross (Minneapolis, 1938), 145.

6. *JR,* 9:91.

7. *New Englands First Fruits* [London, 1643], in Samuel Eliot Morison, *The Founding of Harvard College* (Cambridge, Mass., 1935), 421.

8. *Collections of the Massachusetts Historical Society,* 3d ser. 4 (1834), 90. See also Chrétien Le Clercq, *The First Establishment of the Faith in New France* [Paris, 1691], ed. and trans. John Gilmary Shea, 2 vols. (New York, 1881), 1:111, 141–42.

9. James Sullivan *et al.,* eds., *The Papers of Sir William Johnson,* 14 vols. (Albany, 1921–65), 7:506 (hereafter cited as *Johnson Papers*). See, for example, Le Clercq, *First Establishment of the Faith,* 1:110–11, 214, 222; *Colls. Mass. His. Soc.,* 3d ser. 4 (1834), 14–15; William Hubbard, *The Present State of New-England* (London, 1677), 86–87 (2d pag.); *Ecclesiastical Records, State of New York,* 6 vols. (Albany, 1901–5), 1:398; John R. Bartlett, ed., *Records of the Colony of Rhode Island and Providence Plantations, in New England,* 10 vols. (Providence, 1856–65), 1:297–98.

10. Jean Delanglez, *Frontenac and the Jesuits,* Institute of Jesuit History Publications (Chicago, 1939), 35–65; James Axtell, *The Invasion Within: The Contest of Cultures in Colonial North America* (New York, 1985). ch. 4.

11. William Crashaw, *A Sermon Preached in London before the right honorable the Lord La Warre . . . Febr. 21. 1609* (London, 1610), fols, D4r, K1v.

12. *Johnson Papers,* 5:511.

13. *A Letter from the Rev^d Mr. Sergeant of Stockbridge, to Dr. Colman of Boston* (Boston, 1743), 3, 5; *Collections of the Rhode Island Historical Society,* 4 (1838), 138; Jonathan Edwards to Joshua Paice, Feb. 24, 1752, Andover-Newton Edwards Collection, folder 1752b (transcript), Yale University Library, New Haven, Conn.

14. Le Clercq, *First Establishment of the Faith,* 1:214.

15. Taylor, *Writings of the Hakluyts,* 2:214; Hubbard, *Present State of New-England,* 86 (2d pag.); Farnham, ed., *Farnham Papers,* 24; Nathaniel B. Shurtleff and David Pulsifer, eds., *Records of the Colony of New Plymouth, in New England,* 12 vols. (Boston, 1855–61), 10:285–86, 368; Gray, *Good Speed to Virginia,* fols. C2v, C4r-v; Clayton Colman Hall, ed., *Narratives of Early Maryland, 1633–1684,* Original Narratives of Early American History (New York, 1910), 20, 84, 90; George Washington to Richard Henry Lee, Feb. 8, 1785, American Philosophical Society, Philadelphia, Pa.

16. *A Letter from the Rev^d Mr. Sergeant*, 3; Eleazar Wheelock, *A Continuation of the Narrative of the Indian Charity-School in Lebanon, in Connecticut, From . . . 1768, to . . . 1771* (Hartford, 1771), 20.

17. [George Peckham], *A True Reporte of the late discoveries . . . of the New-found Landes* (London, 1583), fol. F3r; Gray, *Good Speed to Virginia*, fol. D2r.

18. Adriaen Van der Donck, *A Description of the New Netherlands* [Amsterdam, 1655], ed. Thomas F. O'Donnell (Syracuse, N.Y., 1968), 100.

19. *New England Historical and Genealogical Register*, 36 (1882), 296; *Colls. Mass. His. Soc.*, 3d ser. 4 (1834), 126, 137.

20. *Ibid.*, 269.

21. John Josselyn, *An Account of Two Voyages to New-England Made during the years 1638, 1663* [London, 1674] (Boston, 1865), 99.

22. Roger Williams, *A Key into the Language of America* (London, 1643), 46–48; *Colls. Mass. His. Soc.*, 1st ser. 1 (1792), 132; Van der Donck, *New Netherlands*, 81–82.

23. Josselyn, *Account of Two Voyages*, 99; Williams, *Key into the Language of America*, 47.

24. Thomas Morton, *New English Canaan* [Amsterdam, 1637], in Force, *Tracts*, vol. 2, no. 5, p. 20.

25. [Edward] *Johnson's Wonder-Working Providence, 1628–1651*, ed. J. Franklin Jameson, Orig. Narrs. of Early Amer. Hist. (New York, 1910), 162.

26. *Colls. Mass. His. Soc.*, 3d ser. 4 (1834), 50.

27. *Oxford English Dictionary*, s.v. "labour" and "toil."

28. *A Journal of the Pilgrims at Plymouth: Mourt's Relation* [London, 1622], ed. Dwight B. Heath (New York, 1963), 91–92.

29. *Colls. Mass. His. Soc.*, 1st ser. 4 (1795), 63, 71, 73.

30. Hugh Jones, *The Present State of Virginia* [London, 1724], ed. Richard L. Morton (Chapel Hill, 1956), 62.

31. J. Hector St. John de Crèvecoeur, *Letters from an American Farmer* [London, 1782] (London: Everyman's Library, 1912), 215.

32. Force, *Tracts*, vol. 1, no. 12, p. 13.

33. Lyon Gardiner Tyler, ed., *Narratives of Early Virginia, 1606–1625*, Orig. Narrs. of Early Amer. Hist. (New York, 1907), 101; J. Franklin Jameson, ed. *Narratives of New Netherland, 1609–1664*, Orig. Narrs. of Early Amer. Hist. (New York, 1909), 107.

34. *Diary of David McClure . . . 1748–1820*, ed. Franklin B. Dexter (New York, 1899), 68; William Wood, *New Englands Prospect* (London, 1634), 10.

35. Thomas Harriot, *A briefe and true report of the new found land of Virginia* [1588], in David B. Quinn and Alison M. Quinn, eds., *Virginia Voyages from Hakluyt* (London, 1973), 56.

36. *Winthrop Papers* (Boston: Massachusetts Historical Society, 1929–   ), 2:120.

37. Wood, *New Englands Prospect*, 87.

38. Gavin Cochrane, Treatise on the Indians of North America Written in the Year 1764, Ayer MS NA 176, ch. 7, Newberry Library, Chicago, Ill.

39. Samuel Stanhope Smith, *An Essay on the Causes of the Variety of Complexion and Figure in the Human Species* [New Brunswick, N.J., 1810], ed. Winthrop D. Jordan (Cambridge, Mass., 1965), 240.

40. Robert Beverley, *The History and Present State of Virginia* [London, 1705], ed. Louis B. Wright (Chapel Hill, 1947), 233.

41. *The American Magazine and Monthly Chronicle for the British Colonies* (Philadelphia: William Bradford), 1:2 (Nov. 1757), 83.

42. Albert C. Myers, ed., *Narratives of Early Pennsylvania, West New Jersey, and Delaware, 1630–1707,* Orig. Narrs. of Early Amer. Hist. (New York, 1912), 233.

43. Tyler, ed., *Narratives of Early Virginia,* 103.

44. *William Byrd's Histories of the Dividing Line betwixt Virginia and North Carolina,* ed. William K. Boyd (New York, 1967), 116 (my emphasis).

45. Rev. John Heckewelder, *History, Manners, and Customs of the Indian Nations Who Once Inhabited Pennsylvania and the Neighbouring States* [Philadelphia, 1818], rev. ed. Rev. William C. Reichel (Philadelphia, 1876), 141; John Lawson, *A New Voyage to Carolina* [London, 1709], ed. Hugh Talmage Lefler (Chapel Hill, 1967), 204; *Colls. Mass. His. Soc.,* 1st ser. 10 (1809), 108.

46. Beverley, *History of Virginia,* 166.

47. *Colls. Mass. His. Soc.,* 3d ser. 4 (1834), 40.

48. Edward Winslow, *Good Newes from New England* [London, 1624], in Alexander Young, ed., *Chronicles of the Pilgrim Fathers of Plymouth from 1602 to 1625* (2d ed., Boston, 1844), 364. See also Patricia Galloway, "Where Have All the Menstrual Huts Gone? The Invisibility of Menstrual Seclusion in the Late Prehistoric Southeast," in Cheryl Claassen and Rosemary A. Joyce, eds., *Women in Prehistory: North America and Mesoamerica* (Philadelphia, 1997), 47–62.

49. Wood, *New Englands Prospect,* 73.

50. George Alsop, *A Character of the Province of Mary-land* (London, 1666), 72; [James] *Adair's History of the American Indians* [London, 1775], ed. Samuel Cole Williams (Kingsport, Tenn., 1930), 8–9; Bernard Romans, *A Concise Natural History of East and West Florida,* 2 vols. (New York, 1775), 1:42.

51. Wood, *New Englands Prospect,* 72.

52. *Ibid.,* 73.

53. James Axtell, *The School upon a Hill: Education and Society in Colonial New England* (New Haven, 1974), 160–65.

54. Robert G. Pope, ed., *The Notebook of the Reverend John Fiske, 1644–1675,* Publications of the Colonial Society of Massachusetts, 47 (1974), 133; *Proceedings of the Massachusetts Historical Society,* 2d ser. 29 (1895), 99.

55. *Colls. Mass. His. Soc.,* 3d ser. 4 (1834), 50, 109, 142, 178, 208.

56. *Ibid.,* 40, 50; John Eliot, *A Brief Narrative of the Progress of the Gospel amongst the Indians in New England* (London, 1671), 8. See also *JR,* 5:177; 12:61.

57. *Winthrop Papers,* 1:158–59; *Pubs. Col. Soc. of Mass.,* 29 (1933), 147–48. See also *Word from New France: The Selected Letters of Marie de L'Incarnation,* ed. and trans. Joyce Marshall (Toronto, 1967), 77, 84.

58. *Hennepin's Description of Louisiana*, 180.

59. *JR*, 12:169. I have translated *"sauvage"* not as "savage," which has a pejorative ring to modern ears, but as "Indian," which more nearly approximates the neutral descriptive quality of the original. See also *JR*, 3:143, 6:83, 147.

60. *JR*, 14:215.

61. *JR*, 25:113.

62. *JR*, 6:243.

63. *JR*, 12:61.

64. *JR*, 18:101–7, 22:83–85; *Word from New France*, 105–6. See James P. Ronda, "The Sillery Experiment: A Jesuit-Indian Village in New France, 1637–1663," *American Indian Culture and Research Journal*, 3:1 (1979), 1–18. Later Indian *reserves* often protected their members from French justice: see Jan Grabowski, "French Criminal Justice and Indians in Montreal, 1670–1760," *Ethnohistory*, 43:3 (Summer 1996), 405–29.

65. *JR*, 12:61.

66. Alden T. Vaughan, *New England Frontier: Puritans and Indians, 1620–1675* (Boston, 1965), 346–47.

67. *Colls. Mass. His. Soc.*, 3d ser. 4 (1834), 227.

68. Cochrane, Treatise on Indians, Ayer MS NA 176, ch. 7.

69. Delanglez, *Frontenac and the Jesuits*, 35–40; Lucien Campeau, *Les commencements du Collège de Québec (1626–1670)*, Cahiers d'Histoire des Jésuites, 1 (Montreal, 1972), 51–76; Axtell, *The Invasion Within*, 55–57, 68–69.

70. *JR*, 12:63.

71. *An Essay towards Propagating the Gospel among the Neighbouring Nations of Indians in North America* (New London, Conn., 1756), 16; R. A. Brock, ed., *The Official Letters of Alexander Spotswood, Lieutenant-Governor of the Colony of Virginia, 1710–1722, Collections of the Virginia Historical Society*, n.s. 1–2 (1882–85), 1:121–22, 124, 134, 174; *Word from New France*, 223, 233; *JR*, 6:155.

72. *JR*, 5:197, 221, 35:251; Papers of Eleazar Wheelock, MS 762667.2, Dartmouth College Library, Hanover, N.H.

73. James Dow McCallum, ed., *The Letters of Eleazar Wheelock's Indians* (Hanover, N.H., 1932), 287–88. On Indian schools throughout the colonial period, see Axtell, *The Invasion Within*, ch. 8, and Margaret Connell Szasz, *Indian Education in the American Colonies, 1607–1783* (Albuquerque, 1988).

74. Susan M. Kingsbury, ed., *Records of the Virginia Company of London*, 4 vols. (Washington, D.C., 1906–35), 3:557.

75. Thomas Lechford, *Plain Dealing: or, Newes from New-England* [London, 1642], in *Colls. Mass. His. Soc.*, 3d ser. 3 (1833), 80.

76. *JR*, 12:117–25, 33:143–47; Axtell, *The Invasion Within*, 71, 77, 80, 279.

77. *JR*, 23:207–9.

78. *JR*, 53:203–5.

79. See, for example, John Halkett, *Historical Notes Respecting the Indians of North America* (London, 1825), 214, 218–19, 231–32, 256–57, 295; Alexis de Tocqueville,

Democracy in America [Paris, 1835], trans. Henry Reeve and Francis Bowen, ed. Phillips Bradley, 2 vols. (New York, 1945), 1:336–55; [Jeremy Belknap], "Has the Discovery of America Been Useful or Hurtful to Mankind?," *The Boston Magazine* (May 1784), 281–85, esp. 283.

80. Cotton Mather, *The Way to Prosperity* (Boston, 1690), 27.

81. The following paragraphs are based on a large number of primary sources, such as the *Jesuit Relations* and the Eliot tracts. The following secondary works are also pertinent: Anthony F. C. Wallace, *Religion: An Anthropological View* (New York, 1966); Hartley Burr Alexander, *The World's Rim: Great Mysteries of the North American Indians* (Lincoln, 1953); Ruth M. Underhill, *Red Man's Religion: Beliefs and Practices of the Indians North of Mexico* (Chicago, 1965); Ruth Benedict, *The Concept of the Guardian Spirit in North America,* Memoirs of the American Anthropological Association, 29 (Menasha, Wis., 1923); Åke Hultkrantz, *The Religions of the American Indians,* trans. Monica Setterwall (Berkeley, 1979); Werner Müller, "North America," in Walter Krickeberg et al., *Pre-Columbian American Religions,* trans. Stanley Davis (London, 1968), 147–229; Elisabeth Tooker. ed., *Native North American Spirituality of the Eastern Woodlands* (New York, 1979).

82. Wallace, *Religion,* 107.

83. A.F.C. Wallace, *The Death and Rebirth of the Seneca* (New York, 1970), 59–75.

84. See Axtell, *The European and the Indian: Essays in the Ethnohistory of Colonial North America* (New York, 1981), ch. 5.

85. *David Zeisberger's History of the Northern American Indians,* ed. Archer Butler Hulbert and William Nathaniel Schwarze (Columbus: Ohio State Archaeological and Historical Society, 1910), 132–33.

86. John Smith, *Works, 1608–1631,* ed. Edward Arber (Birmingham, Eng., 1884), 564.

87. *JR,* 67:147.

88. *JR,* 20:71; Axtell, *The Invasion Within,* 81–83.

89. *JR,* 10:63, 18:125.

90. *JR,* 3:149, 15:125, 18:125, 23:165, 25:247.

91. For some of the obstacles that the French missionaries had to run, see Alfred G. Bailey, *The Conflict of European and Eastern Algonkian Cultures, 1504–1700* (2d ed., Toronto, 1969), ch. 11; Kennedy, *Jesuit and Savage in New France,* chs. 6–9; Axtell, *The Invasion Within,* chs. 4–6.

92. *JR,* 3:123.

93. *Hennepin's Description of Louisiana,* 178.

94. William M. Beauchamp, ed., *Moravian Journals Relating to Central New York, 1745–66* (Syracuse, N.Y.: Onondaga Historical Association, 1916), 7.

95. Pierre de Charlevoix, *History and General Description of New France* [Paris, 1744], ed. and trans. John Gilmary Shea, 6 vols. (New York, 1870), 2:77; *Hennepin's Description of Louisiana,* 26–27.

96. Albert H. Smyth, ed., *The Writings of Benjamin Franklin,* 10 vols. (New York, 1905–7), 10:100; *JR,* 52:203.

97. Charlevoix, *History of New France,* 2:77–78.

98. *JR,* 1:275.

99. Baron de Lahontan, *New Voyages to North-America* [The Hague, 1703], ed. Reuben Gold Thwaites, 2 vols. (Chicago, 1905), 2:570.

100. Le Clercq, *First Establishment of the Faith,* 1:221–22.

101. James Axtell, "The European Failure to Convert the Indians: An Autopsy," *Papers of the Sixth Algonquian Conference, 1974,* ed. William Cowan, National Museum of Man, Mercury Series, Canadian Ethnology Service, Paper No. 23 (Ottawa, 1975), 274–90, and Axtell, *The Invasion Within,* chs. 10–11.

102. Leonard W. Labaree *et al.,* eds., *The Papers of Benjamin Franklin* (New Haven, 1959–), 4:482–83. No Iroquois children ever attended William and Mary, nor would they have been likely to. There were equally risky schools much closer to New York. See Axtell, *The Invasion Within,* 196–204, on the Stockbridge school and below, Chapter 7, for Eleazar Wheelock's schools in Lebanon, Connecticut, and Hanover, New Hampshire.

103. For the striking contrast between the educational methods of the Indians and the English, see below, Chapters 7 and 8.

104. Frederick L. Weis, "The New England Company of 1649 and Its Missionary Enterprises," *Pubs. Col. Soc. Mass.,* 38 (1947–51), 150.

105. See, for example, John Wolfe Lydekker, *The Faithful Mohawks* (New York, 1938); Elma E. Gray and Leslie Robb Gray, *Wilderness Christians: The Moravian Mission to the Delaware Indians* (Ithaca, 1956); Marion J. Mochon, "Stockbridge-Munsee Cultural Adaptations: 'Assimilated Indians'," *Proceedings of the American Philosophical Society,* 112 (1968), 182–219; Axtell, "Were Indian Conversions *Bona Fide?*" in *After Columbus: Essays in the Ethnohistory of Colonial North America* (New York, 1988), ch. 7.

106. See above, Chapter 1, p. 20.

107. James P. Ronda, "'We Are Well As We Are': An Indian Critique of Seventeenth-Century Christian Missions," *William and Mary Quarterly,* 3d ser. 34 (1977), 66–82.

108. Charles E. Hunter, "The Delaware Nativist Revival of the Mid-Eighteenth Century," *Ethnohistory,* 18 (1971), 39–49; Wallace, *Death and Rebirth of the Seneca,* pt. 3; Alfred A. Cave, "The Delaware Prophet Neolin: A Reappraisal," *Ethnohistory,* 46:2 (Spring 1999), 265–89; Gregory Evans Dowd, *A Spirited Resistance: The North American Indian Struggle for Unity, 1745–1815* (Baltimore, 1992).

109. Tyler, ed., *Narratives of Early Virginia,* 108.

Chapter Seven

1. A convenient copy of the charter may be found in Jere R. Daniell, "Eleazar Wheelock and the Dartmouth College Charter," *Historical New Hampshire,* 24:4 (Winter 1969), 3–44, and in Frederick Chase, *A History of Dartmouth College and the Town of Hanover, New Hampshire (to 1815),* ed. John K. Lord (2d ed., Brattleboro, Vt., 1928), Appendix A.

2. Harry J. Carman, Harold C. Syrett, and Bernard W. Wishy, *A History of the American People,* 2 vols. (3d ed., New York, 1967), 1:104; Richard B. Morris, William

Greenleaf, and Robert H. Ferrell, *America: A History of the People* (Chicago, 1971), 90; Charles Sellers and Henry May, *A Synopsis of American History* (Chicago, 1963), 41; David Hawke, *The Colonial Experience* (Indianapolis, 1966), 443; Edwin Scott Gaustad, *The Great Awakening in New England* (New York, 1957), 105, 108; Alan Heimert and Perry Miller, eds., *The Great Awakening* (Indianapolis, 1967), lvi; Richard L. Bushman, ed., *The Great Awakening* (New York, 1970), 20–21.

3. E. B. O'Callaghan, ed., *The Documentary History of the State of New-York*, 4 vols. (quarto ed., Albany, 1849–51), 4:223.

4. Gaustad, *Great Awakening in New England*, 74–75; James Dow McCallum, *Eleazar Wheelock, Founder of Dartmouth College* (Hanover, N.H., 1939), ch. 2.

5. Harold Blodgett, *Samson Occom* (Hanover, N.H., 1935), chs. 1–3.

6. O'Callaghan, ed., *Doc. His. of N.Y.*, 4:202.

7. WP 760628. WP stands for Papers of Eleazar Wheelock [1728–1779], Dartmouth College Library, Hanover, N.H., and is followed by the calendar number as given in *A Guide to the Microfilm Edition of The Papers of Eleazar Wheelock* (Hanover, N.H.: Dartmouth College Library, 1971). The first three digits indicate the year of the manuscript: e.g., 760628 is 1760.

8. Eleazar Wheelock, *A Continuation of the Narrative of the State, &, of the Indian Charity-School, at Lebanon, in Connecticut; From Nov. 27th, 1762, to Sept. 3d, 1765* (Boston, 1765), 22.

9. Eleazar Wheelock, *A plain and faithful Narrative of the Original Design, Rise, Progress, and Present State of the Indian Charity-School At Lebanon, in Connecticut* (Boston, 1763), 40.

10. WP 762113.

11. WP 761625.1.

12. WP 761602.3.

13. Wheelock, *A plain and faithful Narrative*, 42.

14. WP 761625.1, 762113.

15. WP 761664.3.

16. WP 761404.

17. Eric P. Kelly, "The Dartmouth Indians," *Dartmouth Alumni Magazine* (Dec. 1929), 122–25.

18. Eleazar Wheelock, *A Continuation of the Narrative* . . . (Hartford, 1771), 19–20.

19. Wheelock, *A plain and faithful Narrative*, 28–29.

20. WP 762165.

21. WP 772174.1.

22. Mary Frances Farnham, ed., *The Farnham Papers 1603–1688, Documentary History of the State of Maine, Collections of the Maine Historical Society*, 2d ser. 7 (1901), 21; Edmund S. Morgan, ed., *The Founding of Massachusetts: Historians and the Sources* (Indianapolis, 1964), 453.

23. Morgan, ed., *Founding of Massachusetts*, 320.

24. *Colls. Maine His. Soc.*, 2d ser. 7 (1901), 24; Morgan, ed., *Founding of Massachusetts*, 320.

25. See above, Chapter 6, pp. 144–58.

26. James Sullivan *et al.*, eds., *The Papers of Sir William Johnson,* 14 vols. (Albany, 1921–65), 7:506.

27. WP 762521.1, 764560.1.

28. WP 766504.4.

29. Wheelock, *Continuation of the Narrative* (1771), 22; Eleazar Wheelock, *A Continuation of the Narrative* . . . ([Portsmouth,] N.H., 1773), 13.

30. WP 758618.

31. Eleazar Wheelock, *A Brief Narrative of the Indian Charity-School, in Lebanon in Connecticut, New England* . . . (London, 1766), 9, 21.

32. Wheelock, *Continuation of the Narrative* (1773), 12–13.

33. Wheelock, *A plain and faithful Narrative,* 25.

34. Eleazar Wheelock, *A Continuation of the Narrative* . . . (Hartford, 1775), 11.

35. Wheelock, *A plain and faithful Narrative,* 15. See Margaret Connell Szasz, "Poor Richard Meets the Native American: Schooling for Young Indian Women in Eighteenth-Century Connecticut," *Pacific Historical Review,* 49 (May 1980), 215–35.

36. WP 767427.1; Wheelock, *A plain and faithful Narrative,* 40.

37. Wheelock, *A plain and faithful Narrative,* 44; WP 762667.2.

38. WP 762667.2.

39. James Dow McCallum, ed., *The Letters of Eleazar Wheelock's Indians* (Hanover, N.H., 1932), 287–88.

40. Wheelock, *Continuation of the Narrative* (1771), 5.

41. WP 774657.

42. McCallum, ed., *Letters of Wheelock's Indians,* 231.

43. *Ibid.,* 287.

44. *Ibid.,* 221.

45. *Ibid.,* 65.

46. Wheelock, *Brief Narrative,* 6.

47. WP 756615.

48. WP 764268.1.

49. WP 765164.1.

50. WP 770367.

51. WP 758422.

52. WP 763581.

53. WP 767604.1.

54. WP 763666.2.

55. McCallum, ed., *Letters of Wheelock's Indians,* 255; WP 763666.2.

56. WP 763659, 763666.2.

57. WP 767265.2.

58. WP 767163.

59. WP 762516, 761304.1; Eleazar Wheelock, *A Continuation of the Narrative . . .* (London, 1769), 16.

60. McCallum, ed., *Letters of Wheelock's Indians,* 131, 141, 148, 183. See also Laura J. Murray, ed., *To Do Good to My Indian Brethren: The Writings of Joseph Johnson, 1751–1776* (Amherst, Mass., 1998) and Murray, "'Pray Sir, Consider a Little': Rituals of Subordination and Strategies of Resistance in the Letters of Hezekiah Calvin and David Fowler to Eleazar Wheelock," in Helen Jaskoski, ed., *Early Native American Writing: New Critical Essays* (Cambridge, 1996), 15–41.

61. WP 769209.2.

62. WP 760566.

63. WP 762412.1.

64. WP 769255; Wheelock, *Continuation of the Narrative* (1771), 16.

65. WP 769255, 769274.2.

66. Wheelock, *Continuation of the Narrative* (1775), 11; Gordon M. Day, "Dartmouth and Saint Francis," *Dartmouth Alumni Magazine* (Nov. 1959), 28–30.

67. Wheelock, *Continuation of the Narrative* (1775), 14.

68. WP 764574.

69. Leon Burr Richardson, ed., *An Indian Preacher in England* (Hanover, N.H., 1933); Blodgett, *Samson Occom,* ch. 6.

70. WP 761129.1, 763204, 763407.2.

71. WP 769663.2. See also Daniell, "Eleazar Wheelock and the Dartmouth College Charter," 29.

72. Kelly, "The Dartmouth Indians," 122–25; Leon B. Richardson, "The Dartmouth Indians, 1800–1893," *Dartmouth Alumni Magazine* (June 1930), 524–27.

73. Blodgett, *Samson Occom,* 122–23, 135. See also Dana D. Nelson, "'(I Speak Like a Fool But I am Constrained)': Samson Occom's *Short Narrative* and Economies of the Racial Self," in Jaskoski, ed., *Early Native American Writing,* 42–65.

Chapter Eight

1. See, for example, Samuel Purchas, *Hakluytus Posthumus or Purchas His Pilgrimes* [London, 1625], 20 vols. (Glasgow, 1905–6), 19:406–9, and Merrill Jensen, ed., *American Colonial Documents to 1776,* in David C. Douglas, ed., *English Historical Documents,* 12 vols. (New York, 1955), 9:65, 82, 85, 93.

2. Robert Gray, *A Good Speed to Virginia* (London, 1609), sigs. [C1v]-C2r. See also Michael Wigglesworth, *God's Controversy with New-England* [1662], Massachusetts Historical Society, *Proceedings,* 12 (1873), II. 57–68, 169; H. H. Brackenridge in Archibald Loudon, ed., *A Selection, of Some of the Most Interesting Narratives, of Outrages, Committed by the Indians, in Their Wars, with the White People,* 2 vols. (Carlisle, Pa., 1808–11), 1:v; and [William Smith, D.D.], *Historical Account of Colonel Bouquet's Expedition Against the Ohio Indians, in 1764* [Philadelphia, 1765] (Cincinnati, 1868), 77–78 (hereafter cited as *Bouquet's Expedition*).

3. Cotton Mather, *India Christiana* (Boston, 1721), 28–29. See also Solomon Stoddard, *Question, Whether God is not Angry with the Country for doing so little towards the Conversion of the Indians?* (Boston, 1723), 10.

4. *Bouquet's Expedition,* 80–81.

5. *The Invasion Within: The Contest of Cultures in Colonial North America* (New York, 1985) explores both the Europeans who ran away to join Indian societies and the many reasons for the English—and French—failure to convert the Indians to civilization and Christianity.

6. Cadwallader Colden, *The History of the Five Indian Nations of Canada* (London, 1747), 203–4 (1st pag.).

7. Benjamin Franklin to Peter Collinson, May 9, 1753, in Leonard W. Labaree *et al.,* eds., *The Papers of Benjamin Franklin* (New Haven, 1959–   ), 4:481–82.

8. J. Hector St. John de Crèvecoeur, *Letters from an American Farmer* [1782] (London, 1912), 215. Other contemporaries who recognized the disparity between Indian and European conversion results were Pierre de Charlevoix, *Journal of a Voyage to North-America,* 2 vols. (London, 1761), 2:108; Joseph Doddridge, *Notes on the Settlement and Indian Wars of the Western Parts of Virginia and Pennsylvania, from 1763 to 1783, Inclusive* [Wellsburgh, Va., 1824], ed. Alfred Williams (Albany, 1876), 218; Adolph B. Benson, ed., *Peter Kalm's Travels in North America: The English Version of 1770,* 2 vols. (New York, 1937), 2:456–57; Johann David Schoepf, *Travels in the Confederation* [1783–1784], trans. and ed. Alfred J. Morrison (Philadelphia, 1911), 1:283; J. P. Brissot de Warville, *New Travels in the United States of America, 1788,* trans. Mara Soceanu Vamos and Durand Echeverria, ed. Durand Echeverria (Cambridge, Mass., 1964), 420; John F. Meginness, *Biography of Frances Slocum, the Lost Sister of Wyoming* (Williamsport, Pa., 1891), 196; and Felix Renick, "A Trip to the West," *American Pioneer,* 1 (1842), 79.

Later students of the "white Indians" are John R. Swanton, "Notes on the mental assimilation of races," *Journal of the Washington Academy of Sciences,* 16 (1926), 493–502; Erwin H. Ackerknecht, "'White Indians': Psychological and Physiological Peculiarities of White Children Abducted and Reared by North American Indians," *Bulletin of the History of Medicine,* 15 (1944), 15–36; A. Irving Hallowell, "American Indians, White and Black: The Phenomenon of Transculturalization," *Current Anthropology,* 4 (1963), 519–31; and J. Norman Heard, *White into Red: A Study of the Assimilation of White Persons Captured by Indians* (Metuchen, N.J., 1973). All four draw upon western captives as well as colonial in a search for ethnological generalizations. See also Richard Drinnon's *White Savage: The Case of John Dunn Hunter* (New York, 1972); June Namias, *White Captives: Gender and Ethnicity on the American Frontier* (Chapel Hill, 1993); John Demos, *The Unredeemed Captive: A Family Story from Early America* (New York, 1994).

9. This generalization is based on a reading of over 100 captivity narratives and accounts.

10. [William Walton], *The Captivity and Sufferings of Benjamin Gilbert and His Family, 1780–83* [Philadelphia, 1784], ed. Frank H. Severance (Cleveland, 1904), 27 (hereafter cited as *Captivity of Benjamin Gilbert*).

11. [Susannah] Johnson, *A Narrative of the Captivity of Mrs. Johnson* [Walpole, N.H., 1796], reprint of 3d rev. ed. [1814] (Springfield, Mass., 1907), 36; Emma Lewis

Coleman, *New England Captives Carried to Canada* . . . , 2 vols. (Portland, Me., 1925), 1:120–21, 132, 2:159–60, 261; Samuel G. Drake, ed., *Tragedies of the Wilderness* . . . (Boston, 1846), 100, 168, 280.

12. This is not to say that no expense was involved for the English in securing the release of captive colonists, but it was in the nature of modest presents rather than exorbitant ransoms. Sylvester K. Stevens and Donald H. Kent, eds., *The Papers of Col. Henry Bouquet*, 19 vols. (Harrisburg, Pa., 1940–43), 17:28, 169, 18:182–84 (hereafter cited as *Bouquet Papers*).

13. In the 1770s Guy Johnson and George Croghan, both authorities on the Indians of the Middle Atlantic colonies, thought that the English prisoners had been "generally adopted" rather than put to death ("The Opinions of George Croghan on the American Indian," *Pennsylvania Magazine of History and Biography*, 71 [1947], 157; "Guy Johnson's Opinions on the American Indians," *ibid.*, 77 [1953], 322). See also Mary Jemison's remarks in James E. Seaver, *A Narrative of the Life of Mrs. Mary Jemison* [Canandaigua, N.Y., 1824], ed. Allen W. Trelease (New York, 1961), 46–47 (hereafter cited as *Life of Mary Jemison*). While older men and women could be ransomed from the Middle Atlantic tribes, most Indians who had adopted English children could not be persuaded to "sell [their] own Flesh and Blood," not even for "one thousand Dollars," as the Indian father of twelve-year-old Elizabeth Gilbert put it (*Captivity of Benjamin Gilbert*, 103, 107).

14. "Further Examination of Michael La Chauvignerie, Jun'r, 1757," in Samuel Hazard *et al.*, eds., *Pennsylvania Archives*, 3 (1853), 306; "Examination of Barbara Liningaree and Mary Roy, 1759," *ibid.*, 634; "Narrative of Marie Le Roy and Barbara Leininger, for Three Years Captives Among the Indians," *PMHB*, 29 (1905), 417–20.

15. James Sullivan *et al.*, eds., *The Papers of Sir William Johnson*, 14 vols. (Albany, 1921–62), 11:446, 484–91, 720–21 (hereafter cited as *Johnson Papers*); *Bouquet Papers*, 18:253; William S. Ewing, "Indian Captives Released by Colonel Bouquet," *Western Pennsylvania Historical Magazine*, 39 (1956), 187–203. On his two-month journey to a conference with the western Indians in 1760, John Hays saw 23 English prisoners; at least 14 were children. Their average age was 10 years. Two other prisoners were women, one aged 22 and the other "A[l]most A Woman" (*Pennsylvania Archaeologist*, 24 [1954], 63–83).

16. *Johnson Papers*, 11:466, 728.

17. *Bouquet Papers*, 17:51.

18. *Ibid.*, 38; "Provincial Correspondence: 1750 to 1765," in Samuel Hazard *et al.*, eds., *Register of Pennsylvania*, 4 (1829), 390; *A Narrative of the Captivity of John McCullough, Esq.*, in Loudon, ed., *Selection of Some of the Most Interesting Narratives*, 1:326–27; *Bouquet's Expedition*, 80.

19. "Provincial Correspondence," 390–91; *Johnson Papers*, 11:496–98.

20. *Bouquet's Expedition*, 76, 80; *Johnson Papers*, 4:500; "Provincial Correspondence," 390; "Relation by Frederick Post of Conversation with Indians, 1760," *Pa. Archives*, 3 (1853), 742. I have translated Post's phonetic German spelling.

21. "Prisoners Delivered to Gov., by the Six Nations, 1762," *Pa. Archives*, 4 (1853), 100–101; *Johnson Papers*, 11:720–21; Coleman, *New England Captives*, 1:323, 2:58. In a "List of Prisoners deliv[ere]d up by the Shawanese Nations of Indians at *Fort Pit, 10th May 1765*," the following names were among those given for 14 captives who had

been with the Indians from 2 to 10 years: Wechquessinah ("cant speak Eng[li]sh. knows not from whence taken"), Joseph or Pechyloothume, Jenny or Ketakatwitch, Wapatenaqua, and Nalupeia, sister to Molly Bird (*Johnson Papers*, 11:720–21). In an earlier list were Sour Mouth, Crooked Legs, Pouter or Wynima, David Bighead, Sore Knee, Sour Plumbs (*Bouquet Papers*, 18:248). It would be important to know if these names were given in derision to resistant, older captives, or in good humor to accepting, younger ones.

22. *Johnson Papers*, 11:812; *Bouquet Papers*, 17:39–41.

23. Benson, ed., *Peter Kalm's Travels*, 2:457; Coleman, *New England Captives*, 1:296, 2:11; O. M. Spencer, *The Indian Captivity of O. M. Spencer* [New York, 1835], ed. Milo Milton Quaife, reprint of 1917 ed. (New York, 1968), 168–69; Samuel Stanhope Smith, *An Essay on the Causes of the Variety of Complexion and Figure in the Human Species* [Philadelphia, 1787] (2d ed., New Brunswick, N.J., 1810), 70n–71n. See also Bernard W. Sheehan, *Seeds of Extinction: Jeffersonian Philanthropy and the American Indian* (Chapel Hill, 1973), ch. 1, esp. 40–42; and Doddridge, *Notes on the Settlement and Indian Wars*, 91.

24. Coleman, *New England Captives*, 2:91, 117–18; *Johnson Papers*, 10:160, 11:728. O. M. Spencer's Indian father for "several years" paid him an annual visit (*Indian Captivity of O. M. Spencer*, 171).

25. *Captivity of Benjamin Gilbert*, 181; Thomas Ridout, "An Account of My Capture By the Shawanese Indians . . ." [1788], *Blackwood's Magazine*, 223 (1928), 313.

26. *Bouquet's Expedition*, 80–81.

27. Drake, ed., *Tragedies of the Wilderness*, 128; Stephen Williams, *What Befell Stephen Williams in his Captivity* [Greenfield, Mass., 1837], ed. George Sheldon (Deerfield, Mass., 1889), 5; John Williams, *The Redeemed Captive Returning to Zion* [Boston, 1707] (Springfield, Mass., 1908), 14, 30.

28. Captivity narrative of Joseph Bartlett in Joshua Coffin, *A Sketch of the History of Newbury* . . . (Boston, 1845), 332; *An Account of the Remarkable Occurrences in the Life and Travels of Col. James Smith* [1799], in Howard Peckham, ed., *Narratives of Colonial America, 1704–1765* (Chicago, 1971), 82; Samuel Lee to Nehemiah Grew, 1690, *Publications of the Colonial Society of Massachusetts*, 14 (1911–13), 148.

29. *What Befell Stephen Williams*, 6; Drake, ed., *Tragedies of the Wilderness*, 61.

30. Charles H. Lincoln, ed., *Narratives of the Indian Wars, 1675–1699*, Original Narratives of Early American History (New York, 1913), 30; Drake, *Tragedies of the Wilderness*, 125, 145; Ridout, "Account of My Capture," 303; *Bouquet's Expedition*, 78; "Provincial Correspondence," 390–91.

31. J. Franklin Jameson, ed., *Johnson's Wonder-Working Providence, 1628–1651*, Orig. Narrs. of Early Amer. Hist. (New York, 1910), 150, 263; "Morrell's Poem on New England," *Collections of the Massachusetts Historical Society*, 1st ser. 1 (1792), 135.

32. Charles Thomson in Thomas Jefferson, *Notes on the State of Virginia*, ed. William Peden (Chapel Hill, 1955), 200; "Opinions of George Croghan," 157. See also *Life of Mary Jemison*, 73, and Sylvester K. Stevens *et al.*, eds., *Travels in New France by J. C. B.* (Harrisburg, Pa., 1941), 69.

33. [James] *Adair's History of the American Indians* [London, 1775], ed. Samuel Cole Williams (Kingsport, Tenn., 1930), 171.

34. Jeremy Belknap, *The History of New Hampshire*, 3 vols. (2d ed., Boston, 1813), 1:229.

35. Drake, ed., *Tragedies of the Wilderness*, 61, 115–16, 145, 158; Thomas Hutchinson, *The History of the Colony and Province of Massachusetts-Bay*, ed. Lawrence Shaw Mayo, 2 vols. (Cambridge, Mass., 1936), 2:104n; Mrs. Harriet S. Caswell, *Our Life Among the Iroquois* (Boston, 1892), 53. See also *Life of Mary Jemison*, 47, 57, and Timothy Alden, ed., "An Account of the Captivity of Hugh Gibson . . . ," *Colls. Mass. His. Soc.*, 3d ser. 6 (1837), 153. The source of Hutchinson's information was Williams, *Redeemed Captive*. Jacob Lunenburg was bound so tightly on his captor's back that he was somewhat crippled for life (Coleman, *New England Captives*, 2:215).

36. Johnson, *Narrative of the Captivity of Mrs. Johnson*, 62; [Titus King], *Narrative of Titus King . . .* (Hartford, 1938), 10; Meginness, *Biography of Frances Slocum*, 65. See also Peckham, ed., *Narratives of Colonial America*, 89; Howard H. Peckham, ed., "Thomas Gist's Indian Captivity, 1758–1759," *PMHB*, 80 (1956), 297; [Zadock Steele], *The Indian Captive; or a Narrative of the Captivity and Sufferings of Zadock Steele . . .* [Montpelier, Vt., 1818] (Springfield, Mass., 1908), 68; Loudon, ed., *Selection of Some of the Most Interesting Narratives*, 1:303–4.

37. Johnson, *Narrative of the Captivity of Mrs. Johnson*, 57–58; Drake, ed., *Tragedies of the Wilderness*, 129; King, *Narrative of Titus King*, 8.

38. *A Plain Narrative of the Uncommon Sufferings and Remarkable Deliverance of Thomas Brown, of Charlestown, in New-England* (2d ed., Boston, 1760), in *Magazine of History with Notes and Queries*, Extra Number no. 4 (1908), 8, 12; *The History of the Life and Sufferings of Henry Grace, of Basingstoke in the County of Southampton* [Reading, Eng., 1764] (2d ed., London, 1765), 12. See also Peckham, ed., *Narratives of Colonial America*, 81; Peckham, ed., "Thomas Gist's Indian Captivity," 298; Drake, ed., *Tragedies of the Wilderness*, 269, 272; and *Captivity of Benjamin Gilbert*, 56, 121.

39. Beverley W. Bond, Jr., ed., "The Captivity of Charles Stuart, 1755–57," *Mississippi Valley Historical Review*, 13 (1926–27), 66; "Narrative of John Brickell's Captivity Among the Delaware Indians," *American Pioneer*, 1 (1842), 46.

40. Stevens *et al.*, eds., *Travels in New France by J. C. B.*, 68; Charlevoix, *Journal of a Voyage*, 1:369–70; "Narrative of Marie Le Roy and Barbara Leininger," 409.

41. *Captivity of Benjamin Gilbert*, 56.

42. Peckham, ed., *Narratives of Colonial America*, 81. See also Alden, ed., "Captivity of Hugh Gibson," 143; Loudon, ed., *Selection of Some of the Most Interesting Narratives*, 1:306; and *Life of Mary Jemison*, 44.

43. Steele, *Indian Captive*, 70–71; Johnson, *Narrative of the Captivity of Mrs. Johnson*, 66.

44. Peckham, ed., *Narratives of Colonial America*, 91–92.

45. *Ibid.*, "John Brickell's Captivity," 46; Johnson, *Narrative of the Captivity of Mrs. Johnson*, 68.

46. *Life of Mary Jemison*, 44–47; *Captivity of Benjamin Gilbert*, 107, 123; Loudon, ed., *Selection of Some of the Most Interesting Narratives*, 307; Peckham, ed., "Thomas Gist's Indian Captivity," 299; Luke Swetland, *A Very Remarkable Narrative of Luke Swetland . . . Written by Himself* (Hartford, n.d.), 7–8.

47. *Life of Mary Jemison*, 46; King, *Narrative of Titus King*, 14; Stevens *et al.*, *Travels in New France by J. C. B.*, 73. See also *Johnson Papers*, 13:191, and Charlevoix, *Journal of a Voyage*, 1:373.

48. *Captivity of Benjamin Gilbert*, 126–27, 135.

49. Swetland, *Remarkable Narrative*, 5; Peckham, ed., "Thomas Gist's Indian Captivity," 299; *Life of Mary Jemison*, 47.

50. Johnson, *Narrative of the Captivity of Mrs. Johnson*, 67–68, 71, 76–77.

51. "John Brickell's Captivity," 44; *Bouquet's Expedition*, 78. The Canadian captors of Titus King told him that "I Should never go hum [home] that I was an Indian now and must be and Do as they Did" (King, *Narrative of Titus King*, 14).

52. Ridout, "Account of My Capture"; John Leeth, *A Short Biography of John Leeth* [Lancaster, Ohio, 1831], ed. Reuben Gold Thwaites (Cleveland, 1904), 28; *Captivity of Benjamin Gilbert*, 109; Steele, *Indian Captive*, 72.

53. *Captivity of Benjamin Gilbert*, 81, 83.

54. Peckham, ed., "Thomas Gist's Indian Captivity," 301; "John Brickell's Captivity," 54. Joseph Bartlett also lived with other white captives while a prisoner in Canada (Coffin, *Sketch of the History of Newbury*, 332–33).

55. *Captivity of Benjamin Gilbert*, 74, 87, 124; Alden, ed., "Captivity of Hugh Gibson," 149. Women were not the only captives alarmed by the specter of forced marriage. When Thomas Gist was first brought to the Huron village where he was to be adopted, he was made to stand naked at a post for an hour "while the Indian Ladies was satisfied as to their sight. For my part," he recalled, "I expected they was going to chuse some of the likeliest of us for husbands, by their standing and looking so long at us in this condition" (Peckham, ed., "Thomas Gist's Indian Captivity," 298).

56. *Life of Mary Jemison*, 52–53.

57. Williams, *Redeemed Captive*, 131 (my emphasis); Drake, ed., *Tragedies of the Wilderness*, 125 (my emphasis); "Provincial Correspondence," 390–91.

58. Peckham, ed., "Thomas Gist's Indian Captivity," 301; *Indian Captivity of O. M. Spencer*, 82, 120, 129.

59. Coleman, *New England Captives*, 2:107; *Biography of Leeth*, 39–40; Orlando Allen, "Incidents in the Life of an Indian Captive," *American Historical Record*, 1 (1872), 409. The "8" used by the French in Indian words signifies "w," which did not exist in French.

60. *Captivity of Benjamin Gilbert*, 135; Caswell, *Our Life Among the Iroquois*, 54; Charlevoix, *Journal of a Voyage*, 1:371; *Johnson Papers*, 4:620.

61. *Indian Captivity of O. M. Spencer*, 92–93.

62. Ridout, "Account of My Captivity," 295; Coleman, *New England Captives*, 1:21, 296, 325–26, 2:190–91.

63. Caswell, *Our Life Among the Iroquois*, 54–55.

64. A. Irving Hallowell has coined the unwieldy term "transculturalization" to denote the process whereby individuals, rather than groups, are detached from one society, enter another, and come under the influence of its customs and values ("American Indians, White and Black," 519–31).

65. King, *Narrative of Titus King,* 17; *Life of Mary Jemison,* 57; Peckham, ed., "Thomas Gist's Indian Captivity," 302.

66. Williams, *Redeemed Captive,* 37; Drake, ed., *Tragedies of the Wilderness,* 169–70.

67. *Indian Captivity of O. M. Spencer,* 120–21; Drake, ed., *Tragedies of the Wilderness,* 161.

68. Peckham, ed., "Thomas Gist's Indian Captivity," 300–301.

69. *Life of Mary Jemison,* 48; Peckham, ed., "Thomas Gist's Indian Captivity," 301.

70. Loudon, ed., *Selection of Some of the Most Interesting Narratives,* 1:307; *Indian Captivity of O. M. Spencer,* 65.

71. Renick, "A Trip to the West," 78; *Captivity of Benjamin Gilbert,* 98–100.

72. "Narrative of the Capture of Abel Janney by the Indians in 1782," *Ohio Archaeological and Historical Quarterly,* 8 (1900), 472; *Indian Captivity of O. M. Spencer,* 113, 117–18; Peckham, ed., "Thomas Gist's Indian Captivity," 300; *Life of Mary Jemison,* 55–56. See also James Axtell, ed., *The Indian Peoples of Eastern America: A Documentary History of the Sexes* (New York, 1981), ch. 4.

73. *Bouquet's Expedition,* 81.

74. Roger Williams, *A Key into the Language of America* (London, 1643); "John Brickell's Captivity," 47–49; *Life of Mary Jemison,* 72–73; Douglass Adair and John A. Schutz, ed., *Peter Oliver's Origin & Progress of the American Rebellion: A Tory View* (San Marino, Calif., 1961), 5; Coleman, *New England Captives,* 2:312. In 1758 four pro-English Delaware chiefs accused the English of treaty-breaking and hypocrisy. "We Love you more than you Love us, for when we take any Prisoners from you we treat them as our own children; we are Poor and we cloath them as well as we can, you see our own children are as naked as the first, by this you may see our hearts are better then your heart" ("Journal of Frederick Post," *Pa. Archives,* 3 [1853], 534).

75. "Further Examination of Michael La Chauvignerie," 306; *Narrative of the Life and Adventures of Matthew Bunn . . .* [Providence, *ca.* 1796] (7th rev. ed., Batavia, N.Y.), 11; Loudon, ed., *Selection of Some of the Most Interesting Narratives,* 1:311; *Captivity of Benjamin Gilbert,* 112.

76. *Indian Captivity of O. M. Spencer,* 86; Peckham, ed., *Narratives of Colonial America,* 108.

77. Crèvecoeur, *Letters,* 214.

78. *Ibid.,* 215; Charles S. Grant, *Democracy in the Connecticut Frontier Town of Kent* (New York, 1961); Richard L. Bushman, *From Puritan to Yankee: Character and the Social Order in Connecticut, 1690–1765* (Cambridge, Mass., 1967); Kenneth Lockridge, "Land, Population and the Evolution of New England Society 1630–1790," *Past and Present,* 39 (1968), 62–80; Gary B. Nash, *Quakers and Politics: Pennsylvania, 1681–1726* (Princeton, 1968); Kenneth A. Lockridge, *A New England Town, The First Hundred Years: Dedham, Massachusetts, 1636–1736* (New York, 1970); Patricia U. Bonomi, *A Factious People: Politics and Society in Colonial New York* (New York, 1971); James A. Henretta and Gregory H. Nobles, *Evolution and Revolution: American Society, 1600–1820* (Lexington, Mass., 1987); Gary B. Nash, *Urban Crucible: Social Change, Political Consciousness, and the Origins of the American Revolution* (Cambridge, Mass., 1979); Carla Gardina Pestana and Sharon V. Salinger, eds. *Inequality in Early*

America (Hanover, N. H., 1999). Indeed, it may well be that the adults who chose to become Indians did so for some of the reasons that many of their countrymen turned to revolution.

79. Crèvecoeur, *Letters*, 215.

Chapter Nine

1. Samuel M. Wilson, *Hispaniola: Caribbean Chiefdoms in the Age of Columbus* (Tuscaloosa, 1990).

2. Bruce D. Smith, "The Archaeology of the Southeastern United States: From Dalton to de Soto, 10,500–500 B.P.," *Advances in World Archaeology*, 5 (1986), 53–63; Vincas P. Steponaitis, "Prehistoric Archaeology in the Southeastern United States, 1970–1985," *Annual Review of Anthropology*, 15 (1986), 387–93; Charles Hudson and Carmen Chaves Tesser, eds., *The Forgotten Centuries: Indians and Europeans in the American South, 1521–1704* (Athens, 1994), 17–35, 125–253; Karl T. Steinen, "Ambushes, Raids, and Palisades: Mississippian Warfare in the Interior Southeast," *Southeastern Archaeology*, 11:2 (Winter 1992), 132–39; David H. Dye, "Warfare in the Sixteenth-Century Southeast: The de Soto Expedition in the Interior," in David Hurst Thomas, ed., *Columbian Consequences, Volume 2: Archaeological and Historical Perspectives on the Spanish Borderlands East* (Washington, D.C., 1990), 211–22; Dye, "The Art of War in the Sixteenth-Century Central Mississippi Valley," in Patricia B. Kwachka, ed., *Perspectives on the Southeast: Linguistics, Archaeology, and Ethnohistory*, Southern Anthropological Society Proceedings, No. 27 (Athens, 1994), 44–60.

3. James E. Kelley, Jr., "Juan Ponce de León's Discovery of Florida: Herrera's Narrative Revisited," *Revista de historia de America*, no. 111 (enero-junio 1991), 31–65 at 45, 49.

4. Paul E. Hoffman, *A New Andalucia and a Way to the Orient: The American Southeast During the Sixteenth Century* (Baton Rouge, 1990), chs. 1–2; Jerald T. Milanich, *Florida Indians and the Invasion from Europe* (Gainesville, 1995), 106–113.

5. David B. Quinn, ed., *New American World: A Documentary History of North America to 1612*, 5 vols. (New York, 1979), 1:248 (Gómara); 1:266 (Martyr). See also Paul E. Hoffman on Ayllón in Hudson and Tesser, eds., *Forgotten Centuries*, 36–49.

6. *Cabeza de Vaca's Adventures in the Unknown Interior of America*, ed. and trans. Cyclone Covey (Albuquerque, 1983). The definitive edition is now Rolena Adorno and Patrick Charles Pautz, *Álvar Núñez Cabeza de Vaca: His Account, His Life, and the Expedition of Pánfilo de Narváez*, 3 vols. (Lincoln, 1999). See also Paul E. Hoffman in Hudson and Tesser, eds., *Forgotten Centuries*, 50–73, on the Narváez entrada.

7. Lawrence A. Clayton, Vernon James Knight, Jr., and Edward C. Moore, eds., *The De Soto Chronicles: The Expedition of Hernando De Soto to North America in 1539–1543*, 2 vols. (Tuscaloosa, 1993), 1:48 (Gentleman from Elvas), 360 (royal contract). On Soto's entrada, see Hoffman, *New Andalucia*, ch. 4; Milanich, *Florida Indians and Invasion*, 127–36; Charles Hudson in Hudson and Tesser, eds., *Forgotten Centuries*, 74–103; Hudson, *Knights of Spain, Warriors of the Sun: Hernando de Soto and the South's Ancient Chiefdoms* (Athens, Ga., 1997); Patricia Galloway, ed., *The Hernando de*

Soto Expedition: History, Historiography, and "Discovery" in the Southeast (Lincoln, 1997).

8. See Hoffman, *New Andalucia*, chs. 9–10; Milanich, *Florida Indians and Invasion*, ch. 8; Eugene Lyon, *The Enterprise of Florida: Pedro Menéndez de Avilés and the Spanish Conquest of 1565–1568* (Gainesville, 1976, 1983).

9. Hoffman, *New Andalucia*, ch. 12; David Beers Quinn, *Set Fair for Roanoke: Voyages and Colonies, 1584–1606* (Chapel Hill, 1985).

10. Paul E. Hoffman, "A New Voyage of North American Discovery: Pedro de Salazar's Visit to the 'Island of Giants,'" *Florida Historical Quarterly*, 58:4 (April 1980), 415–26.

11. Quinn, ed., *New American World*, 1:259. See also Hoffman, *New Andalucia*, 3–18.

12. Hoffman, *New Andalucia*, 11, 20, 48 (Oviedo), 67; Lynn Guitar, "Franciscano Chicorano: A North American Indian in King Charles I's Court," *Terrae Incognitae*, 29 (1997), 1–9. See *De Soto Chronicles*, 1:56, 58, for two Florida Indians who were captured by an advance party of Soto's entrada and escaped as soon as they were returned to their homeland.

13. Clifford M. Lewis and Albert J. Loomie, *The Spanish Jesuit Mission in Virginia, 1570–1572* (Chapel Hill, 1953), 15–18, 39–49; Charlotte M. Gradie, "Spanish Jesuits in Virginia: The Mission That Failed," *Virginia Magazine of History and Biography*, 96 (1988), 131–56; Gradie, "The Powhatans in the Context of the Spanish Empire," in Helen C. Rountree, ed., *Powhatan Foreign Relations, 1500–1722* (Charlottesville, 1993), ch. 7.

14. *Cabeza de Vaca's Adventures*, ed. Covey, 32–33; Hugh Honour, *The New Golden Land: European Images of America from the Discoveries to the Present Time* (New York, 1975), 28–29. In the late seventeenth century, coastal Indians were still reaping profits from the material and human salvage of wrecked ships. See *Jonathan Dickinson's Journal; or, God's Protecting Providence* [1696–1697], ed. Evangeline Walker Andrews and Charles McLean Andrews (rev. ed. New Haven, 1961).

15. Laura Branstetter, "Research of the [Montague] Tallant Collection: Final Report" (University of South Florida—New College, senior thesis in Anthropology, May 1989), 9 (Tairona gold man and lizard, Sinu nose ring?), cat. no. A6736 (Colombian cast gold scorpion), A6952 (cast gold eagle pendant); Jonathan Max Leader, "Metal Artifacts from Fort Center: Aboriginal Metal Working in the Southeastern United States" (University of Florida, M.A. thesis in Anthropology, 1985), 74 (Incan jaguar and Quimbaya necklace ornaments).

16. Leader, "Metal Artifacts from Fort Center," 78–80; Branstetter, "Research of the Tallant Collection," 11–13, cat. no. A7041–7064 (silver beads from Spanish coins); Jeffrey M. Mitchem and Dale L. Hutchinson, *Interim Report on Archaeological Research at the Tatham Mound, Citrus County, Florida: Session III* (Misc. Project Report Series No. 30, Florida State Museum, Dept. of Anthropology, 1987), 55–59. For illustrations of reworked silver artifacts, see Jerald T. Milanich and Susan Milbrath, eds., *First Encounters: Spanish Explorations in the Caribbean and the United States, 1492–1570* (Gainesville, 1989), 107, and Milanich, *Florida Indians and Invasion*, 42, 46, 47, 50, 51.

17. *Memoir of D°. d'Escalente Fontaneda Respecting Florida. Written in Spain, About the Year 1575*, ed. and trans. Buckingham Smith (Washington, D.C., 1854; rev. ed. Miami, 1944), 18–20.

18. Gonzalo Solís de Merás, *Pedro Menéndez de Avilés. . . . : Memorial*, ed. and trans. Jeannette Thurber Connor, Publications of the Florida State Historical Society, No. 3 (Deland, 1923; facsimile ed. Gainesville, 1964), 141, 144–45.

19. *Memoir of Fontaneda*, 19; Solís de Merás, *Pedro Menéndez*, 148; *Dickinson's Journal*.

20. *Memoir of Fontaneda*, 19–20.

21. Solís de Merás, *Pedro Menéndez*, 142, 151; Kathleen A. Deagan, "Mestizaje in Colonial St. Augustine," *Ethnohistory*, 20:1 (Winter 1973), 55–65: Eugene Lyon, "Cultural Brokers in Sixteenth-Century Spanish Florida," in *Spanish Borderlands Sourcebooks*, gen. ed. David Hurst Thomas, vol. 24: *Pedro Menéndez de Avilés*, ed. Eugene Lyon (New York, 1995), 329–36.

22. Charles Hudson, *The Juan Pardo Expeditions: Exploration of the Carolinas and Tennessee, 1566–1568* (Washington, D.C., 1990).

23. Herbert I. Priestley, ed. and trans., *The Luna Papers: Documents Relating to the Expedition of Don Tristán de Luna y Arellano for the Conquest of La Florida in 1559–1561*, Publications of the Florida State Historical Society, No. 8, 2 vols. (Deland, 1928); Charles Hudson, Marvin T. Smith, Chester B. DePratter, and Emilia Kelley, "The Tristán de Luna Expedition, 1559–1561," *Southeastern Archaeology*, 8:1 (Summer 1989), 31–45; the letter is also in Milanich and Milbrath, eds., *First Encounters*, ch. 9.

24. Hudson *et al.*, "The Luna Expedition," 32.

25. *De Soto Chronicles*, 1:59, 62, 130 (Gentleman from Elvas), 225 (Biedma), 2:114, 116 (Garcilaso de la Vega).

26. Garcilaso de la Vega, educated and writing in Spain long after the events, said that Indian porters were "called *tamemes* in the language of the island of Española." Historian-editor Buckingham Smith, on the other hand, argued that the word derived from the language of "the Mexican Indians" (Nahuatl, presumably): *tlamama* or *tlamema*, someone who carried loads on the back. *De Soto Chronicles*, 1:194n.110, 2:278.

27. *Ibid.*, 1:154 (Gentleman from Elvas, my emphasis).

28. *Ibid.*, 1:229, 283, 291 (numbers of tamemes), 2:312, 400, 439 (feet crippling).

29. *Ibid.*, 1:74, 150, 153 (Gentleman from Elvas). By contrast, when Captain Pardo set out to "pacify" the territory northwest of Santa Elena twenty-five years later, he took only a hundred-some men and a large quantity of gifts to lubricate the voluntary payment of maize "tribute" to the Spanish and the building of separate lodgings by the Indian villagers he encountered. He even had the foresight to encourage a fertile village not far from Santa Elena to "sow a large quantity of [extra] maize" for future Spanish needs rather than commandeer every kernal they had, as the locust-like Soto entrada was wont to do. Hudson, *Juan Pardo Expeditions*, 293.

30. *De Soto Chronicles*, 1:89, 226, 238, 267, 268, 282–83, 285, 289, 303.

31. *Ibid.*, 1:120, 121 (Gentleman from Elvas), 303 (Rangel).

32. *Ibid.*, 1:289 (Rangel).

33. See above, Chapter 1; also Axtell, *Beyond 1492: Encounters in Colonial North America* (New York, 1992), ch. 2.

34. *De Soto Chronicles,* 1:87, 141 (Gentleman from Elvas), 2:315 (Garcilaso de la Vega).

35. *Ibid.,* 1:94 (Gentleman from Elvas), 285 (Rangel); Woodbury Lowery, *The Spanish Settlements Within the Present Limits of the United States, 1513–1561* (New York, 1911), 365.

36. Quinn, ed., *New American World,* 2:306, 353.

37. *De Soto Chronicles,* 1, 70, 93 (chains), 95, 131, 272, 285, 286–87, 291 (gifts); Hudson, *Juan Pardo Expeditions,* 135–41, 266; Milanich and Milbrath, eds., *First Encounters,* ch. 7; Jeffrey P. Brain, "Artifacts of the Adelantado," *Conference on Historic Site Archaeology Papers,* 8 (1975), 129–38; Kathleen Deagan, *Artifacts of the Spanish Colonies of Florida and the Caribbean, 1500–1800* (Washington, D.C., 1987).

38. *De Soto Chronicles,* 1:279–80 (Rangel). It is possible that Soto's men saw Spanish-style clothing that had been made from local deerskins by the beleaguered colonists themselves; most of their own supplies had been lost in a storm just as they landed.

39. *Ibid.,* 1:265 (Rangel). For its wider use in Spain and Latin America, see Luis Weckmann, *The Medieval Heritage of Mexico,* trans. Frances M. López-Morillas (New York, 1992), 111–13, 115n.20.

40. *De Soto Chronicles,* 1:158, 291, 293; R. B. Cunninghame Graham, *The Horses of the Conquest,* ed. Robert Moorman Denhardt (Norman, 1949); Barbara A. Purdy, "Weapons, Strategies, and Tactics of the Europeans and the Indians in Sixteenth- and Seventeenth-Century Florida," *Florida Historical Quarterly,* 55:3 (January 1977), 259–76 at 267–68.

41. *De Soto Chronicles,* 1:66, 80, 146, 257, 262, 2:150–52, 459–60; Lowery, *Spanish Settlements,* 133–34 (Oviedo); Purdy, "Weapons, Strategies, and Tactics," 268–69; John Grier Varner and Jeannette Johnson Varner, *Dogs of the Conquest* (Norman, 1983), esp. 104–110.

42. Robert L. Blakely, ed., *The King Site: Continuity and Contact in Sixteenth-Century Georgia* (Athens, 1988), chs. 7–9; Blakely and David S. Mathews, "Bioarchaeological Evidence for a Spanish-Native American Conflict in the Sixteenth-Century Southeast," *American Antiquity,* 55:4 (1990), 718–44. At least two Indians interred in the Tatham mound in west-central Florida had been cut by Spanish swords. Mitchem and Hutchinson, *Interim Report on the Tatham Mound,* 9, 41.

43. *De Soto Chronicles,* 1:99, 122, 143, 152, 153, 235, 267, 292. When the Indians retaliated with arrows, Spanish armor—traditional metal and lighter weight quilted cotton and canvas—deflected them. The quilted armor, *escupiles,* was copied from the Aztecs and became the standard defensive gear in sixteenth-century Florida among all Europeans. At the battle of Mabila, Soto's secretary, Rodrigo Rangel, took more than twenty arrows in his "quilted tunic of thick cotton" and suffered no harm. *De Soto Chronicles,* 1:293. See also Purdy, "Weapons, Strategies, and Tactics," 266–67.

44. *De Soto Chronicles,* 1:104, 135 (Gentleman from Elvas).

45. *Ibid.,* 1:145, 146–47, 244, 267.

46. *Ibid.,* 1:106, 150, 155, 229, 241, 256, 264, 301; Charles Hudson, "A Spanish-Coosa Alliance in Sixteenth-Century North Georgia," *Georgia Historical Quarterly,* 72:4 (Winter 1988), 599–626.

47. Dye, "The Art of War in the Mississippi Valley," 60n.16.

48. *Ibid.,* 50–53.

49. *De Soto Chronicles,* 1:106, 153 (Gentleman from Elvas), 2:262–63, 472, 498 (Garcilaso de la Vega). According to Garcilaso, Soto gave a male and a female pig to friendly caciques for breeding. *De Soto Chronicles,* 2:263.

50. Hoffman, *New Andalucia,* 53.

51. Alfred W. Crosby, Jr., *The Columbian Exchange: Biological and Cultural Consequences of 1492* (Westport, Conn., 1972), ch. 3; Crosby, *Germs, Seeds, & Animals: Studies in Ecological History* (Armonk, N.Y., 1994), chs. 2–3; Donna L. Ruhl, "Spanish Mission Paleoethnobotany and Cultural Change: A Survey of the Archaeobotanical Data and Some Speculations on Aboriginal and Spanish Agrarian Interactions in La Florida," in Thomas, ed., *Columbian Consequences,* 2: ch. 35; Ruhl, "Old Customs and Traditions in New Terrain: Sixteenth- and Seventeenth-Century Archaeobotanical Data from *La Florida,*" in C. Margaret Scarry, ed., *Foraging and Farming in the Eastern Woodlands* (Gainesville, 1993), ch. 15; Francis Xavier Luca, "Culture and Ecology: Indians, Europeans, and Animal Husbandry in Colonial Florida," *Southern Historian,* 13 (Spring 1992), 7–23.

52. Menéndez also imported some 3,000 chickens and 2,700 fanegas of corn from Yucatán. Lyon, *Enterprise of Florida,* 183n. 41.

53. The New World had only two chronic infectious diseases of any consequence—tuberculosis and treponematosis, both of which were prevalent in the precontact Southeast. Charles F. Merbs, "A New World of Infectious Disease," *Yearbook of Physical Anthropology,* 35 (1992), 3–42; John W. Verano and Douglas H. Ubelaker, eds., *Disease and Demography in the Americas* (Washington, D.C., 1992), ch. 5.

54. Crosby, *Columbian Exchange,* ch. 2; Crosby, *Germs, Seeds, & Animals,* chs. 2–3, 5–7; Verano and Ubelaker, eds., *Disease and Demography in the Americas,* chs. 4–5, 17; George R. Milner, "Epidemic Disease in the Postcontact Southeast: A Reappraisal," *Midcontinental Journal of Archaeology,* 5:1 (April 1980), 39–56; Robert L. Blakely and Bettina Detweiler-Blakely, "The Impact of European Diseases in the Sixteenth-Century Southeast: A Case Study," *ibid.,* 14:1 (April 1989), 62–89; Noble David Cook, *Born to Die: Disease and New World Conquest, 1492–1650* (Cambridge, 1998). Henry F. Dobyns, *Their Number Become Thinned: Native American Population Dynamics in Eastern North America* (Knoxville, 1983) pertains to sixteenth-century Florida (see esp. 250–74) but is extremely flawed; see critical reviews by Jerald T. Milanich in *Agriculture and Human Values,* 2:3 (Summer 1985), 83–85, James Merrell in *Reviews in American History,* 11:3 (Sept. 1984), 354–58, and David Henige in *Journal of Interdisciplinary History,* 16:4 (Spring 1986), 701–20. Dobyns has written a useful review essay on "Disease Transfer at Contact" in *Annual Review of Anthropology,* 22 (1993), 273–91.

55. *De Soto Chronicles,* 1:83 (Gentleman from Elvas), 2:285, 298, 306 (Garcilaso de la Vega). Chester B. DePratter has argued that the epidemic may never have occurred. Hudson and Tesser, eds., *Forgotten Centuries,* 197–226 at 215–17. Russell Thornton,

Jonathan Warren, and Tim Miller have suggested that the "buffer zones between the chiefdoms of the Southeast may have acted as reservoirs of smallpox, slowing, but not necessarily eliminating the spread of the disease from one chiefdom to another." Verano and Ubelaker, eds., *Disease and Demography in the Americas*, 193.

56. Mitchem and Hutchinson, *Interim Report on the Tatham Mound*, 45–46, 80.

57. Marvin T. Smith, *Archaeology of Aboriginal Culture Change in the Interior Southeast: Depopulation During the Early Historic Period*, Ripley P. Bullen Monographs in Anthropology and History, No. 6 (Gainesville, 1987); Smith, "Aboriginal Depopulation in the Postcontact Southeast," in Hudson and Tesser, eds., *Forgotten Centuries*, 257–75; Smith, "Aboriginal Population Movements in the Early Historic Period Interior Southeast," in Peter H. Wood, Gregory A. Waselkov, and M. Thomas Hatley, eds., *Powhatan's Mantle: Indians in the Colonial Southeast* (Lincoln, 1989), 21–34; Patricia Galloway, *Choctaw Genesis, 1500–1700* (Lincoln, 1995), ch. 4; John E. Worth, *The Timucuan Chiefdoms of Spanish Florida*, Ripley P. Bullen Series, 2 vols. (Gainesville, 1997) Some of the chiefdoms were devolving for ecological, demographic, and/or indigenously political reasons. See David G. Anderson, *The Savannah River Chiefdoms: Political Change in the Late Prehistoric Southeast* (Tuscaloosa, 1994); John F. Scarry, ed., *Political Structure and Change in the Prehistoric Southeastern United States*, Ripley P. Bullen Series, Florida Museum of Natural History (Gainesville, 1996).

58. Milanich, *Florida Indians and Invasion;* Milanich and Samuel Proctor, eds., *Tacachale: Essays on the Indians of Florida and Southeastern Georgia During the Historic Period*, Ripley P. Bullen Monographs in Anthropology and History, No. 1 (Gainesville, 1978).

59. *De Soto Chronicles*, 1:111 (Gentleman from Elvas).

Chapter Ten

1. Christian F. Feest, "Powhatan: A Study in Political Organization," *Wiener Völkerkundliche Mitteilungen*, 13 (1966), 69–83; Feest, "Virginia Algonquians," in William C. Sturtevant, gen. ed., *Handbook of North American Indians*, 15: *Northeast*, ed. Bruce G. Trigger (Washington, D.C.: Smithsonian Institution, 1978), 271–81; Helen C. Rountree and E. Randolph Turner III, "On the Fringe of the Southeast: The Powhatan Paramount Chiefdom in Virginia," in Charles Hudson and Carmen Chaves Tesser eds., *The Forgotten Centuries: Indians and Europeans in the American South, 1521–1704* (Athens, Ga., 1994), 355–72.

2. William Strachey, *The Historie of Travell into Virginia Britania (1612)*, ed. Louis B. Wright and Virginia Freund, Hakluyt Society Publications, 2d ser. 103 (London, 1953), 59.

3. Philip L. Barbour, ed., *The Jamestown Voyages Under the First Charter, 1606–1609*, Hakluyt Soc. Pubs., 2d ser. 136–37 (Cambridge, 1969), 426 (continuous pagination).

4. Clifford M. Lewis and Albert J. Loomie, *The Spanish Jesuit Mission in Virginia, 1570–1572* (Chapel Hill, 1953).

5. See above, Chapter 3.

6. Strachey, *Historie,* 34.

7. Barbour, *Jamestown Voyages,* 191.

8. *Ibid.,* 371.

9. Strachey, *Historie,* 56, 62, 63, 68, 87, 92; Barbour, *Jamestown Voyages,* 370–71.

10. Barbour, *Jamestown Voyages,* 43.

11. *Ibid.,* 51–52.

12. *Ibid.,* 382–83, 397–99, 418–20.

13. *Ibid.,* 80–95, 141, 170–72.

14. *Ibid.,* 88.

15. *Ibid.,* 141.

16. *Ibid.,* 139–40.

17. *Ibid.,* 91. On weapons and armor at Jamestown, see William M. Kelso, Nicholas M. Luccketti, and Beverly A. Straube, *Jamestown Rediscovery IV* (Richmond, Va., 1998), 43–69.

18. *Ibid.,* 216.

19. *Ibid.,* 141.

20. *Ibid.,* 448.

21. *Ibid.,* 426; George Percy, "'A Trewe Relacyon': Virginia from 1609 to 1612," *Tyler's Quarterly Historical and Genealogical Magazine,* 3 (1922), 265.

22. Percy, "Trewe Relacyon," 265.

23. Barbour, *Jamestown Voyages,* 154, 163, 191, 193, 199, 274.

24. *Ibid.,* 154.

25. *Ibid.,* 393–94.

26. Carville V. Earle, "Environment, Disease, and Mortality in Early Virginia," in Thad W. Tate and David L. Ammerman, eds., *The Chesapeake in the Seventeenth Century: Essays on Anglo-American Society* (Chapel Hill, 1979), 96–125; Karen Ordahl Kupperman, "Apathy and Death in Early Jamestown," *Journal of American History,* 66 (1979), 24–40.

27. Barbour, *Jamestown Voyages,* 191–92.

28. *Ibid.,* 194–95. On the trade, see Martin H. Quitt, "Trade and Acculturation at Jamestown, 1607–1609: The Limits of Understanding," *William and Mary Quarterly,* 3rd ser. 52 (April 1995), 227–58. For evidence of the sheet copper cut and traded to the natives, see William M. Kelso, *Jamestown Rediscovery II* (Richmond, Va., 1996), 2, fig. 2.

29. Barbour, *Jamestown Voyages,* 414–15. This may be the famous "Powhatan's mantle" that now resides in the Ashmolean Museum in Oxford, England. An exact copy is displayed at the Jamestown Settlement museum.

30. *Ibid.,* 354, 411.

31. *Ibid.,* 202, 395, 423, 458.

32. Percy, "Trewe Relacyon," 263, 266.

33. Barbour, *Jamestown Voyages,* 426.

34. *Ibid.*, 432–34. On the importance of the scalplock, which represented the native's soul, see below, Chapter 11, p. 262.

35. Barbour, *Jamestown Voyages*, 428.

36. *Ibid.*, 461; Capt. John Smith, *Works, 1608–1631*, ed. Edward Arber (Birmingham, Eng., 1884), 498–99; Percy, "Trewe Relacyon," 266–67; *A Voyage to Virginia in 1609*, ed. Louis B. Wright (Charlottesville, 1964), 99. The severe drought conditions in the Tidewater were established by tree-ring analysis of bald cypress in 1998. See David W. Stahle, "The Lost Colony and Jamestown Droughts," *Science*, 280:5363 (April 24, 1998), 564–67.

37. Samuel M. Bemiss, ed., *The Three Charters of the Virginia Company of London* (Williamsburg, 1957), 55–69. See Helen C. Rountree, ed., *Powhatan Foreign Relations, 1500–1722* (Charlottesville, 1993).

38. Percy, "Trewe Relacyon," 270, 273.

39. *Ibid.*, 271–73.

40. *Ibid.*, 276–77.

41. *Ibid.*, 280; Smith, *Works*, 509–11.

42. Strachey, *Historie*, 85–86.

43. Percy, "Trewe Relacyon," 279–80. See J. Frederick Fausz, "George Thorpe, Nemattanew, and the Powhatan Uprising of 1622," *Virginia Cavalcade*, 28 (1979), 110–17; Fausz, "Opechancanough: Indian Resistance Leader," in David G. Sweet and Gary B. Nash, eds., *Struggle and Survival in Colonial America* (Berkeley and Los Angeles, 1981), 21–37; Fausz, "'An Abundance of Blood Shed on Both Sides': England's First Indian War, 1609–1614," *Virginia Magazine of History and Biography*, 98:1 (Jan. 1990), 3–56.

44. Smith, *Works*, 511–14, 518; Ralph Hamor, *A True Discourse of the Present State of Virginia* [London, 1615], ed. A. L. Rowse (Richmond, 1957), 10–11; Samuel Purchas, *Hakluytus Posthumus, or Purchas His Pilgrimes*, 20 vols. (Glasgow, 1905–07), 19:104–6, 117–18.

45. Smith, *Works*, 530–33. On Pocahontas's treasonable behavior, see Barbour, *Jamestown Voyages*, 459; Smith, *Works*, 455, 531.

46. Smith, *Works*, 533–34; Purchas, *Pilgrimes*, 19:118–19.

47. Susan Myra Kingsbury, ed., *The Records of the Virginia Company of London*, 4 vols. (Washington, D.C., 1906–35), 3:92.

48. Smith, *Works*, 518–19; Hamor, *True Discourse*, 40–42.

49. [James I,] *A Counter-Blaste to Tobacco* [London, 1604] (Emmaus, Pa., 1954), 36.

50. Smith, *Works*, 535.

51. Purchas, *Pilgrimes*, 19:153.

52. Fausz, "George Thorpe"; Alden T. Vaughan, "'Expulsion of the Salvages': English Policy and the Virginia Massacre of 1622," *William and Mary Quarterly*, 3d ser. 35 (1978), 57–84 at 68–71; Eric Gethyn-Jones, *George Thorpe and the Berkeley Company: A Gloucestershire Enterprise in Virginia* (Gloucester, Eng., 1982); James Axtell, *The Invasion Within: The Contest of Cultures in Colonial North America* (New York, 1985), 179–82.

53. Kingsbury, *Va. Co. Recs.*, 3:73.

54. *Ibid.*, 3:128–29, 228.

55. Smith, *Works,* 574–75; Kingsbury, *Va. Co. Recs.,* 3:552.

56. Kingsbury, *Va. Co. Recs.,* 3:446.

57. Smith, *Works,* 564; Bemiss, *Three Charters,* 57–58; Strachey, *Historie,* 90; Kingsbury, *Va. Co. Recs.,* 3:557.

58. Strachey, *Historie,* 91.

59. Smith, *Works,* 574; Kingsbury, *Va. Co. Recs.,* 3:551.

60. Kingsbury, *Va. Co. Recs.,* 3:550–51, 554–55; Purchas, *Pilgrimes,* 19:159, 162–64; Smith, *Works,* 563, 573.

61. Kingsbury, *Va. Co. Recs.,* 3:556–57.

62. Smith, *Works,* 572, 587; J. Frederick Fausz and Jon Kukla, eds., "A Letter of Advice to the Governor of Virginia, 1624," *WMQ,* 3d ser. 34 (1977), 117.

63. Kingsbury, *Va. Co. Recs.,* 3:550, 4:11.

64. *Ibid.*, 3:556, 4:10; Smith, *Works,* 578.

65. Kingsbury, *Va. Co. Recs.,* 3:557–58, 672, 683, 4:71.

66. *Ibid.*, 4:71, 75, 221–22; Barbour, *Jamestown Voyages,* 372. On the scalps, see Axtell, *The European and the Indian: Essays in the Ethnohistory of Colonial North America* (New York, 1981), 26–27.

67. Kingsbury, *Va. Co. Recs.,* 3:665, 4:10, 507–8; W. L. Grant and James Munro, eds., *Acts of the Privy Council of England, Colonial Series, 1613–1680,* 1:pt. 1 (Hereford, Eng., 1908), 54.

68. Gov. Francis Wyatt to [earl of Southampton?], 1624, *WMQ,* 2d ser. 6 (1926), 118; Kingsbury, *Va. Co. Recs.,* 3:683; H. R. McIlwaine, ed., *Minutes of the Council and General Court of Virginia* (Richmond, 1924), 484. See William S. Powell, "Aftermath of the Massacre: The First Indian War, 1622–1632," *Virginia Magazine of History and Biography,* 66 (1958), 44–75, and Michael J. Puglisi, "Revitalization or Extirpation: Anglo-Powhatan Relations, 1622–1644" (M.A. thesis, Dept. of History, College of William and Mary, 1982); Helen C. Rountree, *Pocahontas's People: The Powhatan Indians of Virginia through Four Centuries* (Norman, 1990), chs. 4–7; Frederic W. Gleach, *Powhatan's World and Colonial Virginia: A Conflict of Cultures* (Lincoln, 1997).

69. Robert Beverley, *The History and Present State of Virginia* [London, 1705], ed. Louis B. Wright (Chapel Hill, 1947), 60–62.

70. *Ibid.*, 62.

71. Leo F. Stock, ed., *Proceedings and Debates of the British Parliaments Respecting North America,* 5 vols. (Washington, D.C., 1924), 1:182; Edmund Berkeley and Dorothy Smith Berkeley, eds., *The Reverend John Clayton: . . . His Scientific Writings and Other Related Papers* (Charlottesville, 1965), 39.

Chapter Eleven

1. John Higham, "Beyond Consensus: The Historian as Moral Critic," *American Historical Review,* 67 (1962), 609–25 at 624.

2. For an excellent application of this technique, see W. J. Eccles, *Frontenac, The Courtier Governor* (Toronto, 1959), 182–83, which treats Denonville's enslavement of Iroquois warriors for the king's galleys.

3. Wilcomb Washburn, "Relations between Europeans and Amerindians during the Seventeenth and Eighteenth Centuries: The Epistemological Problem," paper delivered at the International Colloquium on Colonial History, University of Ottawa, Ottawa, Ontario, Nov. 1969, pp. 12–13.

4. Arthur Pound. *Johnson of the Mohawks* (New York, 1930), 243–44.

5. Henry J. Young, "A Note on Scalp Bounties in Pennsylvania," *Pennsylvania History*, 24 (1957), 207–18 at 207–8.

6. Howard Swiggett, *War Out of Niagara: Walter Butler and the Tory Rangers* (New York, 1933), 47.

7. Douglas Edward Leach, *Arms for Empire: A Military History of the British Colonies in North America, 1607–1763* (New York, 1973), 107, 132–33; Pound, *Johnson of the Mohawks*, 243–45.

8. James Oliver Curwood, *The Plains of Abraham* (Garden City, N.Y., 1928), 126n.

9. Alden T. Vaughan, *New England Frontier: Puritans and Indians, 1620–1675* (Boston, 1965), 40–41. The passage is unchanged in the 2nd revised edition (New York, 1979) and the 3rd (Norman, 1994).

10. Francis Jennings, *The Invasion of America: Indians, Colonialism, and the Cant of Conquest* (Chapel Hill, 1975), 160, 163, 166.

11. Rev. John Heckewelder, *History, Manners, and Customs of the Indian Nations Who Once Inhabited Pennsylvania and the Neighbouring States*, rev. ed. Rev. William C. Reichel (Philadelphia, 1876), 215.

12. [William Gerard], *DeBrahm's Report of the General Survey in the Southern District of North America*, ed. Louis DeVorsey, Jr. (Columbia, S.C., 1971), 109.

13. Heckewelder, *History*, 215–16.

14. *Ibid.*, 216.

15. Sir William Johnson to Arthur Lee, Feb. 28, 1771, E. B. O'Callaghan, ed., *The Documentary History of the State of New-York*, 4 vols. (quarto ed., Albany, 1849–51), 4:273.

16. DeVorsey, ed., *DeBrahm's Report*, 111.

17. James Phinney Baxter, ed., *Documentary History of the State of Maine, Collections of the Maine Historical Society*, 2d ser. 23 (1916), 131–32, 139–40 (hereafter cited as *Doc. His. of Maine*). See below, p. 266 for Maryland soldiers who accompanied a Cherokee war party.

18. William Waller Hening, ed., *The Statutes at Large; Being a Collection of all the Laws of Virginia*, 13 vols. (Richmond, 1819–23), 6:565.

19. John Lawson, *A New Voyage to Carolina* [London, 1709], ed. Hugh Talmage Lefler (Chapel Hill, 1967), 10; James W. Covington, "Apalachee Indians, 1704–1763," *Florida Historical Quarterly*, 50 (1972), 366–84 at 369.

20. Thomas Anburey, *Travels through the Interior Parts of America* [London, 1789], 2 vols. (Boston, 1923), 1:170–72.

21. James Sullivan *et al.*, eds., *The Papers of Sir William Johnson*, 14 vols. (Albany, 1921–65), 1:87, 9:8, 25 (hereafter cited as *Johnson Papers*).

22. Captain John Knox, *An Historical Journal of the Campaigns in North America for the Years 1757, 1758, 1759, and 1760* [London, 1769], ed. Arthur G. Doughty, 3 vols. (Toronto: The Champlain Society, 1914–16), 2:348.

23. *Johnson Papers*, 2:375, 9:586–87, 780; see also *ibid.*, 9:28, 2:375, and E. B. O'Callaghan and Berthold Fernouw, eds., *Documents Relative to the Colonial History of the State of New York*, 15 vols. (Albany, 1856–87), 7:134, 152, 864 (hereafter cited as *N.Y. Col. Docs.*). In 1710 the Senecas condoled with Governor Hunter of New York for the loss of one of his lieutenants with a scalp and four beaver pelts (*The Letters and Papers of Cadwallader Colden*, 9, *Collections of the New-York Historical Society*, 68 [1935], 393).

24. *N.Y. Col. Docs.*, 6:363; *Minutes of the Provincial Council of Pennsylvania*, 10 vols. (Philadelphia and Harrisburg, 1851–52), 7:712, 732.

25. *Johnson Papers*, 9:22–31

26. Clifford K. Shipton, *Sibley's Harvard Graduates: Biographical Sketches of Those Who Attended Harvard College* (Cambridge, Mass., 1873–), 7:16; *Journals of the House of Representatives of Massachusetts* (Boston: Massachusetts Historical Society, 1919–), 6:210; William Hand Browne *et al.*, eds., *Archives of Maryland*, 52 (1935), 488–89; Samuel Hazard *et al.*, eds., *Pennsylvania Archives*, 1st ser. 2 (1853), 641.

27. A. C. Goodell, Jr., "The Centennial Anniversary of the Meeting of the Provincial Legislature in Salem, October 5, 1774," Essex Institute, *Historical Collections*, 13 (1875), 26–27.

28. Anburey, *Travels*, 1:237. Perhaps the officer was spared the danger that General George Townshend encountered upon returning to England with a scalp collection. See below, p. 273.

29. *Archives of Maryland*, 6 (1888), 558–63. On the New York frontier in 1777, Timothy Edwards wrote to his commander: "The affair of scalping as relating to Indians is delicate but your knowledge of their disposition will conduct you into such measures as will not deprive them of trophies of warlike achievement" (Gates MSS, microfilm, reel 3, p. 210, New-York Historical Society, New York, N.Y.).

30. *Archives of Maryland*, 9 (1890), 6.

31. *Pa. Archives*, 1st ser. 3 (1853), 185–87, 200.

32. *N.Y. Col. Docs.*, 7:277–78.

33. *Adventure in the Wilderness: The American Journals of Louis Antoine de Bougainville, 1756–1760*, ed. and trans. Edward P. Hamilton (Norman, 1964), 142.

34. *Pa. Archives*, 1st ser. 3 (1853), 200. Harriette Simpson Arnow, *Seedtime on the Cumberland* (New York, 1960), 199, mentions nine scalps made from two during Lord Dunmore's War (1775).

35. *Pa. Archives*, 1st ser. 3 (1853), 199.

36. *Mins. of the Prov. Council of Pa.*, 7:735.

37. *Lieut. Henry Timberlake's Memoirs, 1756–1765* [London, 1765], ed. Samuel Cole Williams (Johnson City, Tenn., 1927), 78.

38. *Pa. Archives*, 1st ser. 3 (1853), 199.

39. Charles Orr, ed., *History of the Pequot War* (Cleveland, 1897), 138; E. B. O'Callaghan, comp., *Laws and Ordinances of New Netherland, 1638–1674* (Albany, 1868), 28–29.

40. Charles H. Lincoln, ed., *Narratives of the Indian Wars, 1675–1699,* Original Narratives of Early American History (New York, 1913), 34.

41. William Hubbard, *The Present State of New-England* (London, 1677), 22; Benjamin Church, *Diary of King Philip's War, 1675–76,* ed. Alan and Mary Simpson (Chester, Conn., 1975), 156.

42. *N.Y. Col. Docs.,* 3:562, 4:150n.

43. *Ibid.,* 10:484.

44. Paul A. W. Wallace, *Conrad Weiser, 1696–1760, Friend of Colonist and Mohawk* (Philadelphia, 1945), 414; *Pa. Archives,* 1st ser. 2 (1853), 511.

45. *Archives of Maryland,* 52 (1935), 176–77; Hening, ed., *Statutes,* 6: 550–51; Leonard W. Labaree *et al.,* eds., *The Papers of Benjamin Franklin* (New Haven, 1959–ㅤ), 6:233, n.7.

46. *Pa. Archives,* 1st ser. 2 (1853), 543, 546, 620; *Johnson Papers,* 2:443–44. See also *Archives of Maryland,* 6 (1888), 435; 52 (1935), 651; Hening, ed., *Statutes,* 7:122; J. Hammond Trumbull and C. J. Hoadly, eds., *The Public Records of the Colony of Connecticut,* 15 vols. (Hartford, 1850–90), 9:228–29; *J. of the Mass. House of Reps.,* 21 (1946), 99; 22 (1947), 71; 32, pt. 1 (1957), 87–88; George Sheldon, *A History of Deerfield, Massachusetts,* 2 vols. (Deerfield, 1895–96), 2:635 (continuous pag.).

47. Richard R. Johnson, "The Search for a Usable Indian: An Aspect of the Defense of Colonial New England," *Journal of American History,* 64 (1977), 623–51 at 643.

48. *Pa. Archives,* 1st ser. 2 (1853), 629.

49. Stanley McCrory Pargellis, *Lord Loudon in North America* (New Haven, 1933), ch. 1; I. K. Steele, *Guerillas and Grenadiers: The Struggle for Canada, 1689–1760* (Toronto, 1969), 69, 123–24. In 1758 a British major under General John Forbes warned a young officer that "the Inhabitants [of Pennsylvania] are very incapable of giveing advice how to Act upon the offensive, as their views are only turn'd how to defend themselves" (Alfred Procter James, ed., *Writings of General John Forbes* [Menasha, Wis., 1938], 186).

50. [John Mitchell], *The Contest in America Between Great Britain and France* (London, 1757), 137; Rev. Benjamin Doolittle, *A Short Narrative of Mischief done by the French and Indian Enemy, on the Western Frontiers of the Province of Massachusetts-Bay* [1744–48] (Boston, 1750), 20.

51. *Archives of Maryland,* 6 (1888), 435; Hening, ed., *Statutes,* 7:122.

52. *Archives of Maryland,* 52 (1935), 651; *Papers of Benjamin Franklin,* 6:455–56; *J. of the Mass. House of Reps.,* 23 (1948), 389; 24 (1949), 14; Nathaniel Bouton, ed., *Provincial Papers: Documents and Records Relating to the Province of New-Hampshire* (Manchester, N.H., 1868), 2:428.

53. *Archives of Maryland,* 9 (1890), 6; 52 (1935), 651; 59 (1942), 64–65.

54. *Pa. Archives,* 1st ser. 8 (1853), 218; *Mins. of the Prov. Council of Pa.,* 9:191–92; *Minutes of the Supreme Executive Council of Pennsylvania,* 6 vols. (Harrisburg,

1852–53), 2:811–12. See also *Pa. Archives,* 1st ser. 7 (1853), 362:8 (1853), 167, 176, 189–90, 227, 283, 393.

55. William Hubbard, *The History of the Indian Wars in New England* [1677], ed. Samuel G. Drake, 2 vols. (Roxbury, Mass., 1865), 1:87; Hamilton, ed., *Adventure in the Wilderness,* 141.

56. William A. Whitehead *et al.,* eds., *Documents Relating to the Colonial, Revolutionary, and post-Revolutionary History of the State of New Jersey, Archives of the State of New Jersey,* 1st ser. 20 (1898), 33, 35 (hereafter cited as *N.J. Archives*).

57. *N.J. Archives,* 1st ser. 19 (1897), 488.

58. Carl Van Doren and Julian P. Boyd, eds., *Indian Treaties Printed by Benjamin Franklin, 1736–1762* (Philadelphia, 1938), lxxiin.

59. See Axtell, *The European and the Indian* (New York, 1981), 328 n.45.

60. Hugh Honour, *The New Golden Land* (New York, 1975), 128.

61. Jeremy Belknap, *History of New Hampshire,* 3 vols. (2d ed., Boston, 1813), 2:52; John Farmer and Jacob Bailey Moore, eds., *Collections, historical and miscellaneous,* 3 vols. (Concord, N.H., 1822–24), 3:151; Autobiographical narrative of Hugh Adams, pp. 15, 43, Belknap MSS, Mass. His. Soc., Boston, Mass. See also *Johnson Papers,* 1:53, and *N.Y. Col. Docs.,* 6:620.

62. Kathryn Whitford, "Hannah Dustin: The Judgement of History," Essex Institute, *Historical Collections,* 108 (1972), 304–25.

63. Henry Bouquet to Anne Willing, Sept. 17, 1759, *The Papers of Henry Bouquet* (Harrisburg, Pa., 1951–   ), 4:115–17.

64. Archibald Kennedy, *Serious Advice to the Inhabitants of the Northern Colonies, on the Present State of Affairs* (New York, 1755), 18–19.

65. *The Acts and Resolves, Public and Private, of the Province of the Massachusetts Bay,* 21 vols. (Boston, 1869–1922), 1:530, 558, 594, 2:259; *Pa. Archives,* 1st ser. 2 (1853), 620 (1756); *Mins. of the Prov. Council of Pa.,* 9:191–92 (1764); *Collections of the New Jersey Historical Society,* 4 (1852), 305–6; Trumbull and Hoadly, eds., *Conn. Col. Recs.,* 9:229.

66. M. Halsey Thomas, ed., *The Diary of Samuel Sewall,* 2 vols. (New York, 1973), 2:691 (June 13, 1712).

67. Van Doren and Boyd, eds., *Indian Treaties Printed by Franklin,* lxxii–lxxiii; *Johnson Papers,* 1:772.

68. *Johnson Papers,* 1:772; *Proposals to Prevent Scalping, & Humbly offered to the Consideration of a Council of War* (New York, 1755), 3.

69. *Doc. His. of Maine,* 9:259; *J. of the Mass. House of Reps.,* 23 (1948), 295–96; Knox, *Journals,* 1:438, 468.

70. Knox, *Journal,* 1:196, n.3; *Pa. Archives,* 1st ser. 7 (1853), 569–70.

71. *Collections of the Connecticut Historical Society,* 15 (1914), 82–83 (Aug. 26, 1747); Sylvester K. Stevens and Donald H. Kent, eds., *Wilderness Chronicles of Northwestern Pennsylvania* (Harrisburg, 1941), 265–66.

72. *Proposals to Prevent Scalping,* 4–5.

73. *Papers of Benjamin Franklin,* 6:382.

74. *Johnson Papers,* 6:102, 11:540.

75. *N.J. Archives,* 1st ser. 20 (1898), 43–44; *Mins. of the Prov. Council of Pa.,* 7:89.

76. Samuel Penhallow, *The History of the Wars of New England, with the Eastern Indians* [1703–22] (Boston, 1726), facs. ed. Edward Wheelock (Williamstown, Mass., 1973), 111 and Notes, 35; Sheldon, *Deerfield,* 637 (1755); *J. of the Mass. House of Reps.,* 24 (1949), 116, 123 (1747); Emma Lewis Coleman, *New England Captives Carried to Canada,* 2 vols. (Portland, Me., 1925), 2:193–95. The few acculturated Indians who hired out to Braddock in 1755 committed a similar breach of their own scalping etiquette because they could not collect the general's £5 bounty without tangible proof (Charles Hamilton, ed., *Braddock's Defeat* [Norman, 1959], 25).

77. *N.J. Archives,* 1st ser. 20 (1898), 243–44.

78. "The Haldiman Papers," *Michigan Pioneer and Historical Collections,* 9 (1886), 501–2.

79. *Sibley's Harvard Graduates,* 6:407–8, 7:176–77.

Chapter Twelve

1. John S. Ezell, ed., *The New Democracy in America: Travels of Francisco de Miranda in the United States, 1783–84,* trans. Judson P. Wood (Norman, 1963), 111.

2. Louis-Philippe, King of France, 1830–1848, *Diary of My Travels in America,* trans. Stephen Becker (New York, 1977), 51.

3. *Moreau de St. Méry's American Journey* [*1793–1798*], ed. and trans. Kenneth Roberts and Anna M. Roberts (Garden City, N.Y., 1947), 293, 300.

4. Johann David Schoepf, *Travels in the Confederation* [*1783–84*], trans. Alfred J. Morrison, 2 vols. (Philadelphia, 1911), 2:40, 149.

5. *Moreau de St. Méry's American Journey,* 309.

6. *Luigi Castiglioni's Viaggio: Travels in the United States of America, 1785–87,* ed. and trans. Antonio Pace (Syracuse, N.Y., 1983), 165.

7. *Moreau de St. Méry's American Journey,* 276.

8. *Chateaubriand's Travels in America,* trans. Richard Switzer (Lexington, Ky., 1969), 175.

9. J. P. Brissot de Warville, *New Travels in the United States of America, 1788,* ed. Durand Echeverria, trans. Maria Soceanu Vamos and Durand Echeverria (Cambridge, Mass., 1964), 82n.6.

10. Marquis de Chastellux, *Travels in North America in the Years 1780, 1781 and 1782,* ed. and trans. Howard C. Rice, Jr., 2 vols. (Chapel Hill, 1963), 1:209.

11. *Historical Statistics of the United States: Colonial Times to 1970,* 2 pts. (Bicentennial ed., Washington, D.C., 1975), Series A 1–5, 43–56, 57–72, 91–104, 335–49; Z 20–23.

12. Peter H. Wood, "The Changing Population of the Colonial South: An Overview by Race and Region, 1685–1790," in Wood, Gregory A. Waselkov, and M. Thomas Hatley, eds., *Powhatan's Mantle: Indians in the Colonial Southeast* (Lincoln, 1989), 38–39.

13. *Historical Statistics of the United States,* Series A 91–104; Z 1–23.

14. Leslie B. Rout, Jr., *The African Experience in Spanish America: 1502 to the Present Day* (Cambridge, 1976), 22.

15. Nicolás Sanchez-Albornez, "The Population of Colonial Spanish America," in Leslie Bethell, ed., *The Cambridge History of Latin America, Volume II: Colonial Latin America* (Cambridge, 1984), 15–19; Magnus Mörner, "Spanish Migration to the New World Prior to 1800: A Report on the State of Research," in Fredi Chiappelli, ed., *First Images of America: The Impact of the New World on the Old*, 2 vols. (Berkeley, 1976), 2:737–82.

16. R. Cole Harris and John Warkentin, *Canada Before Confederation: A Study in Historical Geography* (New York, 1974), 19–21, 32–37; Jacques Henripin and Yves Péron, "The Demographic Transition of the Province of Quebec," in D. V. Glass and Roger Revelle, eds., *Population and Social Change* (London, 1972), 213, 217, 220; Hubert Charbonneau *et al.*, *Naissance d'une population: Les Français établi au Canada au XVIIᵉ siècle*, Institut National d'Études Démographiques, Travaux et Documents, Cahier no. 118 (Montreal, 1987), 15–16: Mario Boleda, "Trente mille Français à la conquête du Saint-Laurent," *Histoire Social-Social History*, 23 (May 1990), 153–77; Leslie Choquette, "Recruitment of French Emigrants to Canada, 1600–1760," in Ida Altman and James Horn, eds., *"To Make America": European Emigration in the Early Modern Period* (Berkeley, 1991), 131–71.

17. *Historical Statistics of the United States*, Series A 91–104; Z 1–23.

18. R. C. Simmons, *The American Colonies: From Settlement to Independence* (New York, 1976), 174–85; A. Roger Ekirch, *Bound for America: The Transportation of British Convicts to the Colonies, 1718–1775* (Oxford, 1987), 26–27.

19. Jim Potter, "Demographic Development and Family Structure," in Jack P. Greene and J. R. Pole, eds., *Colonial British America: Essays in the New History of the Early Modern Era* (Baltimore, 1984), ch. 5; John J. McCusker and Russell R. Menard, *The Economy of British America, 1607–1789* (Chapel Hill, 1985), ch. 10.

20. Benjamin Franklin, *The Interest of Great Britain Considered . . .* [and] *Observations concerning the Increase of Mankind, Peopling of Countries, &c.* [1751] (London, 1760), 51.

21. Simmons, *The American Colonies*, 174, 179–81; Potter, "Demographic Development," 148–50.

22. Carville V. Earle, "Environment, Disease, and Mortality in Early Virginia," in Thad W. Tate and David L. Ammerman, eds., *The Chesapeake in the Seventeenth Century: Essays on Anglo-American Society* (Chapel Hill, 1979), ch. 3; Simmons, *The American Colonies*, 24, 76; Wood, "The Changing Population of the Colonial South," 38; Helen C. Rountree, *Pocahontas's People: The Powhatan Indians of Virginia Through Four Centuries* (Norman, 1990), 96, 104.

23. Simmons, *The American Colonies*, 24, 175, 178.

24. *Ibid.*, 124, 176, 178.

25. John White, *The Planters Plea* (London, 1630), quoted in David Cressy, *Coming Over: Migration and Communication between England and New England in the Seventeenth Century* (Cambridge, 1987), 85.

26. James Axtell, *The Invasion Within: The Contest of Cultures in Colonial North America* (New York, 1985).

27. *Historical Statistics of the United States,* Series A 91–104.

28. William D. Phillips, Jr., *Slavery from Roman Times to the Early Transatlantic Trade* (Minneapolis, 1985); Herbert S. Klein, *The Atlantic Slave Trade* (Cambridge, 1999); David Eltis, *The Rise of African Slavery in the Americas* (Cambridge, 1999).

29. Rout, *The African Experience in Spanish America,* 61–66, ch. 3; Frederick P. Bowser, "Africans in Spanish American Colonial Society," in Bethell, *Cambridge History of Latin America,* 2:357–79.

30. Marcel Trudel, *L'Esclavage au Canada français: Histoire et conditions de l'esclavage* (Quebec, 1960), ch. 3; Robin Winks, *The Blacks in Canada: A History* (Montreal and New Haven, 1971), ch. 1, "Slavery in New France, 1628–1760."

31. Daniel H. Usner, Jr., "From African Slavery to American Slavery: The Introduction of Black Laborers to Colonial Louisiana," *Louisiana History,* 20 (Winter 1979), 25–48; Gwendolyn Midlo Hall, *Africans in Colonial Louisiana: The Development of Afro-Creole Culture in the Eighteenth Century* (Baton Rouge, 1992).

32. Donald R. Wright, *African Americans in the Colonial Era: From African Origins Through the American Revolution* (Arlington Heights, Ill., 1990), ch. 1.

33. *Historical Statistics of the United States,* Series Z 1–23.

34. Simmons, *The American Colonies,* 87, 125, 186; Wright, *African Americans in the Colonial Era,* 17–18, 20.

35. Bernard W. Sheehan, *Seeds of Extinction: Jeffersonian Philanthropy and the American Indian* (Chapel Hill, 1973).

36. Wood, "The Changing Population of the Colonial South," 38–39.

37. Noble David Cook, *Born to Die: Disease and New World Conquest* (Cambridge, 1998); Clark Spencer Larsen and George R. Milner, eds., *In the Wake of Contact: Biological Responses to Conquest* (New York, 1994); John W. Verano and Douglas H. Ubelaker, eds., *Disease and Demography in the Americas* (Washington, D.C., 1992); Russell Thornton, *American Indian Holocaust and Survival: A Population History since 1492* (Norman, 1987), ch. 4.

38. Alexander S. Salley, Jr., ed., *Narratives of Early Carolina, 1650–1708,* Original Narratives of Early American History (New York, 1911), 284–85.

39. John Duffy, "Smallpox and the Indians of the American Colonies," *Bulletin of the History of Medicine,* 25 (1951), 324–41 at 332; Peter H. Wood, "The Impact of Smallpox on the Native Population of the 18th Century South," *New York State Journal of Medicine,* 87 (Jan. 1987), 30–36.

40. [James] *Adair's History of the American Indians* [London, 1775], ed. Samuel Cole Williams (New York, 1966), 244–45.

41. Sherburne F. Cook, "Interracial Warfare and Population Decline Among the New England Indians," *Ethnohistory,* 20:1 (Winter 1973), 1–24.

42. Almon Wheeler Lauber, *Indian Slavery in Colonial Times Within the Present Limits of the United States,* Columbia University Studies in History, Economics, and Public Law, vol. 54, no. 3 (New York, 1913); William Robert Snell, "Indian Slavery in Colonial South Carolina, 1671–1795" (Ph.D. diss., U. of Alabama, 1972); Robert P. Wiegers, "A Proposal for Indian Slave Trading in the Mississippi Valley and Its Impact on the Osage," *Plains Anthropologist,* 33 (May 1988), 187–202.

43. Paul Chrisler Phillips, *The Fur Trade,* 2 vols. (Norman, 1961); above, Chapter 5.

44. William Hand Browne et al., eds., *Archives of Maryland,* 72 vols. to date (Baltimore, 1883–   ), 2:14–15 (Proceedings and Acts of the General Assembly, April 12, 1666).

Chapter Thirteen

1. James Axtell, *The Invasion Within: The Contest of Cultures in Colonial North America* (New York, 1985), ch. 7.

2. See above p. 340n.4.

3. Axtell, *The Invasion Within,* 15–19.

4. *Ibid.,* 9–10, 78–79; James Axtell, *After Columbus: Essays in the Ethnohistory of Colonial North America* (New York, 1988), 132–33.

5. Axtell, *After Columbus,* 134–36.

6. See above Chapter 1, pp. 24–31.

7. See above Chapter 3, pp. 84–86.

8. See above, Chapter 2.

9. See above, Chapter 3, pp. 81–84.

10. Neal Salisbury, "Squanto: Last of the Patuxets," in David G. Sweet and Gary B. Nash, eds., *Struggle and Survival in Colonial America* (Berkeley and Los Angeles, 1981), 228–46; David Beers Quinn, *Set Fair for Roanoke: Voyages and Colonies, 1584–1606* (Chapel Hill, 1985), 233–35. See also Lynn Guitar, "Franciscano Chicorano: A North American Indian in King Charles I's Court," *Terrae Incognitae,* 29 (1997), 1–9.

11. H. P. Biggar, ed. and trans., *The Voyages of Jacques Cartier,* Publications of the Public Archives of Canada, No. 11 (Ottawa, 1924), 187.

12. Clifford M. Lewis and Albert J. Loomie, *The Spanish Jesuit Mission in Virginia, 1570–1572* (Chapel Hill, 1953), 15–18, 39–49.

13. Philip L. Barbour, ed., *The Jamestown Voyages Under the First Charter, 1606–1609,* Hakluyt Society Publications, 2d ser. 136–37 (Cambridge, 1969), 133–34 (continuous pagination).

14. Dwight B. Heath, ed., *A Journal of the Pilgrims at Plymouth: Mourt's Relation* [*1622*] (New York, 1963), 22, 26, 27–29, 35–37, 52; William Bradford, *Of Plymouth Plantation, 1620–1647,* ed. Samuel Eliot Morison (New York, 1952), 65–66, 69–70, 81.

15. James Axtell, *The European and the Indian: Essays in the Ethnohistory of Colonial North America* (New York, 1981), 248–49.

16. *Ibid.,* 249–50.

17. See above, Chapter 8; Daniel K. Richter, "War and Culture: The Iroquois Experience," *William and Mary Quarterly,* 3d ser. 40 (Oct. 1983), 528–59; José António Brandão, *"Your Fyre Shall Burn No More": Iroquois Policy Toward New France and Its Native Allies to 1701* (Lincoln, 1997), ch. 3.

18. Judith Reynolds, "Marriages Between the English and the Indians in Seventeenth Century Virginia," Archaeological Society of Virginia, *Quarterly Bulletin*, 17:2 (Dec. 1962), 19–25; James Hugo Johnston, *Race Relations in Virginia and Miscegenation in the South, 1776–1860* (Amherst, Mass., 1970), ch. 11; J. Leitch Wright, *The Only Land They Knew: The Tragic Story of the American Indians in the Old South* (New York, 1981), 234–37; Cornelius J. Jaenen, "Miscegenation in Eighteenth-Century New France" (Paper presented at the Second Laurier Conference on Ethnohistory and Ethnology, London, Ontario, May 12, 1983); Olive Patricia Dickason, "From 'One Nation' in the Northeast to 'New Nation' in the Northwest: A Look at the Emergence of the Métis," *American Indian Culture and Research Journal*, 6:2 (1982), 1–21; Kathleen A. Deagan, "*Mestizaje* in Colonial St. Augustine," *Ethnohistory*, 20 (1973), 55–65.

19. Salisbury, "Squanto," in Sweet and Nash, *Struggle and Survival*, 235–37.

20. David Landy, "Tuscarora Among the Iroquois," in William C. Sturtevant, gen. ed., *Handbook of North American Indians*, Vol. 15: *Northeast*, ed. Bruce G. Trigger (Washington, D.C., 1978), 518–20.

21. James H. Merrell, *The Indian's New World: Catawbas and Their Neighbors from European Contact through the Era of Removal* (Chapel Hill, 1989), ch. 3.

22. Colin G. Calloway, *The Western Abenakis of Vermont, 1600–1800: War, Migration, and the Survival of an Indian People* (Norman, 1990); Helen C. Rountree, *Pocahontas's People: The Powhatan Indians of Virginia Through Four Centuries* (Norman, 1990), chs. 4–5.

23. Bruce G. Trigger, *Natives and Newcomers: Canada's 'Heroic Age' Reconsidered* (Kingston and Montreal, 1985), 204, 312, 314, 318.

24. Axtell, *The Invasion Within*, chs. 2–6, 11.

25. Richebourg Gaillard McWilliams, ed. and trans., *Fleur de Lys and Calumet: Being the Pénicaut Narrative of French Adventure in Louisiana* (Baton Rouge, 1953), 98, 102–3, 125–26.

26. *Ibid.*, 129–30, 162, 219–20.

27. Daniel H. Usner, Jr., "The Deerskin Trade in French Louisiana," in Philip P. Boucher, ed., *Proceedings of the Tenth Meeting of the French Colonial Historical Society, April 12–14, 1984* (Lanham, Md., 1985), 75–93; Richard White, *Roots of Dependency: Subsistence, Environment, and Social Change Among the Choctaws, Pawnees, and Navajos* (Lincoln, 1983), chs. 3–4; Michael James Forêt, "On the Marchlands of Empire: Trade, Diplomacy, and War on the Southeastern Frontier, 1733–63" (Ph.D. diss., College of William and Mary, Dept. of History, 1990), chs. 2, 4–8.

28. Immanuel Wallerstein, *The Modern World-System: Capitalist Agriculture and the Origins of the European World Economy in the Sixteenth Century* (New York, 1974); Eric R. Wolf, *Europe and the People Without History* (Berkeley and Los Angeles, 1982). See above, Chapter 5.

29. Shepard Krech III, ed., *Indians, Animals, and the Fur Trade: A Critique of KEEPERS OF THE GAME* (Athens, Ga., 1981); Krech, *The Ecological Indian: Myth and History* (New York, 1999).

30. White, *Roots of Dependency*, ch. 3; Anthony F. C. Wallace, *The Death and Rebirth of the Seneca* (New York, 1970), ch. 5; Verner W. Crane, *The Southern Frontier, 1670–1732* (Ann Arbor, 1929); Forêt, "On the Marchlands of Empire"; Allen W. Tre-

lease, *Indian Affairs in Colonial New York: The Seventeenth Century* (Ithaca, N.Y., 1960), 51–58; Denys Delage, *Le Pays renversé: Amérindiens et européens en Amérique du nord-est, 1600–1664* (Montreal, 1985).

31. Peter A. Thomas, "Cultural Change on the Southern New England Frontier, 1630–1665," in William W. Fitzhugh, ed., *Cultures in Contact: The Impact of European Contacts on Native American Cultural Institutions, A.D. 1000–1800* (Washington, D.C., 1985), 131–57 at 157. See also James Warren Springer, "American Indians and the Law of Real Property in Colonial New England," *American Journal of Legal History,* 30 (1986), 25–58.

32. Daniel R. Mandell, "Change and Continuity in a Native American Community: 18th-Century Stockbridge" (M.A. thesis, U. of Virginia, Dept. of History, May 1982), 42–44.

33. K. G. Davies, ed., *Documents of the American Revolution, 1770–1783 (Colonial Office Series),* 21 vols. (Shannon and Dublin, 1972–81), 5:113–17.

34. See, for example, *Records of the Town of East-Hampton, Long Island, Suffolk Co., N.Y.,* vol. 1 (Sag Harbor, N.Y., 1887), 3–4, for a deed of sale dated April 29, 1648, in which the local Indians retain the right to "fish in any or all the cricks and ponds, and hunt up and downe in the woods without Molestation, . . . [and] libertie to fish in all convenient places, for Shells to make wampum."

35. Robert S. Grumet, "An Analysis of Upper Delawaran Land Sales in Northern New Jersey, 1630–1758," in *Papers of the Ninth Algonquian Conference,* ed. William Cowan (Ottawa: Carleton U., Dept. of Linguistics, 1978), 25–35. See also Emerson W. Baker, "'A Scratch with a Bear's Paw,': Anglo-Indian Land Deeds in Early Maine," *Ethnohistory,* 36 (1989), 235–56; Peter S. Leavenworth, "'The Best Title that Indians Can Claime': Native Agency and Consent in the Transferal of Penacook-Pawtucket Land in the Seventeenth Century," *New England Quarterly,* 72:2 (June 1999), 275–300.

36. Arthur J. Ray, *Indians in the Fur Trade: Their Role as Trappers, Hunters, and Middlemen in the Lands Southwest of Hudson Bay, 1660–1870* (Toronto, 1974); Davies, *Documents of the American Revolution,* 2:109; W. L. McDowell, ed., *Journals of the Commissioners of the Indian Trade, September 20, 1710—August 29, 1718,* Colonial Records of South Carolina, Series 2 (Columbia, S.C., 1955), 52, 133, 181, 188, 203, 237.

37. *Collections of the Massachusetts Historical Society,* 4th ser. 6 (1863), 228, Roger Williams to John Winthrop, April 16, 1638.

38. William S. Willis, Jr., "Divide and Rule: Red, White, and Black in the Old South," in Charles M. Hudson, ed., *Red, White, and Black: Symposium on Indians in the Old South* (Athens, Ga., 1971), 99–115.

39. Richard R. Johnson, "The Search for a Usable Indian: An Aspect of the Defense of Colonial New England," *Journal of American History,* 64 (1977), 623–51; I. K. Steele, *Guerillas and Grenadiers: The Struggle for Canada, 1689–1760* (Toronto, 1969); Douglas Edward Leach, *Arms for Empire: A Military History of the British Colonies in North America, 1607–1763* (New York, 1973), index, s. v. "Indians: as allies."

40. Daniel Vickers, "The First Whalemen of Nantucket," *William and Mary Quarterly,* 3d ser. 40 (Oct. 1983), 560–83; T. H. Breen, *Imagining the Past: East Hampton Histories* (Reading, Mass., 1989), 161–89.

41. Axtell, *After Columbus*, 157, 174; Brian L. Evans, "Ginseng: Root of Chinese-Canadian Relations," *Canadian Historical Review*, 66 (1985), 1–26; Russell Magnaghi, "Sassafras and Its Role in Early America, 1562–1662," *Terrae Incognitae*, 29 (1997), 10–21.

42. Edmund B. O'Callaghan and Berthold Fernow, eds., *Documents Relative to the Colonial History of the State of New-York*, 15 vols. (Albany, 1856–87), 2:157; Albert Cook Myers, ed., *Narratives of Early Pennsylvania, West New Jersey, and Delaware, 1630–1707*, Original Narratives of Early American History (New York, 1912), 401.

43. John A. Sainsbury, "Indian Labor in Early Rhode Island," *New England Quarterly*, 48 (1975), 378–93.

44. Theda Perdue, *Cherokee Women: Gender and Culture Change, 1700–1835* (Lincoln, 1998).

45. Wright, *The Only Land They Knew*, 234–37; Merrell, *Indians' New World*, 3, 30–31, 63–64, 86–87; Philippe Jacquin, *Les Indiens blancs: Français et Indiens en Amérique du Nord (XVIe–XVIIIe siècle)* (Paris, 1987), ch. 7.

46. Pierre Pouchot, *Memoir upon the Late War in North America, Between the French and English, 1755–60*, trans. Franklin B. Hough, 2 vols. (Roxbury, Mass., 1866), 2:237; *Travels of William Bartram*, ed. Mark Van Doren (New York, 1955), 215.

47. David Hurst Thomas, ed., *Columbian Consequences. Volume 2: Archaeological and Historical Perspectives on the Spanish Borderlands East* (Washington, D.C., 1990), chs. 24–35; Jerald T. Milanich, *Laboring in the Fields of the Lord: Spanish Missions and Southeastern Indians* (Washington D.C., 1999); Axtell, *The Invasion Within*.

48. Axtell, *The Invasion Within*, 69, 191, 193, 194, 212.

49. Many, perhaps most, tribes called themselves something like "the original people" or "real people [men]"; for example, Lenni Lenape (Delaware), Diné (Navajo), Penobscot, Anishanabe (Chippewa). The Seneca word for "Indians" in general (as distinguished from white or black people) is *ó-gweh 'o-weh*, real men. Wallace L. Chafe, *Seneca Morphology and Dictionary*, Smithsonian Contributions to Anthropology, 4 (Washington, D.C., 1967), 77.

50. Axtell, *After Columbus*, ch. 3; Axtell, *The Invasion Within*, ch. 11; Milanich, *Laboring in the Fields of the Lord*, chs. 5–6.

51. Axtell, *The Invasion Within*, 283–86.

52. *Ibid.*, ch. 8; Margaret Connell Szasz, *Indian Education in the American Colonies, 1607–1783* (Albuquerque, N.M., 1988).

53. Carolyn Thomas Foreman, *Indians Abroad, 1493–1938* (Norman, 1943); Richard N. Ellis and Charlie R. Steen, eds., "An Indian Delegation in France, 1725," *Journal of the Illinois State Historical Society*, 67 (Sept. 1974), 385–405.

54. Davies, *Documents of the American Revolution*, 2:28, John Stuart to Governor Lord Botetourt, Jan. 13, 1770.

55. Lt. Lion Gardener in Charles Orr, ed., *History of the Pequot War* (Cleveland, 1897), 142–43.

56. Axtell, *The European and the Indian*, 257–59; Craig MacAndrew and Robert B. Edgerton, *Drunken Comportment: A Social Explanation* (Chicago, 1969); Thomas W. Hill, "Ethnohistory and Alcohol Studies," in Marc Galanter, ed., *Recent Developments*

in Alcoholism, 2 (New York, 1984), 313–37; Peter C. Mancall, *Deadly Medicine: Indians and Alcohol in Early America* (Ithaca, 1995).

57. Charles E. Hunter, "The Delaware Nativist Revival of the Mid-Eighteenth Century," *Ethnohistory,* 18:1 (Winter 1971), 39–49; Alfred A. Cave, "The Delaware Prophet Neolin: A Reappraisal," *Ethnohistory,* 46:2 (Spring 1999), 265–90. Wallace, *Death and Rebirth of the Seneca,* 114–22.

58. See below Chapter 14. James Axtell, "The Columbian Mosaic in Colonial America," *Humanities* [N.E.H.], 12:5 (Sept./Oct. 1991), 12–18, is a shorter version.

59. Luis Villoro, *Sahagún or the Limits of the Discovery of the Other,* 1992 Lecture Series, Working Papers, No. 2, Dept. of Spanish and Portuguese, U. of Maryland (College Park, 1989), 7, 16.

60. Douglas H. Ubelaker, "North American Indian Population Size, A.D. 1500 to 1985," *American Journal of Physical Anthropology,* 77 (1988), 289–94; Barbara Vobejda, "American Indians' Population Boom," *Washington Post,* Feb. 11, 1991, A1, A4.

Chapter Fourteen

1. Little has been done since 1952 when Bernard DeVoto scolded American historians for making "disastrously little effort to understand how [Indian culture] affected white men and their societies" (Joseph Kinsey Howard, *Strange Empire* [New York, 1952], 9).

2. Edward Eggleston, "The Aborigines and the Colonists," *Century Magazine* (May 1883), 96–114; Alexander F. Chamberlain, "The Contributions of the American Indian to Civilization," *Proceedings of the American Antiquarian Society,* n.s. 16 (1903–4), 91–126; Clark Wissler, "The Influence of Aboriginal Indian Culture on American Life," in *Some Oriental Influences on Western Culture* (New York: American Council of the Institute of Pacific Relations, 1929); Everett E. Edwards, "American Indians' Contribution to Civilization," *Minnesota History,* 15 (1934), 255–72; Felix S. Cohen, "Americanizing the White Man," *The American Scholar,* 21 (1952), 177–91; E. Russell Carter, *The Gift Is Rich* (New York, 1955); A. Irving Hallowell, "The Impact of the American Indian on American Culture," *American Anthropologist,* n.s. 59 (1957), 201–17; Hallowell, "The Backwash of the Frontier: The Impact of the Indian on American Culture," in Walker D. Wyman and Clifton B. Kroeber, eds., *The Frontier in Perspective* (Madison, Wis., 1957), 229–58; Harold E. Driver, *Indians of North America* (2d rev. ed., Chicago, 1969), ch. 29; Wilbur R. Jacobs, *Dispossessing the American Indian: Indians and Whites on the Colonial Frontier* (New York, 1972), 151–72; Margaret C. Szasz and Ferenc M. Szasz, "The American Indian and the Classical Past," *The Midwest Quarterly,* 17:1 (Autumn 1975), 58–70. More but not completely satisfying is Colin G. Calloway, *New Worlds for All: Indians, Europeans, and the Remaking of Early America* (Baltimore, 1997).

3. Cohen, "Americanizing the White Man," 178; C. G. Jung, *Contributions to Analytical Psychology,* trans. H. G. and Cary F. Barnes (New York, 1928), 136–40.

4. Roy Harvey Pearce, *Savagism and Civilization: A Study of the Indian and the American Mind* (rev. ed., Baltimore, 1965).

5. William Hubbard, *The History of the Indian Wars in New England* [1677], ed. Samuel G. Drake, 2 vols. (Roxbury, Mass., 1865), 2:256.

6. [Increase Mather], *The Necessity of Reformation* (Boston, 1679), 7.

7. Joseph Easterbrooks, *Abraham the Passenger* (Boston, 1705), 3; J. Hammond Trumbull and C. J. Hoadly, eds., *The Public Records of the Colony of Connecticut*, 15 vols. (Hartford, 1850–90), 2:328.

8. *Necessity of Reformation*, 5.

9. Cotton Mather, *The Way to Prosperity* (Boston, 1690), 27. See also Kenneth Silverman, ed., *Selected Letters of Cotton Mather* (Baton Rouge, 1971), 398.

10. Franklin B. Dexter, ed., *Diary of David McClure, D.D., 1748–1820* (New York, 1899), 93.

11. Richard J. Hooker, ed., *The Carolina Backcountry on the Eve of the Revolution* (Chapel Hill, 1953), 7, 15, 20, 30–33, 56, 61.

12. Milo Milton Quaife, ed., *John Long's Voyages and Travels in the Years 1768–1788* (Chicago, 1922), 44.

13. Wilbur R. Jacobs, ed., *The Appalachian Indian Frontier: The Edmond Atkin Report and Plan of 1755* (Lincoln, 1967), 8, 22.

14. [James] *Adair's History of the American Indians* [London, 1775], ed. Samuel Cole Williams (Kingsport, Tenn., 1930), 306.

15. John Lawson, *A New Voyage to Carolina* [London, 1709], ed. Hugh Talmage Lefler (Chapel Hill, 1967), 190, 192.

16. Ann Maury, ed., *Memoirs of a Huguenot Family* [1852] (New York, 1907), 349–50.

17. Lawson, *New Voyage to Carolina*, 192.

18. Mrs. Anne Grant, *Memoirs of an American Lady*, ed. James Grant Wilson, 2 vols. (New York, 1901), 1:92, 99–109.

19. *Ibid.*, 1:107–8.

20. *Collections of the Massachusetts Historical Society*, 4th ser. 6 (1863), 215, 222, 245.

21. William Hubbard, *The Present State of New-England* (London, 1677), 59 (2d pag.); Charles H. Lincoln, ed., *Narratives of the Indian Wars, 1675–1699*, Original Narratives of Early American History [hereafter ONEAH] (New York, 1913), 67. See also *Colls. Mass. His. Soc.*, 4th ser. 6 (1863), 307–11. Another renegade, Edward Ashley, drew the fire of Plymouth's William Bradford (*Of Plymouth Plantation, 1620–1647*, ed, Samuel Eliot Morison (New York, 1952), 219, 233). See Colin G. Calloway, "Neither Red Nor White: White Renegades on the American Indian Frontier," *Western Historical Quarterly*, 17 (1986), 43–66.

22. Trumbull and Hoadly, eds., *Pub. Recs. of the Col. of Conn.*, 1:78. Early Virginia also had its share of runaways. See Bernard W. Sheehan, *Savagism and Civility: Indians and Englishmen in Colonial Virginia* (New York, 1980), 110–15.

23. James Axtell, *The European and the Indian* (New York, 1981), ch. 6.

24. John Franklin Meginness, *Biography of Frances Slocum, the Lost Sister of Wyoming* (Williamsport, Pa., 1891), 196. See also Felix Renick, "A Trip to the West," *The Amer-*

ican Pioneer, 1 (1842), 79, and Joseph Doddridge, *Notes on the Settlement and Indian Wars, of the Western Parts of Virginia & Pennsylvania* . . . [1763–1783] (Wellsburgh, Va., 1824), 188.

25. [William Smith, D.D.], *An Historical Account of the Expedition Against the Ohio Indians, in the Year 1764* . . . (Philadelphia, 1765), 29.

26. Silverman, ed., *Selected Letters of Cotton Mather,* 397–99.

27. George W. Corner, ed., *The Autobiography of Benjamin Rush* (Princeton, 1948), 71; J. Hector St. John de Crèvecoeur, *Letters from an American Farmer,* ed. Warren Barton Blake (London: Everyman ed., 1912), 65–66; Samuel Stanhope Smith, *An Essay on the Causes of the Variety of Complexion and Figure in the Human Species,* ed. Winthrop D. Jordan (Cambridge, Mass., 1965), 45n.

28. Smith, *Essay on the Causes,* 12, 17; Crèvecoeur, *Letters from an American Farmer,* 51–52, 222; Alexis de Tocqueville, *Democracy in America,* trans. Henry Reeve and Francis Bowen, ed. Phillips Bradley, 2 vols. (New York, 1945), 1:342–43, 347; Gen. Benjamin Lincoln, in *Colls. Mass. His. Soc.,* 1st ser. 5 (1798), 10. See also Leonard W. Labaree *et al.,* eds., *The Papers of Benjamin Franklin* (New Haven, 1959–   ), 4:481–82, and L. H Butterfield, ed., *Letters of Benjamin Rush,* 2 vols. (Princeton, 1951), 1:400–406, 2:1163.

29. Crèvecoeur, *Letters from an American Farmer,* 47, 52, 55; Smith, *Essay on the Causes,* 15, 17–18.

30. See above, Chapter 2.

31. Capt. John Smith, *Works 1608–1631,* ed. Edward Arber (Birmingham, Eng., 1884), 102, 449, 528, 564, 569, 599; Eleazar Wheelock, *A plain and faithful Narrative of the . . . Indian Charity-School At Lebanon, in Connecticut* (Boston, 1763), 18, 23–24, 27–28, 34.

32. See the recent edition by John T. Teunissen and Evelyn J. Hinz (Detroit, 1973). For linguistic purposes, the heavily annotated edition by J. Hammond Trumbull (Providence, 1860) is still superior.

33. David B. Quinn, ed., "A List of Books Purchased for the Virginia Company," *Virginia Magazine of History and Biography,* 77 (1969), 347–60.

34. Susie M. Ames, ed., *County Court Records of Accomack-Northampton, Virginia, 1632–1640* (Washington, D.C., 1954), 120.

35. Colonel Norwood, *A Voyage to Virginia* [1649], in Peter Force, ed., *Tracts and Other Papers, Relating Principally to the Origin, Settlement, and Progress of the Colonies in North America, from the Discovery of the Country to the Year 1776,* 4 vols. (Washington, D.C., 1836–47), vol. 3, no. 10, pp. 29–30.

36. Alexander F. Chamberlain, "Algonkian Words in American English: A Study in the Contact of the White Man and the Indian," *Journal of American Folklore,* 15 (1902), 240–67, Charles L. Cutler, *O Brave New Words! Native American Loanwords in Current English* (Norman, 1994).

37. Jacobs, *Dispossessing the American Indian,* 164; H. L. Mencken, *The American Language* (4th ed., New York, 1936), 104–13, 530–32; Arthur J. Krim, "Acculturation of the New England Landscape: Native and English Toponymy of Eastern Massachusetts," in Peter Benes, ed., *New England Prospect: Maps, Place Names, and the His-*

torical Landscape, The Dublin Seminar for New England Folklife: Annual Proceedings 1980 (Boston, 1983), 69–88.

38. Edward Eggleston, *The Transit of Civilization from England to America in the Seventeenth Century* [1900] (Boston, 1959), 106.

39. *Ibid.,* 107; Chamberlain, "Algonkian Words in American English," 244.

40. Bradford, *Of Plymouth Plantation,* 61.

41. Eggleston, "The Aborigines and the Colonists," 100.

42. Christopher Levett, *A Voyage into New England* [London, 1628], in Charles Herbert Levermore, ed., *Forerunners and Competitors of the Pilgrims and Puritans,* 2 vols. (Brooklyn, N.Y., 1912), 2:613.

43. [Edward] *Johnson's Wonder-Working Providence, 1628–1651,* ed. J. Franklin Jameson, ONEAH (New York, 1910), 114.

44. George Francis Dow, *Domestic Life in New England in the Seventeenth Century* (Topsfield, Mass., 1925), 4–5; Fiske Kimball, *Domestic Architecture of the American Colonies and of the Early Republic* (New York, 1922), 3–35; Cary Carson, Norman Barka, William Kelso, Garry Stone, and Dell Upton, "Impermanent Architecture in the Southern American Colonies," *Winterthur Portfolio,* 18 (1981).

45. *Johnson's Wonder-Working Providence,* 211.

46. Smith, *Works,* 154–57.

47. Susan Myra Kingsbury, ed., *Records of the Virginia Company of London,* 4 vols. (Washington, D.C., 1906–35), 3:556–57.

48. Bradford, *Of Plymouth Plantation,* 85; William Wood, *New Englands Prospect* (London, 1634), 70.

49. Bradford, *Of Plymouth Plantation,* 85; Dwight B. Heath, ed., *A Journal of the Pilgrims at Plymouth: Mourt's Relation* [1622] (New York, 1963), 82. Lynn Ceci, "Fish Fertilizer: A Native American Practice?" *Science* (April 4, 1975), 26–30; (Sept. 19, 1975), 945–47.

50. Nanepashemet, "It Smells Fishy to Me: An Argument Supporting the Use of Fish Fertilizer by the Native People of Southern New England," in Peter Benes, ed., *Algonkians of New England: Past and Present,* The Dublin Seminar for New England Folklife: Annual Proceedings 1991 (Boston, 1993), 42–50. Archaeologists have also found fish bones in early Indian fields on Cape Cod.

51. *Johnson's Wonder-Working Providence,* 114–15; Edward Everett, ed., *Letters from New England: The Massachusetts Bay Colony, 1629–1638* (Amherst, 1976), 66, 96; 227; Smith, *Works,* 952; Fulmer Mood, "John Winthrop, Jr. on Indian Corn," *New England Quarterly,* 10 (1937), 121–33 at 127–28; Nicholas P. Hardeman, *Shucks, Shocks, and Hominy Blocks: Corn as a Way of Life in Pioneer America* (Baton Rouge, 1981); Esther Louise Larsen, trans., "Pehr Kalm's Description of Maize, How It Is Planted and Cultivated in North America . . . ," *Agricultural History,* 9:2 (April 1935), 98–117.

52. Bradford, *Of Plymouth Plantation,* 178, 181, 202, 380; Darrett B. Rutman, *Husbandmen of Plymouth: Farms and Villages in the Old Colony, 1620–1692* (Boston, 1967), 10–12, 13, 16–17 and n. 33, 37, 42–46, 50–52, 54, 59, 60–61.

53. Charles Hudson, *The Southeastern Indians* (Knoxville, Tenn., 1976), 284.

54. Doddridge, *Notes on the Settlement and Indian Wars,* 156–59; Jeremy Belknap, *The History of New Hampshire,* 3 vols. (2d ed., Boston, 1813), 3:67–69.

55. Rev. Jared Eliot to the Rev. Thomas Prince, June 3, 1729, in *Collections of the Connecticut Historical Society,* 3 (1895), 291–92.

56. Belknap, *History of New Hampshire,* 3:66; Robert Beverley, *The History and Present State of Virginia,* ed. Louis B. Wright (Chapel Hill, 1947), 217–20; Doddridge, *Notes on the Settlement and Indian Wars,* 147–52; Virgil J. Vogel, *American Indian Medicine* (Norman, 1970), 116–19 and *passim,* esp. Appendix.

57. Dr. Benjamin Gale to Eleazar Wheelock, for Samuel Kirkland, July 21, 1769, Wheelock Papers 769421.1, Dartmouth College Library, Hanover, N.H.

58. Doddridge, *Notes on the Settlement and Indian Wars,* 114.

59. Williams, *Key into the Language of America,* 120.

60. Doddridge, *Notes on the Settlement and Indian Wars,* 115.

61. Richard Glover, ed., *David Thompson's Narrative, 1784–1812* (Toronto: The Champlain Society, 1962), 304.

62. Doddridge, *Notes on the Settlement and Indian Wars,* 113; Byron C. Smith, "To Ape the Manner of Savages: Frontier Culture, National Identity, and Rebellion in the Era of the American Revolution" (Directed Research paper, Dept. of History, U. of Richmond, April 1999).

63. Rhys Isaac, "Dramatizing the Ideology of Revolution: Popular Mobilization in Virginia, 1774 to 1776," *William and Mary Quarterly,* [WMQ], 3d ser. 33 (1976), 379–82.

64. Beverley, *History and Present State of Virginia,* 9; Silverman, ed., *Selected Letters of Cotton Mather,* 178, 399; Gottlieb Mittelberger, *Journey to Pennsylvania,* trans. and ed. Oscar Handlin and John Clive (Cambridge, Mass., 1960), 85. See Philip J. Deloria, *Playing Indian* (New Haven, 1998), ch. 1.

65. George Sheldon, *A History of Deerfield, Massachusetts,* 2 vols. (Deerfield, 1895–96), 1:656.

66. Samuel Penhallow, *The History of the Wars of New-England, with the Eastern Indians* (Boston, 1726), 11.

67. Archibald Kennedy, *Serious Advice to the Inhabitants of the Northern-Colonies* (New York, 1755), 6, 15.

68. Peter E. Russell, "Redcoats in the Wilderness: British Officers and Irregular Warfare in Europe and America, 1740 to 1760," *WMQ,* 3d ser. 35 (1978), 629–52.

69. Harold L. Peterson, "The Military Equipment of the Plymouth and Bay Colonies, 1620–1690," *New Eng. Q.,* 20 (1947), 197–208; Kennedy, *Serious Advice,* 14–15.

70. Archibald Kennedy, *The Importance of Gaining and Preserving the Friendship of the Indians to the British Interest Considered* (London, 1752), 43.

71. Alfred Proctor James, ed., *Writings of General John Forbes* (Menasha, Wis., 1938), 125.

72. John K. Mahon, "Anglo-American Methods of Indian Warfare, 1676–1794," *Mississippi Valley Historical Review,* 45 (1958–59), 254–75; Douglas Edward Leach,

Arms for Empire: A Military History of the British Colonies in North America, 1607–1763 (New York, 1973), chs. 9–10, Daniel J. Beattie, "The Adaptation of the British Army to Wilderness Warfare, 1755–1763," in Maarten Ultee, ed., *Adapting to Conditions: War and Society in the Eighteenth Century* (University, Ala., 1986), 56–83; Russell, "Redcoats in the Wilderness."

73. Mahon, "Anglo-American Methods of Indian Warfare," 254–75; Armstrong Starkey, *European and Native American Warfare, 1675–1815* (Norman, 1998); Ian K. Steele, *Warpaths: Invasions of North America* (New York, 1994); Axtell, *The European and the Indian*, 146–47.

74. Charles Francis Adams, ed., *The Works of John Adams,* 10 vols. (Boston, 1850–56), 10:282–83, 288, 313.

75. See above, Chapter 6, p. 146, and Loren E. Pennington, "The Amerindian in English Promotional Literature, 1575–1625," in K. R. Andrews, N. P. Canny, and P. E. H. Hair, eds., *The Westward Enterprise: English Activities in Ireland, the Atlantic, and America 1480–1650* (Detroit, 1979), 175–94.

76. Edmund S. Morgan, *The Puritan Family: Religion and Domestic Relations in Seventeenth-Century New England* (rev. ed., New York, 1966), ch. 7.

77. David D. Hall, *The Faithful Shepherd: A History of the New England Ministry in the Seventeenth Century* (Chapel Hill, 1972), esp. chs. 7, 11.

78. William Kellaway, *The New England Company, 1649–1776: Missionary Society to the American Indians* (London, 1961), ch. 9; R. Pierce Beaver, ed., *Pioneers in Mission: The Early Missionary Ordination Sermons, Charges, and Instructions* (Grand Rapids, Mich., 1966); John Wolfe Lydekker, *The Faithful Mohawks* (New York, 1938); John C. Guzzardo, "The Superintendent and the Ministers: The Battle for Oneida Allegiances, 1761–75," *New York History,* 57 (1976), 255–83; Cedric B. Cowing, *The Great Awakening and the American Revolution: Colonial Thought in the 18th Century* (Chicago, 1971), 77–86.

79. Lawson, *New Voyage to Carolina,* 240.

80. Mather, *The Way to Prosperity,* 27; Rev. John Heckewelder, *History, Manners, and Customs of the Indian Nations Who Once Inhabited Pennsylvania and the Neighbouring States,* rev. ed. Rev. William C. Reichel (Philadelphia, 1876), 223.

81. Cotton Mather, *A Letter to Ungospellized Plantations* (Boston, 1702), 14.

82. Pearce, *Savagism and Civilization,* 5. See also Robert F. Berkhofer, Jr., *The White Man's Indian: Images of the American Indian from Columbus to the Present* (New York, 1978); Gary B. Nash, "The Image of the Indian in the Southern Colonial Mind," *WMQ,* 3d ser. 29 (1972), 197–230; Sheehan, *Savagism and Civility;* Karen Ordahl Kupperman, *Settling with the Indians: The Meeting of English and Indian Cultures in America, 1580–1640* (Totowa, N.J., 1980); James Axtell, "Through a Glass Darkly: Colonial Attitudes Toward the Native Americans," *American Indian Culture and Research Journal,* 1 (1974), 17–28; Gordon M. Sayre, *Les Sauvages Américains: Representations of Native Americans in French and English Colonial Literature* (Chapel Hill, 1997); Kupperman, "Presentment of Civility: English Reading of American Self-Presentation in the Early Years of Colonization," *WMQ,* 3rd ser. 54:1 (Jan. 1997), 193–228; Alden T. Vaughan, "From White Man to Redskin: Changing Anglo-American Perceptions of the American Indian," *American Historical Review,* 86:4 (Oct. 1982), 917–53.

83. Winthrop D. Jordan, *White Over Black: American Attitudes Toward the Negro, 1550–1812* (Chapel Hill, 1968), 40; Michael Zuckerman, "The Fabrication of Identity in Early America," *WMQ*, 3d ser. 34 (1977), 183–214 at 204; Also Zuckerman, "Identity in British America: Unease in Eden," in Nicholas Canny and Anthony Pagden, eds., *Colonial Identity in the Atlantic World, 1500–1800* (Princeton, 1987) ch. 5.

84. Daniel Gookin, "Historical Collections of the Indians in New England" [1674], *Colls. Mass. His. Soc.*, 1st ser. 1 (1792), 131.

85. Michael Kammen, *People of Paradox: An Inquiry Concerning the Origins of American Civilization* (New York, 1972). See the perceptive critique by Carl Degler in *Reviews in American History*, 1 (1973), 470–74.

86. Richard P. Johnson, "The Search for a Usable Indian: An Aspect of the Defense of Colonial New England," *Journal of American History*, 64 (1977), 623–51.

87. Richard Slotkin, *Regeneration Through Violence: The Mythology of the American Frontier, 1600–1860* (Middletown, Conn., 1973); Slotkin, "Dreams and Genocide: The American Myth of Regeneration Through Violence," *Journal of Popular History*, 5:1 (Summer 1971), 38–59; Slotkin, "Massacre," *Berkshire Review*, 14 (1979), 112–32; Robert Shulman, "Parkman's Indians and American Violence," *Massachusetts Review*, 12 (1971), 221–39.

88. Doddridge, *Notes on the Settlement and Indian Wars*, 207. See Patrick M. Malone, *The Skulking Way of War: Technology and Tactics among the New England Indians* (Lanham, Md., 1991) and Starkey, *European and Native American Warfare*, ch. 1.

89. William J. Eccles, *The Canadian Frontier, 1534–1760* (New York, 1969), 42.

90. Diary of Ebenezer Parkman, July 20, 1726, *Proceedings of the American Antiquarian Society*, n.s. 71 (1961), 150–51.

91. Cotton Mather, "A Brand Pluck'd Out of the Burning" [1693], in George Lincoln Burr, ed., *Narratives of the Witchcraft Cases, 1648–1706*, ONEAH (New York, 1914), 255–87.

92. *The Journal of Esther Edwards Burr, 1754–1757*, ed. Carol F. Karlsen and Laurie Crumpacker (New Haven, 1984), 142 (Aug. 8–9, 1755).

93. Ibid., 136 (July 19, 1755).

94. Doddridge, *Notes on the Settlement and Indian Wars*, 210.

95. See above, Chapter 11.

96. See Axtell, *The European and Indian*, 142, 148–49; Axtell, "The Vengeful Women of Marblehead: Robert Roules's Deposition of 1677," *WMQ*, 3d ser. 31 (1974), 647–52.

97. Samuel Davies, *Religion and Patriotism the Constituents of a Good Soldier* (Philadelphia, 1755), 7.

98. Cotton Mather, *Souldiers Counselled and Comforted* (Boston, 1689), 28.

99. James Sullivan *et al.*, eds., *The Papers of Sir William Johnson*, 14 vols. (Albany, 1921–65), 13:198; Frederick Cook, ed., *Journals of the Military Expedition of Major General John Sullivan Against the Six Nations of Indians in 1779* (Auburn, N.Y., 1887), 8.

100. James K. Hosmer, ed., [John] *Winthrop's Journal 'History of New England' 1630–1649*, ONEAH, 2 vols. (New York, 1908), 2:18–19. See also *The Complete Works of Roger Williams*, 7 vols. (New York, 1963), 7:31.

101. *The Poems of Roger Wolcott* (Boston, 1898), 55.

102. R. A. Brock, ed., *The Official Letters of Alexander Spotswood, Collections of the Virginia Historical Society,* n.s. 1 (1882), 134.

103. Bernhard Knollenberg, "General Amherst and Germ Warfare," *Miss. Valley His. Rev.,* 41 (1954–55), 489–94, 762–63; Elizabeth A. Fenn, "Biological Warfare, Circa 1750," *New York Times,* April 11, 1998, A25; Fenn, "Biological Warfare in Eighteenth-Century North America: Beyond Jeffery Amherst," *Journal of American History,* 86:4 (March 2000), 1552–80.

104. Between 1705 and 1708, Massachusetts's defense bills were £30,000 per year, an amount equal to ten times the whole colony budget in the 1680s (Johnson, "Search for a Usable Indian," *J. of Amer. His.,* 64 [1977], 626 n.5).

105. E. McClung Fleming, "The American Image as Indian Princess, 1765–1783," *Winterthur Portfolio,* 2 (1965), 65–81; Hugh Honour, *The New Golden Land: European Images of America from the Discoveries to the Present Time* (New York, 1975), ch. 6.

INDEX